# Fuzzy Sets in Business Management, Finance, and Economics, 2nd Edition

# Fuzzy Sets in Business Management, Finance, and Economics, 2nd Edition

Editors

**Jorge de Andres Sanchez**
**Laura González-Vila Puchades**

Basel • Beijing • Wuhan • Barcelona • Belgrade • Novi Sad • Cluj • Manchester

*Editors*
Jorge de Andres Sanchez
Rovira i Virgili University
Reus
Spain

Laura González-Vila Puchades
University of Barcelona
Barcelona
Spain

*Editorial Office*
MDPI
St. Alban-Anlage 66
4052 Basel, Switzerland

This is a reprint of articles from the Special Issue published online in the open access journal *Mathematics* (ISSN 2227-7390) (available at: https://mdpi.com/si/135764).

For citation purposes, cite each article independently as indicated on the article page online and as indicated below:

Lastname, A.A.; Lastname, B.B. Article Title. *Journal Name* **Year**, *Volume Number*, Page Range.

**ISBN 978-3-7258-1367-4 (Hbk)**
**ISBN 978-3-7258-1368-1 (PDF)**
doi.org/10.3390/books978-3-7258-1368-1

© 2024 by the authors. Articles in this book are Open Access and distributed under the Creative Commons Attribution (CC BY) license. The book as a whole is distributed by MDPI under the terms and conditions of the Creative Commons Attribution-NonCommercial-NoDerivs (CC BY-NC-ND) license.

# Contents

About the Editors . . . . . . . . . . . . . . . . . . . . . . . . . . . . . . . . . . . . . . . . . . . . vii

Preface . . . . . . . . . . . . . . . . . . . . . . . . . . . . . . . . . . . . . . . . . . . . . . . . . . ix

**Jorge de Andres-Sanchez, Ala Ali Almahameed, Mario Arias-Oliva and
Jorge Pelegrin-Borondo**
Correlational and Configurational Analysis of Factors Influencing Potential Patients' Attitudes
toward Surgical Robots: A Study in the Jordan University Community
Reprinted from: *Mathematics* **2022**, *10*, 4319, doi:10.3390/math10224319 . . . . . . . . . . . . . . . 1

**Luciano Barcellos-Paula, Anna María Gil-Lafuente and Aline Castro-Rezende**
Algorithm Applied to SDG13: A Case Study of Ibero-American Countries
Reprinted from: *Mathematics* **2023**, *11*, 313, doi:10.3390/math11020313 . . . . . . . . . . . . . . . . 17

**Fabio Blanco-Mesa, Omar Vinchira and Yesica Cuy**
Forgotten Factors in Knowledge Conversion and Routines: A Fuzzy Analysis of Employee
Knowledge Management in Exporting Companies in Boyacá
Reprinted from: *Mathematics* **2023**, *11*, 412, doi:10.3390/math11020412 . . . . . . . . . . . . . . . . 37

**Giulia Giacomello Pompilio, Tiago F. A. C. Sigahi, Izabela Simon Rampasso,
Gustavo Hermínio Salati Marcondes de Moraes, Lucas Veiga Ávila, Walter Leal Filho and
Rosley Anholon**
Innovation in Brazilian Industries: Analysis of Management Practices Using Fuzzy TOPSIS
Reprinted from: *Mathematics* **2023**, *11*, 1313, doi:10.3390/math11061313 . . . . . . . . . . . . . . . 72

**Zixue Guo and Sijia Liu**
Study on the Selection of Pharmaceutical E-Commerce Platform Considering Bounded
Rationality under Probabilistic Hesitant Fuzzy Environment
Reprinted from: *Mathematics* **2023**, *11*, 1859, doi:10.3390/math11081859 . . . . . . . . . . . . . . . 91

**Phi-Hung Nguyen**
A Fully Completed Spherical Fuzzy Data-Driven Model for Analyzing Employee Satisfaction
in Logistics Service Industry
Reprinted from: *Mathematics* **2023**, *11*, 2235, doi:10.3390/math11102235 . . . . . . . . . . . . . . . 112

**Jorge de Andrés-Sánchez**
Fuzzy Random Option Pricing in Continuous Time: A Systematic Review and an Extension of
Vasicek's Equilibrium Model of the Term Structure
Reprinted from: *Mathematics* **2023**, *11*, 2455, doi:10.3390/math11112455 . . . . . . . . . . . . . . . 146

**Javier Parra-Domínguez, Maria Alonso-García and Juan Manuel Corchado**
Fuzzy Logic to Measure the Degree of Compliance with a Target in an SDG—The Case of
SDG 11
Reprinted from: *Mathematics* **2023**, *11*, 2967, doi:10.3390/math11132967 . . . . . . . . . . . . . . . 167

**Alin Opreana, Simona Vinerean, Diana Marieta Mihaiu, Liliana Barbu and
Radu-Alexandru Șerban**
Fuzzy Analytic Network Process with Principal Component Analysis to Establish a Bank
Performance Model under the Assumption of Country Risk
Reprinted from: *Mathematics* **2023**, *11*, 3257, doi:10.3390/math11143257 . . . . . . . . . . . . . . . 183

**Hongyi Sun, Wenbin Ni and Lanxuan Huang**
Fuzzy Assessment of Management Consulting Projects: Model Validation and Case Studies
Reprinted from: *Mathematics* **2023**, *11*, 4381, doi:10.3390/math11204381 . . . . . . . . . . . . . . . 221

**Xiaoxiang Wang, Songling Wu and Lixiang Zhao**
Research on the Improvement Path of Total Factor Productivity in the Industrial Software
Industry: Evidence from Chinese Typical Firms
Reprinted from: *Mathematics* **2023**, *11*, 4944, doi:10.3390/math11244944 . . . . . . . . . . . . . . . . 243

**Alina Elena Ionașcu, Shankha Shubhra Goswami, Alexandra Dănilă, Maria-Gabriela Horga, Corina Aurora Barbu and Șerban-Comănescu Adrian**
Analyzing Primary Sector Selection for Economic Activity in Romania: An Interval-Valued
Fuzzy Multi-Criteria Approach
Reprinted from: *Mathematics* **2024**, *12*, 1157, doi:10.3390/math12081157 . . . . . . . . . . . . . . . . 269

# About the Editors

**Jorge de Andres Sanchez**

Jorge de Andres Sanchez is a PhD. in Business Management, an Actuary, a Senior Lecturer in Finance at the Rovira i Virgili University (Spain), and a member of the research group, Social and Business Research Laboratory. His main research field is the applications of soft computing in financial and actuarial topics. He is the author of several papers on these topics in academic journals such as *Mathematics, Journal of Risk and Insurance, Insurance: Mathematics and Economics, Fuzzy Sets and Systems* and *Expert Systems with Applications*.

**Laura González-Vila Puchades**

Laura González-Vila Puchades is a PhD. in Economics and Business Sciences and an Actuary. She is currently a Senior Lecturer in the area of financial economics and accounting at the University of Barcelona (Spain) and a member of the research group Actuarial and Financial Modelling. She is the author of several presentations at national and international congresses of finance, insurance and uncertainty, and has published several papers in top-ranked academic journals related to these areas.

# Preface

This reprint collects twelve papers published in the Special Issue of *Mathematics* entitled "Fuzzy Sets in Business Management, Finance, and Economics, 2nd Edition" during the years 2022–2024. It covers a wide range of different tools from fuzzy set theory and applications in many areas of business management, economics, and related fields. More specifically, this reprint contains applications of such instruments as, among others, fuzzy set qualitative comparative analysis (FSQCA), fuzzy multi-criteria decision-making (FMCDM), forgotten effects algorithm, expertons theory, ordered weighted averaging (OWA) operators, and fuzzy expert systems.

The most common topic is the application of FMCDM to business decisions and management. Ionașcu et al. propose the use of FMCDM for decisions linked to the economic primary sector, Nguyen to measure employee satisfaction, and Guo and Liu to select among pharmaceutical e-commerce platforms. Sun et al. demonstrate the usefulness of Dempster–Shafer theory in a project management setting. Finally, Pompilio et al. apply a mixed methodology, combining hierarchical cluster analysis and fuzzy technique for order preference by similarity to ideal solution (TOPSIS), to assess firms' innovation practices.

There are two papers using FSQCA in marketing and managerial topics. Andrés-Sánchez et al. use FSQCA to identify the profiles that lead to the acceptance or rejection of surgical robots. Wang et al. show the usefulness of this technique for identifying antecedents of productivity in the industrial software industry. Blanco-Mesa et al. also use the forgotten effects algorithm and expertons theory within a business management context to show that there are overlooked factors between knowledge conversion and routines related to informal communication and social interactions.

There are three papers dealing with the evaluation of public policies. Opreana et al. use fuzzy analytic network process and principal component analysis to evaluate country risk. Likewise, two of those three papers measure the compliance of countries with sustainable development goals using different approaches. While Parra-Domínguez proposes the use of fuzzy expert systems, Barcellos-Paula et al. use OWA operators.

Finally, Andrés-Sánchez reviews the contributions of fuzzy sets to option pricing and expands Vasicek's model of the yield curve to include fuzzy volatility and reversion speed.

It is hoped that this reprint will be useful not only for business managers, public decision-makers, and researchers in the specific fields of business management, finance, and economics but also in the broader areas of soft mathematics in social sciences. Practitioners will find methods and ideas that could be fruitful in current management issues. Scholars will find novel developments that may inspire further applications in social sciences

**Jorge de Andres Sanchez and Laura González-Vila Puchades**
*Editors*

## Article

# Correlational and Configurational Analysis of Factors Influencing Potential Patients' Attitudes toward Surgical Robots: A Study in the Jordan University Community

Jorge de Andres-Sanchez [1,*], Ala Ali Almahameed [2], Mario Arias-Oliva [3] and Jorge Pelegrin-Borondo [4]

1. Social and Business Research Laboratory, Business Management Department, University Rovira i Virgili, 43002 Tarragona, Spain
2. Social and Business Research Laboratory, Universitat Rovira i Virgili, 43002 Tarragona, Spain
3. Marketing Department, Complutense University of Madrid and Social & Business Research Laboratory, Department of Business Management, Universitat Rovira i Virgili, 43002 Tarragona, Spain
4. Economics and Business Department, University of La Rioja, 26006 Logroño, Spain
* Correspondence: jorge.deandres@urv.cat; Tel.: +34-977759833

**Abstract:** The literature on surgical robots (SRs) usually adopts the perspective of healthcare workers. However, research on potential patients' perceptions and the publics' points of view on SRs is scarce. This fact motivates our study, which assesses the factors inducing the SRs acceptance in the opinion of potential patients. We consider three variables, based on the unified theory of acceptance and the use of technology (UTAUT): the performance expectancy (PE), the effort expectancy (EE), and the social influence (SI); pleasure (PL), arousal (AR), and the perceived risk (PR). To deal with empirical data, we used the ordered logistic regression (OLR) and the fuzzy set comparative qualitative analysis (fsQCA). The OLR allowed us to check for a significant positive average influence of the UTAUT variables and PL, on the intention to undergo robotic surgery. However, the PR had a significant negative impact, and AR was not found to be significant. The FsQCA allowed the identification of the potential patient profiles, linked to acceptance of and resistance to SRs and confirmed that they are not symmetrical. The proposed input variables are presented as core conditions in at least one prime implicate robotic-assisted surgery acceptance. The exception to this statement is the PR, which is affirmed in some recipes and absent in others. The recipes explaining the resistance to SRs were obtained by combining the absence of PE, EE, SI, and PL (i.e., these variables have a negative impact on rejection) and the presence of the PR (i.e., the perceived risk has a positive impact on a resistance attitude toward SRs). Similarly, arousal played a secondary role in explaining the rejection.

**Keywords:** robot services; surgical robots; robot acceptance; unified theory of acceptance and use of technology (UTAUT); smart technologies; regression methods; fuzzy set qualitative comparative analysis (fsQCA)

**MSC:** 62J05; 94D05; 62P25; 91F99

## 1. Introduction

### 1.1. Initial Considerations

The use of surgical robots (SRs) has grown exponentially since the second decade of the 21st century and is now a standard alternative to traditional ordinary surgery (OS) and minimally invasive surgery (MIS) techniques [1]. There is a wide literature displaying health professionals' points of view about the advantages and drawbacks of SRs, with respect to those of OS and MIS [2–5]. However, the successful implantation of SRs does not depend only on health workers' perceptions, but is also linked to public opinion about SRs and to potential and actual patients' willingness to undergo robotic-assisted surgery. So, Boys et al. [4] report from a survey carried out in the USA, about an average positive perception of SRs, by a sample of potential patients. In their sample, most answers indicated that robotic surgery was perceived as safer, faster, less painful, and offered better results than OS or MIS. Jank et al. [6] also reported a positive perception of SRs in a set of patients with a cochlear implantation. However, [7,8] found in their samples a preference of MIS over robotic techniques. Our paper, as [4,7], is focused on the perceptions of potential patients' or the publics' points of view, rather than of actual patients.

The unified theory of acceptance and use of technology (UTAUT) by Venkatesh et al. [9] is a useful instrument to model the attitudes toward the use of SRs, from both professionals' and patients' (actual and potential) perspectives. From the perspective of a surgeon, a UTAUT input factor, such as the easiness expectation, may be focused on his/her perceived job performance (for example, the absence of haptic feedback could be a barrier to SRs). Krishnan et al. [10] and BenMessaoud et al. [11] used this theoretical framework to systematize the advantages and drawbacks of SRs, and assessed their attitudes from the perspective of health workers. UTAUT factors have also been found to be relevant in explaining actual and potential patient attitudes toward robotic surgery [6,8,12]. For example, an issue that may impact the patient performance expectancy, is that robotic surgery usually allows a faster recovery than OS and MIS. Likewise, not only UTAUT factors are significant in explaining the acceptance of robotic-assisted surgery, but also emotional factors [8,12] and cognitive factors, such as the perceived risks [7,12].

The above questions motivated this study to examine how three UTAUT factors (performance expectancy, easiness expectation, and social influence), two affective variables, and the perceived risk influence, combine to influence the intention to undergo surgery that, if needed, will be carried out by a robot. This study used a survey conducted in Jordan's university community. Specifically, we attempted to answer two questions.

RQ1: *What are the average influence and statistical significance of the explanatory variables of intention to undergo, if needed, intervention by a SR?*

RQ2: *How do input variables combine to produce acceptance and induce SR rejection to potential patients?*

To answer RQ1, as in [8,12], we use the ordered logistic regression (OLR). With regard to RQ2, a suitable analytical method to deal with the combinatory effects of factors and their asymmetric influence in inducing and non-inducing a given output is the fuzzy set qualitative comparative analysis (fsQCA) [13,14]. This analytical framework has been applied in several market and business analyses. Thus, whereas [15–18] use fsQCA to evaluate the factors that induce acceptance of new technologies, [19] identified several paths that lead to companies adopting environmental practices in firms. Likewise, fsQCA has been applied to assess risk factors in audit processes [20] and explore the entrepreneurial intention of university students [21]. Moreover, although fsQCA has been used in health research [22–24], all reviewed empirical literature on robot acceptance performs quantitative analyses using correlational methods, such as a regression analysis.

Thus, the novelty of this study can be summarized in two ways. This work contributes to the scarce literature on patients' (actual or potential) attitudes toward robotic surgery. Moreover, to the best of our knowledge, the use of fsQCA as an analytical tool in this context is novel. We show that fsQCA and OLR are complementary analytical tools, because they allow for the analysis of data from two non-excluding focuses. OLR is a variable-oriented technique that allows the measurement of the net incidence of each input variable on the attitude toward SRs. In contrast, fsQCA is case-oriented. Thus, fsQCA will allow us to identify patterns of potential users that are consistently associated with a favorable perception of robotic-assisted surgery, but also profiles that are strongly linked to negative perceptions of SRs.

*1.2. Theoretical Background*

The technology acceptance model (TAM) [25] and UTAUT [10,26] have been used extensively to evaluate the acceptance of new technologies in healthcare settings from a professional perspective [27–30] and from the users' points of view [31–34]. In the more concrete field of SRs, it has been applied to explain the intention to use SRs by doctors and nurses [10,11] and to evaluate the potential and actual patients' attitudes toward SRs [6,8,12]. To explain attitudes toward SRs by potential patients, we use three constructs of the UTAUT model: performance expectancy, easiness expectation, and social influence.

Performance expectancy (PE) is the degree of usefulness perceived by the user of a new technology [25]. Surgical robots provide many advantages, such as a reduced hospital stay, decreased postoperative pain, and a lower incidence of wound infections [2–5,11]. Moreover, SRs are well suited for telesurgery. In this regard, Boys et al. [4] stated that many people prefer telesurgery by a prestigious surgeon to conventional surgery by a less experienced doctor. The positive impact of actual and potential SRs on performance expectancy has been confirmed in several studies [6,8,12]

Effort expectancy (EE) is the perceived simplicity and comfort of using a new technology [25]. Users are more likely to develop a positive attitude toward a new technology if they perceive it to be comfortable, easy to use, and accessible. The relevance of this construct to users' attitudes toward robots was observed in [35–37]. Despite SRs reducing the effective time of surgical intervention, the entire embedded process may be longer [11]. Another factor that may reduce the ease of using SRs is that not all hospitals are equipped with this technology, and this kind of surgery can become less accessible [38]. Likewise, the information provided in an informed consent document is more difficult to understand than that of other surgery types [2]. Several authors have found that EE has a significant positive influence on the perception of SRs [6,11].

Social influence (SI) is the degree to which a person perceives that others believe that they should use a new technology [9]. The opinions of the family and physicians are often relevant when choosing a surgeon and SRs [6,8,12]. Likewise, it must be noted that not all professionals support the use of SRs over conventional techniques [5,11]. However, the presence of SRs is perceived in public opinion as a sign of prestige [5].

While evaluating user attitudes toward robots, several authors have emphasized the importance of cognitive and emotional factors [39–41]. The acceptance of SRs depends not only on rational decision-making, but also on emotions and wishes [6,8,12,42]. We have taken into account these reports in such a way that to explain robotic-assisted surgery, we combine the three UTAUT factors exposed above with a cognitive variable, a perceived risk, and two affective variables, pleasure and arousal.

Perceived risk (PR) has been used to study the acceptance of wearable technologies for healthcare applications [43], attitudes toward cyborg implants [44], and the perception of SRs [7,8,12]. SRs affect surgical risks in several ways. The first is related to the capability of SRs to reduce human risks, such as hand tremors and surgeon imprecision. The second perspective concerns the patient's perception of risk, which is linked to the fact that a SR is a disruptive device and innovation that often induces fear [7]. Notice that any failure of the robot during surgery could expose the patient to serious risk. Furthermore, this variable is connected to trust, since the increase in risk perception could be a result of trust absence [45–48].

Pleasure (PL) expressed during the interaction with robots can significantly impact acceptance, either positively or negatively, as well as a person's emotional state [49,50]. As far as we are concerned, this construct can also be assimilated into less anxiety and post-operative pain, a more pleasant intervention recovery, and better aesthetic results [42].

Arousal (AR) refers to a state of feeling stimulated or active in a certain situation [51]. Its impact on the acceptance of cyborgs is shown by [52]. Furthermore, feelings of arousal promote behavioral engagement, as can be seen in the use of social robots in autism therapy [53].

*1.3. Research Questions and Hypotheses*

As mentioned in Section 1.1. This study aimed to answer two research questions. While the first question, RQ1, inquires about the statistical significance of the assessed input factors to explain the acceptance of SRs, the second query, RQ2, asks about how explanatory variables combine to induce the acceptance and non-acceptance of robotic surgery. Notice that, whereas RQ1 is common in the literature on robots and surgical robot acceptance, RQ2, which asks about how factors combine to produce a willingness and rejection toward robotic-assisted surgery, has still not been addressed. This affirmation can be extended to the literature on the user's attitude toward robots of any kind.

To answer the first question, we evaluated the direction of the relationship between acceptance (ACCEPT) and PE, EE, SI, PR, AR, and PL., accordingly, with the exposition in Section 1.2. Thus, we propose the following hypotheses:

**Hypothesis 1.1 (H1.1).** *Performance Expectancy is linked positively with SRs' acceptance.*

**Hypothesis 1.2 (H1.2).** *Effort Expectancy is linked positively with SRs' acceptance.*

**Hypothesis 1.3 (H1.3).** *Social Influence is linked positively with SRs' acceptance.*

**Hypothesis 1.4 (H1.4).** *Perceived Risk is linked negatively with SRs' acceptance.*

**Hypothesis 1.5 (H1.5).** *Arousal is linked positively with SRs' acceptance.*

**Hypothesis 1.6 (H1.6).** *Pleasure is linked positively with SRs' acceptance.*

To answer the second question, which assesses the combinatorial effects of input variables on SRs' acceptance and rejection, we propose testing the following hypotheses:

**Hypothesis 2.1 (H2.1).** *The combination of the high evaluations (presence) in PE, EE, SI, AR, and PL items, and low evaluations (absence) in PR, produces SRs' acceptance.*

**Hypothesis 2.2 (H2.2).** *The combination of the low evaluations (absence) in PE, EE, SI, AR, and PL items, and high evaluations (presence) in PR, produces SRs' rejection*

**Hypothesis 2.3 (H2.3).** *The combination of the evaluations of PE, EE, SI, PR, AR, and PL to explain the acceptance and rejection is not symmetrical.*

## 2. Material and Methods

### 2.1. Survey Description

The target population of the study was the Jordanian university community, including embedded students, professors, and other workers. The answers were provided using Google Forms, and the hyperlink was provided individually to 1000 individuals. With this selection we tried to attain sex parity, a representation of all collectives of the university community, and reaching quotas by branches of Science. One of the authors of the paper was available to all respondents to answer any question about the research and questionnaire. For example, if the respondent inquires about the content of an informed consent document, an example of that was provided (see https://www.medpro.com/roboticsurgery-informedconsent that could be accessed on 4 November 2022). This also applied, of course, to clarify the nuances in similar questions or giving, if demanded, a more detailed information about robotic surgery by providing studies [2,4]. The survey was conducted in the second half of 2019, using social networks. The final number of responses used in this study was 379, with a success rate of 37.9%. The 62.1% of failed surveys embed those that were not answered and those that did not respond to at least one question. The responses were anonymous. A total of 47% of the respondents were women and 53% were men. Respondents' ages were distributed as follows: between 18 and 24 years (51%), between 25 and 34 years (24%), between 35 and 44 years (13%), and above 44 years (12%). The responses from the public universities and private universities were 64.3% and 35.7%, respectively. Likewise, 26% of individuals were linked to computer and engineering studies, 43% to social sciences, 13% to health sciences, and the rest to arts and humanities studies. Therefore, similar to [4,7,12], the responses used in this study did not come from actual patients but from potential users.

Notice that the use of university community members to develop an assessment of robot acceptance in a non-educational setting has been carried out in several papers [54–56]. We believe that considering Jordan's university community to develop our study, can allow us to obtain relevant results for several reasons. First, the answers must be provided using electronic methods. Practically, all members of the university community are familiar with these procedures and have an easily available electronic device to complain about the survey. Therefore, the success rate may be greater than that of the other collectives.

Taking the university environment as a reference, ensures that the surveyed persons have a cultural status high enough to understand the information in the questionnaire. Surely most of the respondents were aware beforehand about the existence of surgical robots, had an idea about the procedures linked with health services, such as "informed consent", and the complexity that may present an informed consent in a surgery setting.

In any university environment, there is a great diversity of perspectives, regarding technological advances. Members of the community are devoted to health sciences, engineering, basic sciences, humanities, etc. It is expected that their point of view, despite being diverse, has a solid foundation that, of course, could be biased toward technological arguments and philosophical opinions. Moreover, in a university community, it is not difficult to achieve parity between men and women.

We are interested in the opinions of potential patients. Of course, any person could need surgery at any moment, so he/she is a subject of study. However, we also feel that more reliable answers come from persons who, if they needed a surgical intervention, have the possibility to choose between more than one alternative. That freedom embeds choosing hospital and surgeon/surgery techniques, but also has available enough monetary resources to expend in that medical service. Usually, members of the university community belong to families of upper middle and high social classes and/or have/aspire to qualified jobs with considerable wages.

Therefore, we feel that our sample could provide interesting results about SRs acceptance, linked to members of social classes with high cultural status from Jordan, but also from other Middle Eastern countries with similar cultural strata, such as Turkey and Lebanon.

We introduced the survey as follows: *According to recent news published in Newsweek magazine, the smart tissue autonomous robot (STAR), a robot used to perform surgery, has been proven to be more precise than expert human surgeons in performing the same task in laparoscopic surgery. Consider that the robot can perform the required surgery. Indicate the extent to which you agree or disagree with the following statements on a scale of 0 (strongly disagree) to 10 (strongly agree), 5 being neither 'agree nor disagree; "I will accept to use services offered by a robot (if I need a surgery)".* To give enough but not overwhelming information to respondents, the link to the news article was provided in the survey (https://www.newsweek.com/2016/05/20/robot-soft-tissue-surgery-pig-bowels-455765.html, accessed on 2 June 2016). Likewise, if the surveyed person was interested in having more in-depth information on SRs, the references [2,3] were provided. Notice that the success rate was below 40%, i.e., 60% did not complete the survey, surely because they did not feel informed enough, as well as because they had no motivation to gather more information on the issue. Moreover, we suppose that the responses, which come from people with a high cultural status, were given honestly, due to the respondents who felt they were aware enough to give an opinion about the issue, as a potential patient or "public". All items in the questionnaire were rated on a Likert 11-point scale (0–10). Table 1 shows these items and the descriptive statistics of the responses. The measurement scales for PE, EE, and SI were adapted from previous studies on healthcare technology acceptance [34,47]. The measurement scale of the PR was based on that in [57]. Whereas in the question linked to "being risky" it is evaluated if SRs present a risk, i.e., may cause harm; the question linked with "uncertainty about the performance" embeds more aspects: uncertainty about the time needed to recover from the intervention, number of days in the hospital, duration of the surgery, etc. To model the emotional dimensions of arousal and pleasure, we have used the scale in [58]. Table 1 presents the questions and descriptive statistics of the survey.

Table 1. Items in the survey and descriptive statistics.

| Item | Average | Median | Q1 | Q3 | Std. dev. | IV |
|---|---|---|---|---|---|---|
| *Output item: Behavioral intention* | | | | | | |
| ACCEPT = If needed, I will accept being assisted by a surgical robot (SR). | 4.66 | 5 | 1 | 8 | 3.48 | 7 |
| *Input construct: Performance expectancy* | | | | | | |
| PE1 = I find SRs useful. | 4.11 | 4 | 1 | 6.5 | 3.27 | 5.5 |
| PE2 = SRs allow a better recovery from interventions. | 3.97 | 4 | 1 | 6 | 3.23 | 5 |
| PE3 = SRs help to achieve a faster recovery from interventions. | 3.92 | 4 | 1 | 6 | 3.22 | 5 |
| PE4 = SRs allow a more efficient intervention | 4.16 | 4 | 1 | 6 | 3.21 | 5 |
| *Input construct: Effort expectancy* | | | | | | |
| EE1 = The information in the consent document will be easy for me. | 4.97 | 5 | 2 | 7 | 3.26 | 5 |
| EE2 = The intervention by a SR is more comfortable than other types of surgery. | 4.82 | 5 | 2 | 7 | 3.23 | 5 |
| EE3 = It will be easy to access hospitals equipped by SRs. | 5.39 | 6 | 3 | 8 | 3.35 | 5 |
| EE4 = It will be easy to achieve a good interaction with medical services that provide SRs. | 5.47 | 5 | 3 | 8 | 3.19 | 5 |
| *Input construct: Social influence* | | | | | | |
| SI1 = People who influence me think that I should use the services offered by SRs. | 4.61 | 5 | 2 | 7 | 3.11 | 5 |
| SI2 = People who are important to me think that I should use SRs. | 4.60 | 5 | 2 | 7 | 3.11 | 5 |
| SI3 = People whose opinions I value, prefer that I use the services offered by SRs. | 4.66 | 5 | 2 | 7 | 3.12 | 5 |
| *Input construct: Perceived risk* | | | | | | |
| PR1 = The services offered by SRs are risky. | 5.74 | 5 | 3 | 9 | 3.16 | 6 |
| PR2 = There is too much uncertainty in the performance of SRs. | 6.18 | 6 | 4 | 9 | 3.05 | 5 |
| PR3 = Compared with other surgeries, the services offered by SRs is riskier. | 5.84 | 6 | 4 | 8 | 3.12 | 4 |
| *Input construct: Pleasure* | | | | | | |
| PL1 = When I think of the service being provided by a SR, I feel: Unhappy—Happy | 4.89 | 5 | 2 | 8 | 3.38 | 6 |
| PL2 = When I think of the service being provided by a SR, I feel: Annoyed—Pleased | 4.78 | 5 | 2 | 7 | 3.17 | 5 |
| *Input construct: Arousal* | | | | | | |
| AR1 = When I think of the service being provided by a SR, I feel: Relaxed—Stimulated | 4.76 | 5 | 2 | 7 | 3.06 | 5 |
| AR2 = When I think of the service being provided by a SR, I feel: Calm—Excited | 4.93 | 5 | 2 | 8 | 3.17 | 6 |

Note: Q1 and Q3 represent the 1st and 3rd quartile. Std. dev is the standard deviation and IV = Q3−Q1.

### 2.2. Quantitative Analysis

To evaluate the research questions, we used an ordered logistic regression (RQ1) and fsQCA (RQ2). We then proceed sequentially as follows:

Step 1. We checked the reliability of the measurement scale using Cronbach's alpha, the convergent reliability, and the average variance extracted. We also performed the exploratory factor analysis.

Step 2. To answer RQ1, we fitted an ordered logistic regression (OLR) to ACCEPT [8,12] in a similar setting. For the value of the input variables, we took their standardized loadings, obtained in Step 1. The sign of the coefficients and their statistical significance will lead us to assess hypothesis H1.1–H1.6, and so, provide an answer to RQ1.

Step 3. The first step in performing the fsQCA and evaluating RQ2, is to build the membership function of the response variable. It was evaluated on an 11-point Likert scale; therefore, we considered the thresholds for absolute non-membership, indeterminacy, and full membership; the values were 2, 5, and 8, respectively [13]. Therefore, for the $j$th observation of the output variable ACCEPT, $ACC_j$, the membership value is defined in [59] as

$$m_{ACC_j} = \begin{cases} 0 & ACC_j \leq 0.2 \\ \frac{ACC_j - 0.2}{0.6} & 0.2 < ACC_j \leq 0.5 \\ 0.5 + \frac{ACC_j - 0.5}{0.6} & 0.5 < ACC_j \leq 0.8 \\ 1 & ACC_j > 0.8 \end{cases} \quad (1)$$

Step 4. Given that the explanatory variables embed several items, we transformed the factor loadings obtained in Step 1, after performing the exploratory factor analysis into the membership scores using the 5, 50 and 95% percentiles as thresholds [15]. For the $i$th variable $X_i$, the value of the $j$th observation $x_{i,j}$ is transformed into a membership value $m_{x_{i,j}}$, as follows [59]:

$$m_{x_{i,j}} = \begin{cases} 0 & x_{i,j} \leq X_i^{5th} \\ \frac{x_{i,j} - X_i^{5th}}{2(X_i^{50th} - X_i^{5th})} & X_i^{5th} < x_{i,j} \leq X_i^{50th} \\ 0.5 + \frac{x_{i,j} - X_i^{50th}}{2(X_i^{95th} - X_i^{50th})} & X_i^{50th} < x_{i,j} \leq X_i^{95th} \\ 1 & x_{i,j} \leq X_i^{95th} \end{cases} \quad (2)$$

where $X_i^{kth}$ stands for the $k$th percentile of $X_i$.

Step 5. Run the necessity analysis of the input factors for the acceptance and nonacceptance [14]. The presence or absence of a given input factor is considered as a "necessary condition" to generate the presence or absence of the output variable, if the consistency (cons) > 0.9. Otherwise, the factor must be combined with other factors to obtain a sufficient condition. At this step, we define the consistency that a variable $W_i$ produces the response $Y$, whose $j$th observation is $y_j$ as

$$Cons_{W_i \to Y} = \frac{\sum_j \min\{m_{Y_j}; m_{w_{i,j}}\}}{\sum_j m_{Y_j}} \quad (3)$$

where $W_i$ may symbolize $X_i$ or its negation $\sim X_i$, and consequently, $w_{i,j}$ is its $j$th observation. Similarly, $Y$ could be ACCEPT or its negation ($\sim$ACCEPT). It should be noted that the membership degree in the negated variable $\sim X_i$, of the $j$th observation is $m_{\sim x_{ij}} = 1 - m_{x_{ij}}$. Therefore, for $\sim$ACCEPT, we state $m_{\sim ACC_j} = 1 - m_{ACC_j}$.

Step 6. Find the logical implicates that fit the output results by running the Boolean minimization algorithm in [60] on the truth table. If we symbolize the negation of a variable as "$\sim$", we adjust independently the Boolean functions:

$$ACCEPT = f\,(PE,\ EE,\ SI,\ PR,\ PL,\ AR) \quad (4)$$

$$\sim ACCEPT = f\,(PE,\ EE,\ SI,\ PR,\ PL,\ AR) \quad (5)$$

Thus, (1) explains the acceptance of robots and (2) explains the rejection. It implicates that it come directly from the algorithm [60] to conform to the so-called qualitative comparative analysis complex solution (CS).

Step 7. CS is usually difficult to interpret because it is built with no more assumptions than data. A simplified solution, known as a parsimonious solution (PS), is fitted with [33] and any remainder over a non-observed configuration of variables to make the solution as easy as possible [14].

Step 8. To continue the minimization process, it must be supposed for the non-observed configurations that an input variable contributes to the output exclusively when it is present, absent, or in both cases, by using well-founded hypotheses. This step allowed us to obtain an intermediate solution (IS) [14]. In our study, we use the hypotheses tested to answer RQ1, which are displayed in Section 1.3. Therefore, to implement this step, the PE, EE, SI, PL, and AR (PR) have a positive (negative) influence on ACCEPT.

For an in-depth explanation of Boolean minimization procedures in the CS, PS, and IS, see [61].

Step 9. To measure the explanatory power of a given recipe, its consistency (cons) and coverage (cov) must be determined. Let be a possible prime implicate (configuration or recipe) $Z$, that without a loss of generality, we build up as $Z = W_1 \bullet W_2 \bullet \ldots \bullet W_r$, where $1 \leq r \leq n$, $n$ is the number of input variables in the configuration and "*" stands for the Boolean product. Therefore, we obtain, for the $j$th observation

$$m_{Z_j} = min\{m_{w_{1,j}}; m_{w_{2,j}}; \ldots; m_{w_{r,j}}\} \qquad (6)$$

The consistency of recipe $Z$ in producing output $Y$ (ACCEPT or ~ACCEPT) is

$$Cons_{Z \to Y} = \frac{\sum_j min\{m_{Z_j}; m_{Y_j}\}}{\sum_j m_{Z_j}} \qquad (7)$$

The coverage of recipe $Z$ to produce $Y$ is:

$$Cov_{Z \to Y} = \frac{\sum_j min\{m_{Z_j}; m_{Y_j}\}}{\sum_j m_{Y_j}} \qquad (8)$$

The consistency measures the membership degree of a combination of causes (recipe) within the outcome set. This was similar to the statistical measure of significance [62]. There is a wide consensus that, to consider an essential prime implicated as a sufficient condition, cons > 0.75 (or better cons > 0.8). The coverage measures the proportion of outcomes explained by a recipe; that is, it is a measure of empirical relevance similar to $R^2$ [62].

Step 10. To assess the impact of the input variables and their combinations on the acceptance and rejection of robot-assisted surgery, the solutions from the fsQCA must be interpreted. There is no unified point of view regarding which solution (CS, PS, or IS) should be taken into account. CS uses only empirical data; however, the recipes in this solution are often difficult to interpret. In this regard, [13] proposed combining both the IS and PS to state the core (from the PS) and peripheral (present only in the IS) conditions.

## 3. Results

When validating the scales (Table 2), we observed for all the constructs, that while Cronbach's alpha and composite reliability were > 0.7, the average variance extracted was >0.5. Table 2 also shows that in all dimensions, the exploratory factor analysis extracted a significant proportion of the variance in the first factor, since the loadings were >0.7. Thus, we provide robust evidence for the internal consistency of all explanatory constructs.

Table 2. Results of the factor analysis and the scale validation measures.

|  | Factor Loading | Cronbach's Alfa | Composite Reliability | Average Variance Extracted |
|---|---|---|---|---|
| Performance Expectancy |  | 0.941 | 0.957 | 0.849 |
| PE1 | 0.938 |  |  |  |
| PE2 | 0.922 |  |  |  |
| PE3 | 0.934 |  |  |  |
| PE4 | 0.891 |  |  |  |
| Effort Expectancy |  | 0.953 | 0.966 | 0.875 |
| EE1 | 0.927 |  |  |  |
| EE2 | 0.933 |  |  |  |
| EE3 | 0.942 |  |  |  |
| EE4 | 0.940 |  |  |  |
| Social Influence |  | 0.926 | 0.953 | 0.871 |
| SI1 | 0.927 |  |  |  |
| SI2 | 0.945 |  |  |  |
| SI3 | 0.927 |  |  |  |
| Perceived Risk |  | 0.873 | 0.922 | 0.798 |
| PR1 | 0.895 |  |  |  |
| PR2 | 0.885 |  |  |  |
| PR3 | 0.900 |  |  |  |
| Pleasure |  | 0.821 | 0.918 | 0.849 |
| PL1 | 0.921 |  |  |  |
| PL2 | 0.921 |  |  |  |
| Arousal |  | 0.875 | 0.941 | 0.889 |
| AR1 | 0.943 |  |  |  |
| AR2 | 0.943 |  |  |  |

Table 3 presents the results of the regression. The ORL model is significant (pseudo $R^2$ = 23.44%, LR statistic = 402.94, $p < 0.001$). Regarding the explanatory variables, as we expected, we adjusted a positive significant sign for the PE ($p < 0.001$), EE ($p < 0.001$), SI ($p = 0.022$), and PL ($p = 0.005$); therefore, H1.1, H1.2, H1.3, and H1.5 are accepted. For the perceived risk, we also found a negative marginal effect ($p = 0.001$); therefore, H1.4 was also accepted. However, arousal was not found to be significant ($p = 0.9268$); thus, H1.6 was rejected.

Table 3. Results of the ordered logistic regression on intention.

| Variable | Marginal Effect | z-Statistic | p-Value |
|---|---|---|---|
| PE | 0.653 | 5.792 | <0.001 |
| EE | 0.519 | 5.879 | <0.001 |
| SI | 0.245 | 2.297 | 0.0216 |
| PR | −0.243 | −3.889 | 0.0001 |
| PL | 0.246 | 2.816 | 0.005 |
| AR | −0.008 | −0.091 | 0.927 |
| pseudo-$R^2$ | 23.90% |  |  |
| LR-statistic | 402.94 ($p < 0.0001$) |  |  |

Table 4 presents the results of the necessity analysis. With the exception of the PR, the presence of income variables reaches a greater consistency than their negation to explain the acceptance, and the negation of these factors attains a greater consistency than their presence to explain the resistance. With regard to the PR, we observed the opposite result. Therefore, these findings are in accordance with the expected sign of the relationship between variables in H1.1-H1.6. The necessity analysis also revealed that there is no variable whose unique presence/absence is a necessary condition to produce acceptance/resistance, since always cons < 0.9. This fact reinforces the need for further configurational study [13].

Table 4. Necessity analysis of the income variables on ACCEPT and ~ACCEPT.

| | ACCEPT | | | ~ACCEPT | |
|---|---|---|---|---|---|
| Input | Consistency | Coverage | | Consistency | Coverage |
| PE | 0.78 | 0.81 | PE | 0.45 | 0.43 |
| ~PE | 0.41 | 0.43 | ~PE | 0.82 | 0.80 |
| EE | 0.80 | 0.76 | EE | 0.45 | 0.39 |
| ~EE | 0.41 | 0.48 | ~EE | 0.79 | 0.82 |
| SI | 0.78 | 0.76 | SI | 0.47 | 0.41 |
| ~SI | 0.43 | 0.48 | ~SI | 0.79 | 0.81 |
| PR | 0.54 | 0.59 | PR | 0.66 | 0.65 |
| ~PR | 0.62 | 0.63 | ~PR | 0.60 | 0.55 |
| PL | 0.73 | 0.75 | PL | 0.49 | 0.45 |
| ~PL | 0.44 | 0.48 | ~PL | 0.77 | 0.75 |
| AR | 0.73 | 0.74 | AR | 0.50 | 0.46 |
| ~AR | 0.45 | 0.49 | ~AR | 0.76 | 0.75 |

Tables 5 and 6 show the IS results of the fsQCA for ACCEPT and ~ACCEPT. We can check:

1. The consistency and coverage of the IS in ACCEPT and ~ACCEPT are similar and adequate since cons > 0.8 and cov > 0.7 in both cases. Thus, the configurational analysis explains the acceptance and rejection of surgical robots.
2. In the explanatory recipes of ACCEPT, the variables of the PE, EE, SI, PL, and AR were affirmed. Moreover, the PR is negated, as expected, in three recipes; however, it is present within two prime implicates. Therefore, H2.1, is accepted for all explanatory factors, except for the perceived risk. In the configurations explaining ~ACCEPT, the input constructs the PE, EE, SI, PL, and AR always appear negated and the PR affirmed. Therefore, these findings are consistent with H2.2.
3. In Table 5, we can see that the most relevant conditions to explain ACCEPT are the EE, as it is a core variable in six configurations, and the PR, given that it is a core variable in five prime implicates. However, the sign of the influence of the PR is not univocal. However, the performance expectancy seems to be the least relevant factor because its presence is a core condition in only two configurations. The variables of the SI, AR, and PL have an intermediate importance, because they are the core conditions in the three recipes.
4. Table 6 shows that the absence of the PE and the presence of the PR are the most relevant conditions to explain rejection. They come in four prime implicates as the core conditions. The absence of the EE and SI (PL) is the core condition in three (two) recipes, that is, these three variables seem to be less important in explaining a resistance toward SRs than the PE and PR. Finally, arousal is negated in the two recipes but as a peripheral condition. Thus, AR does not seem to be relevant in explaining ~ACCEPT.
5. From the comparison of the configurations in Tables 5 and 6 and our comments in the above paragraph about the most/least relevant variables inducing ACCEPT and ~ACCEPT, we can conclude that there is a clear asymmetry of the effects of the input variables to produce acceptance and to induce rejection. Therefore, H2.3 is accepted.

**Table 5.** fsQCA intermediate solution (IS) ACCEPT = f (PE, EE, SI, PR, PL, AR).

| Recipe | 1 | 2 | 3 | 4 | 5 | 6 | 7 |
|---|---|---|---|---|---|---|---|
| PE | ● |  | ● | ● |  | ● |  |
| EE | ● | ● |  | ● | ● | ● | ● |
| SI | ● | ● | ● |  |  |  | ● |
| PR |  |  | ⊗ | ⊗ | ⊗ | ● | ● |
| PL |  | ● |  | ● | ● | ● | ● |
| AR |  | ● |  | ● | ● |  |  |
| cons | 0.862 | 0.871 | 0.845 | 0.858 | 0.850 | 0.851 | 0.853 |
| cov | 0.656 | 0.607 | 0.457 | 0.457 | 0.429 | 0.488 | 0.479 |
| Cons of IS | 0.829 | | | | | | |
| Cov of IS | 0.739 | | | | | | |

Note: The big circle (●) indicates the presence of a condition, and circles with x (⊗) indicate its absence. Large circle is for the core conditions, small circles are for the peripheral condition and a blank space, is for the "don't care" condition.

**Table 6.** fsQCA intermediate solution ~ACCEPT = f (PE, EE, SI, PR, PL, AR).

| Recipe | 1 | 2 | 3 | 4 | 5 |
|---|---|---|---|---|---|
| PE | ⊗ | ⊗ | ⊗ |  | ⊗ |
| EE |  |  | ⊗ | ⊗ | ⊗ |
| SI | ⊗ | ⊗ | ⊗ | ⊗ | ● |
| PR |  | ● | ● | ● |  |
| PL | ⊗ | ⊗ |  | ⊗ | ⊗ |
| AR |  |  |  | ⊗ | ⊗ |
| cons | 0.880 | 0.874 | 0.876 | 0.872 | 0.882 |
| cov | 0.624 | 0.496 | 0.517 | 0.473 | 0.469 |
| Cons of IS | 0.855 | | | | |
| Cov of IS | 0.704 | | | | |

Note: The big circle (●) indicates the presence of a condition, and circles with x (⊗) indicate its absence. Large circle is for the core conditions, the small circles for the peripheral condition and blank space, for the "don't care" condition.

## 4. Discussion

This paper shows the results of a study about the public/potential patients' perception of robotic-assisted surgery within the Jordan university community. Therefore, our study is in line [4,7,12]. that assess the public's point of view on surgical robots and also close to [54–56], that studied several issues linked to people's attitude toward robotic services in a non-educational setting, within a university context. The survey contained a link to an article in Newsweek magazine on robotic-assisted surgery and, likewise, the target population had a high cultural status. Therefore it is expected that many respondents were aware of the existence of SRs and had some elementary information on the topic. Likewise, one of the authors of the article gave informational assistance to respondents. For example, if it were demanded, in-depth information about SRs [2,3] were provided. It is expected that if any person did not feel that they were aware enough to give an opinion as "public", and also had no motivation to obtain information about it, simply did not answer the survey. In this regard, the response rate of our sample was 40%.

The explanation capability of the ordered logistic regression (OLR) was high, since McFaddens' $R^2 > 20\%$, which in a logistic regression setting could be considered excellent [63]. The results of the OLR showed a significant positive relationship between the performance expectancy (PE), easiness expectation (EE), social influence (SI), and pleasure (PL) with the acceptance of robotic-assisted surgery, if needed (ACCEPT). Similarly, the perceived risk (PR) displays a negative and significant relationship with ACCEPT. However, the results did not show a significant effect on arousal (AR). The values of the coefficients suggest that the PE and EE have the greatest impact on ACCEPT, while the SI, PR, and PL display a similar importance. Therefore, hypotheses H1.1–H1.5 are accepted but H1.6 is rejected.

The fsQCA models fitted for ACCEPT and ~ACCEPT presented satisfactory adjustment measures (cons > 0.8 and cov > 0.7). Even though in all recipes, the sign of the input variables to explain the resistance to SRs is as we expected, this does not follow when fitting ACCEPT. As we expected, the PE, EE, SI, PL and AR are present in the prime implicates, but the PR is present in some recipes and negated in others. These findings lead us to reject H2.1, and accept H2.2. The EE and PR (PE) were the least relevant variables to explain ACCEPT. When fitting ~ACCEPT, the PR and PE (AR) appear to be the most (least) decisive explanatory factors. This suggests that the impact of the input variables on ACCEPT and ~ACCEPT are not mirror opposites, and thus hypothesis H2.3 is not rejected. This is in accordance with the fact that the explanation of the acceptance and resistance of any disruptive technology is not symmetrical [64].

Whereas the results of the OLR quantified the average impact of every variable on the intention to undergo surgical intervention, by means of its marginal effect, the fsQCA displayed how these factors interact to produce acceptance and non-acceptance. Both instruments provided complementary information. Thus, the marginal effects fitted with the OLR indicated that the variables with the greatest impact attitude toward SRs were the PE and EE. The use of the fsQCA allowed us to observe that both variables impacted with the expected sign in both acceptance and resistance to SRs. However, to induce acceptance, the EE, which participated in six of the seven recipes, had a greater influence than the PE, which only participated in two configurations as a core condition. Moreover, when explaining resistance, we found that the absence of the perceived performance was more relevant than the absence of the easiness expectation. While the PE participates as a core condition negated in four out of five recipes, the EE does so in three prime implicates.

The marginal effects fitted for the SI, PR, and PL indicate that the average impact of these variables on acceptance is similar. Moreover, the use of the fsQCA allows us to discover how the impact of social influence and pleasure on attitude and resistance differs from that of the perceived risk. The SI and PL are present (absent) in all primer implicates, in which these constructs are conditions that explain acceptance (rejection). Therefore, the SI and PL have approximately symmetrical effects on the willingness and resistance. With regard to the perceived risk, we can observe that it is negated in three configurations and present in two prime implicates explaining ACCEPT; that is, the net effect of the PR on the favorable attitude toward SRs could be null. Moreover, the PR was present in four of the five configurations, explaining the resistance. Therefore, the negative marginal effect of the impact of the PR on attitudes toward SRs is strictly due to the strong influence of the perceived risk on rejecting robotic surgery. Therefore, the influence of the PR on ACCEPT and ~ACCEPT is clearly asymmetrical.

With the ORL, we have fitted a positive but not significant effect of the AR on attitude toward robotic surgery. Moreover, the use of the fsQCA has shown that the AR has some influence in the attitude toward SRs. In spite of it not being a key variable to explain ACCEPT and ~ACCEPT, its presence is a core condition in three explanatory recipes of acceptance and only a peripheral variable inducing resistance.

We confirmed that the UTAUT variables (PE, EE, and SI) have a significant positive impact on the willingness to use SRs. This finding is in accordance with an important part of the literature on the users' attitudes toward robots and wearable technologies in healthcare services [31–34], concerning social robots [28,35,46,50] and surgical robots [6,8,12]. However, it must be noted that there are several empirical analyses that did not find significant differences in the PE, EE, and/or SI to explain the attitudes in fields, such as healthcare technology acceptance [27,30] and social robots [48].

The perceived risk has a positive impact on the rejection of being operated on by an SR. This finding coincides with that of [7,8,12], who found a relevant negative relation between the PR and the behavioral intention to use SRs. This is also coincident with studies that outline a positive significant link between trust and robot acceptance [28,46,48].

Regarding emotional variables, the fsQCA shows that these factors have a significant relationship with acceptance and rejection of SRs. These results are in accordance with [42,47,48,50].

## 5. Conclusions

To the best of our knowledge, a combinatorial analysis of the variables that induce the acceptance of robot services (in our case, surgical interventions) has not been performed before. In this regard, this study shows that the fsQCA not only helps to understand how input variables influence acceptance and rejection of robotic-assisted surgery, but also allows the evaluation of the usual asymmetrical impact of the factors inducing acceptance and rejection of a new technology.

On the one hand, with regression, we have measured the mean effect of every variable on the intention to use, if needed, robotic-assisted surgery. On the other, the fsQCA displayed that each factor may influence acceptance and non-acceptance attitudes in different ways. So, social influence and pleasure are significant from a statistical point of view and also seem to impact symmetrically on acceptance and resistance attitudes toward SRs. Moreover, the performance expectancy and easiness expectation, that also display significant marginal effects, influence with asymmetric strength, the acceptance and non-acceptance. So, whereas the EE provides its greatest influence on ACCEPT, the strongest impact of the PE comes when this variable is absent contributing to ~ACCEPT. It must be also remarked that in both cases, the influence of the PE and EE on ACCEPT and ~ACCEPT is congruent with the positive marginal effect fitted for both constructs, since the PE and EE always need to be present to produce acceptance and negated to induce resistance.

The way how the perceived risks contribute to ACCEPT and ~ACCEPT is also different to that of the PE, EE, SI and PL. The PR has a significant negative marginal effect in the OLR and impacts asymmetrically on ACCEPT and ~ACCEPT. So, its presence is a key factor to explain the resistance and therefore, this finding is congruent with its negative marginal effect, fitted with the OLR. Moreover, the PR is not a defined sign to induce ACCEPT, since in some recipes it comes affirmed and in others, negated. Notice that the behavior is not coherent with a significant negative impact on attitudes toward SRs.

Our theoretical approach, which combines the UTAUT variables with the perceived risk and emotional variables, has been useful in explaining attitudes toward SRs. While MacFaddens' $R^2$ in OLR shows a good explanation capability of this correlational method; the consistency and coverage of the solutions of the fsQCA for ACCEPT and ~ACCEPT display a good adherence of the configurations to the data. Likewise, note that with the exception of one configuration of ACCEPT, which exclusively presents the three UTAUT constructs, all prime implicates explaining acceptance and resistance need to combine the UTAUT factors with the perceived risk and/or emotional variables.

Our findings have implications for the management and health policies. The combination of correlational and configurational analyses is a powerful instrument for analyzing available data to make decisions. While results from the OLR inform about the overall strength of each variable to explain attitudes toward SRs, the fsQCA discovers profiles of potential users and potential rejecters. Whereas effort expectancy seems to be the key variable to explain acceptance, the lack of a perceived utility and the presence of the perceived risk are of special relevance to explain the resistance toward SRs. Therefore, the successful implantation of any new type of SR needs to show a superior performance and is less risky than more traditional surgery techniques, such as endoscopy or laparoscopy.

Note that in the profiles linked to acceptance, there are two configurations (the sixth and seventh) where the perceived risk is affirmed. Hospital managers must be careful with this information because they do not necessarily imply that these profiles come from risk seekers. Surely, people perceive that the potential advantages of robotic surgery coming from the PE, EE, SI, and PL compensate for the perceived risk.

This study has some limitations of this empirical research. This study was conducted in a single country (Jordan). The research sample was from a university environment where students, professors, and administrative workers participated in the survey, and cultural differences, because of the educational and the social class statuses, may influence potential patients' attitudes toward SRs. Likewise, country cultural stratum is also a relevant variable to explain attitudes toward robots. Therefore, the results obtained in this study could be extrapolated, at least partially, to potential patients from countries of the same geographical area and with a similar culture, such as Turkey, Lebanon, or Kuwait, and similar social groups, but not to countries with different cultures and/or people of lower educational status. Thus, further research that broadens the number of countries and their social or cultural status is required.

Moreover, we analyzed a cross-sectional survey; therefore, our results cannot be generalized in the long run. This issue is relevant because, as mentioned in the introduction, robotic surgery is an active and dynamic field. It could be of interest to carry out a longitudinal study to understand how perceptions of SRs evolve along with their improvement.

**Author Contributions:** Conceptualization, A.A.A.; methodology, J.d.A.-S.; validation, A.A.A., M.A.-O. and J.P.-B.; formal analysis, J.d.A.-S. and A.A.A.; investigation, J.d.A.-S.; resources, A.A.A. and M.A.-O.; data curation, A.A.A.; writing—original draft preparation, J.d.A.-S.; writing—review and editing, A.A.A.; visualization, J.d.A.-S.; supervision J.P.-B.; funding acquisition, M.A.-O. All authors have read and agreed to the published version of the manuscript.

**Funding:** This research was supported by Telefonica and its Telefonica Chair on Smart Cities of the Universitat Rovira i Virgili and Universitat de Barcelona (project number 42. DB.00.18.00).

**Institutional Review Board Statement:** Concerning the ethics approval: (1) all participants were given detailed written information about the study and its procedures; (2) no data directly or indirectly related to the subjects' health were collected, and thus, the Declaration of Helsinki was not generally mentioned when the subjects were informed; (3) the anonymity of the collected data was ensured at all times; (4) no permission was obtained from a board and no approval was obtained from an ethics committee's; it was not required, as the per applicable institutional and national guidelines and regulations; (5) voluntary completion of the questionnaire was taken as consent for the data to be used in research, and informed consent of the participants was implied through survey completion.

**Informed Consent Statement:** Informed consent was obtained from all the subjects. Have been done so.

**Data Availability Statement:** Data is available upon request to any of the authors.

**Acknowledgments:** Authors acknowledge the comments of three anonymous referees that have allow improvements on the paper.

**Conflicts of Interest:** The authors declare no conflict of interest.

## References

1. Chen, R.; Rodrigues-Armijo, P.; Krause, C.; Siu, K.-C.; Oleynikov, D. A comprehensive review of robotic surgery curriculum and training for residents, fellows, and postgraduate surgical education. *Surg. Endosc.* **2020**, *34*, 361–367. [CrossRef] [PubMed]
2. Ashrafian, H.; Clancy, O.; Grover, V.; Darzi, A. The evolution of robotic surgery: Surgical and anaesthetic aspects. *Br. J. Anaesth.* **2017**, *119*, i72–i84. [CrossRef] [PubMed]
3. Martinello, N.; Loshak, H. *Experiences with and Expectations of Robotic Surgical Systems: A Rapid Qualitative Review*; Canadian Agency for Drugs and Technologies in Health: Ottawa, ON, Canada, 2020. Available online: https://www.ncbi.nlm.nih.gov/books/NBK562938 (accessed on 13 July 2022).
4. Boys, J.A.; Alicuben, E.T.; DeMeester, M.J.; Worrell, S.G.; Oh, D.S.; Hagen, J.A.; DeMeester, S.R. Public perceptions on robotic surgery, hospitals with robots, and surgeons that use them. *Surg. Endosc.* **2016**, *30*, 1310–1316. [CrossRef] [PubMed]
5. Beyaz, S. A brief history of artificial intelligence and robotic surgery in orthopedics & traumatology and future expectations. *Jt. Dis. Relat. Surg.* **2020**, *31*, 653. [CrossRef] [PubMed]
6. Jank, B.J.; Haas, M.; Riss, D.; Baumgartner, W.-D. Affiliations expand. Acceptance of patients towards task-autonomous robotic cochlear implantation: An exploratory study. *Int. J. Med. Robot. Comp. Assist. Surg.* **2021**, *17*, 1–6. [CrossRef]
7. Muaddi, H.; Zhao, X.; Leonardelli, G.J.; de Mestral, C.; Nathens, A.; Stukel, T.A.; Guttman, M.P.; Karanicolas, P.J. Fear of innovation: Public's perception of robotic surgery. *Surg. Endosc.* **2022**, *36*, 6076–6083. [CrossRef]

8. Ammer, E.; Mandt, L.S.; Silberdorff, I.C.; Kahl, F.; Hagmayer, Y. Robotic Anxiety—Parents' Perception of Robot-Assisted Pediatric Surgery. *Children* **2022**, *9*, 399. [CrossRef]
9. Venkatesh, V.; Morris, M.G.; Davis, G.B.; Davis, F.B. User Acceptance of Information Technology: Toward a Unified View. *MIS Quart.* **2003**, *27*, 425–478. [CrossRef]
10. Krishnan, G.; Mintz, J.; Foreman, A.; Hodge, J.C.; Krishnan, S. The acceptance and adoption of transoral robotic surgery in Australia and New Zealand. *J. Robot. Surg.* **2019**, *13*, 301–307. [CrossRef]
11. BenMessaoud, C.; Kharrazi, H.; MacDorman, K.F. Facilitators and barriers to adopting robotic-assisted surgery: Contextualizing the unified theory of acceptance and use of technology. *PLoS ONE* **2011**, *6*, e16395. [CrossRef]
12. Torrent-Sellens, J.; Jiménez-Zarco, A.I.; Saigí-Rubió, F. Do People Trust in Robot-Assisted Surgery? Evidence from Europe. *Int. J. Environ. Res. Public Health* **2021**, *18*, 12519. [CrossRef]
13. Pappas, I.O.; Woodside, A.G. Fuzzy-set Qualitative Comparative Analysis (fsQCA): Guidelines for research practice in Information Systems and marketing. *Int. J. Inf. Manag.* **2021**, *58*, 102310. [CrossRef]
14. Ragin, C. *Redesigning Social Inquiry: Fuzzy Sets and Beyond*, 1st ed.; Chicago University Press: Chicago, IL, USA, 2008.
15. Andrés-Sánchez, J.; Arias-Oliva, M.; Pelegrín-Borondo, J.; Almahameed, A.A.M. The influence of ethical judgements on acceptance and non-acceptance of wearables and insideables: Fuzzy set qualitative comparative analysis. *Technol. Soc.* **2021**, *67*, 101689. [CrossRef]
16. Arias-Oliva, M.; de Andrés-Sánchez, J.; Pelegrín-Borondo, J. Fuzzy Set Qualitative Comparative Analysis of Factors Influencing the Use of Cryptocurrencies in Spanish Households. *Mathematics* **2021**, *9*, 324. [CrossRef]
17. Pappas, I.O.; Giannakos, M.N.; Sampson, D.G. Fuzzy set analysis as a means to understand users of 21st-century learning systems: The case of mobile learning and reflections on learning analytics research. *Comput. Hum. Behav.* **2019**, *92*, 646–659. [CrossRef]
18. Zhang, J.; Long, J.; von Schaewen, A.M.E. How Does Digital Transformation Improve Organizational Resilience?—Findings from PLS-SEM and fsQCA. *Sustainability* **2021**, *13*, 11487. [CrossRef]
19. Muñoz-Pascual, L.; Curado, C.; Galende, J. Fuzzy Set Qualitative Comparative Analysis on the Adoption of Environmental Practices: Exploring Technological- and Human-Resource-Based Contributions. *Mathematics* **2021**, *9*, 1553. [CrossRef]
20. Porcuna-Enguix, L.; Bustos-Contell, E.; Serrano-Madrid, J.; Labatut-Serer, G. Constructing the Audit Risk Assessment by the Audit Team Leader When Planning: Using Fuzzy Theory. *Mathematics* **2021**, *9*, 3065. [CrossRef]
21. Castelló-Sirvent, F.; Pinazo-Dallenbach, P. Corruption Shock in Mexico: fsQCA Analysis of Entrepreneurial Intention in University Students. *Mathematics* **2021**, *9*, 1702. [CrossRef]
22. Ragin, C.C. Using qualitative comparative analysis to study causal complexity. *Health Serv. Res.* **1999**, *34*, 1225–1239.
23. Andres-Sanchez, J.; Belzunegui-Eraso, A. Explaining Cannabis Use by Adolescents: A Comparative Assessment of Fuzzy Set Qualitative Comparative Analysis and Ordered Logistic Regression. *Healthcare* **2022**, *10*, 669. [CrossRef] [PubMed]
24. Lee, S.S.-Y. Using fuzzy-set qualitative comparative analysis. *Epidemiol. Health* **2014**, *36*, e2014038. [CrossRef]
25. Davis, F.D. Perceived usefulness, perceived ease of use, and user acceptance of information technology. *MIS Quart.* **1989**, *13*, 319–340. [CrossRef]
26. Venkatesh, V.; Thong, J.Y.L.; Xu, X. Consumer Acceptance and Use of Information Technology: Extending the Unified Theory of Acceptance and Use of Technology. *MIS Quart.* **2012**, *36*, 157–178. [CrossRef]
27. Chow, M.; Chan, L.; Lo, B.; Chu, W.P.; Chan, T.; Lai, Y.M. Exploring the Intention to Use a Clinical Imaging Portal for Enhancing Healthcare Education. *Nurs. Educ. Today* **2013**, *33*, 655–662. [CrossRef]
28. Alaiad, A.; Zhou, L. The Determinants of Home Healthcare Robots Adoption: An Empirical Investigation. *Int. J. Med. Inform.* **2014**, *83*, 825–840. [CrossRef]
29. Abdekhoda, M.; Dehnad, A.; Zarei, J. Determinant factors in applying electronic medical records in healthcare. *East Mediterr. Health J.* **2019**, *25*, 24–33. [CrossRef]
30. Hossain, A.; Quaresma, R.; Rahman, H. Investigating Factors Influencing the Physicians' Adoption of Electronic Health Record (EHR) in Healthcare System of Bangladesh: An Empirical Study. *Int. J. Inform. Manag.* **2019**, *44*, 76–87. [CrossRef]
31. Sun, Y.; Wang, N.; Guo, X.; Peng, Z. Understanding the Acceptance of Mobile Health Services: A Comparison and integration of alternative models. *J. Electron. Commer. Res.* **2013**, *14*, 183–200.
32. Chang, M.Y.; Pang, C.; Michael-Tarn, J.; Liu, T.S.; Yen, D.C. Exploring User Acceptance of an E-hospital Service: An Empirical Study in Taiwan. *Comp. Stand. Inter.* **2015**, *38*, 35–43. [CrossRef]
33. Chu, X.; Lei, R.; Liu, T.; Li, L.; Yang, C.; Feng, Y. An Empirical Study on the Intention to Use Online Medical Service. In Proceedings of the 15th International Conference on Service Systems and Service Management (Icsssm), Hangzhou, China, 21–22 July 2018; pp. 1–7. [CrossRef]
34. Talukder, M.S.; Chiong, R.; Bao, Y.; Malik, B.H. Acceptance and Use Predictors of Fitness Wearable Technology and Intention to Recommend: An Empirical Study. *Ind. Manag. Data Syst.* **2019**, *119*, 170–188. [CrossRef]
35. Heerink, M.; Kröse, B.; Evers, V.; Wielinga, B. Assessing Acceptance of Assistive Social Agent Technology by Older Adults: The Almere Model. *Int. J. Soc. Robot.* **2010**, *2*, 361–375. [CrossRef]
36. Graaf, M.M.; Allouch, S.B.; Klamer, T. Sharing a life with Harvey: Exploring the acceptance of and relationship-building with a social robot. *Comput. Hum. Behav.* **2015**, *43*, 1–14. [CrossRef]
37. Chi, O.; Denton, G.; Gursoy, D. Artificially intelligent device use in service delivery: A systematic review, synthesis, and research agenda. *J. Hosp. Market Manag.* **2020**, *29*, 757–786. [CrossRef]

38. Milner, M.N.; Anania, E.C.; Candelaria-Oquendo, K.; Rice, S.; Winter, S.R.; Ragbir, N.K. Patient perceptions of new robotic technologies in clinical restorative dentistry. *J. Med. Syst.* **2020**, *44*, 33. [CrossRef]
39. Sætra, H.S. The foundations of a policy for the use of social robots in care. *Technol. Soc.* **2020**, *63*, 101383. [CrossRef]
40. Tan, S.Y.; Taeihagh, A.; Tripathi, A. Tensions and antagonistic interactions of risks and ethics of using robotics and autonomous systems in long-term care. *Technol. Forecast. Soc. Chang.* **2021**, *167*, 120686. [CrossRef]
41. Wirtz, J.; Patterson, P.G.; Kunz, W.H.; Gruber, T.; Lu, V.N.; Paluch, S.; Martins, A. Brave New World: Service Robots in the Frontline. *J. Serv. Manag.* **2018**, *29*, 907–931. [CrossRef]
42. McDermott, H.; Choudhury, N.; Lewin-Runacres, M.; Aemn, I.; Moss, E. Gender differences in understanding and acceptance of robot-assisted surgery. *J. Robot. Surg.* **2020**, *14*, 227–232. [CrossRef]
43. Yang, H.; Yu, J.; Zo, H.; Choi, M. User Acceptance of Wearable Devices: An Extended Perspective of Perceived Value. *Telemat. Inform.* **2016**, *33*, 256–269. [CrossRef]
44. Murata, K.; Arias-Oliva, M.; Pelegrín-Borondo, J. Cross-cultural study about cyborg market acceptance: Japan versus Spain. *Eur. Res. Manag. Bus. Econ.* **2019**, *25*, 129–137. [CrossRef]
45. Raigoso, D.; Céspedes, N.; Cifuentes, C.A.; del Alma, A.J.; Múnera, M. Survey on Socially Assistive Robotics: Clinicians' and Patients' Perception of a Social Robot within Gait Rehabilitation Therapies. *Brain Sci.* **2021**, *11*, 738. [CrossRef] [PubMed]
46. Han, J.; Conti, D. The Use of UTAUT and Post Acceptance Models to Investigate the Attitude towards a Telepresence Robot in an Educational Setting. *Robotics* **2020**, *9*, 34. [CrossRef]
47. Graaf, M.M.A.; Allouch, S.B.; van Dijk, J.A.G.M. Why Would I Use This in My Home? A Model of Domestic Social Robot Acceptance. *Hum. Comput. Interact.* **2019**, *34*, 115–173. [CrossRef]
48. Conti, D.; Di Nuovo, S.; Buono, S.; Di Nuovo, A. Robots in Education and Care of Children with Developmental Disabilities: A Study on Acceptance by Experienced and Future Professionals. *Int. J. Soc. Robot.* **2017**, *9*, 51–62. [CrossRef]
49. Damholdt, M.F.; Nørskov, M.; Yamazaki, R.; Hakli, R.; Hansen, C.V.; Vestergaard, C.; Seibt, J. Attitudinal change in elderly citizens toward social robots: The role of personality traits and beliefs about robot functionality. *Front. Psychol.* **2015**, *6*, 1701. [CrossRef]
50. Chen, N. Acceptance of Social Robots by Aging Users: Towards A Pleasure-Oriented View. In *International Conference on Cross-Cultural Design*; Springer: Cham, Switzerland, 2018; pp. 387–397. [CrossRef]
51. Das, G. The Effect of Pleasure and Arousal on Satisfaction and Word-of-Mouth: An Empirical Study of the Indian Banking Sector. *Vikalpa* **2013**, *38*, 95–103. [CrossRef]
52. Reinares-Lara, E.; Olarte-Pascual, C.; Pelegrín-Borondo, J. Do you want to be a cyborg? The moderating effect of ethics on neural implant acceptance. *Comput. Hum. Behav.* **2018**, *85*, 43–53. [CrossRef]
53. Rudovic, O.; Lee, J.; Mascarell-Maricic, L.; Schuller, B.W.; Picard, R.W. Measuring Engagement in Robot-Assisted Autism Therapy: A Cross-Cultural Study. *Front. Robot. AI* **2017**, *4*, 36. [CrossRef]
54. De Graaf, M.M.; Allouch, S.B. Exploring influencing variables for the acceptance of social robots. *Robot. Auton. Syst.* **2013**, *61*, 1476–1486. [CrossRef]
55. Bishop, L.; van Maris, A.; Dogramadzi, S.; Zook, N. Social robots: The influence of human and robot characteristics on acceptance. *Paladyn J. Behav. Robot.* **2019**, *10*, 346–358. [CrossRef]
56. Cormons, L.; Poulet, C.; Pellier, D.; Pesty, S.; Fiorino, H. Testing Social Robot Acceptance. What If You Could Be Assessed for Dementia by a Robot? A Pilot Study. In Proceedings of the 6th International Conference on Mechatronics and Robotics Engineering (ICMRE), IEEE, Barcelona, Spain, 12–15 February 2020; pp. 92–98. [CrossRef]
57. Faqih, K.M.S. An Empirical Analysis of Factors Predicting the Behavioral Intention to Adopt Internet Shopping Technology Among Non-Shoppers in a Developing Country Context: Does Gender Matter? *J. Retail. Cons. Serv.* **2016**, *30*, 140–164. [CrossRef]
58. Mazaheri, E.; Richard, M.O.; Laroche, M. Online consumer behavior: Comparing Canadian and Chinese website visitors. *J. Bus. Res.* **2011**, *64*, 958–965. [CrossRef]
59. Ragin, C. *User's Guide to Fuzzy-Set/Qualitative Comparative Analysis*; Department of Sociology, University of California: Irvine, CA, USA, 2018; Available online: http://www.socsci.uci.edu/~{}cragin/fsQCA/download/fsQCAManual.pdf (accessed on 13 April 2022).
60. McCluskey, E.J. Minimization of Boolean functions. *Bell Syst. Tech. J.* **1956**, *35*, 1417–1444. [CrossRef]
61. Mendel, J.M.; Korjani, M.M. Charles Ragin's fuzzy set qualitative comparative analysis (fsQCA) used for linguistic summarizations. *Inf. Sci.* **2012**, *202*, 1–23. [CrossRef]
62. Thiem, A. Set-relational fit and the formulation of transformational rules in fsQCA. *Compasss WP Ser.* **2010**, *2010*, 61. Available online: http://www.compasss.org/wpseries/Thiem2010.pdf (accessed on 13 April 2022).
63. McFadden, D. *Quantitative Methods for Analyzing Travel Behaviour on Individuals. Some Recent Developments*; Cowles Foundation Discussion Papers 474; Cowles Foundation for Research in Economics, Yale University: New Haven, CT, USA, 1977.
64. Gauttier, S. 'I've got you under my skin'—The role of ethical consideration in the (non-) acceptance of insideables in the workplace. *Technol. Soc.* **2019**, *56*, 93–108. [CrossRef]

 *mathematics*

Article

# Algorithm Applied to SDG13: A Case Study of Ibero-American Countries

Luciano Barcellos-Paula [1,2,*], Anna María Gil-Lafuente [3] and Aline Castro-Rezende [4]

1. Departamento Académico de Posgrado en Negocios, CENTRUM Católica Graduate Business School, Lima 15023, Peru
2. Departamento Académico de Posgrado en Negocios, Pontificia Universidad Católica del Perú, Lima 15088, Peru
3. Department of Business Administration, University of Barcelona, 08034 Barcelona, Spain
4. Faculty of Economics, University of Algarve, 8005-139 Faro, Portugal
* Correspondence: lbarcellosdepaula@pucp.edu.pe

**Abstract:** Scientific studies confirm the existence of a crisis caused by climate change, in which global causes produce local effects. Despite climate agreements, greenhouse gas emissions continue to fall short of targets to limit global warming. There is still a need for comparable data for Sustainable Development Goal (SDG) 13—Climate Action. The motivation of the research is to provide data for decision-making and to propose solutions to address the climate crisis. The article aims to propose a Fuzzy Logic algorithm to evaluate the SDG13 indicators and to deepen the discussion on climate change. The research is applied explanatory with a combined approach (quantitative-qualitative) through modeling, simulation, and case studies. As a result, the OWA operator ranks 10 Ibero-American countries to SDG13, indicating Colombia, Peru, and Cuba in the first positions. The main contributions are the reduction of identified knowledge gaps and proposals for action for policy and decision-makers. A limitation of this study would be the number of participating countries. The authors indicate future lines of research.

**Keywords:** climate change; SDG13; fuzzy logic; OWA operator; Ibero-American countries

**MSC:** 03E75

## 1. Introduction

Climate change is one of the most complex problems we face [1] because its causes and effects are interconnected in various areas, such as economic, social, environmental, political, and health [2]. In addition, it is a dynamic problem marked by increasingly frequent and intense meteorological events [3]. Carbon dioxide ($CO_2$) emissions are the major contributor to global warming [4], and its effects cause sea level rise [5], loss of biodiversity [6], and reduced quality of life [7]. One of the alternative solutions to this problem would be using renewable energy, an effective policy to mitigate global warming in the South Asian region [8].

Approximately 10% of the world's population lives in low-lying coastal regions that may be affected by sea level rise [9], leading to infiltration of seawater into fresh groundwater reserves, degradation of croplands, and accelerated coastal erosion [9]. Research also reveals an increase in concerns about severe heat waves [10], forest fires [11], heavy rains [12], and droughts [13], leading to an increase in casualties [14] and social tensions [15]. In the same direction, research [15] carried out in Sicily, Italy, revealed climatic effects with the constant loss of fertile soil for the agricultural sector and advancing phenomena such as drought and desertification. The same authors warned of the risk of severe socioeconomic consequences for this region shortly [15].

Natural imbalances bring other implications, such as the costs associated with infrastructure destruction [16], floods [3], and reduction of agricultural crop yields [17]. In addition, drought is expected to displace 700 million people by 2030 [18], which may increase social, political, and economic tensions worldwide [19]. The most appropriate measures are to be found in adaptation and mitigation strategies [19], which will generate economic costs. In this direction, it is ratified that proactive adaptation has been less burdensome in life cycle cost than reactive adaptation strategies [16]. Therefore, a crisis caused by climate change is confirmed, in which global causes produce local effects, and we are all affected. The solutions will depend on an urgent effort by all.

As an alternative to solve these problems, the United Nations (UN) launched the 17 Sustainable Development Goals (SDGs) in 2015. These goals seek solutions to significant global environmental, economic and social challenges, designing an agenda for 2030 [20]. SDG13—Climate Action, seeks to adopt urgent measures to address climate change and its effects and is composed of three targets and six specific indicators [21]. Along these lines, this goal has become the primary orientation for countries in this area [20]. Despite the efforts, energy-related $CO_2$ emissions by 2021 increased by 6%, reaching the highest level in history [18]. To avoid the worst consequences of climate change, as stated in the Paris Agreement [22], global greenhouse gas (GHG) emissions should reach zero by 2050. However, GHG emissions will increase by almost 14% by 2030 [18]. Therefore, this research confirms the relevance of SDG13.2.2 (total GHG emissions per year) among the other indicators for minimizing the impacts of global warming [4,22]. However, this relevance needs to be present in the configuration of SDG13 [21] as the indicators have the same weight. A theoretical contribution would be establishing specific weights to the indicators correcting this problem.

The UN [18] acknowledges some progress in data availability for the SDGs, with, for example, SDG3 (health) and SDG7 (energy) having the highest data availability, with more than 80% of countries having at least one data point since 2015. However, despite progress, the need for comparable data for SDG13 persists, as only 20% of countries have data for this target [18]. In this sense, the availability of data on SDG 13 would benefit policymakers in formulating public policies tailored to the reality of each country, and these actions can generate a more significant impact on society. For these reasons, the primary motivation of this article is to provide comparable data on SDG13 and simultaneously propose solutions to address climate change and reduce the first knowledge gap.

On the other hand, studies [20,23] highlight that policy and decision-makers need to understand the correlation between the SDGs, mainly climate change (SDG13), which influences natural resource management (SDG14 and SDG15) and food production (SDG2). Conversely, climate stability (SDG13) and prevention of ocean acidification (SDG14) will support sustainable food production and fisheries (SDG2) [24]. Therefore, the manuscript will seek to moderate this second knowledge gap by broadening the discussion on climate change and its importance among the SDGs, followed by recommendations that positively impact society.

Additionally, researchers [25] have proposed a bounded framework for the planet, identifying a safe operating space for humanity in which climate change and the integrity of the biosphere occupy a central place. However, the framework needs to include how societies should develop. The same authors [25] point out that the human factor should be a priority in public policies concerning climate change. In this sense, this article will advance the frontier of knowledge with proposals to reduce this third identified gap.

Furthermore, this research identified the need to include weightings for the six SDG13 indicators, as each indicator has a different relevance to climate change [4,22]. Including weights would allow a more realistic comparison of SDG13 data and facilitate policymakers in formulating climate strategies and actions. For these reasons, the authors choose Fuzzy Logic [26] as an alternative methodological approach and apply the Ordered Weighted Averaging (OWA) operator [27] to reduce the fourth knowledge gap.

Fuzzy Logic [26] was born to guide decision models that reduce uncertainty and facilitate decision-making [28]. These models have practical applications ranging from consumption to intelligent products [29]. Their effectiveness also responds to new societal needs, such as sustainable development [20], climate change [30], and the COVID-19 pandemic [31]. In the case of the OWA operator, it is a practical algorithm for evaluation and prioritization [32]. It is also flexible in the modeling and simulation process since it is defined by a vector of weights and not by a single parameter [32]. Other researchers claim that this aggregation operator helps merge numerical information and decision-making problems [33]. Scientists applied the OWA operator to facilitate decision-making by public managers in sustainable transport [34]. Another study evaluated companies listed on the Lima Stock Exchange considering the level of compliance with the Principles of Good Corporate Governance [32] and in the decision-making of consumers in the city of Barcelona regarding the selection of groceries by neighborhoods that best suit their needs [35]. Finally, the literature review of this article also showed few publications of the OWA operator applied to climate change, evidencing the fifth knowledge gap and an opportunity for academic contribution. As a drawback, this algorithm depends on the quality of the information received [32], and to overcome this problem, the authors will use data from official sources to perform the calculations. In addition, the results will be validated by three academic specialists from Latin American universities.

This research is applied, explanatory, with a combined approach (quantitative-qualitative) through modeling and simulation, and case studies [36]. As an advantage, the combined method generates added value to the research since the modeling and simulation method is born to understand a real problem and provide solutions [37]. In addition, the case study based on official data is an empirical investigation of a contemporary phenomenon within its actual context [38]. Lastly, the combined research method supports model validation and generates interesting theoretical and practical implications [32]. Figure 1 presents the research classification.

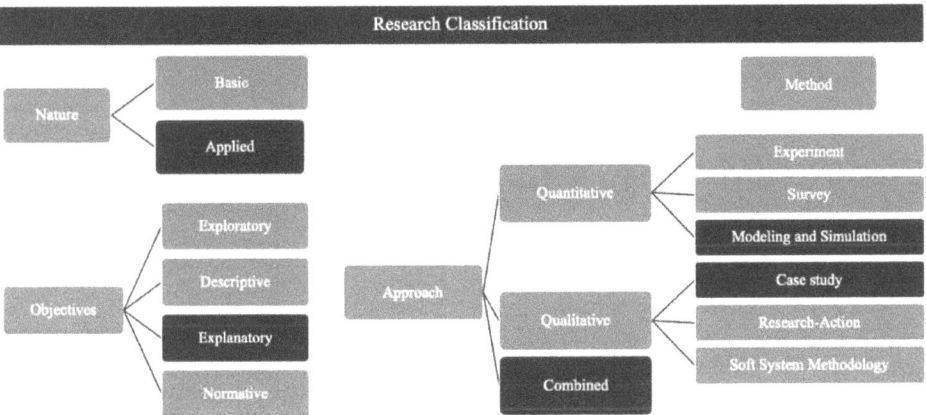

**Figure 1.** Research classification. Source: [36].

In this context, the research aims to propose an algorithm to evaluate SDG13 indicators and to deepen the discussion on climate change. The research is novel because it includes weightings in the SDG13 indicators and evaluates the 10 Ibero-American countries by applying the OWA operator. As was found in the literature review, the OWA operator is the most recommended to meet the research objectives, and this algorithm was little applied to climate change. For these reasons, the research is a scientific novelty for reducing this knowledge gap regarding applying fuzzy logic algorithms to climate change.

The main results reveal a ranking of the countries regarding climate action, with Colombia, Peru, and Cuba in the top positions. As main contributions, at a theoretical level, the research advances the frontier of knowledge on climate change by reducing the five knowledge gaps identified. On a practical level, the study reveals a ranking of 10 Ibero-American countries concerning SDG13 and presents recommendations to policymakers that will positively impact society. A limitation would be the number of countries participating in the study, and future research lines may explore this algorithm's application among other countries. The article is organized as follows. Section 2 explains the materials and methods. Section 3 presents the simulation results applying the OWA operator. Section 4 details a discussion of the results. Finally, Section 5 specifies the conclusions.

## 2. Materials and Methods

The section is organized into six parts to explain the materials and methods of the study. First, a literature review on climate change and OWA operators is presented. Second, the study sample is detailed, followed by the methodology. Next, the variables and measures used, and the data collection process is presented. Finally, the application of the OWA operator to SDG13 in Latin American countries is presented. Figure 2 shows the workflow for conducting scientific research.

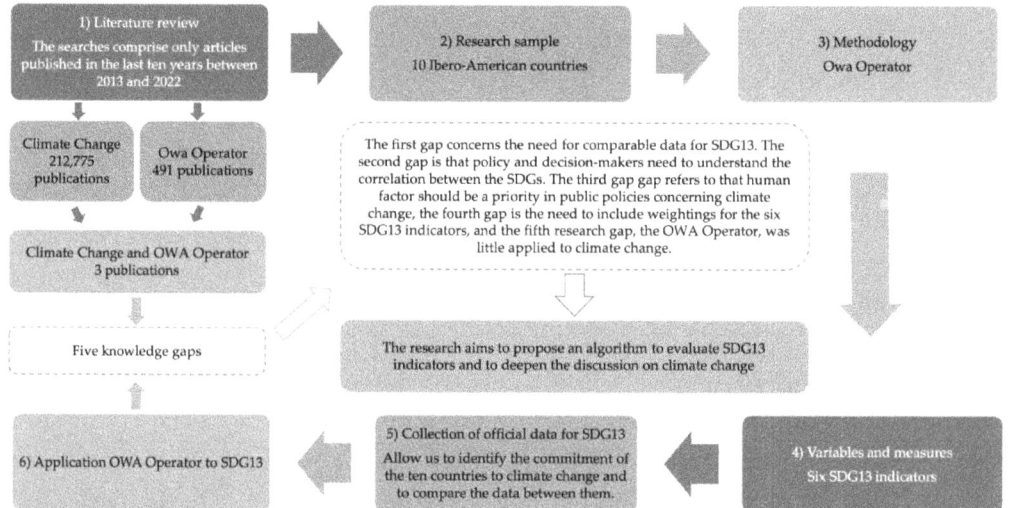

**Figure 2.** Workflow for conducting scientific research. Source: Own elaboration.

### 2.1. Literature Review

The subsection presents the literature review supported by a bibliometric study on Climate Change and OWA operators, and it was conducted on 10 November 2022, through the Web of Science (WoS) database. The searches comprise only articles published in the last ten years between 2013 and 2022, with the keywords "Climate Change", "OWA operator", and the combination between "Climate Change" AND "OWA operator". The results are presented below.

#### 2.1.1. Climate Change

The results show the importance and academic interest in climate change in the last ten years with the number of articles published and citations. Figure 3 shows the distribution of 212,775 publications and 529,686 citations, confirming a positive trend in these two indicators.

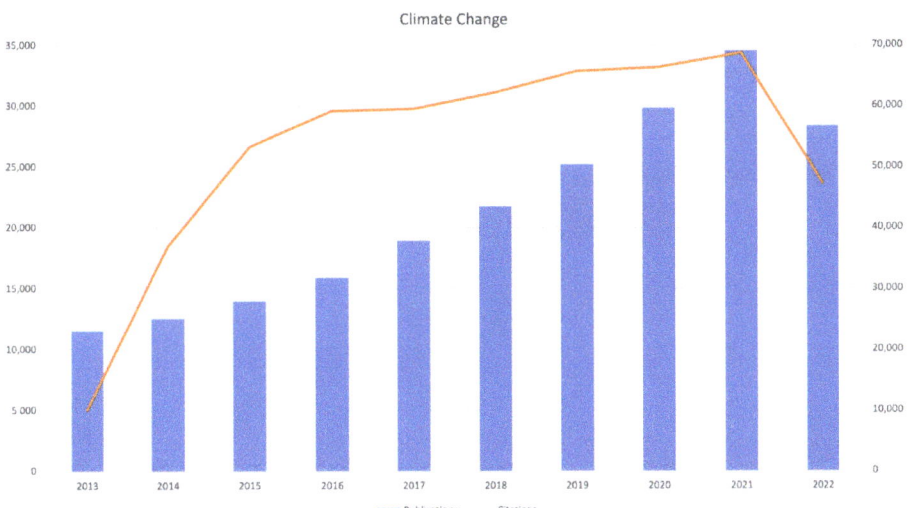

**Figure 3.** Bibliometric study using the keywords "Climate change." Source: WoS (2022).

The main areas of research on climate change are "Environmental Sciences Ecology" in the first instance, with 90,956 published articles. In second place is "Ecology" with 24,760, followed by "Meteorology Atmospheric Sciences" with 24,034 publications. Another bibliometric indicator shows the countries conducting the most research on the subject. In the first position is the USA with 61,941, followed by China with 37,691, and in the third position is England with 21,618 publications. Below is a summary of the three most cited articles on climate change.

First, with 4783 citations, the researchers [25] provide an in-depth analysis of the planetary boundary framework. The results indicate that climate change and biosphere integrity are centrally based on their fundamental importance to the Earth system. These two variables could drive the Earth system to a new state should they be substantially and persistently transgressed. The authors [25] caution that policy decisions must consider human dimensions, including equity. As the main contribution, the research identifies a safe operating space for humanity by establishing a framework of planetary boundaries [25].

Second, with 4480 citations, the authors [39] describe the general configuration of ERA5, which is based on the Integrated Climate Prediction System, which, when completed, will incorporate a detailed record of the global atmosphere, land surface, and ocean waves. The paper also assesses its features and performance, focusing on the publicly available dataset. The results indicate that the higher temporal and spatial resolution allows the detailed evolution of weather systems [39].

Third, with 3045 citations, researchers [40] present systematic analyses of the global disease burden. The results indicate that natural catastrophes claimed thousands of lives in various parts of the world between 2004 and 2015, such as 1870 Hurricane Katrina in the United States in 2005. In 2008, 138,000 by a cyclone in Myanmar, and more than 300 by floods in India in 2015 [40].

In summary, the most cited articles on climate change highlight the limits of the planet [25], the role of policy and decision-makers [25], the improvement in the weather system and climate prediction [39], and the consequences of climate change with deaths caused by natural disasters [40].

Finally, the bibliometric study identified four knowledge gaps in climate change. The first gap concerns the need for comparable data for SDG13 [18]. The second gap is that policy and decision-makers need to understand the correlation between the SDGs [20,23], the third gap refers to that human factor should be a priority in public policies concerning climate change [25], and the fourth gap is the need to include weightings for the six SDG13 indicators [4,22]. In this context, the research is scientifically relevant to reduce the identified gaps and propose solutions to climate change.

2.1.2. OWA Operator

The results of the bibliometric study show academic interest in the OWA operator over the last ten years with the number of articles published and citations. Figure 4 shows the distribution of 491 publications and 8751 citations, which confirms stability in the number of articles published annually and the high number of citations in this period.

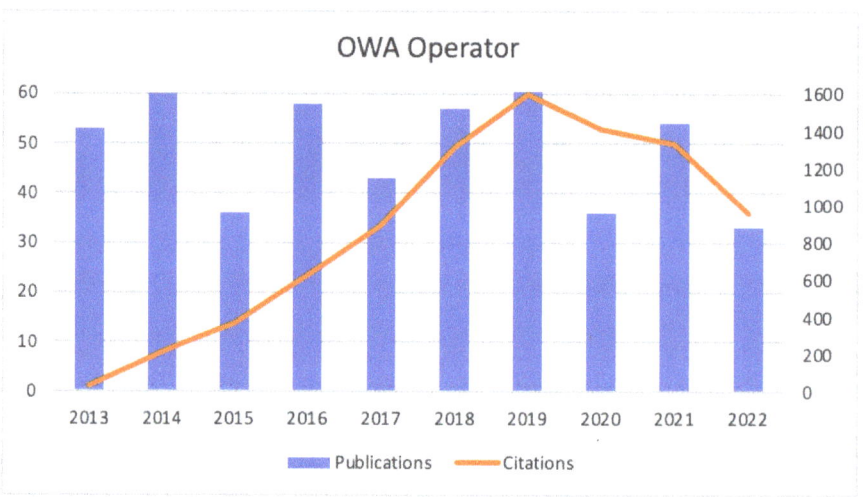

**Figure 4.** Bibliometric study using the keywords "OWA operator." Source: WoS (2022).

The main areas of research on OWA operators are "Computer Science" in the first position with 309 publications, "Engineering" occupies the second position with 100 published articles, and in third place is "Mathematics" with 76 publications. The countries with the most research on OWA operators are China, in first place with 249 published articles, Spain with 78 articles, and Chile, with 48 publications, in third place. Below is a summary of the three most cited articles on OWA operators.

In the first position, with 290 citations, the researchers [41] introduce the Hesitant Fuzzy Linguistic Term Sets (HFLTS) methodology, whose main advantage is facilitating computational processes with words in fuzzy multicriteria decision models. The article also presents a multicriteria decision problem of supplier selection solved with a Technique for Order Preference by Similarity to the Ideal Solution (TOPSIS) model that handles comparative linguistic expressions [41].

In the second position, with 217 citations, the authors [42] develop a method for Pythagorean multicriteria decision-making (MCDM) problems with aggregation operators and distance measures. In addition, the paper introduces a hybrid TOPSIS method for a Pythagorean fuzzy MCDM problem with the proposed operator as the basis. As an advantage, this method reflects the degrees of the attribute's personal information and the decision maker's attitude. It also provides a complete representation of the decision process by considering different scenarios according to their interests [42].

In the third position, with 199 citations, researchers [33] present the 2-tuple induced generalized linguistic generalized 2-tuple OWA (2-TILGOWA) operator. This aggregation operator uses generalized means, order-inducing variables in its argument reordering, and uncertain information evaluated with the 2-tuple linguistic representation model. The article highlights flexibility as the main advantage of this operator since a wide range of specific cases can be included, which allows for considering several different situations and selecting the one that best suits the interests of the decision maker [33].

In summary, the articles on OWA operator show new extensions and applications, such as in word computation processes [41], decision methods considering different scenarios with personal information of the decision maker [42], and finally, method with a qualitative approach based on linguistic evaluations [33].

2.1.3. Climate Change and OWA Operator

The results of the bibliometric study combining the topics "Climate Change" and "OWA operator" indicate only three research. This result shows that there are few studies compared to the searches for the terms separately. A summary of the articles in this combination is presented below.

In the first study, the researchers [43] employed the method to study climate change in some provinces of Iran using data from 15 synoptic stations. The results showed the usefulness of this algorithm, which takes into account the risk attitudes of the decision-maker, and helps environmental managers to cope with climate uncertainties [43]. The OWA operator showed acceptable performance and is recommended by the authors in other climate change studies [43].

In the second research [44] conducted in Spain, the results showed the OWA operator as a robust decision-making tool to assess the performance of future climate projections and to design sustainable policies under uncertainty and risk tolerance [44]. In addition, the methodology made it possible to address stakeholder attitudes and risk preferences regarding actions to be taken and to minimize uncertainties associated with other climate projection methods [44].

In the third study conducted in China, operator OWA measured agricultural carbon emissions in Fujian between 2008 and 2017 [45]. In addition, the present researcher's recommendations to governments to reduce emissions include rational land development and utilization and optimization of land use structure. Other measures would be controlling the total amount of industrial land to avoid the severe shortage of arable land and improving the ecological carrying capacity of agricultural land [45].

Finally, the validity and reliability of the OWA operator applied to climate change, such as in environmental management, climate projections, and carbon measurements in agriculture, are confirmed. It should be noted that all three investigations used accurate data from official sources, which reinforces the use of the OWA operator in this research. Alternative methods or extensions of the OWA operator would be recommended in cases where the available information could be more precise or where numerical data cannot be analyzed [33].

In summary, the bibliometric study indicated 212,775 records for Climate Change, 491 for OWA operators, and three for the combination of two terms. The results reveal a trend of growth in the research over time and an increase in publications and citations. It reinforces the interest in this topic and advances the frontier of knowledge in these lines of research. In addition, the result indicates the existence of a fifth research gap, as the OWA operator was little applied to climate change. Therefore, this algorithm would be recommended to reduce the lack of comparable data to SDG13 [18], another study's scientific merit.

2.2. Research Sample

The research sample comprises 10 Ibero-American countries, and the group comprises Argentina, Brazil, Chile, Colombia, Cuba, Ecuador, Mexico, Peru, Portugal, and Spain. These countries have historical, cultural, scientific, and economic ties and participate in the Ibero-American Intelligent Systems and Expert Computational Models Network project, project number 522RT0130, in the Ibero-American Program of Science and Technology for Development [46]. The project is a 4-year plan (2022–2025) with more than 60 researchers, integrating collaboration, cooperation, and synergy activities that seek to identify areas of competence where the applications of Fuzzy models can beneficially interfere and maximize social and productive benefits in the region with an Ibero-American vision [46]. This project [46] has four phases: Diagnosis and Training (Year 1), Algorithm Production (Year 2), Consolidation and Synergy (Year 3), and Implementation and Transfer (Year 4). In this context, this research is in Phase 1 of diagnosis, and the literature review identified the need for comparable SDG13 data among the ten countries. Therefore, this research is relevant to this project, and the results will be helpful for the participating countries. For these reasons, ten countries were selected for this research.

## 2.3. Methodology

According to other studies [32–34], the OWA operator [27] is a suitable algorithm for evaluation and prioritization, and for these reasons, the authors will apply it in this research. In 1998, Ronald Robert Yager established the OWA aggregation operators, generalizing a model that uses four decision criteria: Optimistic Criterion, Pessimistic Criterion or Wald Criterion, Hurwicz Criterion, and Laplace Criterion [26]. According to the same author [27], an OWA operator of dimension $n$ is an application of de $\mathcal{F}: \mathcal{R}^n \to \mathcal{R}$, which has an associated weighting vector, as:

$$w_i \in [0,1],\ 1 \leq i \leq n \text{ and } \sum_{i=1}^{n} w_i = w_1 + w_2 + \ldots + w_n = 1 \tag{1}$$

where

$$\mathcal{F}(x_1, x_2, \ldots, x_n) = \sum_{k=1}^{n} w_k x_{jk} = w_1 x_1 + w_2 x_2 + \ldots + w_n x_n \tag{2}$$

and $x_{jk}$ is the $k$th largest element of the collection $\{x_1, x_2, \ldots, x_n\}$.

Formula (1) indicates that each element is associated with a weighting vector. In other words, we are evaluating six SDG13 indicators; each indicator is weighted according to the established criteria, and the sum of the weights must equal 1. Table 1 shows the weights ($W_1, W_2, \ldots, W_6$) for each SDG13 indicator. Formula (2) presents the level of adequacy to a given criterion based on the sum of the corresponding weighting vector multiplied by the largest element of collection x, as indicated in Formula (1). In this research, the calculation of the OWA operator is performed by applying Formula (2), using the values presented in Table 1 (weighting vector) and Table 2 (evaluation of each indicator by country). Other researchers [34] agree that a critical aspect of OWA operators is reordering weighting. For, an aggregate $x_i$ is not associated with a weight, but rather the weight is associated with an ordered position $j$ of the arguments. Therefore, this ordering introduces nonlinearity in the aggregation process [34,47].

Table 1. Vector of weights determined of the SDG13 indicators.

| Weights | $W_1$ | $W_2$ | $W_3$ | $W_4$ | $W_5$ | $W_6$ |
|---|---|---|---|---|---|---|
| W= | 0.05 | 0.10 | 0.10 | 0.25 | 0.45 | 0.05 |
| SDG13 Indicators | 13.1.1 | 13.1.2 | 13.1.3 | 13.2.1 | 13.2.2 | 13.3.1 |

Source: Own elaboration based on [4,18,25].

## 2.4. Variables and Measures

The SDG13—Climate Action indicators will be the OWA operator's application variables. SDG13 is composed of three targets and six specific indicators [21]. It should be noted that indicators 13.1.1 and 13.3.1 are composed of four additional indicators. Table A1 presents the SDG13 targets and indicators in detail. The study uses the endecadary scale [48] to facilitate comparability between indicators. Table A2 presents the scale used in the research. Thus, the value closest to 1 expresses an approach to SDG13, and the value closest to 0 shows a move away from this target.

Table 2. Fuzzy subset of the six SDG13 indicators.

| | | SDG13 Indicators | | | | | |
|---|---|---|---|---|---|---|---|
| Code | Countries | 13.1.1 | 13.1.2 | 13.1.3 | 13.2.1 | 13.2.2 | 13.3.1 |
| $C_1$ | Argentina | 0.70 | 0.78 | 0.90 | 1.00 | 0.40 | 0.00 |
| $C_2$ | Brazil | 0.28 | 0.80 | 0.75 | 1.00 | 0.10 | 0.97 |
| $C_3$ | Chile | 0.93 | 0.90 | 0.55 | 1.00 | 0.65 | 0.00 |
| $C_4$ | Colombia | 0.75 | 1.00 | 0.85 | 1.00 | 0.60 | 0.93 |
| $C_5$ | Cuba | 0.20 | 0.75 | 0.70 | 1.00 | 0.85 | 0.99 |
| $C_6$ | Ecuador | 0.71 | 0.68 | 0.45 | 1.00 | 0.75 | 0.00 |
| $C_7$ | Mexico | 0.83 | 0.93 | 0.30 | 1.00 | 0.20 | 0.64 |
| $C_8$ | Peru | 0.54 | 1.00 | 1.00 | 1.00 | 0.70 | 0.75 |
| $C_9$ | Portugal | 0.57 | 0.90 | 0.50 | 1.00 | 0.80 | 0.00 |
| $C_{10}$ | Spain | 0.46 | 1.00 | 0.80 | 1.00 | 0.45 | 0.97 |

Source: Own elaboration based on [49–51].

*2.5. Collection of Official Data for SDG13*

Official data collection [49–51] on the six SDG13 indicators occurred in September and October 2022 and referred to the base year of 2020. The authors chose this baseline for the study as 2020 contemplates more data available for the ten countries. The data obtained are detailed below.

Figure 5 presents the results of each country on the SDG13.1.1 indicator in 2020. In this case, Chile and Mexico present the best results with a comparative approach to SDG13. On the other hand, Cuba and Brazil moved away from this target due to the need for more available data on the additional indicators 13.1.1a and 13.1.1b presented in Table A3. As recommendations, policymakers should keep information on SDG13 updated in official databases [49–51] and invest in information technology systems for data collection and processing [18]. Second, adaptation and mitigation strategies are the most appropriate measures to improve the results of indicator 13.1.1 [19]. In this case, governments should work proactively [16] by strengthening the resilience of communities to natural disasters with investment in protective infrastructure in flood risk areas [52]. Another strategy would be to facilitate the relocation of people living in vulnerable areas to safer places [53,54].

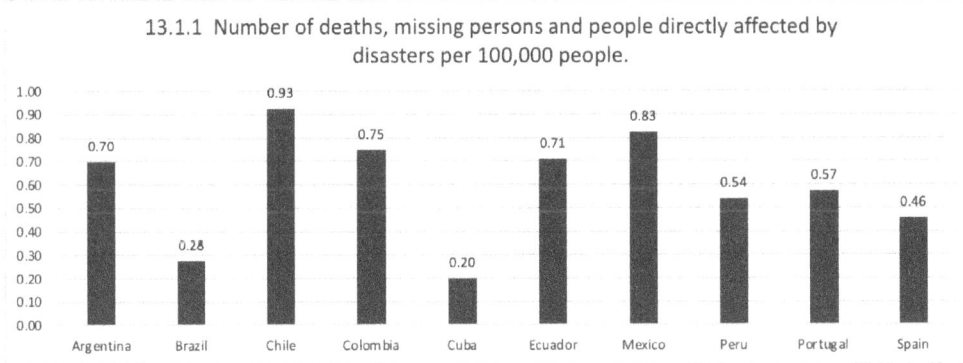

Figure 5. SDG13.1.1 Indicator (2020). Source: Own elaboration based on [49–51].

Figure 6 presents the data for SDG13.1.2 in 2020. In this case, Colombia, Mexico, and Spain show the best results with a coefficient of 1.00, close to SDG13. On the other hand, Ecuador shows a greater distance from this target with a coefficient of 0.68. In terms of strategic planning, the Sendai Framework is essential, as it recognizes the strong connection between health and disasters and promotes the concept of health resilience at all times [55]. However, the same researchers warn that measuring health-related indicators is a challenge, as health data recording in disasters needs to be standardized [55]. For this reason, governments should strengthen care and health data records [18].

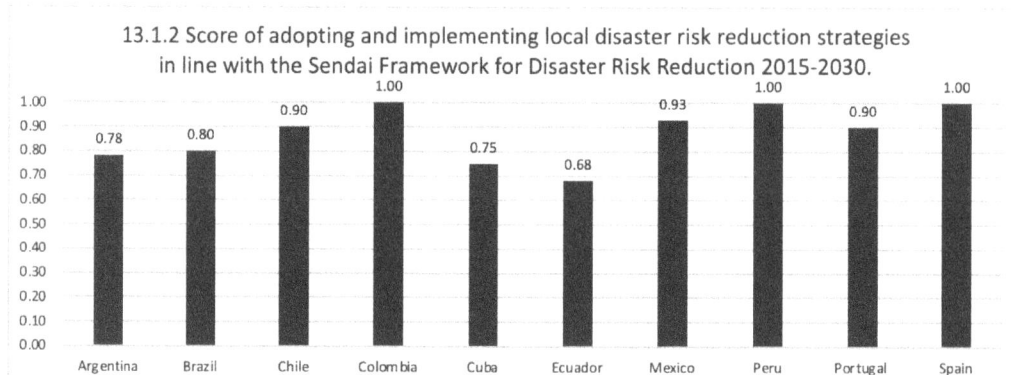

**Figure 6.** SDG13.1.2 Indicator (2020). Source: Own elaboration based on [49–51].

Figure 7 shows each country's information on the SDG13.1.3 indicator in 2020. In this case, Peru presents the best result with a maximum coefficient of 1.00 and a comparative approach to SDG13. On the other hand, Mexico shows a distance from this target with a coefficient of 0.30. One of the reasons for this low performance is the need for more available data. Therefore, recommendations to central governments involve more significant participation of local governments [56] and provide data on this indicator.

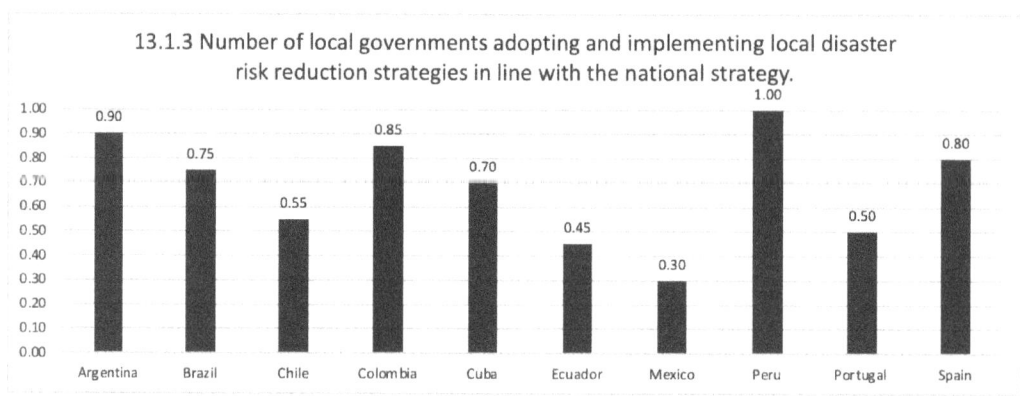

**Figure 7.** SDG13.1.3 Indicator (2020). Source: Own elaboration based on [49–51].

Figure 8 presents each country's data on SDG13.2.1 in 2020. In this case, all ten countries present a comparative approach to SDG13 with the highest score. However, a critical analysis of this result is warranted, as indicator 13.2.1 refers to the establishment or implementation of policy, strategy, or plan and does not identify which countries are in the implementation or planning phase. A recommendation would be to create additional indicators to provide this information in greater detail.

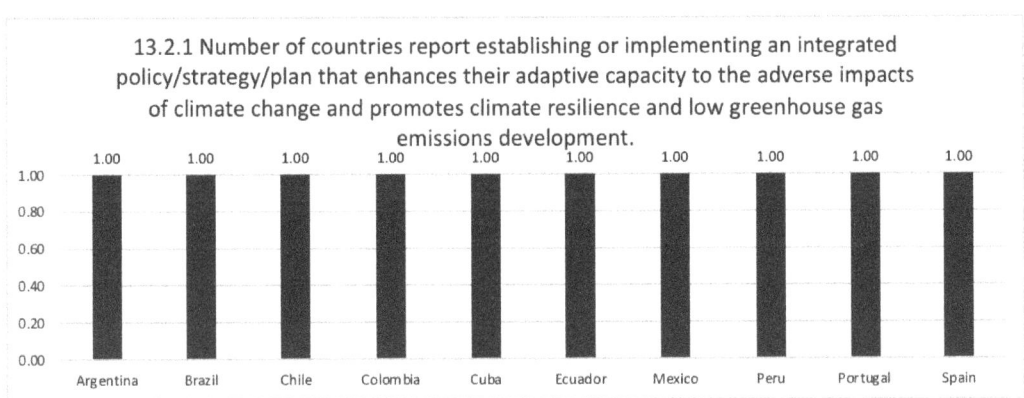

**Figure 8.** SDG13.2.1 Indicator (2020). Source: Own elaboration based on [49–51].

Figure 9 shows the information on the SDG13.2.2 indicator in 2020. In this case, Cuba and Portugal present the best results with a comparative approach to SDG13. On the other hand, Brazil is a move away from this target. According to other research [4,25], this indicator would be the most important to SDG13 since $CO_2$ emissions are responsible for global warming [4] and the climate crisis. Therefore, SDG13.2.2 should be the priority of policy and decision-makers, such as renewable energies [8], circular economy [57], and optimization of agricultural areas [45].

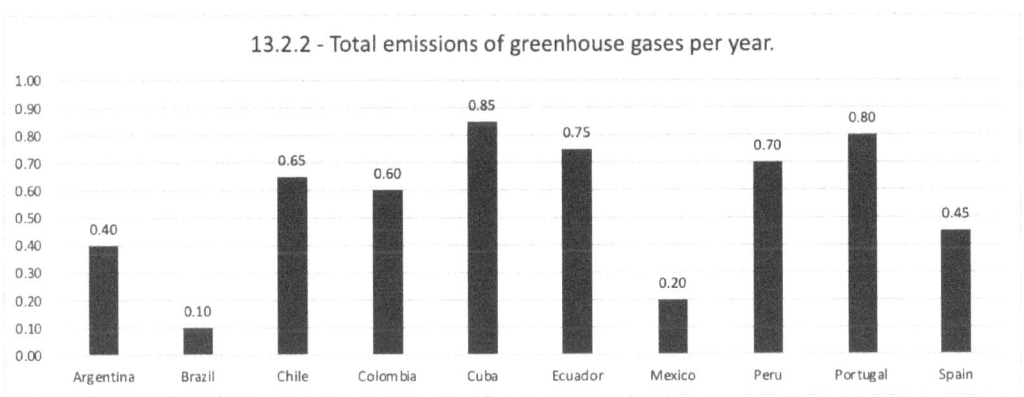

**Figure 9.** SDG13.2.2 Indicator (2020). Source: Own elaboration based on [49–51].

Figure 10 reveals the results of indicator SDG13.3.1 in 2020. In this case, Cuba, Brazil, and Spain present the best results with a comparative approach to SDG13, which shows the importance of education in climate change awareness. On the other hand, countries such as Argentina, Chile, Ecuador, and Portugal presented the worst results due to the need for more available data in the additional indicators presented in Table A4. Proposals for action would be to invest in climate change education curricula [58] and improve data management [59].

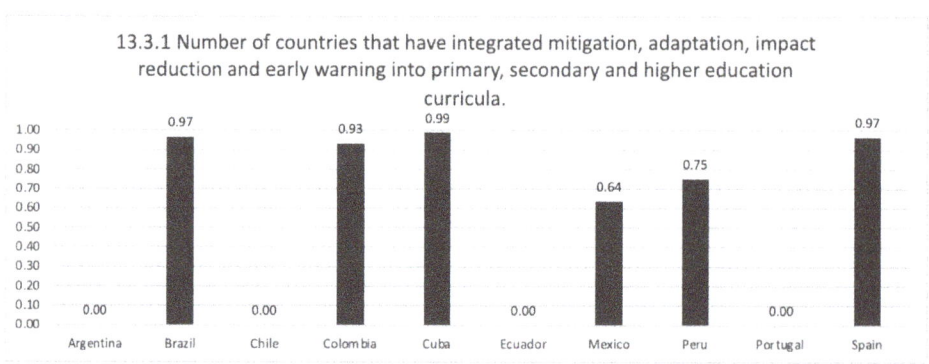

**Figure 10.** SDG13.3.1 Indicator (2020). Source: Own elaboration based on [49–51].

Finally, Figure 11 presents the consolidated data for the ten countries in the three SDG13 targets in 2020. In this case, Colombia presents the best result for target 13.1 with a coefficient of 0.87, followed by Peru with 0.85, Argentina and Chile with 0.79. The result also reveals Cuba leading in target 13.2 with a coefficient of 0.93 and target 13.3 with a coefficient of 0.99.

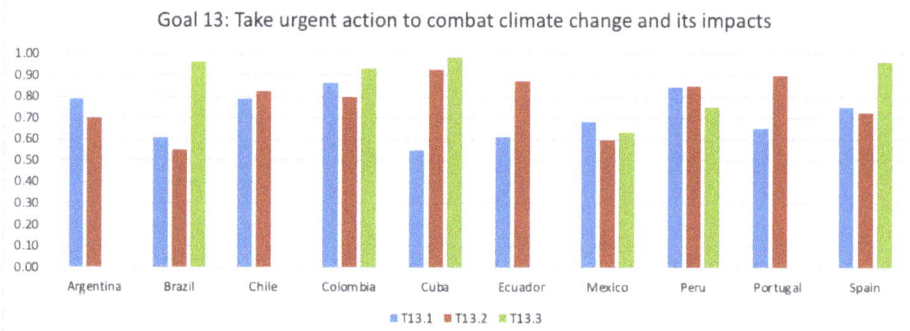

**Figure 11.** SDG13 Targets (2020). Note: T13.1 Strengthen resilience and adaptive capacity to climate-related hazards and natural disasters in all countries; T13.2 Integrate climate change measures into national policies, strategies, and planning; 13.3 Improve education, awareness-raising and human and institutional capacity on climate change mitigation, adaptation, impact reduction, and early warning. Source: Own elaboration based on [49–51].

In summary, the data collected on the SDG13 indicators allow us to identify the commitment of the ten countries to climate change and to compare the data between them. However, the literature review [4,25] showed that each indicator has a different relevance, but they are calculated with the same weight [49–51]. As an opportunity to improve SDG13, the authors propose the inclusion of different weights for each indicator based on official data and scientific studies [4,18,25], which will allow prioritization of the most relevant indicators to climate change and a more realistic ranking of countries. Finally, the results of this proposal can guide policymakers and decision-makers in the solutions to address the climate crisis. The application of the OWA operator to SDG13 is detailed below as the authors' theoretical contribution to climate change.

## 2.6. Application of the OWA Operator to SDG13

First, the weights are established by applying the formula (1) supported by official data [18] and scientific studies [4,25]. Table 1 shows the weights ($W_1, W_2, \ldots W_6$) for each SDG13 indicator.

Secondly, from official sources [49–51], data is collected, with 2020 as a reference year, and each indicator is valued using an endecadary scale [48]. Indicators 13.1.1 and 13.3.1 represent the results of an average value of the additional indicators presented in Tables A3 and A4. Table 2 shows the consolidated result.

Finally, the calculation of the OWA operator is performed by applying the Formula (2), using the values presented in Table 1 (weighting vector) and Table 2 (evaluation of each indicator by country). For example, follow the calculations made for Argentina ($C_1$), Brazil ($C_2$), and Spain ($C_{10}$). OWAC$_i$, for i = 1, 2, …, and 10.

$OWAC_1 = (0.05 * 1.00 + 0.10 * 0.90 + 0.10 * 0.78 + 0.25 * 0.70 + 0.45 * 0.40 + 0.05 * 0.00) = 0.573$

$OWAC_2 = (0.05 * 1.00 + 0.10 * 0.97 + 0.10 * 0.80 + 0.25 * 0.75 + 0.45 * 0.28 + 0.05 * 0.10) = 0.5455$

$OWAC_{10} = (0.05 * 1.00 + 0.10 * 1.00 + 0.10 * 0.97 + 0.25 * 0.80 + 0.45 * 0.46 + 0.05 * 0.45) = 0.6765$

The following section presents the complete results applying the OWA operator.

## 3. Results Applying OWA Operator to SDG13

The result of the algorithm indicates that Colombia ($C_4$) reached the highest coefficient of 0.8230, which means that $C_4$ obtains a better level of adequacy to SDG13. In second place is Peru ($C_8$), with a coefficient of 0.7795, followed by $C_5$ (0.7465), $C_{10}$ (0.6765), and $C_3$ (0.6430), respectively. Countries $C_4$ and $C_8$ are in the top positions, mainly due to the results on targets 13.1, 13.2, and 13.3. Also, these countries due to the availability of data in all indicators. Table 3 presents the complete result and the ranking of the ten countries.

**Table 3.** Ranking of countries applying the OWA operator.

| Code | Countries | OWA | Position |
|---|---|---|---|
| $C_1$ | Argentina | 0.5730 | 7° |
| $C_2$ | Brazil | 0.5455 | 9° |
| $C_3$ | Chile | 0.6430 | 5° |
| $C_4$ | Colombia | 0.8230 | 1° |
| $C_5$ | Cuba | 0.7465 | 3° |
| $C_6$ | Ecuador | 0.5685 | 8° |
| $C_7$ | Mexico | 0.5310 | 10° |
| $C_8$ | Peru | 0.7795 | 2° |
| $C_9$ | Portugal | 0.5875 | 6° |
| $C_{10}$ | Spain | 0.6765 | 4° |

Source: Own elaboration applying the OWA operator based on [49–51].

The second half of the ranking is Portugal ($C_9$), with a coefficient of 0.5875. Followed by Argentina ($C_1$) at 0.5730 and Ecuador ($C_6$) at 0.5685, respectively. On the other hand, Brazil ($C_2$) and Mexico ($C_7$) were in the last positions with coefficients 0.5455 and 0.5310, respectively. The low values can explain these results in indicator 13.2.2. Figure 12 shows the level of adequacy of the ten countries to SDG13.

In addition, the results allow us to classify the countries into sets according to the level of adequacy of SDG13. In this case, the results indicate four groups of countries, the first set being at the strong level $S_3 = \{C_4\}$ represented by Colombia. Two countries form the second set at the considerable level $S_4 = \{C_8, C_5\}$ constituted by Peru and Cuba. The third set is at the fair level $S_5 = \{C_{10}, C_3\}$ with Spain and Chile. Finally, the fourth set $S_6 = \{C_9, C_1, C_6, C_2, C_7\}$ is composed of five countries, Portugal, Argentina, Ecuador, Brazil, and Mexico, and are at the intermediate level. Table 4 presents the classification of countries by level of adequacy to SDG13.

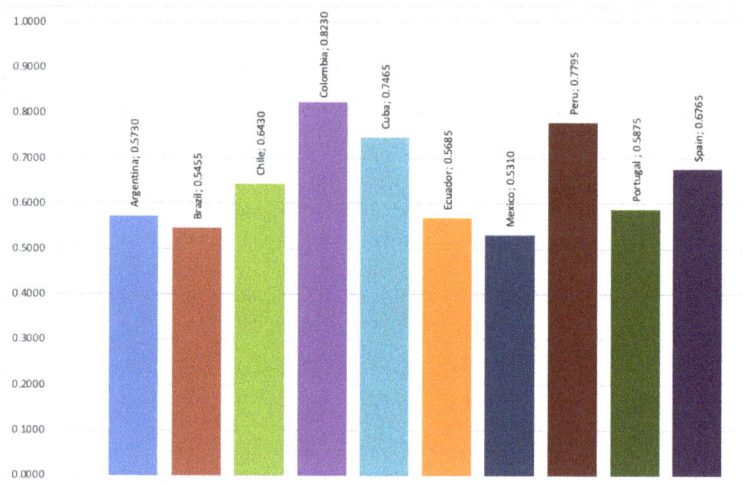

**Figure 12.** Own elaboration applying the OWA operator based on [49–51].

**Table 4.** Classification of countries by adequacy level to the SDG 13.

| Sets | Scale | Adequacy Level | Countries |
|---|---|---|---|
| $S_1$ | [0.90; 0.99] | Absolute | |
| $S_2$ | [0.90; 0.99] | Very strong | |
| $S_3$ | [0.80; 0.89] | Strong | $C_4$ |
| $S_4$ | [0.70; 0.79] | Considerable | $C_8$ and $C_5$ |
| $S_5$ | [0.60; 0.69] | Fair | $C_{10}$ and $C_3$ |
| $S_6$ | [0.50; 0.59] | Intermediate | $C_9, C_1, C_6, C_2$ and $C_7$ |
| $S_7$ | [0.40; 0.49] | Weak | |
| $S_8$ | [0.30; 0.39] | Very weak | |
| $S_9$ | [0.20; 0.29] | Slightly weak | |
| $S_{10}$ | [0.10; 0.19] | Practically null | |
| $S_{11}$ | [0.00; 0.09] | Null | |

Source: Own elaboration applying the OWA operator based on [49–51].

The cluster ranking reveals the degree to which a grouping of countries is on SDG13 and helps to understand each country's progress and weaknesses, facilitating the search for collaborative solutions among countries. Policy and decision-makers can use this information to review national and international plans to combat climate change. The following section is devoted to discussions of the results.

## 4. Discussion of the Results

This research applied the OWA operator in ten Ibero-American nations, which allowed evaluating, ranking, and classifying these countries concerning SDG13. The results can help policymakers review their climate action targets, identify weaknesses, and strengthen actions to address the climate crisis. In addition, the study generated relevant findings for academics, policymakers, and decision-makers.

In response to the authors [18], the research compiled information on SDG13 indicators from Argentina, Brazil, Chile, Colombia, Cuba, Ecuador, Mexico, Peru, Portugal, and Spain from official databases. The OWA operator was then applied using the data collected, considering specific weights for each indicator defined by other studies [4,18,25]. As a result, the article reduced the first concomitance gap [18] by revealing a ranking of the countries and allowing the comparison of data between them on SDG13. However, another alternative prioritization method, such as the Pythagorean Fuzzy Uncertain Environments [60], can be used in future research to compare the results obtained.

The results of the literature review made it possible to warn [25] and raise awareness among policy and decision-makers about the correlation between the SDGs [20] and the urgency of curbing global warming [4], giving priority to the reduction of $CO_2$ emissions through renewable energies [8], circular economy [57], and optimization of agricultural areas [45]. Along these lines, the research narrowed the second knowledge gap [20,23].

The study also confirmed the findings of other researchers [55] by highlighting the importance of the Sendai Framework and recognizing the connection between health and natural disasters [25]. In the same direction, the study highlighted protection solutions in flood-risk areas [52] and social justice by relocating people to safer areas [53,54]. Therefore, the inclusion of the human factor in decision-making is reinforced [25], diminishing the third knowledge gap.

Additionally, in response to other studies [4,22], the authors proposed the inclusion of weights in the SDG13 indicators by applying the OWA operator [27]. As a result, the algorithm generated more reliable data, facilitating policymakers' formulation of climate strategies and reducing the fourth knowledge gap.

Finally, in response to other studies [43–45], the OWA operator was shown to be appropriate for evaluating, prioritizing, and comparing data across countries to SDG13. Determining weights for each indicator based on official data and scientific studies [4,18,25] allowed for prioritizing the most relevant climate change indicators and presenting a more realistic ranking of countries. Besides, the results were validated by three academic specialists from Ibero-American countries. Furthermore, the method enabled it to merge numerical information, contributing to decision-making [33] and minimizing the fifth gap identified.

## 5. Conclusions

The study proposed applying a fuzzy logic algorithm to evaluate the SDG13 indicators and deepened the debate on climate change. The following are the main conclusions of this work:

First, the research broadened the debate on climate change, showing that it is a complex and dynamic problem. It was confirmed that we are going through a climate crisis in which global causes produce local effects and that solutions will depend on an urgent effort by all.

Second, the literature review identified five knowledge gaps related to climate change and the OWA operator. For this reason, the authors applied this algorithm as a methodological alternative to evaluate 10 Ibero-American countries and respond to these gaps.

Thirdly, the research ratified that the OWA operator contributes to decision-making in prioritization processes by ranking Ibero-American countries with SDG13. The study's main results indicated that Colombia with the best level of alignment with SDG13, followed by Peru and Cuba. The last positions are Brazil and Mexico. In addition, the results revealed the importance of having comparable data on SDG13 to identify solutions and contribute to sustainable development with possible action methods.

Fourth, as theoretical contributions, the manuscript advanced the frontier of knowledge on Climate Change and operator OWA from a bibliometric study between 2013 and 2022. The study showed the scientific performance in this period, and the highlighted publications alerted us about the challenges and solutions to address the climate crisis. The study also revealed a growing interest in these lines of research. Moreover, the research reduced the five knowledge gaps identified. Finally, academics can benefit from comparable data on SDG13 to deepen their research on climate change and apply this algorithm to other groups of countries.

Fifth, as practical contributions, the applied study offers governments, society, academia, and decision-makers solutions to address climate change. The research presented a diagnosis of the 10 Ibero-American countries on six SDG13 indicators. It showed proposals for action aimed at policy and decision-makers to strengthen resilience, integrate climate change measures into public policies and improve climate change education. As main recommendations, policymakers should prioritize actions to reduce $CO_2$ emissions, such as renewable energies, circular economy, and optimization of agricultural areas. On the other hand, the authors recommend keeping information on SDG13 updated in official databases and investing in IT systems for data collection and processing. In addition, countries should prioritize climate change adaptation and mitigation strategies, such as strengthening the resilience of communities to natural disasters by investing in protective infrastructure in areas at risk of flooding and facilitating the relocation of people to safer areas. Lastly, the OWA operator helped prioritize and compare data across countries, facilitating the identification of weaknesses and solutions related to SDG Climate Action. Other researchers can use these findings in their research, and policymakers can compare their country's results with those of other participating countries and take urgent action to combat climate change and generate a positive impact on society.

Finally, as the main scientific merit of the study, the manuscript was novel for applying the OWA operator to SDG13 in Ibero-American countries. The authors included different weightings for each indicator based on official data and scientific studies, which allowed prioritization of the most relevant indicators for climate change and a more realistic ranking of countries. Also, it reduced the need for comparable data for the climate action goal. A limitation of the research would be the number of participating countries. As a suggestion, future studies can expand the sample used and explore the application of this algorithm among other countries.

**Author Contributions:** Conceptualization, L.B.-P.; methodology, L.B.-P. and A.M.G.-L.; validation, L.B.-P. and A.M.G.-L.; formal analysis, A.C.-R.; investigation, L.B.-P.; resources, L.B.-P.; writing—original draft preparation, L.B.-P.; writing—review and editing, L.B.-P. and A.C.-R.; supervision, A.M.G.-L. All authors have read and agreed to the published version of the manuscript.

**Funding:** Research supported by Red Sistemas Inteligentes y Expertos Modelos Computacionales Iberoamericanos (SIEMCI), project number 522RT0130 in Programa Iberoamericano de Ciencia y Tecnología para el Desarrollo (CYTED).

**Data Availability Statement:** Not applicable.

**Acknowledgments:** The authors wish to thank The Royal Academy of Economic and Financial Sciences and the University of Barcelona from Spain, and CENTRUM Católica Graduate Business School, Peru.

**Conflicts of Interest:** The authors declare no conflict of interest.

## Appendix A

Table A1. Targets and SDG13 Indicators.

| Targets | SDG13 Indicators |
|---|---|
| 13.1 Strengthen resilience and adaptive capacity to climate-related hazards and natural disasters in all countries. | 13.1.1 Number of deaths, missing persons, and people directly affected by disasters per 100,000 people.<br>a. Deaths—Exposure to forces of nature—Sex: Both—Age: All Ages (Rate).<br>b. Number of deaths and missing persons attributed to disasters per 100,000 population.<br>c. Internally displaced persons, new displacement associated with disasters.<br>d. Number of directly affected persons attributed to disasters per 100,000 population. |
| | 13.1.2 Score of adopting and implementing local disaster risk reduction strategies in line with the Sendai Framework for Disaster Risk Reduction 2015–2030.<br>13.1.3 Number of local governments adopting and implementing local disaster risk reduction strategies in line with the national strategy. |
| 13.2 Integrate climate change measures into national policies, strategies, and planning. | 13.2.1 Number of countries report establishing or implementing an integrated policy/strategy/plan that enhances their adaptive capacity to the adverse impacts of climate change and promotes climate resilience and low greenhouse gas emissions development.<br>13.2.2—Total emissions of greenhouse gases per year. |

**Table A1.** *Cont.*

| Targets | SDG13 Indicators |
|---|---|
| 13.3 Improve education, awareness-raising, and human and institutional capacity on climate change mitigation, adaptation, impact reduction, and early warning. | 13.3.1 Number of countries that have integrated mitigation, adaptation, impact reduction, and early warning into primary, secondary, and higher education curricula.<br>a. Extent to which global citizenship education and education for sustainable development are mainstreamed in curricula.<br>b. Extent to which global citizenship education and education for sustainable development are mainstreamed in national education policies.<br>c. Extent to which global citizenship education and education for sustainable development are mainstreamed in student assessment.<br>d. Extent to which global citizenship education and education for sustainable development are mainstreamed in teacher education. |

Source: Own elaboration based on [61].

**Table A2.** Endecadary scale.

| Adequacy Level | Evaluation |
|---|---|
| Null | 0 |
| Practically null | 0.1 |
| Almost weak | 0.2 |
| Very weak | 0.3 |
| Weak | 0.4 |
| Intermediate | 0.5 |
| Fair | 0.6 |
| Considerable | 0.7 |
| Strong | 0.8 |
| Very strong | 0.9 |
| Absolute | 1 |

Source: Own elaboration based on [48].

**Table A3.** SDG13.1.1 Indicators.

| Indicator/Countries | $C_1$ | $C_2$ | $C_3$ | $C_4$ | $C_5$ | $C_6$ | $C_7$ | $C_8$ | $C_9$ | $C_{10}$ |
|---|---|---|---|---|---|---|---|---|---|---|
| a. | 1 | 0.9 | 0.8 | 0.85 | 0.7 | 0.6 | 1 | 0.2 | 1 | 1 |
| b. | 0 | 0 | 1 | 0.9 | 0 | 0.3 | 0.95 | 0.85 | 0.2 | 0 |
| c. | 0.89 | 0.2 | 0.9 | 0.6 | 0.1 | 0.94 | 0.5 | 0.8 | 0.98 | 0.82 |
| d. | 0.9 | 0 | 1 | 0.65 | 0 | 1 | 0.85 | 0.3 | 0.1 | 0 |
| Total | 0.6975 | 0.275 | 0.925 | 0.75 | 0.2 | 0.71 | 0.825 | 0.5375 | 0.57 | 0.455 |

Note: a. Deaths—Exposure to forces of nature—Sex: Both—Age: All Ages (Rate); b. Number of deaths and missing persons attributed to disasters per 100,000 population; c. Internally displaced persons, new displacement associated with disasters; d. Number of directly affected persons attributed to disasters per 100,000 population.

**Table A4.** SDG13.3.1 Indicators.

| Indicator/Countries | $C_1$ | $C_2$ | $C_3$ | $C_4$ | $C_5$ | $C_6$ | $C_7$ | $C_8$ | $C_9$ | $C_{10}$ |
|---|---|---|---|---|---|---|---|---|---|---|
| a. | 0 | 0.94 | 0 | 0.88 | 1 | 0 | 0 | 0.81 | 0 | 0.91 |
| b. | 0 | 1 | 0 | 1 | 1 | 0 | 0.75 | 1 | 0 | 1 |
| c. | 0 | 0.92 | 0 | 1 | 1 | 0 | 1 | 1 | 0 | 1 |
| d. | 0 | 1 | 0 | 0.85 | 0.95 | 0 | 0.8 | 0.2 | 0 | 0.95 |
| Total | 0 | 0.965 | 0 | 0.9325 | 0.9875 | 0 | 0.6375 | 0.7525 | 0 | 0.965 |

Note: a. Extent to which global citizenship education and education for sustainable development are mainstreamed in curricula; b. Extent to which global citizenship education and education for sustainable development are mainstreamed in national education policies, c. Extent to which global citizenship education and education for sustainable development are mainstreamed in student assessment; d. Extent to which global citizenship education and education for sustainable development are mainstreamed in teacher education.

## References

1. Haeffner, M.; Hames, F.; Barbour, M.M.; Reeves, J.M.; Platell, G.; Grover, S. Expanding collaborative autoethnography into the world of natural science for transdisciplinary teams. *One Earth* **2022**, *5*, 157–167. [CrossRef] [PubMed]
2. Barcellos-Paula, L.; Gil-Lafuente, A.M.; Castro-Rezende, A. Socio-Economic and Health Management of Pandemics Based on Forgotten Effects Theory. *Cybern. Syst.* **2022**, *54*, 1–27. [CrossRef]
3. Yazdani, M.; Mojtahedi, M.; Loosemore, M.; Sanderson, D. A modelling framework to design an evacuation support system for healthcare infrastructures in response to major flood events. *Prog. Disaster Sci.* **2022**, *13*, 100218. [CrossRef]
4. Hu, Y. From global warming to complex physical systems: Reading of the 2021 Nobel Prize in Physics. *Chin. Sci. Bull.* **2022**, *67*, 548–556. [CrossRef]
5. Bernet, M.; Torres Acosta, L. Rising sea level and increasing tropical cyclone frequency are threatening the population of San Andrés Island, Colombia, western Caribbean. *BSGF Earth Sci. Bull.* **2022**, *193*, 4. [CrossRef]
6. Chaika, V.; Lisovyy, M.; Lakyda, M.; Konotop, Y.; Taran, N.; Miniailo, N.; Fedorchuk, S.; Klymenko, T.; Trembitska, O.; Chaika, S. Impact of climate change on biodiversity loss of entomofauna in agricultural landscapes of Ukraine. *J. Cent. Eur. Agric.* **2021**, *22*, 830–835. [CrossRef]
7. Gosens, J.; Lu, Y.; He, G.; Bluemling, B.; Beckers, T.A.M. Sustainability effects of household-scale biogas in rural China. *Energy Policy* **2013**, *54*, 273–287. [CrossRef]
8. Waheed, A.; Tariq, M. The Impact of Renewable Energy on Carbon Dioxide Emissions: An Empirical Analysis of Selected South Asian Countries. *Ukr. J. Ecol.* **2019**, *9*, 527–534. [CrossRef]
9. Siegert, M.; Pearson, P. Reducing Uncertainty in 21st Century Sea-Level Predictions and Beyond. *Front. Environ. Sci.* **2021**, *9*, 751978. [CrossRef]
10. Sánchez-Benítez, A.; Goessling, H.; Pithan, F.; Semmler, T.; Jung, T. The July 2019 European Heat Wave in a Warmer Climate: Storyline Scenarios with a Coupled Model Using Spectral Nudging. *J. Clim.* **2022**, *35*, 2373–2390. [CrossRef]
11. Boccard, N. On the prevalence of forest fires in Spain. *Nat. Hazards* **2022**, *114*, 1043–1057. [CrossRef]
12. Ahmad, D.; Afzal, M. Flood hazards and agricultural production risks management practices in flood-prone areas of Punjab, Pakistan. *Environ. Sci. Pollut. Res.* **2022**, *29*, 20768–20783. [CrossRef] [PubMed]
13. Hochman, A.; Marra, F.; Messori, G.; Pinto, J.G.; Raveh-Rubin, S.; Yosef, Y.; Zittis, G. Extreme weather and societal impacts in the eastern Mediterranean. *Earth Syst. Dyn.* **2022**, *13*, 749–777. [CrossRef]
14. Khraishah, H.; Alahmad, B.; Ostergard, R.L.; AlAshqar, A.; Albaghdadi, M.; Vellanki, N.; Chowdhury, M.M.; Al-Kindi, S.G.; Zanobetti, A.; Gasparrini, A.; et al. Climate change and cardiovascular disease: Implications for global health. *Nat. Rev. Cardiol.* **2022**, *19*, 798–812. [CrossRef] [PubMed]
15. Monforte, P.; Ragusa, M.A. Temperature Trend Analysis and Investigation on a Case of Variability Climate. *Mathematics* **2022**, *10*, 2202. [CrossRef]
16. Swarna, S.T.; Hossain, K. Climate change impact and adaptation for highway asphalt pavements: A literature review. *Can. J. Civ. Eng.* **2022**, *49*, 1109–1120. [CrossRef]
17. Zhu, X.; Liu, T.; Xu, K.; Chen, C. The impact of high temperature and drought stress on the yield of major staple crops in northern China. *J. Environ. Manag.* **2022**, *314*, 115092. [CrossRef]
18. United Nations. *The Sustainable Development Goals Report 2022*, 1st ed.; Jensen, L., Ed.; United Nations Publications: New York, NY, USA, 2022; ISBN 978-92-1-101448-8.
19. Pörtner, H.-O.; Roberts, D.C.; Tignor, M.; Poloczanska, E.S.; Mintenbeck, K.; Alegría, A.; Craig, M.S.; Langsdorf, S.; Löschke, V.; Möller, V. (Eds.) *Climate Change 2022: Impacts, Adaptation and Vulnerability Working Group II Contribution to the Sixth Assessment Report of the Intergovernmental Panel on Climate Change*; Cambridge University Press: New York, NY, USA, 2022.
20. Barcellos-Paula, L.; De la Vega, I.; Gil-Lafuente, A.M. The Quintuple Helix of Innovation Model and the SDGs: Latin-American Countries' Case and Its Forgotten Effects. *Mathematics* **2021**, *9*, 416. [CrossRef]
21. Hwang, H.; An, S.; Lee, E.; Han, S.; Lee, C. Cross-Societal Analysis of Climate Change Awareness and Its Relation to SDG 13: A Knowledge Synthesis from Text Mining. *Sustainability* **2021**, *13*, 5596. [CrossRef]
22. Mitchell, D.; Allen, M.R.; Hall, J.W.; Muller, B.; Rajamani, L.; Le Quéré, C. The myriad challenges of the Paris Agreement. *Philos. Trans. R. Soc. A Math. Phys. Eng. Sci.* **2018**, *376*, 20180066. [CrossRef]
23. Pradhan, P.; Costa, L.; Rybski, D.; Lucht, W.; Kropp, J.P. A Systematic Study of Sustainable Development Goal (SDG) Interactions. *Earth's Futur.* **2017**, *5*, 1169–1179. [CrossRef]
24. Nilsson, M.; Griggs, D.; Visbeck, M. Policy: Map the interactions between Sustainable Development Goals. *Nature* **2016**, *534*, 320–322. [CrossRef] [PubMed]
25. Steffen, W.; Richardson, K.; Rockström, J.; Cornell, S.E.; Fetzer, I.; Bennett, E.M.; Biggs, R.; Carpenter, S.R.; de Vries, W.; de Wit, C.A.; et al. Planetary boundaries: Guiding human development on a changing planet. *Science* **2015**, *347*, 1259855. [CrossRef]
26. Zadeh, L.A. Fuzzy sets. *Inf. Control.* **1965**, *8*, 338–353. [CrossRef]
27. Yager, R.R. On ordered weighted averaging aggregation operators in multicriteria decisionmaking. *IEEE Trans. Syst. Man. Cybern.* **1988**, *18*, 183–190. [CrossRef]
28. Barcellos-Paula, L.; de La Vega, I.; Gil-Lafuente, A.M. Bibliometric review of research on decision models in uncertainty, 1990–2020. *Int. J. Intell. Syst.* **2022**, *37*, 7300–7333. [CrossRef]

29. Năďăban, S. Fuzzy Logic and Soft Computing—Dedicated to the Centenary of the Birth of Lotfi A. Zadeh (1921–2017). *Mathematics* **2022**, *10*, 3216. [CrossRef]
30. Wilberforce, T.; El-Hassan, Z.; Khatib, F.N.; Al Makky, A.; Baroutaji, A.; Carton, J.G.; Olabi, A.G. Developments of electric cars and fuel cell hydrogen electric cars. *Int. J. Hydrog. Energy* **2017**, *42*, 25695–25734. [CrossRef]
31. Melin, P.; Monica, J.C.; Sanchez, D.; Castillo, O. Multiple Ensemble Neural Network Models with Fuzzy Response Aggregation for Predicting COVID-19 Time Series: The Case of Mexico. *Healthcare* **2020**, *8*, 181. [CrossRef]
32. Barcellos-Paula, L.; Agüero-Olivos, C. The strengthening of corporate governance based on applied fuzzy logic. *Corp. Soc. Responsib. Environ. Manag.* **2022**, *29*, 1736–1746. [CrossRef]
33. Merigó, J.M.; Gil-Lafuente, A.M. Induced 2-tuple linguistic generalized aggregation operators and their application in decision-making. *Inf. Sci.* **2013**, *236*, 1–16. [CrossRef]
34. Barcellos de Paula, L.; Marins, F.A.S. Algorithms applied in decision-making for sustainable transport. *J. Clean. Prod.* **2018**, *176*, 1133–1143. [CrossRef]
35. Vizuete-Luciano, E.; Boria-Reverter, S.; Merigó-Lindahl, J.M.; Gil-Lafuente, A.M.; Solé-Moro, M.L. Fuzzy Branch-and-Bound Algorithm with OWA Operators in the Case of Consumer Decision Making. *Mathematics* **2021**, *9*, 3045. [CrossRef]
36. Will, M.; Bertrand, J.; Fransoo, J.C. Operations management research methodologies using quantitative modeling. *Int. J. Oper. Prod. Manag.* **2002**, *22*, 241–264. [CrossRef]
37. Harper, A.; Mustafee, N.; Yearworth, M. Facets of trust in simulation studies. *Eur. J. Oper. Res.* **2021**, *289*, 197–213. [CrossRef]
38. Yin, R. *Case Study Research, Design Methods*, 5th ed.; SAGE Publications Ltd.: Thousand Oaks, CA, USA, 2014; ISBN 978-1452242569.
39. Hersbach, H.; Bell, B.; Berrisford, P.; Hirahara, S.; Horányi, A.; Muñoz-Sabater, J.; Nicolas, J.; Peubey, C.; Radu, R.; Schepers, D.; et al. The ERA5 global reanalysis. *Q. J. R. Meteorol. Soc.* **2020**, *146*, 1999–2049. [CrossRef]
40. Wang, H.; Naghavi, M.; Allen, C.; Barber, R.M.; Bhutta, Z.A.; Carter, A.; Casey, D.C.; Charlson, F.J.; Chen, A.Z.; Coates, M.M.; et al. Global, regional, and national life expectancy, all-cause mortality, and cause-specific mortality for 249 causes of death, 1980–2015: A systematic analysis for the Global Burden of Disease Study 2015. *Lancet* **2016**, *388*, 1459–1544. [CrossRef]
41. Liu, H.; Rodríguez, R.M. A fuzzy envelope for hesitant fuzzy linguistic term set and its application to multicriteria decision making. *Inf. Sci.* **2014**, *258*, 220–238. [CrossRef]
42. Zeng, S.; Chen, J.; Li, X. A Hybrid Method for Pythagorean Fuzzy Multiple-Criteria Decision Making. *Int. J. Inf. Technol. Decis. Mak.* **2016**, *15*, 403–422. [CrossRef]
43. Amir Rahmani, M.; Zarghami, M. A new approach to combine climate change projections by ordered weighting averaging operator; applications to northwestern provinces of Iran. *Glob. Planet Change* **2013**, *102*, 41–50. [CrossRef]
44. Llopis-Albert, C.; Merigó, J.M.; Xu, Y.; Liao, H. Improving Regional Climate Projections by Prioritized Aggregation via Ordered Weighted Averaging Operators. *Environ. Eng. Sci.* **2017**, *34*, 880–886. [CrossRef]
45. Chen, Y.; Li, M.; Su, K.; Li, X. Spatial-Temporal Characteristics of the Driving Factors of Agricultural Carbon Emissions: Empirical Evidence from Fujian, China. *Energies* **2019**, *12*, 3102. [CrossRef]
46. SIEMCI Red Temática Número 522RT0130 en Programa Iberoamericano de Ciencia y Tecnología para el Desarrollo (CYTED) 2022–2025. Available online: https://siemci.org/proyecto/ (accessed on 18 December 2022).
47. Barcellos de Paula, L. Modelos de Gestión Aplicados a la Sostenibilidad Empresarial. Ph.D. Thesis, Universitat de Barcelona, Barcelona, Spain, 2011.
48. Kaufmann, A.; Gil Aluja, J. *Introducción de la Teoría de los Subconjuntos Borrosos a la Gestión de las Empresas*; Milladoiro: Santiago de Compostela, Spain, 1986; ISBN 9788439876304.
49. Ritchie, H.; Roser, M.; Mispy, O.-O. Measuring Progress towards the Sustainable Development Goals. Available online: https://sdg-tracker.org (accessed on 29 September 2022).
50. United Nations UN Office for Disaster Risk Reduction. Available online: https://www.undrr.org (accessed on 28 September 2022).
51. Ritchie, H.; Roser, M.; Rosado, P. $CO_2$ and Greenhouse Gas Emissions. Available online: https://ourworldindata.org/co2-and-other-greenhouse-gas-emissions (accessed on 29 September 2022).
52. Haer, T.; Botzen, W.J.W.; Zavala-Hidalgo, J.; Cusell, C.; Ward, P.J. Economic evaluation of climate risk adaptation strategies: Cost-benefit analysis of flood protection in Tabasco, Mexico. *Atmósfera* **2017**, *30*, 101–120. [CrossRef]
53. Collier, P.; Conway, G.; Venables, T. Climate change and Africa. *Oxf. Rev. Econ. Policy* **2008**, *24*, 337–353. [CrossRef]
54. Lei, Y.; Finlayson, C.; Thwaites, R.; Shi, G.; Cui, L. Using Government Resettlement Projects as a Sustainable Adaptation Strategy for Climate Change. *Sustainability* **2017**, *9*, 1373. [CrossRef]
55. Maini, R.; Clarke, L.; Blanchard, K.; Murray, V. The Sendai Framework for Disaster Risk Reduction and Its Indicators—Where Does Health Fit in? *Int. J. Disaster Risk Sci.* **2017**, *8*, 150–155. [CrossRef]
56. Kelly, S.; Pollitt, M. An assessment of the present and future opportunities for combined heat and power with district heating (CHP-DH) in the United Kingdom. *Energy Policy* **2010**, *38*, 6936–6945. [CrossRef]
57. Zajac, M.; Skocek, J.; Ben Haha, M.; Deja, J. $CO_2$ Mineralization Methods in Cement and Concrete Industry. *Energies* **2022**, *15*, 3597. [CrossRef]
58. Tormey, D.; Dongying, W.; Aixia, F. Geoheritage Education as a Gateway to Developing a Conservation Ethic in High School Students from China and the USA. *Geoheritage* **2022**, *14*, 79. [CrossRef]

59. Fady, B.; Geburek, T.; Scotti, I. Science needs management data for a better prediction of climate change effects on socio-ecosystems. *Ann. For. Sci.* **2019**, *76*, 12. [CrossRef]
60. Wang, L.; Garg, H.; Li, N. Pythagorean fuzzy interactive Hamacher power aggregation operators for assessment of express service quality with entropy weight. *Soft Comput.* **2021**, *25*, 973–993. [CrossRef]
61. United Nations. Goal 13: Take Urgent Action to Combat Climate Change and Its Impacts. Available online: https://www.un.org/sustainabledevelopment/climate-change/ (accessed on 11 October 2022).

**Disclaimer/Publisher's Note:** The statements, opinions and data contained in all publications are solely those of the individual author(s) and contributor(s) and not of MDPI and/or the editor(s). MDPI and/or the editor(s) disclaim responsibility for any injury to people or property resulting from any ideas, methods, instructions or products referred to in the content.

Article

# Forgotten Factors in Knowledge Conversion and Routines: A Fuzzy Analysis of Employee Knowledge Management in Exporting Companies in Boyacá

Fabio Blanco-Mesa *, Omar Vinchira and Yesica Cuy

Facultad de Ciencias Económicas y Administrativas, Escuela de Administración de Empresas, Universidad Pedagógica y Tecnológica de Colombia, Tunja 150003, Colombia
* Correspondence: fabio.blanco01@uptc.edu.co; Tel.: +57-3168644310

**Abstract:** The department of Boyacá accounts for only 0.93% of national exports, which means that the participation of exporting companies in the region is low. One of the most important factors within these organizations is the knowledge of the collaborators, since it is an asset that contributes to the daily activities carried out within an organization. Hence, the objective of this research was to analyze the incidence of the forgotten factors in knowledge management through the conversion of knowledge and the routines of the personnel in Boyacá's exporting companies, by means of causal analysis using fuzzy methodologies. The participants are exporting activity collaborators in the companies, who were consulted as sources of information for the Boyacá chamber of commerce. For the treatment, the forgotten effects theory, the experton method, and the adequacy coefficient are used. The information collected is processed using FuzzyLog software. The findings highlight that there are forgotten factors between the knowledge conversion and routines related to informal communication and social interactions. It is worth noting that it is important to carry out a more in-depth analysis of each of the individual knowledge spiral pillars in exporting companies in different regions of the country, focusing on social interactions (linguistic expression) and informal communication (electronic meetings).

**Keywords:** forgotten effects; knowledge; knowledge management; knowledge conversion; human talent; routines

**MSC:** 03B52

**Citation:** Blanco-Mesa, F.; Vinchira, O.; Cuy, Y. Forgotten Factors in Knowledge Conversion and Routines: A Fuzzy Analysis of Employee Knowledge Management in Exporting Companies in Boyacá. *Mathematics* 2023, 11, 412. https://doi.org/10.3390/math11020412

Academic Editors: Jorge de Andres Sanchez and Laura González-Vila Puchades

Received: 4 November 2022
Revised: 7 January 2023
Accepted: 9 January 2023
Published: 12 January 2023

**Copyright:** © 2023 by the authors. Licensee MDPI, Basel, Switzerland. This article is an open access article distributed under the terms and conditions of the Creative Commons Attribution (CC BY) license (https://creativecommons.org/licenses/by/4.0/).

## 1. Introduction

Knowledge management arises from the need of organizations to know how to create, transmit, and apply knowledge to the processes of each entity [1], which implies the trust and cooperation of the people involved in the organization, who share an organizational vision and develop in an environment that should promote learning [2]. In fact, learning on repeated occasions is centered on transferred knowledge, which is divided into tacit and explicit knowledge. The first refers to personal and subjective knowledge, which is the result of acquired experience; accordingly, it is embedded in people and, thus, difficult to articulate, explain, and learn. The second is objective knowledge that can be codified and systematized, and, for this reason, it is more easily transferable between people [1]. The knowledge management process should include a cyclical development containing the following phases: identification, acquisition (knowledge conversion), classification and storage, distribution, and application. One of the main components of knowledge management is knowledge conversion, which is the process of making available and extending the knowledge created by individuals, as well as crystallizing and connecting it to an organization's knowledge system [3,4]. Here, knowledge is generated by the collaborators (people) themselves, who follow the routines established by the companies. These routines are transformed into stable patterns of behavior that characterize organizational reactions to internal and external stimuli [5]. In fact, a routine is a repeated action sequence, which may have its roots in algorithms and heuristics on how the enterprise achieves things [6,7].

The main problem with the research is the department of Boyacá's low participation in the country's exports, considering that it only represents 0.93% at the national level [8], showing that the companies in the region are at a disadvantage compared with those in other departments. It is important to keep in mind that human capital is the driver of productive activity, and, for this reason, it is relevant to analyze the features and trends in human talent management, which cannot be disengaged from knowledge management to adapt its systems through the nature of that resource [9]. In the same way, companies can gain and understand knowledge, but may not have the skills to transform and exploit it, thus generating profits [10], which demonstrates the low relevance that organizations have given to the creation, conversion, and management of knowledge in a dynamic way [11]. Therefore, it is essential to study and analyze the incidences of knowledge conversion in the routines of exporting company collaborators in Boyacá to understand the factors that can help to improve the flow of knowledge conversion according to the characteristics and environment of the organization. The knowledge spiral is undoubtedly the model that presents the main variables used to determine the relationships between knowledge management and routines, i.e., socialization, internalization, combination, and externalization [12]. Routines are also classified into operational routines and search routines, which are intended to generate current revenues and increase profits in the future, respectively [5]. In fact, the incidence of knowledge conversion in routines may arise from the elements that compose the conversion of tacit and explicit knowledge, the shared context, and/or the set of possible patterns allowed and constrained by a variety of organizational, social, fiscal, and cognitive structures, on the basis of which organizational members carry out certain actions [13]. In this sense, understanding the relationship between knowledge conversion and routines is a complex problem that involves the interrelation among multiple factors, some of which are generally difficult for organizations to perceive, and are critical to the efficiency of data analysis, since they emphasize organizational and human aspects through the application of knowledge conversion theories [14].

On the basis of the above, this study aims to use subjective information to analyze the incidence of neglected factors in knowledge management through knowledge conversion and routines. The study is carried out on exporting companies in Boyacá registered in the Tunja and Sogamoso chambers of commerce. For the treatment of the data and its validity, fuzzy methods, the experton method [15], the adequacy coefficient [16], and the forgotten effects theory [17,18] are used to analyze the second order incidences between the conversion of knowledge and routines to identify an important interrelation between variables that at first seemed nonexistent (see Appendix A, Appendix B, Appendix C). The results show that the key incidence pathways of informal communication and social interactions, belonging to the socialization dimension, present a fracture in the knowledge management related to the incidences of informal communication and social interactions. Furthermore, the research has limitations related to the sample size and the subjective nature of the dataset. Moreover, when using these methodologies, it should be considered that the results obtained depend on the semantic configuration of the research design, even though they do not accurately capture these semantic nuances; hence, a careful design must be made. Here, it is remarkable that these methods give greater relevance to the meaning of the statements than to the measurement that can be derived from them [19]. Lastly, an analysis of the causes and effects is necessary to obtain a better diagnosis and to guide business decision making. Additionally, it is worth noting that a deeper analysis of each of the knowledge spiral pillars individually focusing on social interactions (linguistic expression) and in informal communication (electronic meetings) aids in understanding the particularities of conversion and routines in knowledge management.

The paper is organized as follows: Section 2 deals with the theoretical framework; Section 3 consists of the methodology, the type of approach, the model for finding second-generation relationships, case study, data collection, methods, and direct and indirect causal relationships; Section 4 shows the results; Section 5 comprises the discussion; lastly, Section 6 states the conclusions.

## 2. Theoretical Framework

This section presents a summary of the central characteristics of knowledge management, knowledge conversion, and routines, which were searched for and examined in the Web of Science (WoS) database using the following keywords: knowledge management OR knowledge conversion OR routines. Knowledge management in organizations favors knowledge exchange environments, by means of different models, as well as knowledge conversion, which is based on the relationship between tacit and explicit knowledge that exists in multiple areas of an organization, specifically in the routines of the collaborators that belong to it.

### 2.1. Knowledge Management

Knowledge management contributes to the creation of environments that allow the organization to develop scenarios conducive to the exchange and implementation of its knowledge in each of its departments [20]. The main objective of knowledge management is to facilitate organizations to create or capture critical knowledge, and, in the same way, to make it perceptible and evident for people to use it in an effective time or place. Hence, additional effort is made to generate an applicable knowledge base in datasets [14].

Knowledge management has become a relevant topic for organizations, since it generally deals with various groups of success factors that are oriented to the human being, the organization, technology, and management processes [21]. With respect to the human-oriented factors, which include culture, people, and leadership, it is worth highlighting the important role that people play in an organization, since the future of organizations depends to a great extent on people. This is because those people possess the knowledge and develop the skills and abilities that generate vital economic value for organizations, allowing companies to gain a greater competitive advantage over their rivals through the mastery of information [21].

In addition, the productive factor of excellence is knowledge, which serves as leverage in growing and rapid technological change, where all the information that an individual possesses in their mind is personalized and subjectively related to elements that may or may not be unique, useful, precise, or structural [22]. To test the concept of knowledge management, there is a model that identifies three main components: the linking of people with knowledge to help others, the structuring of processes to synthesize the process of filtering, legitimizing, and sharing knowledge, and the development of robust and enjoyable technologies to improve communication [14].

Similarly, knowledge management strategies can be described in two dimensions, manifesting the knowledge management approach. The first is the exchange of knowledge through interpersonal interaction, and the second is the ability to help create, store, share, and use an organization's explicitly documented knowledge. These strategies also confirm that knowledge creation is associated with cultural factors, such as collaboration, trust, and learning [23].

The theory of organizational knowledge creation is defined as the process of organizationally extending the knowledge created by individuals and crystallizing it as part of an organization's knowledge system, implying the importance of people in the development of knowledge. This process contemplates the distinction between tacit knowledge and explicit knowledge. The first type of knowledge is a cornerstone in the theory of organizational knowledge creation and covers knowledge that is not articulated but is linked to the senses, movement skills, physical experiences, intuition, or implicit rules. The second type of knowledge is transmissible in a formal and systematic language. Consequently, the two types of knowledge have been developed throughout history by individuals and/or collaborators. Therefore, the relationship between tacit and explicit knowledge configures the characteristics of the knowledge conversion model [12].

*2.2. Knowledge Conversion*

Knowledge conversion is based on the fact that human knowledge is created and expanded through the interaction between tacit knowledge and explicit knowledge, which increases both in quality and in quantity through the SECI process, i.e., the four different modes of knowledge conversion: socialization, externalization, combination, and internalization [24,25].

Socialization is the conversion of tacit knowledge to tacit knowledge, which means that it is the process of creating tacit knowledge as shared mental models and technical skills. Externalization is the conversion of tacit knowledge to explicit knowledge, being the process of articulating tacit knowledge into explicit concepts that take the form of metaphors, analogies, concepts, or models. Combination is the conversion of explicit knowledge into explicit knowledge, i.e., the systematization of concepts into a knowledge system, which implies that individuals exchange and combine knowledge through documents, meetings, conversations, or communication networks. Lastly, internalization is the transformation of explicit knowledge into tacit knowledge, which is related to "learning by learning".

The "knowledge spiral" is the interaction between tacit and explicit knowledge, which increases in scale as the ontological levels ascend; the organization must mobilize the tacit knowledge created and accumulated at the individual level, and this is later amplified organizationally through the four modes of knowledge conversion and crystallized at higher ontological levels. Thus, knowledge creation is a spiral process, which starts at the individual level and advances through the expanding community of interactions, overcoming the limits of sections, departments, divisions, and organizations [24].

Individual actions model organizational actions, leading to environmental responses; then, the learning cycle is complete when these environmental responses alter individual representations and, thus, lead to better individual and organizational action [3]. Furthermore, knowledge requires a physical environment and/or context to be created, based on a concept called "Ba" [11], meaning "place", i.e., the interaction space inhabited by different actors, where knowledge is shared, created, and used, in addition to providing the energy and quality to make individual conversions and advance in the spiral of knowledge. This space is not only physical (office, workshop, factory, etc.), but also virtual (email, video calls, etc.) and mental (shared ideals, values, beliefs, etc.) [11].

The authors also describe the four types of Ba. The first is the original Ba, which creates a context for socialization, as it is defined by individual and face-to-face interactions, where experiences, feelings, emotions, and mental models are shared. It is the only way to capture the full range of physical senses and psycho-emotional reactions, which are important elements for sharing tacit knowledge [26]. According to [11], the *socialization dimension* is the process of converting new tacit knowledge through shared experiences. This process derives from group collaborations in which individuals cooperate to share tacit knowledge that has been acquired through the internalization of explicit knowledge gained from information. This correlation results in tacit knowledge that is new to everyone involved (see Table 1) [14].

**Table 1.** The socialization dimension.

| Dimension | Subdimension | Definition |
|---|---|---|
| Socialization | Informal communication | Some researchers discussed the importance of informal communication for feedback and socialization [27]. |
| | Social interactions | From an organizational perspective, experiences are perhaps one of the most significant ways of converting tacit knowledge into tacit knowledge [28]. The epistemology of practice perspective suggests that effective knowledge sharing requires extensive and direct social interactions between people, as only during these processes can the tacit component of knowledge be shared [29]. |

Source: Own elaboration.

The second is the dialog Ba, which provides a context for externalization through collective, face-to-face interaction, where individuals' mental models and skills are shared, converted into common terms, and articulated as concepts. Selecting people with the right combination of specific knowledge and skills is the key to successful knowledge management within the dialog Ba [11]. The *externalization dimension* is the transformation of tacit knowledge into explicit knowledge, being the process of articulating tacit knowledge into explicit concepts, taking the form of metaphors, analogies, concepts, or models (Table 2) [24]. In a multiorganizational context, externalization can become difficult, considering that tacit knowledge is related to culture and context, i.e., it is rooted in individuals [30].

Table 2. The externalization dimension.

| Dimension | Subdimension | Definition |
| --- | --- | --- |
| Externalization | Learning teams | Tacit knowledge can be made explicit at the organizational level through the organization of the company into learning-based teams, where practical experience based on encouragement and a helping attitude predominates [31]. The best way to convert tacit knowledge to explicit knowledge is to organize the company into teams based on learning, considering practical experience based on drive and a predominantly helpful attitude [31]. |

Source: Own elaboration.

The other type of Ba is systematization, defined by collective and virtual interactions, mainly providing a context for the combination of explicit knowledge, and generally supported by information technology. The *combination dimension* is the conversion of explicit-to-explicit knowledge, i.e., the systematization of concepts, which implies that individuals exchange knowledge through documents, meetings, conversations, or communication networks (Table 3) [24]. In this process, aggregated knowledge can become a source of value creation, where participants collaborate to promote and communicate new learning to different teams, such that an organizational knowledge asset is developed [30].

Table 3. The combination dimension.

| Dimension | Subdimension | Definition |
| --- | --- | --- |
| Combination | Information processing | The synthesis and integration of information, whether by means of manuals, documents, and databases, among others, on products, services, processes, etc., in addition to the recovery of material that supports the management or technical information of the entire company [11]. |
| | Dissemination of information | One of the main issues for the management of knowledge resources is the dissemination of knowledge within organizations through computerized communication networks and databases available to the organization. For dissemination to be successful, a process of codification and externalization must first be made [11]. |

Source: Own elaboration.

The last classification of Ba is that of exercise, which is constituted by individual and virtual interactions, offering an internalization context, where individuals incorporate explicit knowledge that is communicated through virtual media, written manuals, and simulation programs, among others, to later convert it into tacit knowledge [11]. The *internalization dimension* is the process of converting explicit knowledge into tacit knowledge. Through internalization, the explicit knowledge created is shared by the whole organization and converted into tacit knowledge by individuals (Table 4) [11]. This procedure changes to an individual dimension, where professionals and operators take explicit knowledge and interpret it according to their own intuition and professional experience, thus internalizing it as tacit knowledge [14].

Table 4. The internalization dimension.

| Dimension | Subdimension | Definition |
|---|---|---|
| Internalization | Learning | In traditional learning, individuals learn the tacit knowledge needed in their trade through practical experience or by reading and analyzing manuals or through simulations and experiments that trigger learning by doing [4]. Collective learning occurs when individuals express their opinions and beliefs, engage in constructive confrontations, and challenge the views of others [32]. |

Source: Own elaboration.

Both tacit and explicit knowledge are important. However, treating them individually, as applied in the process of combination and socialization, can cause problems, since it can result in a superficial interpretation of the existing knowledge that has little to do with the current reality. Furthermore, this knowledge can be limited and difficult to apply in other fields that are different from the specific one in which it was created, respectively [33].

### 2.3. Routines

Routines are one of the keys to understanding organizational functioning [34]. Routines have qualities of both stability and change, and, by means of an analogy, it is understood that an organizational routine is not a single pattern; on the contrary, it is a set of possible patterns allowed and limited by diverse organizational, social, physical, and cognitive structures from which the members of the organization perform certain actions [35].

Considering the above, routines are understood as flows of ideas, actions, and connected results. First, ideas produce actions; subsequently, actions produce results, so that these produce new ideas, generating change [6]. However, the relationship among ideas, actions, and results is not always close, as ideas can generate actions that, in fact, do not execute the ideas; actions can generate results that make possible or necessary new and different actions [13]. On the other hand, some authors oppose considering routines as rules that are definitively established, and propose that routines be understood as adaptive rationality [36].

Routines are stable patterns of behavior that characterize organizational reactions to various internal or external stimuli, with two types of routines demarcated: organizational and accumulation of experience [7]. The former involves the execution of known procedures with the objective of generating current revenues and profits, while the latter seeks to bring about desirable changes in the existing set of operating routines, with the purpose of increasing profits in the future.

The dimension of operational routines: The application of processes that are known by staff to achieve current goals (Table 5) [5]. Team behavioral interaction patterns (TBIP) are a very important feature of team adaptation, as research affirms that, to make groups effective in the performance of stable or routine tasks, long and complex interaction patterns are required to increase team efficiency [37].

Table 5. Dimension of operational routines.

| Dimension | Subdimension | Definition |
|---|---|---|
| Operational routines | Operating frequency | Frequency with which the operating routine is activated and executed in a specific time period [5]. |
| | Heterogeneity | The variation in the characteristics of the task, as it is presented in different events, or how novel the task appears each time to the unit that has to perform it [5]. |

Source: Own elaboration.

The dimension of search routines: The objective of these routines is to elicit and generate desirable alterations to previously established operating routines in such a way as to increase future profits (Table 6) [5]. These can be found as organizational functions aimed at learning and change in a specific department, such as innovation and development, marketing, or human resources, or as processes that are requested in response to a need or problem, so that an individual, a committee, a working group, or a consultant studies and analyzes them [38].

**Table 6.** Dimension of search routines.

| Dimension | Subdimension | Definition |
|---|---|---|
| Search routines | Active search | The search for knowledge can be a time-consuming activity, and managers often end their search for knowledge too early or rely on their own experience [39]. |
| | Knowledge mobilization | Mobilize different knowledge components through the different functions, where several knowledge components are located [40]. |
| | Modification or adaptation | (Re)architecture solutions, which were generated by exploring how to integrate knowledge, leverage, and develop their knowledge architecture competencies, which in turn allows them to design novel solutions [40]. |

Source: Own elaboration.

The previous theoretical review supports the construction of the instrument, since a theoretical framework was developed, from which the dimensions of knowledge conversion and routines emerged. Subsequently, subdimensions are identified to define the statements according to the practices of the organizations and to consider the knowledge spiral. These are evaluated by means of the semantic scale (see Table 9), to capture the subjective perceptions of the companies' collaborators.

Considering that the objective is to analyze the second-degree incidences of knowledge conversion in the routines of the collaborators who provided subjective information by means of the instrument, fuzzy methods are used for its treatment. These allow an understanding and comprehension of the meaning of the results, beyond generating a measurement of the results [19].

## 3. Methodology

This research analyzes the forgotten factors between the conversion of knowledge and the routines of collaborators in exporting companies in Boyacá, using subjective information. Thus, the research type and approach, the model of identification of the second-generation relationships, the description of the case study, and the organization of the subjective data are presented. The methods used to analyze the dataset deal with the subjective information of the collaborators, to correct the underestimation of the data and to obtain the accurate estimates.

### 3.1. Type and Approach

The present research is of an explanatory or causal type since it intends to establish the incidence of the forgotten factors in knowledge management through the conversion of knowledge and the routines of the personnel of the exporting companies of Boyaca. This section presents the model of forgotten or second-generation factors, the description of the case study, the organization of the subjective data and the methods to be used, which are the experton method, the adequacy coefficient, and forgotten effects theory.

### 3.2. Model for Finding Second-Generation Relationship

The realization of the model considered the theoretical review presented in the theoretical framework and the methods studied for the design (data collection, called criteria), the dimensions, the methods, and the results of the relationships, presented in Figure 1, establishing a logical sequence that allows aggregation for the treatment process. This process (Figure 1) contains three elements that determine how to find and establish the forgotten factors. The first is the process, which sets out how second-generation relationships can be established. The second is a description that presents the processing of the information and the creation of the working model, where dimensions and the type of information to be collected were defined. The internal processing then considers the proposed methods; lastly, the new relationships found are shown. The third element describes the stages necessary to obtain the findings [41].

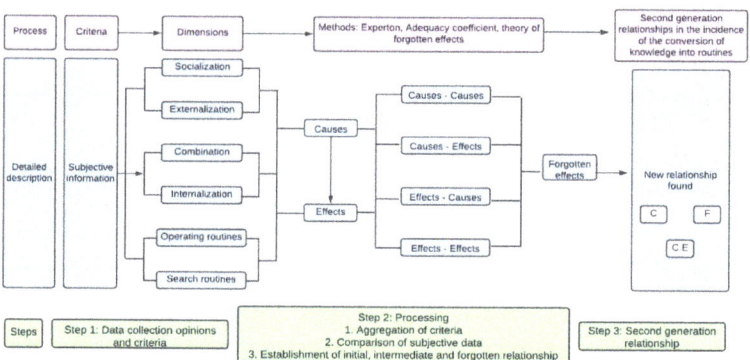

**Figure 1.** A second-generation relationship model in the incidence of the conversion of knowledge into routines. Source: Own elaboration based on the studies of Blanco-Mesa, Leon-Castro, and Castro-Amado [41].

The methods implement calculations and procedures to understand the variations within semantic scales, which are transformed into numerical values representative of the same, generating approximate relationships and relative explanations, creating a large number of possibilities [41].

Models used to search for ignored effects can generate multiple data, since they are often binary-valued systems (i.e., they are evaluated through numbers in [0,1] or confidence intervals of [0,1]), which represent the meaning given to the relationships and not a measure of the relationships in absolute terms [17]; that is, they do not consider the relationship between incidence and the linkage between different arguments that apparently have nothing in common. Indeed, the incidence of relationships is determined by intensity and linkage. Intensity considers the presence of a connecting agent in the relationships, making it possible to analyze the convergence of the boundary, periodicity, and non-standardized situations reflected in elements such as time, space, and possible connections [42]. On the other hand, linkage shows the direct and indirect connections in the relationships, analyzing variations in the intensities and strengths of the relationships to observe the behavior and the links that strengthen or weaken them, either in a period or in a sequence of stages [42].

*3.3. Case Study*

The target population of the study consisted of the collaborators in the exporting companies registered in the chamber of commerce of the department of Boyacá, Colombia. Chambers of commerce are private, nonprofit organizations that represent a group of companies and traders in a region, promoting competitiveness, formalization, and regional development, as well as serving as a consultative body on economic issues, among other characteristics [43]. The exporting companies in this study were registered in the chambers of commerce of Tunja and Sogamoso in the department of Boyacá, and were engaged in different economic activities, such as engineering activities, retail and wholesale trade of different products, legal activities, mixed exploitation (agriculture and livestock), data processing, medical activities, call centers, real estate activities, extraction of emeralds, and the processing and preservation of fruits, vegetables, and legumes.

Initially, the research proposed the participation of all the companies registered in the chambers of commerce in the department of Boyacá, but this was not possible due to different limitations. The first limitation was related to the fact that some companies, even though they are registered, had not carried out any commercial movement, i.e., they were never in operation. On the other hand, there were some difficulties in accessing companies registered with outdated data that prevented face-to-face, telephone, or electronic contact. Similarly, when contacted, some companies showed interest in participating in the research, but postponed the application of the instrument. Consequently, the instrument was applied to 40 collaborators in the 40 companies registered in the Tunja and Sogamoso chambers of commerce.

The instrument was applied in three stages. The first stage involved contacting the chambers of commerce to learn about the exporting companies registered in the region. In the second stage, the first contact was made with the collaborators by telephone and email to confirm their participation and to arrange for the link to the instrument to be sent by email or to be applied by telephone. In the third stage, the survey was carried out via telephone and email, where the link was sent and support was provided in resolving doubts and concerns about the instrument, and in person in some cases. Although the population was small, this did not affect the main objective, which was to analyze the incidence of forgotten factors in knowledge conversion in the routines of the personnel. This objective sought to make sense of the information but not to measure it [19]. Therefore, a fuzzy point of view was used to obtain the expected results.

*3.4. Data Collection*

An instrument was built according to the theory of organizational knowledge creation, which organizationally expands the knowledge created by people and connects it to the knowledge system of an organization, where tacit and explicit knowledge interact dynamically [12]. This instrument was implemented as a scale, considering the forgotten effects theory, since the intention of the study was to establish a causal relationship and to identify forgotten elements that are apparently not related [44–46]. Subsequently, for the treatment of the instrument and its validity, fuzzy methods, the experton method, and the adequacy coefficient were used. The use of fuzzy methods allows us to focus on the meaning of the results rather than on their measurement [19]. The experton method facilitates an understanding of the distribution and trend of the subjective opinions of the individuals, aggregating them to obtain an overall opinion. Lastly, the adequacy coefficient calculates the differences between two elements by neutralizing the real value when it exceeds the ideal value [41]. The causes and effects used in the study are presented below with their respective identifiers and statements (see Tables 7 and 8).

**Table 7.** Causes in the study.

| Dimension | Indicator | Statement | Identifier |
|---|---|---|---|
| Socialization | Informal communication | Extra workspace | CI_EEL |
| | | Spontaneous conversations in workspaces | CI_CEEL |
| | Social interactions | Business meetings | IS_RE |
| | | After work conversations with bosses | IS_CEJ |
| | | Interactions in different areas and positions | IS_IDAC |
| Externalization | Learning teams | Willingness to teach peers | EA_DEC |
| | | Conversation of work topics | EA_CTL |
| | | Teamwork | EA_TE |
| Combination | Information processing | Record of results | TI_RR |
| | | Reports of work completed | TI_ITR |
| | | Supplier knowledge | TI_CP |
| | | Knowledge about clients | TI_CCL |
| | Dissemination of information | Access to organization information | DI_AIO |
| | | Clear and understandable information | DI_ICE |
| | | Access to information from other areas | DI_AIA |

**Table 7.** *Cont.*

| Dimension | Indicator | Statement | Identifier |
|---|---|---|---|
| Operating routines | Operating frequency | Permanent working group | FO_GTP |
| Internalization | Learning | Database discussion<br>Explanation of functions | AP_DBD<br>AP_EF |
| Search routines | Active search | Problem communication<br>Share doubts<br>Ask for help in difficulties<br>Search for continuous improvement | BA_CP<br>BA_CD<br>BA_SAD<br>BA_BMC |
| | Knowledge mobilization | Make some change<br>Interference in a different area | MC_RAC<br>MC_IAD |
| | Modification or adaptation | Freedom to make changes<br>Agreements with the working group | MA_LRC<br>MA_AGT |

Source: Own elaboration.

**Table 8.** Effects in the study.

| Dimension | Indicator | Statement | Identifier |
|---|---|---|---|
| Socialization | Informal communication | Peer relations<br>Linguistic expression<br>Everyday vocabulary | CI_RC<br>CI_EL<br>CI_VC |
| | Social interactions | Virtual meetings<br>Personal conversations with my colleagues | IS_RV<br>IS_CPC |
| Externalization | Learning teams | Trainings<br>Share knowledge to other areas<br>Associate words or images<br>List of known concepts<br>Database | EA_C<br>EA_CCA<br>EA_API<br>EA_RCC<br>EA_BD |
| Combination | Information processing | Use of old reports | TI_UIA |
| | Dissemination of information | Sharing information with other areas<br>Share changes to collaborators | DI_CIA<br>DI_CCC |
| Internalization | Learning | Implementation of manuals and documentation<br>Constant practice of functions<br>Problem resolution | AP_IMD<br>AP_PCF<br>AP_RP |
| Heterogeneity | Operating frequency | Consult the operation manuals<br>Constantly changing roles<br>Change of functions according to the area<br>Change in the way of performing functions | FO_CMO<br>FO_CFC<br>FO_CFA<br>FO_CFRF |
| | Heterogeneity | Excessive number of tasks<br>Error anticipation | H_CET<br>H_AE |
| Search routines | Active search | Identify actions to improve | BA_IAM |
| | Knowledge mobilization | Suggestions are valued<br>A change involves all areas | MC_SV<br>MC_CIA |
| | Modification or adaptation | Improvements help other areas<br>Training improves my work<br>Adaptation of functions | MA_MAA<br>MA_CMT<br>MA_AF |

Source: Own elaboration.

For the evaluation of the elements considered as cause and effect for knowledge conversion, routines and knowledge management are expressed on the scale in Table 9.

Table 9. Semantic scale.

| SS | TD | SD | DI | I | AG | SA | TA |
|---|---|---|---|---|---|---|---|
| SC | 0.14 | 0.29 | 0.43 | 0.57 | 0.71 | 0.86 | 1 |

Source: Own elaboration. SS: semantic scale, SC: standardization criteria, TD: totally disagree, SD: strongly disagree, DI: disagree, I: indifferent, AG: agree, SA: strongly agree, TA: totally agree.

After collecting the information, fuzzy methods, the experton method, and the adequacy coefficient were used for its treatment and validity. The approach was from a fuzzy perspective, using software such as FuzzyLog, which is a calculation program that elaborates and works with models on the basis of uncertainty mathematics to recover the so-called forgotten effects in causality relationships.

To achieve the research aim, three methodological phases are proposed, which give a logical order to the research process. In phase one, a review of the literature on knowledge management is carried out. To observe the context of these topics and their main advances in a holistic way, the Web of Science database is used. The following keywords are used in the search: knowledge creation, routines, and knowledge management. These results are then filtered under the concept of "management" so that the information is closer to the expected field of research. A theory of the creation of organizational knowledge, which has a dynamic model that expands through the interaction between tacit and explicit knowledge, was exposed by Nonaka and Takeuchi. Similarly, Nelson and Winter made important contributions to the concept of routines, which allowed the construction of the theoretical framework and the research methodology. In phase two, a scale instrument is implemented, which is treated with the forgotten effects theory, the experton method, and the adequacy coefficient. The information obtained is analyzed using FuzzyLog software. Lastly, in phase three, with the theoretical review complete, the data treatment is carried out and the preliminary conclusions obtained.

*3.5. Methods*

The present research employed different methods for data analysis, i.e., the experton method, the adequacy coefficient, and the theory of forgotten effects.

3.5.1. Experton Method

The experton method facilitates the addition of close or distant opinions as subjective uncertainty information [15]. The experton is a tool that uses fuzzy set theory and possibility analysis to unify information from different experts using a cumulative distribution function, which is obtained using linguistic expressions from a group of experts on an endecadary scale [0,1]. The experton method is defined as an extension of the probabilistic set, where the probability of each $\alpha$-slice is replaced by a probability interval according to the experts. The structure of the formula is as follows:

$$\forall a \in E : \left[a^{j*}(a)\right], \left[a_{j*}(a)\right] \subset [0,1], \quad (1)$$

where $\subset$ is the inclusion set, and $j$ represents the expert.

Derived from the fact that the experton method is an extension of the probabilistic set, it has the same characteristics, as follows:

- Non-strict horizontal increasing monotonicity property (i.e., the membership characteristic function of the positively sloping function is less than or equal to the characteristic function of the negative slope function).
- Non-strict vertical increasing monotonicity property, except at level 0, which always takes the value 1.

Thus,

$$\forall \alpha \in [0,1] : \alpha_1(a) \leq \alpha_2(a) en\ \alpha_1[\alpha_1(a), \alpha_2(a)], \quad (2)$$

$$\forall \alpha \alpha' \in [0,1] : a' > a \Rightarrow (\alpha_1(a)) \leq \alpha_1 a', \alpha_2(a) < \alpha_2(a'), \tag{3}$$

$$(a = 0) \Rightarrow (a_1(a) = 1, a_2(a) = 1). \tag{4}$$

The variables must be evaluated, using a number $\alpha \in [0,1]$ or through confidence intervals.

- The individual opinions should be converted into an overall opinion of the group of individuals.
- The statistics are generated and the complementary cumulation law is applied.

The importance of the experton method lies in the fact that the distribution and trend of the subjective opinions can be determined and, in the end, aggregated to generate an overall opinion of the group.

3.5.2. Adequacy Coefficient

The notion of distance in the use of fuzzy subsets is based on the premise that every metric is always a distance, but not every distance is a metric [16]. Considering this premise, the adequacy coefficient is a measure of distance called infradistance, which determines appreciable differences by correcting the overestimation of information without being a given metric.

The adequacy coefficient [47,48] is an index that allows us to calculate the differences between two elements, which neutralizes the result when the comparison shows that the real element has a higher value than the ideal element. For the two elements A and B, the adequacy coefficient weight is defined below.

**Definition 1.** *A weighted adequacy coefficient of dimension n has a mapping of* $K : [0,1]^n - x[0,1]^n \to [0,1]$ *which has associated with it a weighting vector w of dimension n with the sum of the weights 1 y* $w_j \in [0,1]$, *such as*

$$K(\langle x_1, y_1 \rangle, \cdots, \langle x_n, y_n, \rangle) = \sum_{i=1}^{n} w_i [1 \wedge (1 - x_i + y_i)], \tag{5}$$

*where* $x_j$, $y$, *and* $y_j$ *are the i-th arguments of the elements X and Y.*

3.5.3. Forgotten Effects Theory

The forgotten effects theory is based on the concept of incidence, which is a subjective notion linked to reasoned action. Incidence is studied based on a network of links that omit several stages and forget conclusions [17].

Therefore, its operation is focused on second-generation effects that make it possible to find the effects forgotten in the first instance. In this way, incidence is a remarkably subjective definition, and its analysis enhances reasoned action and decision making. There is an incidence $a_i$ on $b_j$. Here, the values of the characteristic function of the pair $(a_i, b_j)$ are valued between [0,1]:

$$\forall (a_i, b_j) \Rightarrow M(a_i, b_j) \in [0,1]. \tag{6}$$

The direct incidence matrix is defined by the set of pairs of valued elements, which shows the cause–effect relationship that occurs in different degrees between the elements of set $a$ (causes) and the elements of set $b$ (effects):

$$\widetilde{M} = \begin{array}{c|cccccc} & b_1 & b_2 & \cdots & b_j \\ a_1 & u_{a_1 b_1} & u_{a_1 b_2} & \cdots & u_{a_1 b_j} \\ a_2 & u_{a_2 b_1} & u_{a_2 b_1} & \cdots & u_{a_2 b_j} \\ \vdots & \vdots & \vdots & \vdots & \vdots \\ a_i & u_{a_i b_1} & u_{a_1 b_2} & \cdots & u_{a_i b_j} \end{array}$$

All events show three ways of representing cause–effect relationships, which are denoted within the matrix of direct or first-order events. These relationships are considered when establishing the impact of some elements of one set on those of another.

### 3.6. Direct and Indirect Causal Relationship

It is possible to obtain hidden cause–effect relationships. Causal relationships are given by

$$[\widetilde{M}] = \{Ma_jb_i \in [0,1] / i = 1, 2, \ldots, n; j = 1, 2, \ldots, m\}. \tag{7}$$

According to $M_{a_ib_j}$, the characteristic function of the permanence of the elements of the matrix $[\widetilde{M}]$ is formed by the rows corresponding to the elements of set $a$ (causes) and the columns corresponding to the elements of set $b$ (effects). In fact, the matrix $[M]$ is formed by the effects that the elements of set $a$ have on set $b$. If $[\widetilde{M}]$ shows the first-generation cause–effect relationships, the next step is to obtain an incidence matrix reflecting the indirect relationships. To do this, it must be considered that the different causes can have effects on themselves, and that the effects can have incidences on themselves. Therefore, two additional relationships are created. Consequently, two auxiliary matrices are formulated and defined as square matrices:

$$[\widetilde{A}] = \{Ma_ia_j \in [0,1] \ i, j = 1, 2, \ldots, n\}, \tag{8}$$

$$[\widetilde{B}] = \{Mb_ib_j \in [0,1] \ i, j = 1, 2, \ldots, m\}, \tag{9}$$

where $[\widetilde{A}]$ collects the incidence relationships between the causes, and $[\widetilde{B}]$ does so on the effects. Both matrices are reflexive, and it is satisfied that $M_{a_ia_j} = 1 \ \forall \ i = 1, 2 \ldots, n$ and that $M_{b_ib_j} = 1 \ \forall \ i = 1, 2 \ldots, m$. This implies that any element, whether cause or effect, indicates with the maximum assumption about itself; thus, neither $[\widetilde{A}]$ nor $[\widetilde{B}]$ is a symmetric matrix. With the three matrices defined, the causal relationships between them must be established. Therefore, the maximum–minimum composition of the three matrices is given by $[\widetilde{A}] \circ [\widetilde{M}] \circ [\widetilde{B}] = [\widetilde{M}^*]$.

The degree of neglect of some causal relationships is given by the difference between the matrix of second-generation effects and the matrix of direct incidences: $[\widetilde{O}] = [\widetilde{M}^*] - [\widetilde{M}]$. Therefore, if the value of the characteristic function of the matrix elements $[\widetilde{O}]$ is high, the degree of forgetting in the initial incidence ratio is the highest.

$$[\tilde{O}] = \begin{matrix} & \rightarrow & b_1 & b_2 & \cdots & b_m \\ a_1 & & u^*_{a_1b_1} - u_{a_1b_1} & u^*_{a_1b_2} - u_{a_1b_2} & \cdots & u^*_{a_1b_m} - u_{a_1b_m} \\ a_2 & & u^*_{a_2b_1} - u_{a_2b_1} & u^*_{a_2b_2} - u_{a_2b_2} & \cdots & u^*_{a_2b_m} - u_{a_2b_m} \\ \vdots & & \vdots & \vdots & \vdots & \vdots \\ a_n & & u^*_{a_nb_1} - u_{a_nb_1} & u^*_{a_nb_2} - u_{a_nb_2} & \cdots & u^*_{a_nb_m} - u_{a_nb_m} \end{matrix}$$

## 4. Results

### 4.1. Knowledge Conversion

Figure 2 describes incidences C14 (the information provided by the company is clear and understandable) and E16 (the information provided by the company has allowed me to solve problems and create solutions), which have a forgotten effect equal to one, indicating that there is no direct relationship between cause and effect. The entry of collaborators into companies implies the transfer of explicit knowledge in a clear and understandable way, which requires time, especially in the detailed description of the functions of each collaborator, with the purpose that this becomes tacit knowledge in the future. This is a challenge for organizations; therefore, by structuring the company in teams based on learning, strategies are implemented that relate the thoughts and concepts known by each of the collaborators. It is possible to have a mutual understanding that allows a process to be executed whereby tacit knowledge becomes explicit and permits this information to contribute to problem solving. This is a strategic competitive factor for the exporting companies in Boyacá, in which tacit knowledge plays a fundamental role [14].

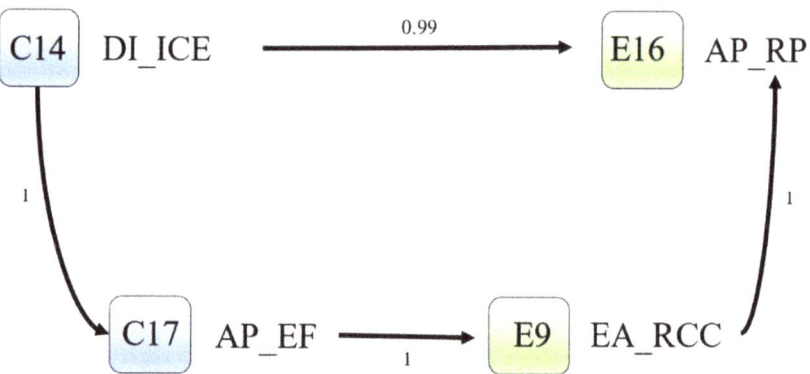

**Figure 2.** Incidence between information dissemination and learning $C_{14} \rightarrow E_{16}$. Source: Own elaboration. $C_{14}$ DI_ICE: The information provided by the company is clear and understandable; $C_{17}$ AP_EF: Upon joining the organization, they took the time to clearly explain my functions to me; $E_9$ EA_RCC: I relate known concepts to express what I know; $E_{16}$ AP_RP: The information provided by the company has allowed me to solve problems and create solutions. Initially estimated value: 0.99. Accumulated value cause–effect: 1. Difference of values (forgotten effect): 1. Relevant interposed key relationship: AP_EF.

Figure 3 describes incidences C16 (I am motivated to discuss databases, documentation, and manuals, among others, with my colleagues) and E2 (sometimes I do not know how to express what I think in words), which have a forgotten effect equal to one, indicating that there is no direct relationship between cause and effect. The starting point is based on the internalization process, where collaborators could transfer explicit knowledge to tacit knowledge through the discussion of codified knowledge [11]. Therefore, the key relationship is the recording of improvements in a database. However, the effect of this process refers to the difficulty for employees to express their thoughts in words, constituting a disadvantage in socialization [12].

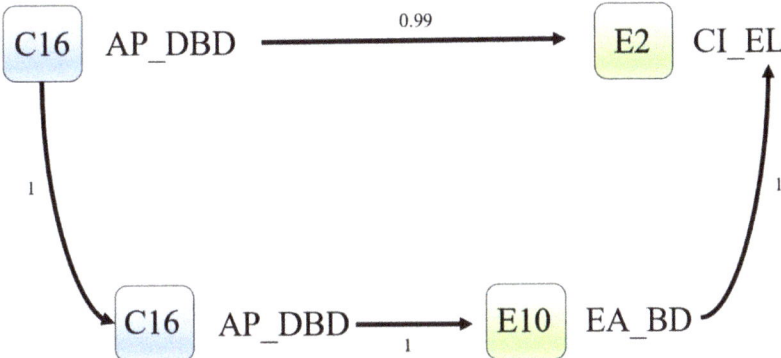

**Figure 3.** Incidence between information dissemination and learning $C_{16} \rightarrow E_2$. Source: Own elaboration. $C_{16}$ AP_DBD: They motivate me to discuss databases, documentation, and manuals, among others, with my colleagues; $E_{10}$ EA_BD: My work team records improvement ideas in a database; $E_2$ CI_EL: Sometimes I do not know how to express what I think in words. Initially estimated value: 0.99. Accumulated value cause–effect: 1. Difference of values (forgotten effect): 1. Relevant interposed key relationship: AP_DBD.

### 4.2. Routines

Figure 4 describes incidences C1 (my work group is always the same) and E9 (when making a change in each area, the company involves all its personnel), which have a forgotten effect close to one (0.8), indicating that there is no direct relationship between cause and effect. The starting point is the high operational frequency of the work group; that is, generally, the collaborators keep the same team in the long term. In this case, when there is freedom to make changes, either because the execution of the routines is not achieving an expected or desired result, or because such results do not reveal new possibilities, the collaborators will try to repair or improve the routine, affecting other areas of the company. This can expand the repertoire of modification or adaptation, considering that there are more environments involved [5].

Figure 5 describes incidences C6 (forbidden to make any change, both in the tasks I perform and in the way I execute them) and E9 (a change involves all the personnel in the area), which have a forgotten effect close to one (0.8), indicating that there is no direct relationship between cause and effect. In organizations, there is an established routine, which does not allow employees to make changes in their functions. However, often, there are both small and large disturbances. The former is absorbed by the different members of the company, and the latter highlights the differences that exist in the interpretations of the routine in each area, considering that these bring with them understandings and motivations. Therefore, interferences, interactions, and the dynamics of knowledge in the different areas are necessary. In addition, organizations have exceptions at specific times and moments, since these changes can shape the adoption, persistence, or mobilization of routines, resulting in improvements that can be useful in other areas and, in the same way, involve the collaborators who interact in them [5].

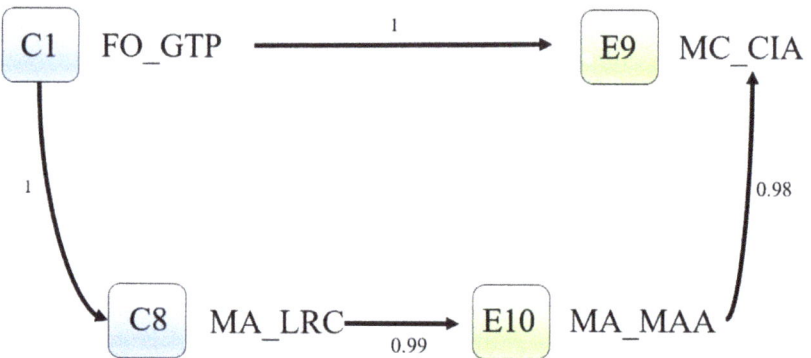

**Figure 4.** Incidences between operating frequency and mobilization of knowledge $C_1 \to E_9$. Source: Own elaboration. $C_1$ FO_GTP: My working group is always the same; $C_8$ MA_LRC: I am free to make changes to my process when I deem it necessary; $E_{10}$ MA_MAA: The improvements that I implemented in my work helped other areas of the company; $E_9$ MC_CIA: When making a change in a certain area, the company involves all its personnel. Initially estimated value: 1. Cumulative cause–effect value: 0.98. Value difference (forgotten effect): 0.8. Relevant interposed key relationship: MA_LRC.

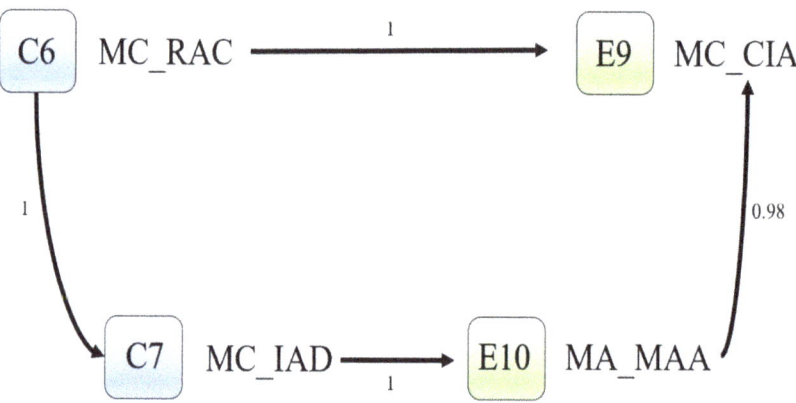

**Figure 5.** Incidence of knowledge mobilization $C_6 \to E_9$. Source: Own elaboration. $C_6$ MC_RAC: I am prohibited from making any changes, both in the tasks I perform and in the way I execute them; $C_7$ MC_IAD: I cannot interfere in an area other than mine, unless the company allows me to; $E_{10}$ MA_MAA: The improvements that I implemented in my work helped other areas of the company; $E_9$ MC_CIA: When making a change in a certain area, the company involves all its personnel. Initially estimated value: 1. Cumulative cause–effect value: 0.98. Value difference (forgotten effect): 0.8. Relevant interposed key relationship: MC_IAD.

### 4.3. Knowledge Management

On the basis of the theoretical concepts and different tests performed in the FuzzyLog program, the dimensions of socialization, internalization, and search routines are found as cause and effect, specifically the variables of informal communication, social interactions, learning, and active search (Table 10). Among them, the causal relationships between knowledge conversion and routines that presented forgotten effects the most are $E_2$ (sometimes I do not know how to express what I think in words) and $E_4$ (in virtual meetings, I feel it is more difficult to express myself than personally).

Table 10. Causes and effects of knowledge management.

| | | | Causes | | | |
|---|---|---|---|---|---|---|
| V | D | I | S | Id | T | Ex |
| Knowledge conversion | Socialization | Informal communication | Extra workspace | CI_EEL | C1 | 0.759 |
| | | | Spontaneous conversations in workspaces | CI_CEEL | C2 | 0.763 |
| | | Social interactions | Business meetings | IS_RE | C3 | 0.806 |
| | | | After work conversations with bosses | IS_CEJ | C4 | 0.753 |
| | | | Interactions in different areas and positions | IS_IDAC | C5 | 0.791 |
| | Internalization | Learning | Database discussion | AP_DBD | C6 | 0.716 |
| | | | Explanation of functions | AP_EF | C7 | 0.825 |
| Routines | Search routines | Active search | Problem communication | BA_CP | C8 | 0.806 |
| | | | Share doubts | BA_CD | C9 | 0.803 |
| | | | Ask for help in difficulties | BA_SAD | C10 | 0.781 |
| | | | Search for continuous improvement | BA_BMC | C11 | 0.797 |
| | | | Effects | | | |
| V | D | I | S | Id | T | Ex |
| Knowledge conversion | Socialization | Informal communication | Peer relations | CI_RC | E1 | 0.781 |
| | | | Linguistic expression | CI_EL | E2 | 0.672 |
| | | Social interactions | Everyday vocabulary | CI_VC | E3 | 0.781 |
| | | | Virtual meetings | IS_RV | E4 | 0.663 |
| | | | Personal conversations with my colleagues | IS_CPC | E5 | 0.800 |
| | Internalization | Learning | Implementation of manuals and documentation | AP_IMD | E6 | 0.759 |
| | | | Constant practice of functions | AP_PCF | E7 | 0.859 |
| | | | Problem resolution | AP_RP | E8 | 0.822 |
| Routines | Search routines | Active search | Identify actions to improve | BA_IAM | E9 | 0.806 |

Source: Own elaboration. V: variable; D: dimension; I: indicator; S: statement; Id: identifier; T: type; Ex: expert.

Consequently, the fractured routes of incidence were identified for each of the effects, i.e., one was chosen for socialization, another for internalization, and one for search routines for both informal communication and social interactions, considering that this is where the greatest number of forgotten effects occurred.

In informal communication, with respect to socialization, case 32 was selected, where the causes are IS_RE and AP_DBD, and the effects are AP_IMD and CI_EL. In the case of internalization, case 33 was chosen, where the causes are AP_DBD and BA_CD, and the effects are AP_RP and CI_EL. In search routines, case 19 was chosen, where the causes are BA_SAD and BA_CD, and the effects are AP_RP and CI_EL. In social interactions, case 4 was selected for socialization, with IS_RE as cause, and IS_CPC and IS_RV as effects. For internalization, case 6 was chosen, in which the cause is AP_DBD, and the effects are AP_IMD and IS_RV. For the search routines, case 4 was chosen, in which the causes are BA_SAD and BA_CD, and the effects are IS_CPC and IS_RV.

## 5. Discussion

The results show the most relevant factors in the knowledge conversion and routines of the collaborators in exporting companies in Boyacá. The incidences between the causes and effects of both knowledge conversion and routines were observed using mathematical tools based on fuzzy models, which establish second-generation relationships between factors that apparently had no evident relationship. The research revealed the incidences in knowledge management by means of the forgotten factors between knowledge conversion and routines, evidencing that the effects that most presented forgetfulness are part of informal communication and social interactions, i.e., that these indicators represent the key route of the incidence, which manifested a fractured route for knowledge management in the Boyacá exporting companies, specifically in the capacity to express linguistically and in a virtual way. This fracture refers to the difficulty of sharing and disseminating tacit knowledge electronically, once it has been produced and appropriated by collaborators. In other words, one of the elements that characterizes tacit knowledge is that people are not aware of its full range, as, once it is internalized, it becomes a natural part of one's behavior or way of thinking [48]; hence, it is more difficult to specify and to express.

*Knowledge Management*

The knowledge management model showed that the effects presenting the highest number of forgotten effects were part of informal communication ($E_2$) and social interactions ($E_4$), and that in these variables, there was a fractured route in the incidences, which hinders the process of knowledge creation. By virtue of this, it can be observed that the system presented 129 alternative routes for $E_2$ and 29 for $E_4$ (see Table 11).

**Table 11.** Number of alternative routes for knowledge management.

|  | Socialization | Internalization | Search Routines | Total |
|---|---|---|---|---|
| Informal communication ($E_2$) | 55 | 44 | 30 | 129 |
| Social interactions ($E_4$) | 13 | 10 | 6 | 29 |

Source: Own elaboration.

According to the FuzzyLog results, one case was selected for socialization, one for internalization, and one for search routines, and, both for informal communication and socialization, considering the cases that were most consistent with the theoretical framework (see Tables 12 and 13). These relationships show that, in informal communication, the causes are part of socialization, internalization, and search routines, which are positive statements, since they refer to situations where employees have the freedom to express their opinions and doubts, discuss codified information, and feel confident enough to ask for help. These causes generated common effects, which are part of learning and informal communication. The effects of learning are favorable, considering that they are based on improvement and problem solving, while the effects that are part of informal communication represent a disadvantage, as it is difficult for employees to express what they think to their colleagues.

This means that organizations have tried to apply collaborative exchange mechanisms that promote the capture, representation, and application of knowledge, improving individual learning [49]. However, the effect of informal communication presented a disadvantage in the linguistic expression of tacit knowledge, evidencing the difficulty of externalizing the level of understanding with words. Consequently, even though the collaborators have the capacity and ability to solve problems, no practices have been developed in socialization for individuals to communicate their ideas, confirming the definition that Michael Polanyi gave to tacit knowledge: "We can know more than we can say" [31].

With respect to relationships in social interactions, the causes reflected are part of social interactions, learning, and active search, showing that there is a deepening in the behavior, emotion (socialization), and cognition (internalization) of the collaborators, which allows an understanding of the daily implementation of routines in the different areas [50]. These causes triggered effects that promoted knowledge conversion and others that limited it. On one hand, the understanding of routines, the discussion of explicit information, and group interactions made possible the connection of individual capabilities with those of employees and managers, resulting in improved functions and spontaneous collaborative exchanges. However, the common effect in the three dimensions reflected the difficulty for employees to express themselves virtually, proving one of the most debated characteristics of tacit knowledge, which states that sharing tacit knowledge through information technology systems is extremely difficult, considering that disseminating tacit knowledge in an explicit and objective way prevents it from being shared electronically [29].

**Table 12.** Alternate routes of informal communication.

| Informal Communication | | |
|---|---|---|
| Socialization | Internalization | Search routines |
| Causes | | |
| IS_RE<br>In business meetings, they allow me to express my opinions and share my experiences | AP_DBD<br>They motivate me to discuss databases, documentation, manuals, among others with my colleagues | BA_SAD<br>I ask my bosses for help when I have difficulties in carrying out my work |
| AP_DBD<br>They motivate me to discuss databases, documentation, manuals, among others with my colleagues | BA_CD<br>I share my doubts with colleagues from other departments to resolve them | BA_CD<br>I share my doubts with colleagues from other departments to resolve them |
| Effects | | |
| AP_IMD<br>Through the implementation of manuals and documentation, among other reports, I have improved the execution of my functions | AP_RP<br>The information provided by the company has allowed me to solve problems and create solutions | AP_RP<br>The information provided by the company has allowed me to solve problems and create solutions |
| CI_EL<br>Sometimes I do not know how to express what I think in words | CI_EL<br>Sometimes I do not know how to express what I think in words | CI_EL<br>Sometimes I do not know how to express what I think in words |

Source: Own elaboration.

**Table 13.** Alternate routes of social interactions.

| Social Interactions | | |
|---|---|---|
| Socialization | Internalization | Search routines |
| Causes | | |
| IS_RE<br>In business meetings, they allow me to express my opinions and share my experiences | AP_DBD<br>They motivate me to discuss databases, documentation, and manuals, among others, with my colleagues | BA_SAD<br>I ask my bosses for help when I have difficulties in carrying out my work |
| | | BA_CD<br>I share my doubts with colleagues from other departments to resolve them |
| Effects | | |
| IS_CPC<br>Personal conversations with my colleagues allow me to give my opinions in a more open and relaxed way | Through the implementation of manuals and documentation, among other reports, I have improved the execution of my functions | IS_CPC<br>Personal conversations with my colleagues allow me to give my opinions in a more open and relaxed way |
| IS_RV<br>In virtual meetings, I feel that it is more difficult to express myself than personally | IS_RV<br>In virtual meetings, I feel that it is more difficult to express myself than personally | IS_RV<br>In virtual meetings, I feel that it is more difficult to express myself than personally |

Source: Own elaboration.

Considering the above relationships, Figure 6 is presented, which exemplifies the second-order incidences for knowledge management. Area one (A1) shows the incidences between knowledge conversion and routines, and the key route of incidence, through informal communication and social interactions. On the other hand, area two (A2) presents a fractured route for knowledge management, i.e., the different constraints found in Boyacá's exporting companies.

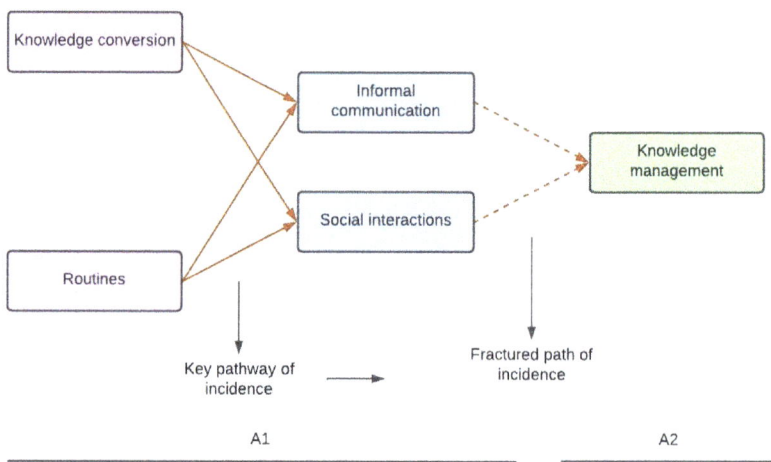

**Figure 6.** Second-order incidents for knowledge management. Source: Own elaboration.

## 6. Conclusions

This research summarizes the theory related to knowledge management, knowledge conversion, and routines. A model is applied to identify the second-degree relationships between knowledge conversion and routines in exporting companies. This model deals with subjective information by means of internal processing, considering the proposed methods, which are the experton method, the adequacy coefficient, and the forgotten effects theory [17]. The notion of expertons contributes to foresight in situations where there is a lack of information [51]. The notion of distance used in the adequacy coefficient, called infradistance, makes it possible to determine the appreciable differences, correcting the overestimation of information without a given metric. The notion of incidences facilitates study of the basis of a network of links that omit several stages and forget the conclusions [17]. In this sense, the methods used make it possible to aggregate the subjective criteria of the collaborators, correct the underestimation of the data to obtain the true estimates, and determine the second-generation incidences.

The case study focused on exporting companies registered with the Tunja and Sogamoso chambers of commerce. The collaborators occupy different positions, reflecting the diversity and heterogeneity in the instrument. The findings allow us to observe incidences in the conversion of knowledge, which show that, in the causes, the four pillars of the knowledge spiral are present. Meanwhile, in the effects generated and the alternative route proposed, socialization, externalization, and internalization prevail in a positive way, specifically informal communication, social interactions, learning teams, and learning.

The relationships found in the routines were revealed as causes of the operational frequency in the routines and the mobilization of knowledge. These triggered favorable common effects that are part of the search routines dimension, showing that the improvements implemented by the collaborators helped other areas and, in the same way, involved the personnel who produced the change. For these relationships, different alternative routes were projected, where the indicators of modification or adaptation, knowledge mobilization, and operational frequency prevailed.

The results obtained can help us to understand both the virtues and the fractures that exist in the knowledge management process, offering a vision of knowledge spiral development within organizations. Thus, the practical implications of the research can help to guide the practices of socialization, externalization, combination, and internalization in the routines of individuals to foster knowledge creation. On the other hand, the theoretical implications of the study refer to the findings of incidence among knowledge management, knowledge conversion, and routines, where a relationship was found among the four components of the SECI model, search routines, and operational routines, showing that knowledge creation is a daily organizational issue, and that it is present in each area of the company.

The advantage of using the proposed method is that it is an effective alternative for dealing with subjective information, which is complex for traditional methods to process. For this reason, this method enables the implementation of subjective criteria, and correction of the overestimates that may occur when comparing the values given with those established to obtain the true estimates. Lastly, it makes it possible to determine second-generation cause–effect incidences to find and analyze hidden relationships.

The limitations of the research are associated with the size of the sample, as the number of respondents was small; therefore, being subjective data, the results are based on the subjective perceptions of the employees, focusing on a specific reality that cannot be generalized. Consequently, the population that could be contacted and that applied the instrument totaled 40 employees in the 40 exporting companies.

When using these methodologies, it should be remembered that the results obtained depend on the semantic configuration of the research design, where academic, cultural, and social aspects influence the manner in which we communicate. In this sense, the methods do not allow us to accurately capture these semantic nuances, and a careful prior design must be made. Similarly, it should be considered that fuzzy methods allow us to deal with soft data; thus, their results are flexible in their interpretation with a solid formal methodological structure. Hence, these methods give greater relevance to the meaning of the statements than to the measurement that can be derived from them [19].

Lastly, as recommendations for future research, from a methodological point of view, an analysis of the causes and effects is necessary to achieve a better diagnosis and guide to business decision making. From an academic perspective, it is important to carry out a deeper analysis of each of the pillars of the knowledge spiral individually in exporting companies belonging to different regions of the country, especially in socialization, social interactions (linguistic expression), and informal communication (electronic meetings).

**Author Contributions:** Conceptualization, Y.C. and O.V.; methodology, F.B.-M.; software, F.B.-M.; validation, F.B.-M., Y.C. and O.V.; formal analysis, F.B.-M.; investigation, Y.C. and O.V.; writing—original draft preparation, F.B.-M.; writing—review and editing, F.B.-M., Y.C. and O.V.; project administration, F.B.-M.; funding acquisition, F.B.-M. All authors have read and agreed to the published version of the manuscript.

**Funding:** This research was funded by Universidad Pedagogica y Tecnologica de Colombia, grant number SGI 3323, and Red Sistemas Inteligentes y Expertos Modelos Computacionales Iberoamericanos (SIEMCI), project number 522RT0130, in Programa Iberoamericano de Ciencia y Tecnología para el Desarrollo (CYTED).

**Data Availability Statement:** Data are available from the authors.

**Conflicts of Interest:** The authors declare no conflict of interest.

# Appendix A. Experton Method Calculus

**Table A1.** Experton method.

| FT | α | C11 | C12 | C13 | C14 | C15 | IS1 | IS2 | IS3 | IS4 | IS5 | EA1 | EA2 | EA3 | EA4 | EA5 | EA6 | EA7 | EA8 | TI1 | TI2 | TI3 | TI4 | TI5 | DI1 | DI2 | DI3 | DI4 | DI5 |
|---|---|---|---|---|---|---|---|---|---|---|---|---|---|---|---|---|---|---|---|---|---|---|---|---|---|---|---|---|---|
| 0 | 0 | 0 | 0 | 0 | 0 | 0 | 0 | 0 | 0 | 0 | 0 | 0 | 0 | 0 | 0 | 0 | 0 | 0 | 0 | 0 | 0 | 0 | 0 | 0 | 0 | 0 | 0 | 0 | 0 |
| 1 | 0.14 | 1 | 1 | 0 | 0 | 0 | 0 | 3 | 1 | 2 | 1 | 1 | 0 | 0 | 0 | 0 | 0 | 1 | 2 | 0 | 0 | 0 | 0 | 0 | 0 | 0 | 0 | 1 | 1 |
| 2 | 0.29 | 2 | 1 | 0 | 0 | 0 | 1 | 3 | 0 | 0 | 1 | 0 | 0 | 0 | 0 | 0 | 0 | 2 | 0 | 1 | 0 | 1 | 0 | 0 | 0 | 0 | 0 | 0 | 0 |
| 3 | 0.43 | 0 | 1 | 2 | 4 | 1 | 0 | 2 | 0 | 1 | 0 | 4 | 0 | 0 | 0 | 0 | 0 | 1 | 0 | 3 | 1 | 4 | 3 | 0 | 0 | 0 | 0 | 0 | 0 |
| 4 | 0.57 | 0 | 1 | 1 | 3 | 1 | 2 | 10 | 0 | 3 | 1 | 1 | 0 | 1 | 0 | 2 | 0 | 6 | 0 | 7 | 6 | 5 | 6 | 2 | 0 | 1 | 0 | 2 | 0 |
| 5 | 0.71 | 28 | 25 | 25 | 22 | 29 | 21 | 16 | 25 | 24 | 24 | 20 | 8 | 12 | 26 | 26 | 25 | 24 | 17 | 21 | 21 | 19 | 25 | 22 | 22 | 18 | 20 | 24 | 22 |
| 6 | 0.86 | 5 | 8 | 9 | 6 | 5 | 9 | 5 | 8 | 6 | 5 | 8 | 23 | 20 | 8 | 6 | 7 | 3 | 11 | 3 | 6 | 3 | 5 | 12 | 9 | 16 | 12 | 9 | 12 |
| 7 | 1 | 4 | 3 | 3 | 0 | 4 | 7 | 1 | 6 | 4 | 8 | 6 | 9 | 7 | 6 | 6 | 8 | 3 | 10 | 5 | 6 | 8 | 1 | 4 | 9 | 5 | 8 | 4 | 5 |
|   |   | 40 | 40 | 40 | 40 | 40 | 40 | 40 | 40 | 40 | 40 | 40 | 40 | 40 | 40 | 40 | 40 | 40 | 40 | 40 | 40 | 40 | 40 | 40 | 40 | 40 | 40 | 40 | 40 |

| RFT | α | C11 | C12 | C13 | C14 | C15 | IS1 | IS2 | IS3 | IS4 | IS5 | EA1 | EA2 | EA3 | EA4 | EA5 | EA6 | EA7 | EA8 | TI1 | TI2 | TI3 | TI4 | TI5 | DI1 | DI2 | DI3 | DI4 | DI5 |
|---|---|---|---|---|---|---|---|---|---|---|---|---|---|---|---|---|---|---|---|---|---|---|---|---|---|---|---|---|---|
| 0 | 0 | 0.000 | 0.000 | 0.000 | 0.000 | 0.000 | 0.000 | 0.000 | 0.000 | 0.000 | 0.000 | 0.000 | 0.000 | 0.000 | 0.000 | 0.000 | 0.000 | 0.000 | 0.000 | 0.000 | 0.000 | 0.000 | 0.000 | 0.000 | 0.000 | 0.000 | 0.000 | 0.000 | 0.000 |
| 1 | 0.1428 | 0.025 | 0.025 | 0.000 | 0.000 | 0.000 | 0.000 | 0.075 | 0.025 | 0.050 | 0.025 | 0.025 | 0.000 | 0.000 | 0.000 | 0.000 | 0.000 | 0.025 | 0.050 | 0.000 | 0.000 | 0.000 | 0.000 | 0.000 | 0.000 | 0.000 | 0.000 | 0.025 | 0.025 |
| 2 | 0.2856 | 0.050 | 0.025 | 0.050 | 0.000 | 0.000 | 0.025 | 0.075 | 0.000 | 0.000 | 0.025 | 0.000 | 0.000 | 0.000 | 0.000 | 0.000 | 0.000 | 0.050 | 0.000 | 0.025 | 0.000 | 0.025 | 0.000 | 0.000 | 0.000 | 0.000 | 0.000 | 0.000 | 0.000 |
| 3 | 0.4284 | 0.000 | 0.025 | 0.025 | 0.100 | 0.025 | 0.000 | 0.050 | 0.000 | 0.025 | 0.000 | 0.100 | 0.000 | 0.025 | 0.000 | 0.000 | 0.000 | 0.025 | 0.000 | 0.075 | 0.025 | 0.100 | 0.075 | 0.000 | 0.000 | 0.000 | 0.000 | 0.000 | 0.000 |
| 4 | 0.5712 | 0.000 | 0.025 | 0.025 | 0.075 | 0.025 | 0.050 | 0.250 | 0.000 | 0.075 | 0.025 | 0.025 | 0.000 | 0.000 | 0.000 | 0.050 | 0.000 | 0.150 | 0.000 | 0.175 | 0.150 | 0.125 | 0.150 | 0.050 | 0.050 | 0.025 | 0.000 | 0.050 | 0.000 |
| 5 | 0.714 | 0.700 | 0.625 | 0.625 | 0.550 | 0.725 | 0.525 | 0.400 | 0.625 | 0.600 | 0.600 | 0.500 | 0.200 | 0.300 | 0.650 | 0.650 | 0.625 | 0.600 | 0.425 | 0.525 | 0.525 | 0.475 | 0.625 | 0.550 | 0.550 | 0.450 | 0.500 | 0.600 | 0.550 |
| 6 | 0.8568 | 0.125 | 0.200 | 0.225 | 0.150 | 0.125 | 0.225 | 0.125 | 0.200 | 0.150 | 0.125 | 0.200 | 0.575 | 0.500 | 0.200 | 0.150 | 0.175 | 0.075 | 0.275 | 0.075 | 0.150 | 0.075 | 0.125 | 0.300 | 0.225 | 0.400 | 0.300 | 0.225 | 0.300 |
| 7 | 1 | 0.100 | 0.075 | 0.075 | 0.000 | 0.100 | 0.175 | 0.025 | 0.150 | 0.100 | 0.200 | 0.150 | 0.225 | 0.175 | 0.150 | 0.150 | 0.200 | 0.075 | 0.250 | 0.125 | 0.150 | 0.200 | 0.025 | 0.100 | 0.225 | 0.125 | 0.200 | 0.100 | 0.125 |

| AFT | α | C11 | C12 | C13 | C14 | C15 | IS1 | IS2 | IS3 | IS4 | IS5 | EA1 | EA2 | EA3 | EA4 | EA5 | EA6 | EA7 | EA8 | TI1 | TI2 | TI3 | TI4 | TI5 | DI1 | DI2 | DI3 | DI4 | DI5 |
|---|---|---|---|---|---|---|---|---|---|---|---|---|---|---|---|---|---|---|---|---|---|---|---|---|---|---|---|---|---|
| 0 | 0 | 1.000 | 1.000 | 1.000 | 1.000 | 1.000 | 1.000 | 1.000 | 1.000 | 1.000 | 1.000 | 1.000 | 1.000 | 1.000 | 1.000 | 1.000 | 1.000 | 1.000 | 1.000 | 1.000 | 1.000 | 1.000 | 1.000 | 1.000 | 1.000 | 1.000 | 1.000 | 1.000 | 1.000 |
| 1 | 0.1428 | 1.000 | 1.000 | 1.000 | 1.000 | 1.000 | 1.000 | 1.000 | 1.000 | 1.000 | 1.000 | 1.000 | 1.000 | 1.000 | 1.000 | 1.000 | 1.000 | 1.000 | 1.000 | 1.000 | 1.000 | 1.000 | 1.000 | 1.000 | 1.000 | 1.000 | 1.000 | 1.000 | 1.000 |
| 2 | 0.2856 | 0.975 | 0.975 | 1.000 | 0.875 | 1.000 | 1.000 | 0.925 | 0.975 | 0.950 | 0.975 | 0.975 | 1.000 | 1.000 | 1.000 | 1.000 | 1.000 | 0.975 | 0.950 | 1.000 | 1.000 | 0.975 | 1.000 | 1.000 | 1.000 | 1.000 | 1.000 | 0.975 | 0.975 |
| 3 | 0.4284 | 0.925 | 0.950 | 1.000 | 0.875 | 1.000 | 0.975 | 0.850 | 0.975 | 0.950 | 0.950 | 0.975 | 1.000 | 1.000 | 1.000 | 1.000 | 1.000 | 0.925 | 0.950 | 0.975 | 1.000 | 0.975 | 1.000 | 1.000 | 1.000 | 1.000 | 1.000 | 0.975 | 0.975 |
| 4 | 0.5712 | 0.925 | 0.925 | 0.950 | 0.775 | 0.975 | 0.975 | 0.800 | 0.975 | 0.925 | 0.950 | 0.875 | 1.000 | 1.000 | 1.000 | 1.000 | 1.000 | 0.900 | 0.950 | 0.900 | 0.975 | 0.875 | 0.925 | 1.000 | 1.000 | 1.000 | 1.000 | 0.975 | 0.975 |

**Table A1.** *Cont.*

| AFT | α | CI1 | CI2 | CI3 | CI4 | CI5 | IS1 | IS2 | IS3 | IS4 | IS5 | EA1 | EA2 | EA3 | EA4 | EA5 | EA6 | EA7 | EA8 | TI1 | TI2 | TI3 | TI4 | TI5 | DI1 | DI2 | DI3 | DI4 | DI5 |
|---|---|---|---|---|---|---|---|---|---|---|---|---|---|---|---|---|---|---|---|---|---|---|---|---|---|---|---|---|---|
| 5 | 0.714 | 0.925 | 0.900 | 0.925 | 0.700 | 0.950 | 0.925 | 0.550 | 0.975 | 0.850 | 0.925 | 0.850 | 1.000 | 0.975 | 1.000 | 0.950 | 1.000 | 0.750 | 0.950 | 0.725 | 0.825 | 0.750 | 0.775 | 0.950 | 1.000 | 0.975 | 1.000 | 0.925 | 0.975 |
| 6 | 0.8568 | 0.225 | 0.275 | 0.300 | 0.150 | 0.225 | 0.400 | 0.150 | 0.350 | 0.250 | 0.325 | 0.350 | 0.800 | 0.675 | 0.350 | 0.300 | 0.375 | 0.150 | 0.525 | 0.200 | 0.300 | 0.275 | 0.150 | 0.400 | 0.450 | 0.525 | 0.500 | 0.325 | 0.425 |
| 7 | 1 | 0.100 | 0.075 | 0.075 | 0.000 | 0.100 | 0.175 | 0.025 | 0.150 | 0.100 | 0.200 | 0.150 | 0.225 | 0.175 | 0.150 | 0.150 | 0.200 | 0.075 | 0.250 | 0.125 | 0.150 | 0.200 | 0.025 | 0.100 | 0.225 | 0.125 | 0.200 | 0.100 | 0.125 |
| Exp | | 0.759 | 0.763 | 0.781 | 0.672 | 0.781 | 0.806 | 0.663 | 0.800 | 0.753 | 0.791 | 0.772 | 0.878 | 0.853 | 0.813 | 0.800 | 0.822 | 0.722 | 0.822 | 0.741 | 0.781 | 0.759 | 0.734 | 0.806 | 0.834 | 0.828 | 0.838 | 0.784 | 0.806 |
| AP1 | AP2 | AP3 | AP4 | AP5 | FC1 | FO2 | FO3 | FO4 | FO5 | H1 | H2 | BA1 | BA2 | BA3 | BA4 | BA5 | MC1 | MC2 | MC3 | MC4 | MA1 | MA2 | MA3 | MA4 | MA5 | | | | |
| 0 | 0 | 0 | 0 | 0 | 0 | 0 | 0 | 0 | 0 | 0 | 0 | 0 | 0 | 0 | 0 | 0 | 0 | 0 | 0 | 1 | 0 | 0 | 0 | 1 | 0 | | | | |
| 0 | 0 | 0 | 0 | 0 | 2 | 2 | 3 | 0 | 4 | 2 | 2 | 0 | 0 | 0 | 0 | 0 | 3 | 1 | 5 | 2 | 0 | 0 | 0 | 1 | 7 | | | | |
| 0 | 0 | 1 | 0 | 0 | 3 | 6 | 3 | 1 | 6 | 6 | 6 | 0 | 0 | 1 | 1 | 1 | 3 | 1 | 1 | 3 | 1 | 2 | 0 | 0 | 5 | | | | |
| 3 | 0 | 3 | 1 | 1 | 14 | 20 | 21 | 13 | 21 | 19 | 17 | 0 | 0 | 0 | 0 | 1 | 4 | 0 | 1 | 3 | 1 | 2 | 0 | 0 | 19 | | | | |
| 7 | 0 | 10 | 1 | 0 | 11 | 7 | 7 | 7 | 7 | 7 | 6 | 0 | 0 | 1 | 0 | 0 | 16 | 11 | 8 | 4 | 17 | 3 | 0 | 7 | 1 | | | | |
| 20 | 14 | 19 | 15 | 18 | 9 | 5 | 6 | 13 | 1 | 5 | 8 | 28 | 28 | 25 | 29 | 25 | 9 | 15 | 21 | 23 | 11 | 23 | 24 | 23 | 8 | | | | |
| 4 | 17 | 6 | 19 | 17 | 1 | 0 | 0 | 4 | 1 | 1 | 0 | 6 | 7 | 9 | 4 | 6 | 1 | 5 | 3 | 3 | 5 | 6 | 10 | 4 | 0 | | | | |
| 6 | 9 | 1 | 4 | 4 | 0 | 0 | 0 | 2 | 0 | 0 | 1 | 6 | 5 | 5 | 5 | 7 | 4 | 7 | 1 | 4 | 6 | 6 | 6 | 5 | 0 | | | | |
| 40 | 40 | 40 | 40 | 40 | 40 | 40 | 40 | 40 | 40 | 40 | 40 | 40 | 40 | 40 | 40 | 40 | 40 | 40 | 40 | 40 | 40 | 40 | 40 | 40 | 40 | | | | |
| AP1 | AP2 | AP3 | AP4 | AP5 | FO1 | FO2 | FO3 | FO4 | FO5 | H1 | H2 | BA1 | BA2 | BA3 | BA4 | BA5 | MC1 | MC2 | MC3 | MC4 | MA1 | MA2 | MA3 | MA4 | MA5 | | | | |
| 0.000 | 0.000 | 0.000 | 0.000 | 0.000 | 0.000 | 0.000 | 0.000 | 0.000 | 0.000 | 0.000 | 0.000 | 0.000 | 0.000 | 0.000 | 0.000 | 0.000 | 0.000 | 0.000 | 0.000 | 0.000 | 0.000 | 0.000 | 0.000 | 0.000 | 0.000 | | | | |
| 0.000 | 0.000 | 0.000 | 0.000 | 0.000 | 0.050 | 0.050 | 0.075 | 0.000 | 0.100 | 0.050 | 0.050 | 0.000 | 0.000 | 0.000 | 0.000 | 0.000 | 0.075 | 0.025 | 0.125 | 0.050 | 0.000 | 0.000 | 0.000 | 0.025 | 0.175 | | | | |
| 0.000 | 0.000 | 0.025 | 0.000 | 0.000 | 0.075 | 0.150 | 0.075 | 0.025 | 0.150 | 0.150 | 0.150 | 0.000 | 0.000 | 0.025 | 0.025 | 0.025 | 0.100 | 0.025 | 0.025 | 0.075 | 0.025 | 0.050 | 0.000 | 0.000 | 0.125 | | | | |
| 0.075 | 0.000 | 0.075 | 0.025 | 0.025 | 0.350 | 0.500 | 0.525 | 0.325 | 0.525 | 0.475 | 0.425 | 0.000 | 0.000 | 0.000 | 0.000 | 0.025 | 0.400 | 0.275 | 0.200 | 0.100 | 0.425 | 0.075 | 0.000 | 0.000 | 0.475 | | | | |
| 0.175 | 0.000 | 0.250 | 0.025 | 0.000 | 0.275 | 0.175 | 0.175 | 0.175 | 0.175 | 0.175 | 0.150 | 0.000 | 0.000 | 0.025 | 0.000 | 0.000 | 0.225 | 0.375 | 0.525 | 0.575 | 0.275 | 0.575 | 0.600 | 0.175 | 0.025 | | | | |
| 0.500 | 0.350 | 0.475 | 0.375 | 0.450 | 0.225 | 0.125 | 0.150 | 0.325 | 0.025 | 0.125 | 0.200 | 0.700 | 0.700 | 0.625 | 0.725 | 0.625 | 0.225 | 0.375 | 0.075 | 0.575 | 0.125 | 0.150 | 0.250 | 0.575 | 0.200 | | | | |
| 0.100 | 0.425 | 0.150 | 0.475 | 0.425 | 0.025 | 0.000 | 0.000 | 0.100 | 0.025 | 0.025 | 0.000 | 0.150 | 0.175 | 0.225 | 0.100 | 0.150 | 0.025 | 0.125 | 0.075 | 0.075 | 0.150 | 0.150 | 0.150 | 0.100 | 0.000 | | | | |
| 0.150 | 0.225 | 0.025 | 0.100 | 0.100 | 0.000 | 0.000 | 0.000 | 0.050 | 0.000 | 0.000 | 0.025 | 0.150 | 0.125 | 0.125 | 0.125 | 0.175 | 0.100 | 0.175 | 0.025 | 0.100 | 0.150 | 0.150 | 0.150 | 0.125 | 0.000 | | | | |
| AP1 | AP2 | AP3 | AP4 | AP5 | FO1 | FO2 | FO3 | FO4 | FO5 | H1 | H2 | BA1 | BA2 | BA3 | BA4 | BA5 | MC1 | MC2 | MC3 | MC4 | MA1 | MA2 | MA3 | MA4 | MA5 | | | | |
| 1.000 | 1.000 | 1.000 | 1.000 | 1.000 | 1.000 | 1.000 | 1.000 | 1.000 | 1.000 | 1.000 | 1.000 | 1.000 | 1.000 | 1.000 | 1.000 | 1.000 | 1.000 | 1.000 | 1.000 | 1.000 | 1.000 | 1.000 | 1.000 | 1.000 | 1.000 | | | | |
| 1.000 | 1.000 | 1.000 | 1.000 | 1.000 | 1.000 | 1.000 | 1.000 | 1.000 | 1.000 | 1.000 | 1.000 | 1.000 | 1.000 | 1.000 | 1.000 | 1.000 | 1.000 | 1.000 | 1.000 | 1.000 | 1.000 | 1.000 | 1.000 | 1.000 | 1.000 | | | | |

Table A1. Cont.

| AFT | α | C11 | C12 | C13 | C14 | C15 | IS1 | IS2 | IS3 | IS4 | IS5 | EA1 | EA2 | EA3 | EA4 | EA5 | EA6 | EA7 | EA8 | T11 | T12 | T13 | T14 | T15 | D11 | D12 | D13 | D14 | D15 |
|---|---|---|---|---|---|---|---|---|---|---|---|---|---|---|---|---|---|---|---|---|---|---|---|---|---|---|---|---|---|
| 1.000 | 1.000 | 1.000 | 1.000 | 1.000 | 0.950 | 0.950 | 0.925 | 1.000 | 0.900 | 0.950 | 0.950 | 1.000 | 1.000 | 1.000 | 1.000 | 1.000 | 0.925 | 0.975 | 0.875 | 0.975 | 1.000 | 1.000 | 1.000 | 0.975 | 0.825 | | | | |
| 1.000 | 1.000 | 0.975 | 1.000 | 1.000 | 0.875 | 0.800 | 0.850 | 0.975 | 0.750 | 0.800 | 0.800 | 1.000 | 1.000 | 1.000 | 0.975 | 0.975 | 0.850 | 0.950 | 0.850 | 0.925 | 1.000 | 1.000 | 1.000 | 0.975 | 0.700 | | | | |
| 0.925 | 1.000 | 0.900 | 0.975 | 0.975 | 0.525 | 0.300 | 0.325 | 0.650 | 0.225 | 0.325 | 0.375 | 1.000 | 1.000 | 1.000 | 0.975 | 0.950 | 0.750 | 0.950 | 0.825 | 0.850 | 0.975 | 0.950 | 1.000 | 0.975 | 0.225 | | | | |
| 0.750 | 1.000 | 0.650 | 0.950 | 0.975 | 0.250 | 0.125 | 0.150 | 0.475 | 0.050 | 0.150 | 0.225 | 1.000 | 1.000 | 0.975 | 0.950 | 0.950 | 0.350 | 0.675 | 0.625 | 0.750 | 0.550 | 0.875 | 1.000 | 0.800 | 0.200 | | | | |
| 0.250 | 0.650 | 0.175 | 0.575 | 0.525 | 0.025 | 0.000 | 0.000 | 0.150 | 0.025 | 0.025 | 0.025 | 0.300 | 0.300 | 0.350 | 0.225 | 0.325 | 0.125 | 0.300 | 0.100 | 0.175 | 0.275 | 0.300 | 0.400 | 0.225 | 0.000 | | | | |
| 0.150 | 0.225 | 0.025 | 0.100 | 0.100 | 0.000 | 0.000 | 0.000 | 0.050 | 0.025 | 0.000 | 0.025 | 0.150 | 0.125 | 0.125 | 0.125 | 0.175 | 0.100 | 0.175 | 0.025 | 0.100 | 0.150 | 0.150 | 0.150 | 0.125 | 0.000 | | | | |
| 0.759 | 0.859 | 0.716 | 0.825 | 0.822 | 0.578 | 0.522 | 0.531 | 0.663 | 0.494 | 0.531 | 0.550 | 0.806 | 0.803 | 0.806 | 0.781 | 0.797 | 0.638 | 0.753 | 0.663 | 0.722 | 0.744 | 0.784 | 0.819 | 0.759 | 0.494 | | | | |

FT: Frequency table; RFT: Relative Frequency Table; AFT: Accumulated Frequency Table; Exp: Experton.

## Appendix B. Adequacy Coefficient Method to Find Cause–Effect, Cause–Cause, and Effect–Effect Matrices to Conversion Knowledge and Routines

Table A2. Cause–effect matrix to conversion knowledge.

| | E1 | E2 | E3 | E4 | E5 | E6 | E7 | E8 | E9 | E10 | E11 | E12 | E13 | E14 | E15 | E16 |
|---|---|---|---|---|---|---|---|---|---|---|---|---|---|---|---|---|
| C1 | 1 | 0.9 | 1 | 0.90 | 1 | 1 | 1 | 1 | 1 | 1 | 1 | 1 | 1 | 1 | 1 | 1 |
| C2 | 1 | 0.9 | 1 | 0.90 | 1 | 1 | 1 | 1 | 1 | 1 | 1 | 1 | 1 | 1 | 1 | 1 |
| C3 | 1 | 0.9 | 1 | 0.9 | 0.99 | 1 | 1 | 0.99 | 1 | 0.9 | 1 | 1 | 1 | 1 | 1 | 1 |
| C4 | 1 | 0.9 | 1 | 0.9 | 1 | 1 | 1 | 1 | 1 | 1 | 1 | 1 | 1 | 1 | 1 | 1 |
| C5 | 1 | 0.9 | 1 | 0.9 | 1 | 1 | 1 | 1 | 1 | 0.9 | 1 | 1 | 1 | 1 | 1 | 1 |
| C6 | 0.90 | 0.8 | 0.90 | 0.8 | 0.92 | 0.9 | 1 | 0.92 | 0.9 | 0.8 | 0.90 | 1 | 0.9 | 0.9 | 1 | 0.9 |
| C7 | 1 | 0.9 | 1 | 0.9 | 0.99 | 1 | 1 | 0.99 | 1 | 0.9 | 1 | 1 | 1 | 0.9 | 1 | 1 |
| C8 | 1 | 0.9 | 1 | 0.8 | 0.98 | 1 | 1 | 0.98 | 1 | 0.90 | 1 | 1 | 1 | 0.9 | 1 | 1 |
| C9 | 1 | 0.9 | 1 | 0.9 | 1 | 1 | 1 | 1 | 1 | 1 | 1 | 1 | 1 | 1 | 1 | 1 |
| C10 | 1 | 0.9 | 1 | 0.90 | 1 | 1 | 1 | 1 | 1 | 1 | 1 | 1 | 1 | 1 | 1 | 1 |
| C11 | 1 | 0.9 | 1 | 0.9 | 1 | 1 | 1 | 1 | 1 | 1 | 1 | 1 | 1 | 1 | 1 | 1 |
| C12 | 1 | 0.9 | 1 | 0.9 | 0.99 | 1 | 1 | 0.99 | 1 | 0.9 | 1 | 1 | 1 | 1 | 1 | 1 |

**Table A2.** Cont.

| | E1 | E2 | E3 | E4 | E5 | E6 | E7 | E8 | E9 | E10 | E11 | E12 | E13 | E14 | E15 | E16 |
|---|---|---|---|---|---|---|---|---|---|---|---|---|---|---|---|---|
| C13 | 0.9 | 0.8 | 0.9 | 0.8 | 0.97 | 0.9 | 1 | 0.97 | 1 | 0.9 | 0.9 | 1 | 1 | 0.9 | 1 | 1 |
| C14 | 1 | 0.8 | 1 | 0.8 | 0.97 | 0.9 | 1 | 0.97 | 1 | 0.9 | 1 | 1 | 1 | 0.9 | 1 | 1 |
| C15 | 1 | 0.9 | 1 | 0.9 | 0.99 | 1 | 1 | 0.99 | 1 | 0.9 | 1 | 1 | 1 | 1 | 1 | 1 |
| C16 | 1 | 1 | 1 | 0.9 | 1 | 1 | 1 | 1 | 1 | 1 | 1 | 1 | 1 | 1 | 1 | 1 |
| C17 | 1 | 0.8 | 1 | 0.8 | 0.98 | 0.9 | 1 | 0.98 | 1 | 0.90 | 1 | 1 | 1 | 0.9 | 1 | 1 |

**Table A3.** Cause–effect matrix to routines.

| | E1 | E2 | E3 | E4 | E5 | E6 | E7 | E8 | E9 | E10 | E11 | E12 |
|---|---|---|---|---|---|---|---|---|---|---|---|---|
| C1 | 0.9 | 0.9 | 0.9 | 0.8 | 0.87 | 0.9 | 1 | 1 | 1 | 1 | 1 | 1 |
| C2 | 0.8 | 0.7 | 0.7 | 0.7 | 0.73 | 0.7 | 1 | 0.95 | 0.9 | 0.9 | 1 | 1 |
| C3 | 0.8 | 0.7 | 0.7 | 0.7 | 0.73 | 0.7 | 1 | 0.95 | 0.9 | 0.9 | 1 | 1 |
| C4 | 0.80 | 0.7 | 0.8 | 0.7 | 0.75 | 0.8 | 1 | 0.97 | 0.9 | 1 | 1 | 1 |
| C5 | 0.8 | 0.7 | 0.7 | 0.70 | 0.73 | 0.8 | 1 | 0.96 | 0.9 | 0.9 | 1 | 1 |
| C6 | 0.9 | 0.9 | 0.9 | 0.9 | 0.89 | 0.9 | 1 | 1 | 1 | 1 | 1 | 1 |
| C7 | 0.9 | 0.9 | 0.9 | 0.9 | 0.87 | 0.9 | 1 | 1 | 1 | 1 | 1 | 1 |
| C8 | 0.8 | 0.8 | 0.8 | 0.8 | 0.77 | 0.8 | 1 | 0.99 | 1 | 1 | 1 | 1 |
| C9 | 1 | 1 | 1 | 1 | 1 | 1 | 1 | 1 | 1 | 1 | 1 | 1 |

**Table A4.** Cause–cause matrix to conversion knowledge.

| | C1 | C2 | C3 | C4 | C5 | C6 | C7 | C8 | C9 | C10 | C11 | C12 | C13 | C14 | C15 | C16 | C17 |
|---|---|---|---|---|---|---|---|---|---|---|---|---|---|---|---|---|---|
| C1 | 1 | 1 | 1 | 1 | 1 | 1 | 1 | 1 | 1 | 1 | 1 | 1 | 1 | 1 | 1 | 1 | 1 |
| C2 | 1 | 1 | 1 | 1 | 1 | 1 | 1 | 1 | 1 | 1 | 1 | 1 | 1 | 1 | 1 | 1 | 1 |
| C3 | 1 | 1 | 1 | 0.9 | 1 | 1 | 1 | 1 | 0.9 | 1 | 0.9 | 1 | 1 | 1 | 1 | 0.9 | 1 |
| C4 | 1 | 1 | 1 | 1 | 1 | 1 | 1 | 1 | 1 | 1 | 1 | 1 | 1 | 1 | 1 | 1 | 1 |

Table A4. Cont.

| | C1 | C2 | C3 | C4 | C5 | C6 | C7 | C8 | C9 | C10 | C11 | C12 | C13 | C14 | C15 | C16 | C17 |
|---|---|---|---|---|---|---|---|---|---|---|---|---|---|---|---|---|---|
| C5 | 1 | 1 | 1 | 1 | 1 | 1 | 1 | 1 | 1 | 1 | 0.9 | 1 | 1 | 1 | 1 | 0.9 | 1 |
| C6 | 0.9 | 0.89 | 0.9 | 0.9 | 0.9 | 1 | 0.9 | 0.9 | 0.9 | 0.9 | 0.9 | 0.9 | 1 | 1 | 0.9 | 0.8 | 0.9 |
| C7 | 0.9 | 1 | 1 | 0.9 | 1 | 1 | 1 | 1 | 0.9 | 0.9 | 0.9 | 1 | 1 | 1 | 1 | 0.90 | 1 |
| C8 | 0.9 | 0.94 | 1 | 0.9 | 1 | 1 | 1 | 1 | 0.9 | 0.9 | 0.9 | 1 | 1 | 1 | 1 | 0.9 | 1 |
| C9 | 1 | 1 | 1 | 1 | 1 | 1 | 1 | 1 | 1 | 1 | 1 | 1 | 1 | 1 | 1 | 1 | 1 |
| C10 | 1 | 1 | 1 | 1 | 1 | 1 | 1 | 1 | 1 | 1 | 1 | 1 | 1 | 1 | 1 | 1 | 1 |
| C11 | 1 | 1 | 1 | 1 | 1 | 1 | 1 | 1 | 1 | 1 | 1 | 1 | 1 | 1 | 1 | 1 | 1 |
| C12 | 1 | 1 | 1 | 0.9 | 1 | 1 | 1 | 1 | 0.9 | 1 | 0.9 | 1 | 1 | 1 | 1 | 0.9 | 1 |
| C13 | 0.9 | 0.93 | 1 | 0.9 | 1 | 1 | 1 | 1 | 0.9 | 0.9 | 0.90 | 1 | 1 | 1 | 1 | 0.9 | 1 |
| C14 | 0.9 | 0.94 | 1 | 0.9 | 1 | 1 | 1 | 1 | 0.9 | 0.9 | 0.9 | 1 | 1 | 1 | 1 | 0.9 | 1 |
| C15 | 1 | 1 | 1 | 0.9 | 1 | 1 | 1 | 1 | 0.9 | 1 | 0.9 | 1 | 1 | 1 | 1 | 0.9 | 1 |
| C16 | 1 | 1 | 1 | 1 | 1 | 1 | 1 | 1 | 1 | 1 | 1 | 1 | 1 | 1 | 1 | 1 | 1 |
| C17 | 0.9 | 0.94 | 1 | 0.9 | 1 | 1 | 1 | 1 | 0.9 | 0.9 | 0.9 | 1 | 1 | 1 | 1 | 0.9 | 1 |

Table A5. Causes–cause matrix to routines.

| | C1 | C2 | C3 | C4 | C5 | C6 | C7 | C8 | C9 |
|---|---|---|---|---|---|---|---|---|---|
| C1 | 1 | 1 | 1 | 1 | 1 | 1 | 1 | 1 | 0.8 |
| C2 | 0.9 | 1 | 1 | 1 | 1 | 0.8 | 0.9 | 1 | 0.7 |
| C3 | 0.9 | 1 | 1 | 1 | 1 | 0.8 | 0.9 | 1 | 0.7 |
| C4 | 0.9 | 1 | 1 | 1 | 1 | 0.9 | 0.9 | 1 | 0.7 |
| C5 | 0.9 | 1 | 1 | 1 | 1 | 0.8 | 0.9 | 1 | 0.70 |
| C6 | 1 | 1 | 1 | 1 | 1 | 1 | 1 | 1 | 0.9 |
| C7 | 1 | 1 | 1 | 1 | 1 | 1 | 1 | 1 | 0.8 |
| C8 | 0.90 | 1 | 1 | 1 | 1 | 0.9 | 0.90 | 1 | 0.7 |
| C9 | 1 | 1 | 1 | 1 | 1 | 1 | 1 | 1 | 1 |

**Table A6.** Effect–effect matrix to conversion knowledge.

|  | E1 | E2 | E3 | E4 | E5 | E6 | E7 | E8 | E9 | E10 | E11 | E12 | E13 | E14 | E15 | E16 |
|---|---|---|---|---|---|---|---|---|---|---|---|---|---|---|---|---|
| E1 | 1 | 0.89 | 1 | 0.9 | 1 | 1 | 1 | 1 | 1 | 0.9 | 1 | 1 | 1 | 1 | 1 | 1 |
| E2 | 1 | 1 | 1 | 1 | 1 | 1 | 1 | 1 | 1 | 1 | 1 | 1 | 1 | 1 | 1 | 1 |
| E3 | 1 | 0.89 | 1 | 0.9 | 1 | 1 | 1 | 1 | 1 | 0.9 | 1 | 1 | 1 | 1 | 1 | 1 |
| E4 | 1 | 1 | 1 | 1 | 1 | 1 | 1 | 1 | 1 | 1 | 1 | 1 | 1 | 1 | 1 | 1 |
| E5 | 1 | 0.87 | 1 | 0.9 | 1 | 1 | 1 | 1 | 1 | 0.9 | 1 | 1 | 1 | 1 | 1 | 1 |
| E6 | 1 | 0.90 | 1 | 0.9 | 1 | 1 | 1 | 1 | 1 | 1 | 1 | 1 | 1 | 1 | 1 | 1 |
| E7 | 0.9 | 0.82 | 0.9 | 0.8 | 0.95 | 0.9 | 1 | 0.95 | 1 | 0.9 | 0.9 | 1 | 0.9 | 0.9 | 1 | 1 |
| E8 | 0.98 | 0.87 | 1 | 0.9 | 1 | 1 | 1 | 1 | 1 | 0.9 | 1 | 1 | 1 | 1 | 1 | 1 |
| E9 | 1 | 0.85 | 1 | 0.8 | 0.98 | 1 | 1 | 0.98 | 1 | 0.90 | 1 | 1 | 1 | 0.9 | 1 | 1 |
| E10 | 1 | 1 | 1 | 0.9 | 1 | 1 | 1 | 1 | 1 | 1 | 1 | 1 | 1 | 1 | 1 | 1 |
| E11 | 1 | 0.89 | 1 | 0.9 | 1 | 1 | 1 | 1 | 1 | 0.9 | 1 | 1 | 1 | 1 | 1 | 1 |
| E12 | 0.9 | 0.83 | 0.9 | 0.8 | 0.96 | 0.9 | 1 | 0.96 | 1 | 0.9 | 0.9 | 1 | 0.9 | 0.9 | 1 | 1 |
| E13 | 1 | 0.89 | 1 | 0.9 | 1 | 1 | 1 | 1 | 1 | 0.9 | 1 | 1 | 1 | 1 | 1 | 1 |
| E14 | 1 | 0.91 | 1 | 0.90 | 1 | 1 | 1 | 1 | 1 | 1 | 1 | 1 | 1 | 1 | 1 | 1 |
| E15 | 0.9 | 0.81 | 0.9 | 0.80 | 0.94 | 0.9 | 1 | 0.94 | 1 | 0.9 | 0.9 | 1 | 0.9 | 0.90 | 1 | 1 |
| E16 | 1 | 0.85 | 1 | 0.9 | 0.98 | 1 | 1 | 0.98 | 1 | 0.90 | 1 | 1 | 1 | 0.9 | 1 | 1 |

**Table A7.** Effect–effect matrix to routines.

|  | E1 | E2 | E3 | E4 | E5 | E6 | E7 | E8 | E9 | E10 | E11 | E12 |
|---|---|---|---|---|---|---|---|---|---|---|---|---|
| E1 | 1 | 0.94 | 1 | 0.9 | 0.95 | 1 | 1 | 1 | 1 | 1 | 1 | 1 |
| E2 | 1 | 1 | 1 | 1 | 1 | 1 | 1 | 1 | 1 | 1 | 1 | 1 |
| E3 | 1 | 1 | 1 | 1 | 1 | 1 | 1 | 1 | 1 | 1 | 1 | 1 |
| E4 | 1 | 1 | 1 | 1 | 1 | 1 | 1 | 1 | 1 | 1 | 1 | 1 |
| E5 | 1 | 1 | 1 | 1 | 1 | 1 | 1 | 1 | 1 | 1 | 1 | 1 |

Table A7. Cont.

|  | E1 | E2 | E3 | E4 | E5 | E6 | E7 | E8 | E9 | E10 | E11 | E12 |
|---|---|---|---|---|---|---|---|---|---|---|---|---|
| E6 | 1 | 1 | 1 | 1 | 1 | 1 | 1 | 1 | 1 | 1 | 1 | 1 |
| E7 | 0.8 | 0.72 | 0.7 | 0.7 | 0.73 | 0.7 | 1 | 0.95 | 0.9 | 0.9 | 1 | 1 |
| E8 | 0.8 | 0.77 | 0.8 | 0.7 | 0.78 | 0.80 | 1 | 1 | 1 | 1 | 1 | 1 |
| E9 | 0.9 | 0.80 | 0.8 | 0.8 | 0.81 | 0.8 | 1 | 1 | 1 | 1 | 1 | 1 |
| E10 | 0.8 | 0.78 | 0.8 | 0.8 | 0.79 | 0.8 | 1 | 1 | 1 | 1 | 1 | 1 |
| E11 | 0.8 | 0.74 | 0.7 | 0.7 | 0.75 | 0.8 | 1 | 0.97 | 0.9 | 1 | 1 | 1 |
| E12 | 0.8 | 0.70 | 0.7 | 0.7 | 0.71 | 0.7 | 1 | 0.93 | 0.90 | 0.9 | 1 | 1 |

## Appendix C. Forgotten Effects Matrices to Conversion Knowledge and Routines

Table A8. Forgotten effects matrices.

Matrix $[\widetilde{M}]$: conversion knowledge

|  | E1 | E2 | E3 | E4 | E5 | E6 | E7 | E8 | E9 | E10 | E11 | E12 | E13 | E14 | E15 | E16 |
|---|---|---|---|---|---|---|---|---|---|---|---|---|---|---|---|---|
| C1 | 1 | 0.91 | 1 | 0.9 | 1 | 1 | 1 | 1 | 1 | 0.96 | 1 | 1 | 1 | 1 | 1 | 1 |
| C2 | 1 | 0.91 | 1 | 0.9 | 1 | 1 | 1 | 1 | 1 | 0.96 | 1 | 1 | 1 | 1 | 1 | 1 |
| C3 | 0.98 | 0.87 | 0.98 | 0.86 | 0.99 | 0.97 | 1 | 0.99 | 1 | 0.92 | 0.98 | 1 | 0.98 | 0.95 | 1 | 1 |
| C4 | 1 | 0.92 | 1 | 0.91 | 1 | 1 | 1 | 1 | 1 | 0.97 | 1 | 1 | 1 | 1 | 1 | 1 |
| C5 | 0.99 | 0.88 | 0.99 | 0.87 | 1 | 0.98 | 1 | 1 | 1 | 0.93 | 0.99 | 1 | 0.99 | 0.97 | 1 | 1 |
| C6 | 0.90 | 0.79 | 0.90 | 0.79 | 0.92 | 0.89 | 0.98 | 0.92 | 0.94 | 0.84 | 0.90 | 0.96 | 0.91 | 0.88 | 0.98 | 0.94 |
| C7 | 0.97 | 0.86 | 0.97 | 0.85 | 0.99 | 0.96 | 1 | 0.99 | 1 | 0.91 | 0.97 | 1 | 0.97 | 0.95 | 1 | 1 |
| C8 | 0.96 | 0.85 | 0.96 | 0.84 | 0.98 | 0.95 | 1 | 0.98 | 1 | 0.90 | 0.96 | 1 | 0.96 | 0.94 | 1 | 1 |
| C9 | 1 | 0.93 | 1 | 0.92 | 1 | 1 | 1 | 1 | 1 | 0.98 | 1 | 1 | 1 | 1 | 1 | 1 |
| C10 | 1 | 0.91 | 1 | 0.90 | 1 | 1 | 1 | 1 | 1 | 0.96 | 1 | 1 | 1 | 1 | 1 | 1 |
| C11 | 1 | 0.94 | 1 | 0.93 | 1 | 1 | 1 | 1 | 1 | 0.99 | 1 | 1 | 1 | 1 | 1 | 1 |
| C12 | 0.98 | 0.87 | 0.98 | 0.86 | 0.99 | 0.97 | 1 | 0.99 | 1 | 0.92 | 0.98 | 1 | 0.98 | 0.95 | 1 | 1 |

Table A8. Cont.

| | E1 | E2 | E3 | E4 | E5 | E6 | E7 | E8 | E9 | E10 | E11 | E12 | E13 | E14 | E15 | E16 |
|---|---|---|---|---|---|---|---|---|---|---|---|---|---|---|---|---|
| | | | | | | Matrix $[\widetilde{M}]$: conversion knowledge | | | | | | | | | | |
| C13 | 0.95 | 0.84 | 0.95 | 0.83 | 0.97 | 0.94 | 1 | 0.97 | 0.99 | 0.89 | 0.95 | 1 | 0.95 | 0.93 | 1 | 0.99 |
| C14 | 0.95 | 0.84 | 0.95 | 0.84 | 0.97 | 0.94 | 1 | 0.97 | 0.99 | 0.89 | 0.95 | 1 | 0.96 | 0.93 | 1 | 0.99 |
| C15 | 0.98 | 0.87 | 0.98 | 0.86 | 0.99 | 0.97 | 1 | 0.99 | 1 | 0.92 | 0.98 | 1 | 0.98 | 0.95 | 1 | 1 |
| C16 | 1 | 0.96 | 1 | 0.95 | 1 | 1 | 1 | 1 | 1 | 1 | 1 | 1 | 1 | 1 | 1 | 1 |
| C17 | 0.96 | 0.85 | 0.96 | 0.84 | 0.98 | 0.95 | 1 | 0.98 | 1 | 0.90 | 0.96 | 1 | 0.96 | 0.93 | 1 | 1 |
| | | | | | | Matrix $[\widetilde{A}] \circ [\widetilde{M}]$ conversion knowledge | | | | | | | | | | |
| | E1 | E2 | E3 | E4 | E5 | E6 | E7 | E8 | E9 | E10 | E11 | E12 | E13 | E14 | E15 | E16 |
| C1 | 1 | 0.96 | 1 | 0.95 | 1 | 1 | 1 | 1 | 1 | 0.98 | 1 | 1 | 1 | 1 | 1 | 1 |
| C2 | 1 | 0.95 | 1 | 0.95 | 1 | 1 | 1 | 1 | 1 | 0.98 | 1 | 1 | 1 | 1 | 1 | 1 |
| C3 | 1 | 0.93 | 1 | 0.93 | 1 | 1 | 1 | 1 | 1 | 0.96 | 1 | 1 | 1 | 1 | 1 | 1 |
| C4 | 1 | 0.96 | 1 | 0.95 | 1 | 1 | 1 | 1 | 1 | 0.98 | 1 | 1 | 1 | 1 | 1 | 1 |
| C5 | 1 | 0.94 | 1 | 0.93 | 1 | 1 | 1 | 1 | 1 | 0.96 | 1 | 1 | 1 | 1 | 1 | 1 |
| C6 | 0.95 | 0.89 | 0.95 | 0.89 | 0.96 | 0.95 | 0.98 | 0.96 | 0.96 | 0.92 | 0.95 | 0.96 | 0.95 | 0.94 | 0.98 | 0.96 |
| C7 | 1 | 0.93 | 1 | 0.92 | 1 | 1 | 1 | 1 | 1 | 0.96 | 1 | 1 | 1 | 1 | 1 | 1 |
| C8 | 0.98 | 0.92 | 0.98 | 0.92 | 0.99 | 0.97 | 1 | 0.99 | 1 | 0.94 | 0.98 | 1 | 0.98 | 0.97 | 1 | 1 |
| C9 | 1 | 0.96 | 1 | 0.95 | 1 | 1 | 1 | 1 | 1 | 0.99 | 1 | 1 | 1 | 1 | 1 | 1 |
| C10 | 1 | 0.96 | 1 | 0.95 | 1 | 1 | 1 | 1 | 1 | 0.98 | 1 | 1 | 1 | 1 | 1 | 1 |
| C11 | 1 | 0.96 | 1 | 0.95 | 1 | 1 | 1 | 1 | 1 | 0.99 | 1 | 1 | 1 | 1 | 1 | 1 |
| C12 | 1 | 0.93 | 1 | 0.93 | 1 | 1 | 1 | 1 | 1 | 0.96 | 1 | 1 | 1 | 1 | 1 | 1 |
| C13 | 0.97 | 0.92 | 0.97 | 0.91 | 0.98 | 0.97 | 1 | 0.98 | 0.99 | 0.93 | 0.97 | 1 | 0.97 | 0.96 | 1 | 0.99 |
| C14 | 0.98 | 0.92 | 0.98 | 0.91 | 0.99 | 0.97 | 1 | 0.99 | 1 | 0.94 | 0.98 | 1 | 0.98 | 0.96 | 1 | 1 |
| C15 | 1 | 0.93 | 1 | 0.93 | 1 | 1 | 1 | 1 | 0 | 0.96 | 1 | 1 | 1 | 1 | 1 | 1 |
| C16 | 1 | 0.96 | 1 | 0.95 | 1 | 1 | 1 | 1 | 1 | 1 | 1 | 1 | 1 | 1 | 1 | 1 |
| C17 | 0.98 | 0.92 | 0.98 | 0.92 | 0.99 | 0.97 | 1 | 0.99 | 1 | 0.94 | 0.98 | 1 | 0.98 | 0.97 | 1 | 1 |

Table A8. Cont.

Matrix $[\tilde{A}] \circ [\tilde{M}] \circ [\tilde{B}]$ conversion knowledge

| | E1 | E2 | E3 | E4 | E5 | E6 | E7 | E8 | E9 | E10 | E11 | E12 | E13 | E14 | E15 | E16 |
|---|---|---|---|---|---|---|---|---|---|---|---|---|---|---|---|---|
| C1 | 1 | 0.98 | 1 | 0.96 | 1 | 1 | 1 | 1 | 1 | 0.98 | 1 | 1 | 1 | 1 | 1 | 1 |
| C2 | 1 | 0.98 | 1 | 0.95 | 1 | 1 | 1 | 1 | 1 | 0.98 | 1 | 1 | 1 | 1 | 1 | 1 |
| C3 | 1 | 0.96 | 1 | 0.94 | 1 | 1 | 1 | 1 | 1 | 0.96 | 1 | 1 | 1 | 1 | 1 | 1 |
| C4 | 1 | 0.98 | 1 | 0.96 | 1 | 1 | 1 | 1 | 1 | 0.98 | 1 | 1 | 1 | 1 | 1 | 1 |
| C5 | 1 | 0.96 | 1 | 0.94 | 1 | 1 | 1 | 1 | 1 | 0.96 | 1 | 1 | 1 | 1 | 1 | 1 |
| C6 | 0.96 | 0.92 | 0.96 | 0.92 | 0.96 | 0.96 | 0.98 | 0.96 | 0.97 | 0.95 | 0.96 | 0.98 | 0.96 | 0.96 | 0.98 | 0.97 |
| C7 | 1 | 0.96 | 1 | 0.94 | 1 | 1 | 1 | 1 | 1 | 0.96 | 1 | 1 | 1 | 1 | 1 | 1 |
| C8 | 0.98 | 0.94 | 0.98 | 0.94 | 0.99 | 0.98 | 1 | 0.99 | 1 | 0.96 | 0.98 | 1 | 0.98 | 0.98 | 1 | 1 |
| C9 | 1 | 0.99 | 1 | 0.96 | 1 | 1 | 1 | 1 | 1 | 0.99 | 1 | 1 | 1 | 1 | 1 | 1 |
| C10 | 1 | 0.98 | 1 | 0.96 | 1 | 1 | 1 | 1 | 1 | 0.98 | 1 | 1 | 1 | 1 | 1 | 1 |
| C11 | 1 | 0.99 | 1 | 0.96 | 1 | 1 | 1 | 1 | 1 | 0.99 | 1 | 1 | 1 | 1 | 1 | 1 |
| C12 | 1 | 0.96 | 1 | 0.94 | 1 | 1 | 1 | 1 | 1 | 0.96 | 1 | 1 | 1 | 1 | 1 | 1 |
| C13 | 0.98 | 0.93 | 0.98 | 0.93 | 0.98 | 0.97 | 1 | 0.98 | 0.99 | 0.96 | 0.98 | 1 | 0.98 | 0.97 | 1 | 0.99 |
| C14 | 0.98 | 0.94 | 0.98 | 0.94 | 0.99 | 0.98 | 1 | 0.99 | 1 | 0.96 | 0.98 | 1 | 0.98 | 0.98 | 1 | 1 |
| C15 | 1 | 0.96 | 1 | 0.94 | 1 | 1 | 1 | 1 | 0 | 0.96 | 1 | 1 | 1 | 1 | 1 | 1 |
| C16 | 1 | 1 | 1 | 0.96 | 1 | 1 | 1 | 1 | 1 | 1 | 1 | 1 | 1 | 1 | 1 | 1 |
| C17 | 0.98 | 0.94 | 0.98 | 0.94 | 0.99 | 0.98 | 1 | 0.99 | 1 | 0.96 | 0.98 | 1 | 0.98 | 0.98 | 1 | 1 |

Matrix $[\tilde{O}]$ conversion knowledge

| | E1 | E2 | E3 | E4 | E5 | E6 | E7 | E8 | E9 | E10 | E11 | E12 | E13 | E14 | E15 | E16 |
|---|---|---|---|---|---|---|---|---|---|---|---|---|---|---|---|---|
| C1 | 0 | 0 | 0 | 0 | 0 | 0 | 0 | 0 | 0 | 0 | 0 | 0 | 0 | 0 | 0 | 0 |
| C2 | 0 | 0 | 0 | 0 | 0 | 0 | 0 | 0 | 0 | 0 | 0 | 0 | 0 | 0 | 0 | 0 |
| C3 | 1 | 0 | 1 | 0 | 1 | 1 | 0 | 1 | 0 | 0 | 1 | 0 | 1 | 1 | 0 | 0 |
| C4 | 0 | 0 | 0 | 0 | 0 | 0 | 0 | 0 | 0 | 0 | 0 | 0 | 0 | 0 | 0 | 0 |
| C5 | 1 | 0 | 1 | 0 | 0 | 1 | 0 | 0 | 0 | 0 | 1 | 0 | 1 | 1 | 0 | 0 |
| C6 | 0 | 0 | 0 | 0 | 0 | 0 | 0 | 0 | 0 | 0 | 0 | 0 | 0 | 0 | 0 | 0 |

**Table A8.** *Cont.*

| | \multicolumn{16}{c}{Matrix $[\widetilde{O}]$ conversion knowledge} |
|---|---|---|---|---|---|---|---|---|---|---|---|---|---|---|---|---|
| | E1 | E2 | E3 | E4 | E5 | E6 | E7 | E8 | E9 | E10 | E11 | E12 | E13 | E14 | E15 | E16 |
| C7 | 1 | 0 | 1 | 0 | 1 | 1 | 0 | 1 | 0 | 0 | 1 | 0 | 1 | 1 | 0 | 0 |
| C8 | 0 | 0 | 0 | 0 | 0 | 0 | 0 | 0 | 0 | 0 | 0 | 0 | 0 | 0 | 0 | 0 |
| C9 | 0 | 0 | 0 | 0 | 0 | 0 | 0 | 0 | 0 | 0 | 0 | 0 | 0 | 0 | 0 | 0 |
| C10 | 0 | 0 | 0 | 0 | 0 | 0 | 0 | 0 | 0 | 0 | 0 | 0 | 0 | 0 | 0 | 0 |
| C11 | 0 | 0 | 0 | 0 | 0 | 0 | 0 | 0 | 0 | 0 | 0 | 0 | 0 | 0 | 0 | 0 |
| C12 | 1 | 0 | 1 | 0 | 1 | 1 | 0 | 1 | 0 | 0 | 1 | 0 | 1 | 1 | 0 | 0 |
| C13 | 0 | 0 | 0 | 0 | 0 | 0 | 0 | 0 | 0 | 0 | 0 | 0 | 0 | 0 | 0 | 0 |
| C14 | 0 | 0 | 0 | 0 | 0 | 0 | 0 | 0 | 1 | 0 | 0 | 0 | 0 | 0 | 0 | 1 |
| C15 | 1 | 0 | 1 | 0 | 1 | 1 | 0 | 1 | 0 | 0 | 1 | 0 | 1 | 1 | 0 | 0 |
| C16 | 0 | 1 | 0 | 0 | 0 | 0 | 0 | 0 | 0 | 0 | 0 | 0 | 0 | 0 | 0 | 0 |
| C17 | 0 | 0 | 0 | 0 | 0 | 0 | 0 | 0 | 0 | 0 | 0 | 0 | 0 | 0 | 0 | 0 |

| | \multicolumn{12}{c}{Matrix $[\widetilde{M}]$ routines} |
|---|---|---|---|---|---|---|---|---|---|---|---|---|
| | E1 | E2 | E3 | E4 | E5 | E6 | E7 | E8 | E9 | E10 | E11 | E12 |
| C1 | 0.92 | 0.86 | 0.87 | 0.83 | 0.87 | 0.89 | 1 | 1 | 1 | 1 | 1 | 1 |
| C2 | 0.77 | 0.72 | 0.73 | 0.69 | 0.73 | 0.74 | 1 | 0.95 | 0.92 | 0.94 | 0.98 | 1 |
| C3 | 0.78 | 0.72 | 0.73 | 0.69 | 0.73 | 0.75 | 1 | 0.95 | 0.92 | 0.94 | 0.98 | 1 |
| C4 | 0.80 | 0.74 | 0.75 | 0.7 | 0.75 | 0.77 | 1 | 0.97 | 0.94 | 0.96 | 1 | 1 |
| C5 | 0.78 | 0.73 | 0.73 | 0.70 | 0.73 | 0.75 | 1 | 0.96 | 0.93 | 0.95 | 0.99 | 1 |
| C6 | 0.94 | 0.88 | 0.89 | 0.86 | 0.89 | 0.91 | 1 | 1 | 1 | 1 | 1 | 1 |
| C7 | 0.92 | 0.86 | 0.87 | 0.83 | 0.87 | 0.89 | 1 | 1 | 1 | 1 | 1 | 1 |
| C8 | 0.82 | 0.76 | 0.77 | 0.74 | 0.77 | 0.79 | 1 | 0.99 | 0.96 | 0.99 | 1 | 1 |
| C9 | 1 | 1 | 1 | 1 | 1 | 1 | 1 | 1 | 1 | 1 | 1 | 1 |

| | \multicolumn{12}{c}{Matrix $[\widetilde{A}] \circ [\widetilde{M}]$ routines} |
|---|---|---|---|---|---|---|---|---|---|---|---|---|
| | E1 | E2 | E3 | E4 | E5 | E6 | E7 | E8 | E9 | E10 | E11 | E12 |
| C1 | 0.94 | 0.88 | 0.89 | 0.86 | 0.89 | 0.91 | 1 | 1 | 1 | 1 | 1 | 1 |

Table A8. Cont.

Matrix $[\tilde{A}] \circ [\tilde{M}]$ routines

| | E1 | E2 | E3 | E4 | E5 | E6 | E7 | E8 | E9 | E10 | E11 | E12 |
|---|---|---|---|---|---|---|---|---|---|---|---|---|
| C2 | 0.86 | 0.86 | 0.86 | 0.83 | 0.86 | 0.86 | 1 | 0.97 | 0.95 | 0.96 | 0.99 | 1 |
| C3 | 0.86 | 0.86 | 0.86 | 0.84 | 0.86 | 0.86 | 1 | 0.97 | 0.96 | 0.96 | 0.99 | 1 |
| C4 | 0.88 | 0.86 | 0.87 | 0.86 | 0.87 | 0.88 | 1 | 0.98 | 0.96 | 0.98 | 1 | 1 |
| C5 | 0.87 | 0.86 | 0.87 | 0.84 | 0.87 | 0.87 | 1 | 0.97 | 0.96 | 0.96 | 0.99 | 1 |
| C6 | 0.94 | 0.88 | 0.89 | 0.86 | 0.89 | 0.91 | 1 | 1 | 1 | 1 | 1 | 1 |
| C7 | 0.94 | 0.88 | 0.89 | 0.86 | 0.89 | 0.91 | 1 | 1 | 1 | 1 | 1 | 1 |
| C8 | 0.90 | 0.88 | 0.88 | 0.86 | 0.88 | 0.89 | 1 | 0.99 | 0.96 | 0.99 | 1 | 1 |
| C9 | 1 | 1 | 1 | 1 | 1 | 1 | 1 | 1 | 1 | 1 | 1 | 1 |

Matrix $[\tilde{A}] \circ [\tilde{M}] \circ [\tilde{B}]$ routines

| | E1 | E2 | E3 | E4 | E5 | E6 | E7 | E8 | E9 | E10 | E11 | E12 |
|---|---|---|---|---|---|---|---|---|---|---|---|---|
| C1 | 0.94 | 0.94 | 0.94 | 0.92 | 0.94 | 0.94 | 1 | 1 | 0.98 | 1 | 1 | 1 |
| C2 | 0.86 | 0.86 | 0.86 | 0.86 | 0.86 | 0.86 | 1 | 0.97 | 0.97 | 0.97 | 0.99 | 1 |
| C3 | 0.86 | 0.86 | 0.86 | 0.86 | 0.86 | 0.86 | 1 | 0.97 | 0.97 | 0.97 | 0.99 | 1 |
| C4 | 0.88 | 0.88 | 0.88 | 0.88 | 0.88 | 0.88 | 1 | 0.98 | 0.98 | 0.98 | 1 | 1 |
| C5 | 0.87 | 0.87 | 0.87 | 0.87 | 0.87 | 0.87 | 1 | 0.97 | 0.97 | 0.97 | 0.99 | 1 |
| C6 | 0.94 | 0.94 | 0.94 | 0.92 | 0.94 | 0.94 | 1 | 1 | 0.98 | 1 | 1 | 1 |
| C7 | 0.94 | 0.94 | 0.94 | 0.92 | 0.94 | 0.94 | 1 | 1 | 0.98 | 1 | 1 | 1 |
| C8 | 0.90 | 0.90 | 0.90 | 0.90 | 0.90 | 0.90 | 1 | 0.99 | 0.98 | 0.99 | 1 | 1 |
| C9 | 1 | 1 | 1 | 1 | 1 | 1 | 1 | 1 | 1 | 1 | 1 | 1 |

Matrix $[\tilde{O}]$ routines

| | E1 | E2 | E3 | E4 | E5 | E6 | E7 | E8 | E9 | E10 | E11 | E12 |
|---|---|---|---|---|---|---|---|---|---|---|---|---|
| C1 | 0 | 0 | 0 | 0 | 0 | 0 | 0 | 0 | 0.8 | 0 | 0 | 0 |
| C2 | 0 | 0 | 0 | 0 | 0 | 0 | 0 | 0 | 0 | 0 | 0 | 0 |
| C3 | 0 | 0 | 0 | 0 | 0 | 0 | 0 | 0 | 0 | 0 | 0 | 0 |
| C4 | 0 | 0 | 0 | 0 | 0 | 0 | 0 | 0 | 0 | 0 | 0 | 0 |

**Table A8.** *Cont.*

| | Matrix $[\tilde{O}]$ routines | | | | | | | | | | | |
|---|---|---|---|---|---|---|---|---|---|---|---|---|
| | E1 | E2 | E3 | E4 | E5 | E6 | E7 | E8 | E9 | E10 | E11 | E12 |
| C5 | 0 | 0 | 0 | 0 | 0 | 0 | 0 | 0 | 0 | 0 | 0 | 0 |
| C6 | 0 | 0 | 0 | 0 | 0 | 0 | 0 | 0 | 0.8 | 0 | 0 | 0 |
| C7 | 0 | 0 | 0 | 0 | 0 | 0 | 0 | 0 | 0.8 | 0 | 0 | 0 |
| C8 | 0 | 0 | 0 | 0 | 0 | 0 | 0 | 0 | 0 | 0 | 0 | 0 |
| C9 | 0 | 0 | 0 | 0 | 0 | 0 | 0 | 0 | 0 | 0 | 0 | 0 |

## References

1. Mejia-Rocha, M.I.; Colin-Salgado, M. Gestión del conocimiento: Una aproximación teórica y propuesta para su observación. *Desarro. Gerenc.* **2013**, *5*, 145–170.
2. Levin, D.Z.; Cross, R. The strength of weak ties you can trust: The mediating role of trust in effective knowledge transfer. *Manag. Sci.* **2004**, *50*, 1477–1490. [CrossRef]
3. Nonaka, I.; von Krogh, G. Tacit knowledge and knowledge conversion: Controversy and advancement in organizational knowledge creation theory. *Organ. Sci.* **2009**, *20*, 635–652. [CrossRef]
4. Chang, H.C.; Tsai, M.-T.; Tsai, C.L. Complex organizational knowledge structures for new product development teams. *Knowl. Based Syst.* **2011**, *24*, 652–661. [CrossRef]
5. Zollo, M.; Winter, S.G. Deliberate learning and the evolution of dynamic capabilities. *Organ. Sci.* **2002**, *13*, 339–351. [CrossRef]
6. Teece, D.J. Dynamic Capabilities: Routines versus Entrepreneurial Action. *J. Manag. Stud.* **2012**, *49*, 1395–1401. [CrossRef]
7. Becker, M.C. The concept of routines: Some clarifications. *Camb. J. Econ.* **2005**, *29*, 249–262. [CrossRef]
8. Ministerio de Comercio, I. y T. Perfiles económicos y comerciales por departamentos | MINCIT—Ministerio de Comercio, Industria y Turismo. Available online: https://www.mincit.gov.co/estudios-economicos/perfiles-economicos-por-departamentos (accessed on 29 May 2022).
9. Ramirez, R.; Chacon, H.; El Kadi Janbeih, O. *Gestión Estratégica Del Talento Humano en Las PYMES*, 1st ed.; Corporación CIMTED: Barranquilla, Columbia, 2018.
10. Zahra, S.A.; George, G. Absorptive capacity: A review, reconceptualization, and extension. *Acad. Manag. Rev.* **2002**, *27*, 185. [CrossRef]
11. Nonaka, I.; Toyama, R.; Konno, N. SECI, Ba and leadership: A unified model of dynamic knowledge creation. *Long Range Plan.* **2000**, *33*, 5–34. [CrossRef]
12. Nonaka, I. The Knowledge-Creating Company. *Harv. Bus. Rev.* **2007**, *85*, 162–170.
13. Feldman, M.S. Organizational routines as a source of continuous change. *Organ. Sci.* **2000**, *11*, 611–629. [CrossRef]
14. Schaefer, C.; Makatsaria, A. Framework of data analytics and integrating knowledge management. *Int. J. Intell. Netw.* **2021**, *2*, 156–165. [CrossRef]
15. Kaufmann, A.; Gil-Aluja, J. *Técnicas Especiales Para La Gestión de Expertos*; Villadoiro: Vigo, Spain, 1993; ISBN 84-604-7564-6.
16. Gil-Aluja, J. *Elementos Para Una Teoría De La Decisión en La Incertidumbre*; Milladoiro: Santiago de Compostela, Spain, 1999; ISBN 8460594378.
17. Kaufmann, A.; Gil-Aluja, J. *Modelos Para La Investigación de Efectos Olvidados*; Milladoiro: Vigo, Spain, 1988.
18. Gil-Lafuente, A.M.; Molina, L.A.; Martínez, A.T. Modelo de efectos olvidados en el análisis estratégico de medios de comunicación. *Inquietud Empres.* **2020**, *20*, 73–85. [CrossRef]
19. Blanco-Mesa, F.; Merigó, J.M.; Gil-Lafuente, A.M. Fuzzy decision making: A bibliometric-based review. *J. Intell. Fuzzy Syst.* **2017**, *32*, 2033–2050. [CrossRef]
20. Kianto, A.; Vanhala, M.; Heilmann, P. The impact of knowledge management on job satisfaction. *J. Knowl. Manag.* **2016**, *20*, 621–636. [CrossRef]
21. Hussinki, H.; Ritala, P.; Vanhala, M.; Kianto, A. Intellectual capital, knowledge management practices and firm performance. *J. Intellect. Cap.* **2017**, *18*, 904–922. [CrossRef]
22. Arbonies Ortiz, A.L. *Conocimiento Para Innovar. Cómo Evitar La Miopía en La Gestión Del Conocimiento*, 2nd ed.; Ediciones Díaz de Santos: Bogotá, Colombia, 2006; ISBN 84-7978-755-4.
23. Lee, H.; Choi, B. Knowledge management enablers, processes, and organizational performance: An integrative view and empirical examination. *J. Manag. Inf. Syst.* **2014**, *20*, 179–228. [CrossRef]
24. Nonaya, I.; Takehuchi, H.; Umemoto, K. A theory of organizational knowledge creation. *Int. J. Technol. Manag.* **2014**, *11*, 833–845.
25. Ben Arfi, W.; Hikkerova, L. Corporate entrepreneurship, product innovation, and knowledge conversion: The role of digital platforms. *Small Bus. Econ.* **2021**, *56*, 1191–1204. [CrossRef]
26. Lu, H.; Lee, H.I. Case study on four patterns of knowledge conversion: Behavioural competency and social learning theory perspectives. *Knowl. Manag. Res. Pract.* **2017**, *14*, 270–279. [CrossRef]
27. Sarbaugh-Thompson, M.; Feldman, M.S. Electronic mail and organizational communication: Does saying "Hi" really matter? *Organ. Sci.* **1998**, *9*, 685–698. [CrossRef]
28. Nonaka, I.; Konno, N. The concept of "Ba": Building a foundation for knowledge creation. *Calif. Manag. Rev.* **1998**, *40*, 40–54. [CrossRef]
29. Hislop, D. Mission impossible? communicating and sharing knowledge via information technology. *J. Inf. Technol.* **2002**, *17*, 165–177. [CrossRef]
30. Rice, J. The applicability of the SECI model to multi-organisational endeavours: An integrative review. *Int. J. Organ. Behav.* **2002**, *9*, 671–682.
31. Johannessen, J.A.; Olaisen, J.; Olsen, B. Mismanagement of tacit knowledge: The importance of tacit knowledge, the danger of information technology, and what to do about it. *Int. J. Inf. Manag.* **2001**, *21*, 3–20. [CrossRef]
32. Argyris, C.; Schön, D.A. Organizational learning: A theory of action perspective. In *Reis: Revista Española de Investigaciones Sociológicas*; Centro de Investigaciones Sociologicas: Madrid, Spain, 1997; pp. 345–348. [CrossRef]
33. Nonaka, I. A dynamic theory of organizational knowledge creation. *Organ. Sci.* **1994**, *5*, 14–37. [CrossRef]

34. Nelson, R.; Winter, S. *An Evolution Theory of Economic Change*; Harvard University Press: Cambridge, MA, USA, 1985.
35. Pentland, B. Grammatical models of organizational processes. *Organ. Sci.* **1995**, *6*, 541–556. [CrossRef]
36. March, J.G.; Simon, H.A. "Classical" Organization Theory. In *Organizations*; Blackwell: Massachusetts, MA, USA, 1993; pp. 31–52. ISBN 978-0-631-18631-1.
37. Hoogeboom, M.A.M.G.; Wilderom, C.P.M. A complex adaptive systems approach to real-life team interactions patterns, task context, information sharing and effectiveness. *Gr. Organ. Manag.* **2019**, *45*, 3–42. [CrossRef]
38. Hilliard, R.; Goldstein, D. Identifying and measuring dynamic capability using search routines. *Strateg. Organ.* **2018**, *17*, 210–240. [CrossRef]
39. Lechner, C.; Floyd, S.W. Searching, processing, codifying and practicing—Key learning activities in exploratory initiatives. *Long Range Plan.* **2007**, *40*, 9–29. [CrossRef]
40. Tippmann, E.; Sharkey Scott, P.; Mangematin, V. Stimulating knowledge search routines and architecture competences: The role of organizational context and middle management. *Long Range Plan.* **2014**, *47*, 206–223. [CrossRef]
41. Blanco-Mesa, F.; Leon-Castro, E.; Bermudez-Mondragon, D.; Castro-Amado, M. Forgotten Motivational Factors of Boyacense Colombian Entrepreneurs: A Subjective Analysis of Second-Generation Incidences. *Mathematics* **2021**, *9*, 973. [CrossRef]
42. Blanco-Mesa, F.; Gil-Lafuente, A.M.; Merigó, J.M. Subjective stakeholder dynamics relationships treatment: A methodological approach using fuzzy decision-making. *Comput. Math. Organ. Theory* **2018**, *24*, 441–472. [CrossRef]
43. Datacredito Experian ¿Qué Son Las Cámaras de Comercio y sus Principales Funciones? Available online: https://www.datacreditoempresas.com.co/blog-datacredito-empresas/que-son-las-camaras-de-comercio-y-sus-principales-funciones/ (accessed on 29 May 2022).
44. Ruiz, G.E.S.; Flores, V.V.; Gil-Lafuente, A.M.; Valenzuela, K.S. Los efectos olvidados en las cooperativas pesqueras de la bahía de Altata. *Inquietud Empres.* **2022**, *22*, 35–56. [CrossRef]
45. Velazquez-Cazares, M.G.; Gil-Lafuente, A.M.; Leon-Castro, E.; Blanco-Mesa, F. Innovation capabilities measurement using fuzzy methodologies: A Colombian SMEs case. *Comput. Math. Organ. Theory* **2021**, *27*, 384–413. [CrossRef]
46. Gil-Lafuente, A.M.; Blanco-Mesa, F.; Castillo, C. The forgotten effects of sport. In *Proceedings of the Soft Computing in Management and Business Economics*; Gil-Lafuente, A.M., Gil-Lafuente, J., Merigó-Lindahl, J.M., Eds.; Springer: Berlin/Heidelberg, Germany, 2012; Volume 287, pp. 375–391.
47. Kaufmann, A.; Gil-Aluja, J. *Introducción de la Teoría de Los Subconjuntos Borrosos a la Gestión de Las Empresas*; Milladoiro: Santiago de Compostela, Spain, 1986.
48. Kaufmann, A.; Gil-Aluja, J. *Técnicas Operativas de Gestión Para el Tratamiento de la Incertidumbre*; Hispano Europea: Barcelona, Spain, 1987; ISBN 84-255-0775-8.
49. Patnayakuni, R.; Ruppel, C.P. Managing the complementarity of knowledge integration and process formalization for systems development performance. *J. Assoc. Inf. Syst.* **2006**, *7*, 545–567. [CrossRef]
50. Parmigiani, A.; Howard-Grenville, J. Routines revisited: Exploring the capabilities and practice perspectives. *Acad. Manag. Ann.* **2011**, *5*, 413–453. [CrossRef]
51. Haldin-Herrgard, T. Difficulties in diffusion of tacit knowledge in organizations. *J. Intellect. Cap.* **2000**, *1*, 357–365. [CrossRef]

**Disclaimer/Publisher's Note:** The statements, opinions and data contained in all publications are solely those of the individual author(s) and contributor(s) and not of MDPI and/or the editor(s). MDPI and/or the editor(s) disclaim responsibility for any injury to people or property resulting from any ideas, methods, instructions or products referred to in the content.

 *mathematics*

Article

# Innovation in Brazilian Industries: Analysis of Management Practices Using Fuzzy TOPSIS

Giulia Giacomello Pompilio [1], Tiago F. A. C. Sigahi [1,*], Izabela Simon Rampasso [2], Gustavo Hermínio Salati Marcondes de Moraes [3,4], Lucas Veiga Ávila [5], Walter Leal Filho [6,7] and Rosley Anholon [1]

[1] School of Mechanical Engineering, State University of Campinas, Campinas 13083-970, Brazil; v225551@dac.unicamp.br (G.G.P.); rosley@unicamp.br (R.A.)
[2] Departamento de Ingeniería Industrial, Universidad Católica del Norte, Antofagasta 1240000, Chile; izabela.rampasso@ucn.cl
[3] School of Applied Science, State University of Campinas, Limeira 13484-350, Brazil; salati@unicamp.br
[4] School of Management Sciences, North-West University, Vanderbijlpark 1900, South Africa
[5] Center for Social Sciences and Humanities, Federal University of Santa Maria, Santa Maria 97105-900, Brazil; lucas.avila@ufsm.br
[6] Faculty of Life Sciences, Hamburg University of Applied Sciences, 20099 Hamburg, Germany; walter.leal2@haw-hamburg.de
[7] School of Science and the Environment, Manchester Metropolitan University, Manchester M15 6BH, UK
* Correspondence: sigahi@unicamp.br

**Abstract:** This study examined the practices of innovation management used by Brazilian industries. A survey was carried out with specialists that assessed 27 practices (PR) proposed by ISO 56002, considering two types of firms: small and medium-sized industries (SMI) and large industries (LI). The methodological approach included Hierarchical Cluster Analysis to identify the similarities between the specialists and define levels of specialists, as well as Fuzzy TOPSIS and frequency and sensitivity analyses to examine their responses. PR1 (analysis of internal and external issues that impact innovation management) was deemed the best practice for LIs, whereas PR10 (adequate assessment of potential partnerships) was best evaluated for SMIs. The PR27 (periodic audits to identify opportunities for improvement) received the lowest rating from both LIs and SMIs. In general, SMIs in the Brazilian context have more severe deficiencies in terms of applying innovation management practices than LIs. A broad overview of the innovation practices adopted in the Brazilian industrial scenario is provided. The study's findings may assist managers and policymakers to develop initiatives and actions to improve the capacity of Brazilian industries to innovate. This research can also support future studies aimed at better understanding specific practices related to the topic.

**Keywords:** fuzzy sets in business management; multiple criteria decision making; mathematics applied to business; fuzzy TOPSIS; Hierarchical Cluster Analysis; innovation management; ISO 56002; Brazilian industries

**MSC:** 03B52; 03E72

## 1. Introduction

Innovation processes are directly related to business evolution, since they are what drive industries to improve their products and services, enhance performance and expand market share [1–3]. Innovation enables organisations to explore new businesses and services, allowing access to external knowledge [4,5] and, at its limit, it is the factor that determines the survival of a company in an environment with increasing complexity, dynamics and competitiveness [6–8].

Through the innovation process, firms can gain a competitive advantage over time [9]. Openness to change and the implementation of innovation is an excellent way to increase performance, as it reduces the response time for customers and increases satisfaction rates [10]. Santoro et al. [11] and Nwankpa et al. [12] argue that resources are only transformed into a competitive advantage when used strategically and wisely and that innovation management can greatly contribute in this regard. Innovation management is an extremely powerful tool in a context of rapid technological change, high flow of information, increasing production costs and pressure for corporate responsibility [6,13]. Innovation plays an important role in the growth of both rich and developing economies [14,15], being a crucial factor for the social and economic development of the latter [16–19].

For innovation management to work, there must be tangible factors that measure effectiveness and success rate, an issue that proves to be a challenge [20]. Benraouane and Harrington [21] reinforce this idea and state that the clear definition of practices within a well-organised operational innovation management system is a differentiating factor between failure and sustained growth. In addition, it is important to emphasise that innovation management must be sensitive to the specifics of each firm, since factors such as size, pre-existing levels of technological advancement, type of industry, consumer market, strategies and organisational factors, greatly interfere in the approach to be adopted [22,23]. Thus, innovation management practices have a great impact on the results achieved by the organisation and, therefore, must be very well structured [9].

In this context, the ISO 56002 standard [24] has been regarded as an important instrument for the structuring, implementation, maintenance and continuous improvement of innovation management systems [21,25]. Hyland and Karlsson [26] state that ISO 56002 provided a common language and framework for building an innovation capability, while Mir et al. [27] highlight that there was no international consensus about how to manage innovation until prior to their publication. Anholon et al. [28] discussed the importance of the ISO 56002 standard in the context of COVID-19 in Brazil, arguing that it is critical that managers adopt the concepts and guidelines presented in this standard in order to recover organisations and their innovative approach, which is a vital component in this country's economic recovery. Khan et al. [6] support this view and state that the COVID-19 pandemic is the perfect example which clearly shows that innovative companies can survive and continue their business due to innovation and technology.

Despite its importance, the literature on ISO 56002 is still quite scarce [6]. Considering its relatively recent launch and the importance of innovation management for the competitiveness and long-term survival of companies, studies that shed light on the process of implementing the ISO 56002 standard can be of great value [26,28]. In this setting, the objective of this article was to examine the innovation management practices adopted in the Brazilian industrial sector, using the ISO 56002 standard as a framework of analysis. This research is relevant to the spread of information about this key instrument and to the managers who can enhance innovation management practices based on ISO 56002. It is also relevant for companies that can improve their competitiveness and for developing countries whose economic development is heavily reliant on their ability to innovate. These factors were the primary motivation for conducting this study, which could contribute to debates and other research about the topic, regardless of the area of expertise.

It is important to note that this study is part of a larger project whose main goal was to conduct exploratory research in three areas in the Brazilian industrial context: (i) business continuity management; (ii) innovation management; and (iii) competence management. Each study used as a framework the corresponding ISO standard, namely ISO 22301, ISO 56002 and ISO 10015, respectively. In all studies, data was collected via survey from specialists with extensive academic and professional experience in the specific area (i, ii or iii). Regarding the data analysis, all studies used an adapted version of Fuzzy TOPSIS (Technique for Order Preference by Similarity to Ideal Solution), in which specialists were used as criteria and their responses were weighted based on their level of knowledge and experience in the area, as well as Hierarchical Cluster Analysis (HCA) to group the specialists according to their characteristics, frequency analysis and sensitivity analysis. The first study of this macro-project was published in the Mathematics journal with the title, "Analysis of the Level of Adoption of Business Continuity Practices by Brazilian Industries: An Exploratory Study Using Fuzzy TOPSIS" [29]. It featured in a special edition called, "Advances in Fuzzy Logic and Artificial Neural Networks". In the present paper, the study concerning innovation management is presented.

## 2. Background
*2.1. Innovation Management and the Growing Need for Structured Systems*

Innovation management has great potential to add value to businesses and society as a whole [6,30]. In order to enhance innovation capacity, organisations need systemic changes that encompass not only the products offered, but also the way business is carried out [31]. Thus, innovation management systems need to be adaptable and sensitive to new knowledge [14].

According to Albors-Garrigos et al. [22], an organisation will successfully implement innovation processes if three key points are followed: (1) an innovation principle that challenges a previous obsolete model; (2) systematisation of innovation with well-defined phases and processes; and (3) transformation of innovation into a continuous process within the company. Rajapathirana and Hui [32] emphasise that innovation management incorporates well-established tools to support strategic decisions, in order to enable the integration of new technologies into key activities of the organisation. Tools, practices and management systems are critical components for organisations seeking to innovate. Without them, it is difficult to address the uncertainties and risks involved in the technological environment [22,23,33].

The innovation environment has been characterised by volatility, uncertainty, complexity and ambiguity (VUCA). Each aspect was pursued independently for a long period by academics in the strategy arena [34]. These characteristics arise because of several factors, among which are volatility, associated with unstable economic factors, uncertainty of rapid technological advances, complexity surrounding the emergence of multifactorial issues in an increasingly globally connected world and ambiguity due to the difficulty of choosing approaches suitable for specific situations [35]. The VUCA world, while posing significant challenges to companies seeking innovation, also represents an opportunity to innovate, as it produces conditions for the generation of ideas and technological evolution, thereby boosting the development of new systems and practices for managing innovation [36].

In this context, there is a growing need for structured innovation management systems (IMS) [25,26]. Mir et al. [37] studied the impacts of standardised IMS and found a significant positive relationship between a company's innovative capability and business performance. Idris and Durmuşoğlu [38] added that the standardisation of IMS is essential to provide a common language, terminology, credibility, facilitated implementation and a benchmarking basis. Finally, the importance of IMS guidelines in systematically and efficiently managing innovation should be emphasized, with a focus on understanding the effects of innovation processes not only on R&D departments, but the whole company [37].

*2.2. Innovation Management from the Perspective of ISO 56002 Standard*

An important instrument in the search for systematic innovation is the ISO 56002 standard, since it makes it possible to manage innovation processes in a more integrated, systemic and effective way, thus adding value to companies' business models [21,30].

According to the International Organization for Standardization [24], ISO 56002 provides guidance for the establishment, implementation, maintenance and continuous improvement of an innovation management system for use in all organisations. It is important to mention that it does not impose detailed methods for its implementation, such as tools or requirements, but rather establishes an overview for guidance [25].

In addition to an introductory section, ISO 56002 has ten other sections. The first three sections cover scope, normative references, and terminology and definitions. Section 4.1 of

ISO 56002 introduces essential elements for businesses to have a good understanding of external (e.g., socioeconomic, geopolitical and market) and internal (e.g., strategic objectives, leadership, individual and organisational competencies) factors that affect innovation management. These factors must be evaluated on a regular basis to ensure that innovation management is successful and that the results are long-lasting [21].

Section 4.4 of ISO 56002 is concerned with the establishment of the IMS, which must be continually reviewed and improved. To accomplish this, organisations should foster an innovation culture within the business environment, as well as a strategy for managing internal and external collaborations [24].

For these efforts to be effective, it is essential that the leadership has a clear focus, vision and innovation strategy [6]. This entails demonstrating a willingness to take risks and tolerance for failure. Communication across all sectors and hierarchies is also essential. Section 5 of ISO 56002 addresses these concerns [24].

Another important part of ISO 56002 to be highlighted is Section 6.2, which proposes that, when commencing system planning, it is necessary to keep in mind: the goals to be achieved; how this will be done; who will be involved with each task; deadlines to be met; required resources; parameters for evaluating the results; and methods for communicating and recording them [24].

Throughout the entire process of planning, developing and implementing the ISO 56002 guidelines, the organisation must provide support, such as managing people, time, financial resources, infrastructure and knowledge [28]. Those in charge of the organisation must ensure that everyone involved is aware of the strategies to be used, objectives, the importance of innovation and the importance of each individual to this process [21]. Furthermore, the activities must be documented, updated as needed and controlled. Section 7 of the standard, specifically Sections 7.1 and 7.5, contains a description of these elements [24].

Section 8 of ISO 56002 focuses on the innovation process itself, proposing the following steps: identifying opportunities (8.3.2); creating concepts (8.3.3); validating concepts (8.3.4); developing solutions (8.3.5); and implementing solutions (8.3.6) [24]. It is important to emphasise that, in this standard, the innovation process is conceived in a non-linear manner, as illustrated in Figure 1.

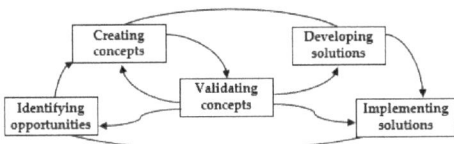

**Figure 1.** Innovation processes and their interactions. Source: Elaborated based on ISO 56002 [24].

Finally, based on Sections 9 and 10 of the standard, the performance achieved must be evaluated in order to implement improvements. This process is encouraged to go through an internal audit as well as a leadership critical review [26], and improvement must occur on an ongoing basis for the IMS to be implemented effectively [24].

*2.3. Innovation Management and Firm Size in the Brazilian Industrial Context*

In the industrial sector of emerging countries such as Brazil, adaptability is regarded as an important characteristic to overcome the various daily problems, and the presence of an innovation management system can greatly contribute to this context [16]. Vrchota and Řehoř [39] state that firms without investments in innovation become much more limited, especially in terms of a qualified workforce. Innovating is, therefore, an essential process for overcoming crises and distinguishing those companies that will survive from those that will go bankrupt [6].

Literature has shown that firm size influences innovation management and the decisions involved in its implementation [19,40,41]. According to the National Confederation of Industry [42], the main representative entity of Brazilian industry, large industries (LI) have an advantage in managing risks because an unsuccessful investment or one with a slow return has less impact. Brazilian LIs are characterised by R&D strategies that are already validated and well-structured, as well as significant capital commitments for this purpose. Overall, they have a large consumer market and a large number of employees, and their operations have a national and even global impact [42].

In the case of medium-sized industries, innovation can lead to reaching new markets and overcoming crises [43], being a decisive factor in launching them into the global market [44]. However, there are several obstacles along the way, notably the company's need to distinguish itself from so many other companies with similar characteristics. For Brazilian medium-sized enterprises, factors such as economic instability and investment uncertainty in the industry impose barriers to innovation. In addition, the capital allocated for innovation in this type of industry is scarce, increasing the risk and pressure to make the right decisions [42].

With regard to small industries in Brazil, the discussion on innovation is also necessary. While it is clear that management approaches and organisational objectives are different from those adopted by large and medium-sized companies, the reasons for innovating remain the same. Many of the challenges for small Brazilian industries, however, arise even before there is any financial return, necessitating constant re-elaboration of the business plan, redirection of monetary and technological efforts and high resilience on the part of all involved [42].

All types of businesses, companies and industries, regardless of their size, can benefit from well-structured innovation management systems [25,37,38]. Managers, firms and society as a whole may benefit from innovation, particularly in emerging economies, as is the case for Brazil [17,28].

### 2.4. Fuzzy Set Theory and Its Application in Innovation Management

There are several types of related uncertainties in the context of innovation management. Thus, Fuzzy Set Theories are a powerful tool with which to investigate topics in this field and they are increasingly used by researchers interested in the subject. Table 1 displays studies that used various fuzzy approaches to investigate topics related to innovation management.

**Table 1.** Applications of fuzzy approaches to innovation management research.

| Author(s) | Methodological Approach | Description |
|---|---|---|
| Alfaro-García et al. [45] | Expertons models, fuzzy sets, intervals of confidence and random sets | An innovation management measurement approach is presented to manufacturing SMIs |
| Ju et al. [46] | Intuitionistic fuzzy set | A divergence-based distance measure of intuitionistic fuzzy sets is applied to decision-making in innovation management |
| Yue [47] | Interval-valued intuitionistic fuzzy sets | A decision-making method for knowledge innovation management is proposed |
| Hessami [48] | Fuzzy DEMATEL and fuzzy ANP | An open innovation management model was formulated considering the elements that influence innovation diffusion |
| Dinesh and Sushil [49] | Total Interpretive Structural Modeling (TISM) | A simulation-based study was conducted to investigate hierarchical models of strategic innovation |

Table 1. *Cont.*

| Author(s) | Methodological Approach | Description |
|---|---|---|
| Yang et al. [50] | Triangular Fuzzy AHP | A study was conducted to determine a risk factor set of collaborative innovation in the context of environmental protection equipment manufacturing enterprises |
| Yin et al. [51] | VIKOR method, intuitional fuzzy entropy and TOPSIS | A framework for collaboration in digital green innovation management was developed |
| Poorkavoos et al. [52] | Fuzzy-set Qualitative Comparative Analysis (fsQCA) | The study examined how SMIs' inter-organisational knowledge transfer networks and organisations' internal capabilities impact types of innovation |
| Kumar et al. [53] | Fuzzy Delphi and DEMATEL | This study evaluated the technology and human resources innovation capabilities of Indian real estate firms |
| Li and Wang [54] | K-means clustering, Ordinary Least Squares (OLS), Coupling coordination metrics | This study applied a fuzzy approach to investigate the technological innovation diffusion behaviour in industrial clusters |
| García and Velásquez [55] | Fuzzy inference system method | A methodology to evaluate technological innovation capabilities in universities is proposed |
| Jing et al. [56] | Fuzzy proximity method | A framework for selecting management strategies and enterprise life cycle periods was created |
| Velazquez-Cazares et al. [57] | Expertons model, adequacy coefficient and forgotten effects theory | This study looked into the hidden occurrences that can help beekeeper SMIs improve specific aspects of their innovation capabilities. |

Source: Elaborated by the authors.

More specifically, Fuzzy TOPSIS is a widely used research approach that has been used in a wide range of management-related areas, including, for example, business resilience [29], technology [58], environment [59] and team performance [60].

Fuzzy TOPSIS, proposed by Chen [61], is defined as a multi-criteria decision method that, in addition to providing an approximation of the Positive Ideal Solution (PIS) and the greatest possible distance from the Negative Ideal Solution (NIS), incorporates the factor of uncertainty of the numbers obtained, i.e., fuzzy logic [62].

Lima Junior and Carpinetti [63] conducted a study comparative analysis of TOPSIS and Fuzzy TOPSIS. The advantages of Fuzzy TOPSIS, according to these authors, are its appropriateness for investigating qualitative criteria and weights, for modelling quantitative criteria in situations of uncertainty, and the fact that the inclusion or exclusion of alternatives does not cause inversion in the generated ranking. In terms of its disadvantages, Fuzzy TOPSIS presents greater data collection complexity, needs additional judgments to parameterize fuzzy numbers and requires greater computational complexity [63].

Lima Junior et al. [64] conducted a study comparing Fuzzy TOPSIS and Fuzzy AHP. These authors pointed out that Fuzzy TOPSIS produces consistent preference order in terms of adequacy to changes of alternatives. When it comes to decision-making agility, Fuzzy TOPSIS outperforms Fuzzy AHP in most cases, except when there are very few criteria and alternatives. In terms of time complexity, Fuzzy AHP performs better than Fuzzy TOPSIS in most cases. Finally, it is critical to consider the number of criteria and alternatives in the problem under consideration, as Fuzzy TOPSIS has no such limitation, whereas Fuzzy AHP does [64].

## 3. Methodological Approach

For a better understanding of the research steps, Figure 2 depicts the sequence of activities performed and, subsequently, a more detailed description of them is presented.

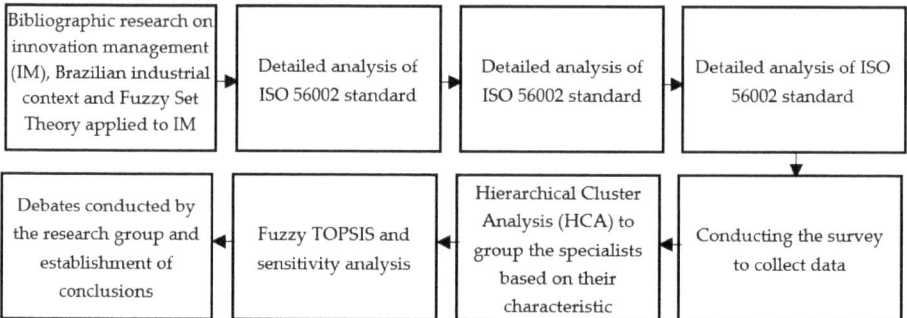

**Figure 2.** Research steps and activities. Source: Elaborated by the authors.

*3.1. Survey Design and Research Questionnaire Creation*

In order to establish a panorama of the adoption of innovation management guidelines by Brazilian firms, a survey was carried out with specialists with extensive knowledge and experience in innovation management activities in Brazilian industries. This research was evaluated and approved by the university's Research Ethics Committee (CAAE No. 50589321.2.0000.5404). In Brazil, all research involving information provided by human beings, even in terms of opinions, must be approved by a Research Ethics Committee. The CAAE is the protocol number that designates that this research has been approved to be conducted in Brazil. The survey addressed 27 practices related to the innovation management system proposed by ISO 56002 (Table 2).

**Table 2.** The innovation management practices considered for analysis.

| Practice | Description |
|---|---|
| PR1 | Firms frequently analyse internal and external issues that may compromise results related to innovation management |
| PR2 | Firms monitor, interact with all interested parties and constantly review their desires and needs in order to incorporate such information into innovation initiatives |
| PR3 | Firms clearly define the scope of innovation management, that is, the limits and applicability of their processes, as well as functions, collaboration interest and willingness to face uncertainty |
| PR4 | Firms promote a culture of innovation, allowing creative attitudes and behaviours to coexist with others focused on operations |
| PR5 | Firms seek to develop leaders committed to innovation at all levels of the hierarchical hierarchy |
| PR6 | Firms' top management constantly supports and commits to activities in favour of innovation, as well as providing the necessary resources so that initiatives can take place and the desired results can be achieved |
| PR7 | Firms' top management conducts critical analyses of initiatives related to innovation management on a regular basis, covering topics such as value generated, goals achieved, successes and failures and performance indicators; following that, it takes actions to continuously improve innovation management |
| PR8 | The roles and responsibilities associated with managing innovation in organisations are correctly defined and understood by all employees |
| PR9 | Firms value the diversity of employees when forming teams to develop activities related to innovation in order to capitalise on experiences and ideas and generate positive results |
| PR10 | Firms have a system to correctly assess the need for collaboration to innovate (including innovation in terms of knowledge, competence, infrastructure and resources) and, if relevant, adopt guidelines to improve the selection process of partners |

Table 2. *Cont.*

| Practice | Description |
|---|---|
| PR11 | Firms have established procedures to correctly measure risks and support debates about their acceptability when analysing opportunities related to innovation |
| PR12 | Firms assess existing deficiencies in terms of organisational competencies for innovation (individual or team competencies) and offer training programs to employees in order to achieve better performance in initiatives |
| PR13 | Firms clearly define the innovation objectives to be achieved in each initiative in a coherent and easy-to-monitor way, and then communicate those objectives to all stakeholders |
| PR14 | Firms have flexible and adaptable innovation strategies, so that they can be adjusted based on the performance and feedback of innovation activities |
| PR15 | Firms correctly define plans to achieve innovation goals, including what will be done, who will be involved, the timeline, how the results will be evaluated and how communication will occur |
| PR16 | Firms manage their innovation portfolios properly, that is, they check how each initiative contributes to the achievement of the strategic objectives on a regular basis, analyse synergies between initiatives and communicate the progress of initiatives to stakeholders |
| PR17 | Firms develop innovation management in tandem with knowledge management; they seek to understand the external context, apply lessons learned, facilitate access and reuse of acquired knowledge and maintain mechanisms for knowledge flow, throughout the entire innovation process |
| PR18 | Firms have a documentation control system in place to assist with innovation management |
| PR19 | Firms correctly develop intellectual property management associated with innovation management, seeking to understand the assets they should or should not protect, creating an inventory of the firms' intellectual assets |
| PR20 | Firms continually review their innovation initiatives in terms of adequacy of scope and expected results |
| PR21 | Managers debate and reflect on the best approach to implementing innovation initiatives before putting them into action, whether through internal implementation or collaborative agreements or outsourcing |
| PR22 | Firms clearly communicate to employees that innovation processes are not always linear. Identifying opportunities, developing and validating concepts, developing and implementing solutions may necessitate feedback and non-direct connections in both directions |
| PR23 | Firms have well-structured activities and use tools and methods such as scanning, prospective analysis, benchmarking, internal and external research, ethnography, forecasting activities and dynamic models to identify opportunities to innovate |
| PR24 | Firms have well-structured activities that allow them to leverage the initial ideas, analyse the most viable ones and determine the associated uncertainties, in addition to defining technical, financial and organisational aspects relevant to this phase |
| PR25 | Firms have well-structured activities that allow for greater added value in the development of solutions and their implementation in the innovation process, such as solution delivery, customer feedback, identification of new implications for intellectual property and lessons learned |
| PR26 | Firms are clear about how they measure the performance of their innovation initiatives, taking into account critical parameters, frequency of monitoring and responsible workers |
| PR27 | Firms audit their innovation management processes on a regular basis to identify areas for improvement, seeking to document the entire cycle so that such data can support decision-making and/or be used as lessons learned |

Source: Elaborated by the authors based on ISO 56002:2020 [24].

For each of the practices presented in Table 2, specialists were asked about their adoption considering two types of firms: small and medium-sized industries (SMI) and large industries (LI).

The first part of the questionnaire was dedicated to sampling characterisation, including questions about the specialist's research area, academic titles and professional and research experience in innovation management.

The second part assessed the level of adoption of ISO 56002 innovation management practices by Brazilian LIs and SMIs. The questions in the research instrument (questionnaire) were the practices from PR1 to PR27. The methodological approach proposed by Bobel et al. [29] was used as follows: For each practice and each category, specialists should evaluate based on a five-point Likert scale: 'Not applied' (NA); 'Applied superficially' (AS); 'Applied reasonably' (AR); 'Applied properly' (AP); or 'Applied in a well-structured way' (AW). Each practice was analysed considering the type of firm (LI and SMI).

Sampling was done through a non-probabilistic and judgmental procedure, following the recommendations of Apostolopoulos and Liargovas [65], in which the researchers chose the audience based on the research purpose, conceptual and practical knowledge of the specialists that qualifies them to participate in the research, and relevance of the information to be obtained. The invitation to participate in the study was sent to potential participants identified based on the information available in the Brazilian National Council for Scientific and Technological Development Researchers Platform [66], obtaining 26 acceptances.

### 3.2. Procedures and Methods for Data Analysis

Following the completion of data collection, data analysis was carried out using HCA, Fuzzy TOPSIS and frequency and sensitivity analysis.

The HCA allowed defining how the data are grouped according to the characteristics of the specialists, resulting in a hierarchy that can be represented by a dendrogram [67]. In this study, the HCA was applied to understand specialists' similarities and group them according to their academic titles and professional experience in the innovation management field. These aspects were chosen for analysis because the researchers considered they were the most relevant to the purpose of allocating the specialists in levels of ability to express opinions about the topics under investigation. The HCA produced seven groups of specialists (see Section 4.1 for a detailed explanation).

The percentage indicated by specialists for each of the 27 innovation management practices evaluated according to the type of firms (i.e., SMI and LI) was analyzed using frequency analysis. Fuzzy TOPSIS was employed to order the practices in Table 2 based on their level of application in Brazilian LIs and SMIs.

Following the methodological procedures proposed by Chen [61], the innovation management practices represented the alternatives ($A_i$) and the specialists the criteria ($C_j$), with weights ($w_j$) based on their level of expertise (groups defined by the HCA). The matrix $\tilde{D}$ composed of the fuzzy numbers $\tilde{x}_{ij}$ and the vector $\tilde{E}$, which represents the fuzzy weights of the specialists, are presented below.

$$\tilde{D} = \begin{bmatrix} \tilde{x}_{11} & \tilde{x}_{12} & \cdots & \tilde{x}_{1n} \\ \tilde{x}_{21} & \tilde{x}_{22} & \cdots & \tilde{x}_{2n} \\ \cdots & \cdots & \cdots & \cdots \\ \tilde{x}_{m1} & \tilde{x}_{m2} & \cdots & \tilde{x}_{mn} \end{bmatrix} ; \tilde{x}_{ij} = [a_{ij}, b_{ij}, c_{ij}] ; \tilde{E} = [\tilde{w}_1, \tilde{w}_2, \ldots \tilde{w}_n] ; \tilde{w}_j = [w_1, w_2, w_3]$$

Figure 3 depicts the fuzzy version of the scales used (Figure 3a) and the levels for allocating specialists based on their educational level, experience and knowledge of innovation management (Figure 3b).

Following Chen's [61] recommendations, the matrix $\tilde{D}$ was normalised based on the highest value, obtaining the matrix $\tilde{R}$, which was then weighted by the vector $\tilde{E}$, generating the matrix $\tilde{V}$. The equations used in the calculation are shown in the sequence.

$$\tilde{R} = [\tilde{r}_{ij}]_{m \times n} \text{ where } \tilde{r}_{ij} = \left( \frac{a_{ij}}{C_j^*}, \frac{b_{ij}}{C_j^*}, \frac{c_{ij}}{C_j^*} \right) ; C_j^* = \max{(i)} c_{ij}$$

$$\tilde{V} = [\tilde{v}_{ij}]_{m \times n} ; \tilde{v}_{ij} = \tilde{r}_{ij} (.) \tilde{w}_j$$

The next step was to calculate the distances $d(\tilde{m}, \tilde{n})$ between each element of the matrix $\tilde{V}$ and the PIS (unit vector) and NIS (null vector).

$$(\tilde{m}, \tilde{n}) = \sqrt{\frac{1}{3}[(m_1 - n_1)^2 + (m_2 - n_2)^2 + (m_3 - n_3)^2]}$$

The sum of distances—positive ($d_i^*$) and negative ($d_i^-$)—related to each alternative was calculated using the partial distances, allowing the structuring of the ranking of the alternatives based on the proximity coefficient ($CC_i$).

$$d_i^* = \sum_{j=1}^{n} d(\tilde{v}_{ij}, \tilde{v}_j^*) \; ; \; d_i^- = \sum_{j=1}^{n} d(\tilde{v}_{ij}, \tilde{v}_j^-) \; ; \; CC_i = \frac{d_i^-}{(d_i^* + d_i^-)}$$

In the last step, a sensitivity analysis was performed to determine the impact of removing each group of specialists in the final comparative ranking of innovation management practices generated by Fuzzy TOPSIS. Seven scenarios for the sensitivity analysis were considered, each with a different group of specialists defined by the HCA removed: scenario 1 (remove Group 1 and keep the others); scenario 2 (remove Group 2 and keep the others); scenario 3 (remove Group 3 and keep the others); scenario 4 (remove Group 4 and keep the others); scenario 5 (remove Group 5 and keep the others); scenario 6 (remove Group 6 and keep the others); and scenario 7 (remove Group 7 and keep the others).

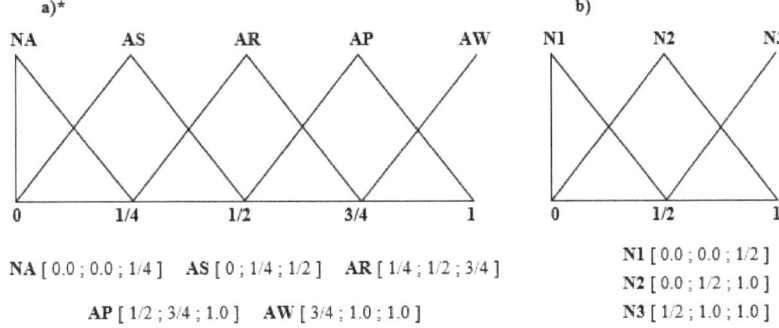

Figure 3. Fuzzyfication of the evaluation scale of practices and levels for allocation of specialists. (a) depicts the fuzzy version of the scales used and (b) shows the levels for allocating specialists based on their educational level, experience and knowledge of innovation management. * Note: The scales used were based on Bobel et al. [29] as follows: Not applied (NA); Applied superficially (AS); Applied reasonably (AR); Applied properly (AP); Applied in a well-structured way (AW).

## 4. Results

### 4.1. Hierarchical Cluster Analysis

The specialists' characteristics were assessed based on time working with innovation (years), research projects in the field of innovation management and experience in educating and developing innovation management professionals. The application of HCA resulted in the classification of the 26 specialists into seven groups, as shown in Figure 4.

The groups of specialists were then assigned in ascending order in levels 1 (Group 5), 2 (Groups 2, 3 and 7) and 3 (Groups 1, 4 and 6) (Table 3).

Table 3. Classification of specialists based on their similarities.

| Level | Specialists |
| --- | --- |
| N1 | S1, S7 and S8 |
| N2 | S3, S5, S6, S15, S16, S20 and S25 |
| N3 | S2, S4, S9, S10, S11, S12, S13, S14, S17, S18, S19, S21, S22, S23, S24 and S26 |

Based on the characteristics of the specialists, N1, N2 and N3 correspond, respectively, to groups of those with lower, intermediate and high educational levels, experience and knowledge. It should be highlighted that the sample is composed of 84.6% of participants with a PhD, with an average of 17.7 years of experience in teaching and research in the area of innovation management. Moreover, it is important to note that this grouping used the fuzzy numbers technique, as explained in Section 3.2, which allowed for the incorporation of uncertainty in the allocation of specialists to levels through weighting.

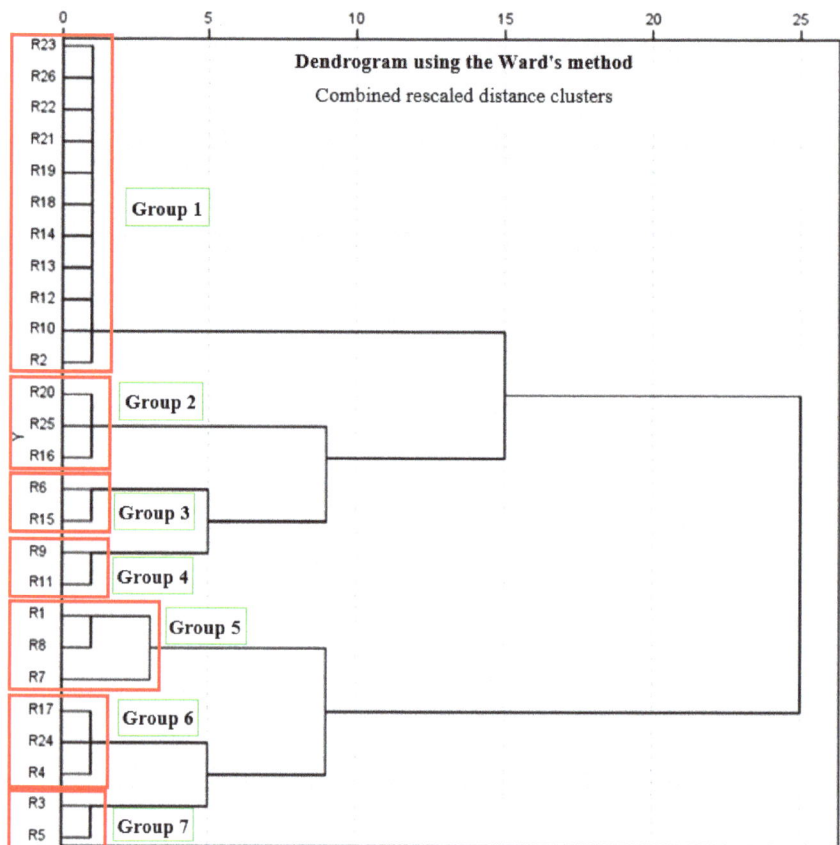

**Figure 4.** Dendrogram from the Hierarchical Cluster Analysis.

*4.2. Frequency Analysis of the Specialists' Responses*

For each of the 27 practices evaluated (see Table 2), the frequency of responses was calculated and the analysis was performed considering the types of firms (LI and SMI) and the groups of specialists (N1, N2, N3).

4.2.1. Adoption of Innovation Management Practices in Large Industries (LI)

The results for LIs are examined in this section. Following an analysis of the responses provided by the specialists considering the levels determined through the HCA (N1, N2 and N3), the unified global frequencies for LIs are analyzed.

Considering Brazilian LIs, none of the N1 specialists chose the response 'Not applied' (NA) for any of the 27 practices. In general, the most common responses in this group were distributed between the alternatives 'Applied reasonably' (AR) and 'Applied properly' (AP). Concerning PR3 (firms clearly define the scope of innovation management, that is, the limits and applicability of their processes, as well as functions, collaboration interest and willingness to face uncertainty), there was unanimous agreement in N1 on the alternative

'Applied properly' (AP). For N2, the option 'Not applied' (NA) was also not selected for any of the 27 practices. The option 'Applied in a well-structured way' (AW) was selected for fewer practices in N2 compared to N1. In terms of overall response distribution, N2 demonstrated greater homogeneity amongst the three intermediate options of the scale, namely AS, AR and AP, with emphasis on the latter two. N3 was the only group to provide answers that covered all five levels of practice application, focusing on intermediate alternatives (AS, AR and AP).

These findings show that, despite the perceived differences between N1, N2 and N3, specialists believe that Brazilian LIs have well-structured and consolidated innovation management practices. Based on the global frequency analysis, the LIs in Brazil present practices that are consistent with the literature on organisations with high revenue streams and high innovation performance.

Table 4 shows the global frequency of the evaluation of practices for LIs.

**Table 4.** Level of adoption of innovation management practices in LIs.

| Practices | Level of Application | | | | |
|---|---|---|---|---|---|
| | NA | AS | AR | AP | AW |
| PR1 | 0.000 | 0.077 | 0.462 | 0.346 | 0.115 |
| PR2 | 0.000 | 0.154 | 0.462 | 0.308 | 0.077 |
| PR3 | 0.000 | 0.231 | 0.231 | 0.500 | 0.038 |
| PR4 | 0.000 | 0.269 | 0.308 | 0.385 | 0.038 |
| PR5 | 0.000 | 0.346 | 0.385 | 0.231 | 0.038 |
| PR6 | 0.000 | 0.385 | 0.192 | 0.385 | 0.038 |
| PR7 | 0.000 | 0.346 | 0.308 | 0.308 | 0.038 |
| PR8 | 0.038 | 0.462 | 0.346 | 0.115 | 0.038 |
| PR9 | 0.038 | 0.308 | 0.231 | 0.346 | 0.077 |
| PR10 | 0.000 | 0.269 | 0.346 | 0.346 | 0.038 |
| PR11 | 0.077 | 0.346 | 0.192 | 0.346 | 0.038 |
| PR12 | 0.038 | 0.154 | 0.538 | 0.192 | 0.077 |
| PR13 | 0.000 | 0.269 | 0.423 | 0.269 | 0.038 |
| PR14 | 0.000 | 0.308 | 0.385 | 0.269 | 0.038 |
| PR15 | 0.038 | 0.115 | 0.346 | 0.423 | 0.077 |
| PR16 | 0.038 | 0.269 | 0.385 | 0.192 | 0.115 |
| PR17 | 0.038 | 0.385 | 0.308 | 0.231 | 0.038 |
| PR18 | 0.038 | 0.192 | 0.462 | 0.269 | 0.038 |
| PR19 | 0.000 | 0.154 | 0.538 | 0.231 | 0.077 |
| PR20 | 0.000 | 0.192 | 0.462 | 0.308 | 0.038 |
| PR21 | 0.038 | 0.231 | 0.423 | 0.192 | 0.115 |
| PR22 | 0.077 | 0.346 | 0.269 | 0.269 | 0.038 |
| PR23 | 0.000 | 0.231 | 0.462 | 0.269 | 0.038 |
| PR24 | 0.038 | 0.115 | 0.500 | 0.308 | 0.038 |
| PR25 | 0.000 | 0.346 | 0.308 | 0.231 | 0.115 |
| PR26 | 0.038 | 0.192 | 0.462 | 0.192 | 0.115 |
| PR27 | 0.154 | 0.192 | 0.423 | 0.192 | 0.038 |

4.2.2. Adoption of Innovation Management Practices in Small and Medium-Sized Industries (SMI)

The results for SMIs are examined in this section. Following an analysis of the responses provided by the specialists considering the levels determined through the HCA (N1, N2 and N3), the unified global frequencies for SMIs are analyzed.

In the scenario of SMIs in Brazil, the N1 specialists did not mark the options 'Applied reasonably' (AR) and 'Applied properly' (AP) for any of the 27 practices, while 'Not applied' (NA) was selected only for PR16 (firms manage their innovation portfolios properly, that is, they check how each initiative contributes to the achievement of the strategic objectives on a regular basis, analyse synergies between initiatives and communicate the progress of initiatives to stakeholders) by only one specialist. Thus, for N1, there is a significant concentration on the alternatives 'Applied superficially' (AS) and 'Applied reasonably' (AR), with complete agreement for several practices, which was not observed for the LIs. In the case of N2, there was also a clear concentration on the AS and AR, with only the alternative 'Applied in a well-structured way' (AW) not being chosen for any of the evaluated practices, a fact that also occurred for N3. These findings are consistent with those obtained for N1.

In general, the frequency analysis reveals a trend in which specialists at all levels (N1, N2 and N3) believe that there is no well-implemented innovation management practice in Brazilian SMIs. In addition, it is worth noting that the alternative 'Applied properly' (AP) was only chosen for a few practices and by a few specialists, causing the highest frequencies observed to be in the initial levels of application (NA, AS and AR).

Table 5 shows the global frequency of the evaluation of practices for SMIs.

**Table 5.** Level of adoption of innovation management practices in SMIs.

| Practices | Level of Application | | | | |
|---|---|---|---|---|---|
| | NA | AS | AR | AP | AW |
| PR1 | 0.154 | 0.615 | 0.154 | 0.077 | 0.000 |
| PR2 | 0.231 | 0.500 | 0.231 | 0.038 | 0.000 |
| PR3 | 0.154 | 0.577 | 0.231 | 0.038 | 0.000 |
| PR4 | 0.154 | 0.538 | 0.308 | 0.000 | 0.000 |
| PR5 | 0.231 | 0.462 | 0.308 | 0.000 | 0.000 |
| PR6 | 0.115 | 0.538 | 0.308 | 0.038 | 0.000 |
| PR7 | 0.231 | 0.423 | 0.308 | 0.038 | 0.000 |
| PR8 | 0.269 | 0.538 | 0.115 | 0.077 | 0.000 |
| PR9 | 0.231 | 0.423 | 0.269 | 0.077 | 0.000 |
| PR10 | 0.115 | 0.538 | 0.308 | 0.038 | 0.000 |
| PR11 | 0.269 | 0.500 | 0.231 | 0.000 | 0.000 |
| PR12 | 0.077 | 0.615 | 0.308 | 0.000 | 0.000 |
| PR13 | 0.154 | 0.538 | 0.308 | 0.000 | 0.000 |
| PR14 | 0.154 | 0.577 | 0.269 | 0.000 | 0.000 |
| PR15 | 0.231 | 0.423 | 0.269 | 0.077 | 0.000 |
| PR16 | 0.231 | 0.654 | 0.115 | 0.000 | 0.000 |
| PR17 | 0.269 | 0.654 | 0.077 | 0.000 | 0.000 |
| PR18 | 0.192 | 0.615 | 0.192 | 0.000 | 0.000 |
| PR19 | 0.231 | 0.615 | 0.154 | 0.000 | 0.000 |
| PR20 | 0.154 | 0.577 | 0.231 | 0.038 | 0.000 |
| PR21 | 0.154 | 0.577 | 0.231 | 0.038 | 0.000 |
| PR22 | 0.192 | 0.615 | 0.154 | 0.038 | 0.000 |
| PR23 | 0.231 | 0.577 | 0.192 | 0.000 | 0.000 |
| PR24 | 0.154 | 0.577 | 0.231 | 0.038 | 0.000 |
| PR25 | 0.231 | 0.462 | 0.308 | 0.000 | 0.000 |
| PR26 | 0.192 | 0.577 | 0.231 | 0.000 | 0.000 |
| PR27 | 0.385 | 0.500 | 0.115 | 0.000 | 0.000 |

*4.3. Ranking of Adoption of Innovation Management Practices via Fuzzy TOPSIS*

Based on Chen's [61] approach to Fuzzy TOPSIS (see Section 3.2 for a step-by-step description), a ranking was obtained ordering the practices according to their level of adoption in LIs and SMIs.

4.3.1. Ordering Practices for Large Industries (LI)

Table 6 displays the outcomes of the innovation management practices ordering and the sensitivity analysis for LIs.

Table 6. Ordering of practices via Fuzzy TOPSIS and sensitivity analysis for LIs.

| Practices | $CC_i$ | All Groups | Group Excluded for Sensitivity Analysis | | | | | | |
|---|---|---|---|---|---|---|---|---|---|
| | | | G1 | G2 | G3 | G4 | G5 | G6 | G7 |
| PR1 | 0.4916 | 1st | 1st | 1st | 1st | 1st | 1st | 1st | 1st |
| PR2 | 0.4613 | 6th | 4th | 8th | 6th | 10th | 8th | 3rd | 7th |
| PR3 | 0.4719 | 3rd | 2nd | 3rd | 4th | 3rd | 3rd | 5th | 3rd |
| PR4 | 0.4615 | 5th | 8th | 5th | 3rd | 8th | 6th | 9th | 4th |
| PR5 | 0.4288 | 21st | 22nd | 18th | 19th | 21st | 21st | 21st | 21st |
| PR6 | 0.4340 | 19th | 12th | 21st | 15th | 20th | 19th | 19th | 17th |
| PR7 | 0.4305 | 20th | 19th | 20th | 21st | 18th | 20th | 14th | 16th |
| PR8 | 0.3844 | 26th | 24th | 26th | 26th | 27th | 26th | 26th | 26th |
| PR9 | 0.4427 | 13th | 5th | 14th | 14th | 17th | 14th | 15th | 14th |
| PR10 | 0.4611 | 7th | 16th | 6th | 5th | 5th | 4th | 4th | 6th |
| PR11 | 0.4137 | 22nd | 10th | 23rd | 22nd | 24th | 23rd | 25th | 22nd |
| PR12 | 0.4470 | 11th | 21st | 10th | 11th | 6th | 12th | 12th | 10th |
| PR13 | 0.4474 | 10th | 11th | 11th | 9th | 13th | 11th | 11th | 12th |
| PR14 | 0.4460 | 12th | 18th | 12th | 12th | 11th | 10th | 13th | 11th |
| PR15 | 0.4810 | 2nd | 3rd | 2nd | 2nd | 2nd | 2nd | 2nd | 2nd |
| PR16 | 0.4414 | 14th | 20th | 13th | 13th | 12th | 13th | 17th | 13th |
| PR17 | 0.4007 | 24th | 23rd | 24th | 24th | 25th | 24th | 23rd | 25th |
| PR18 | 0.4369 | 17th | 13th | 17th | 17th | 19th | 18th | 10th | 19th |
| PR19 | 0.4599 | 8th | 9th | 7th | 8th | 7th | 7th | 6th | 8th |
| PR20 | 0.4640 | 4th | 7th | 4th | 7th | 4th | 5th | 7th | 5th |
| PR21 | 0.4385 | 16th | 14th | 15th | 18th | 15th | 16th | 20th | 18th |
| PR22 | 0.3986 | 25th | 25th | 25th | 25th | 23rd | 25th | 24th | 24th |
| PR23 | 0.4107 | 23rd | 27th | 22nd | 23rd | 22nd | 22nd | 22nd | 23rd |
| PR24 | 0.4536 | 9th | 6th | 9th | 10th | 14th | 9th | 8th | 9th |
| PR25 | 0.4356 | 18th | 15th | 19th | 20th | 16th | 17th | 16th | 20th |
| PR26 | 0.4411 | 15th | 17th | 16th | 16th | 9th | 15th | 18th | 15th |
| PR27 | 0.3802 | 27th | 26th | 27th | 27th | 26th | 27th | 27th | 27th |

The first place in the scenario of Brazilian LIs—i.e., the practice with the highest level of adoption—was PR1 (Firms frequently analyse internal and external issues that may compromise results related to innovation management), while the last place was PR27 (firms conduct periodic audits of their innovation management processes in order to identify opportunities for improvement; they seek to document the entire cycle so that such data can support decision-making and/or be used as lessons learned).

The group that had the most influence was G1, showing that the assignment of different weights to the three levels was done properly, as N3 (which encompasses G1, G4 and G6) should always be the one with the greatest impact.

4.3.2. Ordering Practices for Small and Medium-Sized Industries (SMI)

Table 7 shows the results of the innovation management practices ordering and the sensitivity analysis for SMIs.

In the scenario of SMIs in Brazil, it was observed that PR10 (firms have a system to correctly assess the need for collaboration to innovate—including innovation in terms of knowledge, competence, infrastructure and resources—and, if relevant, adopt guidelines to improve the selection process of partners) is the most well-established, while PR27 remained the least applied. Although PR10 was in first place in most of the tested scenarios and in the overall ranking, the sensitivity analysis revealed a fluctuation in the first position in the following cases: PR20 (firms continually review their innovation initiatives in terms of adequacy of scope and expected results) when G1 is excluded; PR6 (firms top management constantly supports and commits to activities in favour of innovation, as well as providing the necessary resources so that initiatives can take place and the desired results can be achieved) when G3 is excluded; and PR12 (firms assess existing deficiencies in terms of organisational competencies for innovation (individual or team competencies) and offer training programs to employees in order to achieve better performance in initiatives) when G7 is excluded.

The G6 was the most influential group, also belonging to the N3, which is methodologically consistent as it corresponds to specialists with the highest educational level, experience and knowledge in the area of innovation management.

Table 7. Ordering of practices via Fuzzy TOPSIS and sensitivity analysis for SMIs.

| Practices | $CC_i$ | All Groups | Group Excluded for Sensitivity Analysis | | | | | | |
|---|---|---|---|---|---|---|---|---|---|
| | | | G1 | G2 | G3 | G4 | G5 | G6 | G7 |
| PR1 | 0.3924 | 10th | 20th | 11th | 10th | 9th | 7th | 3rd | 10th |
| PR2 | 0.3819 | 15th | 21st | 15th | 11th | 15th | 13th | 5th | 15th |
| PR3 | 0.3936 | 7th | 10th | 7th | 5th | 5th | 8th | 11th | 8th |
| PR4 | 0.3952 | 6th | 4th | 6th | 4th | 12th | 6th | 9th | 6th |
| PR5 | 0.3726 | 16th | 16th | 16th | 16th | 17th | 19th | 17th | 16th |
| PR6 | 0.4099 | 2nd | 2nd | 2nd | 1st | 4th | 3rd | 2nd | 3rd |
| PR7 | 0.3847 | 14th | 9th | 14th | 14th | 14th | 15th | 14th | 11th |
| PR8 | 0.3592 | 22nd | 13th | 22nd | 23rd | 22nd | 22nd | 24th | 20th |
| PR9 | 0.3955 | 5th | 3rd | 5th | 7th | 11th | 5th | 6th | 5th |
| PR10 | 0.4109 | 1st | 8th | 1st | 2nd | 1st | 1st | 1st | 2nd |
| PR11 | 0.3528 | 23rd | 15th | 23rd | 22nd | 24th | 23rd | 26th | 23rd |
| PR12 | 0.4080 | 3rd | 5th | 3rd | 3rd | 2nd | 2nd | 4th | 1st |
| PR13 | 0.3856 | 13th | 18th | 13th | 13th | 13th | 14th | 7th | 14th |
| PR14 | 0.3860 | 12th | 19th | 12th | 12th | 8th | 12th | 12th | 13th |
| PR15 | 0.3933 | 8th | 14th | 8th | 8th | 6th | 9th | 8th | 7th |
| PR16 | 0.3426 | 25th | 26th | 25th | 25th | 25th | 25th | 23rd | 25th |
| PR17 | 0.3321 | 26th | 27th | 26th | 26th | 26th | 26th | 25th | 26th |
| PR18 | 0.3647 | 20th | 22nd | 20th | 17th | 21st | 20th | 18th | 21st |
| PR19 | 0.3480 | 24th | 24th | 24th | 24th | 23rd | 24th | 22nd | 24th |
| PR20 | 0.3888 | 11th | 1st | 10th | 15th | 10th | 11th | 15th | 12th |
| PR21 | 0.3956 | 4th | 11th | 4th | 6th | 3rd | 4th | 13th | 4th |
| PR22 | 0.3715 | 17th | 7th | 17th | 18th | 18th | 16th | 21st | 17th |
| PR23 | 0.3616 | 21st | 23rd | 21st | 20th | 20th | 21st | 20th | 22nd |
| PR24 | 0.3931 | 9th | 6th | 9th | 9th | 7th | 10th | 10th | 9th |
| PR25 | 0.3706 | 19th | 12th | 19th | 21st | 16th | 18th | 19th | 19th |
| PR26 | 0.3712 | 18th | 17th | 18th | 19th | 19th | 17th | 16th | 18th |
| PR27 | 0.3173 | 27th | 25th | 27th | 27th | 27th | 27th | 27th | 27th |

## 5. Discussion

In general, SMIs in the Brazilian context have more severe deficiencies in terms of applying innovation management practices than LIs. SMIs did not have any of the 27 practices evaluated at the highest level of application, indicating that there is still much work to be done. Regardless of the fact that a number of barriers to SMIs' innovation have been documented in the literature [16,42], it is critical that managers and policymakers pay attention to this issue, since innovation capacity can be a determining factor not only for SMIs' growth [3,43,44], but also for their survival [6,21].

Although the results indicated that there is room for improvement in terms of innovation management in LIs, it is clear that the consolidation of practices is already much more evident when compared to SMIs. In the context of LIs, the corporate structure, materials, technologies and people are superior and can be adapted to market demands, the firm's objectives and unexpected changes in a VUCA world [30,35,36]. This flexibility and reliability present in LIs, together with the willingness to take risks, are vital for the consolidation and effectiveness of an innovation management system [21].

When considering the ordering of practices based on their level of application, the results obtained spark important discussions. Although PR1 ranked first in all tested scenarios for Brazilian LIs, it is worth noting that three practices (PR3, PR15 and PR20) related to planning, scope definition and supervision of innovation management rank immediately after. Such practices express, respectively, the need to: identify the limits and applicability of innovation management; define plans for the innovation management process; and review the innovation initiatives put in place. These three practices are considered essential for the proper operation of the innovation management cycle, and it is significant that the results of this research are consistent with the qualified literature [26,28]. Furthermore, precisely because it is characterised as a cycle, it is necessary to consider the importance of feedback for the innovation management process, and it is concerning that PR27—related to the audit to identify opportunities for change and improvement—has received the lowest ratings, a result observed for both LIs and SMIs.

## 6. Conclusions

Based on the structure of the ISO 56002 standard and the opinions of specialists in the field, the goal of this study was to examine the level of adoption of innovation management practices in the Brazilian industrial sector. PR1 was regarded as having the highest application rate for LIs. In turn, PR10 was evaluated as the most adopted by SMIs. PR27 received the lowest rating from both LIs and SMIs. Taking into account all scenarios tested through sensitivity analysis, PR27 ranked last in 13 of the 16 cases.

Despite ISO 56002 being recently published and companies still working to comply with its guidelines, the recommended innovation management practices have seen some adherence in the reality of Brazilian LIs, while SMIs continue to be in more deficient circumstances. For Brazilian managers seeking to establish a structured innovation management system and/or consolidate current practices in their companies, the study's findings may be helpful. Since innovation is a crucial component of the economic growth of countries, particularly in emerging economies like Brazil, it is also important to emphasize the systemic impact that improvements in a firm's innovative capacity can have.

Although exploratory in nature, the findings of this study contribute to a better understanding of the reality of Brazilian industries in terms of innovation management and correlated practices, allowing for the expansion of the scientific literature in the field. The methodological approach developed in this study (i.e., survey, Fuzzy TOPSIS, HCA, frequency and sensitivity analysis) can be applied in other contexts to understand how industries are leading with innovation management systems. Thus, the research instruments and methods can be useful to advance a scholar and practitioner's knowledge on innovation management by conducting studies or actions that compare their reality (including both developing and developed countries) with the findings of this study. The results and discussions presented in this paper can also be used to inform future studies aimed at better understanding specific practices related to the topic.

The limitations of the study are related to the specific context studied and the methods used. Regarding the method, it should be noted that triangular functions were used in the application of the Fuzzy TOPSIS method to determine both the scale of variables and the level of experience of the specialists (other types of functions could have been used), and that the weight vector was defined in three categories (N1, N2 and N3). It should be noted, however, that this study was designed with an exploratory purpose in mind, with the goal of better understanding the Brazilian industrial reality in terms of innovation management.

It is suggested that future research delve deeper into the innovation management practices in the Brazilian context, employing qualitative methods and expanding the sample of specialists. An interesting possibility is to use the Delphi method to refine debates on specific practices. Another suggestion is to compare the results using other multi-criteria decision-making approaches, providing more information for discussion.

Finally, it is worth noting that the ISO 56002 standard serves as an important reference for firms looking to implement practices related to innovation management, and researchers can be excellent partners in this regard.

**Author Contributions:** Conceptualization, G.G.P. and R.A.; methodology, G.G.P. and R.A.; validation, G.G.P. and R.A.; formal analysis, G.G.P., T.F.A.C.S. and R.A.; investigation, G.G.P. and R.A.; resources, T.F.A.C.S., I.S.R., G.H.S.M.d.M., L.V.Á., W.L.F. and R.A.; writing—original draft preparation, G.G.P., T.F.A.C.S. and R.A.; writing—review and editing, T.F.A.C.S., I.S.R., G.H.S.M.d.M., L.V.Á., W.L.F. and R.A.; supervision, R.A.; project administration, R.A. All authors have read and agreed to the published version of the manuscript.

**Funding:** The authors are grateful for the support of the National Council for Scientific and Technological Development (CNPq/Brazil) under the grants No. 304145/2021-1, No. 303924/2021-7 and No. 150662/2022-0.

**Data Availability Statement:** Not applicable.

**Conflicts of Interest:** The authors declare no conflict of interest. The funders had no role in the design of the study; in the collection, analyses, or interpretation of data; in the writing of the manuscript; or in the decision to publish the results.

## References

1. Gyedu, S.; Heng, T.; Ntarmah, A.H.; He, Y.; Frimppong, E. The Impact of Innovation on Economic Growth among G7 and BRICS Countries: A GMM Style Panel Vector Autoregressive Approach. *Technol. Forecast. Soc. Chang.* **2021**, *173*, 121169. [CrossRef]
2. Skare, M.; Porada-Rochon, M. The Role of Innovation in Sustainable Growth: A Dynamic Panel Study on Micro and Macro Levels 1990–2019. *Technol. Forecast. Soc. Chang.* **2022**, *175*, 121337. [CrossRef]
3. Oltra, M.J.; Flor, M.L.; Alfaro, J.A. Open Innovation and Firm Performance: The Role of Organizational Mechanisms. *Bus. Process Manag. J.* **2018**, *24*, 814–836. [CrossRef]
4. Riad Shams, S.M.; Vrontis, D.; Chaudhuri, R.; Chavan, G.; Czinkota, M.R. Stakeholder Engagement for Innovation Management and Entrepreneurial Development: A Meta-Analysis. *J. Bus. Res.* **2020**, *119*, 67–86. [CrossRef] [PubMed]
5. Nguyen, H.; Harrison, N. Leveraging Customer Knowledge to Enhance Process Innovation. *Bus. Process Manag. J.* **2019**, *25*, 307–322. [CrossRef]
6. Khan, P.A.; Johl, S.K.; Johl, S.K. Does Adoption of ISO 56002-2019 and Green Innovation Reporting Enhance the Firm Sustainable Development Goal Performance? An Emerging Paradigm. *Bus. Strateg. Environ.* **2021**, *30*, 2922–2936. [CrossRef]
7. Martínez-Costa, M.; Jimenez-Jimenez, D.; del Castro-del-Rosario, Y.P. The Performance Implications of the UNE 166.000 Standardised Innovation Management System. *Eur. J. Innov. Manag.* **2019**, *22*, 281–301. [CrossRef]
8. Trabucchi, D.; Sanasi, S.; Ghezzi, A.; Buganza, T. Idle Asset Hunters—The Secret of Multi-Sided Platforms. *Res. Manag.* **2021**, *64*, 33–42. [CrossRef]
9. Hwang, W.-S.; Choi, H.; Shin, J. A Mediating Role of Innovation Capability between Entrepreneurial Competencies and Competitive Advantage. *Technol. Anal. Strateg. Manag.* **2020**, *32*, 1–14. [CrossRef]
10. Veiga, P.M.; Teixeira, S.J.; Figueiredo, R.; Fernandes, C.I. Entrepreneurship, Innovation and Competitiveness: A Public Institution Love Triangle. *Socioecon. Plann. Sci.* **2020**, *72*, 100863. [CrossRef]
11. Santoro, G.; Vrontis, D.; Thrassou, A.; Dezi, L. The Internet of Things: Building a Knowledge Management System for Open Innovation and Knowledge Management Capacity. *Technol. Forecast. Soc. Chang.* **2018**, *136*, 347–354. [CrossRef]
12. Nwankpa, J.K.; Roumani, Y.; Datta, P. Process Innovation in the Digital Age of Business: The Role of Digital Business Intensity and Knowledge Management. *J. Knowl. Manag.* **2022**, *26*, 1319–1341. [CrossRef]
13. Ahmed, W.; Najmi, A.; Ikram, M. Steering Firm Performance through Innovative Capabilities: A Contingency Approach to Innovation Management. *Technol. Soc.* **2020**, *63*, 101385. [CrossRef]
14. Vujanović, N.; Radošević, S.; Stojčić, N.; Hisarciklilar, M.; Hashi, I. FDI Spillover Effects on Innovation Activities of Knowledge Using and Knowledge Creating Firms: Evidence from an Emerging Economy. *Technovation* **2022**, *118*, 102512. [CrossRef]
15. Ma, D.; Zhu, Q. Innovation in Emerging Economies: Research on the Digital Economy Driving High-Quality Green Development. *J. Bus. Res.* **2022**, *145*, 801–813. [CrossRef]
16. Matos, L.M.; Rampasso, I.S.; Quelhas, O.L.G.; Leal Filho, W.; Anholon, R. Technological Innovation Management: Understanding Difficulties in an Emerging Country to Enhance Manufacturers Performance. *Int. J. Product. Perform. Manag.* **2021**, *ahead-of-print*. [CrossRef]
17. De Araujo, T.R.; Jugend, D.; Pimenta, M.L.; Jesus, G.M.K.; Barriga, G.D.D.C.; de Toledo, J.C.; Mariano, A.M. Influence of New Product Development Best Practices on Performance: An Analysis in Innovative Brazilian Companies. *J. Bus. Ind. Mark.* **2022**, *37*, 266–281. [CrossRef]
18. Martinez, C.; Zuniga, P. Contracting for Technology Transfer: Patent Licensing and Know-How in Brazil. *Ind. Innov.* **2017**, *24*, 659–689. [CrossRef]
19. Silva, D.R.d.M.; Lucas, L.O.; Vonortas, N.S. Internal Barriers to Innovation and University-Industry Cooperation among Technology-Based SMEs in Brazil. *Ind. Innov.* **2020**, *27*, 235–263. [CrossRef]
20. Meissner, D.; Kergroach, S. Innovation Policy Mix: Mapping and Measurement. *J. Technol. Transf.* **2021**, *46*, 197–222. [CrossRef]

21. Benraouane, S.; Harrington, H.J. *Using the ISO 56002 Innovation Management System*; Productivity Press: New York, NY, USA, 2021; ISBN 9781000373318.
22. Albors-Garrigos, J.; Igartua, J.I.; Peiro, A. Innovation Management Techniques and Tools: Its Impact on Firm Innovation Performance. *Int. J. Innov. Manag.* **2018**, *22*, 1850051. [CrossRef]
23. Niroumand, M.; Shahin, A.; Naghsh, A.; Peikari, H.R. Frugal Innovation Enablers, Critical Success Factors and Barriers: A Systematic Review. *Creat. Innov. Manag.* **2021**, *30*, 348–367. [CrossRef]
24. *ISO 56002*; Innovation Management—Innovation Management System—Guidance. International Organization for Standardization: Genève, Switzerland, 2020.
25. Tidd, J. A Review and Critical Assessment of the ISO 56002 Innovation Management Systems Standard: Evidence and Limitations. *Int. J. Innov. Manag.* **2021**, *25*, 2150049. [CrossRef]
26. Hyland, J.; Karlsson, M. Towards a Management System Standard for Innovation. *J. Innov. Manag.* **2021**, *9*, XI–XIX. [CrossRef]
27. Mir, R.A.; Rameez, R.; Tahir, N. Measuring Internet Banking Service Quality: An Empirical Evidence. *TQM J.* **2022**, *32*, 492–518. [CrossRef]
28. Anholon, R.; Serafim, M.P.; Dibbern, T.; Leal, W. The Importance of ISO Management System Standards in a Scenario of Profound Changes Caused by the COVID-19 Pandemic to Brazilian Companies. *Braz. J. Oper. Prod. Manag.* **2022**, *19*, e20221248. [CrossRef]
29. Bobel, V.A.d.O.; Sigahi, T.F.A.C.; Rampasso, I.S.; de Moraes, G.H.S.M.; Ávila, L.V.; Leal Filho, W.; Anholon, R. Analysis of the Level of Adoption of Business Continuity Practices by Brazilian Industries: An Exploratory Study Using Fuzzy TOPSIS. *Mathematics* **2022**, *10*, 4041. [CrossRef]
30. Abdulkader, B.; Magni, D.; Cillo, V.; Papa, A.; Micera, R. Aligning Firm's Value System and Open Innovation: A New Framework of Business Process Management beyond the Business Model Innovation. *Bus. Process Manag. J.* **2020**, *26*, 999–1020. [CrossRef]
31. Kraśnicka, T.; Głód, W.; Wronka-Pośpiech, M. Management Innovation and Its Measurement. *J. Entrep. Manag. Innov.* **2016**, *12*, 95–122. [CrossRef]
32. Rajapathirana, R.P.J.; Hui, Y. Relationship between Innovation Capability, Innovation Type, and Firm Performance. *J. Innov. Knowl.* **2018**, *3*, 44–55. [CrossRef]
33. Milan, E.; Ulrich, F.; Faria, L.G.D.; Li-Ying, J. Exploring the Impact of Organisational, Technological and Relational Contingencies on Innovation Speed in the Light of Open Innovation. *Ind. Innov.* **2020**, *27*, 804–836. [CrossRef]
34. Millar, C.C.J.M.; Groth, O.; Mahon, J.F. Management Innovation in a VUCA World: Challenges and Recommendations. *Calif. Manage. Rev.* **2018**, *61*, 5–14. [CrossRef]
35. Taskan, B.; Junça-Silva, A.; Caetano, A. Clarifying the Conceptual Map of VUCA: A Systematic Review. *Int. J. Organ. Anal.* **2022**, *ahead-of-print*. [CrossRef]
36. Allahar, H. A Management Innovation Approach to Project Planning. *Technol. Innov. Manag. Rev.* **2019**, *9*, 4–13. [CrossRef]
37. Mir, M.; Casadesús, M.; Petnji, L.H. The Impact of Standardized Innovation Management Systems on Innovation Capability and Business Performance: An Empirical Study. *J. Eng. Technol. Manag.* **2016**, *41*, 26–44. [CrossRef]
38. Idris, M.-C.; Durmuşoğlu, A. Innovation Management Systems and Standards: A Systematic Literature Review and Guidance for Future Research. *Sustainability* **2021**, *13*, 8151. [CrossRef]
39. Vrchota, J.; Řehoř, P. Project Management and Innovation in the Manufacturing Industry in Czech Republic. *Procedia Comput. Sci.* **2019**, *164*, 457–462. [CrossRef]
40. Leal-Rodríguez, A.L.; Eldridge, S.; Roldán, J.L.; Leal-Millán, A.G.; Ortega-Gutiérrez, J. Organizational Unlearning, Innovation Outcomes, and Performance: The Moderating Effect of Firm Size. *J. Bus. Res.* **2015**, *68*, 803–809. [CrossRef]
41. Forés, B.; Camisón, C. Does Incremental and Radical Innovation Performance Depend on Different Types of Knowledge Accumulation Capabilities and Organizational Size? *J. Bus. Res.* **2016**, *69*, 831–848. [CrossRef]
42. NCI. *To Innovate Is to Develop the Industry of the Future*; CNI/SESI/ SENAI/SEBRAE: Brasília, Brazil, 2019.
43. Limaj, E.; Bernroider, E.W.N. The Roles of Absorptive Capacity and Cultural Balance for Exploratory and Exploitative Innovation in SMEs. *J. Bus. Res.* **2019**, *94*, 137–153. [CrossRef]
44. Falahat, M.; Ramayah, T.; Soto-Acosta, P.; Lee, Y.-Y. SMEs Internationalization: The Role of Product Innovation, Market Intelligence, Pricing and Marketing Communication Capabilities as Drivers of SMEs' International Performance. *Technol. Forecast. Soc. Chang.* **2020**, *152*, 119908. [CrossRef]
45. Alfaro-García, V.G.; Gil-Lafuente, A.M.; Alfaro Calderón, G.G. A Fuzzy Methodology for Innovation Management Measurement. *Kybernetes* **2017**, *46*, 50–66. [CrossRef]
46. Ju, F.; Yuan, Y.; Yuan, Y.; Quan, W. A Divergence-Based Distance Measure for Intuitionistic Fuzzy Sets and Its Application in the Decision-Making of Innovation Management. *IEEE Access* **2020**, *8*, 1105–1117. [CrossRef]
47. Yue, Q. Bilateral Matching Decision-Making for Knowledge Innovation Management Considering Matching Willingness in an Interval Intuitionistic Fuzzy Set Environment. *J. Innov. Knowl.* **2022**, *7*, 100209. [CrossRef]
48. Hessami, F. Formulation and Explanation of a Success Model in Innovation Management and Its Diffusion at Sports Federations. *Manag. Sci. Lett.* **2018**, *8*, 69–78. [CrossRef]
49. Dinesh, K.K. Sushil Fuzzy Predictive Modeling for the Hierarchical Structure of Strategic Innovation Management. *IEEE Trans. Eng. Manag.* **2023**, *early access*. [CrossRef]
50. Yang, T.A.O.; Bao, J.; Fu, Q.; Yang, B.O.; Chen, W.E.I. Risk Sharing Strategy for Collaborative Innovation Management of Environmental Protection Equipment Manufacturing Enterprises. *J. Environ. Prot. Ecol.* **2022**, *23*, 1928–1937.

51. Yin, S.; Dong, T.; Li, B.; Gao, S. Developing a Conceptual Partner Selection Framework: Digital Green Innovation Management of Prefabricated Construction Enterprises for Sustainable Urban Development. *Buildings* **2022**, *12*, 721. [CrossRef]
52. Poorkavoos, M.; Duan, Y.; Edwards, J.S.; Ramanathan, R. Identifying the Configurational Paths to Innovation in SMEs: A Fuzzy-Set Qualitative Comparative Analysis. *J. Bus. Res.* **2016**, *69*, 5843–5854. [CrossRef]
53. Kumar, A.; Kaviani, M.A.; Hafezalkotob, A.; Zavadskas, E.K. Evaluating Innovation Capabilities of Real Estate Firms: A Combined Fuzzy Delphi and DEMATEL Approach. *Int. J. Strateg. Prop. Manag.* **2017**, *21*, 401–416. [CrossRef]
54. Li, J.; Wang, Y. Coupling Effect of Regional Industrial Cluster and Innovation Based on Complex System Metric and Fuzzy Mathematics. *J. Intell. Fuzzy Syst.* **2019**, *37*, 6115–6126. [CrossRef]
55. García, J.S.; Velásquez, J.R. Methodology for Evaluating Innovation Capabilities at University Institutions Using a Fuzzy System. *J. Technol. Manag. Innov.* **2013**, *8*, 101–102. [CrossRef]
56. Jing, S.; Yang, Y.; Ho, Z.-P.; Yan, J.; Huang, H.-T. The Development of a Frame Model for Management Strategies Selection Using Fuzzy Proximity. *Cluster Comput.* **2017**, *20*, 141–153. [CrossRef]
57. Velazquez-Cazares, M.G.; Gil-Lafuente, A.M.; Leon-Castro, E.; Blanco-Mesa, F. Innovation Capabilities Measurement Using Fuzzy Methodologies: A Colombian SMEs Case. *Comput. Math. Organ. Theory* **2021**, *27*, 384–413. [CrossRef]
58. Abdul, D.; Wenqi, J. Evaluating Appropriate Communication Technology for Smart Grid by Using a Comprehensive Decision-Making Approach Fuzzy TOPSIS. *Soft Comput.* **2022**, *26*, 8521–8536. [CrossRef]
59. Chen, D.; Faibil, D.; Agyemang, M. Evaluating Critical Barriers and Pathways to Implementation of E-Waste Formalization Management Systems in Ghana: A Hybrid BWM and Fuzzy TOPSIS Approach. *Environ. Sci. Pollut. Res.* **2020**, *27*, 44561–44584. [CrossRef]
60. Wen, T.-C.; Chang, K.-H.; Lai, H.-H.; Liu, Y.-Y.; Wang, J.-C. A Novel Rugby Team Player Selection Method Integrating the TOPSIS and IPA Methods. *Int. J. Sport Psychol.* **2021**, *52*, 137–158. [CrossRef]
61. Chen, C.-T. Extension of Fuzzy TOPSIS Method Based on Interval-Valued Fuzzy Sets". *Appl. Soft Comput. J.* **2000**, *26*, 513–514. [CrossRef]
62. Nădăban, S.; Dzitac, S.; Dzitac, I. Fuzzy TOPSIS: A General View. *Procedia Comput. Sci.* **2016**, *91*, 823–831. [CrossRef]
63. Lima Junior, F.R.; Carpinetti, L.C.R. A Comparison between TOPSIS and Fuzzy-TOPSIS Methods to Support Multicriteria Decision Making for Supplier Selection. *Gestão Produção* **2015**, *22*, 17–34. [CrossRef]
64. Lima Junior, F.R.; Osiro, L.; Carpinetti, L.C.R. A Comparison between Fuzzy AHP and Fuzzy TOPSIS Methods to Supplier Selection. *Appl. Soft Comput.* **2014**, *21*, 194–209. [CrossRef]
65. Apostolopoulos, N.; Liargovas, P. Regional Parameters and Solar Energy Enterprises. *Int. J. Energy Sect. Manag.* **2016**, *10*, 19–37. [CrossRef]
66. National Council for Scientific and Technological Development Lattes Platform 2022. Available online: https://lattes.cnpq.br (accessed on 1 February 2023).
67. Subramaniyan, M.; Skoogh, A.; Muhammad, A.S.; Bokrantz, J.; Johansson, B.; Roser, C. A Generic Hierarchical Clustering Approach for Detecting Bottlenecks in Manufacturing. *J. Manuf. Syst.* **2020**, *55*, 143–158. [CrossRef]

**Disclaimer/Publisher's Note:** The statements, opinions and data contained in all publications are solely those of the individual author(s) and contributor(s) and not of MDPI and/or the editor(s). MDPI and/or the editor(s) disclaim responsibility for any injury to people or property resulting from any ideas, methods, instructions or products referred to in the content.

*Article*

# Study on the Selection of Pharmaceutical E-Commerce Platform Considering Bounded Rationality under Probabilistic Hesitant Fuzzy Environment

Zixue Guo [1,2] and Sijia Liu [1,*]

1 School of Management, Hebei University, Baoding 071002, China
2 Center for Common Prosperity Research, Hebei University, Baoding 071002, China
* Correspondence: liu_sj@stumail.hbu.edu.cn

**Abstract:** The selection of a pharmaceutical e-commerce platform is a typical multi-attribute group decision-making (MAGDM) problem. MAGDM is a common problem in the field of decision-making, which is full of uncertainty and fuzziness. A probabilistic hesitant fuzzy multi-attribute group decision-making method based on generalized TODIM is proposed for the selection of pharmaceutical e-commerce under an uncertain environment. Firstly, the credibility of a probabilistic hesitant fuzzy element is defined, and a credibility-based method for adjusting the weights of decision-makers and determining attribute weights is proposed, which fully considers the reliability of information provided by the decision-makers. Secondly, the power average (PA) operator is extended to the probabilistic hesitant fuzzy environment. The probabilistic hesitant fuzzy power average (PHFPA) operator and the probabilistic hesitant fuzzy power weighted average (PHFPWA) operator are defined, and their properties are discussed. Thirdly, considering the usual information expression of decision-makers in real life and the different risk attitudes towards gain and loss, the generalized TODIM method is extended to the probabilistic hesitant fuzzy environment to construct a prospect theory-based group decision-making method in the probabilistic hesitant fuzzy environment. Finally, the feasibility of the method in this paper is proved through the case of pharmaceutical e-commerce platform selection, and the stability of the method in this paper is verified by sensitivity analysis.

**Keywords:** multi-attribute group decision-making; probabilistic hesitant fuzzy sets; selection of pharmaceutical e-commerce platform; TODIM; credibility

**MSC:** 90B50

**Citation:** Guo, Z.; Liu, S. Study on the Selection of Pharmaceutical E-Commerce Platform Considering Bounded Rationality under Probabilistic Hesitant Fuzzy Environment. *Mathematics* **2023**, *11*, 1859. https://doi.org/10.3390/math11081859

Academic Editors: Jorge de Andres Sanchez and Laura González-Vila Puchades

Received: 7 March 2023
Revised: 4 April 2023
Accepted: 11 April 2023
Published: 13 April 2023

**Copyright:** © 2023 by the authors. Licensee MDPI, Basel, Switzerland. This article is an open access article distributed under the terms and conditions of the Creative Commons Attribution (CC BY) license (https://creativecommons.org/licenses/by/4.0/).

## 1. Introduction

With the development of China's Internet technology and e-commerce, online shopping has become an important channel for consumer spending. In 2020, under the influence of COVID-19, the demand for pharmaceutical e-commerce platforms increased significantly, and the demand for online drug sales became prominent. According to the 49th Statistical Report on the Development of the Internet in China [1] released by the Internet Information Center, the number of online medical users in China reached 298 million by December 2021, which is an increase of 83.08 million compared to December 2020, accounting for 28.9% of the total Internet users. Online pharmacies provide people with more choices and practical convenience. By purchasing drugs online, consumers can greatly save time and transportation costs. At the same time, online medical care and online pharmacies have effectively distributed outpatient services, alleviating the current situation of difficulty in getting medical service. Consumers have realized the advantages of e-commerce in many aspects, and the public has a greater demand and expectation for pharmaceutical e-commerce platforms. For pharmaceutical enterprises, if they can choose an appropriate high-quality pharmaceutical e-commerce platform and carry out long-term cooperation, they can fully seize the opportunity, expand the coverage of drugs to achieve digital marketing, and improve the development speed of enterprises. Therefore, it is of great practical significance to study the selection of pharmaceutical e-commerce platform.

Since the evaluation of pharmaceutical e-commerce platforms needs to consider multiple indicators, the selection of a pharmaceutical e-commerce platform belongs to a multi-attribute decision-making problem. A single decision-maker may make mistakes in decision-making due to insufficient understanding of pharmaceutical e-commerce platforms or personal preferences. In order to reduce the risk of decision-making, several decision-makers are selected to evaluate and choose pharmaceutical e-commerce platform, and multi-attribute group decision-making method is used to study the selection of pharmaceutical e-commerce platform. There are two important difficulties in the multi-attribute group decision-making process, one of which is the representation of uncertain information. Professor Zadeh proposed the fuzzy set theory in 1965 [2]. Subsequently, the theory of fuzzy sets is extended by some scholars, such as trapezoidal fuzzy sets [3–6], intuitionistic fuzzy sets [7], interval intuitionistic fuzzy sets [8–10], Pythagorean fuzzy sets [11], hesitant fuzzy sets (HFS) [12], probabilistic hesitant fuzzy sets (PHFS) [13], etc. Among them, PHFS, as one of the extended forms of fuzzy sets, adds probability information to each membership degree, which can well express the different importance levels between different membership degrees and effectively describe the preferences of decision-makers. Therefore, PHFS can retain more original information and can express the uncertain preference information of decision-makers in a more comprehensive and detailed way, which can well enhance the rationality and credibility of decision results and be more in line with objective reality and the human way of thinking. In the multi-attribute group decision-making problem of selecting pharmaceutical e-commerce platforms, it is inaccurate to use accurate numbers to evaluate pharmaceutical e-commerce platforms due to the subjective evaluation factors involved in the evaluation indicators. In order to make the expression of decision information more accurate, this article chooses to use probability hesitant fuzzy sets to evaluate pharmaceutical e-commerce platforms.

Another important difficulty in multi-attribute group decision-making is the procedure of aggregating the decision-making information provided by decision-makers. Considering the correlation between indicators, many scholars choose to use aggregation operators such as Heronian mean operator, Bonferroni mean operator, Maclaurin symmetric mean operator, and other operators to aggregate information, but these operators cannot deal with outliers in the evaluation information. In the real multi-attribute group decision-making problem, the decision-maker's evaluation of the alternative is often subjective due to the influence of the decision-maker's personal preference and the fuzziness of the decision environment. However, from an objective point of view, the evaluation of multiple decision-makers on the same alternative under various attributes should be similar. Therefore, when decision-makers have bias or wrong information collection, abnormal data may appear, which may easily lead to unreasonable decision results. To solve this problem, Yager [14] proposed the Power Average (PA) operator in 2001. The PA operator can not only express the relationship between a single evaluation value and other evaluation values through the degree of support, but also obtain the corresponding harmonic weight through the degree of support so as to reduce the influence of unreasonable data on the final decision result. Subsequently, Xu and Yager [15] further developed the PA operator and defined the power ordered weighted average (POWA) operator. Since then, many scholars have studied the extension of the PA operator, resulting in the PA operator becoming rapidly developed and widely used [16–20].

After reviewing the literature, we find that there are some problems in the current research on multi-attribute group decision-making: (1) Compared with the classical hesitant fuzzy set, the probabilistic hesitant fuzzy set has better performance in expressing the hesitation of decision-makers, but there are few studies on the multi-attribute group decision-making problem with the evaluation information of a probabilistic hesitant fuzzy set. (2) As one of the classical aggregation operators, the PA operator has not been extended to the probabilistic hesitant fuzzy set; (3) In the process of multi-attribute group decision-making, decision-makers are not completely rational people, and their behaviors in the decision-making process will have an impact on the decision-making results.

To address the above problems, this study aims to propose a multi-attribute group decision-making method considering bounded rationality in a probabilistic hesitant fuzzy environment. The main work of this study is as follows: (1) In order to improve the reliability of group opinions, the credibility of probabilistic hesitant fuzzy element is defined, and the weights of decision-makers are adjusted according to the credibility. (2) The PA operator is extended to the probabilistic hesitant fuzzy environment, and the probabilistic hesitant fuzzy power average operator is defined for information aggregation of the decision-makers. (3) Taking into account the bounded rationality of decision-makers, the generalized TODIM method developed from prospect theory is extended to the probabilistic hesitant fuzzy environment. (4) The effectiveness and feasibility of the method in this paper are illustrated through a case study of pharmaceutical e-commerce selection.

The rest of this paper is organized as follows. Some basic concepts of PHFS are introduced in Section 2. The credibility of probabilistic hesitant fuzzy elements and the method for adjusting weights of decision-makers based on credibility are described in Section 3. The probabilistic hesitant fuzzy power average operator and its weighted form are defined, and their properties are explored in Section 4. A generalized TODIM multi-attribute group decision-making method in a probabilistic hesitant fuzzy environment is proposed in Section 5. A numerical example of pharmaceutical e-commerce platform selection is analyzed by the proposed method in Section 6 to demonstrate its validity and applicability. Finally, this paper is concluded in Section 7.

## 2. Preliminaries

In this section, some basic definitions and concepts associated with PHFS will be overviewed briefly.

### 2.1. Concept of PHFS

PHFS, as one of the important extended forms of fuzzy sets, take into full consideration both the different membership degrees and the probability of each membership degree, effectively taking into account the preferences of the decision-makers. The basic concept of PHFS is defined as follows:

**Definition 1** ([21]). *Let X be a fixed set, then a PHFS on X is expressed by a mathematical symbol:*

$$H = \{\langle x, h(p)\rangle | x \in X\} \tag{1}$$

*where the set* $h(p) = \{\gamma^\lambda(p^\lambda), \lambda = 1, 2, \ldots, l\}$ *is the basic tool to describe PHFS H, which is usually called probabilistic hesitant fuzzy element (PHFE). Membership degree* $\gamma^\lambda \in [0, 1]$ *represents the possibility that the element* $x \in X$ *belongs to the PHFS H.* $p^\lambda \in [0, 1]$ *indicates the possibility of* $\gamma^\lambda$, *and meets* $\sum_{\lambda=1}^{l} p^\lambda = 1$. *In particular, when* $p^\lambda = \frac{1}{l}$, *the PHFS degenerates into HFS.*

### 2.2. The Ranking Method of PHFE

In order to compare the size of PHFE, the score function, deviation function and comparison law of PHFE are defined as follows:

**Definition 2** ([21]). *Generally, the elements in all PHFE* $h(p)$ *are sorted from small to large according to the membership degree. For a PHFE* $h(p) = \{\gamma^\lambda(p^\lambda), \lambda = 1, 2, \ldots, l\}$, *then its score function is defined as follows:*

$$s(h(p)) = \sum_{\lambda=1}^{l} \gamma^\lambda \cdot p^\lambda \tag{2}$$

*where* $\gamma^\lambda$ *denotes the smallest value of* $\lambda$ *in the PHFE.*

**Definition 3 ([21]).** Let $h(p) = \{\gamma^\lambda(p^\lambda), \lambda = 1, 2, \ldots, l\}$ be the PHFE, then the deviation function is defined as follows:

$$D(h(p)) = \sum_{\lambda=1}^{l} \left(\gamma^\lambda p^\lambda - s(h(p))\right)^2 \tag{3}$$

**Definition 4 ([21]).** According to the score function and the deviation function, the comparison rules of the two PHFE $h_1(p), h_2(p)$ can be presented as follows:

If $s(h_1(p)) > s(h_2(p))$, then $h_1(p)$ is greater than $h_2(p)$ which is denoted by $h_1(p) \succ h_2(p)$;
If $s(h_1(p)) = s(h_2(p))$, then:
if $D(h_1(p)) > D(h_2(p))$, then $h_2(p)$ is greater than $h_1(p)$ which is denoted by $h_2(p) \succ h_1(p)$;
if $D(h_1(p)) = D(h_2(p))$, then $h_1(p)$ and $h_2(p)$ represent the same information which is denoted by $h_1(p) \sim h_2(p)$.

Since the element dimension will increase when PHFE is operated, which leads to a geometric growth in calculation, a new type of PHFE operation rule is proposed in the literature.

**Definition 5 ([22]).** Let $h(p), h_1(p), h_2(p)$ be three PHFE, $\lambda > 0$, then:

$$h^C(p) = \left\{\left[1 - \gamma^\lambda\right](p^\lambda), \lambda = 1, 2, \cdots, l\right\} \tag{4}$$

$$\alpha h(p) = \left\{\left[1 - \left(1 - \gamma^\lambda\right)^\alpha\right](p^\lambda), \lambda = 1, 2, \cdots, l\right\}, \alpha > 0 \tag{5}$$

$$(h(p))^\alpha = \left\{\left[\left(\gamma^\lambda\right)^\alpha\right](p^\lambda), \lambda = 1, 2, \cdots, l\right\}, \alpha > 0 \tag{6}$$

$$h_1(p) \oplus h_2(p) = \left\{\left[\gamma_1^\lambda + \gamma_2^\lambda - \gamma_1^\lambda \gamma_2^\lambda\right]\overline{\left(p_1^\lambda + p_2^\lambda\right)}, \lambda = 1, 2, \cdots, l\right\} \tag{7}$$

$$h_1(p) \otimes h_2(p) = \left\{\left[\gamma_1^\lambda \gamma_2^\lambda\right]\overline{\left(p_1^\lambda + p_2^\lambda\right)}, \lambda = 1, 2, \cdots, l\right\} \tag{8}$$

where the normalized probability $\overline{p_1^\lambda + p_2^\lambda} = \frac{p_1^\lambda + p_2^\lambda}{\sum_{\lambda=1}^{l}(p_1^\lambda + p_2^\lambda)}, \lambda = 1, 2, \cdots, l$, therefore $\sum_{\lambda=1}^{l}(p_1^\lambda + p_2^\lambda) = 1$. The calculation rules defined in this way allow the number of elements contained in the integrated result to remain unchanged, avoiding an increase in computational effort due to the increase in the number of dimensions during the PHFE operation.

### 2.3. The Distance Measure of PHFE

In the probabilistic hesitant fuzzy environment, a new probabilistic hesitant fuzzy distance measure is defined as follows:

**Definition 6 ([23]).** Let $h_1 = \{\gamma_1^\lambda(p_1^\lambda), \lambda = 1, 2, \ldots, l\}$ and $h_2 = \{\gamma_2^\lambda(p_2^\lambda), \lambda = 1, 2, \ldots, l\}$ be two PHFEs elements that are equal. The probabilistic hesitant fuzzy distance measure can be defined as:

$$d(h_1, h_2) = |f(h_1) - f(h_2)| + q(h_1, h_2) \tag{9}$$

where $f(h_i)$ is the hesitancy degree of PHFE $h_i$, $q(h_1, h_2)$ is the difference measure between the PHFEs $h_1, h_2$, and the hesitancy and difference measure of PHFE are defined as follows:

$$f(h_i) = \frac{1}{2}\left(\frac{1}{l}\sum_{\lambda=1}^{l}\left[\gamma_i^\lambda p_i^\lambda - \left(\frac{1}{l}\sum_{\lambda=1}^{l}\gamma_i^\lambda p_i^\lambda\right)\right]^2 + \sqrt{\left(1 - \frac{1}{1 + \ln l}\right)}\right) \tag{10}$$

$$q(h_1, h_2) = \frac{1}{2l}\sum_{\lambda=1}^{l}\left(\left|\gamma_1^\lambda p_1^\lambda - \gamma_2^\lambda p_2^\lambda\right| + \left|\gamma_1^\lambda - \gamma_2^\lambda\right| \cdot \left|p_1^\lambda - p_2^\lambda\right|\right) \tag{11}$$

## 3. Credibility of PHFE

In this section, the concept of credibility of PHFE is defined, the method of adjusting the weights of the decision-makers based on credibility, and the method of determining attribute weights based on credibility are proposed. Credibility is applied to the selection of pharmaceutical e-commerce platforms to eliminate the influence of decision-makers on decision-making results due to personal bias or insufficient access to information.

### 3.1. Concept of Credibility of PHFE

With the gradual refinement of the social division of labor, in order to ensure the rationality and accuracy of the evaluation provided by decision-makers in the multi-attribute decision-making process, the level of knowledge of decision-makers with the domain being decided needs to be taken into account. In order to measure the reliability of evaluation information, the concept of credibility of PHFE is defined in this section, which indicates the familiarity of decision-makers with the domain to be decided. The higher the hesitancy degree of an alternative under a particular attribute, the more uncertain the evaluation of the decision-maker under this attribute and the lower the credibility of this decision-maker is. Therefore, the credibility of PHFE is defined as follows.

**Definition 7.** Let $h(p) = \{\gamma^\lambda(p^\lambda), \lambda = 1, 2, \ldots, l\}$ be a PHFE, then the credibility of PHFE is defined as:
$$R(h(p)) = 1 - f(h(p)) \quad (12)$$
where $f(h(p))$ is the hesitancy degree of $h(p)$.

**Property 1.** According to the properties of hesitancy degree, credibility has the following properties:
(1) $0 \leq R(h(p)) \leq 1$;
(2) When there is only one membership degree in the PHFE, $R(h(p)) = 1$.

**Proof.** (1) Since $l \geq 1$, so $1 - \frac{1}{1+\ln l} \leq 1$ and therefore $\sqrt{\left(1 - \frac{1}{1+\ln l}\right)} \leq 1$. Because $\gamma^\lambda \in [0,1], p^\lambda \in [0,1]$, then $\gamma_i^\lambda p_i^\lambda \in [0,1]$, therefore $\frac{1}{l}\sum_{\lambda=1}^{l} \gamma_i^\lambda p_i^\lambda \in [0,1]$, we can get $\frac{1}{l}\sum_{\lambda=1}^{l}\left[\gamma_i^\lambda p_i^\lambda - \left(\frac{1}{l}\sum_{\lambda=1}^{l}\gamma_i^\lambda p_i^\lambda\right)\right]^2 \in [0,1]$. Then the hesitancy degree is $f(h_i) = \frac{1}{2}\left(\frac{1}{l}\sum_{\lambda=1}^{l}\left[\gamma_i^\lambda p_i^\lambda - \left(\frac{1}{l}\sum_{\lambda=1}^{l}\gamma_i^\lambda p_i^\lambda\right)\right]^2 + \sqrt{\left(1 - \frac{1}{1+\ln l}\right)}\right) \in [0,1]$, and according to Equation (14) we can get $R(h(p)) \in [0,1]$.

(2) When there is only one membership degree in the PHFE, it is obtained that:
$$\begin{cases} \gamma_i^\lambda p_i^\lambda = \frac{1}{l}\sum_{\lambda=1}^{l}\gamma_i^\lambda p_i^\lambda \\ 1 - \frac{1}{1+\ln l} = 0 \end{cases}$$

Then $f(h_i) = 0$, $R(h(p)) = 1$.
Thus, we complete the proof of properties of credibility of PHFE. □

### 3.2. Adjustment for Weights of the Decision-Makers

Due to the different knowledge level and expertise of each decision-maker, there will be some bias in the evaluation of pharmaceutical e-commerce platforms. Excessive trust in the evaluation of one decision-maker will lead to one-sided decision results. Therefore, the weights of decision-makers need to be adjusted in the multi-attribute group decision-making process. Generally, decision-maker weights are subjectively determined, representing the importance of the decision information provided by that decision-maker in the decision-making process. How to determine the decision-maker weights effectively has a huge impact on the decision result. Therefore, a method to adjust the decision-maker's weight based on the decision-maker's credibility in the probabilistic hesitant fuzzy environment is proposed in this paper. On the basis of considering the subjective weight of decision-makers, the original weight of the decision-makers is adjusted according to the credibility of the decision-makers. A higher weight is assigned to decision-makers with high credibility and a lower weight is assigned to decision-makers with low credibility, so as to obtain decision-maker weights that are more in line with the actual situation. Considering the above ideas, the formula for adjusting decision-maker weights based on credibility is defined as:

$$\eta'_k = \frac{\eta_k}{1 + \eta_k - \frac{1}{mn}\sum_{i=1}^{m}\sum_{j=1}^{n} R\left(h_{ij}^k\right)} \tag{13}$$

where $\eta'_k$ is the adjusted weight of the decision-maker, which can be regarded as the degree of support provided by the decision-maker, and meets $\eta'_k \in [0,1]$; $\frac{1}{mn}\sum_{i=1}^{m}\sum_{j=1}^{n} R\left(h_{ij}^k\right)$ is the average credibility of the decision-maker.

The final weight of decision-maker $d_k$ is obtained by normalizing $\eta'_k$:

$$\eta''_k = \frac{\eta'_k}{\sum_{k=1}^{t} \eta'_k} \tag{14}$$

Equation (13) can adjust the weight of the decision-maker according to the credibility of the decision-maker. When the credibility of decision-maker $d_k$ is high, but the weight assigned to it is low, the decision-maker weight will be adjusted. The denominator of Equation (13) is less than 1, so the adjusted decision-maker weight is higher than the original decision-maker weight ($\eta'_k > \eta_k$). Thus, this decision-maker will receive more attention in the process of decision-making aggregation, which is more conducive to obtaining scientific and objective decision-making opinions. Similarly, when the credibility of a decision-maker is low, but the original weight is high, the above formula can also reduce the influence of his preference in the decision-making process.

### 3.3. Attribute Weight Determination Model Based on Credibility

According to the credibility defined in this paper, the higher the credibility, the better the real situation of the alternative can be reflected. Therefore, in order to ensure the rationality of the results, this paper determines the attribute weight of each pharmaceutical e-commerce platform according to the credibility of the evaluation of the decision-maker. That is, the higher the credibility of the evaluation of the alternative under attribute $C_j$, the more important the attribute is, and the higher the weight assigned to it. On the contrary, the lower the credibility, the lower the weight assigned to the attribute. According to the above ideas, the maximum deviation method is used to determine the attribute weights, and the PHFS is combined with the TODIM method to construct a selection method of pharmaceutical e-commerce platform. By extending the maximum deviation method to the probabilistic hesitant fuzzy environment to determine attribute weight, the objective function can be constructed as follows:

$$\begin{cases} \max \sum_{i=1}^{m}\sum_{j=1}^{n} \omega_j R\left(h_{ij}\right) \\ \sum_{j=1}^{n} \omega_j^2 = 1, 0 \leq \omega_j \leq 1 \end{cases} \tag{15}$$

where $\omega_j$ are the attribute weights, and $R\left(h_{ij}\right)$ is the credibility of $h_{ij}$.

In order to solve the above maximization deviation model, a Lagrangian function needs to be constructed.

$$L(\omega_j, \xi) = \sum_{i=1}^{m}\sum_{j=1}^{n} \omega_j R(h_{ij}) + \frac{1}{2}\xi\left(\sum_{j=1}^{n}\omega_j^2 - 1\right) \quad (16)$$

where $\xi$ is the Lagrangian multiplier.

Let the partial derivatives of both $\omega_j$ and $\xi$ be 0, then we can get:

$$\begin{cases} \frac{\partial L(\omega_j,\xi)}{\partial \omega_j} = \sum_{i=1}^{m} R(h_{ij}) + \xi\omega_j = 0 \\ \frac{\partial L(\omega_j,\xi)}{\partial \xi} = \sum_{j=1}^{n} \omega_j^2 - 1 = 0 \end{cases} \quad (17)$$

The optimal solution of attribute weight can be obtained as follows:

$$\omega_j^* = \frac{\sum_{i=1}^{m} R(h_{ij})}{\sqrt{\sum_{j=1}^{n}\left(\sum_{i=1}^{m} R(h_{ij})\right)^2}} \quad (18)$$

By normalizing the above equation, the final weight of the evaluation index $C_j$ can be written as follows:

$$\omega_j = \frac{\omega_j^*}{\sum_{j=1}^{n}\omega_j^*} = \frac{\sum_{i=1}^{m} R(h_{ij})}{\sum_{i=1}^{m}\sum_{j=1}^{n} R(h_{ij})}, j = 1, 2, \ldots, n \quad (19)$$

## 4. Probabilistic Hesitant Fuzzy Information Aggregation Operators

In this section, the PA operator is introduced into the probabilistic hesitant fuzzy environment, the probabilistic hesitant fuzzy power average (PHFPA) operator and the probabilistic hesitant fuzzy power weighted average (PHFPWA) operator are defined, and their properties including idempotence, boundedness, and permutation invariance are discussed. The PHFPWA operator is applied to the selection of pharmaceutical e-commerce platforms to eliminate the impact of extreme values on the decision results in the process of information aggregation.

### 4.1. PHFPA Operator

Firstly, the degree of support of PHFEs is defined.

**Definition 8.** *Let* $h_i(p) = \{\gamma_i^\lambda(p_i^\lambda), \lambda = 1, 2, \ldots, l\} (i = 1, 2)$ *be two PHFEs and the degree of support between them is defined as:*

$$sup(h_1(p), h_2(p)) = 1 - d(h_1(p), h_2(p)) \quad (20)$$

where $d(h_1(p), h_2(p))$ represents the distance between PHFE $h_1(p)$ and $h_2(p)$.

**Property 2.** *The degree of support meets following three properties:*
(1) $sup(h_i(p), h_j(p)) \subset [0, 1]$;
(2) $sup(h_i(p), h_j(p)) = sup(h_j(p), h_i(p))$;
(3) If $d(h_i(p), h_j(p)) < d(h_j(p), h_i(p))$, then $sup(h_i(p), h_j(p)) \geq sup(h_j(p), h_i(p))$.

According to the distance measure in Definition 6, Property 2 is easy to prove and will not be discussed here.

Based on Definition 8, the PHFPA operator is defined as follows:

**Definition 9.** Let $h_i(p) = \{\gamma_i^\lambda(p_i^\lambda), \lambda = 1, 2, \ldots, l\}$ be a set of PHFEs, then the probabilistic hesitant fuzzy power average (PHFPA) operator can be defined as:

$$PHFPA(h_1(p), h_2(p), \ldots, h_n(p)) = \frac{\oplus_{i=1}^n (1 + T(h_i(p)))h_i(p)}{\sum_{i=1}^n (1 + T(h_i(p)))} \quad (21)$$

where $T(h_i(p)) = \sum_{j=1, j \neq i}^n \sup(h_i(p), h_j(p))$, and $\sup(h_i(p), h_j(p))$ denotes the degree of support of $h_i(p)$ and $h_j(p)$.

From Definitions 5 and 9, we can get the following result by using mathematical in-duction.

**Theorem 1.** Let $h_i(p) = \{\gamma_i^\lambda(p_i^\lambda), \lambda = 1, 2, \ldots, l\}$ be a set of PHFEs, then the aggregated value by the PHFPA operator is also a PHFE, and

$$\begin{aligned}
&PHFPA(h_1(p), h_2(p), \ldots, h_n(p)) \\
&= \frac{\oplus_{i=1}^n (1+T(h_i(p)))h_i(p)}{\sum_{i=1}^n (1+T(h_i(p)))} \\
&= \left\{ \left[1 - \prod_{i=1}^n (1 - \gamma_i^\lambda)^{\frac{1+T(h_i(p))}{\sum_{i=1}^n (1+T(h_i(p)))}}\right] \left(\sum_{i=1}^n p_i^\lambda\right), \lambda = 1, 2, \cdots, l \right\}
\end{aligned} \quad (22)$$

**Proof.** Firstly, prove the following formula using mathematical induction:

$$\oplus_{i=1}^n (1 + T(h_i(p)))h_i(p) = \left\{ \left[1 - \prod_{i=1}^n (1 - \gamma_i^\lambda)^{1+T(h_i(p))}\right] \left(\sum_{i=1}^n p_i^\lambda\right), \lambda = 1, 2, \cdots, l \right\},$$

When $n = 2$, then

$$\begin{aligned}
&\oplus_{i=1}^2 (1 + T(h_i(p)))h_i(p) \\
&= (1 + T(h_1(p)))h_1(p) \oplus (1 + T(h_2(p)))h_2(p) \\
&= \left\{ \left[1 - (1 - \gamma_1^\lambda)^{1+T(h_1(p))}\right] (p_1^\lambda) \right\} \oplus \left\{ \left[1 - (1 - \gamma_2^\lambda)^{1+T(h_2(p))}\right] (p_2^\lambda) \right\} \\
&= \left\{ \left[1 - (1 - \gamma_1^\lambda)^{1+T(h_1(p))} (1 - \gamma_2^\lambda)^{1+T(h_2(p))}\right] (p_1^\lambda + p_2^\lambda), \lambda = 1, 2, \cdots, l \right\},
\end{aligned}$$

Assume that when $n = k$, the following equation is established:

$$\oplus_{i=1}^k (1 + T(h_i(p)))h_i(p) = \left\{ \left[1 - \prod_{i=1}^k (1 - \gamma_i^\lambda)^{1+T(h_i(p))}\right] \left(\sum_{i=1}^k p_i^\lambda\right), \lambda = 1, 2, \cdots, l \right\}$$

Then, when $n = k + 1$,

$$\begin{aligned}
&\oplus_{i=1}^{k+1} (1 + T(h_i(p)))h_i(p) \\
&= \oplus_{i=1}^k (1 + T(h_i(p)))h_i(p) \oplus (1 + T(h_{k+1}(p)))h_{k+1}(p) \\
&= \left\{ \left[1 - \prod_{i=1}^k (1 - \gamma_i^\lambda)^{1+T(h_i(p))}\right] \left(\sum_{i=1}^k p_i^\lambda\right) \right\} \oplus \left\{ \left[1 - (1 - \gamma_{k+1}^\lambda)^{1+T(h_{k+1}(p))}\right] (p_{k+1}^\lambda) \right\} \\
&= \left\{ \left[1 - \prod_{i=1}^{k+1} (1 - \gamma_i^\lambda)^{1+T(h_i(p))}\right] \left(\sum_{i=1}^{k+1} p_i^\lambda\right), \lambda = 1, 2, \cdots, l \right\},
\end{aligned}$$

Secondly, according to the Definition 4 on PHFE operation rule, the result can be obtained as:

$$\begin{aligned}
&\frac{\oplus_{i=1}^{n}(1+T(h_i(p)))h_i(p)}{\sum_{i=1}^{n}(1+T(h_i(p)))} \\
&= \frac{1}{\sum_{i=1}^{n}(1+T(h_i(p)))}\left\{\left[1-\prod_{i=1}^{n}\left(1-\gamma_i^{\lambda}\right)^{1+T(h_i(p))}\right]\left(\sum_{i=1}^{n}p_i^{\lambda}\right), \lambda=1,2,\cdots,l\right\} \\
&= \left\{\left[1-\prod_{i=1}^{n}\left(\left(1-\gamma_i^{\lambda}\right)^{1+T(h_i(p))}\right)^{\frac{1}{\sum_{i=1}^{n}(1+T(h_i(p)))}}\right]\left(\sum_{i=1}^{n}p_i^{\lambda}\right), \lambda=1,2,\cdots,l\right\} \\
&= \left\{\left[1-\prod_{i=1}^{n}\left(1-\gamma_i^{\lambda}\right)^{\frac{1+T(h_i(p))}{\sum_{i=1}^{n}(1+T(h_i(p)))}}\right]\left(\sum_{i=1}^{n}p_i^{\lambda}\right), \lambda=1,2,\cdots,l\right\},
\end{aligned}$$

where $\gamma_i^{\lambda} \in [0,1]$, $\frac{1+T(h_i(p))}{\sum_{i=1}^{n}(1+T(h_i(p)))} \in [0,1]$, then $\prod_{i=1}^{n}\left(1-\gamma_i^{\lambda}\right)^{\frac{1+T(h_i(p))}{\sum_{i=1}^{n}(1+T(h_i(p)))}} \in [0,1]$. Therefore, the aggregation result of membership degree is $1-\prod_{i=1}^{n}\left(1-\gamma_i^{\lambda}\right)^{\frac{1+T(h_i(p))}{\sum_{i=1}^{n}(1+T(h_i(p)))}} \in [0,1]$, which meets the property of membership degree of PHFE.

Furthermore, because of the definition of standardized probability in Definition 4, we can obtain that $\overline{\sum_{i=1}^{n}p_i^{\lambda}} \in [0,1]$, and then $\sum_{\lambda=1}^{l}\overline{\sum_{i=1}^{n}p_i^{\lambda}}=1$, which meets the requirement of probability of PHFE.

Therefore, the result after aggregation by using $PHFPA$ is still a PHFE.

Thus, we complete the proof of Theorem 1. □

Based on Theorem 1, the basic properties of the HPFPA operator are as follows:

**Property 3** (Idempotence). *Let $h_i(p) = \{\gamma_i^{\lambda}(p_i^{\lambda}), \lambda=1,2,\ldots,l\}$ be a set of PHFEs, if for all $i=1,2,\cdots,n$, we have $h_i(p)=h(p)=\{\gamma^{\lambda}(p^{\lambda}), \lambda=1,2,\ldots,l\}$, then:*

$$PHFPA(h_1(p), h_2(p), \ldots, h_n(p)) = h(p) \tag{23}$$

**Proof.**

$$\begin{aligned}
&PHFPA(h_1(p), h_2(p), \ldots, h_n(p)) \\
&= PHFPA(h(p), h(p), \ldots, h(p)) \\
&= \left\{\left[1-\prod_{i=1}^{n}\left(1-\gamma^{\lambda}\right)^{\frac{1+T(h_i(p))}{\sum_{i=1}^{n}(1+T(h_i(p)))}}\right]\left(\sum_{i=1}^{n}p_i^{\lambda}/\sum_{\lambda=1}^{l}\sum_{i=1}^{n}p_i^{\lambda}\right), \lambda=1,2,\cdots,l\right\} \\
&= \left\{\left[1-\left(1-\gamma^{\lambda}\right)^{\sum_{i=1}^{n}\frac{1+T(h_i(p))}{\sum_{i=1}^{n}(1+T(h_i(p)))}}\right]\left(\sum_{i=1}^{n}p_i^{\lambda}/\sum_{i=1}^{n}\sum_{\lambda=1}^{l}p_i^{\lambda}\right), \lambda=1,2,\cdots,l\right\} \\
&= \left\{\left[1-\left(1-\gamma^{\lambda}\right)^{1}\right]\left(np^{\lambda}/\sum_{i=1}^{n}1\right), \lambda=1,2,\cdots,l\right\} \\
&- \{\gamma^{\lambda}(p^{\lambda}), \lambda-1,2,\cdots,l\} \\
&= h(p)
\end{aligned}$$

Thus, we complete the proof of idempotence. □

**Property 4** (Boundedness). *Let $h_i(p) - \{\gamma_i^{\lambda}(p_i^{\lambda}), \lambda-1,2,\ldots,l\}$ be a set of PIIFLs, if $h^{-}(p) = \left\{\min_i \gamma_i^{\lambda}\left(\min_i p_i^{\lambda}\right), \lambda=1,2,\ldots,l\right\}$, $h^{+}(p) = \left\{\max_i \gamma_i^{\lambda}\left(\max_i p_i^{\lambda}\right), \lambda=1,2,\ldots,l\right\}$, then:*

$$h^{-}(p) \leq PHFPA(h_1(p), h_2(p), \ldots, h_n(p)) \leq h^{+}(p) \tag{24}$$

**Proof.** Let $h(p) = PHFPA(h_1(p), h_2(p), \ldots, h_n(p))$, and $\omega_i = \frac{1+T(h_i(p))}{\sum_{i=1}^{n}(1+T(h_i(p)))}$, then

$$s(h(p)) = \sum_{\lambda=1}^{l}\left\{\left[1 - \prod_{i=1}^{n}\left(1-\gamma_i^\lambda\right)^{\omega_i}\right] \cdot \overline{\sum_{i=1}^{n} p_i^\lambda}\right\},$$

According to Definition 2 of the score function, it can be obtained that:

$$s_{h^-(p)} = \sum_{\lambda=1}^{l} \min_i \gamma_i^\lambda \cdot \min_i p_i^\lambda, \quad s_{h^+(p)} = \sum_{\lambda=1}^{l} \max_i \gamma_i^\lambda \cdot \max_i p_i^\lambda,$$

Since $0 \leq \min_i \gamma_i^\lambda \leq \gamma_i^\lambda \leq \max_i \gamma_i^\lambda \leq 1$, it can be obtained that:

$$1 - \min_i \gamma_i^\lambda \geq 1 - \gamma_i^\lambda \geq 1 - \max_i \gamma_i^\lambda,$$

Thus,

$$\prod_{i=1}^{n}\left(1 - \min_i \gamma_i^\lambda\right)^{\omega_i} \geq \prod_{i=1}^{n}\left(1 - \gamma_i^\lambda\right)^{\omega_i} \geq \prod_{i=1}^{n}\left(1 - \max_i \gamma_i^\lambda\right)^{\omega_i},$$

Hence,

$$1 - \prod_{i=1}^{n}\left(1 - \min_i \gamma_i^\lambda\right)^{\omega_i} \leq 1 - \prod_{i=1}^{n}\left(1 - \gamma_i^\lambda\right)^{\omega_i} \leq 1 - \prod_{i=1}^{n}\left(1 - \max_i \gamma_i^\lambda\right)^{\omega_i},$$

Therefore,

$$\min_i \gamma_i^\lambda \leq 1 - \prod_{i=1}^{n}\left(1 - \gamma_i^\lambda\right)^{\omega_i} \leq \max_i \gamma_i^\lambda,$$

Furthermore, because of $0 \leq \min_i p_i^\lambda \leq p_i^\lambda \leq \max_i p_i^\lambda \leq 1$, it can be obtained that:

$$\overline{\sum_{i=1}^{n} \min_i p_i^\lambda} \leq \overline{\sum_{i=1}^{n} p_i^\lambda} \leq \overline{\sum_{i=1}^{n} \max_i p_i^\lambda}$$

Thus,

$$\min_i p_i^\lambda \leq \overline{\sum_{i=1}^{n} p_i^\lambda} \leq \max_i p_i^\lambda$$

Hence,

$$\sum_{\lambda=1}^{l} \min_i \gamma_i^\lambda \cdot \min_i p_i^\lambda \leq \sum_{\lambda=1}^{l}\left\{\left[1 - \prod_{i=1}^{n}\left(1-\gamma_i^\lambda\right)^{\omega_i}\right] \cdot \overline{\sum_{i=1}^{n} p_i^\lambda}\right\} \leq \sum_{\lambda=1}^{l} \max_i \gamma_i^\lambda \cdot \max_i p_i^\lambda$$

Therefore,

$$h^-(p) \leq PHFPA(h_1(p), h_2(p), \ldots, h_n(p)) \leq h^+(p)$$

Thus, we complete the proof of boundedness. □

**Property 5** (Permutation invariance). *Let $h_i(p) = \{\gamma_i^\lambda(p_i^\lambda), \lambda = 1, 2, \ldots, l\}$ be a set of PHFEs, if $(h'_1(p), h'_2(p), \cdots, h'_n(p))$ is any permutation of $(h_1(p), h_2(p), \cdots, h_n(p))$, then:*

$$PHFPA(h_1(p), h_2(p), \ldots, h_n(p)) = PHFPA(h'_1(p), h'_2(p), \cdots, h'_n(p)) \quad (25)$$

**Proof.** Since $(h'_1(p), h'_2(p), \cdots, h'_n(p))$ is the permutation of $(h_1(p), h_2(p), \cdots, h_n(p))$, there must exist a unique $h'_j(p)$ for each $h_i(p)$, then $h'_j(p) = h_i(p)$ and vice versa. Thus, $T\left(h'_j(p)\right) = T(h_i(p))$. It can be obtained that:

$$\begin{aligned} PHFPA(h_1(p), h_2(p), \ldots, h_n(p)) &= \frac{\oplus_{i=1}^n (1+T(h_i(p)))h_i(p)}{\sum_{i=1}^n (1+T(h_i(p)))} \\ &= \frac{\oplus_{j=1}^n \left(1+T\left(h'_j(p)\right)\right)h'_j(p)}{\sum_{j=1}^n \left(1+T\left(h'_j(p)\right)\right)} \\ &= PHFPA\left(h'_1(p), h'_2(p), \ldots, h'_n(p)\right) \end{aligned}$$

Thus, we complete the proof of permutation invariance. □

### 4.2. PHFPWA Operator

According to the definition of PHFPA operator, the probabilistic hesitant fuzzy power weighted average operator is defined as below.

**Definition 10.** *Let* $h_i(p) = \{\gamma_i^\lambda(p_i^\lambda), \lambda = 1, 2, \ldots, l\}$ *be a set of PHFEs, and* $\omega = (\omega_1, \omega_2, \cdots, \omega_n)^T$ *be a vector of weights, which meets* $\sum_{i=1}^n \omega_i = 1, \omega_i \geq 0 (i = 1, 2, \cdots, n)$, *then the probabilistic hesitant fuzzy power weighted average (PHFPWA) operator can be defined as:*

$$PHFPWA(h_1(p), h_2(p), \ldots, h_n(p)) = \frac{\oplus_{i=1}^n \omega_i(1+T(h_i(p)))h_i(p)}{\sum_{i=1}^n \omega_i(1+T(h_i(p)))} \qquad (26)$$

**Theorem 2.** *Let* $h_i(p) = \{\gamma_i^\lambda(p_i^\lambda), \lambda = 1, 2, \ldots, l\}$ *be a set of PHFEs, then the aggregated value by the PHFPWA operator is also a PHFE, and*

$$\begin{aligned} &PHFPWA(h_1(p), h_2(p), \ldots, h_n(p)) \\ &= \frac{\oplus_{i=1}^n \omega_i(1+T(h_i(p)))h_i(p)}{\sum_{i=1}^n \omega_i(1+T(h_i(p)))} \\ &= \left\{ \left[ 1 - \prod_{i=1}^n (1-\gamma_i^\lambda)^{\frac{\omega_i(1+T(h_i(p)))}{\sum_{i=1}^n \omega_i(1+T(h_i(p)))}} \right] \left( \prod_{i=1}^n p_i^\lambda \right) \right\} \end{aligned} \qquad (27)$$

The proof of Theorem 2 is similar to Theorem 1 and it is therefore omitted.

Let $h_i(p) = \{\gamma_i^\lambda(p_i^\lambda), \lambda = 1, 2, \ldots, l\}$ be a set of PHFEs, then the $PHFPWA$ operator satisfies the following properties:

**Property 6** (Idempotence). *If* $h_i(p) = h(p) = \{\gamma^\lambda(p^\lambda), \lambda = 1, 2, \ldots, l\}(i = 1, 2, \cdots, n)$, *then:*

$$PHFPWA(h_1(p), h_2(p), \ldots, h_n(p)) = h(p) \qquad (28)$$

**Property 7** (Boundedness). *If we make* $h^-(p) = \left\{ \min_i \gamma_i^\lambda \left( \min_i p_i^\lambda \right), \lambda = 1, 2, \ldots, l \right\}$, $h^+(p) = \left\{ \max_i \gamma_i^\lambda \left( \max_i p_i^\lambda \right), \lambda = 1, 2, \ldots, l \right\}$, *then:*

$$h^-(p) \leq PHFPWA(h_1(p), h_2(p), \ldots, h_n(p)) \leq h^+(p) \qquad (29)$$

**Property 8** (Permutation invariance). If $(h'_1(p), h'_2(p), \cdots, h'_n(p))$ is any permutation of $(h_1(p), h_2(p), \cdots, h_n(p))$, then:

$$PHFPWA(h_1(p), h_2(p), \ldots, h_n(p)) = PHFPWA(h'_1(p), h'_2(p), \cdots, h'_n(p)) \quad (30)$$

The above three properties are proved in a similar way to Properties 3–5 and they are therefore omitted.

## 5. A Method of Pharmaceutical E-Commerce Platform Selection Based on Generalized TODIM under Probabilistic Hesitant Fuzzy Environment

### 5.1. Description of the Problem

For the selection of a pharmaceutical e-commerce platform, it is assumed that there are $m$ pharmaceutical e-commerce platforms, and then the pharmaceutical e-commerce platform set is expressed as $A = \{A_1, A_2, \ldots, A_m\}(i = 1, 2, \ldots, m)$. There are $n$ evaluation indexes in the evaluation index system of the pharmaceutical e-commerce platform, then the evaluation index set is $C = \{C_1, C_2, \ldots, C_n\}(j = 1, 2, \ldots, n)$, and the attribute weight vector is $\omega = (\omega_1, \omega_2, \ldots, \omega_n)^T$, which satisfies $\sum_{j=1}^{n} \omega_j = 1, \omega_j \geq 0 (i = 1, 2, \cdots, n)$. Let $D = \{d_1, d_2, \cdots, d_t\}$ be the set of decision-makers, and the weights of the decision-makers satisfies $\sum_{k=1}^{t} \eta_k = 1, \eta_k \geq 0 (k = 1, 2, \cdots, t)$. The decision-maker evaluates the pharmaceutical e-commerce platforms using PHFE, which is denoted as $h(p) = \{\gamma^\lambda(p^\lambda), \lambda = 1, 2, \ldots, l\}$. For the $k$-th decision-maker $d_k$, the evaluation value of the pharmaceutical e-commerce platform $A_i$ on the evaluation index $C_j$ is represented by the PHFE $h'^k_{ij}(p_{ij}) = \left\{\gamma'^{k\lambda}_{ij}\left(p'^{k\lambda}_{ij}\right), i = 1, 2, \ldots, m; j = 1, 2, \ldots, n; k = 1, 2, \cdots, t; \lambda = 1, 2, \ldots, l\right\}$, then the $k$-th decision-maker's probabilistic hesitant fuzzy multi-attribute decision-making matrix $H'^k(P) = \left(h'^k_{ij}(p_{ij})\right)_{m \times n}$ can be expressed as:

$$H'^k(P) = \begin{bmatrix} h'^k_{11}(p_{11}) & h'^k_{12}(p_{12}) & \cdots & h'^k_{1n}(p_{1n}) \\ h'^k_{21}(p_{21}) & h'^k_{22}(p_{22}) & \cdots & h'^k_{2n}(p_{2n}) \\ \vdots & \vdots & \ddots & \vdots \\ h'^k_{m1}(p_{m1}) & h'^k_{m2}(p_{m2}) & \cdots & h'^k_{mn}(p_{mn}) \end{bmatrix} \quad (31)$$

When dealing with practical problems, different attributes have different physical scales. The evaluation attributes of pharmaceutical e-commerce platforms are generally classified as two types: benefit-type $J_1$ and cost-type $J_2$. For the benefit-type attributes, the corresponding probability hesitant fuzzy information remains unchanged. For the cost-type attributes, the membership degree in the probabilistic hesitant fuzzy information is complemented and the corresponding probability remains unchanged. Then the standardized matrix $E^k(P) = \left(e^k_{ij}(p_{ij})\right)_{m \times n}$ can be shown as:

$$e^k_{ij}(p_{ij}) = \begin{cases} \left\{\gamma^{k,\lambda}_{ij}\left(p^{k,\lambda}_{ij}\right) \middle| \lambda = 1, 2, \cdots, l\right\}, C_j \in J_1 \\ \left\{\left(1 - \gamma^{k,\lambda}_{ij}\right)\left(p^{k,\lambda}_{ij}\right) \middle| \lambda = 1, 2, \cdots, l\right\}, C_j \in J_2 \end{cases} \quad (32)$$

### 5.2. Probabilistic Hesitant Fuzzy Generalized TODIM Method

The TODIM (Tomada de decisao interativae multicritévio) method, as a multi-attribute decision-making method proposed on the basis of prospect theory, can take into account the different psychological behaviors of decision-makers on losses and gains, affecting the decision-making results. In the traditional TODIM method, the results may be contrary to the facts in some cases. Therefore, a simplified model of the TODIM method was proposed by Llamazares [24], and two examples were given to illustrate the results contrary to the expectations caused by the change of attribute weights, and then the concepts of weight consistency and weight monotonicity were proposed. By using the non-decreasing function in the definition of dominance, a generalized TODIM method is proposed, which avoids the violation of the results and facts caused by weight changes in some cases.

In the generalized TODIM method, the dominance of pharmaceutical e-commerce platform $A_i$ to pharmaceutical e-commerce platform $A_k$ under attribute $C_j$ is defined as:

$$\Phi_j(A_i, A_k) = \begin{cases} g_1(\omega_k) f_1\left(y_{ij} - y_{kj}\right), & \left(y_{ij} - y_{kj}\right) \geq 0 \\ -g_2(\omega_k) f_2\left(y_{kj} - y_{ij}\right), & \left(y_{ij} - y_{kj}\right) < 0 \end{cases} \quad (33)$$

Among them, $g_1, g_2 : (0,1) \to (0, +\infty), f_1, f_2 : [0,1] \to [0, +\infty), f_1(0) = f_2(0) = 0$.

In this paper, the generalized TODIM method is extended to the probabilistic hesitant fuzzy environment, and the probabilistic hesitant fuzzy generalized TODIM method is constructed based on credibility. Then, the dominance of pharmaceutical e-commerce platform $A_i$ to pharmaceutical e-commerce platform $A_k$ under attribute $C_j$ is defined as:

$$\Phi_j(A_i, A_k) = \begin{cases} g_1(\omega_j) f_1\left(R_{ij} - R_{kj}\right), & R_{ij} > R_{kj} \\ -g_2(\omega_j) f_2\left(R_{ij} - R_{kj}\right), & R_{ij} < R_{kj} \end{cases} \quad (34)$$

where $R_{ij}$ is the credibility of pharmaceutical e-commerce platform $A_i$ under attribute $C_j$, $g_1, g_2 : (0,1) \to (0, +\infty), f_1, f_2 : [0,1] \to [0, +\infty)$ and $f_1(0) = f_2(0) = 0$.

The total dominance degree of pharmaceutical e-commerce platform $A_i$ is calculated according to the relative dominance degree, and the pharmaceutical e-commerce platforms are sorted according to the value of $\Phi(A_i)$. The total dominance degree of pharmaceutical e-commerce platform $A_i$ is defined as:

$$\Phi(A_i) = \sum_{k=1}^{m} \sum_{j=1}^{n} \Phi_j(A_i, A_k) \quad (35)$$

The basic principle of the generalized TODIM method is consistent with that of the traditional TODIM method, but the calculation steps are simplified in the process of processing, making the calculation more concise. This paper assumes $g_1(x) = f_1(x) = x^\alpha$, $g_2(x) = \frac{1}{\theta} x^\beta$, $f_2(x) = x^\beta$, $\alpha = \beta = 0.5$, $\theta = 2.25$, which is consistent with the traditional TODIM method.

### 5.3. Decision-Making Process

Based on the above analysis, we give the specific steps of the selection method of a pharmaceutical e-commerce platform under a probabilistic hesitant fuzzy environment:

Step 1: The performance of each pharmaceutical e-commerce platform under each attribute is evaluated by each decision-maker using PHFE, and $t$ probabilistic hesitant fuzzy decision-making matrices $H^k (k = 1, 2, \cdots, t)$ are obtained.

Step 2: Considering the cost attributes, the initial probabilistic hesitant fuzzy matrix is normalized according to Equation (32) to obtain the matrix $E^k(P)$.

Step 3: The hesitancy degree $f\left(h_{ij}^k\right)$ and credibility $R\left(h_{ij}^k\right)$ of PHFE $h_{ij}^k$ are calculated by Equations (10) and (12), respectively, and adjust the subjective weights of decision-makers by Equations (13) and (14) to obtain the adjusted weights of decision-makers $\eta_k''$.

Step 4: Integrate the information of decision-makers using the $PHFPWA$ operator to obtain the comprehensive decision matrix $H = [h_{ij}]_{m \times n}$.

Step 5: The credibility of the comprehensive decision matrix is calculated, and the attribute weight determination model is built based on the credibility. The attribute weight vector $W = (\omega_1, \omega_2, \cdots, \omega_n)^T$ is obtained by Equations (18) and (19).

Step 6: Calculate the dominance $\Phi_j(A_i, A_s)$ of each pharmaceutical e-commerce platform for attribute $C_j$ according to Equation (34), and the dominance matrix is obtained.

Step 7: Calculate the total dominance $\Phi(A_i)$ of pharmaceutical e-commerce platform $A_i$ by Equation (35), and sort the pharmaceutical e-commerce platforms according to the size of $\Phi(A_i)$.

## 6. Numerical Example

### 6.1. Background

With the continuous promotion of the "Healthy China" strategy, the "Internet + medical health" model represented by pharmaceutical e-commerce platform is becoming a new trend. On 6 September 2022, the Ministry of Commerce released the 2021 Statistical Report on Pharmaceutical Circulation Industry. The report pointed out that in 2021, the total sales volume of seven categories of medical commodities in China reached CNY 2.6 trillion, and the total sales volume of pharmaceutical e-commerce platform direct reporting enterprises in 2021 reached CNY 216.2 billion (including the transaction volume of third-party trading service platform), accounting for 8.3% of the total scale of the national pharmaceutical market in the same period [25]. Since the outbreak of the COVID-19, the pharmaceutical e-commerce platform industry has developed rapidly, and the recognition of consumers of the pharmaceutical e-commerce platform has gradually increased. S Online consultation, self-testing, and drug sales have brought a lot of convenience to residents, and the demand for online drug sales has grown significantly. According to relevant data, during the epidemic, the number of daily online active users of pharmaceutical e-commerce platforms such as JD and Alibaba increased significantly from the previous month, and the peak could even rise to 1.48 million, with a maximum growth rate of 10% in the same period in 2019. According to data, based on the development of digital medical industry, China's pharmaceutical e-commerce platform and online consultation will enter a stage of rapid growth, and the market size is expected to reach CNY 1.2 trillion and CNY 407 billion, respectively, in 2030.

After a period of exploration and cultivation, China's pharmaceutical e-commerce platform industry has been basically formed, and a number of representative enterprises have emerged in their fields. Since 2018, the government has issued a series of policies to support the development of Internet hospitals, and has gradually liberalized the online sales of some prescription medicine, bringing a bright light to the development of pharmaceutical e-commerce platforms. In the future, compliant pharmaceutical e-commerce platforms are expected to establish a matching licensed pharmacist remote prescription examination system and prescription drug distribution system. The vigorous development of pharmaceutical e-commerce platforms has also brought new opportunities for pharmaceutical enterprises. The new Internet channels have broadened the sales scope of pharmaceutical enterprises, and the area covered by consumers is not limited by time and space. At the same time, through the management of the intelligent supply chain system and the unified deployment of medical storage and transportation, pharmaceutical enterprises have developed into low-cost modern green logistics to reduce the circulation cost. Therefore, it is of great practical significance for pharmaceutical enterprises to select an appropriate pharmaceutical e-commerce platform.

### 6.2. Research Hypothesis

Take pharmaceutical company A as an example. The enterprise has developed a new drug, and the management of the company plans to cooperate with a pharmaceutical e-commerce platform to promote the new drug. At present, there are four pharmaceutical e-commerce platforms $A = \{A_1, A_2, A_3, A_4\}$ for a company to choose from. We will evaluate these four platforms in five aspects, including type of drugs ($C_1$), price ($C_2$), response speed ($C_3$), level of medical personnel ($C_4$), and company qualification ($C_5$). The evaluation committee is composed of three decision-makers $d_i (i = 1, 2, 3)$, and the weight vector of the decision-makers is $\omega = (0.5, 0.3, 0.2)$. The evaluation value given by invited decision-makers is expressed by PHFE, and the initial evaluation results are shown in Tables 1–3.

**Table 1.** Original evaluation matrix of Expert 1 ($d_1$).

|       | $A_1$                  | $A_2$                  |
|-------|------------------------|------------------------|
| $c_1$ | {0.2(0.3), 0.8(0.7)}   | {0.3(0.2), 0.7(0.8)}   |
| $c_2$ | {0.3(0.8), 0.8(0.2)}   | {0.2(0.7), 0.9(0.3)}   |
| $c_3$ | {0.4(0.4), 0.5(0.6)}   | {0.3(0.2), 0.6(0.8)}   |
| $c_4$ | {0.1(0.3), 0.4(0.7)}   | {0.3(0.4), 0.6(0.6)}   |
| $c_5$ | {0.2(0.4), 0.6(0.6)}   | {0.4(0.3), 0.5(0.7)}   |
|       | $A_3$                  | $A_4$                  |
| $c_1$ | {0.6(0.9), 0.9(0.1)}   | {0.4(0.4), 0.6(0.6)}   |
| $c_2$ | {0.3(0.4), 0.6(0.6)}   | {0.6(0.4), 0.8(0.6)}   |
| $c_3$ | {0.5(0.7), 0.8(0.3)}   | {0.7(0.4), 0.8(0.6)}   |
| $c_4$ | {0.3(0.4), 0.9(0.6)}   | {0.2(0.6), 0.7(0.4)}   |
| $c_5$ | {0.2(0.4), 0.6(0.6)}   | {0.2(0.4), 0.5(0.6)}   |

**Table 2.** Original evaluation matrix of Expert 2 ($d_2$).

|       | $A_1$                  | $A_2$                  |
|-------|------------------------|------------------------|
| $c_1$ | {0.5(0.3), 0.8(0.7)}   | {0.3(0.2), 0.6(0.8)}   |
| $c_2$ | {0.3(0.8), 0.8(0.2)}   | {0.4(0.7), 0.9(0.3)}   |
| $c_3$ | {0.4(0.3), 0.5(0.7)}   | {0.3(0.4), 0.7(0.6)}   |
| $c_4$ | {0.2(0.4), 0.5(0.6)}   | {0.4(0.3), 0.6(0.7)}   |
| $c_5$ | {0.3(0.5), 0.6(0.5)}   | {0.4(0.3), 0.5(0.7)}   |
|       | $A_3$                  | $A_4$                  |
| $c_1$ | {0.6(0.7), 0.8(0.3)}   | {0.3(0.3), 0.6(0.7)}   |
| $c_2$ | {0.2(0.3), 0.3(0.7)}   | {0.5(0.4), 0.8(0.6)}   |
| $c_3$ | {0.4(0.4), 0.7(0.6)}   | {0.5(0.7), 0.8(0.3)}   |
| $c_4$ | {0.4(0.4), 0.9(0.6)}   | {0.2(0.6), 0.7(0.4)}   |
| $c_5$ | {0.5(0.4), 0.8(0.6)}   | {0.2(0.6), 0.6(0.4)}   |

**Table 3.** Original evaluation matrix of Expert 3 ($d_3$).

|       | $A_1$                  | $A_2$                  |
|-------|------------------------|------------------------|
| $c_1$ | {0.4(0.3), 0.8(0.7)}   | {0.3(0.2), 0.6(0.8)}   |
| $c_2$ | {0.3(0.8), 0.9(0.2)}   | {0.4(0.7), 0.9(0.3)}   |
| $c_3$ | {0.4(0.4), 0.5(0.6)}   | {0.4(0.4), 0.6(0.6)}   |
| $c_4$ | {0.1(0.4), 0.4(0.6)}   | {0.3(0.6), 0.7(0.4)}   |
| $c_5$ | {0.2(0.4), 0.6(0.6)}   | {0.4(0.4), 0.5(0.6)}   |
|       | $A_3$                  | $A_4$                  |
| $c_1$ | {0.5(0.6), 0.8(0.4)}   | {0.4(0.3), 0.6(0.7)}   |
| $c_2$ | {0.5(0.2), 0.8(0.8)}   | {0.2(0.4), 0.8(0.6)}   |
| $c_3$ | {0.3(0.4), 0.6(0.6)}   | {0.7(0.4), 0.8(0.6)}   |
| $c_4$ | {0.5(0.4), 0.6(0.6)}   | {0.4(0.6), 0.7(0.4)}   |
| $c_5$ | {0.3(0.4), 0.5(0.6)}   | {0.3(0.3), 0.5(0.7)}   |

### 6.3. Data Processing and Alternative Ranking

Step 1: Data normalization processing. According to Equation (32), the decision matrix of the three decision-makers $H'^k(P)$ were transformed into $E^k(P)$, and the transformed results are shown in Tables 4–6.

**Table 4.** Standardized evaluation matrix of Expert 1 ($d_1$).

|       | $A_1$ | $A_2$ |
|-------|-------|-------|
| $c_1$ | {0.2(0.3), 0.8(0.7)} | {0.3(0.2), 0.7(0.8)} |
| $c_2$ | {0.2(0.2), 0.7(0.8)} | {0.1(0.3), 0.8(0.7)} |
| $c_3$ | {0.4(0.4), 0.5(0.6)} | {0.3(0.2), 0.6(0.8)} |
| $c_4$ | {0.1(0.3), 0.4(0.7)} | {0.3(0.4), 0.6(0.6)} |
| $c_5$ | {0.2(0.4), 0.6(0.6)} | {0.4(0.3), 0.5(0.7)} |
|       | $A_3$ | $A_4$ |
| $c_1$ | {0.6(0.9), 0.9(0.1)} | {0.4(0.4), 0.6(0.6)} |
| $c_2$ | {0.4(0.6), 0.7(0.4)} | {0.2(0.6), 0.4(0.4)} |
| $c_3$ | {0.5(0.7), 0.8(0.3)} | {0.7(0.4), 0.8(0.6)} |
| $c_4$ | {0.3(0.4), 0.9(0.6)} | {0.2(0.6), 0.7(0.4)} |
| $c_5$ | {0.2(0.4), 0.6(0.6)} | {0.2(0.4), 0.5(0.6)} |

**Table 5.** Standardized evaluation matrix of Expert 2 ($d_2$).

|       | $A_1$ | $A_2$ |
|-------|-------|-------|
| $c_1$ | {0.5(0.3), 0.8(0.7)} | {0.3(0.2), 0.6(0.8)} |
| $c_2$ | {0.2(0.2), 0.7(0.8)} | {0.1(0.3), 0.6(0.7)} |
| $c_3$ | {0.4(0.3), 0.5(0.7)} | {0.3(0.4), 0.7(0.6)} |
| $c_4$ | {0.2(0.4), 0.5(0.6)} | {0.4(0.3), 0.6(0.7)} |
| $c_5$ | {0.3(0.5), 0.6(0.5)} | {0.4(0.3), 0.5(0.7)} |
|       | $A_3$ | $A_4$ |
| $c_1$ | {0.6(0.7), 0.8(0.3)} | {0.3(0.3), 0.6(0.7)} |
| $c_2$ | {0.7(0.7), 0.8(0.3)} | {0.2(0.6), 0.5(0.4)} |
| $c_3$ | {0.4(0.4), 0.7(0.6)} | {0.5(0.7), 0.8(0.3)} |
| $c_4$ | {0.4(0.4), 0.9(0.6)} | {0.2(0.6), 0.7(0.4)} |
| $c_5$ | {0.5(0.4), 0.8(0.6)} | {0.2(0.6), 0.6(0.4)} |

**Table 6.** Standardized evaluation matrix of Expert 3 ($d_3$).

|       | $A_1$ | $A_2$ |
|-------|-------|-------|
| $c_1$ | {0.4(0.3), 0.8(0.7)} | {0.3(0.2), 0.6(0.8)} |
| $c_2$ | {0.1(0.2), 0.7(0.8)} | {0.1(0.3), 0.6(0.7)} |
| $c_3$ | {0.4(0.4), 0.5(0.6)} | {0.4(0.4), 0.6(0.6)} |
| $c_4$ | {0.1(0.4), 0.4(0.6)} | {0.3(0.6), 0.7(0.4)} |
| $c_5$ | {0.2(0.4), 0.6(0.6)} | {0.4(0.4), 0.5(0.6)} |
|       | $A_3$ | $A_4$ |
| $c_1$ | {0.5(0.6), 0.8(0.4)} | {0.4(0.3), 0.6(0.7)} |
| $c_2$ | {0.2(0.8), 0.5(0.2)} | {0.2(0.6), 0.8(0.4)} |
| $c_3$ | {0.3(0.4), 0.6(0.6)} | {0.7(0.4), 0.8(0.6)} |
| $c_4$ | {0.5(0.4), 0.6(0.6)} | {0.4(0.6), 0.7(0.4)} |
| $c_5$ | {0.3(0.4), 0.5(0.6)} | {0.3(0.3), 0.5(0.7)} |

Step 2: Firstly, according to Equations (10) and (12), the hesitancy and credibility of decision-maker $d_k$ about pharmaceutical e-commerce platform $A_i$ under attribute $C_j$ are obtained. Then, the weight of decision-maker is adjusted by Equations (13) and (14). The adjusted weight of decision-maker is as follows:

$$\eta_k'' = (0.4126, 0.3272, 0.2602)^T$$

Step 3: Integrate the information of decision-makers using the $PHFPWA$ operator to obtain the comprehensive decision matrix $H = [h_{ij}]_{m \times n}$ (Table 7):

**Table 7.** Evaluation matrix $H$.

|       | $A_1$ | $A_2$ |
|-------|-------|-------|
| $c_1$ | {0.364(0.300), 0.800(0.700)} | {0.300(0.200), 0.645(0.800)} |
| $c_2$ | {0.175(0.200), 0.700(0.800)} | {0.100(0.300), 0.699(0.700)} |
| $c_3$ | {0.400(0.367), 0.500(0.633)} | {0.327(0.333), 0.636(0.667)} |
| $c_4$ | {0.134(0.367), 0.435(0.633)} | {0.334(0.433), 0.629(0.567)} |
| $c_5$ | {0.234(0.433), 0.600(0.567)} | {0.400(0.333), 0.500(0.667)} |
|       | $A_3$ | $A_4$ |
| $c_1$ | {0.567(0.733), 0.849(0.267)} | {0.369(0.333), 0.600(0.667)} |
| $c_2$ | {0.484(0.700), 0.700(0.300)} | {0.200(0.600), 0.575(0.400)} |
| $c_3$ | {0.420(0.500), 0.725(0.500)} | {0.647(0.500), 0.800(0.500)} |
| $c_4$ | {0.390(0.400), 0.857(0.600)} | {0.257(0.600), 0.700(0.400)} |
| $c_5$ | {0.337(0.400), 0.661(0.600)} | {0.227(0.433), 0.535(0.567)} |

Step 4: The credibility of the comprehensive decision matrix is calculated according to Equations (10) and (12), and then the reliability-based attribute weight determination model is built. The attribute weight is calculated according to Equations (18) and (19):

$$\omega_j = (0.1982, 0.1983, 0.2016, 0.2008, 0.2011)^T$$

Step 5: According to Equation (34), the dominance matrix $\Phi_j$ under attribute $C_j$ can be obtained.

$$\Phi_1 = \begin{bmatrix} 0 & 0 & 0 & 0 & 0 \\ 0.0103 & -0.2019 & 0.0421 & -0.0283 & -0.0456 \\ -0.1433 & -0.4034 & -0.0260 & 0.0441 & 0.0172 \\ -0.1256 & -0.4069 & -0.0531 & -0.0659 & -0.0430 \end{bmatrix}$$

$$\Phi_2 = \begin{bmatrix} -0.0232 & 0.0401 & -0.0928 & 0.0128 & 0.0206 \\ 0 & 0 & 0 & 0 & 0 \\ -0.1452 & -0.1555 & -0.0964 & 0.0459 & 0.0269 \\ -0.1277 & -0.1573 & -0.1069 & -0.0596 & 0.0069 \end{bmatrix}$$

$$\Phi_3 = \begin{bmatrix} 0.0639 & 0.0801 & 0.0118 & -0.0976 & -0.0381 \\ 0.0647 & 0.0694 & 0.0437 & -0.1016 & -0.0594 \\ 0 & 0 & 0 & 0 & 0 \\ 0.0308 & -0.0237 & -0.0463 & -0.1178 & -0.0574 \end{bmatrix}$$

$$\Phi_4 = \begin{bmatrix} 0.0560 & 0.0808 & 0.0241 & 0.0298 & 0.0195 \\ 0.0569 & 0.0702 & 0.0485 & 0.0269 & -0.0152 \\ -0.0691 & 0.0106 & 0.0210 & 0.0532 & 0.0260 \\ 0 & 0 & 0 & 0 & 0 \end{bmatrix}$$

Step 6: The total dominance degree of pharmaceutical e-commerce platform $A_i$ is calculated by Equation (35) as follows:

$$\Phi(A_1) = -1.4292, \Phi(A_2) = -0.8113$$
$$\Phi(A_3) = -0.1773, \Phi(A_4) = 0.4391$$

Finally, according to the size of $\Phi(A_i)$, the order of pharmaceutical e-commerce platforms can be obtained: $A_4 \succ A_3 \succ A_2 \succ A_1$, and $A_4$ should be selected as the cooperative pharmaceutical e-commerce platform.

### 6.4. Analysis of Sensitivity

Three different parameters are involved in this paper, which are risk preference coefficient $\theta$ and sensitivity coefficient $\alpha, \beta$. In order to verify the robustness of the method proposed in this paper, different parameter values are calculated in this section.

(1) When $\alpha = \beta = 0.5$, by selecting different risk preference coefficients $\theta$, the total dominance of each pharmaceutical e-commerce platform was calculated and ranked, and the result was shown in Figure 1.

(2) When $\theta = 2.25, \beta = 0.5$, by selecting different parameters $\alpha$, the total dominance of each pharmaceutical e-commerce platform was calculated and ranked, and the result was shown in Figure 2a.

(3) When $\theta = 2.25, \alpha = 0.5$, by selecting different parameters $\beta$, the total dominance of each pharmaceutical e-commerce platform was calculated and ranked, and the result was shown in Figure 2b.

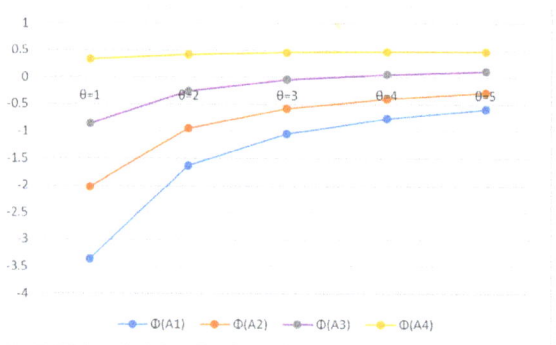

**Figure 1.** Influence of different values of $\theta$ on pharmaceutical e-commerce platform ranking.

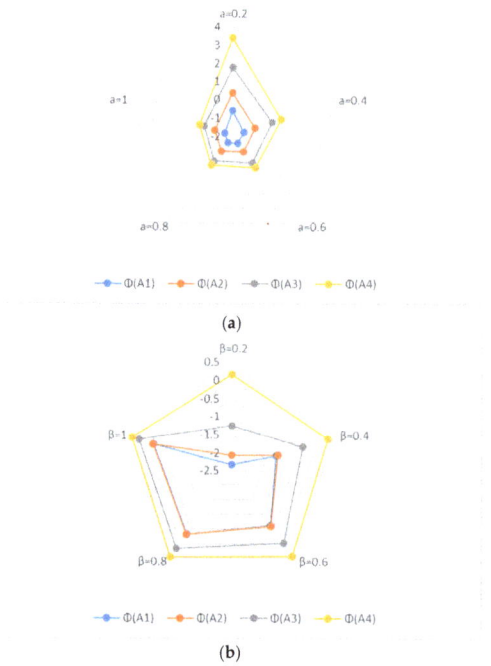

**Figure 2.** Influence of different values of $\alpha$ and $\beta$ on pharmaceutical e-commerce platform ranking. (**a**) Influence of different values of $\alpha$ on pharmaceutical e-commerce platform ranking. (**b**) Influence of different values of $\beta$ on pharmaceutical e-commerce platform ranking.

It can be clearly seen from Figures 1 and 2 that:

(1) In the case study of this paper, when parameters $\theta$, $\alpha$, and $\beta$ are changed, respectively, the optimal pharmaceutical e-commerce platform is always $A_4$.

(2) The difference between different parameter values is that the total dominance degree of pharmaceutical e-commerce platforms is different with different parameters, and the degree of differentiation between pharmaceutical e-commerce platforms is also different. According to Figure 1, the total dominance of each pharmaceutical e-commerce platform increases as $\theta$ increases. $\theta$ reflects the degree of sensitivity of the decision-maker to risk. The greater $\theta$ is, the lower the degree of risk aversion of the decision-maker is. That is, when facing risk, the smaller the impact of loss of the decision-makers and the smaller the gap of dominance degree between pharmaceutical e-commerce platforms will be. On the contrary, the smaller $\theta$ is, the higher the degree of risk aversion of decision-maker and the greater the gap of dominance degree between pharmaceutical e-commerce platforms. According to Figure 2a, with the increase of $\alpha$, the total dominance of pharmaceutical e-commerce platforms gradually decreases, and the gap between pharmaceutical e-commerce platforms is also gradually narrowed. Similarly, according to Figure 2b, the total dominance of pharmaceutical e-commerce platforms increases with the increase of $\beta$, and the gap between pharmaceutical e-commerce platforms is also narrowed.

From the above analysis, it can be seen that the changes of $\theta$, $\alpha$ and $\beta$ will affect the total dominance degree, but the impact on the final ranking results of the pharmaceutical e-commerce platform is not obvious, which proves that the method proposed in this paper has stability within a certain range.

*6.5. Comparative Analysis*

In order to illustrate the reliability and rationality of the method proposed in this paper, a comparative analysis will be conducted with the PHFWBM operator and PHFWGBM operator proposed in Ref. [22], the PHFWMGSM operator proposed in Ref. [26], and the PHFOWA operator and PHFOWG operator proposed in Ref. [27]. The results are shown in Table 8.

**Table 8.** The combined score and sorting results obtained by using different operators.

| Operator | $A_1$ | $A_2$ | $A_3$ | $A_4$ | Ranking Results |
|---|---|---|---|---|---|
| PHFPWA | −1.4292 | −0.8113 | −0.1773 | 0.4391 | $A_4 \succ A_3 \succ A_2 \succ A_1$ |
| PHFWBM [22] | 0.218 | 0.202 | 0.232 | 0.251 | $A_4 \succ A_3 \succ A_1 \succ A_2$ |
| PHFWGBM [22] | 0.372 | 0.357 | 0.394 | 0.425 | $A_4 \succ A_3 \succ A_1 \succ A_2$ |
| PHFWMGSM [26] | 0.956 | 0.947 | 0.961 | 0.967 | $A_4 \succ A_3 \succ A_1 \succ A_2$ |
| PHFOWA [27] | 0.404 | 0.433 | 0.419 | 0.453 | $A_4 \succ A_2 \succ A_3 \succ A_1$ |
| PHFOWG [27] | 0.331 | 0.364 | 0.349 | 0.380 | $A_4 \succ A_2 \succ A_3 \succ A_1$ |

It can be seen from Table 8 that the method proposed in this paper and the optimal pharmaceutical e-commerce platform obtained in Refs. [22,26,27] are all $A_4$, that is, the pharmaceutical company A should cooperate with pharmaceutical e-commerce platform $A_4$, indicating that the multi-attribute group decision-making method constructed in this paper is reasonable. The ranking results of PHFWBM operator, PHFWGBM operator, and PHFWMGSM operator are $A_4 \succ A_3 \succ A_1 \succ A_2$, and the ranking results of PHFOWA operator and PHFOWG operator are $A_4 \succ A_2 \succ A_3 \succ A_1$, which are different from the ranking results proposed by this paper ($A_4 \succ A_3 \succ A_2 \succ A_1$).

The main reasons for this difference are:

(1) Different comparison methods: The score function and deviation function defined in Ref. [21] are used in this paper to compare the size of the PHFE, while Ref. [22] used the distance of the PHFE proposed in it to compare the size of the PHFE, and the calculation is more complicated. Refs. [26,27] used score function and deviation function to compare the size of PHFE, but the function formulas used are different from those in this paper and are more outdated than those in this paper.

(2) Different aggregation methods: The above methods only focus on the relation between attributes when aggregating information, ignoring the influence of extreme value in group decision-making on the decision results. However, this paper not only considers the relation between attributes, but also pays attention to the extreme value in evaluation information, which is more consistent with reality.

(3) The irrationality of decision-makers can have an impact on decision results. The method proposed in this paper is a generalized TODIM multi-attribute group decision-making model, while the TODIM method is an effective tool for dealing with the multi-attribute decision-making problem considering the preference of the DMs. However, Refs. [22,26,27] did not consider the impact of decision-maker irrationality on decision results.

In fact, according to the assessment information in the original evaluation matrix of the experts, the values of pharmaceutical e-commerce platform $A_3$ are higher than pharmaceutical e-commerce platform $A_2$, and the values of pharmaceutical e-commerce platform $A_2$ are higher than pharmaceutical e-commerce platform $A_1$, namely $A_4 \succ A_3 \succ A_2 \succ A_1$, which agree with the decision results proposed in this paper. However, the results obtained in Refs. [22,26,27] are inconsistent with the original data, so the decision method proposed in this paper is more reliable.

## 7. Conclusions

In this paper, a probabilistic hesitant fuzzy pharmaceutical e-commerce platform selection method based on prospect theory is proposed. In the probabilistic hesitant fuzzy environment, firstly, the credibility of the decision-makers is proposed. Based on the credibility, the weights of the decision-makers are adjusted to eliminate the influence of insufficient information acquisition or personal bias on the decision results. Secondly, the PHFPA operator and PHFPWA operator are defined for information aggregation to eliminate the influence of extreme values on the decision results. Thirdly, considering that the decision-makers are not completely rational, a generalized TODIM method developed from prospect theory is introduced to construct a probabilistic hesitant fuzzy generalized TODIM multi-attribute group decision-making model. Finally, the method is applied to the selection of a pharmaceutical e-commerce platform.

In the future, we will further extend the model proposed in this paper from the two following aspects: (1) This paper used a single PA operator to assemble information. In the future, the PA operator will be considered to integrate with other operators with different characteristics, such as Bonferroni mean operator and Heronian mean operator, to solve the multi-attribute group decision-making problem more comprehensively. (2) This paper proved the effectiveness of the method with a numerical example. In order to more fully prove the feasibility and innovation of the method, actual data will be obtained for empirical research in the future.

**Author Contributions:** Conceptualization, S.L. and Z.G.; methodology, S.L. and Z.G.; writing—original draft preparation, S.L.; writing—review and editing, S.L. and Z.G. All authors have read and agreed to the published version of the manuscript.

**Funding:** This research was supported by the National Social Science Foundation of China [grant number: 20BTJ012]; Post-graduate's Innovation Fund Project of Hebei University [grant number: HBU2021bs003].

**Data Availability Statement:** Data is contained within the article.

**Conflicts of Interest:** The authors declare no conflict of interest.

## References

1. China Internet Network Information Center. The 49th Statistical Report on China's Internet Development[R/OL]. 25 February 2022. Available online: https://www.cnnic.net.cn/NMediaFile/old_attach/P020220721404263787858.pdf (accessed on 3 April 2023).
2. Zadeh, L.A. Fuzzy sets. *Inf. Control.* **1965**, *8*, 338–353. [CrossRef]
3. Webb, L. Green Purchasing: Forging a New Link in the Supply Chain. *Resource* **1994**, *6*, 14–18.
4. Handfield, R.B. Green Supply Chain: Best Practices from the Furniture Industry. *Proc.-Annu. Meet. Decis. Sci. Inst.* **1996**, *3*, 1295–1297.

5. Wu, J. A new approach for priorities trapezoidal fuzzy number reciprocal judgement matrix. *Chin. J. Manag. Sci.* **2010**, *3*, 95–100. [CrossRef]
6. Gao, X.L.; Wang, H.L.; Gan, W.H. Group decision model for green supplier selection based on trapezoidal fuzzy soft sets. *Comput. Eng. Appl.* **2017**, *1*, 265–270.
7. Li, L.; Zhang, S.Y. Aggregation method of intuitionistic fuzzy numbers with minimized maximal compromise under consensus condition. *Chin. J. Manag. Sci.* **2021**, *29*, 168–176.
8. Liu, J.B.; Peng, L.S.; Li, H.X.; Huang, B.; Zhou, X.Z. Interval-valued intuitionistic fuzzy three-way group decisions considering the unknown weight information. *Oper. Res. Manag. Sci.* **2022**, *31*, 50–57.
9. Peng, Y.; Liu, X.H.; Sun, J.B. Interval-valued intuitionistic fuzzy multi-attribute group decision making approach based on the hesitancy degrees and correlation coefficient. *Chin. J. Manag. Sci.* **2021**, *29*, 229–240.
10. Pan, F.P.; Gong, R.Z.; Tan, K.X. Multi-attribute group decision-making method for tourism projects under interval intuitionistic fuzzy information. *Stat. Decis.* **2021**, *37*, 173–176.
11. Shi, M.H.; Xiao, Q.X. Pythagorean group decision making method and its application in green supplier selection. *Oper. Res. Manag. Sci.* **2019**, *28*, 47–56.
12. Torra, V. Hesitant fuzzy sets. *Int. J. Intell. Syst.* **2010**, *25*, 529–539. [CrossRef]
13. Zhu, B. *Research and Application of Decision-Making Method Based on Preference Relation*; Southeast University: Nanjing, China, 2014.
14. Yager, R.R. The power average operator. *IEEE Trans. Syst. Man Cybern. Part A Syst. Hum.* **2001**, *31*, 724–731. [CrossRef]
15. Xu, Z.S.; Yager, R.R. Power-geometric operators and their use in group decision making. *IEEE Trans. Fuzzy Syst.* **2010**, *18*, 94–105.
16. Wan, B.T.; Lu, R.Y.; Lai, Z.Q. Interval-valued Pythagorean fuzzy power-weighted averaging operator and group decision method. *Comput. Appl. Res.* **2020**, *37*, 183–187.
17. Liu, P.D.; Liu, X. The neutrosophic number generalized weighted power averaging operator and its application in multiple attribute group decision making. *Int. J. Mach. Learn. Cybern.* **2018**, *9*, 347–358. [CrossRef]
18. Liang, D.C.; Darko, A.P.; Zeng, J. Interval-valued pythagorean fuzzy power average-based MULTIMOORA method for multi-criteria decision-making. *J. Exp. Theor. Artif. Intell.* **2020**, *32*, 845–874. [CrossRef]
19. Wang, J.; Shang, X.P.; Bai, K.Y.; Xu, Y. A new approach to cubic q-rung orthopair fuzzy multiple attribute group decision-making based on power Muirhead. *Neural Comput. Appl.* **2020**, *32*, 14087–14112. [CrossRef]
20. Li, L.; Ji, C.J.; Wang, J. A Novel Multi-attribute Group Decision-Making Method Based on q-Rung Dual Hesitant Fuzzy Information and Extended Power Average Operators. *Cogn. Comput.* **2021**, *13*, 1345–1362. [CrossRef]
21. Xu, Z.S.; Zhou, W. Consensus building with a group of decision makers under the hesitant probabilistic fuzzy environment. *Fuzzy Optim. Decis. Mak.* **2017**, *16*, 481–503. [CrossRef]
22. Wu, J.; Liu, X.D.; Zhang, S.T.; Wang, Z.Z. Probabilistic hesitant fuzzy Bonferroni mean operators and their application in decision making. *Fuzzy Syst. Math.* **2019**, *33*, 116–126.
23. Liu, S.J.; Guo, Z.X. Probabilistic hesitant fuzzy multi-attribute decision-making method based on improved distance measurement. *J. Intell. Fuzzy Syst.* **2022**, *43*, 5953–5964. [CrossRef]
24. Llamazares, B. An analysis of the generalized TODIM method. *Eur. J. Oper. Res.* **2018**, *269*, 1041–1049. [CrossRef]
25. Ministry of Commerce of the People's Republic of China. 2021 Statistical Report on Pharmaceutical Circulation Industry[R/OL]. 6 September 2022. Available online: http://images.mofcom.gov.cn/scyxs/202209/20220906181153114.pdf (accessed on 3 April 2023).
26. Wu, W.Y.; Li, Y.; Ni, C.W.; Zhu, X.H.; Wu, Z.J. Probabilistic hesitant fuzzy Maclaurin geometric symmetric averaging operator and its group decision model. *Syst. Sci. Math.* **2020**, *40*, 1074–1089.
27. Wu, W.Y.; Li, Y.; Jin, F.F.; Ni, Z.W.; Zhu, X.H. Group Decision Making Model Based on Probabilistic Hesitant Fuzzy Information Aggregation Operations. *Pattern Recognit. Artif. Intell.* **2017**, *30*, 894–906.

**Disclaimer/Publisher's Note:** The statements, opinions and data contained in all publications are solely those of the individual author(s) and contributor(s) and not of MDPI and/or the editor(s). MDPI and/or the editor(s) disclaim responsibility for any injury to people or property resulting from any ideas, methods, instructions or products referred to in the content.

Article

# A Fully Completed Spherical Fuzzy Data-Driven Model for Analyzing Employee Satisfaction in Logistics Service Industry

Phi-Hung Nguyen

Research Center of Applied Sciences, Faculty of Business, FPT University, Hanoi 100000, Vietnam; hungnp30@fe.edu.vn

**Abstract:** This study proposes a two-stage MCDM model that combines Delphi and decision-making trial and evaluation laboratory methods based on spherical fuzzy sets (SF-Delphi and SF-DEMATEL) to analyze the motivation and demotivation factors affecting employee satisfaction in the Vietnamese logistics service industry. In the first stage, the SF-Delphi approach is used to gather expert opinions and develop consensus on the significance of criteria. In the second stage, the SF-DEMATEL technique explores causal linkages between the criteria and identifies root causes of the issues. Based on a comprehensive literature review and feedback from 40 experts, this study identified crucial factors affecting employee satisfaction related to both motivation and demotivation aspects. The findings of this study provide recommendations for managers to improve employee satisfaction, such as establishing clear and detailed wage and bonus rules, offering training courses, developing a positive work culture, recognizing employee efforts, and addressing poor treatment by supervisors and inadequate leadership support. Furthermore, the proposed model accurately identifies essential elements, represents uncertainty, adapts to various contexts, has resilience and accuracy, and has practical implications for mitigating demotivating factors and enhancing motivation, thereby positively influencing employee satisfaction in the logistics service industry.

**Keywords:** motivation; demotivation; employee satisfaction; logistics service industry; spherical fuzzy sets; Delphi; DEMATEL; Vietnam

**MSC:** 97M30; 91B02; 62P05; 91B84

Citation: Nguyen, P.-H. A Fully Completed Spherical Fuzzy Data-Driven Model for Analyzing Employee Satisfaction in Logistics Service Industry. *Mathematics* **2023**, *11*, 2235. https://doi.org/10.3390/math11102235

Academic Editors: Jorge de Andres Sanchez and Laura González-Vila Puchades

Received: 13 April 2023
Revised: 6 May 2023
Accepted: 8 May 2023
Published: 10 May 2023

**Copyright:** © 2023 by the author. Licensee MDPI, Basel, Switzerland. This article is an open access article distributed under the terms and conditions of the Creative Commons Attribution (CC BY) license (https://creativecommons.org/licenses/by/4.0/).

## 1. Introduction

Logistics is a crucial aspect of commercial and economic systems, playing a significant role in the global economy. In Vietnam, the logistics industry is thriving and productive, with an average annual growth rate of 14–16% and a value of around USD 40–42 billion per year. Vietnam's status as an emerging logistics market was confirmed by Agility's 2022 ranking, which placed it as the 11th top market out of 50 [1]. Additionally, Vietnam's logistics performance index (LPI) ranking by the World Bank in 2023 places it at 43rd out of 139 countries and fourth in the ASEAN region, following Singapore, Malaysia, and Thailand [2].

It is vital to approach the logistics industry with caution, diligence, and foresight due to its vast and varied activities worldwide. Challenges can arise depending on the job's stage and type, such as meeting deadlines for document completion, complying with new import/export regulations, ensuring transportation compliance, meeting transparency requirements in goods production, and navigating time zones or cultural differences with agents [3]. Handling these complex and demanding challenges requires highly skilled individuals who can work under pressure. As such, human resource management (HRM) plays a critical role in understanding employee satisfaction, which significantly impacts the success of service sectors such as logistics [4].

To optimize productivity and engagement within a workforce, leaders and managers must understand the factors contributing to employee satisfaction. However, numerous previous studies [5–8] have shown that using quantitative analysis to study employee satisfaction can be challenging due to the intangible nature of employee motivation and demotivation [9]. Furthermore, quantitative analysis fails to account for the inherent uncertainty and imprecision of human behavior, leading to a limited ability to comprehend the complexity of employee satisfaction. Qualitative analysis, on the other hand, can provide more profound comprehension of the underlying factors that influence employee behavior, but it can be resource-intensive and struggles to quantify the interrelationships among various factors [10]. Consequently, a comprehensive research approach is necessary to identify and quantify the interrelationships among factors related to employee motivation and demotivation.

To address this problem, multiple criteria decision making (MCDM) presents a viable solution by developing and implementing decision-making models for issues that incorporate multiple criteria or decision attributes in situations where uncertainties and incomplete information exist. The features commonly utilized can be imprecise and capable of being represented as fuzzy information [11]. Fuzzy set theory, initially proposed by Zadeh [12], has received significant attention from researchers worldwide who have explored its theoretical and practical aspects. Researchers have extended general fuzzy sets since 1965, resulting in various extensions, such as type-2 fuzzy sets by Zadeh [13], intuitionistic fuzzy sets by Atanassov [14], neutrosophic sets by Smarandache [15], hesitant fuzzy sets by Torra [16], Pythagorean fuzzy sets by Yager [17], picture fuzzy sets by Cuong [18], and spherical fuzzy sets by Mahmood et al. [19] and Kahraman and Gündoğdu [20], which have gained popularity in the literature. Spherical fuzzy sets (SFSs) are the recent extension of fuzzy sets, allowing experts to express their indeterminacy, membership, and non-membership degrees as long as they are within the unit sphere, which is a notable feature that distinguishes SFSs from other fuzzy set models [4]. As a result, MCDM-model-based SFSs have been applied in various fields, such as international trade [21], vaccination [22], supply chain management [23], tourism and hospitality management [4], etc.

In the context of HRM problems, it is appropriate to employ an MCDM approach that utilizes SFSs to capture the uncertainty and ambiguity inherent in expert evaluations. Among the various MCDM models, the Delphi and decision-making trial and evaluation laboratory (DEMATEL) methods represent a balanced approach between quantitative and qualitative analysis, including subjective judgments and linguistic variables typically ignored by conventional research methods [24]. Notably, the Delphi method serves as a useful MCDM tool for verifying crucial factors before evaluating them. The DEMATEL model is better suited than the analytic hierarchy process (AHP) and analytic network process (ANP) models for exploring the interrelationships among the various factors. The DEMATEL model evaluates the interrelationships among factors, capturing both direct and indirect relationships, leading to a more comprehensive understanding of the factors influencing employee motivation and demotivation. Unlike previous studies reviewed in this literature, this study aims to better reflect the interrelationships between criteria that directly affect the decision-making process. Rather than treating criteria as independent concepts, this research proposes a two-stage, data-driven approach that combines SFS and MCDM models to comprehensively analyze and evaluate the significant factors that impact employee satisfaction in the Vietnamese logistics service industry from both motivational and demotivational perspectives.

The research questions guiding this study are as follows:

(i) What are the critical factors that impact employee satisfaction from both motivation and demotivation perspectives in the logistics service industry in Vietnam?
(ii) What is the nature of the interrelationships between these from both motivation and demotivation perspectives in the logistics service industry in Vietnam?

The following research goals are expected to be realized by this study:

(i) Identify the critical factors that impact employee satisfaction from both motivation and demotivation perspectives in the logistics service industry in Vietnam.

(ii) Quantify the interrelationships among these factors from both motivation and demotivation perspectives in the logistics service industry in Vietnam.

Remarkably, in contrast to prior studies such as [25–28], the proposed model, which comprises SF-Delphi and SF-DEMATEL, involves fully computing SFSs to detect and measure the interdependencies among the critical factors impacting employee satisfaction in the Vietnamese logistics service industry, thereby leveraging the strengths of both SFS and MCDM models.

The structure of this study is organized into several sections. Section 2 presents a comprehensive literature review covering related theories, employee motivation and demotivation perspectives, and previous research that applied MCDM models in HRM. Section 3 describes spherical fuzzy sets and the proposed method. Section 4 presents a case study from Vietnam, including the main results and discussion. Finally, conclusions, implications, and suggestions for further investigation are summarized in Section 5.

## 2. Literature Review
### 2.1. Theoretical Frameworks

Employee satisfaction is crucial to any organization's success, and various theories have been proposed to understand it better.

Maslow's hierarchy of needs theory [29] is often used in HRM research to understand employee behavior, which states that human needs can be organized into a hierarchy, starting with basic physiological needs, such as food, water, and shelter, and progressing to higher needs, such as safety, love and belonging, esteem, and self-actualization. Maslow suggests that employees are motivated by fulfilling these needs, and once a lower-level need is met, the employee is motivated by the next higher need [30]. Additionally, it can provide a valuable framework for understanding the different levels of needs that must be met to increase employee satisfaction and motivation. By including this theory in the theoretical framework, this study can provide a comprehensive understanding of the factors that impact employee satisfaction in the Vietnamese logistics service industry.

Herzberg's two-factor theory [31] is another popular theory that explains the impact of hygiene and motivators on employee motivation and satisfaction. Hygiene factors are associated with the work environment, such as salary, working conditions, and company policies, and although they can prevent dissatisfaction, they do not necessarily motivate employees. On the other hand, motivators are linked to the nature of the work, such as job recognition, growth opportunities, and achievement, and can lead to satisfaction and motivation [32]. This theory is relevant to the present study as it emphasizes the importance of both environmental and intrinsic factors in influencing employee satisfaction. Additionally, equity theory [33] suggests that employees are motivated by the perceived fairness of their treatment in the workplace. Employees compare their inputs (effort, skills, experience) to their outputs (salary, recognition, promotion) with their peers. If they perceive inequity, they may become demotivated, leading to lower productivity and satisfaction [34]. This theory highlights the importance of fairness and the negative impact of perceived inequity on employee motivation and satisfaction.

Similarly, Victor Vroom's expectancy theory [35] implies that employees are motivated by the expectation that their efforts will lead to desired outcomes. The theory proposes that employees make decisions based on their belief that their efforts will lead to good performance, which leads to rewards such as recognition, promotion, and pay raises. Thus, employees are more motivated when they perceive a clear relationship between their efforts, performance, and rewards [36]. Moreover, self-determination theory highlights that people are naturally motivated to pursue their goals and interests and that autonomy, competence, and relatedness are essential for intrinsic motivation. Autonomy refers to the need for control over one's work and environment, competence refers to the need to feel competent and capable of achieving goals, and relatedness refers to the need for social connection and belongingness [37].

By integrating these theories into the theoretical framework, the study can thoroughly examine the factors that affect employee satisfaction, encompassing both motivational and demotivational aspects. The suggested approach can aid stakeholders in devising strategies and implementing practices that increase employee motivation while mitigating demotivation. This, in turn, can lead to improvements in HRM practices in the Vietnamese logistics service sector.

*2.2. Employee Satisfaction, Motivation and Demotivation*

Employee satisfaction refers to an employee's level of contentment or fulfilment with their job and work environment [38]. It encompasses various aspects, such as job satisfaction, pay and benefits, opportunities for growth and development, recognition and appreciation, workplace relationships, and work-life balance. High employee satisfaction can increase motivation, productivity, and organizational commitment. It can also result in lower employee turnover rates and absenteeism, as satisfied employees are more likely to remain with their current employer. Employee satisfaction is essential for the success of any organization as it plays a significant role in attracting and retaining talented employees, maintaining a positive organizational culture, and ultimately achieving business objectives. Therefore, organizations must prioritize employee satisfaction and implement strategies to ensure employees feel valued and supported in their roles.

Employee motivation is the driving force that propels individuals to take action and make decisions to achieve their goals [39]. In the workplace, motivation is the willingness of employees to exert and maintain an effort towards reaching organizational goals. There are two types of motivation: intrinsic and extrinsic [40]. Extrinsic motivation includes external incentives, such as salary, promotions, benefits, and work environment, while intrinsic motivation includes the internal drive to use one's talents, meet challenges, and receive recognition for accomplishments. High levels of employee motivation are linked with increased job satisfaction and engagement. The concept of motivation is complex and influenced by various factors, including working conditions, resource availability, infrastructure, supervision, training, and career advancement opportunities [40,41]. The interactions between employees and their workplaces affect the development of motivation, making it a psychological and transactional process [6,42].

Employee demotivation refers to the state of lowered motivation or even the absence of motivation among employees, which can negatively impact their job performance, health, and overall well-being [43]. It can be caused by poor leadership, lack of organizational support, unfulfilled needs and expectations, or a hostile work environment [44]. Demotivated employees experience frustration, disappointment, and low morale, leading to decreased productivity, absenteeism, and turnover [45]. Therefore, management must identify and address the causes of employee demotivation by implementing various policies and strategies to improve their job satisfaction, well-being, and engagement.

*2.3. Motivation Categories*

(A) Compensation and benefits: This dimension includes salary, bonuses, benefits, and perks. Intrinsically motivated employees (i.e., who genuinely enjoy their work) and those who are motivated by extrinsic rewards (i.e., pay and perks) both perform better for both themselves and their companies, with lesser burnout, fewer physical symptoms, and higher levels of commitment [46].

(B) Career growth and development: This dimension includes factors such as opportunities for advancement, training, and development. Employees who feel they have opportunities to grow and develop their skills may be more motivated and invested in their work. Opportunities for training are generally linked to greater motivation levels, are widely seen as motivators, and are favorably correlated with satisfaction [41,47,48]. According to workers' employment intentions, the likelihood of receiving a promotion is a negative predictor of their intention to quit, indicating that extrinsic incentives also favorably affect their levels of commitment [49].

(C) Work environment and culture: This dimension includes workplace safety, cleanliness, and culture. Employees who work in a positive and supportive environment may be more motivated and engaged. The interactions between people and their work environment lead to motivation, which is a psychological and transactional process [6]. According to [50,51], workplace improvement can impact performance and behaviors by encouraging self-motivated actions and demoralizing ineffective personnel.

(D) Recognition and feedback: This dimension includes positive feedback, constructive criticism, and recognition for good performance. This is when someone is acknowledged for a job well done, feels appreciated for accomplishing or finishing a task, and is given the appropriate credit for it [8]. Employees who receive regular feedback and recognition for their work may be more motivated and engaged.

(E) Organizational support: This dimension includes organizational communication, organizational justice, organizational commitment, and employee retention strategies. When an organization supports employees, they may feel more inspired and committed [52].

(F) Management style: This dimension includes leadership, trust in management and purposeful work. The motivation of employees is directly impacted by management style [5]. People may feel more motivated when they work with appropriate leadership and trust the organization's governance.

Reviewing previous research papers and referring to experts' recommendations, our study proposes 38 factors divided into six dimensions. The names and meanings of the factors are presented in Table 1.

Table 1. Employees' motivation factors.

| Dimension | | Factor | Description | References |
|---|---|---|---|---|
| A<br>Compensation and benefits | M1 | Equity in pay | The fairness and equality in pay between employees who perform similar work. | [46,50,51] |
| | M2 | Base salary | The fixed amount of money paid to an employee for their work. | |
| | M3 | Compensation | Providing fair and competitive wages and benefits. For example, offering a bonus or salary increase to an employee who consistently meets or exceeds performance goals. | |
| | M4 | Relaxation allowances | A part of the time is added to the primary time to allow workers or operators to recover after fatigue. | |
| | M5 | Bonus structure | A system of extra payments given to employees based on their performance or company profits. | |
| | M6 | Performance-based pay | The compensation given to employees based on their individual or team performance. | |
| | M7 | Health insurance | The coverage provided to employees to help pay for medical expenses. | |
| | M8 | Retirement benefits | The financial benefits given to employees after they retire from the company. | |
| | M9 | Benefits package | The collection of benefits offered to employees, including health insurance, retirement plans, and other perks. | |
| B<br>Career growth and development | M10 | Professional development | Offering opportunities for skill-building and career advancement. For example, providing training programs, mentorship, or tuition reimbursement for further education | [47,48] |
| | M11 | Opportunities for creativity and innovation | Providing opportunities for employees to share their ideas and implement new strategies. | |
| | M12 | Training | Providing opportunities for employees to learn and grow. | |
| | M13 | Opportunities for social connection | Providing opportunities for employees to connect and build relationships with their colleagues. | |
| | M14 | Challenging work | Providing opportunities for employees to work on challenging projects and assignments that stretch their skills and abilities. For example, assigning a complex project that requires problem-solving and creativity | |

Table 1. Cont.

| Dimension | | Factor | Description | References |
|---|---|---|---|---|
| C<br>Work environment and culture | M15 | Work-life balance | Supporting employees' personal lives and well-being and, for example, offering flexible work arrangements or generous vacation time. | [6,50,51] |
| | M16 | Flexibility | Being responsive to changing circumstances and accommodating employees' needs by, for example, allowing employees to adjust their work schedule or take a leave of absence when needed. | |
| | M17 | Resources and support | Refers to the resources and support employees required to perform their job duties. | |
| | M18 | Job security | Providing a stable and secure work environment. For example, communicating clearly about the company's plans for growth and stability and providing fair and consistent employment policies. | |
| | M19 | Teamwork | Fostering a culture of collaboration and teamwork. For example, encouraging employees to work together on projects and providing opportunities for team-building activities. | |
| | M20 | Workload | Refers to the amount of work an employee is responsible for completing. | |
| | M21 | Positive work culture | Fostering a culture of trust, respect, and collaboration. For example, encouraging open communication and teamwork and recognizing and addressing toxic behavior. | |
| | M22 | Social support | Refers to the support employees receive from colleagues and supervisors. | |
| | M23 | Physical environment | Refers to the conditions in which employees work, such as lighting, noise levels, and temperature. | |
| | M24 | Autonomy | It gives employees the freedom to make decisions and take ownership of their work, empowering them to work on projects that align with their strengths and interests. | |
| D<br>Recognition and feedback | M25 | Positive feedback and constructive criticism | Providing constructive feedback and encouragement to employees. | [8,50,51] |
| | M26 | Recognition | Acknowledging employees' contributions and achievements. For example, publicly thanking an employee who went above and beyond on a project. | |
| | M27 | Employee empowerment | Giving employees the authority to make decisions and take responsibility for their work allows them to make decisions independently without needing approval from higher-ups. | |
| | M28 | Recognition of individual differences | Understanding and valuing each employee's unique perspectives, backgrounds, and experiences. For example, providing accommodations for employees with disabilities and celebrating diversity and inclusion in the workplace. | |
| E<br>Organizational support | M29 | Perceived organizational support | The degree to which employees perceive the company as supportive of their well-being and success. | [50–52] |
| | M30 | Employee satisfaction surveys | Surveys are used to measure employee satisfaction with various aspects of their job. | |
| | M31 | Organizational support | The support provided to employees to help them succeed in their roles. | |
| | M32 | Organizational communication | The degree to which communication is effective and efficient within the company. | |
| | M33 | Employee retention strategies | The strategies used to retain employees within the company. | |
| | M34 | Organizational commitment | The degree to which employees are committed to the company's goals and values. | |
| | M35 | Organizational justice | The fairness and equality in the treatment of employees within the company. | |
| F<br>Management style | M36 | Trust in management | The degree to which employees trust and have confidence in the company's management. | [50,51] |
| | M37 | Leadership | Providing effective leadership that inspires and guides employees. For example, modeling the behavior they want to see in their employees and providing clear direction and feedback. | |
| | M38 | Purposeful work | Providing employees with a sense of purpose and meaning in their work. | |

*2.4. Demotivation Categories*

Likewise, there are several broad categories into which the demotivating causes for workers in the logistic service industry can be divided. The following examples of dimensions are possible:

(G) Poor Management: This dimension includes factors such as lack of supervisor support, poor communication, and inadequate management. It is believed that three main organizational management theories have been supported [53–56]. These include the "distributive justice theory", which emphasizes equity in resource distribution; the "procedural justice theory", which emphasizes fairness in the procedures and decisions that lead to results; and the "interactional justice theory", which emphasizes the fairness that employees experience at work when interacting with others. Employees under poor management may feel undervalued and unsupported, decreasing motivation and engagement. Particularly, inadequate leadership support affects employees' perceptions regarding insufficient support from their leaders. It is related to the organization's overall management and how leaders are perceived in their roles. Demotivation in a workplace can also result from people's perceptions of organizational politics, in which people behave to further their interests at the expense of others or in opposition to organizational aims [57].

(H) Inadequate compensation and benefits: This dimension includes low pay, lack of benefits, and inadequate perks. The biggest issue causing employee demotivation is the issue of low pay and salaries [58]. Poor pay leads to discontent and a lack of motivation. Employees who feel they are not fairly compensated for their work may become demotivated and disengaged.

(I) Lack of career growth and development opportunities: This dimension includes limited opportunities for advancement, lack of training and development, and poor career paths [59]. The ability to advance one's career inside an organization is provided by career development. A lack of professional development would make it difficult for logistics and supply chains to hold onto their critical human assets in a growing market where logistical knowledge is in short supply [60].

(J) Poor work environment and culture: This dimension includes workplace safety, cleanliness, job security, workload pressure, and culture. All organizations have traditions that shape their culture and affect employees' behavior. Demotivating factors in this category include those specific to the organization, including organizational culture and ethics, leadership, and decision-making [43]. Furthermore, a lack of freedom can undermine control and ownership over one's work. High workloads can positively or negatively impact creativity and performance at work. On the positive side, the intellectually demanding nature of a project can make up for excessive workloads. On the negative side, when employees are under too much pressure to complete their tasks, it can result in stress, mistakes, and a general drop in productivity [61]. On the other hand, inept leadership behavior can have a negative impact on employee satisfaction. It refers to the inappropriate behavior of leaders, such as disrespect, discrimination, or favoritism, which can create a hostile work environment and culture. This is similar to the way that poor physical surroundings can impact inspiration for creativity and depress morale if they are not viewed as attractive [62]. Employees who work in a harmful or toxic work environment may become demotivated and disengaged from their work.

(K) Lack of recognition and feedback: This dimension includes factors such as lack of feedback, criticism without guidance, and lack of recognition for good performance [63]. Employees will become demotivated in a workplace with a feedback system that only emphasizes the poor aspects of their job and does not praise the good or provide constructive criticism [64].

After evaluating prior research publications and consulting expert recommendations, our analysis suggests 21 factors broken down into the five dimensions mentioned earlier. Table 2 lists the names and definitions of the factors.

Table 2. Employees' demotivation factors.

| Dimension | | Factor | Description | References |
|---|---|---|---|---|
| G<br>Poor management | DM1 | Poor organization ethics | False accounting, data privacy, nepotism, and discrimination are just some of the ethical dilemmas in the workplace. | [53–56] |
| | DM2 | Inadequate leadership support | Leaders do not provide support and guidance. | |
| | DM3 | Poor management | Bad management practices, such as micromanagement, and lack of communication and support, can demotivate employees. | |
| | DM4 | Bad treatment by supervisors | Employees who feel treated unfairly or differently than their colleagues can become demotivated. Employers need to ensure that policies and procedures are applied consistently and fairly to all employees. | |
| | DM5 | Working excessively long hours | Working 12 or more hours per day (Dembe et al., 2005). | |
| H<br>Inadequate compensation and benefits | DM6 | Back pay | Workers do not receive wages according to the company's commitment time. | [58] |
| | DM7 | Inadequate salaries and rewards | Salary and bonuses are paid below the capacity and efficiency of the employee. | |
| | DM8 | Unfair pay in comparison to colleagues | Some businesses pay men more than women in the same job position | |
| I<br>Lack of career growth and development opportunities | DM9 | Inadequate opportunity for career promotion | Lack of advancement opportunities is the most commonly cited reason for employees to seek new jobs elsewhere. Lack of advancement creates morale problems when employees realize they are stuck in a dead-end position. | [59,60] |
| | DM10 | Underutilization of skills | Workers have skills beyond those needed to do their work. | |
| | DM11 | Inadequate training and development | Employees without the necessary training and resources to perform their job effectively can become demotivated. Employers need to ensure that employees are trained and supported. | |
| | DM12 | Inadequate freedom in the day-to-day conduct of work | Employees do not have a chance to propose and coordinate the work freely or have adequate autonomy to execute project deliverables | |
| J<br>Poor work environment and culture | DM13 | Lack of job security | Employees who feel their job is insecure can become demotivated and may not feel invested in their work. Employers need to provide job security and stability. | [43,61,62] |
| | DM14 | Poor working environment | Employees who work in unpleasant or unsafe conditions can become demotivated and may not feel valued by their employer. Employers must ensure the workplace is safe, clean, and comfortable. | |
| | DM15 | Inept leadership personal behaviors | Leaders ignoring employees' opinions and suggestions can negatively impact their motivation. | |
| | DM16 | Unsafe work conditions | Employees who work in unacceptable conditions, such as lack of proper personal protective equipment, unqualified personnel working with dangerous tools, improper workstation layout, and poorly maintained equipment, can become demotivated. | |
| | DM17 | Unhealthy competition among co-workers | If the goal is for every individual to win on their own, then individuals will do whatever it takes to win against their 'competition'. The result is that people are always trying to sabotage one another. | |
| | DM18 | Excessive workload pressure | Employees who are overworked and overwhelmed can become demotivated and burnt out. Employers must ensure that the workload is reasonable and that employees have the resources and support to manage their work effectively. | |
| K<br>Lack of recognition and feedback | DM19 | Poor feedback and inappropriate evaluation system | Employees would work harder if they felt their efforts were being recognized. When managers offer little or no feedback, it can lead to employees feeling ignored by their manager and not feeling valued by their employer. | [63,64] |
| | DM20 | Low participation in decision making | Workers who are less involved in decision-making may feel their capacity is not recognized. Their opinions may be seen as less valuable for managers. | |
| | DM21 | Lack of recognition | Employees who feel their work is not appreciated or acknowledged can become demotivated. Lack of recognition can lead to feelings of unimportance and low morale. | |

## 2.5. MCDM Methods in HRM Sector

In recent years, MCDM methods have gained popularity in human resource management to achieve organizational sustainability. MCDM models are of value in HRM due to the complexity of the decision-making processes involved in managing employees, such as employee selection, promotion, training, performance evaluation, and compensation. By employing MCDM techniques, HR managers can make more informed and objective decisions, considering the various criteria and trade-offs involved. AHP has been applied in various HRM-related decision-making processes, such as recruitment and selection [65], performance evaluation [66] and employee retention [67].

Among commonly used MCDM models in HRM, the technique for order preference by similarity to ideal solution (TOPSIS) has been widely applied. For instance, Saeidi et al. [68] introduced a new approach that combines stepwise weight assessment ratio analysis (SWARA) and TOPSIS methods to prioritize factors and alternatives in sustainable HRM problems. Similarly, Lai et al. [69] applied MCDM methods to identify potential talents in a high-tech company's sales and marketing team, while Stević et al. [70] used MCDM to evaluate and motivate drivers in an international transport company.

Regarding employee productivity and selection, Knežević et al. [71] integrated fuzzy sets and TOPSIS to analyze employee productivity in selected D-electrical power supply companies operating in Serbia. Thus, Safari et al. [72] ranked bank branches based on employee empowerment using fuzzy AHP and Vlse Kriterijumska Optimizacija Kompromisno Resenje (VIKOR) methods to determine the weights of the criteria and rank the branches based on eight indexes that have a significant impact on employee empowerment. These studies provide valuable insights into the practical application of MCDM methods in real-world employee productivity and selection scenarios.

To evaluate different aspects of HRM, Kalvakolanu et al. [73] applied a combination of Entropy, CRiteria Importance Through Inter-criteria Correlation (CRITIC), and TOPSIS methods to measure job satisfaction levels of airport employees through a shorter variant of the Minnesota Satisfaction Questionnaire (MSQ). Esangbedo et al. [66] used two new hybrid MCDM methods to evaluate human resource information systems provided by different vendors. Grey-PA-FUCOM combines the simple point-allocation method and the advanced FUCOM method. At the same time, the grey regime is an extension of the classical regime method based on grey system theory, while Malebye et al. [74] proposed an objective selection sequence for job candidates, which involves a quantitative/mathematical measure and two other independent measures to validate the decision taken. The approach combines statistics and operations research (StoR) methods, such as SAW, TOPSIS, and WP. SAW is used in the first-cut selection process, while TOPSIS and WP validate selections.

In summary, the existing literature has demonstrated the potential of MCDM methods to solve various HRM problems. MCDM methods offer a flexible and practical decision-making approach in complex situations where multiple criteria must be considered. Incorporating multiple criteria and decision-makers' preferences can help organizations make informed and objective decisions, improve their productivity, and enhance their competitiveness in the marketplace. These studies illustrate the various applications and benefits of MCDM in HRM contexts, including sustainable HRM, talent identification, employee motivation, productivity analysis, recruitment, and supplier selection.

## 2.6. Research Gaps

Despite the growing popularity of MCDM methods in HRM contexts, there is a lack of research on the application of MCDM in analyzing motivation and demotivation factors impacting employee satisfaction in the logistics service sector, particularly in Vietnam. Therefore, there is a need for a comprehensive MCDM model that can identify and prioritize critical factors and how they affect employee satisfaction in the logistics service industry in Vietnam.

In addition, there is a gap in the literature on combining SFS and MCDM models in HRM contexts. Furthermore, established MCDM models have limitations in handling complex and multidimensional problems, such as employee satisfaction. In particular, pairwise comparisons among various factors can be time-consuming and prone to errors, and the assumption of independence among decision criteria is often not valid in real-world situations. Thus, it is necessary to investigate the efficacy of the spherical fuzzy decision-making approach in the field of HRM. To overcome these limitations, this study proposes a two-stage Delphi and DEMATEL method based on spherical fuzzy sets for analyzing the motivation and demotivation factors affecting employee satisfaction in the Vietnamese logistics service.

The proposed method can incorporate subjective judgments and linguistic variables often overlooked in traditional research methods, and it can capture both direct and indirect relationships among factors, providing a more comprehensive understanding of the factors influencing employee satisfaction. In the first stage, the SF-Delphi method is applied to identify the vital motivation and demotivation factors affecting employee satisfaction. The SF-Delphi method helps to remove unsuitable factors effectively and reach a consensus among experts, and the use of SFSs can handle uncertainty and imprecision in the experts' judgments. In the second stage, the SF-DEMATEL method evaluates the interrelationships among the identified factors.

The proposed research can contribute to the existing literature by providing insights into the application of MCDM and SFSs in HRM contexts and its potential benefits for organizations in the Vietnamese logistics service industry context.

## 3. Methodology

### 3.1. Spherical Fuzzy Sets (SFSs)

According to Mahmood et al. [19] or Kahraman and Gündoğdu [20], when it comes to complex issues, individuals tend to convey their level of satisfaction, abstention, and dissatisfaction in different ways. In response to this, the concept of SFSs was developed, which includes the degree of membership $\alpha(x)$, the neutral-membership degree $\beta(x)$, and the non-membership degree $\gamma(x)$, ultimately providing a more comprehensive understanding of the situation. Spherical fuzzy linguistic scales are presented in Figure 1 and Table 3.

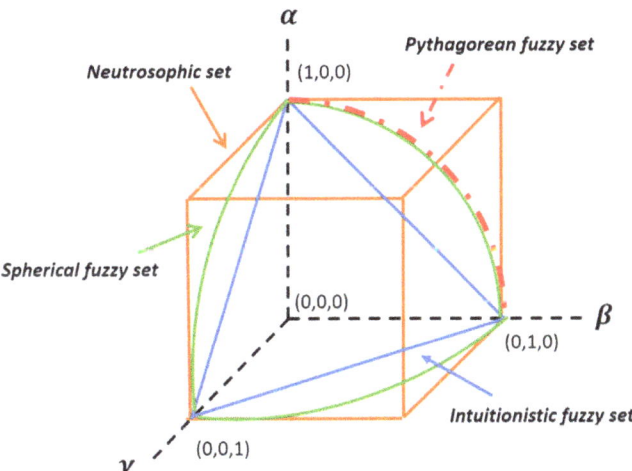

**Figure 1.** Representations of SFSs [4].

**Table 3.** Linguistic scales.

| Scales | (α, β, γ) | Score Index (SI) |
|---|---|---|
| Absolutely more importance (AMI) | (0.9, 0.1, 0.1) | 9 |
| Very high importance (VHI) | (0.8, 0.2, 0.2) | 7 |
| High importance (HI) | (0.7, 0.3, 0.3) | 5 |
| Slightly more importance (SMI) | (0.6, 0.4, 0.4) | 3 |
| Equal importance (EI) | (0.5, 0.5, 0.5) | 1 |
| Slightly low importance (SLI) | (0.4, 0.6, 0.4) | 1/3 |
| Low importance (LI) | (0.3, 0.7, 0.3) | 1/5 |
| Very low importance (VLI) | (0.2, 0.8, 0.2) | 1/7 |
| Absolutely low importance (ALI) | (0.1, 0.9, 0.1) | 1/9 |

**Definition 1.** *Spherical fuzzy set $\widetilde{F}_S$ of the universe X is denoted as follows:*

$$\widetilde{F}_S = \{x, (\alpha_{\widetilde{F}_S}(x), \beta_{\widetilde{F}_S}(x), \gamma_{\widetilde{F}_S}(x)) | x \in X\} \quad (1)$$

$$\alpha_{\widetilde{F}_S}(x) : X \to [0,1], \beta_{\widetilde{F}_S}(x) : X \to [0,1], \gamma_{\widetilde{F}_S}(x) : X \to [0,1] \quad (2)$$

*and*

$$0 \leq \alpha_{\widetilde{F}_S}^2(x) + \beta_{\widetilde{F}_S}^2(x) + \gamma_{\widetilde{F}_S}^2(x) \leq 1 \quad (3)$$

*with $\forall x \in X$, for each $x$, $\alpha_{\widetilde{F}_S}(x)$ for membership, $\beta_{\widetilde{F}_S}(x)$ for non − membership and $\gamma_{\widetilde{F}_S}(x)$ for hesitancy levels of $x$ to $\widetilde{F}_S$.*

**Definition 2.** *Basic operations of SFS are presented as follows. Let $\widetilde{S}_s = (\alpha_{\widetilde{S}_s}, \beta_{\widetilde{S}_s}, \gamma_{\widetilde{S}_s})$ and $F_s = (\alpha_{F_s}, \beta_{F_s}, \gamma_{F_s})$ be two SFSs.*
*Union operation*

$$\widetilde{S}_s \cup \widetilde{F}_s = \left\{ max\{\alpha_{\widetilde{S}_s}, \alpha_{\widetilde{F}_s}\}, min\{\beta_{\widetilde{S}_s}, \beta_{\widetilde{F}_s}\}, min\left\{ \left(1 - \left((max\{\alpha_{\widetilde{S}_s}, \alpha_{\widetilde{F}_s}\})^2 + (min\{\beta_{\widetilde{S}_s}, \beta_{\widetilde{F}_s}\})^2\right)\right)^{\frac{1}{2}}, max\{\gamma_{\widetilde{S}_s}, \gamma_{\widetilde{F}_s}\}\right\}\right\} \quad (4)$$

*Intersection operation*

$$\widetilde{S}_s \cap \widetilde{F}_s = \left\{ min\{\alpha_{\widetilde{S}_s}, \alpha_{\widetilde{F}_s}\}, max\{\beta_{\widetilde{S}_s}, \beta_{\widetilde{F}_s}\}, max\left\{ \left(1 - \left((min\{\alpha_{\widetilde{S}_s}, \alpha_{\widetilde{F}_s}\})^2 + (max\{\beta_{\widetilde{S}_s}, \beta_{\widetilde{F}_s}\})^2\right)\right)^{\frac{1}{2}}, min\{\gamma_{\widetilde{S}_s}, \gamma_{\widetilde{F}_s}\}\right\}\right\} \quad (5)$$

*Addition operation*

$$\widetilde{S}_s \oplus \widetilde{F}_s = \left\{ \left(\alpha_{\widetilde{S}_s}^2 + \alpha_{\widetilde{F}_s}^2 - \alpha_{\widetilde{S}_s}^2 \alpha_{\widetilde{F}_s}^2\right)^{\frac{1}{2}}, \beta_{\widetilde{S}_s}\beta_{\widetilde{F}_s}, \left((1 - \alpha_{\widetilde{F}_s}^2)\gamma_{\widetilde{S}_s}^2 + (1 - \alpha_{\widetilde{S}_s}^2)\gamma_{\widetilde{F}_s}^2 - \gamma_{\widetilde{S}_s}^2 \gamma_{\widetilde{F}_s}^2\right)^{\frac{1}{2}}\right\} \quad (6)$$

*Multiplication operation*

$$\widetilde{S}_s \otimes \widetilde{F}_s = \left\{ \alpha_{\widetilde{S}_s}\alpha_{\widetilde{F}_s}, \left(\beta_{\widetilde{S}_s}^2 + \beta_{\widetilde{F}_s}^2 - \beta_{\widetilde{S}_s}^2 \beta_{\widetilde{F}_s}^2\right)^{\frac{1}{2}}, \left((1 - \beta_{\widetilde{F}_s}^2)\gamma_{\widetilde{S}_s}^2 + (1 - \beta_{\widetilde{S}_s}^2)\gamma_{\widetilde{F}_s}^2 - \gamma_{\widetilde{S}_s}^2 \gamma_{\widetilde{F}_s}^2\right)^{\frac{1}{2}}\right\} \quad (7)$$

*Multiplication by $\lambda$ scalar; $\lambda > 0$*

$$\lambda.\widetilde{S}_s = \left\{ \left(1 - \left(1 - \alpha_{\widetilde{S}_s}^2\right)^{\lambda}\right)^{\frac{1}{2}}, \beta_{\widetilde{S}_s}^{\lambda}, \left(\left(1 - \alpha_{\widetilde{S}_s}^2\right)^{\lambda} - \left(1 - \alpha_{\widetilde{S}_s}^2 - \gamma_{\widetilde{S}_s}^2\right)^{\lambda}\right)^{\frac{1}{2}}\right\} \quad (8)$$

*Power of $F_S$; $\lambda > 0$*

$$\widetilde{S}_s^{\lambda} = \left\{ \alpha_{\widetilde{S}_s}^{\lambda}, \left(1 - \left(1 - \beta_{\widetilde{S}_s}^2\right)^{\lambda}\right)^{\frac{1}{2}}, \left(\left(1 - \beta_{\widetilde{S}_s}^2\right)^{\lambda} - \left(1 - \beta_{\widetilde{S}_s}^2 - \gamma_{\widetilde{S}_s}^2\right)^{\lambda}\right)^{\frac{1}{2}}\right\} \quad (9)$$

**Definition 3.** For these SFSs $\widetilde{S}_s = (\alpha_{\widetilde{S}_s}, \beta_{\widetilde{S}_s}, \gamma_{\widetilde{S}_s})$ and $\widetilde{F}_s = (\alpha_{\widetilde{F}_s}, \beta_{\widetilde{F}_s}, \gamma_{\widetilde{F}_s})$, the following are valid under the condition $\mu, \mu_1, \mu_2 > 0$:

$$\widetilde{S}_s + \widetilde{F}_s = \widetilde{F}_s + \widetilde{S}_s \tag{10}$$

$$\widetilde{S}_s . \widetilde{F}_s = \widetilde{F}_s . \widetilde{S}_s \tag{11}$$

$$\mu\left(\widetilde{S}_s + \widetilde{F}_s\right) = \mu \widetilde{S}_s + \mu \widetilde{F}_s \tag{12}$$

$$\mu_1 \widetilde{S}_s + \mu_2 \widetilde{S}_s = (\mu_1 + \mu_2) \widetilde{S}_s \tag{13}$$

$$\left(\widetilde{S}_s . \widetilde{F}_s\right)^\mu = \widetilde{S}_s^\mu . \widetilde{F}_s^\mu \tag{14}$$

$$\widetilde{S}_s^{\mu_1} . \widetilde{S}_s^{\mu_2} = \widetilde{S}_s^{\mu_1 + \mu_2} \tag{15}$$

**Definition 4.** Spherical weighted arithmetic mean (SWAM) concerning $w = (w_1, w_2, \ldots, w_n)$; $w_i \in [0, 1]$; $\sum_{i=1}^n w_i = 1$, SWAM is defined as follows:

$$\begin{aligned}
SWAM_w\left(\widetilde{S}_{S1}, \ldots, \widetilde{S}_{Sn}\right) &= w_1 \widetilde{S}_{S1} + w_2 \widetilde{S}_{S2} + \ldots + w_n \widetilde{S}_{Sn} \\
&= \left\{ \left[1 - \prod_{i=1}^n (1 - \alpha_{\widetilde{S}_{Si}}^2)^{w_i}\right]^{0.5}, \right. \\
&\left. \prod_{i=1}^n \beta_{\widetilde{S}_{Si}}^{w_i}, \left[\prod_{i=1}^n (1 - \alpha_{\widetilde{S}_{Si}}^2)^{w_i} - \prod_{i=1}^n (1 - \alpha_{\widetilde{S}_{Si}}^2 - \gamma_{\widetilde{S}_{Si}}^2)^{w_i}\right]^{1/2} \right\}
\end{aligned} \tag{16}$$

**Definition 5.** Spherical weighted geometric mean (SWGM) concerning $w = (w_1, w_2 \ldots, w_n;$ $w_i \in [0, 1]$; $\sum_{i=1}^n w_i = 1$, SWGM is defined as follows:

$$\begin{aligned}
SWGM_w(\widetilde{S}_{S1}, \ldots, \ddot{S}_{Sn}) &= \widetilde{S}_{S1}^{w_1} + \widetilde{S}_{S2}^{w_2} + \ldots + \widetilde{S}_{Sn}^{w_n} \\
&= \left\{ \prod_{i=1}^n \alpha_{\widetilde{S}_{Si}}^{w_i}, \left[1 - \prod_{i=1}^n (1 - \beta_{\widetilde{S}_{Si}}^2)^{w_i}\right]^{0.5}, \left[\prod_{i=1}^n (1 - \beta_{\widetilde{S}_{Si}}^2)^{w_i} \right. \right. \\
&\left. \left. - \prod_{i=1}^n (1 - \beta_{\widetilde{S}_{Si}}^2 - \gamma_{\widetilde{S}_{Si}}^2)^{w_i}\right]^{1/2} \right\}
\end{aligned} \tag{17}$$

### 3.2. Proposed Model of SF-Delphi and SF-DEMATEL

#### 3.2.1. Research Process

The proposed model includes a two-stage procedure of the SF-Delphi and SF-DEMATEL methods, as shown in Figure 2.

The research process began with the author establishing research goals and conducting a literature review on HRM and employee satisfaction from both motivation and demotivation aspects.

A panel of experts was then selected based on their expertise and background in the logistic service industry, and university scholars researched HRM to obtain expert opinions. The experts were questioned about the dimensions and factors that enhance employee satisfaction from both the motivation and demotivation aspects.

The SF-Delphi technique was used in the first analysis stage to determine the most crucial dimensions and factors. In the second stage, the SF-DEMATEL method was utilized to identify the causal connections between the factors and dimensions of preference and to determine the degree of impact of each dimension and factor related to employee motivation and demotivation.

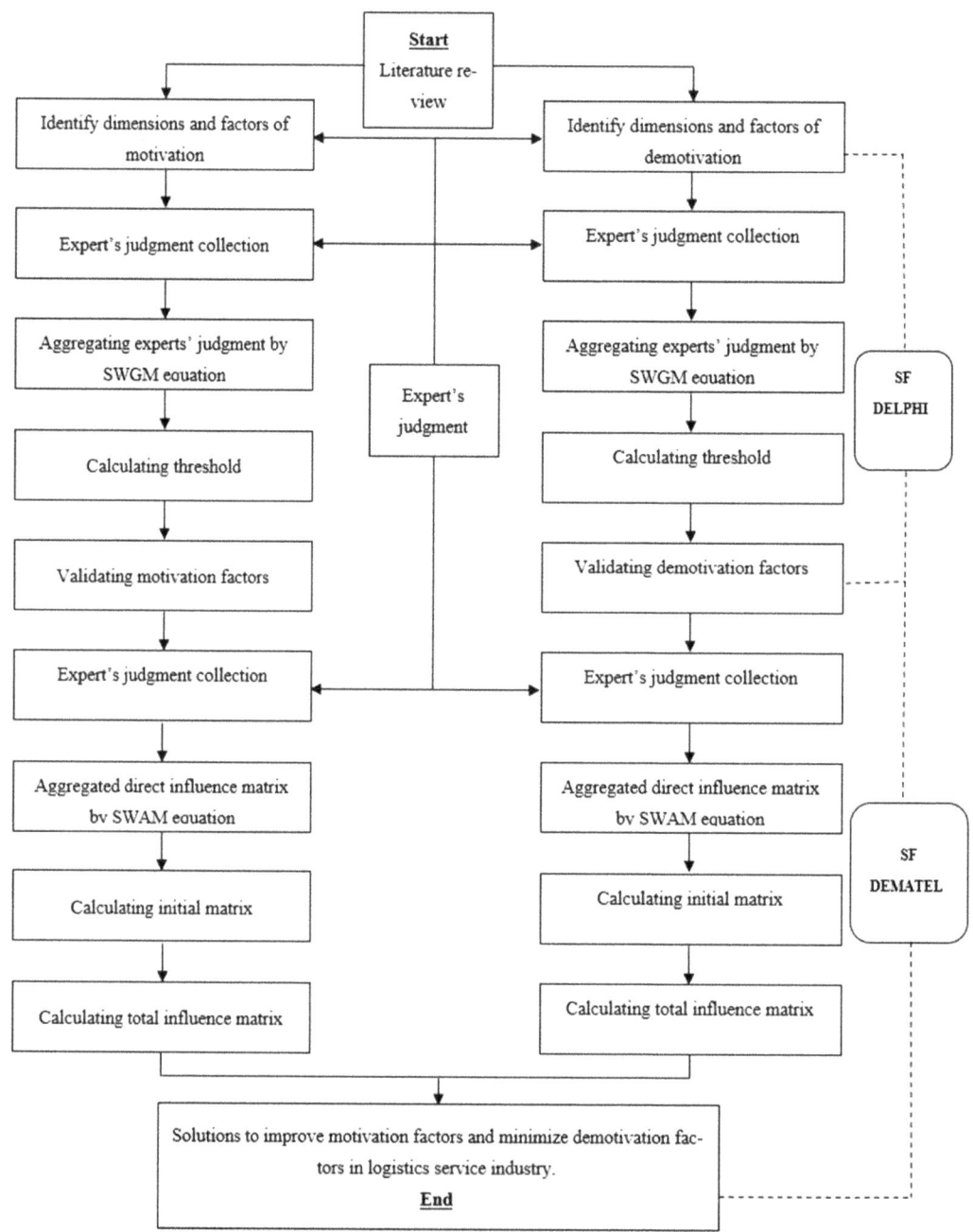

**Figure 2.** Proposed research framework.

The data was processed using Microsoft Office 2021's Excel functions, and Origin 2022 software was used to create visual representations of the study's results.

### 3.2.2. SF-Delphi Method

The details of the SF-Delphi technique proposed by Nguyen [4] in 2022 are demonstrated below:

Step 1: To aggregate experts' opinions.

The experts use the linguistic terms in Table 2 to evaluate the list of potential dimensions and factors in the context of this study. The SWAM operator is used to obtain the significance vector for each indicator [20], and it is shown in Equations (17) and (18):

$$\tilde{U}^{agg} = \begin{bmatrix} \alpha_{11}, \beta_{11}, \gamma_{11} & \cdots & \alpha_{1m}, \beta_{1m}, \gamma_{1m} \\ \vdots & \ddots & \vdots \\ \alpha_{n1}, \beta_{n1}, \gamma_{n1} & \cdots & \alpha_{nm}, \beta_{nm}, \gamma_{nm} \end{bmatrix} \quad (18)$$

Step 2: To defuzzy the aggregated criteria score.

Equation (19) is applied to obtain the score of each criterion.

$$Score(d_i) = (2\alpha_{ij} - \gamma_{ij})^2 - (\beta_{ij} - \gamma_{ij})^2 \quad (19)$$

Step 3: A threshold is attained using Equation (20) to validate the list of critical criteria. If $d_i < D$, criterion $C_i$ is removed, and if $d_i > D$, criterion $C_i$ is valid.

$$D_i = \sum_{i=1}^{n} \frac{d_i}{m} \quad (20)$$

### 3.2.3. SF-DEMATEL Method

This study introduces a new approach to the SF-DEMATEL method that employs full spherical fuzzy operators in the computation process without the normalization step used in previous studies [25–28]. The steps of the extended SF-DEMATEL method are outlined as follows:

Step 1: Creating direct influence matrices following the expert's evaluation.

To describe the expert's assessment of the influence of the criteria, Equation (21) is applied to obtain the score index (SI) value using the linguistic scales in Table 4.

$$SI = \sqrt{|100 * [(\mu - \pi)^2 - (v - \pi)^2]|} \quad (21)$$

Table 4. Linguistics scales of SF-DEMATEL.

| Linguistic Scales | ($\alpha$, $\beta$, $\gamma$) | Index (SI) |
|---|---|---|
| No influence (NI) | (0, 0.3, 0.2) | 0 |
| Weak influence (WI) | (0.35, 0.25, 0.25) | 1 |
| Moderate influence (MI) | (0.6, 0.2, 0.35) | 2 |
| Strong influence (SI) | (0.85, 0.15, 0.45) | 3 |

The direct influence matrix form ($D^e$) is created in Equation (22) based on the expert pairwise comparisons:

$$D^e = \left[d_{ij}^e\right]_{n \times n} = \left[\alpha_{ij}^e, \beta_{ij}^e, \gamma_{ij}^e\right]_{n \times n} \quad i,j = 1,\ldots, n \text{ and } e = 1,\ldots, k \quad (22)$$

where $n$ is a factor, $D^e$ is the direct influence matrix and $\left[d_{ij}^e\right]_{n \times n} = \left[\alpha_{ij}^e, \beta_{ij}^e, \gamma_{ij}^e\right]_{n \times n}$ is the spherical fuzzy value of the impact of factor $i$th to $j$th by $e^{th}$ expert.

Step 2: Creating a matrix of pooled direct influence ($D^{agg}$).

To combine the individual judgments of the decision-makers, the next step involves creating a matrix of pooled direct influence ($D^{agg}$). The SWAM process is employed using

Equation (16) as the basis to generate the aggregated direct influence matrix ($D^{agg}$) in Equation (23).

$$(D^{agg}) = \begin{bmatrix} 0 & (\alpha_{12}^{agg}, \beta_{12}^{agg}, \gamma_{12}^{agg}) & \cdots & (\alpha_{1n}^{agg}, \beta_{1n}^{agg}, \gamma_{1n}^{agg}) \\ (\alpha_{21}^{agg}, \beta_{21}^{agg}, \gamma_{21}^{agg}) & 0 & \cdots & (\alpha_{2n}^{agg}, \beta_{2n}^{agg}, \gamma_{2n}^{agg}) \\ \vdots & \vdots & \ddots & \vdots \\ (\alpha_{n1}^{agg}, \beta_{n1}^{agg}, \gamma_{n1}^{agg}) & (\alpha_{n2}^{agg}, \beta_{n2}^{agg}, \gamma_{n2}^{agg}) & \cdots & 0 \end{bmatrix} \quad (23)$$

where $(\alpha_{ij}^{agg}, \beta_{ij}^{agg}, \gamma_{ij}^{agg})$ is the aggregated SF value of the impact of criterion $i$th to $j$th.

Step 3: Building the initial direct influence matrix ($X$).

The SF value of each comparison contains three dimensions, including membership ($\alpha$), non-membership ($\beta$), and hesitancy level ($\gamma$). The normalization of matrix ($D$) will be carried out to produce the initial direct influence matrix ($X$), after dividing them into three submatrices Equation (24). Equation (25) describes the final matrix form in this stage.

$$X = sD \text{ where } s = \min\left[\frac{1}{\max_i \sum_{j=1}^n |d_{ij}|}, \frac{1}{\max_j \sum_{i=1}^n |d_{ij}|}\right] \quad (24)$$

where $s$ is the normalization index

$$X^\alpha = \begin{bmatrix} 0 & \alpha_{12} & \cdots & \alpha_{1n} \\ \alpha_{21} & 0 & \cdots & \alpha_{21} \\ \vdots & \vdots & \ddots & \vdots \\ \alpha_{n1} & \alpha_{n2} & \cdots & 0 \end{bmatrix}, X^\beta = \begin{bmatrix} 0 & \beta_{12} & \cdots & \beta_{1n} \\ \beta_{21} & 0 & \cdots & \beta_{21} \\ \vdots & \vdots & \ddots & \vdots \\ \beta_{n1} & \beta_{n2} & \cdots & 0 \end{bmatrix}, X^\gamma = \begin{bmatrix} 0 & \gamma_{12} & \cdots & \gamma_{1n} \\ \gamma_{21} & 0 & \cdots & \gamma_{21} \\ \vdots & \vdots & \ddots & \vdots \\ \gamma_{n1} & \gamma_{n2} & \cdots & 0 \end{bmatrix} \quad (25)$$

Step 4: Calculating the total influence matrix ($T$).

Using Equation (26), the submatrices of $X$ are changed into the submatrices of ($T$). The ($T$) matrix in Equation (27) is created by combining these matrices.

$$T = X + X' = X(1-X) = \begin{bmatrix} t_{11} & \cdots & t_{1n} \\ \vdots & \ddots & \vdots \\ t_{i i 1} & \cdots & t_{nn} \end{bmatrix} \quad i,j = 1,\ldots,n \quad (26)$$

$$(T) = \begin{bmatrix} (\alpha_{11}^T, \beta_{11}^T, \gamma_{11}^T) & (\alpha_{11}^T, \beta_{11}^T, \gamma_{11}^T) & \cdots & (\alpha_{11}^T, \beta_{11}^T, \gamma_{11}^T) \\ (\alpha_{21}^T, \beta_{21}^T, \gamma_{21}^T) & (\alpha_{21}^T, \beta_{21}^T, \gamma_{21}^T) & \cdots & (\alpha_{21}^T, \beta_{21}^T, \gamma_{21}^T) \\ \vdots & \vdots & \ddots & \vdots \\ (\alpha_{n1}^T, \beta_{n1}^T, \gamma_{n1}^T) & (\alpha_{n1}^T, \beta_{n1}^T, \gamma_{n1}^T) & \cdots & (\alpha_{n1}^T, \beta_{n1}^T, \gamma_{n1}^T) \end{bmatrix} \quad (27)$$

The impact from factor $i$th to $j$th is represented by the SF value of the ($T$) matrix, where ($T$) is the total influence matrix, ($X$) is the direct influence matrix, ($X'$) is the indirect influence matrix, and $(\alpha_{ij}^T, \beta_{ij}^T, \gamma_{ij}^T)$ is the SF value of the ($T$) matrix.

Step 5: The spherical fuzzy column ($c_i$) and row sum ($r_i$) calculation.

Row sum ($r_i$) and column sum ($c_i$) spherical fuzzy values are computed using Equations (28) and (29), respectively.

$$r_i = \sum_{i=1}^n \left(\alpha_{ij}^T, \beta_{ij}^T, \gamma_{ij}^T\right) \quad i,j = 1,\ldots,n \quad (28)$$

$$c_i = \sum_{j=1}^n \left(\alpha_{ij}^T, \beta_{ij}^T, \gamma_{ij}^T\right) \quad i,j = 1,\ldots,n \quad (29)$$

Step 6: Evaluating the significance of relation and prominence.

Defuzzification into crisp numbers, shown as score values using Equation (19).

The ($r_i + c_i$) value describes the degree of importance of factors and the $r_i - c_i$ values describe the cause and effect among factors.

If ($r_i - c_i$) value greater than zero, the factor belongs to the "cause" group.
If ($r_i - c_i$) value lower than zero, the factor belongs to the "effect" group.
Step 7: Drawing Network Relations Map (NRM).

In this research, establishing a threshold value is crucial for obtaining the digraph from the total influence matrix (T), which provides information about the impact of one factor on another. The decision-maker must determine the threshold value to filter out insignificant effects, ensuring that only effects greater than the threshold value are displayed in the digraph. The average of the elements in the matrix (T) is computed to establish the threshold value. The NRM visualizes the relationship between factors based on their prominence and relation in Step 6. The NRM consists of two axes, the "Prominence" axis and the "Relation" axis, which are horizontal and vertical, respectively. In the NRM, a single arrow represents a one-way impact of one factor on another, while a double arrow represents a two-way interrelationship between two factors. This distinction is important because it can help identify feedback loops and other complex relationships between factors. By analyzing the NRM, decision-makers can gain insights into the relationships between different factors and identify which factors are most influential in the system.

## 4. Case Study
### 4.1. Expert Selection

The SF-Delphi survey participants are not selected randomly; instead, they are carefully chosen based on their knowledge and experience in a specific field relevant to the research topic [75]. While there is no established rule for the panel size, it is generally believed that a larger panel will lead to more reliable group judgments [76,77]. It has been suggested that each area of expertise should have a minimum of 10 to 18 panel members [78,79]. Given the complexity of the dimensions and factors involved in this study, the author aimed for a minimum sample size of 40 participants. The survey was created using Google Forms and distributed via email to 56 specialists. Out of those, 40 responses were received and included in the research. The selected experts had at least 15 years of experience in the logistics industry and worked in some well-known universities in Vietnam; their profiles are presented in Table 5.

**Table 5.** Experts' Profiles.

| Gender | | Education | | Working Years | Position | |
|---|---|---|---|---|---|---|
| Male | Female | Master | PhD | Average | University Scholars | Managers |
| 23 persons | 17 persons | 27 persons | 13 persons | 18.7 years | 11 persons | 29 persons |

### 4.2. Results of the SF-Delphi Technique
#### 4.2.1. Results of Motivation Categories

In this study, secondary sources and experts' feedback were used to list 38 potential indicators. It was anticipated that the test would take 30 min to complete and was split into two parts. Section 1 collected demographic data, such as position, years of experience, education, and industry sector. The questionnaire was only circulated once permission had been obtained, and the invites were initially delivered by email. Data were gathered from November 2022 to February 2023 utilizing an online survey using Google Forms in both English and Vietnamese. Experts' opinions after collection were converted from linguistic to spherical fuzzy numbers (Table 3). The SWAM operator was then used to integrate the experts' judgments, and then score functions were calculated by Equation (19) to determine the threshold value. The SF-Delphi method results are displayed in Table 6. Based on comparisons between the score values ($Sd_i$) of each criterion and the threshold ($D_i$), seven motivation factors, including M3, M6, M8, M16, M19, M27, and M30 were rejected.

Table 6. The SF-Delphi method results in motivation categories.

| Factor | α | β | γ | Score | Decision |
|---|---|---|---|---|---|
| M1 | 0.721 | 0.310 | 0.320 | 1.256 | Accepted |
| M2 | 0.683 | 0.347 | 0.323 | 1.089 | Accepted |
| M3 | 0.555 | 0.456 | 0.420 | 0.475 | Rejected |
| M4 | 0.647 | 0.374 | 0.360 | 0.872 | Accepted |
| M5 | 0.649 | 0.388 | 0.338 | 0.921 | Accepted |
| M6 | 0.563 | 0.451 | 0.428 | 0.487 | Rejected |
| M7 | 0.654 | 0.366 | 0.369 | 0.880 | Accepted |
| M8 | 0.618 | 0.392 | 0.383 | 0.727 | Rejected |
| M9 | 0.654 | 0.377 | 0.368 | 0.882 | Accepted |
| M10 | 0.644 | 0.391 | 0.348 | 0.884 | Accepted |
| M11 | 0.652 | 0.364 | 0.375 | 0.861 | Accepted |
| M12 | 0.648 | 0.384 | 0.361 | 0.874 | Accepted |
| M13 | 0.652 | 0.371 | 0.377 | 0.858 | Accepted |
| M14 | 0.645 | 0.371 | 0.356 | 0.874 | Accepted |
| M15 | 0.655 | 0.367 | 0.363 | 0.895 | Accepted |
| M16 | 0.551 | 0.462 | 0.423 | 0.459 | Rejected |
| M17 | 0.645 | 0.375 | 0.355 | 0.874 | Accepted |
| M18 | 0.656 | 0.366 | 0.360 | 0.906 | Accepted |
| M19 | 0.573 | 0.432 | 0.409 | 0.544 | Rejected |
| M20 | 0.688 | 0.340 | 0.324 | 1.107 | Accepted |
| M21 | 0.666 | 0.366 | 0.366 | 0.933 | Accepted |
| M22 | 0.644 | 0.388 | 0.362 | 0.857 | Accepted |
| M23 | 0.644 | 0.370 | 0.361 | 0.859 | Accepted |
| M24 | 0.674 | 0.352 | 0.349 | 0.998 | Accepted |
| M25 | 0.651 | 0.372 | 0.370 | 0.869 | Accepted |
| M26 | 0.659 | 0.364 | 0.354 | 0.930 | Accepted |
| M27 | 0.558 | 0.450 | 0.411 | 0.497 | Rejected |
| M28 | 0.655 | 0.366 | 0.368 | 0.889 | Accepted |
| M29 | 0.653 | 0.385 | 0.340 | 0.933 | Accepted |
| M30 | 0.544 | 0.466 | 0.431 | 0.430 | Rejected |
| M31 | 0.648 | 0.382 | 0.357 | 0.879 | Accepted |
| M32 | 0.650 | 0.366 | 0.368 | 0.867 | Accepted |
| M33 | 0.657 | 0.369 | 0.360 | 0.910 | Accepted |
| M34 | 0.678 | 0.352 | 0.330 | 1.053 | Accepted |
| M35 | 0.651 | 0.379 | 0.360 | 0.889 | Accepted |
| M36 | 0.661 | 0.352 | 0.378 | 0.889 | Accepted |
| M37 | 0.659 | 0.363 | 0.366 | 0.904 | Accepted |
| M38 | 0.673 | 0.343 | 0.356 | 0.980 | Accepted |
| Threshold | | | | 0.850 | |

4.2.2. Results of Demotivation Categories

The experts also assessed a list of 21 factors of demotivation factors. As a result, only M15 was rejected because the score function value (0.419) was lower than the threshold value (0.878), as shown in Table 7.

Table 7. The SF-Delphi method results in demotivation categories.

| Factor | α | β | γ | Score | Decision |
|---|---|---|---|---|---|
| DM1 | 0.672 | 0.344 | 0.354 | 0.980 | Accepted |
| DM2 | 0.651 | 0.372 | 0.359 | 0.890 | Accepted |
| DM3 | 0.649 | 0.370 | 0.355 | 0.888 | Accepted |
| DM4 | 0.656 | 0.371 | 0.365 | 0.898 | Accepted |
| DM5 | 0.646 | 0.387 | 0.354 | 0.879 | Accepted |
| DM6 | 0.652 | 0.370 | 0.356 | 0.898 | Accepted |
| DM7 | 0.656 | 0.368 | 0.365 | 0.896 | Accepted |
| DM8 | 0.659 | 0.354 | 0.360 | 0.918 | Accepted |
| DM9 | 0.662 | 0.368 | 0.369 | 0.913 | Accepted |

Table 7. Cont.

| Factor | α | β | γ | Score | Decision |
|---|---|---|---|---|---|
| DM10 | 0.656 | 0.364 | 0.340 | 0.944 | Accepted |
| DM11 | 0.652 | 0.365 | 0.368 | 0.878 | Accepted |
| DM12 | 0.652 | 0.378 | 0.363 | 0.886 | Accepted |
| DM13 | 0.652 | 0.376 | 0.358 | 0.894 | Accepted |
| DM14 | 0.648 | 0.368 | 0.351 | 0.893 | Accepted |
| DM15 | 0.542 | 0.469 | 0.436 | 0.419 | Rejected |
| DM16 | 0.661 | 0.359 | 0.353 | 0.940 | Accepted |
| DM17 | 0.647 | 0.374 | 0.354 | 0.884 | Accepted |
| DM18 | 0.653 | 0.369 | 0.364 | 0.886 | Accepted |
| DM19 | 0.651 | 0.369 | 0.363 | 0.883 | Accepted |
| DM20 | 0.648 | 0.372 | 0.359 | 0.878 | Accepted |
| DM21 | 0.658 | 0.374 | 0.374 | 0.889 | Accepted |
| Threshold | | | | 0.878 | |

## 4.3. Results of SF-DEMATEL Method

### 4.3.1. SF-DEMATEL Results of Employee Motivation Factors

The second poll was conducted with 40 experts who participated in the first phase after using the Delphi approach to identify 31 significant elements affecting employee motivation. The survey asked experts to evaluate the impact of each pair of factors using the linguistic scale shown in Table 3. The SF-DEMATEL method results of motivation are presented in Tables 8–13, and the influence relation maps is displayed in Figures 3–9.

Table 8. The SF-DEMATEL results of employee motivation dimensions.

| Dimension | $(r_i+c_i)$ | $(r_i-c_i)$ | Classification |
|---|---|---|---|
| A Compensation and benefits | 1.916 | 0.037 | Cause |
| B Career growth and development | 1.842 | 0.007 | Cause |
| C Work environment and culture | 1.903 | 0.075 | Cause |
| D Recognition and feedback | 1.895 | 0.105 | Cause |
| E Organizational support | 1.849 | −0.121 | Effect |
| F Management | 1.854 | −0.103 | Effect |

Based on the data presented in Table 8, it can be seen that A was the most important causal factor affecting the motivation of employees because it had the largest $(r_i + c_i)$ value and had a positive value $(r_i - c_i)$. Furthermore, C was the second-most significant causal factor, followed by D and B, respectively. Considering that E and F had low $(r_i - c_i)$ values, they are two effect factors. E and F are two factors that were impacted by all four factors, according to the influence relationship map among the dimensions in Figure 3.

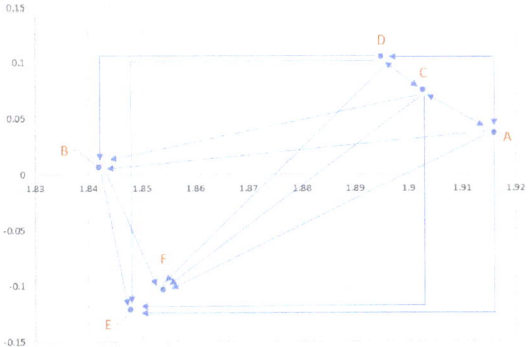

Figure 3. Network relations map of employee motivation dimensions.

However, E and F did not have an impact on one another. In addition, in the cause group, factors A, C, and D. A and D had mutual effects and impacted on factor B. Therefore, to improve the motivation of employees, it is necessary to focus resources on improving A, C, and D, and then factors B, E, and F will be simultaneously addressed.

Next, Table 9 presents SF-Dematel results between factors in compensation and benefits, and Figure 4 presents an impact relationship among them. The results show that, M2, M5 and M7 are cause factors by the positive $(r_i - c_i)$ values, in which M2 is the most significant factor with the greatest $(r_i + c_i)$ value. Similarly, due to their $(r_i - c_i)$ value lower than 0, M1, M4 and M8 are the affected factors.

Table 9. The SF-DEMATEL results of compensation and benefits.

| Factor |                      | $(r_i + c_i)$ | $(r_i - c_i)$ | Classification |
|--------|----------------------|---------------|---------------|----------------|
| M1     | Equity in pay        | 1.4349        | −0.2188       | Effect         |
| M2     | Base salary          | 1.7833        | 0.2167        | Cause          |
| M4     | Relaxation allowances| 1.4966        | −0.0443       | Effect         |
| M5     | Bonus structure      | 1.5713        | 0.0349        | Cause          |
| M7     | Health insurance     | 1.5047        | 0.1408        | Cause          |
| M8     | Retirement benefits  | 1.3897        | −0.1294       | Effect         |

Considering the direction of the arrow, it can be seen that M2 and M7 affect all the remaining factors and affect each other. Therefore, it is necessary to concentrate on exploiting these two factors to have a suitable compensation and benefits system.

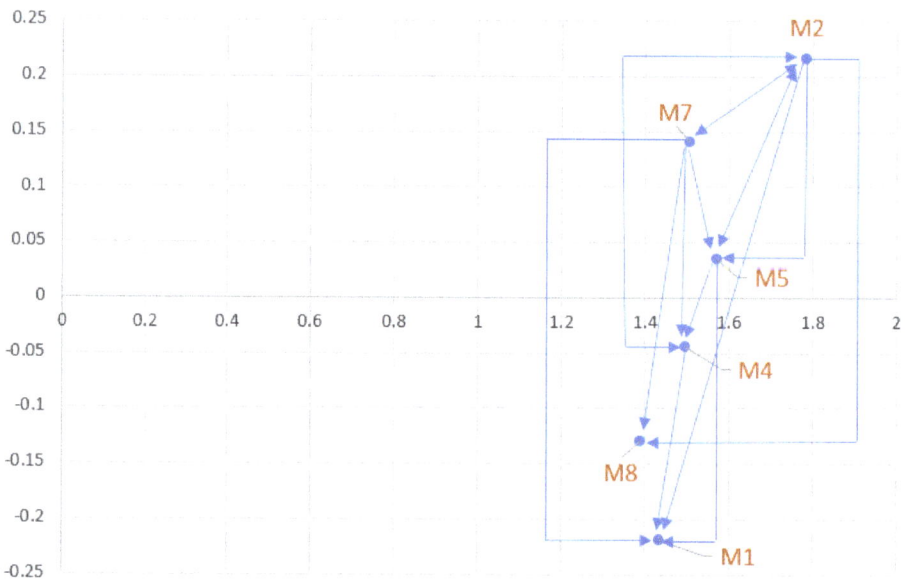

Figure 4. Network relations map of compensation and benefits.

Similarly, in the dimension of career growth and development, M10, M11, and M12 are the primary factors that contribute to a rise in employee motivation due to the positive $(r_i - c_i)$ values. In particular, M10 is the most critical factor, followed by M11 and M12, respectively. The factors of the affected group include M13 and M14; all three cause factors influence these factors. The results are shown in Table 10 and Figure 5.

Table 10. The SF-DEMATEL results in career growth and development.

| Factor | | $(r_i+c_i)$ | $(r_i-c_i)$ | Classification |
| --- | --- | --- | --- | --- |
| M10 | Professional development | 1.9232 | 0.0768 | Cause |
| M11 | Opportunities for creativity and innovation | 1.9098 | 0.0221 | Cause |
| M12 | Training | 1.8797 | 0.0714 | Cause |
| M13 | Opportunities for social connection | 1.8410 | −0.0575 | Effect |
| M14 | Challenging work | 1.8312 | −0.1128 | Effect |

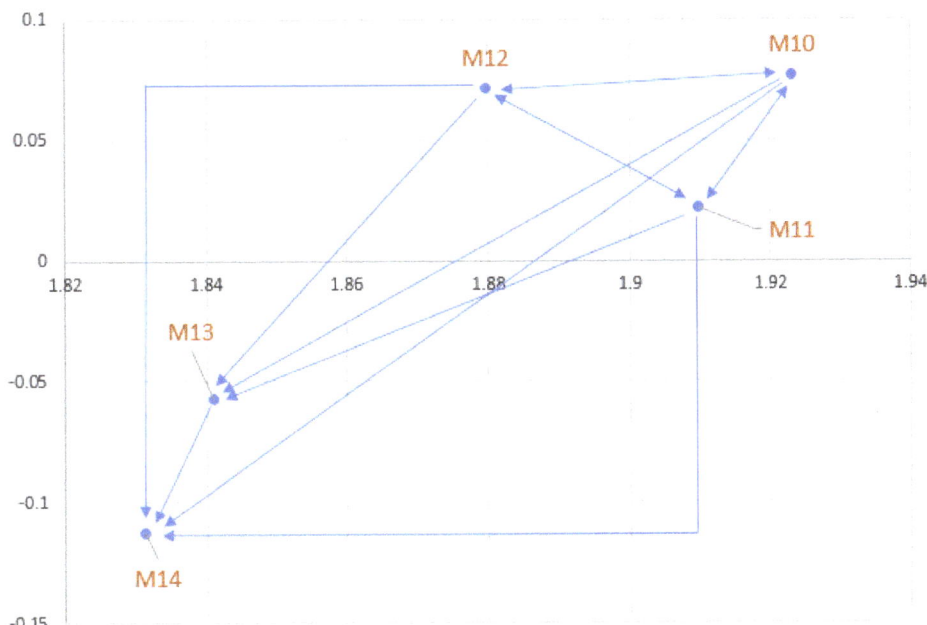

Figure 5. Network relations map of career growth and development.

The work environment and culture dimension has eight factors, as listed in Table 11; the results show that M15, M18, M20, M21, M22, and M23 are cause factors, in which the three most important reasons are M21, M15, and M20, respectively. The other two factors are M17 and M24, acting as factors affected by negative $(r_i - c_i)$ values. The direction of the arrow in Figure 6 shows how the M21 influences all the other variables. Hence, this aspect must be highlighted most when attempting to create a pleasant work environment for staff members.

Table 11. The SF-DEMATEL results of work environment and culture.

| Factor | | $(r_i+c_i)$ | $(r_i-c_i)$ | Classification |
| --- | --- | --- | --- | --- |
| M15 | Work-life balance | 1.9099 | 0.0051 | Cause |
| M17 | Resources and support | 1.8094 | −0.0825 | Effect |
| M18 | Job security | 1.8916 | 0.0334 | Cause |
| M20 | Workload | 1.9099 | 0.0208 | Cause |
| M21 | Positive work culture | 1.9592 | 0.0408 | Cause |
| M22 | Social support | 1.8605 | 0.0442 | Cause |
| M23 | Physical environment | 1.831 | 0.0685 | Cause |
| M24 | Autonomy | 1.8582 | −0.1303 | Effect |

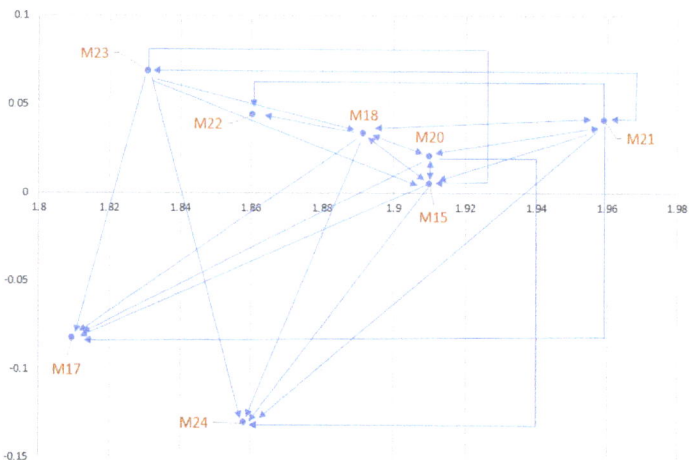

**Figure 6.** Network relations map of work environment and culture.

One of the critical dimensions for motivation is the dimension of recognition and feedback. The measurement findings and the relationships between the factors are displayed in Table 12 and Figure 7 below.

**Table 12.** The SF-DEMATEL results of recognition and feedback.

| Factor | | $(r_i+c_i)$ | $(r_i-c_i)$ | Classification |
|---|---|---|---|---|
| M25 | Positive feedback and constructive criticism | 1.8404 | 0.1596 | Cause |
| M26 | Recognition | 1.8628 | 0.0976 | Cause |
| M28 | Employee empowerment | 1.7272 | −0.2575 | Effect |

The results show that M25 and M26 are the cause factors because of positive $(r_i - c_i)$ values. M25 and M26 impact the remaining factors and impact each other. In particular, M26 is the most crucial factor, with the largest $(r_i + c_i)$ value. The factor acting as an affected factor is M28.

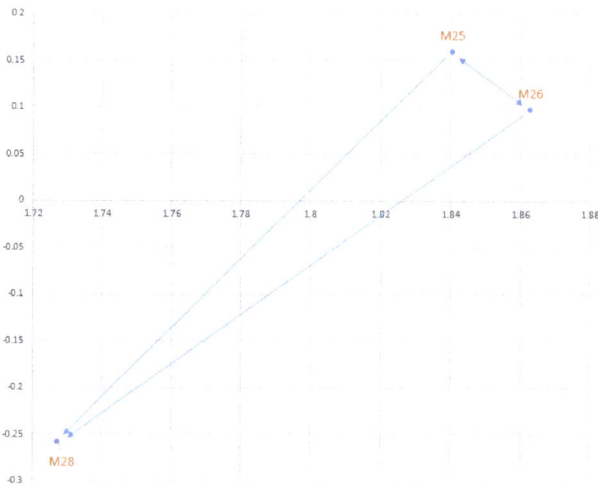

**Figure 7.** Network relations map of recognition and feedback.

Likewise, Table 13 and Figure 8 demonstrate the outcomes of the organizational support dimension. M29 is the most significant factor because it has the highest $(r_i + c_i)$ value, but because it has a negative $(r_i - c_i)$ value, M29 belongs to the effect group. With positive $(r_i - c_i)$, M31, M33, M34 and M35 are identified as cause factors. As a result, it is crucial to concentrate on enhancing the components that contribute to the problem, particularly the M35 factor, because it has the second highest $(r_i + c_i)$ value and affects the other factors, including M29.

Table 13. The SF-DEMATEL results of organizational support.

| Factor | | $(r_i+c_i)$ | $(r_i-c_i)$ | Classification |
| --- | --- | --- | --- | --- |
| M29 | Perceived organizational support | 1.964 | −0.020 | Effect |
| M31 | Organizational support | 1.916 | 0.030 | Cause |
| M32 | Organizational communication | 1.868 | −0.100 | Effect |
| M33 | Employee retention strategies | 1.859 | 0.010 | Cause |
| M34 | Organizational commitment | 1.804 | 0.013 | Cause |
| M35 | Organizational justice | 1.933 | 0.067 | Cause |

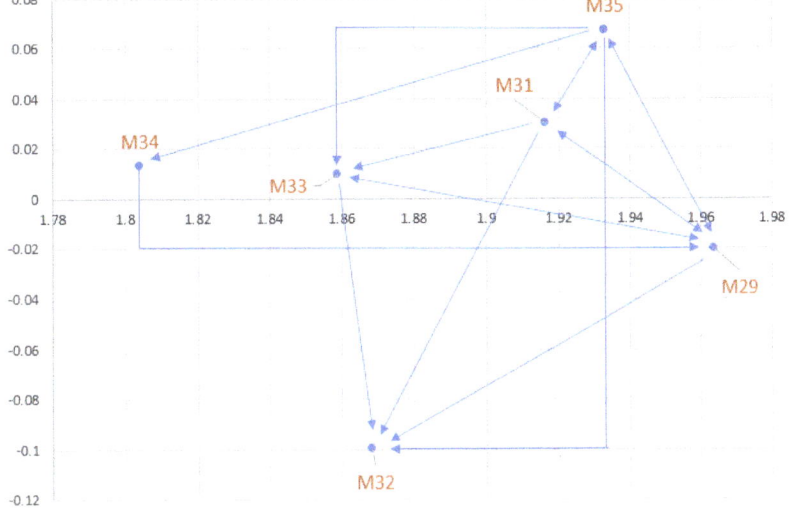

Figure 8. Network relations map of organizational support.

Lastly, Table 14 illustrates the management style dimension's measurement results. The outcome demonstrates that M37 is this dimension's sole and most significant element. M37 influences the other two factors in the group, while M36 and M38 also have the opposite effect, as shown in Figure 9.

Table 14. The SF-DEMATEL results of management.

| Factor | | $(r_i+c_i)$ | $(r_i-c_i)$ | Classification |
| --- | --- | --- | --- | --- |
| M36 | Trust in management | 1.577 | −0.023 | Effect |
| M37 | Leadership | 1.922 | 0.079 | Cause |
| M38 | Purposeful work | 1.602 | −0.056 | Effect |

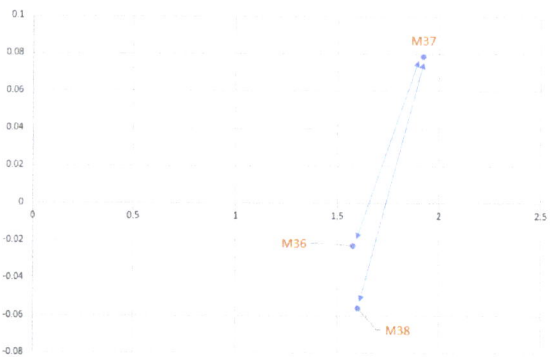

**Figure 9.** Network relations map of management style.

### 4.3.2. SF-DEMATEL Results of Employee Demotivation Dimension

The results of the SF-DEMATEL method for 20 factors belonging to the demotivation categories are presented in Tables 15–20 and in Figures 10–15.

First, five dimensions are investigated for their importance and relationship. J and K are recognized as the effect dimensions since the $(r_i - c_i)$ values are less than zero. G, H, and I, however, are the cause dimensions. G is the most significant factor because its $(r_i + c_i)$ value is the highest.

**Table 15.** The SF-DEMATEL results of employee demotivation dimensions.

| Dimension | $(r_i+c_i)$ | $(r_i-c_i)$ | Classification |
|---|---|---|---|
| G Inadequate compensation and benefits | 1.8808 | 0.0527 | Cause |
| H Poor management | 1.6910 | 0.0018 | Cause |
| I Lack of career growth and development opportunities | 1.8155 | 0.1845 | Cause |
| J Poor work environment and culture | 1.6431 | −0.1870 | Effect |
| K Lack of recognition and feedback | 1.6764 | −0.0520 | Effect |

Regarding the arrow direction of the factors, it can be seen that all causal factors influence K and J. In contrast, G, H, and I affect all other factors, and they have a reciprocal relationship. Therefore, decision-makers should address the cause factors, especially G, to minimize employee demotivation, as shown in Table 15 and Figure 10.

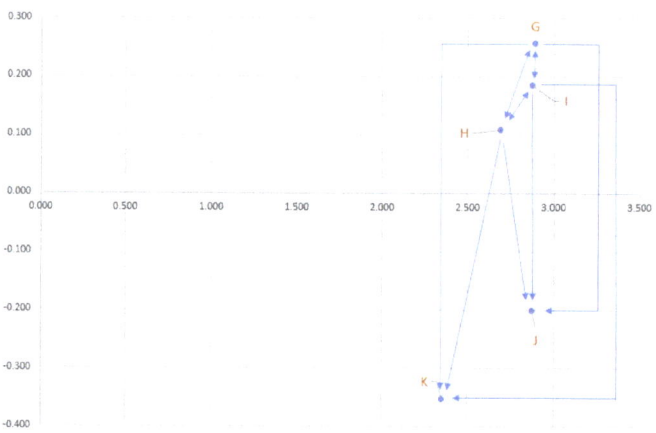

**Figure 10.** Network relations map of employee demotivation dimensions.

For the first dimension, Table 16 and Figure 11 indicate the outcomes of an inadequate compensation and benefits dimension. DM1 and DM2 are causative factors because the (r − c) values are higher than zero. Moreover, considering the direction of the arrow, DM2 not only has the largest $(r_i + c_i)$ value, but also affects all factors in the group. Therefore it is necessary to focus on solving DM2.

Table 16. The SF-DEMATEL results for inadequate compensation and benefits.

| Factor | | $(r_i+c_i)$ | $(r_i-c_i)$ | Classification |
|---|---|---|---|---|
| DM1 | Back pay | 1.806 | 0.029 | Cause |
| DM2 | Inadequate salaries and rewards | 1.972 | 0.028 | Cause |
| DM3 | Unfair pay in comparison to colleagues | 1.832 | −0.057 | Effect |

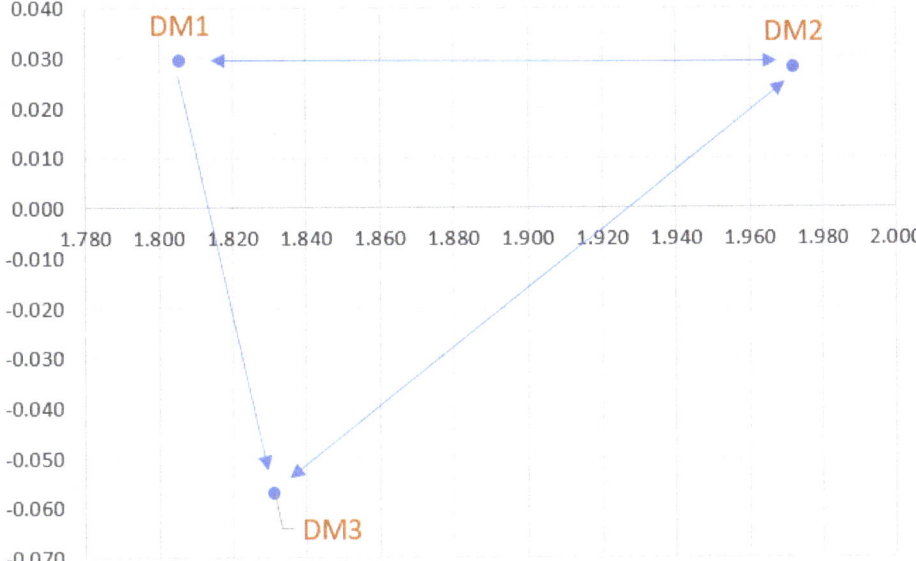

Figure 11. Network relations map of inadequate compensation and benefits.

Moreover, DM5, DM6, and DM7 belong to the cause group due to the positive $(r_i - c_i)$ values and DM4 and DM8 belong to the effect group because of the negative $(r_i - c_i)$ values. Because DM7 is the causal factor with the highest $(r_i + c_i)$ value, it is essential to pay attention to it if management is to be improved. In Table 17 and Figure 12, the results are displayed.

Table 17. The SF-DEMATEL results from poor management (H).

| Factor | | $(r_i+c_i)$ | $(r_i-c_i)$ | Classification |
|---|---|---|---|---|
| DM4 | Poor organization ethics | 1.506 | −0.062 | Effect |
| DM5 | Inadequate leadership support | 1.585 | 0.030 | Cause |
| DM6 | Poor management | 1.583 | 0.069 | Cause |
| DM7 | Bad treatment by supervisors | 1.834 | 0.166 | Cause |
| DM8 | Working excessively long hours | 1.617 | −0.203 | Effect |

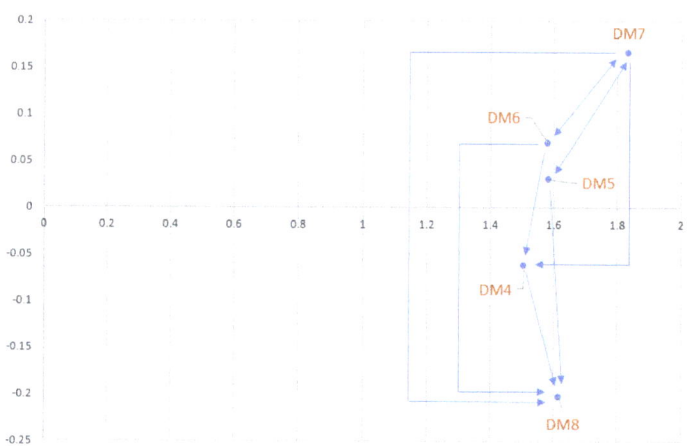

**Figure 12.** Network relations map of poor management.

Similarly, the lack of career growth and development opportunities has three factors, and DM9 is both the cause and the most essential factor that needs to be improved. DM10 and DM11, the other two factors, are the effect factors. Table 18 and Figure 13 show the measurement results.

**Table 18.** The SF-DEMATEL results for a lack of career growth and development opportunities (I).

| Factor |  | $(r_i+c_i)$ | $(r_i-c_i)$ | Classification |
|---|---|---|---|---|
| DM9 | Inadequate opportunity for career promotion | 1.859 | 0.141 | Cause |
| DM10 | Underutilization of skill | 1.524 | −0.019 | Effect |
| DM11 | Inadequate training and development | 1.456 | −0.122 | Effect |

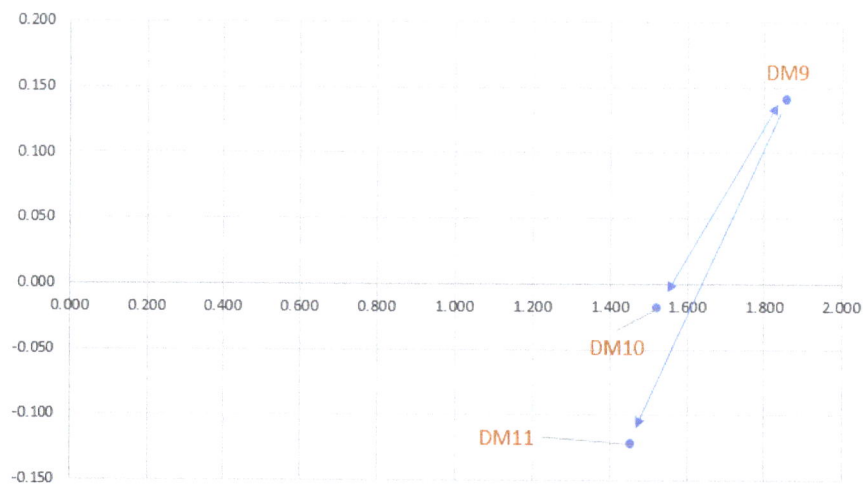

**Figure 13.** Network relations map of a lack of career growth and development opportunities.

The next crucial dimension to be investigated is poor work environment and culture (Table 19). Due to the positive $(r_i - c_i)$ value, the factors DM13, DM14 and DM17 are the influencing factors; on the other hand, DM12, DM 16 and DM18 are the factors affected by the negative $(r_i - c_i)$ value. DM13 was identified as the most critical factor and should be improved because it affects all the remaining factors in the group, as shown in Figure 14.

Table 19. The SF-DEMATEL results for poor work environment and culture (J).

| Factor | | $(r_i+c_i)$ | $(r_i-c_i)$ | Classification |
|---|---|---|---|---|
| DM12 | Inadequate freedom in the day-to-day conduct of work | 1.844 | −0.036 | Effect |
| DM13 | Lack of job security | 1.926 | 0.075 | Cause |
| DM14 | Poor working environment | 1.856 | 0.111 | Cause |
| DM16 | Unsafe work conditions | 1.869 | −0.126 | Effect |
| DM17 | Unhealthy competition among co-workers | 1.872 | 0.041 | Cause |
| DM18 | Excessive workload pressure | 1.868 | −0.064 | Effect |

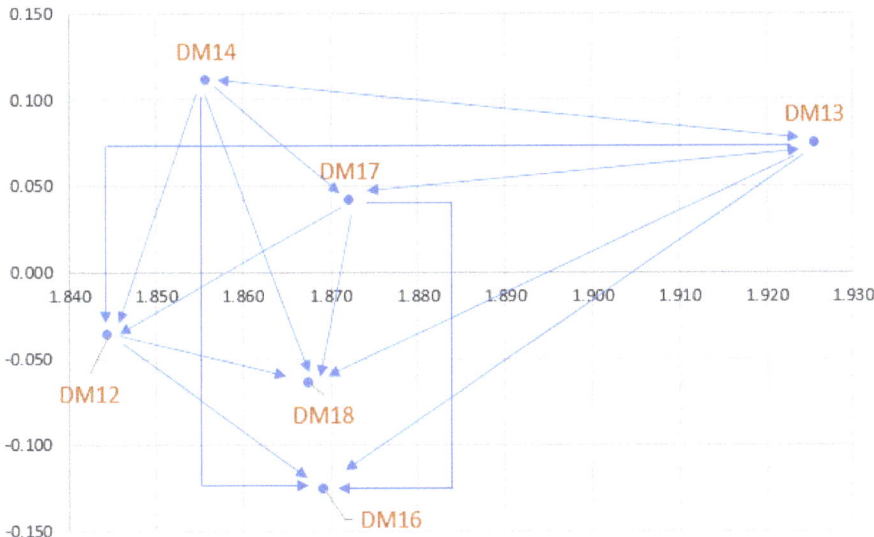

Figure 14. Network relations map of poor work environment and culture.

Finally, the measurement results of lack of recognition and feedback dimension are presented in Table 20. The group's most significant causal element was found to be DM21; nevertheless, when the arrow's direction was considered in Figure 15, it became clear that DM21 had no impact on DM19. On the other hand, DM19 affects DM21 and DM20. Decision-makers must be concerned not just with DM21 but also with DM19 to improve this dimension because DM19 is a causal factor.

Table 20. The SF-DEMATEL results for a lack of recognition and feedback (K).

| Factor | | $(r_i+c_i)$ | $(r_i-c_i)$ | Classification |
|---|---|---|---|---|
| DM19 | Poor feedback and inappropriateevaluation system | 2.086 | 0.086 | Cause |
| DM20 | Low participation in decision making | 2.248 | −0.116 | Effect |
| DM21 | Lack of recognition | 2.383 | 0.030 | Cause |

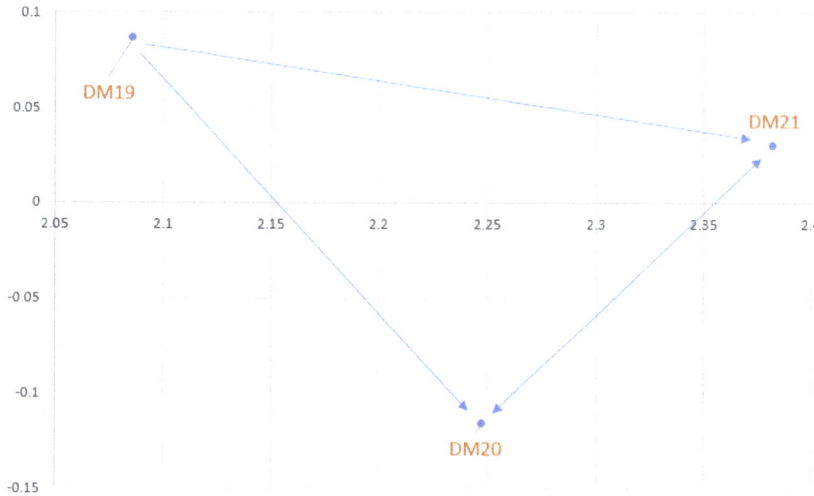

**Figure 15.** Network relations map of lack of recognition and feedback (K).

*4.4. Discussion*

In the first stage, this study identified motivation categories, including six dimensions affecting employee satisfaction. The dimensions of compensation and benefits (A), career growth and development (B), work environment and culture (C), and recognition and feedback (D) were classified under the cause group. Conversely, organizational support (E) and management (F) fell under the effect group. Based on the study results, managers in logistics service firms should prioritize recognition and feedback (D) as it has the highest relationship compared to other dimensions, such as compensation and benefits (A), career growth and development (B), and work environment and culture (C). This prioritization is crucial in enhancing employee motivation as recognition and feedback (D) have a significant causal effect.

Compensation and benefits (A) have the most substantial impact within the cause group and are essential for enhancing employees' work performance. Previous studies [5,80] have supported this by showing that high-income employees contribute more to the organization, and higher salaries lead to increased job satisfaction. Therefore, it is crucial for companies to establish a reasonable salary and bonus system that takes into account employees' demands and regularly investigates them [81].

In addition, career growth and development (B) is also critical for retaining top talent. According to Deloitte, employees who receive regular career development opportunities are ten times more likely to stay with their current organization than those who do not receive such opportunities [82]. Employees who feel they have a future in the organization and opportunities for career advancement are more motivated to work harder and remain loyal to the company [83]. Therefore, investing in employee training and development programs can improve employee motivation and the organization's overall retention rate.

The impact of the work environment and culture (C) on employee motivation is undeniable, as it directly affects the organization's performance. Research consistently shows that a positive work environment, which includes safety, proper facilities and equipment, and a healthy atmosphere, enhances job satisfaction and boosts employee motivation [6,84,85]. However, creating an ideal workplace is a significant investment for organizations, as it requires substantial financial and human capital. Despite this, organizations must prioritize creating a positive and supportive work environment to retain employees, ensure motivation, and promote overall job satisfaction. These efforts can substantially impact the organization's long-term success and growth.

Furthermore, recognition and feedback (D) is vital in developing a positive work culture where employees feel appreciated and valued. Maslow's theory suggests that recognition encourages employees to exceed their duties and to take the initiative [29]. By recognizing their achievements, employees feel a sense of accomplishment and are motivated to continue performing at a high level. Additionally, recognition and feedback can improve employee retention rates, as employees are more likely to stay with an organization that values and appreciates their work. Therefore, organizations must establish a formal recognition program that acknowledges and rewards employees for their hard work and dedication.

In the second stage, it is essential to identify the factors that contribute to employee demotivation, as these factors can harm a company's productivity and performance. The study reveals that insufficient compensation and benefits (G), poor management (H) and a lack of career growth and development opportunities (I) are the primary drivers of employee demotivation. On the other hand, poor work environment and culture (J) and inadequate recognition and feedback (K) are lesser causes of demotivation. Therefore, companies must prioritize addressing inadequate compensation and benefits, poor management, and a lack of career growth and development opportunities to eradicate employee demotivation. By doing so, firms can foster a positive work environment that promotes employee satisfaction and motivation, resulting in heightened productivity and performance.

The role of compensation and benefits in employee motivation and demotivation cannot be overstated, particularly in industries such as logistics that involve high workloads and require professional competence. This aligns with the theories of Maslow and Herzberg [86], which stress the importance of financial incentives in motivating employees. However, while sufficient compensation and benefits can boost employee motivation, inadequate ones can also lead to demotivation. As such, firms must establish a fair and just system of salary and bonuses to prevent employee demotivation. Beyond insufficient compensation and benefits (G), addressing poor work environment and culture (J) and lack of career growth and development opportunities (I) are also vital in preventing employee demotivation. Such factors can have a significant impact on employee satisfaction and motivation, which, in turn, can influence productivity and performance. Therefore, logistics service firms should prioritize developing positive work environments that promote employee satisfaction, address poor management practices, and offer opportunities for career growth and development.

Finally, it is widely recognized that the absence of career advancement and growth opportunities is a critical factor in employee demotivation in the Vietnamese logistics industry [3]. As the majority of workers in this industry are young adults, they have a strong desire for training and development opportunities that can help them progress in their careers. The lack of such opportunities can lead to disengagement and a decline in motivation among employees. To address this issue, HR professionals must provide employees with opportunities for growth and development that can keep them motivated and committed to their work. This can not only improve retention rates but also contribute to the overall success of the organization [59].

The optimal functioning of an organization is significantly contingent upon its human resources. Consequently, it is essential for managers to possess a comprehensive understanding of the factors that influence employee performance. Critical determinants of employee satisfaction include personal motivators and demotivators. Therefore, this study made three substantial contributions to the HRM literature as follows:

Firstly, this study proposed a novel approach that considers multiple criteria to synthesize the principal dimensions and factors of employee satisfaction from both motivation and demotivation perspectives. This leads to a more comprehensive understanding of HRM problems and ultimately enhances employee satisfaction. The use of SFSs sets them apart from other fuzzy sets because they define membership, non-membership, and hesitant degrees independently. Furthermore, the membership functions are defined on a spherical surface, providing a wider range of options for experts to express their preferences compared to other fuzzy sets. This feature enables accounting for uncertain and ambiguous information in the process of rating the relative importance of factors, leading to more accurate results.

Secondly, this study contributed to the advancement of the methodological calculation process by developing a fully completed spherical fuzzy MCDM technique (SF-Delphi-SF-DEMATEL), which is an improvement over previous studies that only applied partial SFS operations, thereby, leading to a more robust and data-driven decision-making process.

Thirdly, this study made significant contributions to the theoretical and methodological development of the HRM field, providing insights into effective decision-making across various contexts. These insights are valuable not only for HRM but also for other fields, such as finance and economics, where complex decisions require careful consideration.

## 5. Conclusions, Implications, Limitations, and Future Work

### 5.1. Conclusions

In this study, the spherical fuzzy MCDM model, which integrates multiple decision-making techniques, successfully achieved all the research objectives. Firstly, the model's distinct features, such as the use of fully completed spherical fuzzy operations, set it apart from previous decision-making methods. Secondly, the SF-Delphi approach was employed in the preliminary phase to validate 31 critical factors of employee motivation and 20 factors of demotivation based on the consensus opinions of 40 experts. Thirdly, the SF-DEMATEL technique identified the root causes of motivators and demotivators affecting employee satisfaction in the Vietnamese logistics service industry by exploring the causal linkages among both nominated dimensions and factors. Finally, the insights gained from the proposed model has provided guidance for developing effective interventions and policies to enhance employee satisfaction in the logistics service industry. In summary, the effectiveness of the proposed model highlights its potential to improve decision-making in various fields, including HRM, finance, and economics.

### 5.2. Theoretical Implications

The theoretical implications of this study are significant for both researchers and practitioners in HRM.

Firstly, this study's identification of the 11 main dimensions that impact employee satisfaction related to both motivation and demotivation perspectives provides valuable insights for managers and HR professionals in the logistics industry. Focusing on these critical areas can effectively improve employee motivation and reduce demotivation, ultimately enhancing overall employee satisfaction and organizational performance.

Secondly, this study provides additional evidence to support the significance of specific dimensions of employee motivation, such as compensation and benefits, work environment and culture, and recognition and support. While previous research has identified these factors as necessary, this study reinforces their importance in the logistics service industry. This information can guide future research to investigate further and confirm the impact of these factors on employee satisfaction and retention, leading to improved productivity and overall organizational success.

Thirdly, this study provides insights into the factors that have causal relationships with employee motivation and demotivation in the logistics industry. These findings can help stakeholders identify potential areas for improving employee satisfaction and develop appropriate interventions to address any issues.

Finally, drawing on related theories of employee satisfaction, this study provides valuable insights into the complex nature of employee satisfaction in the logistics industry. Specifically, it emphasizes the importance of addressing both physical and psychological factors in the workplace and highlights the need for significant financial and human resources investments to enhance employee motivation and reduce demotivators in further analysis.

*5.3. Managerial Implications*

The findings of the study have significant managerial implications for the logistics sector. To improve employee engagement and motivation, human resource managers must focus on several key elements related to pay and bonuses, including base salary, bonus structure, inadequate salaries and rewards, and back pay.

Firstly, regarding pay and bonuses, it is essential to establish a clear and detailed system of wage and bonus rules and make timely payments. Inadequate salaries and rewards, as well as back pay, can significantly demotivate employees, leading to reduced job satisfaction and employee turnover. To retain and motivate employees, human resource managers should prioritize developing a competitive compensation structure that includes base salary and bonus structures.

Secondly, career growth and development opportunities are another crucial factor in enhancing employee motivation. Logistics service firms must provide employees with opportunities for professional development, creativity, and innovation and offer career advancement opportunities. Lack of growth and development opportunities can lead to employees feeling undervalued, leading to reduced job satisfaction and employee turnover.

Thirdly, the working environment and culture play a critical role in employee motivation. A positive work culture, work-life balance, and workload are essential factors in this dimension. Managers in the logistics service sector must develop a collaborative, trusting, and respectful workplace atmosphere, provide flexible work arrangements, good vacation time, and manage workloads in a sensible manner to keep employees motivated and engaged.

Fourth, recognition, positive feedback, and constructive feedback also motivate employees. Therefore, companies must consistently recognize and reward employees' efforts and create a reward system for their contributions. This can include offering incentives for meeting performance targets, providing bonuses, and creating a culture of appreciation through positive feedback and constructive criticism.

Finally, to mitigate employee demotivation, organizations must address issues related to poor treatment by supervisors, inadequate leadership support, and ineffective management. This requires providing management-level members with capacity-building training and fostering a charismatic leadership image. Effective leadership involves appropriate delegation, evaluating and rewarding constructive alternatives, and fostering team engagement, while charismatic leadership involves setting an example for subordinates and creating a sense of pride in being part of the team. By improving management practices and fostering positive leadership, organizations can increase employee motivation and ultimately improve overall performance.

*5.4. Limitations and Future Work*

Although the fully completed two-stage spherical fuzzy MCDM model made significant contributions in identifying the main factors that affect employee satisfaction and their causal relationships in the logistics service industry, the study has certain limitations that require attention.

Firstly, the study did not consider the "weight" of the experts in the analysis, relying only on their subjective evaluations without considering their years of experience and expertise. To enhance the validity of the findings, increasing the number of experts and considering their weights in future research is necessary. Secondly, while involving experts (e.g., master's and Ph.D.s) is valuable, involving employees directly in the testing process could provide a more accurate representation of the proposed method's effectiveness and practicality in real-world situations. Future studies may consider involving employees to further validate the model's effectiveness in the logistics service industry. Thirdly, the study only focused on the logistics service sector in Vietnam, limiting the generalizability of the results to other industries and countries. Future research can use a similar approach to analyze employee motivation and demotivation in different businesses, nations, or areas to address this issue. Fourthly, the study did not consider other potential factors influencing employee satisfaction, such as technological advancements and the effects of globalization. Therefore, exploring these factors in future research can improve the accuracy and applicability of the proposed model. Finally, while the proposed model provides a valuable tool, further research is necessary to overcome the identified limitations and improve the model's accuracy and applicability in different contexts.

**Funding:** This research received no external funding.

**Data Availability Statement:** All the data generated or analyzed during the study are available upon request.

**Conflicts of Interest:** The authors declare no conflict of interest.

## References

1. Vietnam Logistics Business Association. Vietnam International Logistics. Available online: https://vilog.vn/en/overview/ (accessed on 11 April 2023).
2. World Bank. Logistics Performance Index 2023. Available online: https://lpi.worldbank.org/international/global (accessed on 11 April 2023).
3. Nguyen, H.P. Human Resource Management of Logistics in Vietnam: Status and Policy Solutions. *Int. J. Innov. Creat. Chang.* **2020**, *11*, 569–583.
4. Nguyen, P.-H. Spherical Fuzzy Decision-Making Approach Integrating Delphi and TOPSIS for Package Tour Provider Selection. *Math. Probl. Eng.* **2022**, *2022*, 29. [CrossRef]
5. Smithers, G.L.; Walker, D.H.T. The Effect of the Workplace on Motivation and Demotivation of Construction Professionals. *Constr. Manag. Econ.* **2000**, *18*, 833–841. [CrossRef]
6. Thi Hoai Thu, N.; Wilson, A.; McDonald, F. Motivation or Demotivation of Health Workers Providing Maternal Health Services in Rural Areas in Vietnam: Findings from a Mixed-Methods Study. *Hum. Resour. Health* **2015**, *13*, 91. [CrossRef]
7. Kikulwe, E.M.; Okurut, S.; Ajambo, S.; Nowakunda, K.; Stoian, D.; Naziri, D. Postharvest Losses and Their Determinants: A Challenge to Creating a Sustainable Cooking Banana Value Chain in Uganda. *Sustainability* **2018**, *10*, 2381. [CrossRef]
8. Anisah, C.; Wisesa, A. The Impact of Covid-19 towards Employee Motivation and Demotivation Influence Employee Performance: A Study of Sayurmoms. *Eqien J. Ekon. Dan Bisnis* **2021**, *8*, 371–380. [CrossRef]
9. Sukamolson, S. Fundamentals of Quantitative Research. *Lang. Inst. Chulalongkorn Univ.* **2007**, *1*, 1–20.
10. Yauch, C.A.; Steudel, H.J. Complementary Use of Qualitative and Quantitative Cultural Assessment Methods. *Organ. Res. methods* **2003**, *6*, 465–481. [CrossRef]
11. Butdee, S.; Phuangsalee, P. Uncertain Risk Assessment Modelling for Bus Body Manufacturing Supply Chain Using AHP and Fuzzy AHP. *Procedia Manuf.* **2019**, *30*, 663–670. [CrossRef]
12. Zadeh, L.A. Fuzzy Sets. *Inf. Control.* **1965**, *8*, 338–353. [CrossRef]
13. Zadeh, L.A. The Concept of a Linguistic Variable and Its Application to Approximate Reasoning—I. *Inf. Sci.* **1975**, *8*, 199–249. [CrossRef]
14. Atanassov, K.T. Intuitionistic Fuzzy Sets. *Intuit. Fuzzy Sets* **1999**, *35*, 1–137.
15. Smarandache, F. Neutrosophy: Neutrosophic Probability, Set, and Logic: Analytic Synthesis & Synthetic Analysis. *Am. Res. Press* **1998**, *105*, 97–99.
16. Torra, V. Hesitant Fuzzy Sets. *Int. J. Intell. Syst.* **2010**, *25*, 529–539. [CrossRef]
17. Yager, R.R. Pythagorean Fuzzy Subsets. In Proceedings of the 2013 Joint IFSA World Congress and NAFIPS Annual Meeting (IFSA/NAFIPS), Edmonton, AB, Canada, 24–28 June 2013; pp. 57–61.
18. Cuong, B.C.; Kreinovich, V. Picture Fuzzy Sets. *J. Comput. Sci. Cybern.* **2014**, *30*, 409–420.
19. Mahmood, T.; Ullah, K.; Khan, Q.; Jan, N. An Approach toward Decision-Making and Medical Diagnosis Problems Using the Concept of Spherical Fuzzy Sets. *Neural Comput. Appl.* **2019**, *31*, 7041–7053. [CrossRef]
20. Kutlu Gündoğdu, F.; Kahraman, C. Spherical Fuzzy Sets and Decision Making Applications. In Proceedings of the International Conference on Intelligent and Fuzzy Systems, Istanbul, Turkey, 23–25 July 2019; pp. 979–987.
21. Nguyen, P.-H.; Dang, T.-T.; Nguyen, K.-A.; Pham, H.-A. Spherical Fuzzy WASPAS-Based Entropy Objective Weighting for International Payment Method Selection. *Comput. Mater. Contin.* **2022**, *72*, 2055–2075. [CrossRef]
22. Nguyen, P.H.; Tsai, J.F.; Dang, T.T.; Lin, M.H.; Pham, H.A.; Nguyen, K.A. A Hybrid Spherical Fuzzy MCDM Approach to Prioritize Governmental Intervention Strategies against the COVID-19 Pandemic: A Case Study from Vietnam. *Mathematics* **2021**, *9*, 2626. [CrossRef]
23. Nguyen, T.-L.; Nguyen, P.-H.; Pham, H.-A.; Nguyen, T.-G.; Nguyen, D.-T.; Tran, T.-H.; Le, H.-C.; Phung, H.-T. A Novel Integrating Data Envelopment Analysis and Spherical Fuzzy MCDM Approach for Sustainable Supplier Selection in Steel Industry. *Mathematics* **2022**, *10*, 1897. [CrossRef]
24. Gabus, A.; Fontela, E. World Problems, an Invitation to Further Thought within the Framework of DEMATEL. *Battelle Geneva Res. Cent. Geneva Switz.* **1972**, 1–8.

25. Gündogdu, F.K.; Kahraman, C. (Eds.) Optimal Site Selection of Electric Vehicle Charging Station by Using Spherical Fuzzy TOPSIS Method. In *Decision Making with Spherical Fuzzy Sets*; Springer: Berlin/Heidelberg, Germany, 2021; pp. 201–216.
26. Özdemirci, F.; Yüksel, S.; Dinçer, H.; Eti, S. An Assessment of Alternative Social Banking Systems Using T-Spherical Fuzzy TOP-DEMATEL Approach. *Decis. Anal. J.* **2023**, *6*, 100184. [CrossRef]
27. Erdoğan, M.; Kaya, İ.; Karaşan, A.; Çolak, M. Evaluation of Autonomous Vehicle Driving Systems for Risk Assessment Based on Three-Dimensional Uncertain Linguistic Variables. *Appl. Soft Comput.* **2021**, *113*, 107934. [CrossRef]
28. Gül, S. Spherical Fuzzy Extension of DEMATEL (SF-DEMATEL). *Int. J. Intell. Syst.* **2020**, *35*, 1329–1353. [CrossRef]
29. Maslow, A.H. A Theory of Human Motivation. *Psychol. Rev.* **1943**, *50*, 370–396. [CrossRef]
30. Rasskazova, E.; Ivanova, T.; Sheldon, K. Comparing the Effects of Low-Level and High-Level Worker Need-Satisfaction: A Synthesis of the Self-Determination and Maslow Need Theories. *Motiv. Emot.* **2016**, *40*, 541–555. [CrossRef]
31. Hinton, B.L. An Empirical Investigation of the Herzberg Methodology and Two-Factor Theory. *Organ. Behav. Hum. Perform.* **1968**, *3*, 286–309. [CrossRef]
32. Lee, B.; Lee, C.; Choi, I.; Kim, J. Analyzing Determinants of Job Satisfaction Based on Two-Factor Theory. *Sustain.* **2022**, *14*, 12557. [CrossRef]
33. Pritchard, R.D. Equity Theory: A Review and Critique. *Organ. Behav. Hum. Perform.* **1969**, *4*, 176–211. [CrossRef]
34. Watters, E.R. Factors in Employee Motivation: Expectancy and Equity Theories. *J. Color. Polic. Off. J. Color. Assoc. Chiefs Police* **2021**, *6*, 970.
35. Heneman, H.G.; Schwab, D.P. Evaluation of research on expectancy theory predictions of employee performance. *Psychol. Bull.* **1972**, *78*, 1–9. [CrossRef]
36. Matthews, B.; Daigle, J.; Cooper, J. Causative Effects of Motivation to Transfer Learning among Relational Dyads: The Test of a Model. *Eur. J. Manag. Bus. Econ.* **2020**, *29*, 297–314. [CrossRef]
37. Allah Pitchay, A.; Aboue Eliz, N.M.; Ganesan, Y.; Mydin, A.A.; Ratnasari, R.T.; Mohd Thas Thaker, M.A. Self-Determination Theory and Individuals' Intention to Participate in Donation Crowdfunding. *Int. J. Islam. Middle East. Financ. Manag.* **2022**, *15*. [CrossRef]
38. Richmond, V.P.; McCroskey, J.C. Management Communication Style, Tolerance for Disagreement, and Innovativeness as Predictors of Employee Satisfaction: A Comparison of Single-Factor, Two-Factor, and Multiple-Factor Approaches. *Ann. Int. Commun. Assoc.* **1979**. [CrossRef]
39. Yusoff, W.F.W.; Kian, T.S.; Idris, M.T.M. Herzberg's Two Factors Theory on Work Motivation: Does Its Work for Todays Environment. *Glob. J. Commer. Manag.* **2013**, *2*, 18–22.
40. Franco, L.M.; Bennett, S.; Kanfer, R. Health Sector Reform and Public Sector Health Worker Motivation: A Conceptual Framework. *Soc. Sci. Med.* **2002**, *54*, 1255–1266. [CrossRef] [PubMed]
41. Dieleman, M.; Cuong, P.V.; Anh, L.V.; Martineau, T. Identifying Factors for Job Motivation of Rural Health Workers in North Viet Nam. *Hum. Resour. Health* **2003**, *1*, 10. [CrossRef]
42. Adair, J.E. *Leadership and Motivation: The Fifty-Fifty Rule and the Eight Key Principles of Motivating Others*; Kogan Page Publishers: London, UK, 2006; ISBN 0749447982.
43. Oyedele, L.O. Analysis of Architects' Demotivating Factors in Design Firms. *Int. J. Proj. Manag.* **2013**, *31*, 342–354. [CrossRef]
44. Kakepoto, I.; Hadina, H.; Omar, N.O.M.; Omar, H. Conceptions on Low Motivation of Engineers in Engineering Workplace of Pakistan. *Eur. J. Bus. Manag.* **2012**, *4*, 149.
45. Aung, Z.M.; San Santoso, D.; Dodanwala, T.C. Effects of Demotivational Managerial Practices on Job Satisfaction and Job Performance: Empirical Evidence from Myanmar's Construction Industry. *J. Eng. Technol. Manag.* **2023**, *67*, 101730. [CrossRef]
46. Dill, J.; Erickson, R.J.; Diefendorff, J.M. Motivation in Caring Labor: Implications for the Well-Being and Employment Outcomes of Nurses. *Soc. Sci. Med.* **2016**, *167*, 99–106. [CrossRef]
47. Mbaruku, G.M.; Larson, E.; Kimweri, A.; Kruk, M.E. What Elements of the Work Environment Are Most Responsible for Health Worker Dissatisfaction in Rural Primary Care Clinics in Tanzania? *Hum. Resour. Health* **2014**, *12*, 38. [CrossRef] [PubMed]
48. Mutale, W.; Ayles, H.; Bond, V.; Mwanamwenge, M.T.; Balabanova, D. Measuring Health Workers' Motivation in Rural Health Facilities: Baseline Results from Three Study Districts in Zambia. *Hum. Resour. Health* **2013**, *11*, 8. [CrossRef] [PubMed]
49. Tourangeau, A.E.; Cummings, G.; Cranley, L.A.; Ferron, E.M.; Harvey, S. Determinants of Hospital Nurse Intention to Remain Employed: Broadening Our Understanding. *J. Adv. Nurs.* **2010**, *66*, 22–32. [CrossRef] [PubMed]
50. Jex, S.M.; Britt, T.W. *Organizational Psychology: A Scientist-Practitioner Approach*; John Wiley & Sons: Hoboken, NJ, USA, 2014; ISBN 1118724070.
51. Mitchell, T.R.; Daniels, D. Observations and Commentary on Recent Research in Work Motivation. *Motiv. Work Behav.* **2003**, *7*, 225–254.
52. Chillakuri, B.; Vanka, S. Understanding the Effects of Perceived Organizational Support and High-Performance Work Systems on Health Harm through Sustainable HRM Lens: A Moderated Mediated Examination. *Empl. Relations* **2022**, *44*. [CrossRef]
53. Bies, R.J. Interactional Justice: Communication Criteria of Fairness. *Res. Negot. Organ.* **1986**, *1*, 43–55.
54. Colquitt, J.A. On the Dimensionality of Organizational Justice: A Construct Validation of a Measure. *J. Appl. Psychol.* **2001**, *86*, 386. [CrossRef]

55. Rose, T.; Manley, K. Motivation toward Financial Incentive Goals on Construction Projects. *J. Bus. Res.* **2011**, *64*, 765–773. [CrossRef]
56. Umphress, E.E.; Labianca, G.; Brass, D.J.; Kass, E.; Scholten, L. The Role of Instrumental and Expressive Social Ties in Employees' Perceptions of Organizational Justice. *Organ. Sci.* **2003**, *14*, 738–753. [CrossRef]
57. Kacmar, K.M.; Bozeman, D.P.; Carlson, D.S.; Anthony, W.P. An Examination of the Perceptions of Organizational Politics Model: Replication and Extension. *Hum. Relat.* **1999**, *52*, 383–416. [CrossRef]
58. Kaming, P.F.; Olomolaiye, P.O.; Holt, G.D.; Harris, F.C. What Motivates Construction Craftsmen in Developing Countries? A Case Study of Indonesia. *Build. Environ.* **1998**, *33*, 131–141. [CrossRef]
59. Pak, K.; Kooij, D.T.A.M.; De Lange, A.H.; Van Veldhoven, M.J.P.M. Human Resource Management and the Ability, Motivation and Opportunity to Continue Working: A Review of Quantitative Studies. *Hum. Resour. Manag. Rev.* **2019**, *29*, 336–352. [CrossRef]
60. Ding, M.J.; Kam, B.H.; Zhang, J.Y.; Jie, F. Effects of Human Resource Management Practices on Logistics and Supply Chain Competencies–Evidence from China Logistics Service Market. *Int. J. Prod. Res.* **2015**, *53*, 2885–2903. [CrossRef]
61. Amabile, T.; Gryskiewicz, S.S. *Creativity in the R & D Laboratory*; Center for Creative Leadership: Greensboro, NC, USA, 1987; ISBN 0912879289.
62. Haner, U. Spaces for Creativity and Innovation in Two Established Organizations. *Creat. Innov. Manag.* **2005**, *14*, 288–298. [CrossRef]
63. Laub, J.A. Assessing the Servant Organization; Development of the Organizational Leadership Assessment (OLA) Model. Dissertation Abstracts International. *Procedia Soc. Behav. Sci.* **1999**, *60*, 308.
64. Moss, S.E.; Sanchez, J.I. Are Your Employees Avoiding You? Managerial Strategies for Closing the Feedback Gap. *Acad. Manag. Perspect.* **2004**, *18*, 32–44. [CrossRef]
65. Nguyen, P.H. GA-GDEMATEL: A Novel Approach to Optimize Recruitment and Personnel Selection Problems. *Math. Probl. Eng.* **2022**, *2022*, 1–17. [CrossRef]
66. Esangbedo, M.O.; Bai, S.; Mirjalili, S.; Wang, Z. Evaluation of Human Resource Information Systems Using Grey Ordinal Pairwise Comparison MCDM Methods. *Expert Syst. Appl.* **2021**, *182*, 115151. [CrossRef]
67. Yildiz, D.; Temur, G.T.; Beskese, A.; Bozbura, F.T. A Spherical Fuzzy Analytic Hierarchy Process Based Approach to Prioritize Career Management Activities Improving Employee Retention. *J. Intell. Fuzzy Syst.* **2020**, *39*, 6603–6618. [CrossRef]
68. Saeidi, P.; Mardani, A.; Mishra, A.R.; Cajas Cajas, V.E.; Carvajal, M.G. Evaluate Sustainable Human Resource Management in the Manufacturing Companies Using an Extended Pythagorean Fuzzy SWARA-TOPSIS Method. *J. Clean. Prod.* **2022**, *370*, 133380. [CrossRef]
69. Lai, Y.L.; Ishizaka, A. The Application of Multi-Criteria Decision Analysis Methods into Talent Identification Process: A Social Psychological Perspective. *J. Bus. Res.* **2020**, *109*, 637–647. [CrossRef]
70. Stević, Ž.; Brković, N. A Novel Integrated FUCOM-MARCOS Model for Evaluation of Human Resources in a Transport Company. *Logistics* **2020**, *4*, 4. [CrossRef]
71. Knežević, S.P.; Mandić, K.; Mitrović, A.; Dmitrović, V.; Delibašić, B. An FAHP-TOPSIS Framework for Analysis of the Employee Productivity in the Serbian Electrical Power Companies. *Manag. Sustain. Bus. Manag. Solut. Emerg. Econ.* **2017**, *22*, 47. [CrossRef]
72. Safari, H.; Cruz-Machado, V.A.; Faghih, A.; Heidari, M.; Rabor, F.M. Assessment Employee Empowerment through Combination of FAHP and VIKOR Methods. In *Advances in Intelligent Systems and Computing*; Janusz, K., Ed.; Systems Research Institute: Warszawa, Poland, 2014.
73. Kalvakolanu, S.; Sama, H.R.; Mathew, M.; Somasekhar, D. Measuring Job Satisfaction Levels of Airport Employees Using Entropy, Critic and TOPSIS Methods. *Int. J. Bus. Excell.* **2022**, *27*, 1–22. [CrossRef]
74. Malebye, W.P.R.; Seeletse, S.M.; Rivera, M.A. Merit Measures and Validation in Employee Evaluation and Selection. *Probl. Perspect. Manag.* **2015**, *13*, 66–78.
75. Akins, R.B.; Tolson, H.; Cole, B.R. Stability of Response Characteristics of a Delphi Panel: Application of Bootstrap Data Expansion. *BMC Med. Res. Methodol.* **2005**, *5*, 37. [CrossRef]
76. Murphy, M.K.; Black, N.A.; Lamping, D.L.; McKee, C.M.; Sanderson, C.F.; Askham, J.; Marteau, T. Consensus Development Methods, and Their Use in Clinical Guideline Development. *Health Technol. Assess.* **1998**, *2*, 1–88. [CrossRef]
77. Nguyen, P.; Tran, L.; Nguyen, H.B.; Ho, T.P.; Duong, Q.; Tran, T. Unlocking the Potential of Open Innovation through Understanding the Interrelationship among Key Determinants of FDI Attractiveness. *J. Open Innov. Technol. Mark. Complex.* **2023**, *9*, 100021. [CrossRef]
78. Okoli, C.; Pawlowski, S.D. The Delphi Method as a Research Tool: An Example, Design Considerations and Applications. *Inf. Manag.* **2004**, *42*, 15–29. [CrossRef]
79. Nguyen, P.H.; Nguyen, T.L.; Le, H.Q.; Pham, T.Q.; Nguyen, H.A.; Pham, C.V. How Does the Competitiveness Index Promote Foreign Direct Investment at the Provincial Level in Vietnam? An Integrated Grey Delphi–DEA Model Approach. *Mathematics* **2023**, *11*, 1500. [CrossRef]
80. Delaney, J.T.; Huselid, M.A. The Impact of Human Resource Management Practices on Perceptions of Organizational Performance. *Acad. Manag. J.* **1996**, *39*, 949–969. [CrossRef]
81. Davidescu, A.A.; Apostu, S.-A.; Paul, A.; Casuneanu, I. Work Flexibility, Job Satisfaction, and Job Performance among Romanian Employees—Implications for Sustainable Human Resource Management. *Sustainability* **2020**, *12*, 6086. [CrossRef]

82. Zhou, A.J.; Fey, C.; Yildiz, H.E. Fostering Integration through HRM Practices: An Empirical Examination of Absorptive Capacity and Knowledge Transfer in Cross-Border M&As. *J. World Bus.* **2020**, *55*, 100947.
83. Rao, K.; Stenger, A.J.; Wu, H.-J. Training Future Logistics Managers: Logistics Strategies within the Corporate Planning Framework. *J. Bus. Logist.* **1994**, *15*, 249.
84. Chatterjee, S.; DuttaGupta, S.; Upadhyay, P. Sustainability of Microenterprises: An Empirical Analysis. *Benchmarking An Int. J.* **2018**, *25*, 919–931. [CrossRef]
85. Chang, R.-D.; Zuo, J.; Zhao, Z.-Y.; Soebarto, V.; Lu, Y.; Zillante, G.; Gan, X.-L. Sustainability Attitude and Performance of Construction Enterprises: A China Study. *J. Clean. Prod.* **2018**, *172*, 1440–1451. [CrossRef]
86. Aghayeva, K.; Ślusarczyk, B. Analytic Hierarchy of Motivating and Demotivating Factors Affecting Labor Productivity in the Construction Industry: The Case of Azerbaijan. *Sustainability* **2019**, *11*, 5975. [CrossRef]

**Disclaimer/Publisher's Note:** The statements, opinions and data contained in all publications are solely those of the individual author(s) and contributor(s) and not of MDPI and/or the editor(s). MDPI and/or the editor(s) disclaim responsibility for any injury to people or property resulting from any ideas, methods, instructions or products referred to in the content.

*Review*

# Fuzzy Random Option Pricing in Continuous Time: A Systematic Review and an Extension of Vasicek's Equilibrium Model of the Term Structure

Jorge de Andrés-Sánchez

Social and Business Research Lababoratory, University Rovira i Virgili, Campus Bellissens, 43203 Reus, Spain; jorge.deandres@urv.cat

**Abstract:** Fuzzy random option pricing in continuous time (FROPCT) has emerged as an active research field over the past two decades; thus, there is a need for a comprehensive review that provides a broad perspective on the literature and identifies research gaps. In this regard, we conducted a structure review of the literature by using the WoS and SCOPUS databases while following the PRISMA criteria. With this review, we outline the primary research streams, publication outlets, and notable authors in this domain. Furthermore, the literature review revealed a lack of advancements for the equilibrium models of the yield curve. This finding serves as a primary motivation for the second contribution of this paper, which involves an extension of Vasicek's yield curve equilibrium model. Specifically, we introduce the existence of fuzzy uncertainty in the parameters governing interest rate movements, including the speed of reversion, equilibrium short-term interest rate, and volatility. By incorporating fuzzy uncertainty, we enhance the model's ability to capture the complexities of real-world interest rate dynamics. Moreover, this paper presents an empirical application of the proposed extension to the term structure of fixed-income public bonds in European Union. The empirical analysis suggests the suitability of the proposed extension of Vasicek's model for practical applications.

**Keywords:** option pricing; fuzzy random variables; fuzzy numbers; fuzzy random option pricing; Vasicek's model of term structure

**MSC:** 62A88; 91G20; 91G30

Citation: Andrés-Sánchez, J.d. Fuzzy Random Option Pricing in Continuous Time: A Systematic Review and an Extension of Vasicek's Equilibrium Model of the Term Structure. *Mathematics* 2023, *11*, 2455. https://doi.org/10.3390/math11112455

Academic Editor: Chuangyin Dang

Received: 21 April 2023
Revised: 19 May 2023
Accepted: 24 May 2023
Published: 25 May 2023

**Copyright:** © 2023 by the author. Licensee MDPI, Basel, Switzerland. This article is an open access article distributed under the terms and conditions of the Creative Commons Attribution (CC BY) license (https://creativecommons.org/licenses/by/4.0/).

## 1. Introduction

Option pricing mathematics started its development at the end of the 19th century [1] and has been an active research field since the second half of the 20th century [2]. The Black–Scholes–Merton option pricing model [3,4] (the BSM model hereinafter) is commonly considered a milestone, not only in the constrained field of option pricing, but also in the financial arena [2]. The value of the model [3,4] is twofold. From a strict perspective of the options on financial asset pricing, the BSM model provides a very operational formula, as the parameters required for its implementation are easy to obtain and do not depend on subjective risk attitudes. From a more general setting of pricing any asset, valuation through the so-called "arbitrage argument", which is generalized by the concepts of "risk-neutral valuation" and "equivalent martingale measure", allows for any asset to be valued according to the mathematical expectation of the present value of its future cash flows [5].

Thus, the BSM model can be applied to options on stocks but also to any asset that includes some type of optionality. Therefore, it can be used to determine the price of assets such as convertible bonds and develop formulas for new types of options such as exotic options or novel derivative assets such as catastrophe bonds [2]. Additionally, the model has also been applied to traditional assets such as mortgage-backed loans or life insurance policies with guaranteed returns [2] and real assets by using real option theory [6]. In fact, Black and Scholes [3] explicitly state in their work that their formula can be used to value companies.

The analytical framework of the BSM model has been particularly productive at modeling the term structure of interest rates with arbitrage-based models, and it has provided a solid mathematical foundation for pricing interest rate derivative instruments such as bond options, caps, floors, or other options, and also to assess the dynamics of the yield curve. Following [7], the BSM model can be differentiated into models whose parameters do not depend on time [8–10] and those with time-varying parameters [11]. The first type of development, while providing a valuable analytical framework to conduct economic analyses on the yield curve, does not capture its empirical shapes especially well. Thus, due to its parsimony, it is very useful to conduct a great deal of financial and economic analyses, but when valuing interest rate derivatives, their usefulness is limited [7]. On the other hand, time-dependent parameter models are calibrated based on the actual observed prices of zero-coupon instruments, which results in perfect adherence to the observed temporal structure forms, but they suffer from a lack of parsimony [7].

Option valuation models, since their early stages in the late 19th century, have been grounded in the analytical framework of statistics and stochastic calculus. Therefore, they assume a strict risk environment where probabilities of alternative event realizations can be established [12]. Undoubtedly, these models provide a valuable analytical framework. However, financial activities are conducted with information that involves different degrees of knowledge, and these models can combine risk with other sources of uncertainty, such as imprecision or vagueness. Fuzzy set theory (FST) has provided tools for option pricing when modeling nonprobabilistic uncertainty, such as fuzzy measures, fuzzy numbers, or fuzzy regression, since the early 2000s [13]. While stochastic models provide rigorous analytical groundwork, the addition of fuzzy tools can improve their results by allowing for the introduction of additional sources of uncertainty to risk [12,13].

Among the various ways in which FST has been applied to option valuation (FOP), the most fruitful is what we can label as fuzzy random option pricing (FROP) [13]. This set of contributions extends conventional option valuation models to the hypothesis that knowledge of the parameters governing financial asset price movements is not crisp, as they could be affected by issues such as fuzziness or imprecision [12]. The uncertainty existing in these parameters, such as volatility, observed price of the underlying asset, or discount rates, is modeled by using fuzzy numbers [12]. Thus, FROP can be applied to continuous time models by using the BSM framework or to discrete-time models [12]. The first approach, which is the scope of this paper, will be referred to as FROP in continuous time (FROPCT).

This work has two research objectives within the field of FROPCT:

1. The first objective is to present the results of a systematic literature review on FROP that covers the period from the first work up to March 2023 by using Web of Knowledge (WoS) and SCOPUS. We will focus on contributions related to FROPCT. This systematic review aims to offer a valuable perspective on the main contributions and developments in FROPCT and to identify research gaps. Among these research gaps, we have observed that FROPCT has achieved significant development in the context of equity [14–18] and real options [19–21]. However, extensions to the context of fixed-income markets and interest-rate-sensitive instruments are relatively scarce.

2. The aforementioned research gap motivated the second research objective of this study, which involves developing a fuzzy random extension of Vasicek's yield curve model [8]. In this regard, we will assume that the uncertainty about the parameters governing interest rates (mean reverting rate, long-term mean, and volatility) is modeled by using fuzzy numbers. Our extension will be applied to the zero-coupon curve published by the European Central Bank for bonds with the highest credit rating in Europe.

We believe that this paper provides three contributions to FROPCT. The structured literature review serves as a foundation for subsequent advancements in this field by identifying several research gaps. The introduction of a FROP focus to model uncertainty in parameters that describe the yield curve is a novelty. Additionally, the proposed methodology for estimating these parameters by using objective information from fixed-income markets is an original approach that combines autoregressive time series with a coherent probability–possibility transformation criterion [22] instead of a fuzzy regression method such as those proposed in [23] in a fuzzy option pricing setting.

The rest of the paper is structured as follows: In Section 2, we present the results of a comprehensive review of related works framed within FROPCT, following the PRISMA criteria. The findings of this section motivated Section 3, which proposes an extension of Vasicek's equilibrium model for the term structure [8]. This extension will be applied to the curve fitting of coupon bonds in the risk-free bond market of European Union issuers. In Section 4, we discuss the main results obtained in this study. We conclude by highlighting the main limitations of the presented work and suggesting future lines of research.

## 2. Bibliographical Analysis

### 2.1. Methodology

The bibliographic review was conducted following the PRISMA guidelines [24]. Its implementation required us to specify the methodology used to search for the documents to be reviewed, the databases where these documents should be found, the types of documents that will be considered, etc. Subsequently, how the obtained documents have been compiled must be determined. The next step is to classify the papers identifying the sources, authors, and main areas of application of FROP in continuous time.

Regarding the eligible studies, we only considered articles written in English and published as journal articles or book chapters until 31 March 2023. We did not consider other types of documents that are typically categorized as "grey literature," such as conference proceedings or documents in digital repositories. The reason is that normally, after a peer review process, these types of contributions are usually published as articles or book chapters. Additionally, we only analyzed works written in English. We chose to combine two databases, SCOPUS and WoS, in this review, as they are commonly used in bibliographic reviews, and it is recommended to combine more than one bibliographic source when the topic is not very broad [13].

The search was executed on titles, abstracts, and keywords using the following search: ("option pricing" OR "arbitrage model" OR "risk neutral pricing" OR "equivalent martingale measure") AND ("fuzzy sets" OR "fuzzy mathematics" OR "fuzzy numbers"). Figure 1 graphically shows how we proceeded.

There were a total of 117 documents reported by SCOPUS and 144 by WoS. We eliminated duplicate works and examined the title, abstract, keywords, and, if necessary, the full document to ensure that the papers were effectively related to FROP.

Finally, we identified 104 documents related to FROP. We found 83 documents common to both databases; 7 were exclusively provided by WoS, and SCOPUS provided 15. At this stage, the Meyer's index, which quantifies the level of coverage attributable to each database, recorded a rate of 46.15% for WoS and 53.85% for SCOPUS. The degree of overlap, i.e., the redundancy rate of a database, was 92.13% for WoS and 84.54% for SCOPUS.

Our bibliographic exploration showed that FROPCT was developed in 77 articles. Within these documents, 2 came exclusively from the WoS database and 11 from SCOPUS. Therefore, 64 documents were common to both SCOPUS and WoS. At this step, Meyer's index was 55.84% for SCOPUS and 44.16% for WoS. We verified an overlap level of 85.33% for SCOPUS and 96.97% for WoS.

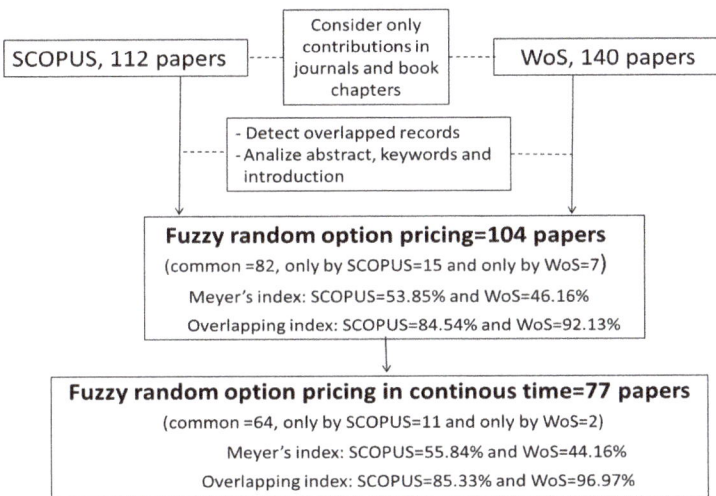

**Figure 1.** Protocol used to select articles on FROP and FROPCT for review. Source: own elaboration by following PRISMA guidelines [22].

*2.2. Classification*

Figure 2 shows the evolution of the production of FROPCT by year of publication. The first works were published in the years 2001–2003, which means that the introduction of fuzzy numbers in option valuation started in the beginning of the 21st century. We could observe a trend until 2013 that, although not monotonic, was clearly increasing. In that year, the maximum number of published works (8) was reached. From that year, works on FROPCT remained within a fluctuation range of 3 to 8 annual contributions. Therefore, although FROP is not a mainstream topic in fuzzy mathematics, it can be considered a consolidated topic within the applications of fuzzy logic.

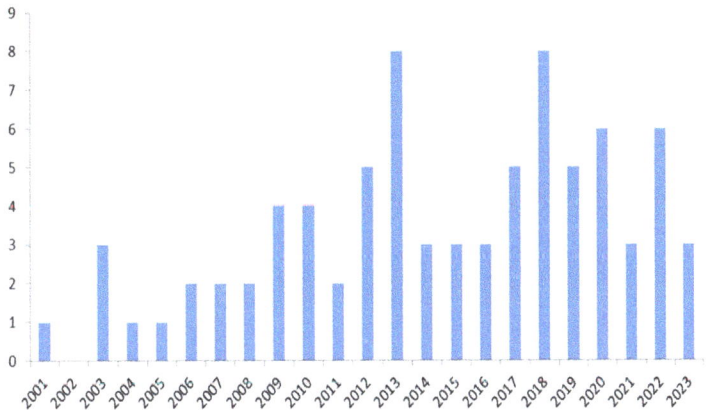

**Figure 2.** Evolution of the papers on fuzzy random option pricing in continuous time published during 2003–2023. Source: own elaboration based on the WoS and Scopus databases.

Table 1 displays the works reviewed in this article that were published in 2015 or received more than 25 citations in the WoS or SCOPUS databases. These were classified in columns according to the stochastic process that serves as the basis for fuzzy extensions.

**Table 1.** Revised papers on fuzzy stochastic option pricing in continuous time from 2015 or at least with 25 citations in the WoS or Scopus databases.

|  | Geometric Brownian Process (BSM) | Geometric Brownian Process (More than One Asset) | Other Brownian Processes |
|---|---|---|---|
| All papers in the table | [14,15,21,25–50] | [19,20,51–53] | [48,54] |
| Fuzzy numbers of higher degree | [42,47] |  | [48] |
| Non-European options | [38,49] | [19,20,51–53] | [48,54] |
| Hedging | [14,28,31,33,35] |  | [54] |
| Application to financial markets | [23,25,26,36,37] |  |  |
| Real Options | [21,30,42] | [19,20,51–53] | [54] |
| Other financial applications | [45,47,50] |  | [48] |

|  | Jump diffusion | Heston | Fractional | Levy |
|---|---|---|---|---|
| All papers in the table | [55,56] | [57] | [18,58–63] | [16,17,55,64–71] |
| Fuzzy numbers of higher degree |  |  | [61] |  |
| Non-European options |  |  | [60,61] | [17,70] |
| Hedging |  |  |  |  |
| Application to financial markets |  | [57] | [18] | [17,71] |
| Real Options |  |  |  |  |
| Other financial applications |  |  |  | [67,69] |

Source: own elaboration based on WoS and Scopus databases.

Table 1 shows that the majority of works (29) assumed a single underlying asset and geometric Brownian motion. Thus, the majority were based on the application of the Black–Scholes–Merton (BSM) model. However, there are several nuances to consider in this regard. For example, ref. [49] extended the Asian option valuation formula of Kemma and Vorst [72]. Additionally, within the framework of geometric Brownian motion, there were 5 works that assumed that various parameters of the Margrabe exchange valuation model [73] and Geske's compound option model pricing formula [74] are given by fuzzy numbers.

In the framework of more complex stochastic models, fractional Brownian motion (7 works) and the more general Levy modeling (11 works) have been extensively addressed. It is also worth mentioning that Merton's jump-diffusion model [75] and the Heston formula [76] have been objects of attention in the FROPCT literature.

In most cases, the analyzed topics are technical aspects that emerge from the juxtaposition of stochastic calculus with fuzzy mathematics. The most common mathematical issue is the application of fuzzy arithmetic, which quantifies certain parameters of the generalized option formula. Without being exhaustive, we can indicate that [43,44] quantified these parameters in the context of the BSM model, refs. [20,51] quantified them by using a multiple underlying asset options framework that was governed by Brownian motion, ref. [55] quantified them by using the framework of a diffusion and jump model, ref. [57] quantified them via the fuzzification of Heston's model, and ref. [58] quantified them via fuzzy fractional models or the fuzzy extension to Levy stochastic processes [16,71]. In some cases, especially in articles that were based on the standard BSM model, issues associated with fuzzy analysis were refined. These issues may embed in areas such as defuzzification [39,40,48] or the construction of membership functions for the inputs of the pricing formula or the final price of the asset [26,27,36,37].

The first row of Table 1 indicates that the modeling of uncertainty in the parameters of the valuation formula is usually conducted by using type-1 fuzzy numbers (i.e., conventional fuzzy numbers). Exceptions are [42,61], which model uncertain parameters with type-2 fuzzy numbers, and [47], which use intuitionistic fuzzy numbers. In most cases, the assumed form of the fuzzy magnitude is linear, i.e., triangular or trapezoidal. However, within type-1 fuzzy numbers, the literature has also used other shapes, such as adaptive fuzzy numbers [14,39,40], Gaussian fuzzy numbers [28], or parabolic fuzzy numbers [17]. The parameters that are considered crisp and those that are considered fuzzy are established ad hoc depending on the problem being addressed. In options on financial assets traded in financial markets, the volatility (always), risk-free interest rate, and underlying asset value (in most cases) are assumed to be estimated with fuzzy numbers. However, the strike price and expiration are crisp parameters because they are clearly defined in the contract. However, in terms of real options, the strike price [21] or even the expiration [13] may not be known with precision and, therefore, are susceptible to being quantified with fuzzy numbers.

Starting from the second row (included), relevant topics on financial pricing addressed by concrete papers are indicated. A great proportion of papers price European options. However, other types of options, such as American [17], binary [60,66], exchange [19,20,51], or compound [53,63,70] options, were analyzed. A sensitivity analysis of the option prices from the perspective of the BSM model has been the subject of attention of various authors [28,31]. Likewise, while fuzzy Malliavin calculus has been applied in [33,54], ref. [26] showed that the use of Greeks can be useful in the linear approximation of the membership functions of fuzzy option prices.

We must acknowledge that there is a relative scarcity of empirical applications of FROPCT [12,13]. Among these works, notable contributions include [27], which proposes the utilization of congruent probability–possibility transformations [27] to model option volatility based on empirical data, and [23,36,37], which employ fuzzy regression models to estimate the volatility, kurtosis, and skewness of the asset returns. The papers [25,26] demonstrated the good adherence of the fuzzy version of the standard BSM formula to the traded prices on the Spanish stock index IBEX-35. Additionally, ref. [57], which is an extension of [76]; ref. [18], which explored the fuzzy extension of the geometric fractional Brownian motion; and [17,71], who conducted fuzzy Levy modeling, present comprehensive empirical applications for options regarding indexes such as the SSE 50 or Standard and Poor's indexes.

Beyond the options for stocks or indexes traded on stock exchanges, a very fruitful field of FROPCT has been real options. In a sense, it is logical since for this type of option, the underlying asset is usually an investment project, and the data on it are often given by subjective estimates from experts that can be well represented through trapezoidal or triangular numbers [19,21]. While the simplest real options can be valued by using a fuzzy version of the BSM formula [21,30,41,42], other works [19,20,51–53,63,70] extend more complex option valuation frameworks to real asset-related optionality.

Other residual applications of FROPCT to asset valuation include assessing the firms' value [50], as suggested by the seminal work of Black and Scholes [3]; credit default swaps [47,48]; bank deposit insurance [45]; catastrophe bonds [69]; and forward contracts in energy markets [67].

Table 2 shows the main outlets where the contributions of FROPCT have been published. We only included journals with two or more contributions. Undoubtedly, the main journal was Fuzzy Sets and Systems (10 contributions), which was one of the principal academic references in fuzzy mathematics. Other journals whose scope was fuzzy logic and where FROP had a significant impact were the International Journal of Fuzzy Systems (4 contributions), IEEE Transactions on Fuzzy Systems, Fuzzy Optimization and Decision Making, and Journal of Intelligent and Fuzzy Systems (2 contributions). Other types of journals that publish a large proportion of studies of the contributions of FROPCT are more generalist journals dedicated to computing and/or soft computing (for example, Journal of Computational and Applied Mathematics, 4 contributions; Soft Computing, 3 contributions; or International Journal of Intelligent Systems, 2 contributions). Likewise, generalist journals of operational research have also been a vehicle for relevant productions of FROPCT (e.g., European Journal of Operational Research with 4 contributions; International Journal of Information Technology and Decision Making and Journal of Applied Mathematics and Statistics with 2 contributions).

Table 2. Principal outlets of fuzzy random option pricing in continuous time.

| Journal | Number of Items |
|---|---|
| Fuzzy Sets and Systems | 10 |
| Journal of Computational and Applied Mathematics | 4 |
| International Journal of Fuzzy Systems | 4 |
| European Journal of Operational Research | 4 |
| Soft Computing | 3 |
| IEEE Transactions on Fuzzy Systems | 2 |
| Fuzzy Optimization and Decision Making | 2 |
| Journal of Intelligent and Fuzzy Systems | 2 |
| Computers and Mathematics with Applications | 2 |
| Discrete Dynamics in Nature and Society | 2 |
| International Journal of Information Technology and Decision Making | 2 |
| International Journal of Intelligent Systems | 2 |
| International Journal of Applied Mathematics and Statistics | 2 |
| Journal of Applied Mathematics | 2 |

Source: own elaboration based on WoS and Scopus databases.

Table 3a,b list the most relevant works according to the WoS (Table 3a) and SCOPUS (Table 3b) databases. We determined the relevance based on the number of citations, and we included works referenced at least 25 times. We observed that both databases essentially included the same works, and the ordering, although not identical, was very similar. It can also be noted that works were usually more cited in SCOPUS than in WoS, which was expected since the SCOPUS database is more comprehensive. The most cited works were usually the oldest works that fell between 2001 and 2010 and were all within the framework of the BSM formula.

Table 3. (a) Papers with at least 25 citations in the WoS database. (b) Papers with at least 25 citations in the Scopus database.

| (a) | | | | |
|---|---|---|---|---|
| Year | Authors | Article Title | Source Title | Citations |
| 2003 | Carlsson, C; Fuller, R. [21] | A fuzzy approach to real option valuation | Fuzzy Sets and Systems | 168 |
| 2003 | Yoshida, Y. [15] | The valuation of European options in uncertain environment | European Journal of Operational Research | 119 |
| 2004 | Wu, H.C. [43] | Pricing European options based on the fuzzy pattern of Black-Scholes formula | Computers and Operations Research | 105 |
| 2001 | Zmeskal, Z. [50] | Application of the fuzzy-stochastic methodology to appraising the firm value as an European call option | European Journal of Operational Research | 81 |
| 2007 | Wu, H.C. [44] | Using fuzzy sets theory and Black-Scholes formula to generate pricing boundaries of European options | Applied Mathematics and Computation | 80 |
| 2009 | Chrysafis, K.A.; Papadopoulos, BK. [14] | On theoretical pricing of options with fuzzy estimators | Journal of Computational and Applied Mathematics | 50 |

Table 3. Cont.

| (a) | | | | |
|---|---|---|---|---|
| Year | Authors | Article Title | Source Title | Citations |
| 2009 | Thavaneswaran, A.; Appadoo, S.S.; Paseka, A. [39] | Weighted possibilistic moments of fuzzy numbers with applications to GARCH modeling and option pricing | Mathematical and Computer Modeling | 50 |
| 2007 | Thiagarajah, K.; Appadoo, S.S.; Thavaneswaran, A. [40] | Option valuation model with adaptive fuzzy numbers | Computers and Mathematics with Applications | 49 |
| 2005 | Wu, H.C. [53] | European option pricing under fuzzy environments | International Journal of Intelligent Systems | 36 |
| 2010 | Nowak, P.; Romaniuk, M. [16] | Computing option price for Levy process with fuzzy parameters | European Journal of Operational Research | 35 |
| 2013 | Thavaneswaran, A.; Appadoo, S.S.; Frank, J. [38] | Binary option pricing using fuzzy numbers | Applied Mathematics Letters | 33 |
| 2015 | Muzzioli, S.; Ruggieri, A.; De Baets, B. [23] | A comparison of fuzzy regression methods for the estimation of the implied volatility smile function | Fuzzy Sets and Systems | 31 |
| 2009 | Xu, W.; Wu, C.; Xu, W.; Li, H. [55] | A jump-diffusion model for option pricing under fuzzy environments | Insurance Mathematics and Economics | 31 |
| 2014 | Nowak, P.; Romaniuk, M. [68] | Application of Levy processes and Esscher transformed martingale measures for option pricing in fuzzy framework | Journal of Computational and Applied Mathematics | 29 |
| 2012 | Zhang, L.H.; Zhang, W.G.; Xu, W.J.; Xiao, W.J. [56] | The double exponential jump diffusion model for pricing European options under fuzzy environments | Economic Modeling | 29 |
| 2017 | Muzzioli, S.; De Baets, B. [12] | Fuzzy Approaches to Option Price Modeling | IEEE Transactions on Fuzzy Systems | 28 |
| (b) | | | | |
| Year | Author | Tittle | Source Title | Citations |
| 2003 | Carlsson, C., Fullér, R. [21] | A fuzzy approach to real option tvaluation | Fuzzy Sets and Systems | 195 |
| 2003 | Yoshida, Y. [15] | The valuation of European options in uncertain environment | European Journal of Operational Research | 122 |
| 2004 | Wu, H.C. [43] | Pricing European options based on the fuzzy pattern of Black-Scholes formula | Computers and Operations Research | 112 |
| 2007 | Wu, H.C. [44] | Using fuzzy sets theory and Black-Scholes formula to generate pricing boundaries of European options | Applied Mathematics and Computation | 76 |
| 2001 | Zmeškal, Z. [50] | Application of the fuzzy-stochastic methodology to appraising the firm value as an European call option | European Journal of Operational Research | 73 |

Table 3. Cont.

| (b) | | | | |
|---|---|---|---|---|
| Year | Author | Tittle | Source Title | Citations |
| 2009 | Thavaneswaran, A., Appadoo, S.S., Paseka, A. [39] | Weighted possibilistic moments of fuzzy numbers with applications to GARCH modeling and option pricing | Mathematical and Computer Modeling | 55 |
| 2009 | Chrysafis, K.A., Papadopoulos, B.K. [14] | On theoretical pricing of options with fuzzy estimators | Journal of Computational and Applied Mathematics | 51 |
| 2007 | Thiagarajah, K., Appadoo, S.S., Thavaneswaran, A. [40] | Option valuation model with adaptive fuzzy numbers | Computers and Mathematics with Applications | 51 |
| 2005 | Wu, H.C., [53] | European option pricing under fuzzy environments | International Journal of Intelligent Systems | 46 |
| 2015 | Muzzioli, S.; Ruggieri, A.; De Baets, B. [23] | A comparison of fuzzy regression methods for the estimation of the implied volatility smile function | Fuzzy Sets and Systems | 31 |
| 2010 | Nowak, P., Romaniuk, M., [16] | Computing option price for Levy process with fuzzy parameters | European Journal of Operational Research | 36 |
| 2017 | Muzzioli, S., De Baets, B. [12] | Fuzzy Approaches to Option Price Modeling | IEEE Transactions on Fuzzy Systems | 32 |
| 2009 | Xu, W., Wu, C., Xu, W., Li, H. [55] | A jump-diffusion model for option pricing under fuzzy environments | Insurance: Mathematics and Economics | 32 |
| 2013 | Thavaneswaran, A., Appadoo, S.S., Frank, J. [38] | Binary option pricing using fuzzy numbers | Applied Mathematics Letters | 31 |
| 2014 | Nowak, P., Romaniuk, M. [68] | Application of Levy processes and Esscher transformed martingale measures for option pricing in fuzzy framework | Journal of Computational and Applied Mathematics | 29 |
| 2012 | Zhang, L.-H., Zhang, W.-G., Xu, W.-J., Xiao, W.-L. [56] | The double exponential jump diffusion model for pricing European options under fuzzy environments | Economic Modeling | 29 |
| 2011 | Guerra, M.L., Sorini, L., Stefanini, L. [31] | Option price sensitivities through fuzzy numbers | Computers and Mathematics with Applications | 27 |

(a) Source: own elaboration based on WoS database. (b) Source: own elaboration based on the Scopus database.

Within the WoS database (Table 3a), the most cited paper was [21], which applied a fuzzy version of the BSM model to real options, followed by [15,43], which developed the valuation of European-style options with the BSM model on stocks. The papers [14,15,39,40,43,44,50] also fell within the scope of the BSM model and value European-style options, but some of them introduced new nuances related to nonlinear fuzzy numbers [14,40], defuzzification [39], sensitivity analysis of prices [14], or valuation of companies [50]. It was not until the tenth work [16] that we observed an analytical framework different from that provided by the geometric Brownian motion; specifically, it was a more general Levy stochastic process. In the eleventh cited contribution, ref. [38], a different type of option from the European binary options was evaluated. In later positions, there were several contributions whereby more alternative fuzzy stochastic modeling was used to model stock prices movements such as in [55,56], whereby the authors addressed the jump-diffusion processes, and in [68], whereby the authors used fuzzy Levy processes. Additionally, noteworthy are the contributions of [23], who applied fuzzy regression in the adjustment of implied volatility, and [12], who provided a review of fuzzy random option pricing in both continuous and discrete time. The patterns observed in the SCOPUS database (Table 3b) were very similar to those in WoS, although there may have been small changes. Changes in the ranking were not very pronounced in any case. The top three most cited works continued to be [15,21,43]. However, starting from the fourth work, the order underwent subtle modifications. For example, in the SCOPUS database, ref. [50] was the fifth most referenced work instead of the fourth. On the other hand, ref. [44] went from being the fifth in SCOPUS to the fourth in WoS.

Table 4 shows that the authors who, as of March 2023, had the highest indexed production in WoS and SCOPUS in the field of FROPCT were Nowak (7 contributions), followed by Muzzioli, Romaniuk, and Guerra (4 contributions). These 4 authors were followed by 11 authors with 3 papers.

**Table 4.** Authors with at least 3 items.

| Author | Country | Items | Author | Country | Items |
| --- | --- | --- | --- | --- | --- |
| Nowak, P. | Poland | 7 | Liu, S. | China | 3 |
| Muzzioli, S. | Italy | 4 | Pawlowski, M. | Poland | 3 |
| Romaniuk, M. | Poland | 4 | Sorini, L. | Italy | 3 |
| Guerra, M.L. | Italy | 4 | Stefanini, L. | Italy | 3 |
| Andres-Sanchez, J. | Spain | 3 | Thavaneswaran, A. | Canada | 3 |
| Appadoo, S.S. | Canada | 3 | Vilani, G. | Italy | 3 |
| de Baets, B. | Belgium | 3 | Wu, H.C. | Taiwan | 3 |
| Figa-Talamanca, G. | Italy | 3 | | | |

Source: own elaboration based on WoS and Scopus databases.

## 3. Fuzzy Random Extension to Vasicek's Equilibrium Term Model

### 3.1. Preeliminary Questions

Table 1 shows that the main focus of fuzzy random option pricing in continuous time is on options on stocks, primarily European-style options and real options. However, we did not find any fuzzy random approaches to equilibrium models of yield rates or option pricing formulas derived from these models. We can only mention [48], which assumes a crisp model of the term structure by using the Cox–Ingersoll and Ross model [10] to determine the risk-free interest rate to evaluate credit default swaps. However, the observed short rate is considered a fuzzy number. This observation motivates the extension developed in this section, which applies the one-factor model for the yield curve by Vasicek [8] to incorporate fuzziness in the parameters. This extension is based on the following hypotheses:

1. The evolution of short rates can be described by using a mean-reverting process with a constant mean. This hypothesis is commonly employed in practical applications, such as in [77], whereby it was employed in the context of life insurance.
2. Uncertainty regarding the parameters governing interest rate movements can be represented by using fuzzy numbers. Following the concept commonly adopted in FROPCT, we consider fuzzy parameters as epistemic fuzzy numbers, assuming they are disjunctive sets [78].
3. A fuzzy number can represent an ill-defined deterministic value and provide a rough approximation of information about the population being observed [79]. This can be achieved through an appropriate transformation of a probability distribution function into a possibility distribution [22].
4. In the empirical application presented in this paper, the fuzzy parameters are constructed based on objective information obtained from bond markets.

The fuzzy extension of [8] presented in this section was applied to the prices of default-free zero-coupon bonds in European Union fixed income markets, which serve as the main reference for investors of euro-denominated fixed-income assets and for the European Central Bank when assessing the evolution of long-term interest rates.

## 3.2. The Equilibrium Model of the Yield Curve by Vasicek

As with any one-factor model, in ref. [8] it is assumed that the stochastic variability comes from short-term interest rate ($r$) fluctuations. The ultimate goal of equilibrium models is to obtain the price that would be agreed upon at $t$ for a risk-free zero-coupon bond that pays one monetary unit (u.m) at $T \geq t$, $P(t, T)$. In term structure models, stochastic variation does not directly apply to $P(t, T)$, as in the case of stocks, but rather to the interest rate ($r$), which is directly connected to $P(t, T)$. In general, one-factor models suppose that $r$ follows an Ito process such as [8]:

$$dr = m(r,t)dt + \sigma(r,t)dz, \quad (1)$$

where $m(r,t)$ and $\sigma(r,t)$ are the instantaneous drift and variance, respectively, and $dz$ is a Wiener process with a standard deviation of $dt$. The price of any asset affected by $r$ (bonds, derivatives on fixed-income assets, etc.), $P$, must accomplish:

$$\frac{\partial P}{\partial t} + m(r,t)\frac{\partial P}{\partial r}dt + \frac{1}{2}\frac{\partial^2 P}{\partial r^2}\sigma^2(r,t) = rP, \quad (2)$$

and thus, to obtain $P(t, T)$, we have to consider the condition $P(T, T) = 1$.

Among the many models proposed for $dr$ (see Hull [80]), we extend the classical Vasicek's model [8]. It supposes that the fluctuations in the short interest rate follow a mean-reverting process:

$$dr = a(b-r)dt + \sigma dz, \quad (3)$$

where $a \geq 0$ is the reversion rate, i.e., the speed at which the interest rates return to equilibrium, and the $b$ is the equilibrium short rate. By naming $r_T$ the short interest rate in year $T$ and $r_t$ to that rate in $t \leq T$, the expectation of $r_T$ in $t$ $E_t(r_T)$ is

$$E_t(r_T) = b + (r_t - b)e^{-a(T-t)}, \quad (4a)$$

and the variance $V_t(r_T)$ is

$$V_t(r_T) = \frac{\sigma^2}{2a}\left(1 - e^{-2a(T-t)}\right). \quad (4b)$$

Note that for $\to \infty$, $E_t(r_T) = b$, i.e., $r_T$ is increasing with respect to $b$. Likewise, (4b) suggests that the variance in the short-term rate is affected by an exponential decay at rate $a$. That decreasing behavior can be easily checked by the limit because if $T \to \infty$, $V_t(r_T) = \frac{\sigma^2}{2a}$, and the long-term variance is decreasing with respect to $a$ and of course increasing with respect to $\sigma$.

Therefore, in the mean-reverting groundwork (3), the general Equation (2) becomes

$$\frac{\partial P}{\partial t} + a(b-r)\frac{\partial P}{\partial r}dt + \frac{1}{2}\frac{\partial^2 P}{\partial r^2}\sigma^2 = rC. \quad (5)$$

Thus, for the zero-coupon bond, we find

$$P(t, T, a, b, \sigma, r_t) = A(t, T, a, b, \sigma)e^{-B(t,T,a) \cdot r_t}, \quad (6a)$$

where

$$B(t, T, a) = \frac{1 - e^{-a(T-t)}}{a}, \quad (6b)$$

$$A(t,T,a,b,\sigma) = \exp\left[\frac{(B(t,T,a) - T + t)\left(a^2 b - \frac{\sigma^2}{2}\right)}{a^2} - \frac{\sigma^2 B^2(t,T,a)}{4a}\right]. \quad (6c)$$

Note that the fact that $b$ and $r_t$ are the discount rates of the zero-coupon bond implies that the partial derivatives must be $\frac{\partial P}{\partial b} < 0$ and $\frac{\partial P}{\partial r_t} < 0$. Likewise, the price of a bond is a decreasing function of the interest rate volatility because its profit is positively linked with volatility [81]. Therefore, $\frac{\partial P}{\partial \sigma} < 0$ and $\frac{\partial P}{\partial a} > 0$ since $a$ basically negatively affects the volatility of the short-term interest rate (see (4b)).

### 3.3. An Extension of Vasicek's Yield Curve with Fuzzy Parameters

In the following, we will suppose that with the exception of the maturities $t$ and $T$, all the parameters of (6a)–(6c) are imprecise and are given by means of fuzzy numbers (FNs). A FN is a fuzzy set $\tilde{f}$ defined on the reference set $\mathbb{R}$ and is normal (i.e., $\max_{x \in \mathbb{R}} \mu_f(x) = 1$, where $\mu_f(x)$ is its membership function) and convex, i.e., all its $\alpha$-cuts are convex and compact sets. Therefore, the fuzzy set can be represented as confidence intervals (so-called $\alpha$-cuts or $\alpha$-level sets) $f_\alpha = \left[\underline{f_\alpha}, \overline{f_\alpha}\right]$, where $\underline{f_\alpha}$ ($\overline{f_\alpha}$) are continuously increasing (decreasing) functions of $\alpha$. A FN can be interpreted as a fuzzy quantity that is approximately equal to the value $x \in \mathbb{R}$ whose membership function is one, $f_1$.

Therefore, the parameters $a, b, \sigma$, and $r_t$ are now the imprecise quantities $\tilde{a}, \tilde{b}, \tilde{\sigma}$, and $\tilde{r}_t$ whose $\alpha$-cuts are denoted as $a_\alpha = \left[\underline{a_\alpha}, \overline{a_\alpha}\right]$, $b_\alpha = \left[\underline{b_\alpha}, \overline{b_\alpha}\right]$, $\sigma_\alpha = \left[\underline{\sigma_\alpha}, \overline{\sigma_\alpha}\right]$ and $r_{t\alpha} = \left[\underline{r_{t\alpha}}, \overline{r_{t\alpha}}\right]$.

Therefore, under our hypothesis, the mean-reverting process (3) turns into a fuzzy random process where the parameters that rule the interest rate movements are fuzzy numbers. In the fuzzy random approach setting of the FOP, the differential Equation (5) has fuzzy parameters but a crisp boundary condition $P(T, T) = 1$.

Studies in the FROPCT literature obtain fuzzy option prices by evaluating the crisp pricing formula that comes from the assumed stochastic process (e.g., the BSM model after accepting that geometrical Brownian motion explains the price movements of subjacent assets) with fuzzy numbers by using the rules in [82]. This procedure is theoretically supported by the concept of the solution of differential equations with fuzzy coefficients [83]. Thus, in our case, the assumption of fuzzy parameters in (3) leads to the need to solve (6a)–(6c) with FNs. Therefore, the price of a zero-coupon bond turns into a fuzzy number $\tilde{P}(t, T) = P\left(t, T, \tilde{a}, \tilde{b}, \tilde{\sigma}, \tilde{r}_t\right)$ whose $\alpha$-levels $P(t, T)_\alpha = \left[\underline{P(t, T)_\alpha}, \overline{P(t, T)_\alpha}\right]$ can be obtained by evaluating (6a)–(6c) in $a_\alpha$, $b_\alpha$, $\sigma_\alpha$, and $r_{t\alpha}$:

$$P(t,T)_\alpha = \left\{x \middle| x = P(t,T,a,b,\sigma,r_t) = A(t,T,a,b,\sigma)e^{-B(t,T,a)\cdot r_t}, \, a \in a_\alpha, b \in b_\alpha, \sigma \in \sigma_\alpha, r_t \in r_{t\alpha}\right\}, \quad (7a)$$

and given that $\frac{\partial P}{\partial b} < 0$, $\frac{\partial P}{\partial r_t} < 0$, $\frac{\partial P}{\partial \sigma} < 0$, and $\frac{\partial P}{\partial a} > 0$, we can obtain the extremes of the $\alpha$-cuts by evaluating (6a)–(6c) in the extremes of $a_\alpha$, $b_\alpha$, $\sigma_\alpha$, and $r_{t\alpha}$ as

$$\underline{P(t,T)_\alpha} = P\left(t, T, \underline{a_\alpha}, \overline{b_\alpha}, \overline{\sigma_\alpha}, \overline{r_{t\alpha}}\right) = A\left(t, T, \underline{a_\alpha}, \overline{b_\alpha}, \overline{\sigma_\alpha}\right) e^{-B(t,T,\underline{a_\alpha})\cdot \overline{r_{t\alpha}}}, \quad (7b)$$

and

$$\overline{P(t,T)_\alpha} = P\left(t, T, \overline{a_\alpha}, \underline{b_\alpha}, \underline{\sigma_\alpha}, \underline{r_{t\alpha}}\right) = A\left(t, T, \overline{a_\alpha}, \underline{b_\alpha}, \underline{\sigma_\alpha}\right) e^{-B(t,T,\overline{a_\alpha})\cdot \underline{r_{t\alpha}}}. \quad (7c)$$

### 3.4. Empirical Application of Fuzzy Vasicek's Model in the Public Debt Bond Market of Europe

The empirical application developed in this work estimates the theoretical yield curve by using the Vasicek model [8] for European public bonds with the highest rating (AAA) on April 18, 2023. The data we worked with were obtained from the website of the European Central Bank (https://www.ecb.europa.eu/home/html/index.en.html accessed on 18 April 2023). The short-term interest rate considered was the 3-month interest rate, which was the lowest term published in the public bond market by the European Central Bank.

We will use the parameters in (3) as the fuzzy numbers $\tilde{a}, \tilde{b}, \tilde{\sigma}$ by using the probability–possibility criterion exposed in [22], in which these FN will be modeled by means of symmetrical fuzzy numbers, which we will also suppose are triangular. A triangular symmetrical fuzzy number (TSFN) can be represented as $\tilde{f} = (f_C, f_R)$, where $f_C$ is the center of the FN and $f_R$ is the spread. Its membership function is $\mu_f(x) = \max\left\{0, \frac{|x - f_C|}{f_R}\right\}$, and its α-cut representation $f_\alpha = \left[\underline{f_\alpha}, \overline{f_\alpha}\right] = [f_C - f_R(1-\alpha), f_C + f_R(1-\alpha)]$. Therefore, its support is $f_0 = \left[\underline{f_0}, \overline{f_0}\right] = [f_C - f_R, f_C + f_R]$. For example, for the equilibrium short-term rate $\tilde{b} = (3\%, 0.5\%)$, it can be interpreted that the most reliable value for that rate is 3%, but deviations of approximately 0.5% are viewed as possible.

To fit the parameters, we used the ground of the conventional AR(1) model that serves as the basis to empirically estimate (3) [7]. Therefore, the time series model to fit is [7]

$$r_{t+1} = \gamma + \beta r_t + \varepsilon_{t+1}, \ t = 1, 2, \ldots, n. \tag{8}$$

where $\gamma$ is the intercept, $\beta$ is the slope, and $\varepsilon_{t+1}$ is the normal white noise and i.i.d. with mean 0 and standard deviation $\sigma_\varepsilon$. A commonly used methodology to adjust (8) is ordinary least squares. In this regard, it is easy to check that the relations between the parameters of (3), (4a), and (8) are $a = -\ln \beta \cdot h$, $b = \frac{\gamma}{1-\beta}$, and $\sigma = \sigma_\varepsilon \sqrt{h}$, where $h$ is the frequency of the data. Thus, for daily data, $h = 252$.

To fit the temporal structure in the calendar date $m$, we adjusted (8) in the moments $i = 1, 2, \ldots, m$ in all cases by using $n$ observations. Therefore, for the $i$th adjustment of (8), we obtain point estimates in (8) $\hat{\gamma}^{(i)}$, $\hat{\beta}^{(i)}$, $\hat{\sigma}_\varepsilon^{(i)}$, $i = 1, 2, \ldots, m$, and consequently, $\hat{a}^{(i)}$, $\hat{b}^{(i)}$, $\hat{\sigma}^{(i)}$, $i = 1, 2, \ldots, m$.

After fitting the $m$ AR(1) models (8), we can fit an empirical probability distribution for every parameter; for the parameter $f$, we symbolize it as $\hat{f}$, an its outcomes are $\hat{f}^{(i)}$, $i = 1, 2, \ldots, m$. Therefore, we can calculate the mean and the standard deviation of $f$ simply as

$$\hat{f}_{mean} = \frac{\sum_i \hat{f}^{(i)}}{m} \ \text{and} \ \hat{f}_{sd} = \sqrt{\frac{\sum_i \left(\hat{f}^{(i)} - \hat{f}_{mean}\right)^2}{m}}. \tag{9}$$

A natural way to adjust a fuzzy number to an unimodal probability distribution $f$ with mean $\hat{f}_{mean}$ and standard deviation $\hat{f}_{sd}$ is to fit an STFM $\tilde{f} = (f_C, f_R)$ with a center $f_C = \hat{f}_{mean}$ and fit the spread $f_R$ by considering the Chebyshev inequality [22]. Specifically, given that

$$P\left(x \in \left[\hat{f}_{mean} - k \cdot \hat{f}_{sd}, \hat{f}_{mean} + k \cdot \hat{f}_{sd}\right]\right) \geq 1 - \frac{1}{2.25 \cdot k^2}, \ k \geq 1, \tag{10}$$

where $P(\cdot)$ is a probability measure, and we choose $f_R$ such that $P(x \in [\hat{f}_{mean} - f_R, \hat{f}_{mean} + f_R]) \geq 1 - \frac{1}{2.25 \cdot k^2}$, after fixing $k$, $f_R = k \cdot \hat{f}_{sd}$.

In our empirical application, to implement the set of regressions (8), we considered $n = 50$ and $s = 25$ so that all the observations from the year 2023 until 18 April were used. The data used had a daily periodicity, so $h = 252$. Figure 3a–c show the estimated empirical distribution functions for the parameters ruling the model. The coefficients must be quantified through fuzzy numbers that must be coherent with the empirical distribution function of these parameters. Although there are various criteria for this purpose [22], we used the one described in Equations (9) and (10). We found it interesting to analyze whether the observations were compatible with a unimodal probability distribution, as it was the underlying hypothesis in Equations (9) and (10). In this regard, by using a Chi-square test, we tested whether the observations of parameters $a$ and $\sigma$ were compatible with a normal probability distribution while parameter $b$ was compatible with a Gamma distribution which, in any case, is also a unimodal distribution.

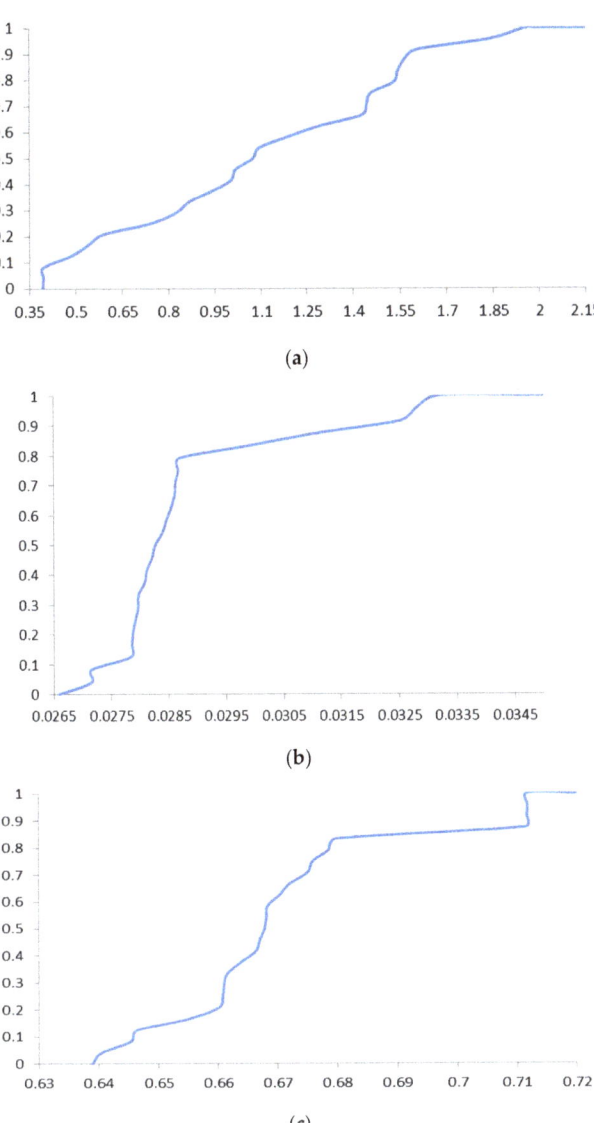

**Figure 3.** (a) Empirical distribution function of the speed of adjustment rate $a$; (b) empirical distribution function of the equilibrium interest rate $b$; (c) empirical distribution function of the parameter $\sigma$. Source: own elaboration-based data from the European Central Bank.

Table 5 displays the center of the fuzzy numbers $\tilde{a}$, $\tilde{b}$, and $\tilde{\sigma}$, as well as their possible spreads for $k = 2, 3, 4$, considering Equation (10). Note that there is no optimal value for $k$. On the one hand, a higher value of $k$ results in more uncertain and imprecise estimates of zero-coupon bond prices, but on the other hand, it allows for a better fit of the real yield curve shapes.

**Table 5.** Estimates of $\tilde{a}$, $\tilde{b}$, and $\tilde{\sigma}$ on 18 April 2023.

|   |          | $\hat{a}$ | $\hat{b}$ | $\hat{\sigma}$ |
|---|----------|-------|---------|-----------|
|   | mean     | 1.117 | 0.02882 | 0.0067075 |
|   | std. dev.| 0.245 | 0.00174 | 0.0002121 |
| k |          | $\tilde{a}$ | $\tilde{b}$ | $\tilde{\sigma}$ |
|   | center   | 1.117 | 0.02882 | 0.0067075 |
| 2 | spread   | 0.491 | 0.00349 | 0.0004242 |
| 3 | spread   | 0.736 | 0.00523 | 0.0006363 |
| 4 | spread   | 0.982 | 0.00697 | 0.0008484 |

Source: own elaboration-based data from the European Central Bank.

Table 6 presents the observed prices of zero-coupon bonds with a face value of 100, ranging from 3 months to 20 years, as well as the fuzzy estimations of these prices using the proposed extension to [8]. At the given date, the 3-month interest rate was $r_0 = 2.877\%$. Despite one of the main criticisms of one-factor models with fixed parameters being their inability to capture all possible shapes of the term structure [7], the proposed fuzzy extension to [8] successfully generated predictions of zero-coupon bond prices that aligned with the observed prices. Therefore, ref. [8] can be considered valuable for explaining term structure equilibria and conducting economic analyses that require a parametric and parsimonious estimation of the yield rates. It can be observed that the 0 cut of Equations (7a) and (7b) adequately captured the prices of the zero-coupon bonds across various maturities, with the exception of the bonds maturing in 3, 4, and 5 years. However, even in these cases, the maximum deviation between the 0-cut predictions and the actual prices was consistently less than 0.5%. For instance, for the 4-year maturity bond, the deviation was $\frac{90.56-90.37}{90.56} = 0.002$.

**Table 6.** Spot prices of zero-coupon bonds with face value 100 monetary units on 18 April 2023 in the European Union public debt market and α-cuts of the estimates (α = 0, 0.5, 1) from fuzzy Vasicek's model.

|          | Observed | Estimated by Vasicek's Model | | | | |
|----------|----------|-------|-------|-------|-------|-------|
|          |          | 1-Cut | 0.5-Cut | | 0-Cut | |
| T        | $P(0,T)$ | $P(0,T)_1$ | $\underline{P(0,T)}_{0.5}$ | $\overline{P(0,T)}_{0.5}$ | $\underline{P(0,T)}_0$ | $\overline{P(0,T)}_0$ |
| 3 months | 99.29    | 99.28 | 99.27 | 99.29 | 99.25 | 99.29 |
| 1 year   | 97.04    | 97.16 | 97.00 | 97.26 | 96.79 | 97.28 |
| 2 years  | 94.62    | 94.40 | 93.96 | 94.72 | 93.44 | 94.81 |
| 3 years  | 92.57    | 91.72 | 90.98 | 92.31 | 90.16 | 92.52 |
| 4 years  | 90.56    | 89.12 | 88.09 | 89.98 | 86.99 | 90.37 |
| 5 years  | 88.49    | 86.59 | 85.29 | 87.72 | 83.93 | 88.32 |
| 6 years  | 86.36    | 84.13 | 82.58 | 85.53 | 80.98 | 86.35 |
| 7 years  | 84.20    | 81.74 | 79.96 | 83.39 | 78.14 | 84.45 |
| 8 years  | 82.02    | 79.42 | 77.42 | 81.31 | 75.39 | 82.61 |
| 9 years  | 79.86    | 77.17 | 74.96 | 79.28 | 72.74 | 80.82 |
| 10 years | 77.73    | 74.98 | 72.57 | 77.30 | 70.18 | 79.07 |
| 11 years | 75.64    | 72.85 | 70.27 | 75.37 | 67.72 | 77.37 |
| 12 years | 73.61    | 70.78 | 68.03 | 73.48 | 65.34 | 75.70 |
| 13 years | 71.64    | 68.77 | 65.87 | 71.65 | 63.04 | 74.08 |
| 14 years | 69.73    | 66.82 | 63.78 | 69.86 | 60.82 | 72.49 |
| 15 years | 67.90    | 64.92 | 61.75 | 68.12 | 58.69 | 70.93 |
| 16 years | 66.13    | 63.08 | 59.79 | 66.41 | 56.62 | 69.41 |
| 17 years | 64.44    | 61.29 | 57.89 | 64.76 | 54.63 | 67.93 |

**Table 6.** *Cont.*

| | Observed | Estimated by Vasicek's Model | | | | |
|---|---|---|---|---|---|---|
| | | 1-Cut | 0.5-Cut | | 0-Cut | |
| $T$ | $P(0,T)$ | $P(0,T)_1$ | $\underline{P(0,T)}_{0.5}$ | $\overline{P(0,T)}_{0.5}$ | $\underline{P(0,T)}_0$ | $\overline{P(0,T)}_0$ |
| 18 years | 62.82 | 59.55 | 56.05 | 63.14 | 52.71 | 66.47 |
| 19 years | 61.27 | 57.86 | 54.27 | 61.56 | 50.86 | 65.05 |
| 20 years | 59.79 | 56.22 | 52.54 | 60.03 | 49.07 | 63.65 |

Note: The spread of parameters used in the estimation of prices was stated as $k = 4$. Likewise, the 3-month rate at that date was 2.877%. Source: own elaboration-based data from the European Central Bank.

## 4. Discussion and Implications

*4.1. Discussion of Findings*

This paper presents a double contribution. On the one hand, we systematically reviewed a set of contributions that we can label as fuzzy random option prices in continuous time (FROPCT), which is the dominant approach within fuzzy option pricing [13]. On the other hand, we extended the fuzzy random approach to model the term structure with an equilibrium model. We concretely extended the classical model [12] to the existence of imprecise parameters in the mean-reverting process.

We checked that journals of soft computing and fuzzy mathematics were the most burgeoning outlets of FROPCT. However, journals devoted to the wider fields of computational mathematics and operational research have also actively published papers on FROPCT. We checked that the contributions to FROPCT grew continuously from early 2000 to 2013. In the mid 2010s, the literature on FROPCT stopped having a growing constant production; thus, FROPCT can be labeled as a small but well-established branch of fuzzy mathematics.

The mainstream FROPCT models have imprecise knowledge of the parameters that govern the subjacent random movements of subjacent assets with type-1 fuzzy numbers that are often triangular and trapezoidal. More complex forms of uncertain quantities such as type-2 fuzzy numbers or intuitionistic fuzzy numbers are rarely applied.

The main applications of FROPCT have focused on the development of the valuation of stocks on stock and stock market indexes. Most developments take the analytical framework of the Black–Scholes–Merton (BSM) formula as a reference [3,4], which is based on the consideration of the geometric Brownian motion of the subjacent asset price. However, the literature has also provided other approaches with more complex stochastic processes such as jump diffusion [55,56], stochastic variance [57], fractional stochastic movements (e.g., [58,59,66]), or Levy processes (e.g., [64,65,71]). The development of real options with fuzziness in the parameters has been another relevant stream of FROPCT. The reviewed developments of fuzzy real options are based on the assumption of conventional geometric Brownian motion. Thus, when it comes to the modeling of the simplest options, the FROPCT literature uses the BSM framework (e.g., [21]), but in the case of options on options or compound options, the analytical frameworks that support contributions such as [19,20,42,51,52] are option-pricing models [73,74]. The use of fuzzy subset theory has been more extensive than the approach through FROPCT, as other tools such as fuzzy measures or fuzzy inference systems have been applied [13]. In our opinion, the combination of game theory and fuzzy inference systems in the assessment of real options can be particularly fruitful, as it has already been applied to similar business problems such as the establishment of hotel pricing policies within the Stackelberg game framework [84].

The no-arbitrage approach to option valuation initiated in [3,4] has been particularly fruitful when modeling the term structure of interest rates [7,80]. Surprisingly, we observed that developments by the FROPCT literature in this setting have been scarce, if not nonexistent. In this regard, we highlight [85], which does not use a fuzzy random approach but rather uncertain Liu processes. This lack of the no-arbitrage approach has motivated the second contribution of the paper, in which we extended the equilibrium model of the yield rate curve by Vasicek [8] to fuzziness in the reverting rate, long-term equilibrium short-term rate, and volatility.

A key aspect in the fuzzy random modeling of asset prices is the calibration of the fuzzy parameters that govern their variation [7]. Naturally, since the parameters that govern the movements of short-term interest rates have a clear economic interpretation, it could be assumed that they can be set intuitively by experts. Alternatively, following [14,17,18,23,25–27,57,71], we can adjust the parameters that are assumed to be fuzzy numbers based on existing evidence in financial markets. Likewise, it should be noted that the existence of studies that empirically apply FROPCT developments is relatively scarce [12,13]. Both considerations motivate the parameter adjustment methodology of the mean reversion process outlined in this study, which is also a novelty. The speed of the return to equilibrium, the asymptotic short-term interest rate, and the volatility are fitted by using symmetric triangular fuzzy numbers that are obtained by combining the conventional autoregressive modeling of the Ornstein–Uhlenbeck process [7] and the application of a consistent probability–possibility transformation criterion [22].

The empirical application developed in the European public debt market suggests that the extension of model [8] can reasonably capture the prices of zero-coupon bonds for all analyzed maturities (up to 20 years); this is performed by using only the fuzzy random modeling of the 3-month interest rate as the input with a fuzzy stochastic process with mean reversion and constant volatility. This finding is in accordance with the reviewed literature. In Spanish option markets, it has been observed that the introduction of fuzzy uncertainty on the parameters governing market prices yields good estimates of observed prices of valued assets [25,26]. Similarly, in the option market of Shanghai [18] and over options on Standard and Poor's index [18,57,71], similar results have been obtained.

*4.2. Practical Implications*

In our opinion, this work presents various consequences both from a theoretical perspective and from the perspective of financial practice. From an academic point of view, we provided an overview of the contributions of FROPCT to the field of option theory, which allows for the identification of research gaps. In this regard, we can highlight the additional use of comprehensive fuzzy modeling of uncertainty over type-1 fuzzy numbers, the further development of FROPCT in equilibrium models of the term structure and the valuation of interest-sensitive instruments, or the increased applications of FROPCT with empirical data from financial derivative markets.

The results of this paper have practical implications as well. We observed the viability of a parametric interest rate model such as Vasicek [8], which has wide practical applications, such as modeling the returns obtained by life insurance companies [77] while considering the fact that the uncertainty governing the movement of interest rates is modeled through fuzzy numbers. The proposed extension, which allows for the uncertainty of risk-free interest rates to be captured with fuzzy numbers based on market data, is particularly applicable in fuzzy capital budgeting [86]. Furthermore, the implementation of the presented developments and their interpretation from the perspective of a nonexpert professional in fuzzy logic is straightforward. For the interpretation of the results, while the endpoints of the 0 cut provide an understanding of the values of zero-coupon bonds in the most extreme scenarios regarding equilibrium interest rates, the equilibrium return ratio, and volatility, the 1 cut quantifies the price in the most plausible scenario. In all cases, the calculations were performed by using formulas widely known to practitioners.

We believe that the proposed methodology of adjusting the parameters governing the movement of short-term interest rates also has potential implications. We constructed a method for estimating the fuzzy parameters of the mean-reverting process which, starting from the widely used autoregressive modeling and a coherent probability–possibility transformation criterion, allows us to capture the uncertainty of the parameters governing the mean-reversion process through fuzzy numbers. Of course, this method can be applied to any variable whose fluctuations may exhibit mean reversion, such as commodity prices [87].

## 5. Conclusions and Further Research

Given that the majority of the literature in the field of FROPCT has introduced uncertainty when using type-1 fuzzy numbers, the application of such more complex fuzzy numbers in FROPCT may be a natural and fruitful research field. However, it must also be taken into account that the introduction of these more sophisticated forms of imprecise quantities could also be a source of drawbacks. Note that defining their shape requires estimating more parameters than for conventional fuzzy numbers, and their arithmetical handle is less parsimonious in such a way that the developments of FROPCT with this type of uncertainty may be more difficult to put into practice.

The fuzzy random extension of the model [8] has been applied in an empirical application in the European market for public debt bonds with the highest credit rating. We are aware that one of the main criticisms of [8] is that the model allows negative interest rates that, from an economic perspective, have no meaning. However, the empirical evidence in European fixed-income markets, such as that of public debt assets, contradicts this alleged disadvantage because in 2010, the internal rate of returns was consistently negative.

Of course, there are better alternatives to equilibrium term structure models if the only objective is to obtain the best adjustment of the yield curve. For example, econometric models usually provide better results, and some of them have been implemented with fuzzy regression [88]. However, in our empirical application, we were interested in demonstrating that the extension of the FROPCT in [8], which is a parsimonious parametric model, can be useful in further analytical developments, not only because of its good properties and ease of interpretation but also because it is coherent with empirical evidence.

A natural extension of this paper involves extending the possibility of fuzziness in the coefficients that govern the movement of interest rates to other yield curve models based on arbitrage arguments; these models can be either single factor [10] or multifactorial [9], and this extension can occur in continuous time, such as in [10], or in discrete time [11]. It should be noted that while models with fixed parameters, such as those in [8–10], which were built simply on the basis of a no-arbitrage argument, do not necessarily provide a perfect fit for the term structure, they are very useful in a wide variety of economic and financial analyses. Conversely, models that are referred to as consistent with variable parameters such as [11] require a greater number of parameters to be estimated, which allows them to perfectly fit the zero-coupon yield curve existing on a particular date; however, they are less parsimonious, and their application is usually limited to the valuation of interest-rate-sensitive instruments such as swaptions, options on bonds, cap and floor options, etc.

**Funding:** This research received no external funding.

**Data Availability Statement:** The data used in this paper are freely available at https://www.ecb.europa.eu/home/html/index.en.html (accessed on 18 April 2023).

**Conflicts of Interest:** The author declares no conflict of interest.

## References

1. Dotsis, G. Option pricing methods in the City of London during the late 19th century. *Quant. Financ.* **2020**, *20*, 709–719. [CrossRef]
2. Merton, R.C. Applications of option-pricing theory: Twenty-five years later. *Am. Econ. Rev.* **1998**, *88*, 323–349. Available online: http://www.jstor.org/stable/116838 (accessed on 29 March 2023).
3. Black, F.; Scholes, M. The pricing of options and corporate liabilities. *J. Political Econ.* **1973**, *81*, 637–654. Available online: http://www.jstor.org/stable/1831029 (accessed on 29 March 2023). [CrossRef]
4. Merton, R.C. Theory of rational option pricing. *Bell J. Econ. Manag. Sci.* **1973**, *4*, 141–183. [CrossRef]
5. Broadie, M.; Detemple, J.B. Option pricing: Valuation models and applications. *Manag. Sci.* **2004**, *50*, 1145–1177. [CrossRef]
6. Trigeorgis, L.; Reuer, J.J. Real options theory in strategic management. *Strateg. Manag. J.* **2017**, *38*, 42–63. [CrossRef]
7. Chen, R.R. *Understanding and Managing Interest Rate Risks (Vol. 1)*; World Scientific: Singapore, 1996.
8. Vasicek, O. An equilibrium characterization of the term structure. *J. Financ. Econ.* **1977**, *5*, 177–188. [CrossRef]
9. Brennan, M.J.; Schwartz, E.S. A continuous time approach to the pricing of bonds. *J. Bank. Financ.* **1979**, *3*, 133–155. [CrossRef]

10. Cox, J.C.; Ingersoll, J.E., Jr.; Ross, S.A. An intertemporal general equilibrium model of asset prices. *Econometrica* **1985**, *53*, 363–384. [CrossRef]
11. Hull, J.; White, A. One-factor interest-rate models and the valuation of interest-rate derivative securities. *J. Financ. Quant. Anal.* **1993**, *28*, 235–254. [CrossRef]
12. Muzzioli, S.; De Baets, B. Fuzzy approaches to option price modelling. *IEEE Trans. Fuzzy Syst.* **2016**, *25*, 392–401. [CrossRef]
13. Andrés-Sánchez, J. A systematic review of the interactions of fuzzy set theory and option pricing. *Expert Syst. Appl.* **2023**, *223*, 119868. [CrossRef]
14. Chrysafis, K.A.; Papadopoulos, B.K. On theoretical pricing of options with fuzzy estimators. *J. Comput. Appl. Math.* **2009**, *223*, 552–566. [CrossRef]
15. Yoshida, Y. The valuation of European options in uncertain environment. *Eur. J. Oper. Res.* **2003**, *145*, 221–229. [CrossRef]
16. Nowak, P.; Romaniuk, M. Computing option price for Levy process with fuzzy parameters. *Eur. J. Oper. Res.* **2010**, *201*, 206–210. [CrossRef]
17. Zhang, H.M.; Watada, J. Fuzzy Levy-GJR-GARCH American Option Pricing Model Based on an Infinite Pure Jump Process. *IEICE Trans. Inf. Syst.* **2018**, *101*, 1843–1859. [CrossRef]
18. Zhang, W.G.; Li, Z.; Liu, Y.J.; Zhang, Y. Pricing European Option Under Fuzzy Mixed Fractional Brownian Motion Model with Jumps. *Comput. Econ.* **2021**, *58*, 483–515. [CrossRef]
19. Anzilli, L.; Villani, G. Cooperative R&D investment decisions: A fuzzy real option approach. *Fuzzy Sets Syst.* **2022**, *458*, 143–164. [CrossRef]
20. Biancardi, M.; Villani, G. A fuzzy approach for R&D compound option valuation. *Fuzzy Sets Syst.* **2017**, *310*, 108–121. [CrossRef]
21. Carlsson, C.; Fuller, R. A fuzzy approach to real option valuation. *Fuzzy Sets Syst.* **2003**, *139*, 297–312. [CrossRef]
22. Dubois, D.; Folloy, L.; Mauris, G.; Prade, H. Probability–possibility transformations, triangular fuzzy sets, and probabilistic inequalities. *Reliab. Comput.* **2004**, *10*, 273–297. [CrossRef]
23. Muzzioli, S.; Ruggieri, A.; De Baets, B. A comparison of fuzzy regression methods for the estimation of the implied volatility smile function. *Fuzzy Sets Syst.* **2015**, *266*, 131–143. [CrossRef]
24. Belle, A.B.; Zhao, Y. Evidence-based decision-making: On the use of systematicity cases to check the compliance of reviews with reporting guidelines such as PRISMA 2020. *Expert Syst. Appl.* **2023**, *217*, 119569. [CrossRef]
25. Andres-Sanchez, J. An empirical assessment of fuzzy Black and Scholes pricing option model in Spanish stock option market. *J. Intell. Fuzzy Syst.* **2017**, *33*, 2509–2521. [CrossRef]
26. Andres-Sanchez, J. Pricing European Options with Triangular Fuzzy Parameters: Assessing Alternative Triangular Approximations in the Spanish Stock Option Market. *Int. J. Fuzzy Syst.* **2018**, *20*, 1624–1643. [CrossRef]
27. Capotorti, A.; Figà-Talamanca, G. SMART-or and SMART-and fuzzy average operators: A generalized proposal. *Fuzzy Sets Syst.* **2020**, *395*, 1–20. [CrossRef]
28. Chen, H.M.; Hu, C.F.; Yeh, W.C. Option pricing and the Greeks under Gaussian fuzzy environments. *Soft Comput.* **2019**, *23–24*, 13351–13374. [CrossRef]
29. Dash, J.K.; Panda, S.; Panda, G.B. A new method to solve fuzzy stochastic finance problem. *J. Econ. Stud.* **2022**, *49*, 243–258. [CrossRef]
30. Gao, H.; Ding, X.H.; Li, S.C. EPC renewable project evaluation: A fuzzy real option pricing model. *Energy Sources Part B Econ. Plan. Policy* **2018**, *13*, 404–413. [CrossRef]
31. Guerra, M.L.; Sorini, L.; Stefanini, L. Option price sensitivities through fuzzy numbers. *Comput. Math. Appl.* **2011**, *61*, 515–526. [CrossRef]
32. Guerra, M.L.; Sorini, L.; Stefanini, L. Value Function Computation in Fuzzy Models by Differential Evolution. *Int. J. Fuzzy Syst.* **2017**, *19*, 1025–1031. [CrossRef]
33. Jafari, H. Sensitivity of option prices via fuzzy Malliavin calculus. *Fuzzy Sets Syst.* **2022**, *434*, 98–116. [CrossRef]
34. Kim, Y.; Lee, E.B. Optimal Investment Timing with Investment Propensity Using Fuzzy Real Options Valuation. *Int. J. Fuzzy Syst.* **2018**, *20*, 1888–1900. [CrossRef]
35. Li, H.; Ware, A.; Di, L.; Yuan, G.; Swishchuk, A.; Yuan, S. The application of nonlinear fuzzy parameters PDE method in pricing and hedging European options. *Fuzzy Sets Syst.* **2018**, *331*, 14–25. [CrossRef]
36. Muzzioli, S.; Gambarelli, L.; De Baets, B. Indices for Financial Market Volatility Obtained through Fuzzy Regression. *Int. J. Inf. Technol. Decis. Mak.* **2018**, *17*, 1659–1691. [CrossRef]
37. Muzzioli, S.; Gambarelli, L.; De Baets, B. Option implied moments obtained through fuzzy regression. *Fuzzy Optim. Decis. Mak.* **2020**, *19*, 211–238. [CrossRef]
38. Thavaneswaran, A.; Appadoo, S.S.; Frank, J. Binary option pricing using fuzzy numbers. *Appl. Math. Lett.* **2013**, *26*, 65–72. [CrossRef]
39. Thavaneswaran, A.; Appadoo, S.S.; Paseka, A. Weighted possibilistic moments of fuzzy numbers with applications to GARCH modelling and option pricing. *Math. Comput. Model.* **2009**, *49*, 352–368. [CrossRef]
40. Thiagarajah, K.; Appadoo, S.S.; Thavaneswaran, A. Option valuation model with adaptive fuzzy numbers. *Comput. Math. Appl.* **2007**, *53*, 831–841. [CrossRef]
41. Tolga, A.C. Real options valuation of an IoT based healthcare device with interval Type-2 fuzzy numbers. *Socio-Econ. Plan. Sci.* **2020**, *69*, 100693. [CrossRef]

42. Wang, X.D.; He, J.M.; Li, S.W. Compound Option Pricing under Fuzzy Environment. *J. Appl. Math.* **2014**, *2014*, 875319. [CrossRef]
43. Wu, H.C. Pricing European options based on the fuzzy pattern of Black-Scholes formula. *Comput. Oper. Res.* **2004**, *31*, 1069–1081. [CrossRef]
44. Wu, H.C. Using fuzzy sets theory and Black-Scholes formula to generate pricing boundaries of European options. *Appl. Math. Comput.* **2007**, *185*, 136–146. [CrossRef]
45. Wu, S.L.; Yang, S.G.; Wu, Y.F.; Zhu, S.Z. Interval Pricing Study of Deposit Insurance in China. *Discret. Dyn. Nat. Soc.* **2020**, *2020*, 1531852. [CrossRef]
46. Xu, J.X.; Tan, Y.H.; Gao, J.G.; Feng, E.M. Pricing Currency Option Based on the Extension Principle and Defuzzification via Weighting Parameter Identification. *J. Appl. Math.* **2013**, *2013*, 623945. [CrossRef]
47. Wu, L.; Liu, J.F.; Wang, J.T.; Zhuang, Y.M. Pricing for a basket of LCDS under fuzzy environments. *SpringerPlus* **2016**, *5*, 1747. [CrossRef] [PubMed]
48. Wu, L.; Mei, X.B.; Sun, J.G. A New Default Probability Calculation Formula an Its Application under Uncertain Environments. *Discret. Dyn. Nat. Soc.* **2018**, *2018*, 3481863. [CrossRef]
49. Zhang, W.G.; Xiao, W.L.; Kong, W.T.; Zhang, Y. Fuzzy pricing of geometric Asian options and its algorithm. *Appl. Soft Comput.* **2015**, *28*, 360–367. [CrossRef]
50. Zmeskal, Z. Application of the fuzzy-stochastic methodology to appraising the firm value as an European call option. *Eur. J. Oper. Res.* **2001**, *135*, 303–310. [CrossRef]
51. Anzilli, L.; Villani, G. Real R&D options under fuzzy uncertainty in market share and revealed information. *Fuzzy Sets Syst.* **2021**, *434*, 117–134. [CrossRef]
52. Tang, W.; Cui, Q.; Zhang, F.; Chen, Y. Urban Rail-Transit Project Investment Benefits Based on Compound Real Options and Trapezoid Fuzzy Numbers. *J. Constr. Eng. Manag.* **2019**, *145*, 05018016. [CrossRef]
53. Wu, H.C. European option pricing under fuzzy environments. *Int. J. Intell. Syst.* **2005**, *20*, 89–102. [CrossRef]
54. Liu, K.; Chen, J.; Zhang, J.; Yang, Y. Application of fuzzy Malliavin calculus in hedging fixed strike lookback option. *AIMS Math.* **2023**, *8*, 9187–9211. [CrossRef]
55. Xu, W.D.; Wu, C.F.; Xu, W.J.; Li, H.Y. A jump-diffusion model for option pricing under fuzzy environments. *Insur. Math. Econ.* **2009**, *44*, 337–344. [CrossRef]
56. Zhang, L.H.; Zhang, W.G.; Xu, W.J.; Xiao, W.L. The double exponential jump diffusion model for pricing European options under fuzzy environments. *Econ. Model.* **2012**, *29*, 780–786. [CrossRef]
57. Figa-Talamanca, G.; Guerra, M.L.; Stefanini, L. Market Application of the Fuzzy-Stochastic Approach in the Heston Option Pricing Model. *Financ. Uver-Czech J. Econ. Financ.* **2012**, *62*, 162–179.
58. Bian, L.; Li, Z. Fuzzy simulation of European option pricing using subfractional Brownian motion. *Chaos Solitons Fractals* **2021**, *153*, 111442. [CrossRef]
59. Ghasemalipour, S.; Fathi-Vajargah, B. Fuzzy simulation of European option pricing using mixed fractional Brownian motion. *Soft Comput.* **2019**, *23*, 13205–13213. [CrossRef]
60. Qin, X.Z.; Lin, X.W.; Shang, Q. Fuzzy pricing of binary option based on the long memory property of financial markets. *J. Intell. Fuzzy Syst.* **2020**, *38*, 4889–4900. [CrossRef]
61. Wang, T.; Zhao, P.P.; Song, A.M. Power Option Pricing Based on Time-Fractional Model and Triangular Interval Type-2 Fuzzy Numbers. *Complexity* **2022**, *2022*, 5670482. [CrossRef]
62. Zhang, J.K.; Wang, Y.Y.; Zhang, S.M. A New Homotopy Transformation Method for Solving the Fuzzy Fractional Black-Scholes European Option Pricing Equations under the Concept of Granular Differentiability. *Fractal Fract.* **2022**, *6*, 286. [CrossRef]
63. Zhao, P.P.; Wang, T.; Xiang, K.L.; Chen, P.M. N-Fold Compound Option Fuzzy Pricing Based on the Fractional Brownian Motion. *Int. J. Fuzzy Syst.* **2022**, *24*, 2767–2782. [CrossRef]
64. Feng, Z.Y.; Cheng, J.T.S.; Liu, Y.H.; Jiang, I.M. Options pricing with time changed Levy processes under imprecise information. *Fuzzy Optim. Decis. Mak.* **2015**, *65*, 2348–2362. [CrossRef]
65. Nowak, P.; Pawlowski, M. Option Pricing with Application of Levy Processes and the Minimal Variance Equivalent Martingale Measure Under Uncertainty. *IEEE Trans. Fuzzy Syst.* **2017**, *25*, 402–416. [CrossRef]
66. Nowak, P.; Pawlowski, M. Pricing European options under uncertainty with application of Levy processes and the minimal L-q equivalent martingale measure. *J. Comput. Appl. Math.* **2019**, *345*, 416–433. [CrossRef]
67. Nowak, P.; Pawłowski, M. Application of the Esscher Transform to Pricing Forward Contracts on Energy Markets in a Fuzzy Environment. *Entropy* **2023**, *25*, 527. [CrossRef]
68. Nowak, P.; Romaniuk, M. Application of Levy processes and Esscher transformed martingale measures for option pricing in fuzzy framework. *J. Comput. Appl. Math.* **2014**, *263*, 129–151. [CrossRef]
69. Nowak, P.; Romaniuk, M. Catastrophe bond pricing for the two-factor Vasicek interest rate model with automatized fuzzy decision making. *Soft Comput.* **2017**, *21*, 2575–2597. [CrossRef]
70. Wang, X.D.; He, J.M. A geometric Levy model for n-fold compound option pricing in a fuzzy framework. *J. Comput. Appl. Math.* **2016**, *306*, 248–264. [CrossRef]
71. Zhang, H.M.; Watada, J. An European call options pricing model using the infinite pure jump levy process in a fuzzy environment. *IEEJ Trans. Electr. Electron. Eng.* **2018**, *13*, 1468–1482. [CrossRef]
72. Kemma, A.G.C.; Vorst, A.C.F. A pricing method for options based on average asset values. *J. Bank. Financ.* **1990**, *4*, 121–168.

73. Margrabe, W. The value of an exchange option to exchange one asset for another. *J. Financ.* **1978**, *33*, 177–186. [CrossRef]
74. Geske, R. The valuation of compound options. *J. Financ. Econ.* **1979**, *7*, 63–81. [CrossRef]
75. Merton, R.C. Option pricing when underlying stock returns are discontinuous. *J. Financ. Econ.* **1976**, *3*, 125–144. [CrossRef]
76. Heston, S.L. A closed-form solution for options with stochastic volatility with applications to bond and currency options. *Rev. Financ. Stud.* **1993**, *6*, 327–343. [CrossRef]
77. Clemente, G.P.; Della Corte, F.; Savelli, N. A Bridge between Local GAAP and Solvency II Frameworks to Quantify Capital Re-quirement for Demographic Risk. *Risks* **2021**, *9*, 175. [CrossRef]
78. Romaniuk, M.; Hryniewicz, O. Interval-based, nonparametric approach for resampling of fuzzy numbers. *Soft Comput.* **2019**, *23*, 5883–5903. [CrossRef]
79. Couso, I.; Dubois, D. Statistical reasoning with set-valued information: Ontic vs. epistemic views. *Int. J. Approx. Reason.* **2014**, *55*, 1502–1518. [CrossRef]
80. Hull, J.C. *Options Futures and Other Derivatives*; Pearson Education: Noida, India, 2008.
81. Longstaff, F.A.; Schwartz, E.S. Interest rate volatility and bond prices. *Financ. Anal. J.* **1993**, *49*, 70–74. [CrossRef]
82. Buckley, J.J.; Qu, Y. On using α-cuts to evaluate fuzzy equations. *Fuzzy Sets Syst.* **1990**, *38*, 309–312. [CrossRef]
83. Buckley, J.J.; Feuring, T. Fuzzy differential equations. *Fuzzy Sets Syst.* **2000**, *110*, 43–54. [CrossRef]
84. Ahmadi, S.A.; Ghasemi, P. Pricing strategies for online hotel searching: A fuzzy inference system procedure. *Kybernetes* **2022**, *ahead of print.* [CrossRef]
85. Bo, L.; You, C. Fuzzy Interest Rate Term Structure Equation. *Int. J. Fuzzy Syst.* **2020**, *22*, 999–1006. [CrossRef]
86. Kuchta, D. Fuzzy capital budgeting. *Fuzzy Sets Syst.* **2000**, *111*, 367–385. [CrossRef]
87. Lawal, A.I.; Omoju, O.E.; Babajide, A.A.; Asaleye, A.I. Testing mean-reversion in agricultural commodity prices: Evidence from wavelet analysis. *J. Int. Stud.* **2019**, *12*, 100–114. [CrossRef]
88. Andres-Sanchez, J.; Gómez, A.T. Estimating a term structure of interest rates for fuzzy financial pricing by using fuzzy regression methods. *Fuzzy Sets Syst.* **2003**, *139*, 313–331. [CrossRef]

**Disclaimer/Publisher's Note:** The statements, opinions and data contained in all publications are solely those of the individual author(s) and contributor(s) and not of MDPI and/or the editor(s). MDPI and/or the editor(s) disclaim responsibility for any injury to people or property resulting from any ideas, methods, instructions or products referred to in the content.

 *mathematics*

Article

# Fuzzy Logic to Measure the Degree of Compliance with a Target in an SDG—The Case of SDG 11

Javier Parra-Domínguez [1,*], Maria Alonso-García [2] and Juan Manuel Corchado [1,2]

1. BISITE Research Group, University of Salamanca, Espejo, S/N, 37007 Salamanca, Spain; corchado@usal.es
2. AIR Institute, 47011 Valladolid, Spain; marialonsogar@air-institute.com
* Correspondence: javierparra@usal.es

**Abstract:** Sustainable development and its significant challenges motivate various international organisations in a way that has never been seen before. With Europe at the forefront, countries such as the United States want to be included in the progress and what a clear and determined commitment to sustainability means for future generations. Our study aimed to go deeper into the follow-up and monitoring of the development of reliable indicators that make the continuous improvement process in sustainability robust. To this end, and using the fuzzy logic methodology, we applied it to one of the indices that have been developed to date, the "Sustainable Development Report" (in its 2022 edition), working on the specific application of SDG 11. Our results show favourable positions for countries such as Brunei Darussalam, Tonga, Tuvalu, Andorra, and the Netherlands and provide robustness when there is a lack of data quality and improvements in the implementation of the process when experts intervene.

**Keywords:** sustainability; fuzzy logic; SDGs; smart cities

**MSC:** 03B52; 91B76; 91D10

**Citation:** Parra-Domínguez, J.; Alonso-García, M.; Corchado, J.M. Fuzzy Logic to Measure the Degree of Compliance with a Target in an SDG—The Case of SDG 11. *Mathematics* **2023**, *11*, 2967. https://doi.org/10.3390/math11132967

Academic Editors: Michael Voskoglou, Laura González-Vila Puchades and Jorge de Andres Sanchez

Received: 14 April 2023
Revised: 28 June 2023
Accepted: 30 June 2023
Published: 3 July 2023

**Copyright:** © 2023 by the authors. Licensee MDPI, Basel, Switzerland. This article is an open access article distributed under the terms and conditions of the Creative Commons Attribution (CC BY) license (https://creativecommons.org/licenses/by/4.0/).

## 1. Introduction

Humanity's continuous challenges are characteristic of a developing world [1]. Technology, and working together with it, is part of this development, making the pace of development faster [2] and giving rise to currents of thought that have to work towards measuring the reaction to the high speed of progress while taking care of the possible negative impacts that may result [3]. The objectives as a society are not only set for the present, but the challenge is to work towards the best objectives and quality of life for future generations. Reflection on progress must be based on homogenisation to have the capacity for objective criteria. In this sense, the SDGs [1] and, in our case, the concern for their fulfilment have been developed. Once homogeneous measurement criteria are in place, it is time to move on to interpretation and work on concrete improvements where objectivity accompanies a rigorous and necessary subjectivity in approximating the reality of human beings' experiences of the fact of the space that surrounds us. This research will focus on establishing criteria to measure, control, and favour decision-making motivated by the treatment of fuzzy logic as a method since it is an approach capable of involving objectivity and subjectivity in an indicator. It is essential to emphasise that this will be undertaken from a theoretical point of view and will not be overdimensioned, based on the model proposed for SDG 11 (sustainable cities and communities: making cities and human settlements inclusive, safe, resilient, and sustainable), which represents one of the significant challenges of the world's population, which is none other than the existence of cities that, as ecosystems, bring together a large part of the population. All of the above highlights the novelty of in the current study, which is none other than the incorporation of fuzzy logic systems in the expert judgement that participates in an improvement of the homogeneous measurement of sustainability based on the SDGs. The development was carried out on SDG 11 and was based on a use case. To develop the research, the link between the SDGs and sustainable development was first explored in depth, and the reality of fuzzy logic systems as a support for decision-making was introduced. The second section examined the progress of different SDG measurement and monitoring systems, focusing on SDG 11. The third section incorporated the proposed fuzzy logic system for action on SDG 11. Subsequently, comparative results will be presented, and finally, the discussion and conclusions will be included.

*1.1. The SDGs and Sustainable Development*

In today's changing world, knowing where we are heading is essential. There are various tools for monitoring humanity's progress in its sustainable development, one of the most relevant at present being compliance with the Sustainable Development Goals (SDGs) [4].

At this point, it is essential to highlight the current SDGs and their implication for recent development, especially for what is considered sustainable development [5,6]. There are 17 SDGs and the United Nations classifies them as "No poverty", "Zero hunger", "Good health and well-being", "Quality education", "Gender quality", "Clean water and sanitation", "Affordable and clean energy", "Decent work and economic growth", "Industry, innovation and infrastructure", "Reduced inequalities", "Sustainable cities and communities", "Responsible consumption and production", "Climate action", "Life below water", "Life on land", "Peace, justice and strong institutions", and "Partnerships for the goals".

The 17 SDGs were established in 2015 [7], when world leaders established them as a set of global goals to eradicate poverty, protect the planet, and ensure prosperity for all as part of the new sustainable development agenda. The deadline for achieving these goals was set at 15 years [8].

To introduce the historical context, it is essential to point out that concern for the environment began to emerge at the end of the Second World War [9], which is the period when concerns about the significant problems of that period became evident. At this stage, we should highlight the First Report of the Club of Rome, dated 1972, called "the limits of growth" [10], which concluded that the planet would reach the limits of its growth over the next one hundred years. It was in 1987 that the concept of sustainable development came into existence [11], which had international repercussions thanks to the Brundtland Report presented by the World Commission on Environment and Development [12]. The idea in question, defined in 1983 by the Commission, created by the United Nations (UN), was limited to *"development that meets the needs of the present without compromising the ability of future generations to meet their own needs"*[13]. Although this may be one of the broadest conceptions of sustainability to date, it can be refined by clearly distinguishing, for example, between development and sustainability, which is not entirely clear. While development is based on cultural uniformity and the destruction of natural resources [14], sustainability leans towards conservation and the rational use of the environment [15].

The above evolution shapes the so-called 2030 agenda [16], an initiative taken forward by UN country leaders. Previously, 189 leaders formed and signed the so-called Millennium Declaration [17], the objective of which was to be achieved by 2015 and was made up of the so-called Millennium Development Goals (MDGs) [18]. It should be noted that, at the end of the period, essential conclusions were drawn for the United Nations, and this led to a commitment by these leaders to the achievement of future goals to make global action work while at the same time pushing for the adoption of new ambitions to meet global needs better [19–21]. With 193 countries now signatories, the MDGs were replaced by the action plan *"Transforming our World: The 2030 Agenda for Sustainable Development"*, which set out the 17 known SDGs and 169 associated targets [22].

Of the 17 SDGs, this article will focus on SDG 11. SDG 11 focuses on sustainable cities and communities in an increasingly urbanised world [23]. The article will link SDG 11 with the mathematical methodology of fuzzy logic [24,25], allowing us to take into account aspects of mainstreaming in the measurement given the characterisation of systems and society and the economy [26,27]. With the representation of the theoretical model to be introduced, the aim was to respond to the challenge posed by the fact that, since 2007, more of the world's population has been living in cities, a trend that is expected to reach 60 per cent by 2030 [28]. The importance of SDG 11 is evident in addressing challenges ranging from protecting cultural heritage to constructing sustainable and resilient buildings [29]. These challenges could also improve air quality or transport efficiency by expanding public transport services and enhancing their accessibility and safety. The targets of SDG 11, in concrete terms, are "11.1 Ensuring access to adequate, safe, affordable housing and essential services, and slum upgrading", "11.2 Providing access to safe, affordable, accessible, and sustainable transport systems for all and improving road safety", "11.3 Increasing inclusive and sustainable urbanisation and capacity for participatory planning and management", "11.4 Increased efforts to protect and safeguard the world's cultural and natural heritage", "11.5 Reducing the number of deaths caused by disasters, including water-related disasters", "11.6 Reducing the negative per capita environmental impact of cities", "11.7 Providing universal access to safe, inclusive and accessible green spaces and public spaces", "11.a Supporting positive economic, social and environmental linkages between urban, peri-urban and rural areas", "11.b Significantly increase the number of cities and human settlements adopting and implementing integrated policies and plans to promote inclusiveness, resource efficiency, climate change mitigation and adaptation, and disaster resilience", and "11.c Provide support to least developed countries for more efficient building construction".

As will be described when introducing the methodological framework and the theoretical model developed, fuzzy logic will also link measurable variables to each of the targets involved in the monitoring of SDG 11.

*1.2. Fuzzy Systems for Decision Making*

The theory of fuzzy logic based systems approximates the behaviour of a system when there are no analytical functions or numerical relations to define it. Social or political problems are complex systems for which it is often not possible to capture analytically the information required to represent them. The more complex a system is, the more imprecise or inaccurate the knowledge available to characterise it. The uncertainty surrounding a problem can be caused by its complexity, the lack of knowledge, the inability to make adequate measurements, or the inherent vagueness of natural language. Using vagueness to describe a system allows some intuitive information or inaccuracies to be incorporated, for example, by determining whether the biodiversity of an area is "adequate". Ragin's seminal work [30] critiqued the conventional approach to social research and proposed the use of set-theoretic methods to overcome its limitations. In his book, Ragin argues for the integration of fuzzy-set analysis, a set-theoretic method, as a means to strengthen the connection between qualitative researchers' deep case knowledge and quantitative researchers' exploration of cross-case patterns. Schneider and Wageman [31] provide an extensive guide to Qualitative Comparative Analysis (QCA), a set-theoretic method that has gained popularity in social science research. This book covers both basic and advanced issues in set-theoretic methods, equipping researchers with a comprehensive understanding of QCA. The authors also offer practical tips on software handling and exercises to facilitate the application of QCA in empirical research. Another article [32] highlights the use of Qualitative Comparative Analysis (QCA), encompassing crisp and fuzzy sets, in the field of business and management research. The authors emphasize the significance of incorporating contextual information and cognitive aspects into the analysis, which leads to a more comprehensive understanding of the subject matter. By utilizing QCA, researchers in business and management can gain valuable insights into complex phenomena. Pappas and Woodside's article [33] focuses on providing guidelines for using Fuzzy-set Qualitative Comparative Analysis (fsQCA) in Information Systems and marketing research. The authors discuss the distinctions between fsQCA and variance-based approaches, as well as structured equation modeling. Moreover, they offer a summary of thresholds and guidelines for practical implementation. The article also emphasizes how existing papers employing variance-based approaches can benefit from integrating fsQCA into their research.

In the case of the SDGs, many countries lack data and some variables cannot be measured accurately, suggesting that the assessment of the SDGs should be modelled assuming some uncertainty. The idea of thinking of this problem as a mathematical model based on fuzzy logic has been raised before to apply it to the study of human trafficking or to score test policies [34]. Establishing such frameworks provides great flexibility and allows for subsequent adaptation and continuous improvement. In decision-making, it is important to highlight the work of fuzzy logic in approximating complex assignments when the data set is to be decided upon, and the decision rules need to be clarified [35]. In addition to the examples mentioned earlier and the referenced handbook that evaluates the role of fuzzy logic in the field of decision-making, all of the above is reinforced due to the strong links in the field of medical sciences [36,37] and widely referenced fields such as engineering [38] or social sciences [39], specifically within business development [40].

## 2. The Current Implementation and Monitoring of the SDGs—The SDG 11 Case

As previously introduced, one of the main difficulties in approximating effective compliance with sustainability is the lack of robust and, above all, homogeneous criteria for follow-up and monitoring of the variables that give rise to knowing [41,42], for example, the position of each country or region concerning sustainability. There are even voices in favour of the scientific community considering whether the SDGs are suitable for measuring progress on the 2030 Agenda. In any case, they are also the ones that allow us to go beyond merely economic measurements.

Following Díaz-Sarachaga et al. (2017) [43], the indicators that already motivated, in one way or another, the provision of monitoring criteria important for humanity, were as follows:

- The Human Development Index (HDI) reflects three important human aspects: the pursuit of a long and healthy life, access to knowledge, and a good standard of living. This index, developed by the Human Development Report Office of the United Nations Development Programme (UNDP) in 2016, is calculated from the geometric mean of three normalised sub-indices representing the life expectancy index, the education index, and the gross national income index [44].
- The Ecological Footprint (EF) is an indicator that aims to determine the area of land required to cover the consumption of natural resources by a defined population [45]. It is a helpful measure developed by the University of British Columbia to quickly compare the demand for nature required to meet the needs of a given human settlement. Another indicator motivated by environmental sustainability monitoring is the Living Planet Index developed by the Worldwide Wildlife Foundation (WWF) and the Zoological Society of London (ZSL) [46].
- Another key indicator that has accompanied society in its well-being assessment is the result of collaboration between the International Union for Conservation of Nature (IUCN) and the International Development Research Centre (IDRC). It began with the birth of the Sustainability Barometer tool [47]. It led to what is known as the Well-being Assessment Method [48], which has been applied in 180 countries as the first global assessment of sustainability. Importantly, sustainable development is measured by combining four indices: the Human Well-being Index (HWI), the Ecosystem Well-being Index (EWI), the Well-being Index (WI), and the Well-being Stress Index (WSI).
- Focusing on current research, there are also indices and indicators related to the concern for the advancement of cities. The so-called Urban Development Index (UDI) classifies cities according to their urban development based on criteria of liveability, poverty, traffic congestion, inclusion and different sustainability factors. Also noteworthy is the emergence, in 2012, of City Prosperity. This indicator promotes and integrates other elements such as those supporting local, regional, and national decision-makers

in productivity, infrastructure, quality of life, equity, and inclusion, environmental sustainability and factors related to governance and legislation. It is divided into four scenarios:

1. Global City Ranking for global and regional monitoring.
2. Basic CPI provides the first internationally comparable diagnosis.
3. Extended CPI, consisting of a comparable in-depth analysis within the country.
4. Contextual CPI serves as an urban monitoring tool that includes national urban policies.

- In addition to the above, and already related to purely economic criteria, there are indices of a financial nature such as the Gross Domestic Product (GDP) [49], which evaluates economic well-being and for which alternatives emerged, such as the Economic Well-being Measure, which adjusted GDP by adding values relating to leisure time, unpaid work, and subtracting the importance of environmental damage due to industrial production and consumption. Another alternative is the Genuine Progress Indicator (GPI) [50], which considers income inequality, crime costs, environmental damage, and reduced leisure time. Finally, another of the highlights is the Adjusted Net Savings Index (ANSI), also known as the Genuine Savings Index (GSI) [51], which measures the change in annual net national wealth, taking into account the human, natural and economic dimensions. The latter indicator is also concerned with the wealth that future generations may receive; otherwise, sustainability would not be guaranteed.

In addition to the above indicators, the so-called SDG index describes the progress towards the SDGs of different countries, i.e., it works at the aggregate country level, establishing critical points where progress may be considered insufficient. This is an optimal representation of development represented through percentages in what is indicated as an SDG index. This index works by establishing a series of differences between any given country's score and the maximum value given, 100, and establishing this as the distance in percentage points that each country is from the development optimum. Of course, the SDG index uses the same indicators for all countries and tracks them by ranking against the particular index. Details on the applied statistics can be found in Papadimitriou et al. (2019) [52], within their studies conducted at the Joint Research Centre of the European Commission (EU JCR), and the methodology developed in the latest report can be found in Lafortune et al. (2018) [53], also developed within the EU JCR. All of the above was developed and can be visualised in the dashboard, which allows the development of the different countries concerning the 17 SDGs to be visualised by colour. The index in question has limitations that have been observed and expressed in the different annual reports that have been developed, among which we would highlight the following:

- The change in some of the metrics or the indicators developed annually may cause the indicator to be affected by a lack of complete comparability concerning the previous year.
- The index incorporates data from official and non-official sources. Official sources include FAO, ILO, OECD, UNICEF, WHO, and The World Bank. At this point, what is noteworthy as a possible gap is the non-availability of weights and aggregation criteria by experts, as there is no consensus, given the disaggregation and idiosyncrasies of each area at the global level. In this sense, the index favours the existence of equal weights for each of the variables mentioned.

After the first strategic step, where a five-step decision tree is established, the normalisation criterion is followed by the equation

$$x' = \frac{x - \min.(x)}{\max.(x) - \min.(x)} 100, \qquad (1)$$

where $x$ is the raw data value, the min. and max. denote the lower and upper bounds, respectively and, therefore, $x'$ is the normalized value. The requirements already mentioned for the weights and rankings are then selected and the dashboard is generated, where the different trends in the measurement of the SDGs can be observed. Specifically, concerning SDG 11, which is the one we worked on in this theoretical study, the indicators included in the latest Sustainable Development Report are as follows [54]:

- Proportion of urban population living in a slum, in percentage terms.
- Annual mean concentration of particulate matter of less than 2.5 microns in diameter (PM2.5) (mg/m$^3$).
- Access to improved water source, in percentage terms of urban population.
- Satisfaction with public transport, in percentage.
- Population with rent overburden, in percentage.

In order, each of the above corresponds to the following optimal criteria:

- Proportion of urban population living in a slum. Zero is the optimum and is justified by the premise "leave no one behind".
- Annual mean concentration of particulate matter of less than 2.5 microns in diameter (PM2.5) (mg/m$^3$); 6.3 is the optimum and is justified on the premise "average of five best performers".
- Access to improved water source. One hundred is the optimum and is justified by the premise "leave no one behind".
- Satisfaction with public transport; 82.6 is the optimum and is justified by the premise "average of five best performers".
- Population with rent overburden; 4.6 is the optimum and is justified by the premise "average of three best OECD performers".

With all of the above, and as has been introduced, we will work on optimising the incorporation of fuzzy logic systems which, for cities, as units of vital development, favour the incorporation of expert criteria. Furthermore, the automation in the homogenisation of the process will allow for agility in compiling different sources in different cities.

## 3. The Proposed Fuzzy Assessment System

The diagram in the Figure 1 represents the steps to be followed to define the fuzzy logic system [55]. The first phase consists of identifying the variables that govern the system (input and output) and set criteria indicating the interaction between them. In a fuzzy logic system, the association between input and output variables is determined by a collection of fuzzy rules. These rules delineate the manner in which inputs are linked to outputs, taking into account their linguistic terms and accompanying membership functions. Input variables are commonly characterized by fuzzy sets, representing varying degrees of membership for each linguistic term. Likewise, output variables are also defined by fuzzy sets that encompass linguistic terms and their respective membership functions. Fuzzy rules elucidate the behavior of the system by establishing logical connections between input and output variables. Each rule comprises an antecedent (input) and a consequent (output). The antecedent evaluates the extent to which the input variables fulfill the conditions specified by linguistic terms and membership functions. The consequent determines the degree to which output variables are assigned to specific linguistic terms and their corresponding membership functions. The process of mapping inputs to outputs in a fuzzy logic system entails fuzzification, rule evaluation, aggregation, and defuzzification. Fuzzification converts precise input values into fuzzy sets, associating them with appropriate linguistic terms and membership degrees. Rule evaluation quantifies the degree of activation for each rule based on the membership values of the input variables. Aggregation combines the activated rules to ascertain the overall output membership functions. Finally, defuzzification converts the fuzzy output sets into precise output values by calculating a representative value, such as the centroid or maximum membership, derived from the aggregated membership functions. Finally, if data are available, they are fed into the system to obtain output values. The last phase consists of the interpretation and validation by experts of the results obtained. Each of these steps is detailed below as applied to the particular case of defining a fuzzy logic system that assesses compliance with SDG 11.

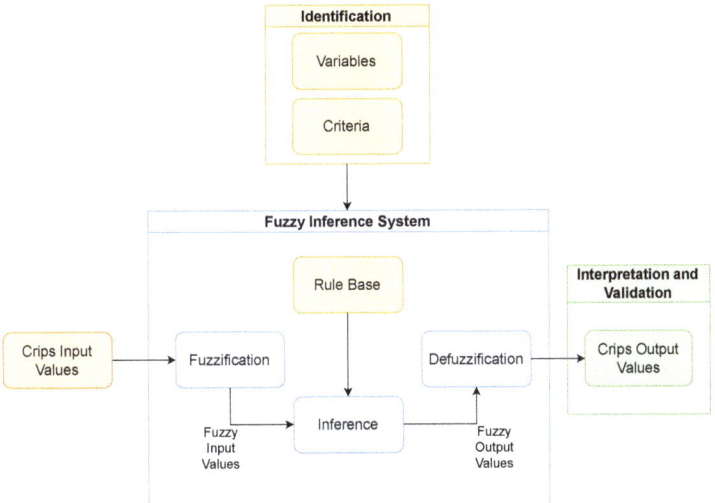

**Figure 1.** Fuzzy logic evaluation system architecture.

First, the system must be defined by identifying the variables governing the system and how the input variables are related to each other and to the output variable. In this study, the indicators included in the Sustainable Development Report 2022 for SDG 11 (Table A.5) [54], which will be described in detail below, are taken as input variables and mathematically denoted as follows. Let $\{v_i\}_{i=1}^{5}$ be the set of the fuzzy input variables, where $v_1$ is the proportion of urban population living in slums (%); $v_2$ is the annual mean concentration of particulate matter of less than 2.5 microns in diameter (PM2.5) ($\mu g/m^3$); $v_3$ is the access to improved source, piped (% of urban population); $v_4$ is the satisfaction with public transport (%); and $v_5$ is the population with rent overburden (%). Each fuzzy variable is fully characterised in the following paragraphs in terms of its universe of discourse and fuzzy subsets.

Let $X_i$ be the universe of discourse, that is, the set of real values $x \in X_i$ for which a variable $v_i$, $\forall i \in \{1, ..., 5\}$ is defined. In practice, it could be defined by giving the minimum $a_i$, maximum $b_i$ and number of points contained between these two extremes $s_i$ (in theory it is possible to define a real interval with infinite values between the points defining an interval but in any practical implementation it is necessary to define some way to discretise the domain, in this case, it is proposed to fix the number of intermediate points contained between extremes). The universe of discourse for the indicators measured in percentages will be $[0, 100]$ by definition of percentage and we take $X_2 = [5, 107]$ as these are the floor of the minimum and ceiling of the maximum values for $v_2$ found by studying the available data per country obtained from the Sustainable Development Report 2022. For example, the annual mean concentration of particulate matter of less than 2.5 microns in diameter ($v_2$) for a country could be any value between 5 and 107, including both.

Currently, each variable is divided exactly into subsets defined by quantitative thresholds that map each value of an indicator to a colour code (green, yellow, orange, red, or grey). These colour codes represent how far a country is from meeting a given SDG [54]. The colour legend used is illustrated in Figure 2 and associates a colour with a linguistic description of the progress of a country towards achieving an SDG [56].

**Legend**

- SDG achieved
- Challenges remain
- Significant challenges remain
- Major challenges remain
- Information unavailable

**Figure 2.** Colour scales to benchmark progress towards achieving the SDGs.

The colour green should not be taken to mean that the state has achieved the SDG indicator but rather that it is on track to do so by 2030 [56]. A range is associated with each colour so that, if an indicator takes values in that range, the corresponding colour is associated with it. The limits of each interval have been defined by experts, scientifically determined levels, or using summary statistics of data when the previous options are not possible [56]. This definition of the ranges suggests that the fuzzy logic approach to the problem may be more suitable due to factors such as possible discrepancies between expert judgement or future changes in the data that would shift the thresholds. For SDG 11 indicators, the current ranges $A_j^i$ associated with each variable $v_i$ are shown in the Table 1. For example, if the proportion of the urban population living in slums ($v_1$) is 3% for a country, then it is considered as SDG-achieved or green ($A_1^1$).

**Table 1.** Defined bounds per indicator for SDG 11.

|  | $v_1$ | $v_2$ | $v_3$ | $v_4$ | $v_5$ |
|---|---|---|---|---|---|
| Universe of discourse ($X_i$) | [0, 100] | [5, 107] | [0, 100] | [0, 100] | [0, 100] |
| SDG achieved—Green—($A_1^i$) | [0, 5] | [5, 10] | [98, 100] | [72, 100] | [0, 7] |
| Challenges remain—Yellow—($A_2^i$) | (5, 15] | (10, 17.5] | [86.5, 98) | [57.5, 72) | (7, 12] |
| Significant challenges remain—Orange—($A_3^i$) | (15, 25] | (17.5, 25] | [75, 86.5) | [43, 57.5) | (12, 17] |
| Major challenges remain—Red—($A_4^i$) | (25, 100] | (25, 107] | [0, 75) | [0, 43) | (17, 100] |

At this point, it is important to mention a drawback related to data availability: some countries are not fully characterised, this is, the corresponding value of $v_i$ is not available for one or more $i \in \{1, ..., 5\}$. Therefore, to deal with this, we proposed to create the system dynamically according to the input variables for which information is available, provided that the number of available input variables is equal to or greater than two. In case a country has no information for any variable or has information for only one, the current criterion—identifying SDG 11 compliance with grey as information not available—is maintained. As a consequence, it will not be possible to define a single system but there will be as many as there are combinations of two or more variables. This is equivalent to saying that the number of fuzzy logic systems, #FLS, resulting from this approach are the number of possible combinations formed by two or more unordered and non-repeating variables:

$$\#\text{FLS} \leq \sum_{k=2}^{5} C_k(n) = 26, \quad C_k(n) = \binom{n}{k} = \frac{n!}{k!(n-k)!}, \tag{2}$$

where $n = 5$ is the maximum number of variables.

To conclude with the identification of variables, we define the output variable, $\eta$, as the degree of SDG compliance, measured as a percentage. The universe of discourse and the ranges we have considered for the output variable are shown in Table 2.

Table 2. Crisp bounds for the output variable.

| | $\eta$ |
|---|---|
| Universe of discourse ($X_6$) | [0, 100] |
| SDG achieved—Green—($A_1^6$) | (80, 100] |
| Challenges remain—Yellow—($A_2^6$) | (50, 80] |
| Significant challenges remain—Orange—($A_3^6$) | (20, 50] |
| Major challenges remain—Red—($A_4^6$) | [0, 20] |

Finally, the relationships of the input variables to each other and to the output variable must be established. One simple rule block is defined per variable present in the system plus two additional rules combining multiple variables. Each simple block consists of four rules—one for each interval of values defined in each input variable—and each rule relates each interval of an input variable to an interval of those of the output variable following a relationship of direct proportionality. Let $\xi_j, j = \{1, 2, 3, 4\}$ denote each qualitative range of values that defines a variable, such that $\xi_1 :=$ SDG achieved (Green), $\xi_2 :=$ Challenges remain (Yellow), $\xi_3 :=$ Significant challenges remain (Orange), and $\xi_4 :=$ Major challenges remain (Red). Then, a simple block of rules for a variable $v_i$ is given by:

$$\text{If } (v_i = \xi_j), \text{ then } (\eta = \xi_j), \forall j = 1, .., 4. \tag{3}$$

Examples of these rules inside a block in natural language include "if slum population is SDG-achieved, then compliance degree is SDG-achieved" or "if matter concentration is that significant challenges remain, then compliance degree is that significant challenges remain". These rule blocks establish the relationships between the input variables and the output variable based on the defined qualitative ranges (Green, Yellow, Orange, Red). Each input variable's interval is mapped to an interval of the output variable, maintaining a direct proportionality relationship.

The other two additional rules can be deduced from the following extract:

*"Averaging across all indicators for an SDG might hide areas of policy concern if a country performs well on most indicators but faces serious shortfalls on one or two metrics within the same SDG (often called the "substitutability" or "compensation" issue). [...] We applied the added rule that a red rating is given only if the country scores red on both of its worst-performing indicators for that goal. Similarly, to score green, both of these indicators had to be green [54]."*

This implies that $\eta = \xi_4$ for a country if at least two of its indicators are red and that it is green if and only if all its indicators are green. These rules are transformed into implication type for inclusion in the rule base:

$$\text{If } \Big(((v_1 = \xi_4) \text{ and } (v_2 = \xi_4)) \text{ or } ((v_1 = \xi_4) \text{ and } (v_3 = \xi_4)) \text{ or } \tag{4}$$

$$((v_1 = \xi_4) \text{ and } (v_4 = \xi_4)) \text{ or } ((v_2 = \xi_4) \text{ and } (v_3 = \xi_4)) \text{ or }$$

$$((v_2 = \xi_4) \text{ and } (v_4 = \xi_4)) \text{ or } ((v_3 = \xi_4) \text{ and } (v_4 = \xi_4))\Big), \text{ then } (\eta = \xi_4)$$

$$\text{If } \Big((v_1 = \xi_1) \text{ and } (v_2 = \xi_1) \text{ and } (v_3 = \xi_1) \text{ and } (v_4 = \xi_1)\Big), \text{ then } (\eta = \xi_1). \tag{5}$$

That is: "If (((((((((slum population is Major challenges remain) and (matter concentration is Major challenges remain)) or ((slum population is Major challenges remain) and (water access is Major challenges remain))) or ((slum population is Major challenges remain) and (public transport satisfaction is Major challenges remain))) or ((slum population is Major challenges remain) and (rent overburden population is Major challenges remain))) or ((matter concentration is Major challenges remain) and (water access is Major challenges remain))) or ((matter concentration is Major challenges remain) and (public transport satisfaction is Major challenges remain))) or ((matter concentration is Major challenges remain) and (rent overburden population is Major challenges remain))) or ((water access is Major challenges remain) and (public transport satisfaction is Major challenges remain))) or ((water access is Major challenges remain) and (rent overburden population is Major challenges remain))) or ((public transport satisfaction is Major challenges remain) and (rent overburden population is Major challenges remain)), then compliance degree is Major challenges remain"; and "If ((((slum population is SDG achieved) and (matter concentration is SDG achieved)) and (water access is SDG achieved)) and (public transport satisfaction is SDG achieved)) and (rent overburden population is SDG achieved), then compliance degree is SDG achieved". In what follows, we will refer to these rules as "red rule" and "green rule".

By incorporating these two additional rules along with the previous rule blocks for each input variable, a complete set of rules is defined to evaluate the degree of compliance (output variable) based on the given input variables. This concludes the identification phase and leads to the construction of a fuzzy logic system.

Fuzzification can be described as the process of transforming crisp input values into fuzzy sets, which are completely characterized by the set of pairs:

$$\tilde{\zeta}_j^i = \left\{ \left(x, \mu_{\tilde{\zeta}_j^i}(x)\right), x \in X_i \right\}, \quad i = \{1, ..., 6\}, j = \{1, ..., 4\}, \tag{6}$$

where $\mu_{\tilde{\zeta}_j^i}$ denotes the membership function that associates a degree of membership to each $x \in \tilde{\zeta}_j^i$ such that $\mu_{\tilde{\zeta}_j^i}(x) \in [0,1]$. The membership functions are intended to describe vagueness and ambiguity: if the degree of membership is one, $x \in \tilde{\zeta}_j^i$; if it is zero, $x \notin \tilde{\zeta}_j^i$; any value between zero and one indicates the degree of uncertainty associated with the value being in a given set.

For this phase, we have taken the limits defined in Tables 1 and 2 and blurred their boundaries to incorporate uncertainty. This is justified by the difficulty of defining precise upper and lower limits in practice. We chos S-shaped, Z-shaped, and bell-shaped membership functions as shown in the Figure 3. However, this choice is not unique and other types of functions, such as trapezoidal or triangular, can be considered. Each fuzzy set has an associated description in linguistic terms, as described above. For example, the membership functions for the slum population variable can be defined formally as follows:

$$\mu_{\tilde{\zeta}_1^1}(x) = \begin{cases} 0 & \text{if } x \leq 3 \\ 1 - 2\left(\frac{x-3}{5-3}\right)^2 & \text{if } 3 \leq x \leq 4 \\ 1 & \text{if } x \geq 5 \end{cases} \tag{7}$$

$$\mu_{\tilde{\zeta}_2^1}(x) = \frac{1}{1 + \left|\frac{x-10}{5}\right|^{10}} \tag{8}$$

$$\mu_{\tilde{\zeta}_3^1}(x) = \frac{1}{1 + \left|\frac{x-20}{5}\right|^{10}} \tag{9}$$

$$\mu_{\tilde{\zeta}_4^1}(x) = \begin{cases} 0 & \text{if } x \leq 23 \\ 2\left(\frac{x-23}{30-23}\right)^2 & \text{if } 23 \leq x \leq 26.5 \\ 1 - 2\left(\frac{x-30}{30-23}\right)^2 & \text{if } 26.5 \leq x \leq 30 \\ 1 & \text{if } x \geq 30 \end{cases} \tag{10}$$

These equations represent the membership functions that associate a degree of membership $\mu_{\tilde{\zeta}_{ij}}(x)$ to each value $x$. The membership functions of the other variables are defined analogously.

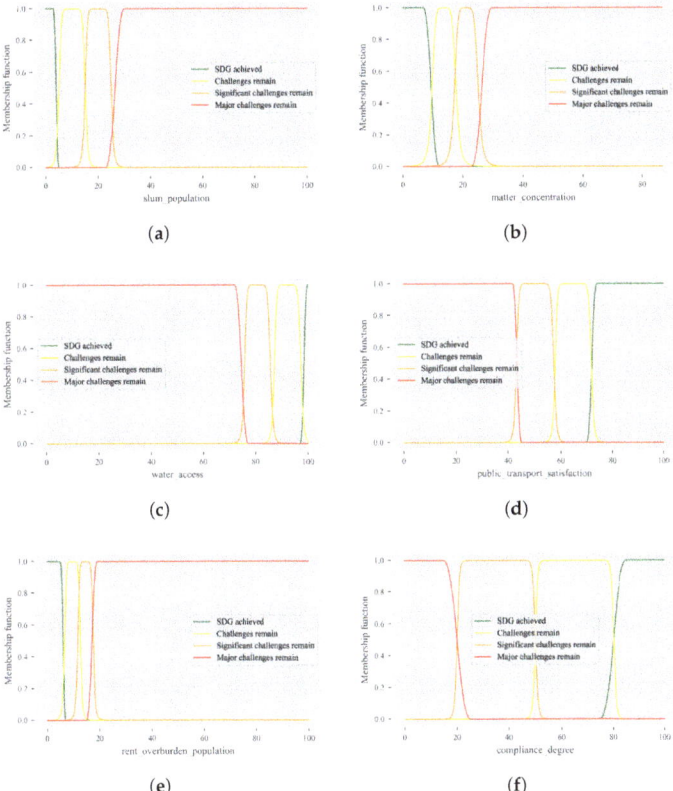

**Figure 3.** Fuzzy membership functions per variable. (a) $\tilde{\zeta}^1_j$; (b) $\tilde{\zeta}^2_j$; (c) $\tilde{\zeta}^3_j$; (d) $\tilde{\zeta}^4_j$; (e) $\tilde{\zeta}^5_j$; (f) $\tilde{\zeta}^6_j$.

The rule set in the identification phase indicates how to relate the input variables to the output variable. In terms of fuzzy logic, each block of simple rules is converted into:

$$\text{If } (v_i = \tilde{\zeta}^i_j), \text{ then } (\eta = \tilde{\zeta}^6_j), \forall j = 1,..,4, \qquad (11)$$

where $v_i$ and $\eta$ are now fuzzy variables, $\tilde{\zeta}^i_j$ is the $j$-th fuzzy set of the variable $v_i$, and $\tilde{\zeta}^6_j$ is the $j$-th fuzzy set of the variable $\eta$. The remaining two rules (4) and (5) are translated analogously. The operations of *or* and *and* of the last two rules are the Zadeh logical operators of fuzzy logic, where $(x \text{ or } y) := \max(x,y)$ and $(x \text{ and } y) := \min(x,y)$. In addition, each rule is weighted with a $\omega_k \in (0,1], k \in \{1,...,22\}$, according to the importance assigned to it in relation to the other rules. Note that if the current approach is to be respected, the last two rules should have considerably more weight than the other simple rules. Consequently, we tentatively assign $\omega_k = 0.1$ for each simple rule and $\omega_k = 1$ for red and green rules.

After evaluating each rule in a fuzzy inference system, a fuzzy set is obtained as output. These outputs are aggregated using the maximum aggregation function to produce another fuzzy set. Defuzzification converts this aggregate fuzzy set into a single number by selecting the best possible crisp value. For this, the centroid method was applied, which gives the value of the centre of the area under the curve.

The output is precisely the degree of compliance with SDG 11 for each country, obtained after combining the values of the input variables collected with the rule base.

The current implementation of the method can be found in the following repository: https://github.com/marialonsogar/fuzzy-compliance-SDG11, (accessed on 20 May 2023).

## 4. Results

The results of the previous research are now presented. The first outcome of the research is the identification of the lack of data and the limitations this places on any further analysis or modelling.

Ideally, all countries covered by the report should have values for each of the five indicators. However, in the data used for the report, only 28 countries (14.51%) have complete information. On the other hand, there are 11 countries (5.7%) that have only one non-missing value—marked as grey, meaning information unavailable.

As indicated by Equation (2), there is one model for each possible combination of indicators available. Theoretically, there are 26 possible combinations but in practice this dataset contains only eight of them. Therefore, the same number of fuzzy logic-based models is defined. After applying this method, the best and worst ranked countries are collected in Tables 3 and 4, respectively, along with their corresponding input values.

Table 3. Best ranked countries for SDG 11.

| Country | $v_1$ | $v_2$ | $v_3$ | $v_4$ | $v_5$ | FIS Evaluation |
|---|---|---|---|---|---|---|
| Brunei Darussalam | - | 5.102 | 99.60 | - | - | 89.771 |
| Tonga | - | 10.117 | 99.75 | - | - | 83.243 |
| Tuvalu | - | 10.251 | 100.00 | - | - | 82.202 |
| Andorra | - | 11.189 | 100.00 | - | - | 75.114 |
| Netherlands | 0 | 11.411 | 100.00 | 78.0 | 6.144 | 74.950 |

Table 4. Worst ranked countries for SDG 11.

| Country | $v_1$ | $v_2$ | $v_3$ | $v_4$ | $v_5$ | FIS Evaluation |
|---|---|---|---|---|---|---|
| Togo | 53.3 | 41.082 | 41.827 | 29.0 | - | 10.079 |
| South Sudan | 97.3 | 46.141 | 10.489 | 18.0 | - | 10.079 |
| Afghanistan | 73.5 | 54.950 | 41.859 | 34.0 | - | 10.078 |
| Equatorial Guinea | 66.1 | 59.020 | 48.115 | - | - | 10.078 |
| Central African Republic | 98.5 | 61.733 | 32.291 | 25.0 | - | 10.078 |

Brunei Darussalam, the country with the highest score, aligns with the current report's classification and has been assigned a green colour. This country is the only one to receive a green colour designation within the report. It is crucial to note that this evaluation came from having only some green indicators but rather from having two green ones and the rest not reported. This could suggest that the model might favour information gaps, a trend in other top-ranking countries. On the other hand, countries with the lowest scores correspond with those assigned a red colour in the report, indicating their two worst indicators as red. A clear pattern emerged in the analysis, showing a superior overall performance from countries in Asia, Oceania, and Europe. At the same time, Africa and the notable outlier, Afghanistan in Asia, demonstrate comparatively unfavourable results. Sustainable Development Goal 11 (SDG 11) currently focuses on cities as unique units within countries and continents. As cities are a significant driving force for societal progression, they play a critical role in fostering social development. Therefore, adopting a holistic perspective and actively engaging in discussions regarding this indicator is vital, as it provides an all-encompassing evaluation of sustainability progress.

## 5. Discussion

In this paper, a dynamic method based on fuzzy logic was proposed to translate human criteria involving some uncertainty into technical and computational language in order to define a robust evaluation system for SDGs accomplishment degree. This approach should be understood as an initial proposal for understanding and automating the evaluation of policies where human reasoning is involved in some way. Several limitations have been identified herein, primarily stemming from the availability of data. In this particular instance, the absence of certain indicators may potentially yield overly optimistic scores for certain countries. Furthermore, the comparison between countries lacks complete precision, as not all cases consider identical information, despite being a commendable approximation. Consequently, the scarcity of information necessitates a penalization mechanism, either through the inclusion of a new rule or by subsequent adjustment of the results. Moreover, all rules pertaining to individual indicators were regarded as equally significant in this study, implying that each indicator carries the same weightage in the final evaluation. To address this, it is imperative to incorporate expert judgment in order to discern the relative importance of various indicators. For instance, prioritizing the minimization of the population residing in suburban areas may be deemed more significant than evaluating satisfaction with public transportation.

On the other hand, fuzzy logic, despite its usefulness in handling imprecision and uncertainty, faces several limitations that need to be considered. Firstly, the subjectivity involved in designing membership functions introduces inconsistencies and potential bias in the system, as different experts may have varying opinions. Additionally, fuzzy logic systems can be sensitive to small changes in input values, leading to unexpected outputs. Furthermore, the absence of universally accepted standards for system design, rule formulation, and performance evaluation makes it challenging to compare and benchmark different fuzzy logic systems, hindering widespread adoption. Addressing these limitations by experts is crucial for ensuring the effective and reliable use of fuzzy logic systems.

Beyond the possible future lines of work in mathematics, future studies must move forward in transferring this study to other SDGs by generating a monitoring system to support decision-making that acquires the operation for complex fields of fuzzy logic. Furthermore, in the work of the cities themselves, it is also possible to observe the scope of the measurements, not only in terms of a specific indicator such as SDG 11 but also because the activity in the cities can affect the following SDGs:

- Good health and well-being;
- Clean water and sanitation;
- Affordable and clean energy;
- Industry, innovation, and infrastructure;
- Sustainable cities and communities;
- Responsible consumption and production;
- Climate action;
- Life on land.

In addition to the application to other SDGs as future lines, future research may benefit from exploring extensions to research more complex types of fuzzy subsets, allowing for further deepening of the analysis. Still, it is essential to note that using more complex types requires more parameter tuning, which may result in a more parsimonious analysis.

## 6. Conclusions

Several international organisations and institutions are concerned about sustainable development and its consequences. In addition to the different organisations and institutions, there is a notable concern on the part of experts and academics in the sense of accompanying and monitoring this sustainable development. The primary motivation for our study lies precisely in the capacity of governments and institutions to generate sustainability reports based on the necessary expert judgement. Sustainability must comply with the premises observed in the 2030 Agenda, which, disaggregated, can be found in the different Sustainable Development Goals that currently exist. With this research, working on an already completed "Sustainable Development Report" (in its 2022 edition), it is possible to incorporate the field of fuzzy logic to the necessary progress in the marking of sustainability criteria that robustly make the systems ready not only to issue reporting information but also to take this information as information that can be monitored and can be subjected to comparability criteria.

This study highlights some of the current limitations in assessing compliance with the SDGs and, in particular, with SDG 11. The lack of data for some indicators makes it impossible to provide a fully objective and comparable assessment. In addition, the information collected is not necessarily up to date: the reference years may be earlier than 2022. However, the approach presented here provides a way of assessing a country's performance while respecting the current reporting guidelines and is intended to serve as a basis for evaluating future policies. As the Sustainable Development Report (2022) sets out certain rules for evaluating an SDG, it seems natural to provide a fuzzy logic-based system that incorporates precisely this rule engine. As indicated above, the importance assigned to each defined rule must be refined by experts.

As a result, a ranking of countries was obtained, where the best rated country with our method—Brunei Darussalam—coincides with the best rated country with the current evaluation method and analogously for the worst scoring countries. Some results change as all available information is incorporated into this system and not only the information from the two worst indicators, as had been the case in the past. We have also highlighted some limitations of the system, caused mainly by the quality of the data collected so far. The technical limitations encountered are in line with the current monitoring system. A greater homogenisation of criteria through techniques such as fuzzy logic will allow the correct monitoring so that, in later phases such as verification, cities can make use of it in their progress concerning key factors such as:

- Mobility
    1. Air quality;
    2. Noise measurement;
    3. Parking and access;
    4. Low emission zone;
- Environment
    1. Intelligent irrigation;
    2. Waste monitoring;
- Energy
    1. Renewable energy;
    2. Smart lighting;
    3. Energy efficiency;
- Water
    1. Remote meter reading;
    2. Industrial water management.

**Author Contributions:** Conceptualization, J.P.-D.; methodology, J.P.-D., M.A.-G. and J.M.C.; software, M.A.-G. and J.M.C.; validation, J.P.-D., M.A.-G. and J.M.C.; formal analysis, J.P.-D., M.A.-G. and J.M.C.; investigation, J.P.-D., M.A.-G. and J.M.C.; resources, M.A.-G. and J.M.C.; data curation, M.A.-G. and J.M.C.; writing—original draft preparation, J.P.-D., M.A.-G. and J.M.C.; writing—review and editing, J.P.-D.; visualization, M.A.-G. and J.M.C.; supervision, J.P.-D.; project administration, J.P.-D.; funding acquisition, J.M.C. All authors have read and agreed to the published version of the manuscript.

**Funding:** This work has been partially supported by the project FARMS4CLIMATE (PRIMA S1 2021 FARMING SYSTEMS): Smart governance and operational models for agroecological carbon farming.

**Data Availability Statement:** Not applicable.

**Acknowledgments:** The authors would like to thank Deep Intelligence for the willingness and freedom to use the deepint software.

**Conflicts of Interest:** The authors declare no conflict of interest.

## References

1. Mensah, J. Sustainable development: Meaning, history, principles, pillars, and implications for human action: Literature review. *Cogent Soc. Sci.* **2019**, *5*, 1653531. [CrossRef]
2. Bayer, J.B.; LaRose, R. Technology habits: Progress, problems, and prospects. *Psychol. Habit* **2018**, *2018*, 111–130. [CrossRef]
3. Gao, Q.; Fang, C.; Cui, X. Carrying capacity for SDGs: A review of connotation evolution and practice. *Environ. Impact Assess. Rev.* **2021**, *91*, 106676. [CrossRef]
4. Reyers, B.; Stafford-Smith, M.; Erb, K.H.; Scholes, R.J.; Selomane, O. Essential variables help to focus sustainable development goals monitoring. *Curr. Opin. Environ. Sustain.* **2017**, *26*, 97–105. [CrossRef]
5. Pizzi, S.; Caputo, A.; Corvino, A.; Venturelli, A. Management research and the UN sustainable development goals (SDGs): A bibliometric investigation and systematic review. *J. Clean. Prod.* **2020**, *276*, 124033. [CrossRef]
6. United Nations. Sustainable Development Goals. 2015. Available online: https://www.un.org/sustainabledevelopment/inequality (accessed on 20 May 2023).
7. Kumar, S.; Kumar, N.; Vivekadhish, S. Millennium development goals (MDGS) to sustainable development goals (SDGS): Addressing unfinished agenda and strengthening sustainable development and partnership. *Indian J. Community Med. Off. Publ. Indian Assoc. Prev. Soc. Med.* **2016**, *41*, 1. [CrossRef]
8. Leal Filho, W.; Azeiteiro, U.; Alves, F.; Pace, P.; Mifsud, M.; Brandli, L.; Caeiro, S.S.; Disterheft, A. Reinvigorating the sustainable development research agenda: The role of the sustainable development goals (SDG). *Int. J. Sustain. Dev. World Ecol.* **2018**, *25*, 131–142. [CrossRef]
9. Lipschutz, R.D. Reconstructing world politics: The emergence of global civil society. *Millennium* **1992**, *21*, 389–420. [CrossRef]
10. Turner, G.M. A comparison of The Limits to Growth with 30 years of reality. *Glob. Environ. Chang.* **2008**, *18*, 397–411. [CrossRef]
11. Redclift, M. Sustainable development (1987–2005): An oxymoron comes of age. *Sustain. Dev.* **2005**, *13*, 212–227. [CrossRef]
12. Hauff, V. Brundtland Report: A 20 Years Update. In Proceedings of the Keynote Speech Presented at the European Sustainability: Linking Policies, Implementation, and Civil Society Action Conference, Berlin, Germany, 3–5 June 2007; Volume 7.
13. Emas, R. The concept of sustainable development: Definition and defining principles. *Brief Gsdr 2015*, 2015. [CrossRef]
14. Barnett, H.J.; Morse, C. *Scarcity and Growth: The Economics of Natural Resource Availability*; Routledge: Abingdon-on-Thames, UK, 2013.
15. Hopwood, B.; Mellor, M.; O'Brien, G. Sustainable development: Mapping different approaches. *Sustain. Dev.* **2005**, *13*, 38–52. [CrossRef]
16. Scholte, J.A.; Söderbaum, F. A Changing Global Development Agenda? In *Proceedings of the Forum for Development Studies*; Routledge: Abingdon-on-Thames, UK, 2017; Volume 44, pp. 1–12.
17. UN. *United Nations Millennium Declaration*; UN: New York, NY, USA, 2000.
18. Lomazzi, M.; Borisch, B.; Laaser, U. The Millennium Development Goals: Experiences, achievements and what's next. *Glob. Health Action* **2014**, *7*, 23695. [CrossRef] [PubMed]
19. Parnell, S. Defining a global urban development agenda. *World Dev.* **2016**, *78*, 529–540. [CrossRef]
20. Beynaghi, A.; Trencher, G.; Moztarzadeh, F.; Mozafari, M.; Maknoon, R.; Leal Filho, W. Future sustainability scenarios for universities: Moving beyond the United Nations Decade of Education for Sustainable Development. *J. Clean. Prod.* **2016**, *112*, 3464–3478. [CrossRef]
21. Savaresi, A. The Paris Agreement: A new beginning? *J. Energy Nat. Resour. Law* **2016**, *34*, 16–26. [CrossRef]
22. Sachs, J.D. From millennium development goals to sustainable development goals. *Lancet* **2012**, *379*, 2206–2211. [CrossRef]
23. Küfeoğlu, S. *SDG-11: Sustainable Cities and Communities*; Springer: Berlin/Heidelberg, Germany, 2022; pp. 385–408.
24. Mordeson, J.N.; Mathew, S. Fuzzy Logic Applied to Sustainable Development Goals and Human Trafficking. *Symmetry* **2020**, *12*, 87. [CrossRef]
25. Mordeson, J.N.; Mathew, S. Sustainable Development Goals: Analysis by the Stakeholder Method. In *Sustainable Development Goals: Analysis by Mathematics of Uncertainty*; Springer: Berlin/Heidelberg, Germany, 2021; pp. 61–105.
26. Alonso, J.M.; Magdalena, L. Special issue on interpretable fuzzy systems. *Inf. Sci.* **2011**, *181*, 4331–4339. [CrossRef]
27. Ganga, G.M.D.; Carpinetti, L.C.R. A fuzzy logic approach to supply chain performance management. *Int. J. Prod. Econ.* **2011**, *134*, 177–187. [CrossRef]
28. Zlotnik, H. World Urbanization: Trends and Prospects. In *New Forms of Urbanization*; Routledge: Abingdon-on-Thames, UK, 2017; pp. 43–64.
29. Arslan, T.V.; Durak, S.; Aytac, D.O. Attaining SDG11: Can Sustainability Assessment Tools be Used for Improved Transformation of Neighbourhoods in Historic City Centers? In *Natural Resources Forum*; Blackwell Publishing Ltd.: London, UK, 2016; Volume 40, pp. 180–202.
30. Ragin, C. *Redesigning Social Inquiry: Fuzzy Sets and Beyond*; Bibliovault OAI Repository, the University of Chicago Press: Chicago, IL, USA, 2008. [CrossRef]
31. Schneider, C.Q.; Wagemann, C. *Set-Theoretic Methods for the Social Sciences: A Guide to Qualitative Comparative Analysis*; Cambridge University Press: Cambridge, UK, 2012. [CrossRef]
32. Roig-Tierno, N.; Huarng, K.H.; Ribeiro-Soriano, D. Qualitative comparative analysis: Crisp and fuzzy sets in business and management. *J. Bus. Res.* **2015**, *69*, 1261–1264. [CrossRef]
33. Pappas, I.O.; Woodside, A.G. Fuzzy-set Qualitative Comparative Analysis (fsQCA): Guidelines for research practice in Information Systems and marketing. *Int. J. Inf. Manag.* **2021**, *58*, 102310. [CrossRef]

34. Cisneros-Montemayor, A.M.; Singh, G.G.; Cheung, W.W. A fuzzy logic expert system for evaluating policy progress towards sustainability goals. *Ambio* **2018**, *47*, 595–607. [CrossRef]
35. Lootsma, F.A. *Fuzzy Logic for Planning and Decision Making*; Springer Science & Business Media: Berlin/Heidelberg, Germany, 2013; Volume 8.
36. Korenevskiy, N. Application of fuzzy logic for decision-making in medical expert systems. *Biomed. Eng.* **2015**, *49*, 46–49. [CrossRef]
37. Bates, J.H.; Young, M.P. Applying fuzzy logic to medical decision making in the intensive care unit. *Am. J. Respir. Crit. Care Med.* **2003**, *167*, 948–952. [CrossRef]
38. Jane, J.B.; Ganesh, E. A Review on Big Data with Machine Learning and Fuzzy Logic for Better Decision Making. *Int. J. Sci. Technol. Res.* **2019**, *8*, 1121–1125.
39. Hoskova-Mayerova, S.; Maturo, A. Decision-Making Process Using Hyperstructures and Fuzzy Structures in Social Sciences. In *Soft Computing Applications for Group Decision-Making and Consensus Modeling*; Springer: Berlin/Heidelberg, Germany, 2018; pp. 103–111.
40. Büyüközkan, G.; Feyzioglu, O. A fuzzy-logic-based decision-making approach for new product development. *Int. J. Prod. Econ.* **2004**, *90*, 27–45. [CrossRef]
41. Sikdar, S.K.; Sengupta, D.; Mukherjee, R. *Measuring Progress towards Sustainability*; Springer: Berlin/Heidelberg, Germany, 2017; Volume 10, pp. 978–983.
42. De Guimarães, J.C.F.; Severo, E.A.; Júnior, L.A.F.; Da Costa, W.P.L.B.; Salmoria, F.T. Governance and quality of life in smart cities: Towards sustainable development goals. *J. Clean. Prod.* **2020**, *253*, 119926. [CrossRef]
43. Diaz-Sarachaga, J.M.; Jato-Espino, D.; Castro-Fresno, D. Is the Sustainable Development Goals (SDG) index an adequate framework to measure the progress of the 2030 Agenda? *Sustain. Dev.* **2018**, *26*, 663–671. [CrossRef]
44. Lind, N. Values reflected in the human development index. *Soc. Indic. Res.* **2004**, *66*, 283–293. [CrossRef]
45. Van den Bergh, J.C.; Grazi, F. Ecological footprint policy? Land use as an environmental indicator. *J. Ind. Ecol.* **2014**, *18*, 10–19. [CrossRef]
46. WWF. *Living Planet Report—2018: Aiming Higher*; Grooten, M., Almond, R.E.A., Eds.; WWF: Gland, Switzerland, 2018.
47. Prescott-Allen, R. *Barometer of Sustainability: Measuring and Communicating Wellbeing and Sustainable Development*; IUCN: Gland, Switzerland, 1997.
48. Pavot, W.; Diener, E.; Oishi, S.; Tay, L. The Cornerstone of Research on Subjective Well-Being: Valid Assessment Methodology. In *Handbook of Well-Being. Noba Scholar Handbook Series: Subjective Well-Being*; DEF Publishers: Salt Lake City, UT, USA, 2018.
49. Frugoli, P.; Almeida, C.; Agostinho, F.; Giannetti, B.; Huisingh, D. Can measures of well-being and progress help societies to achieve sustainable development? *J. Clean. Prod.* **2015**, *90*, 370–380. [CrossRef]
50. Lawn, P.A. A theoretical foundation to support the Index of Sustainable Economic Welfare (ISEW), Genuine Progress Indicator (GPI), and other related indexes. *Ecol. Econ.* **2003**, *44*, 105–118. [CrossRef]
51. Strezov, V.; Evans, A.; Evans, T.J. Assessment of the economic, social and environmental dimensions of the indicators for sustainable development. *Sustain. Dev.* **2017**, *25*, 242–253. [CrossRef]
52. Papadimitriou, E.; Neves, A.R.; Becker, W. *JRC Statistical Audit of the Sustainable Development Goals Index and Dashboards*; Publications Office of the European Union: Brussels, Belgium, 2019.
53. Sachs, J.; Schmidt-Traub, G.; Kroll, C.; Lafortune, G.; Fuller, G. *SDG Index and Dashboards Report 2018*; Bertelsmann Stiftung and Sustainable Development Solutions Network (SDSN): New York, NY, USA, 2018.
54. Sachs, J.; Kroll, C.; Lafortune, G.; Fuller, G.; Woelm, F. *Sustainable Development Report 2022*; Cambridge University Pres: Cambridge, UK, 2022. [CrossRef]
55. Ross, T.J. Fuzzy Systems Simulation. In *Fuzzy Logic with Engineering Applications*; John Wiley & Sons, Ltd.: New York, NY, USA, 2010; Chapter 8, pp. 245–275.
56. Sachs, J.; Kroll, C.; Lafortune, G.; Fuller, G.; Woelm, F. *Sustainable Development Report 2021*; Cambridge University Pres: Cambridge, UK, 2021. [CrossRef]

**Disclaimer/Publisher's Note:** The statements, opinions and data contained in all publications are solely those of the individual author(s) and contributor(s) and not of MDPI and/or the editor(s). MDPI and/or the editor(s) disclaim responsibility for any injury to people or property resulting from any ideas, methods, instructions or products referred to in the content.

Article

# Fuzzy Analytic Network Process with Principal Component Analysis to Establish a Bank Performance Model under the Assumption of Country Risk

Alin Opreana [1,*], Simona Vinerean [1], Diana Marieta Mihaiu [2], Liliana Barbu [2] and Radu-Alexandru Șerban [1]

1   Department of Management, Marketing and Business Administration, Lucian Blaga University of Sibiu, 550024 Sibiu, Romania; simona.vinerean@ulbsibiu.ro (S.V.); radu.serban@ulbsibiu.ro (R.-A.Ș.)
2   Department of Finance and Accounting, Lucian Blaga University of Sibiu, 550024 Sibiu, Romania; diana.mihaiu@ulbsibiu.ro (D.M.M.); liliana.barbu@ulbsibiu.ro (L.B.)
*   Correspondence: alin.opreana@ulbsibiu.ro

**Abstract:** In recent years, bank-related decision analysis has reflected a relevant research area due to key factors that affect the operating environment of banks. This study's aim is to develop a model based on the linkages between the performance of banks and their operating context, determined by country risk. For this aim, we propose a multi-analytic methodology using fuzzy analytic network process (fuzzy-ANP) with principal component analysis (PCA) that extends existing mathematical methodologies and decision-making approaches. This method was examined in two studies. The first study focused on determining a model for country risk assessment based on the data extracted from 172 countries. Considering the first study's scores, the second study established a bank performance model under the assumption of country risk, based on data from 496 banks. Our findings show the importance of country risk as a relevant bank performance dimension for decision makers in establishing efficient strategies with a positive impact on long-term performance. The study offers various contributions. From a mathematic methodology perspective, this research advances an original approach that integrates fuzzy-ANP with PCA, providing a consistent and unbiased framework that overcomes human judgement. From a business and economic analysis perspective, this research establishes novelty based on the performance evaluation of banks considering the operating country's risk.

**Keywords:** fuzzy-ANP; principal component analysis; bank performance; country risk

**MSC:** 90B50; 62C86

## 1. Introduction

Worldwide, there are increasing concerns based on political and economic unrest. Escalating geopolitical differences in various areas of the world, international threat of financial crisis and economic downturn, increasing income inequality, and many other factors affect the operating environment of banks. Globalization enhances the propagation of these factors based on the interconnectedness of "economic structures, financial markets, and political institutions" [1], thus increasing the urgency of examining country risk and its connection to bank performance.

Initial investigations have described country risk as the potential incapacity of a sovereign state to generate sufficient foreign exchange to reimburse its external debt [2–4]. Explaining the primary "risk factors, causes, levels, and development trends" in a country or region represents the main goal of country risk investigation and assessment [4]. As a multifaceted topic, previous empirical investigations have explored country risk in relation to various contexts, such as environmental issues [5–9], supply chain contexts [10–12], and energy [13,14], as well as business contexts related to process effectiveness [15] and firm exposure [16].

Country risk has also proven to be highly relevant in assessing performance and related activities of banks and financial institutions [1,17–20]. To examine country risk and its potential impact on business operations, previous empirical investigations have used a wide range of data analysis techniques, such as Copula [21], regression [6–8,10,14,16,17], analytic hierarchy process (AHP) [15], fuzzy sets [8,15,22], Bayesian Belief Network [11], Grey-TOPSIS Model [23], artificial neural networks [24], and principal component analysis [12,25,26]. Nonetheless, no consensus has been reached in proposing a specific methodology and framework. Therefore, it is of great significance to further develop new methodologies and data analysis techniques to assess country risk and evaluate bank performance.

Examining the core factors that affect country risk and bank performance is critical given their relevance to business practices and decision making. Thus, this study's primary objective is to establish a model based on the linkages between the performance of banks and their operating context, determined by country risk. Despite the existence of various research on these matters [1,27], there is a need to advance empirical evidence for the evaluation of bank performance, while incorporating country risk.

This study aims to offers multiple contributions to the existing literature. By extending previous methodologies [12,26], this paper proposes a new framework by using fuzzy analytic network process (fuzzy-ANP) with principal component analysis (PCA) in a multi-analytic model, as a form of widening decision-making approaches. This newly proposed framework fills the gap regarding mathematical methodologies applied in country risk assessment and bank performance evaluation, by providing a consistent and unbiased technique that overcomes human judgement. This novel approach effectively addressed the recurrent issues of prejudices and discrepancies that have been prevalent in the broader implementation of fuzzy-ANP by contributing a new mathematical framework that proposes the combination of secondary data in fuzzy-ANP with PCA.

This study also aims to provide new additions to the relevant literature by proposing a new methodology for applying fuzzy-ANP in country risk assessment. Fuzzy-ANP is regarded as a valuable research methodology [28] directed at reducing and overcoming regression-associated limitations. Specifically, ANP offers a framework that explores interdependences between elements, whereas regression does not account for interdependency [27]. Fuzzy-logic implies human assessment based on linguistic expressions, with a focus on minimizing ambiguity and imprecision associated with human judgements [27,28]. Furthermore, as another original development, this study aims to utilize fuzzy-ANP for examining bank performance considering interdependent indicators and incorporating country risk scores. Thus, the results of this research aim to provide a novel basis for bank managers to allow for better decision-making processes.

The remainder of this manuscript is consolidated as follows. Section 2 provides theoretical framework regarding the country risk assessment, bank performance evaluation, and existing methodologies. Section 3 details the paper's methodology and its innovative frameworks. Section 4 presents the empirical analysis and includes the validation of the proposed methodology in two studies (country risk assessment and bank performance evaluation under the assumption of country risk). Section 5 addresses the results of the analysis and Section 6 highlights the conclusions and the practical recommendations associated with the study's results.

## 2. Literature Review

### 2.1. Country Risk Assessment

The concept of risk assessment gained momentum starting from 1950s due to the risk implied in foreign lending and financing initiatives of international banks [4]. Especially during this period, commercial banks and international institutions adopted country risk evaluation as an essential analysis method aimed at detecting debt issues in a specific nation [2]. The increase in international loans provided by financial institutions from developed countries to underdeveloped and developing countries was supplemented by debt defaults, restructuring, and refinancing [4].

Thus, a well-recognized definition of country risk was provided by Nagy [3], explaining it as follows: "Country risk is the possibility of loss in cross-border loans, which is caused by events in a particular country, not by private enterprises or individuals". Broadly, country risk reflects the likelihood that certain events occurring within a nation could lead to negative impacts on specific organizations' operations or individual behaviors [29]. As a result, a growing set of academic research emphasizes the importance of country risk assessment in decision-making processes, highlighting resource allocation in different markets [30]. Previous authors have classified country risks in terms of sociopolitical risk (associated with government, political policy, and social aspects), economic risk (at macroeconomic and microeconomic levels), and natural risk [31]. Another classification of country risk includes political, economic, and criminal dimensions [32]. Considering this multi-attribute structure, a generally accepted framework [4] highlights that for a country $i$, country risk as time $t$ can be identified as a function of multiple factors ($r_{ij}$), based on the available information set $\Omega$: "$CR_{it} = f(r_{i1}, r_{i2}, \ldots r_{ij}, \Omega)$" [4].

To comprehend the primary risk factors, main triggers, and causes, along with progression patterns of a particular nation or group of countries, it is necessary to perform a country risk assessment, based on multiple dimensions and relevant variables. Bouchet et al. [31] proposed three methodological frameworks for addressing country risk assessment: (1) qualitative analysis focused on "economic, financial and socio-political fundamentals that can affect the investment return prospects in a foreign country" and highlighting the abilities and deficiencies in a country's structure and advancement prospects [31] (p. 50); (2) ratings approach, highlighting either global country risk rankings or country credit ratings [31] (p. 79), [32]; and (3) econometric and mathematical methods. For this latter framework, Bouchet et al. [31] outlined a wide range of country risk assessment techniques used for investment strategies, including discriminant analysis, logit and probit models, regression analysis, Monte Carlo simulations, value at risk (VaR), artificial neural networks, multicriteria, and principal components analysis (PCA). Bouchet et al. [31] noted value in using PCA to establish new factors that provide the basis for additional analyses.

Despite the wide range of techniques available, prior empirical analyses have mainly explored country risk based on regression models. For instance, Lee, Lin, and Lee [1] developed a regression model for country risk based on globalization indexes (considering "economic, political, and overall globalization dimensions") and macroeconomic control variables, specifically "real GDP per capita, the ratio of government consumption against GDP, capital formation as investment proxy, percentage change in GDP deflator as inflation proxy, and secondary gross enrollment rate as a human capital proxy" [1]. Similarly, Peiró-Signes et al. [8] explored a regression model based on environmental performance indicators (environmental health and ecosystem vitality) and country risk. Their study discovered that environmental performance index scores reflected connections with country risk scores [8]. Still in line with the environmental context, Li et al. [10] investigated the impact of country risk on the cobalt trade pattern (as a strategic mineral used in batteries), considering a panel regression. Despite the popularity of this technique, previous authors have recommended extending mathematical techniques to explore country risk in innovative frameworks [25,29,31].

*2.2. Bank Performance and Country Risk*

A new strand of research has focused on exploring the impact of country risk on bank performance. Banks frequently base their decisions on the overall context of a nation and the prospects of their operating environment. According to Gelemerova et al. [33], banks' decision-making process and overall strategy consider a country's history, culture, political climate, macroeconomic environment, and legislation, which highlight the overall country risk.

Considering a macroeconomic perspective on country risk assessment, various studies have detected a connection between financial crises and lingering economic growth [17]. According to Roe and Siegel [34], Lehkonen and Heimonen [35], and Lee and Lee [17], country risk factors could display a negative effect on economic activity, leading to an inferior performance in the banking sector. Similarly, several studies have highlighted that political instability, a key country risk factor, had a prominent effect on the performance of banks [1,27,30].

From a microeconomic point of view, country risk, especially reflected in the economic environment, has an adverse impact on the resource allocation and FDIs of international companies [36,37] and on the investment opportunities and private consumption of consumers [38]. Subsequently, these aspects have negative implications for the adoption of banking services and overall bank performance [17].

Thus, various empirical investigations have demonstrated that banking activities and country risk should be explored in the same settings [1]. For instance, Lee et al. [1] incorporated bank-related indicators (such as return of assets and bank concentration) to explore the association between banks and country risk. In a model considering 36 countries, Simpson [20] formulated a risk-scoring model based on "historical bank-country economic development, bank-country economic, and country-bank financial data". Specifically, Simpson [20] used bank-related indicators (liquidity, profitability, capitalization, and bank size) and country-related factors (industrialization, trade, GDP growth rate, short-term debt, and long-term external debt). In addition, while addressing the effect of country risk on bank stability, Huang and Lin [39] examined 500 banks from 39 countries (developed and emerging nations). In their empirical investigation, the authors incorporated multiple analyses, including a PCA for establishing bank-related factors (based on 25 CAMEL indicators). Huang and Lin [39] discovered that "political, economic and financial risks, as well as country risk have a negative and significant effect on bank stability", with a more prominent impact observed for emerging countries.

Despite escalating studies on 'country risk' and 'bank performance', authors have highlighted the need to develop novel methods for integrating country-specific risk traits into bank performance evaluation to help with better decision-making frameworks [40]. Considering the wide spectrum of available methodologies, fuzzy-ANP could be extended and incorporated in the evaluation of bank performance under the assumption of country risk. ANP depicts a "decision-making problem as a network of elements" (namely, criteria and alternatives) that are gathered into clusters [41]. As the expanded version of AHP, ANP reflects a flexible and comprehensive framework [28,42,43] that evaluates "factors, sub-factors, goals, and alternatives weight through a single matrix called supermatrix" [44]. ANP overcomes the limitations of AHP due to its capacity to model network structure and for prioritizing clusters of items.

The general application of ANP involves human judgment using linguistic expressions. Incorporating fuzzy logic in ANP tackles the issues of ambiguity and imprecision associated with human judgements, which further lead to inconsistencies in developing the pairwise comparison matrices [45,46]. Fuzzy-ANP has been applied in an expansive set of contexts, ranging from supplier choice [45], to the selection of an outsourcing provider [47], to engineering decisions [48]. Moreover, fuzzy-ANP provides a flexible method that has been extended in different frameworks, including DEMATEL [45,47,49–51], TOPSIS [45], and ELECTRE-IS [52]. Considering these validated extensions, in this research, we propose a new framework based on fuzzy-ANP with PCA to assess bank performance and country risk. This newly proposed method is presented in the following section.

### 3. Method

To establish a bank performance model under the assumption of country risk, this mathematical methodology included a multi-analytic and integrated effort, focused on combining fuzzy analytic network process (fuzzy-ANP) with principal component analysis (PCA). This multi-analytic effort (fuzzy-ANP and PCA) was implemented in two phases:

(1) firstly, the analysis developed a country risk assessment model (presented in Section 3.2.), (2) secondly, the results from the country risk assessment were integrated in the banks' performance evaluation (presented in Section 3.3). Section 3.1 presents the general application of this new proposed framework.

### 3.1. Proposed Method of Fuzzy-ANP with PCA

As previously mentioned, fuzzy-ANP depicts any decision-making problem as a network of elements arranged in clusters [49]. Nonetheless, general implementation of this method implies human judgements, which may lead to prejudiced outcomes. Moreover, due to the complexity of fuzzy-ANP, Ergu [46] emphasized the need to solve the issues with inconsistencies in the matrices. To solve these issues of biases and inconsistencies, this newly proposed methodology integrates an important and objective phase of principal component analysis. The PCA results are then integrated in the fuzzy-ANP framework. Although the methods of PCA [25,39] and fuzzy-ANP [53,54] are widely known and applied in terms of the evaluation of bank-related activities for decision selection, they have been investigated separately. General application of fuzzy-ANP involves collecting the primary data from decision making. In this newly proposed framework of using secondary data for fuzzy-ANP with PCA, this method aims to reduce the risk of information gaps and/or biases that may occur in methodologies relying exclusively on primary data. In this paper, we propose an innovative integration of these techniques for a multi-analytical fuzzy-ANP with PCA approach. For this newly established multi-analytic and unbiased methodology, the following steps are proposed (Figure 1):

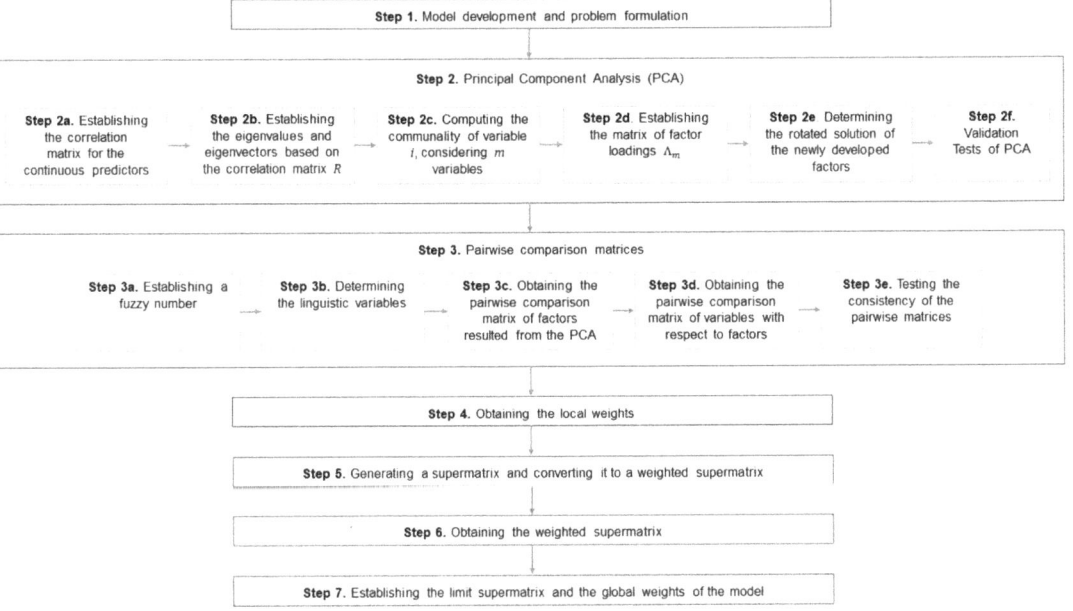

**Figure 1.** Proposed method of fuzzy-ANP with PCA (source: own computation).

**Step 1.** Model development and problem formulation

This developing model aims to establish the relative importance weights of the variables proposed for evaluating a bank performance model under the assumption of country risk. Considering an innovative and multi-analytic dual-phase model, existing studies provided the foundation for variable selection, whereas the principal component analysis was applied to reduce the variables in every phase to a lower number of factors. The resulting

PCA factors, together with the initial variables collected from the secondary data, represent the interconnected elements in a hierarchical network structure (Figure 2).

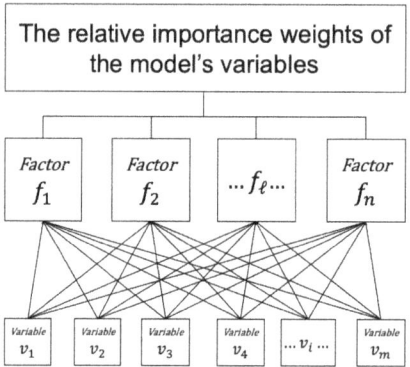

**Figure 2.** Hierarchical network structure (source: own computation).

**Step 2.** Principal Component Analysis (PCA)

Initially introduced by Pearson in 1901 [55], principal component analysis is applied when the main objective is to establish a minimum number of factors that aim to explain the highest level of variance observed in the data, with the intention to use these newly developed factors in subsequent analyses [56,57]. In other words, PCA generates new variables, i.e., principal components or factors, from "linear combinations of the original variables" [58]. As an interdependent procedure, PCA aims to "define the underlying structure among the variables in the analysis" [59]. Thus, PCA focuses on minimizing the information loss and adequately representing the original dataset [59,60]. Previous studies support the inclusion of PCA in country risk assessment and bank evaluation [25,31,39]. For PCA, the following steps are relevant for the analysis.

**Step 2a.** Establishing the correlation matrix for the continuous predictors

Let $X_1, X_2, \ldots, X_m$ be $m$ observed variables. The starting point of PCA involves the development of the correlation matrix $R$ [61–63]:

$$R = \begin{bmatrix} r_{11} & r_{12} & \cdots & r_{1m} \\ r_{21} & r_{21} & \cdots & r_{21} \\ \vdots & \vdots & r_{ij} & \vdots \\ r_{m1} & r_{m2} & \cdots & r_{mm} \end{bmatrix} \quad (1)$$

where

$$r_{ij} = \frac{\sum_{k=1}^{n}\left(X_{i_k} - X_i\right)\left(X_{j_k} - X_j\right)}{\sqrt{\sum_{k=1}^{n}\left(X_{i_k} - X_i\right)^2 \times \sum_{k=1}^{n}\left(X_{j_k} - X_j\right)^2}} \quad (2)$$

**Step 2b.** Establishing the eigenvalues and eigenvectors based on the correlation matrix $R$

For the next step, we compute $\lambda_1 \geq \lambda_2 \geq \ldots \geq \lambda_m$ as the eigenvalues (sorted in descending order) and $\omega_1, \omega_2, \ldots, \omega_m$ as their corresponding eigenvectors of $R$. The eigenvalues are calculated based on the following [64]:

$$|R - \lambda I| = 0 \quad (3)$$

The corresponding eigenvectors of $R$ are computed as follows:

$$(R - \lambda_i I)\omega_j = 0 \quad (4)$$

**Step 2c.** Computing the communality of variable $i$, considering $m$ variables

For PCA, a communality represents the "estimate of its shared, or common, variance among the variables as represented by the derived factors" [59], calculated as follows [61,65]:

$$h_i = \sum_{j=1}^{m} |\lambda_j| \omega_{ij}^2 \tag{5}$$

For each variable included in the PCA, the communality should adhere to a recommended threshold of 0.5 [59].

**Step 2d.** Establishing the matrix of factor loadings $\Lambda_m$ considering the following equation [61,65]:

$$\Lambda_m = \Omega_m \Gamma_m^{1/2} \tag{6}$$

where
$\Omega_m = (\omega_1, \omega_2, \ldots, \omega_m)$, $\Gamma_m = diag(|\lambda_1|, |\lambda_2|, \ldots, |\lambda_m|)$

Factor loadings reflect the correlation between the examined variables and the developed factor [59,65]. To establish the number of relevant extracted factors, previous studies have recommended retaining all of the factors that have eigenvalues greater than 0.7 [64], while considering the percentage of variance criterion of a 60% suggested threshold [59]. Thus, by applying principal component analysis in IBM SPSS Statistics v.26 (IBM Corp., Armonk, NY, USA), we obtained the following component matrix, corresponding to Equation (6):

$$\Lambda = \begin{bmatrix} \lambda_{11}^{1/2} & \cdots & \lambda_{1n}^{1/2} \\ \vdots & \lambda_{i\ell}^{1/2} & \vdots \\ \lambda_{m1}^{1/2} & \cdots & \lambda_{mn}^{1/2} \end{bmatrix} \tag{7}$$

where Eigenvalue $\lambda_\ell > 0.7$ [64] associated with factor $\ell$ is

$$\lambda_\ell = \sum_{i=1}^{m} \lambda_{i\ell}^{1/2} \tag{8}$$

and communality $h_i$, based on corresponding Equation (5), can be expressed by

$$h_i = \sum_{\ell=1}^{m} \lambda_{i\ell}^{1/2}, \text{where } h_i > 0.5 \tag{9}$$

**Step 2e.** Determining the rotated solution of the newly developed factors

After establishing and retaining the number of principal components based on recommended frameworks, the next step in PCA involves the rotation. The rotated solutions of the factor matrix reflect a more meaningful and significant factor pattern, which is achieved by redistributing the variance from earlier components to subsequent ones [59]. Varimax rotation is recommended [58,65] as it "maximizes the sum of variances of required loadings of the factor matrix" [66]. Factor matrix is normalized by the square root of communalities [58,61,64,65], considering:

$$\Lambda_m^* = H^{-1/2} \Lambda_m \tag{10}$$

where
$\Lambda_m = (\underline{\lambda}_1, \underline{\lambda}_2, \ldots, \underline{\lambda}_m)$ is the factor pattern matrix;
$H = diag(h_1, h_2, \ldots, h_n)$ is the diagonal matrix of communalities.

Varimax generates $i$ iterations by searching for linear combinations, until the variance of the square loadings is maximized:

$$SV_{(i)} = \sum_{j=1}^{m} \left( n \sum_{k=1}^{n} \lambda_{kj(i)}^{*4} - \left( \sum_{k=1}^{n} \lambda_{kj(i)}^{*2} \right)^2 \right) / n^2 \tag{11}$$

where the initial $\Lambda^*_{m(1)}$ indicates the original factor pattern matrix. Considering successive iterations, the primary value represents the final value of $\Lambda^*_{m(i-1)}$, once factor pairs showcase rotation [61].

After rotation, we rearrange the rotated factors so that [61]

$$\sum_{i=1}^{m} \tilde{\lambda}_{i1}^2 \geq \ldots \geq \sum_{i=1}^{m} \tilde{\lambda}_{in}^2 \qquad (12)$$

Based on Equations (10)–(12), we have the following rotated matrix with $n$ rotated factors and $m$ variables:

$$\tilde{\Lambda}_{m \times n} = \begin{bmatrix} \tilde{\lambda}_{11} & \cdots & \tilde{\lambda}_{1n} \\ \tilde{\lambda}_{21} & \cdots & \tilde{\lambda}_{2n} \\ \vdots & \tilde{\lambda}_{i\ell} & \vdots \\ \tilde{\lambda}_{m1} & \cdots & \tilde{\lambda}_{mn} \end{bmatrix} \qquad (13)$$

From this matrix, the following $n$ factors are obtained:

$$f_\ell = \sum_{i=1}^{m} \tilde{\lambda}_{i\ell}^2 = \sum_{i=1}^{m} v_{\ell_i} \qquad (14)$$

Derived from Equation (14), we have variable $v_{\ell_i}$ with respect to every factor $f_\ell$ determined by the following expression:

$$v_{\ell_i} = \tilde{\lambda}_{i\ell}^2 \qquad (15)$$

As the results of PCA, all factors $f_\ell$ and variables $v_{\ell_i}$ are integrated into fuzzy-ANP to construct pairwise comparison matrices.

**Step 2f. Validation Tests of PCA**

Before proceeding to the next phase of the fuzzy-ANP, the accuracy of PCA needs to be assessed based on relevancy tests. First, Chi-square value for Bartlett's test of sphericity (and its associated significance test) tests the presence of relevant correlations for the set of examined variables [59,61,62,65,66]:

$$\chi^2 = -\left(W - 1 - \frac{2p+5}{6}\right) \log|C| \qquad (16)$$

with $p(p-1)/2$ degrees of freedom.

Second, Kaiser–Mayer–Olkin measure of sample adequacy identifies the appropriateness of the solution, based on values higher than 0.7 [61,67,68]:

$$KMO_j = \frac{\sum_{i \neq j} r_{ij}^2}{\sum_{i \neq j} r_{ij}^2 + \sum_{i \neq j} a_{ij}^{2*}} \qquad (17)$$

$$KMO = \frac{\sum_{i \neq j} \sum r_{ij}^2}{\sum_{i \neq j} \sum r_{ij}^2 + \sum_{i \neq j} \sum a_{ij}^{2*}} \qquad (18)$$

where $a_{ij}^*$ is the anti-image correlation coefficient.

**Step 3. Pairwise comparison matrices**

After validating the PCA, we proceed to the fuzzy-ANP phase. As a widely popular technique [41,47,48], fuzzy-ANP has shown versatility in a broad spectrum of contexts. For the fuzzy-ANP method, first, we define a fuzzy number and corresponding linguistic variables.

**Step 3a. Establishing a fuzzy number**

At this phase in the mathematical technique, a fuzzy number [69] is established:

$$\tilde{A}_i^* = \begin{cases} (x_i - l_i)/(m_i - l_i), & l_i \leq x_i \leq m_i \\ (u_i - x_i)/(u_i - m_i), & m_i \leq x_i \leq u_i \\ 0, & otherwise \end{cases} \quad (19)$$

In Equation (19), $l_i$ and $u_i$ reflect the lower and upper bounds for the fuzzy number $\tilde{A}_i^*$, and $m_i$ indicates the modal value for $\tilde{A}_i^*$. The triangular fuzzy number (TFN0) [70,71], is expressed as follows

$$\tilde{A}_i^* = (l_i, m_i, u_i) \quad (20)$$

while the reciprocal of the fuzzy number is as follows:

$$\tilde{A}_i^{*^{-1}} = (l_i, m_i, u_i)^{-1} = (1/u_i, 1/m_i, 1/l_i) \quad (21)$$

**Step 3b.** Determining the linguistic variables

The relative importance of the elements is measured based on Saaty's nine-point scale [42, 43,72–74]. This scale is further transformed to a fuzzy triangular scale, according to Table 1.

**Table 1.** Linguistic terms and their corresponding triangular fuzzy numbers [28].

| Saaty's Scale | Linguistic Terms | Fuzzy Triangular Scale |
|---|---|---|
| 9 | Extremely importance | (9, 9, 9) |
| 8 | Very, very strong | (7, 8, 9) |
| 7 | Very strong importance | (6, 7, 8) |
| 6 | Strong plus | (5, 6, 7) |
| 5 | Strong importance | (4, 5, 6) |
| 4 | Moderate plus | (3, 4, 5) |
| 3 | Moderate importance | (2, 3, 4) |
| 2 | Weak | (1, 2, 3) |
| 1 | Equal importance | (1, 1, 1) |

**Step 3c.** Obtaining the pairwise comparison matrix of factors resulted from the PCA

Let $f_1, f_2, \ldots, f_n$ be $n$ factors resulting from PCA, sorted in descending order, $f_1 \geq f_2 \geq \ldots \geq f_n$. To transform the data for pairwise comparison based on Saaty's scale [28,43], the following min–max normalization formula is applied [74–76]:

$$f_\ell^* = \frac{f_\ell - min_F}{max_F - min_F}(new\_max_F - new\_min_F) + new\_min_F \quad (22)$$

where

$$\begin{aligned} max_F &= \max(f_1, f_2, \ldots, f_n) \\ min_F &= \min(f_1, f_2, \ldots, f_n) \\ new\_max_F &= 9 \\ new\_min_F &= 1 \end{aligned} \quad (23)$$

Following this step, we obtain values $f_{ij}^*$ that are assigned to fuzzy number $\tilde{f}_{ij}^*$.

$$\begin{aligned} f_{ij}^* &= \frac{f_i^*}{f_j^*}, \text{where } f_i^* \geq f_j^* \\ f_{ji}^* &= \frac{1}{f_{ij}^*} \end{aligned} \quad (24)$$

Linguistic terms to the pairwise comparisons are assigned by using Equations (19)–(24), and based on Table 1, the resulting fuzzy pairwise comparison matrix $\tilde{F}$ is developed:

$$\tilde{F} = \begin{bmatrix} 1 & \tilde{f}_{12}^* & \cdots & \tilde{f}_{1n}^* \\ 1/\tilde{f}_{21}^* & 1 & \cdots & \tilde{f}_{2n}^* \\ \vdots & \vdots & \ddots & \vdots \\ 1/\tilde{f}_{1n}^* & 1/\tilde{f}_{2n}^* & \cdots & 1 \end{bmatrix} \quad (25)$$

**Step 3d.** Obtaining the pairwise comparison matrix of variables with respect to factors

Let $v_{\ell_1}, v_{\ell_2}, \ldots, v_{\ell_n}$ be $m$ variables with respect to factor $f_\ell$ resulting from PCA. We use the following min–max normalization formula [74–76] to transform the data:

$$v_{\ell_i}^* = \frac{v_{\ell_i} - min_{V_\ell}}{max_{V_\ell} - min_{V_\ell}} \left(new\_max_{V_\ell} - new\_min_{V_\ell}\right) + new\_min_{V_\ell} \quad (26)$$

where

$$\begin{aligned} max_{V_\ell} &= \max(v_{\ell_1}, v_{\ell_2}, \ldots, v_{\ell_3}) \\ min_{V_\ell} &= \min(v_{\ell_1}, v_{\ell_2}, \ldots, v_{\ell_3}) \\ new\_max_{V_\ell} &= 9 \\ new\_min_{V_\ell} &= 1 \end{aligned} \quad (27)$$

Following this, we obtain values $v_{c_{ij}}^*$ that are assigned to fuzzy number $\tilde{v}_{c_{ij}}^*$.

$$\begin{aligned} v_{\ell_{ij}}^* &= \frac{v_{\ell_i}^*}{v_{\ell_j}^*}, \text{ where } v_{\ell_i}^* \geq v_{\ell_j}^* \\ v_{\ell_{ji}}^* &= \frac{1}{v_{\ell_{ij}}^*} \end{aligned} \quad (28)$$

Fuzzy pairwise comparison matrix $\tilde{V}_\ell$ is constructed in the same manner as the matrix from Step 3c.

$$\tilde{V}_\ell = \begin{bmatrix} 1 & \tilde{v}_{\ell_{12}}^* & \cdots & \tilde{v}_{\ell_{1n}}^* \\ 1/\tilde{v}_{\ell_{12}}^* & 1 & \cdots & \tilde{v}_{\ell_{2n}}^* \\ \vdots & \vdots & \ddots & \vdots \\ 1/\tilde{v}_{\ell_{1n}}^* & 1/\tilde{v}_{\ell_{2n}}^* & \cdots & 1 \end{bmatrix} \quad (29)$$

**Step 3e.** Testing the consistency of the pairwise matrices

The most well-known consistency test [46,77] for the pairwise comparison matrices in ANP is the consistency ratio by Saaty [28,43]:

$$CR = \frac{\lambda_{max} - n}{(n-1)RI} \quad (30)$$

where $\lambda_{max}$ is the maximum eigenvalue of a matrix, $n$ is the order of the matrix, and $RI$ is the average random matrix index proposed by Saaty [28,43]. The comparison matrix is consistent if the value of CR is less than 0.1 [28,41,43,46,77]. By integrating PCA, consistency is assured for the matrices obtained in the preceding steps associated with fuzzy-ANP.

**Step 4.** Obtaining the local weights

Let $X = \{x_1, x_2, \ldots, x_t\}$ be an object and $U = \{u_1, u_2, \ldots, u_p\}$ be the goal set. As stated by Chang's extent analysis method [69], each object is considered, and extent analysis is applied for each goal $u_i$. Then, for each $p$ from Chang's extent analysis, each object can be expressed by $M_{g_i}^1, M_{g_i}^2, \ldots, M_{g_i}^p, i = 1, 2, \ldots, t$, where all of the $M_{g_i}^j (j = 1, 2, \ldots, p)$ represent TFNs.

First, the value of fuzzy synthetic extent with respect to $i$-th object is as follows [69]:

$$S_i = \sum_{j=1}^{p} M_{g_i}^j \otimes \left[\sum_{i=1}^{t}\sum_{j=1}^{p} M_{g_i}^j\right]^{-1} \tag{31}$$

where

$$\sum_{j=1}^{p} M_{g_i}^j = \left(\sum_{j=1}^{p} l_j, \sum_{j=1}^{p} m_j, \sum_{j=1}^{p} u_j\right) \tag{32}$$

$$\left[\sum_{i=1}^{t}\sum_{j=1}^{p} M_{g_i}^j\right]^{-1} = \left(\frac{1}{\sum_{i=1}^{t}\sum_{j=1}^{p} u_{ij}}, \frac{1}{\sum_{i=1}^{t}\sum_{j=1}^{p} m_{ij}}, \frac{1}{\sum_{i=1}^{t}\sum_{j=1}^{p} l_{ij}}\right) \tag{33}$$

Hence,

$$S_i = \left(\sum_{j=1}^{p} l_j, \sum_{j=1}^{p} m_j, \sum_{j=1}^{p} u_j\right) \otimes \left(\frac{1}{\sum_{i=1}^{t}\sum_{j=1}^{p} u_{ij}}, \frac{1}{\sum_{i=1}^{t}\sum_{j=1}^{p} m_{ij}}, \frac{1}{\sum_{i=1}^{t}\sum_{j=1}^{p} l_{ij}}\right) \tag{34}$$

Second, the degree possibility $S_2 = (l_2, m_2, u_2) \geq S_1 = (l_1, m_1, u_1)$ is expressed as follows [48,69,78]:

$$V(S_2 \geq S_1) = sup[min(\mu_{S_1}(x), \mu_{S_2}(y))] = \begin{cases} 1, & if\ m_2 \geq m_1 \\ 0, & if\ l_1 \geq l_2 \\ \frac{l_1 - u_2}{(m_2 - u_2) - (m_1 - l_1)} \end{cases} \tag{35}$$

According to Chang [69]: "the degree possibility for a convex fuzzy number to be greater than $k$ convex fuzzy numbers $S_i(i = 1, 2, \ldots, k)$", is defined by the following [69]:

$$V(S \geq S_1, S_2, \ldots, S_k)$$
$$= V[(S \geq S_1)\ and\ (S \geq S_2)\ and\ \ldots\ and\ (S \geq S_k)] \tag{36}$$
$$= minV(S \geq S_i),\ i = 1, 2, \ldots, k$$

Assuming that

$$d'(A_i) = minV(S_i \geq S_k),\ for\ k = 1, 2, \ldots, n; k \neq i. \tag{37}$$

we obtain the following weight vector:

$$W' = (d'(A_1), d'(A_2), \ldots, d'(A_t))^T,\ where\ A_i(i = 1, 2, \ldots, t)\ are\ t\ elements. \tag{38}$$

Through normalization, we find the normalized weight vectors:

$$W_i = (d(A_1), d(A_2), \ldots, d(A_t))^T \tag{39}$$

where $W_i$ indicates a nonfuzzy number.

**Step 5.** Generating a supermatrix and converting it to a weighted supermatrix

A supermatrix illustrates the impact of a network's distinct elements on the other elements in the same network [41]. The columns of the supermatrix are populated with the weights obtained from previous steps [28]. To attain overall priorities in a system's interaction, internal importance vectors are included into columns, based on the connection between elements [72]. In this model, the supermatrix representation is provided as follows [47,79]:

$$W = \begin{bmatrix} 0 & 0 & 0 \\ W_{21} & 0 & 0 \\ 0 & W_{32} & I \end{bmatrix} \tag{40}$$

The vector of $W_{21}$ represents the local weights vector of the factors with respect to the goal, the vector of $W_{32}$ represents the local weights vector of the variables with respect to each factor, and $I$ represents the identity matrix [47].

**Step 6.** Obtaining the weighted supermatrix

To obtain the weighted supermatrix, entries of the initial supermatrix are divided by the sum of the weights of their corresponding column. The following weighted supermatrix is obtained [44]:

$$W_n = \begin{bmatrix} \frac{W_{11}}{d_1} & \cdots & \frac{W_{1n}}{d_n} \\ \vdots & \ddots & \vdots \\ \frac{W_{n1}}{d_1} & \cdots & \frac{W_{nn}}{d_n} \end{bmatrix} \quad (41)$$

where

$$d_j = \sum_{j=1}^{n} W_{ij} \quad (42)$$

**Step 7.** Establishing the limit supermatrix and the global weights of the model

The limit supermatrix is computed by multiplying the weighted supermatrix by itself until the values are stabilized [28,44].

$$L = \lim_{g \to \infty} (W_n^\alpha)^g \quad (43)$$

The limit supermatrix yields the relative importance weights for each variable included in the model. [28].

### 3.2. Method for Country Risk Assessment

The fuzzy-ANP with PCA method proposed in Section 3.1. is adapted for a country risk assessment model. To establish this model, this empirical analysis involved data collection and variable explanations from Refinitiv Thomson Reuters, considering a set of 172 countries with complete data for the variables considered. A set of 17 variables were selected based on previous examinations [1,4,20,25,27,30,36,39]. The collected data followed the measurement scale proposed by Refinitiv, ranging from 1 (very low risk) to 5 (very high risk). This model assessed a 2016–2022 timeframe, for a total of 1204 observations. Further details on these variables are presented in Table 2.

Table 2. Country risk variables.

| Environment | | Variable | Variable Description | Mean | SD |
|---|---|---|---|---|---|
| Political environment | $X_1$ | Type of governance | Progress and transformation process towards democracy and market economy | 2.7749 | 1.0648 |
| | $X_2$ | Civil liberties & political rights | Freedom of individuals in terms of individual rights and personal autonomy, and government functioning along with electoral and political participation | 2.8978 | 1.1917 |
| | $X_3$ | Freedom of the press | Journalistic freedom and free flow of news | 2.9111 | 1.0568 |
| | $X_4$ | Political stability | Likelihood of political destabilization and interferences in governmental jurisdiction | 2.9045 | 0.9760 |
| | $X_5$ | Regulatory quality | Sound policies to support private sector activity | 2.9668 | 0.9583 |
| | $X_6$ | Rule of law | Aggregated individual governance indicators of economies | 3.0291 | 0.9836 |
| | $X_7$ | Armed conflict | Potential conflict based on clashing interests | 2.9203 | 0.9880 |
| | $X_8$ | Human rights | State respect regarding human rights indicators | 2.9543 | 1.0333 |
| | $X_9$ | Voice & accountability | Perceptions of citizens' freedom of expression and association | 2.9668 | 1.0414 |
| Economic environment | $X_{10}$ | Average earnings | Economy classification based on Gross National Income per capita | 3.0739 | 1.1713 |
| | $X_{11}$ | Economic freedom | Benchmarks highlighting freedom of trade, business, investment, etc. | 2.9344 | 1.0168 |
| | $X_{12}$ | Sovereign credit ratings | Risk level of debt that is guaranteed by the sovereign | 3.0033 | 0.9181 |
| | $X_{13}$ | Competitiveness | Economic classification based on the Global Competitiveness Index | 3.0008 | 1.0351 |
| Criminal environment | $X_{14}$ | Corruption | Abuse level of power for personal gain | 2.9236 | 1.0495 |
| | $X_{15}$ | Natural resources industry controls | Assessment of industry controls in resource-rich countries | 2.8887 | 1.1694 |
| | $X_{16}$ | Terrorism | Assessment of country terrorism fatalities and threats | 2.9618 | 0.8074 |
| | $X_{17}$ | Absence of violence | Assessment of 'peace' level based on internal and external conflicts | 2.8912 | 0.9738 |

The fuzzy-ANP with PCA provides the mathematical framework for this proposed model's country risk assessment. Conceptually, in this paper, the country risk model is described as a system of 17 dimensions (variables) that interact with each dimension with respect to $n$ factors obtained with PCA. The fuzzy-ANP with PCA provides a multicriteria model of country risk assessment based on the steps presented in Section 3.1. This section provides the basis for model validation in Section 4.1.

3.2.1. Extracting Country Risk Factors with PCA

To start, we apply the PCA mathematical technique for variables $X_1, X_2, \ldots, X_{17}$ (Table 2). Following Steps 2a–f and applying the algorithm based on Equations (1)–(18), the analysis extracts $n$ factors. In the following step, the 17 variables $X_i$ are pairwise compared with respect to each factor $f_\ell$.

3.2.2. Constructing Pairwise Comparison Matrices for Factors and Variables: Obtaining the Local Weights for the Country Risk Model

From PCA, we obtain factors $f_1, f_2, \ldots, f_n$, with each factor $f_\ell$ corresponding to variables $v_{\ell_1}, v_{\ell_2}, \ldots, v_{\ell_{17}}$. Based on the previously mentioned Steps 3a–3e and Equations (19)–(30), pairwise comparison matrices for the factors and their associated variables are obtained.

Considering Chang's [69] extent analysis (Step 4), we apply Equations (31)–(39). Based on this process, the normalized weight vectors are obtained. These vectors showcase the local weights for the country risk model.

### 3.2.3. Determining the Unweighted Supermatrix and Converting It to a Weighted Supermatrix

The weights obtained in previous steps are used to construct the unweighted supermatrix, based on Step 5. This matrix is normalized by applying Equation (42) to obtain the weighted supermatrix (Step 6).

### 3.2.4. Establishing the Limit Supermatrix and the Global Weights for the Country Risk Model

By applying Equation (43), the weighted supermatrix of the country risk model's variables is multiplied by itself and the limit supermatrix is generated. This aspect provides the basis for extraction from the limit supermatrix of the global weights $w_1, w_2, \ldots, w_{17}$ associated with the country risk model's variables. Thus, based on weights $w_i$, we obtain the country risk score ($R_k$ score), for each country $k$ from the 172 considered countries, by applying the following formula:

$$R_k = \sum_{i=1}^{17} w_i X_{ik} \tag{44}$$

*3.3. Method for Bank Performance Model under the Assumption of Country Risk*

In this section, the fuzzy-ANP with PCA method proposed in Section 3.1. is adapted for the bank performance model. The country risk assessment results (namely, country risk scores $R_1, R_2, \ldots, R_{172}$) were further integrated in the next phase of this model to establish a bank performance evaluation model. For this proposed model, the data analysis included previously established country risk scores (based on fuzzy-ANP with PCA) and a set of bank-related variables collected from Refinitiv Thomson Reuters and International Monetary Fund (IMF) (Table 3). The data collection process involved filtering the set by public and listed companies, with the available data on the selected set of variables, for the timeframe of 2016–2022. For the bank performance assessment, this study included a set of commonly used indicators selected from the banking literature [1,20,27,30]. The final sample comprised 496 banks operating across 58 countries. Compared with the previous study of 172 countries for country risk assessment, this bank performance model retained a set of 58 countries based on bank-related data availability.

To examine bank performance, we opted for a straightforward approach. Two sets of variables were taken into account as the model's explanatory variables. Firstly, we established a set of variables relative to the bank's characteristics, based on previous research. Consistent with prior research [27,80,81], this study focused on return-on-assets (ROA) as the primary variable to illustrate bank performance. Following previous investigations [27,82], variables related to the financial profile of banks were considered, such as asset quality (AQ), earnings and profitability (E&P), capitalization and leverage (C&L), and funding and liquidity (F&L). Moreover, using direction from previous empirical studies [27,83,84], this analysis included other variables that showcased the characteristics of banks, namely ratio of equity to total assets (EQUITY) and bank size using the logarithm of total assets [SIZE]. Secondly, to reflect the impacts connected to economic conditions, two frequently applied indicators from banking investigations were selected, i.e., a country's growth rate (GDP) and inflation rate (INF) [1,27,39]. Table 3 addresses the bank-specific variables used in this research.

**Table 3.** Variables of bank performance model under the assumption of country risk.

| $U_{v_\beta} \mid U_{v_k}$ | $v_\beta^*$ | $max_v$ | $min_v$ | $v_\beta$ | Description | Mean | SD |
|---|---|---|---|---|---|---|---|
| $U_{ROA_\beta} = ROA_\beta^* e^{-R_k}$ | $ROA_\beta^* = \frac{ROA_\beta - 7.83}{7.83 - (-0.12)}$ | 7.83 [b] | −0.12 [b] | ROA | Ratio of net profit to total assets (%, 4-year average) | 1.12 | 0.62 |
| $U_{AQ_\beta} = AQ_\beta^* e^{-R_k}$ | $AQ_\beta^* = 1 - \frac{AQ_\beta - 0.25}{14 - 0.25}$ | 14 [a] | 0.25 [a] | AQ | Ratio of impaired loans to gross loans (%, 4-year average) | 2.17 | 3.34 |
| $U_{E\&P_\beta} = E\&P_\beta^* e^{-R_k}$ | $E\&P_\beta^* = \frac{E\&P_\beta - (-0.25)}{5 - (-0.25)}$ | 5 [a] | −0.25 [a] | E&P | Ratio of operating profit to risk-weighted assets (%, 4-year average) | 4.14 | 36.78 |
| $U_{C\&L_\beta} = C\&L_\beta^* e^{-R_k}$ | $C\&L_\beta^* = \frac{C\&L_\beta - 6}{22 - 6}$ | 22 [a] | 6 [a] | C&L | Core capital ratio (%) | 15.09 | 4.54 |
| $U_{F\&L_\beta} = F\&L_\beta^* e^{-R_k}$ | $F\&L_\beta^* = 1 - \frac{F\&L_\beta - 45}{250 - 45}$ | 250 [a] | 45 [a] | F&L | Ratio of loans to customer deposits (%, 4-year average) | 109.20 | 63.12 |
| $U_{SIZE_\beta} = SIZE_\beta^* e^{-R_k}$ | $SIZE_\beta^* = \frac{SIZE_\beta - 18.94}{19.14 - 18.94}$ | 29.14 [b] | 18.94 [b] | SIZE | Natural logarithm of total assets (%, 4-year average) | 23.19 | 1.98 |
| $U_{EQUITY_\beta} = EQUITY_\beta^* e^{-R_k}$ | $EQUITY_\beta^* = \frac{EQUITY_\beta - 2.46}{46.65 - 2.46}$ | 46.65 [b] | 2.46 [b] | EQUITY | Ratio of equity to total assets (%, 4-year average) | 10.71 | 3.39 |
| $U_{GDP_k} = GDP_k^* e^{-R_k}$ | $GDP_k^* = \frac{GDP_k - 13.55}{13.55 - (-15.70)}$ | 13.55 [b] | −15.70 [b] | GDP | GDP growth rate of the country (%) | 2.07 | 3.89 |
| $U_{INF_k} = INF_k^* e^{-R_k}$ | $INF_k^* = 1 - \frac{INF_k - 2}{64.27 - 2}$ | 64.27 [b] | 2 | INF | Inflation rate of the country (%) | 4.66 | 5.96 |

Note: [a] minimum and maximum levels are provided in accordance with the Fitch Rating methodology for rating banks [82]; [b] minimum and maximum of the values set.

Considering the existing framework [74–76], data were preprocessed and standardized for analysis by applying the min–max normalization formula [74–76] for every variable in Table 3:

$$v_\beta^* = \frac{v_\beta - min_v}{max_v - min_v} \quad \text{normalized by maximizing} \quad (45)$$

$$v_\beta^* = 1 - \frac{v_\beta - min_v}{max_v - min_v} \quad \text{normalized by minimazing} \quad (46)$$

where $v_\beta$ refers to variable $v$ of bank $\beta$.

To evaluate bank performance, we determined a model under the assumption of country risk based on the following utility functions:

$$U_{v_\beta} = v_\beta e^{-R_k}, \text{ for banking variables} \quad (47)$$

$$U_{v_k} = v_k e^{-R_k}, \text{ for country variables} \quad (48)$$

The fuzzy-ANP with PCA provides a multicriteria model of bank performance under the assumption of country risk based on the steps presented in Section 3.1. This section provides the basis for model validation in Section 4.2.

3.3.1. Extracting Bank Performance Factors with PCA

To begin with, we applied PCA for variables $U_{ROA_\beta}, U_{AQ_\beta}, U_{E\&P_\beta}, U_{C\&L_\beta}, U_{F\&L_\beta}, U_{EQUITY_\beta}, U_{SIZE_\beta}, U_{GDP_k}, U_{INF_k}$ (Table 3). Following Steps 2a–e and the algorithm reflected in Equations (1)–(15), the analysis showed $n$ number of factors. In the following step, the nine variables were pairwise compared with respect to each factor $f_\ell$.

### 3.3.2. Constructing the Pairwise Comparison Matrices for Factors and Variables: Obtaining Local Weights for the Bank Performance Model under the Assumption of Country Risk

Factors $f_1, f_2, \ldots, f_n$ result from PCA, and each factor $f_\ell$ has a corresponding variable from $v_{\ell_1}, v_{\ell_2}, \ldots, v_{\ell_9}$. Considering Steps 3a–e and Equations (19)–(30), pairwise comparison matrix for factors and variables are obtained. Considering Chang's [69] extent analysis (Step 4), we apply Equations (31)–(39) to obtain the normalized local weight vectors for the bank performance model.

### 3.3.3. Determining the Unweighted Supermatrix and Converting It to a Weighted Supermatrix

Based on the local weights, we construct the unweighted supermatrix (Step 5), and after normalization (Step 6), we determine the weighted supermatrix.

### 3.3.4. Establishing the Limit Supermatrix and the Global Weights of the Bank Performance Model under Assumption of Country Risk

By applying Equation (43), the weighted supermatrix of the model's variables is multiplied by itself and the limit supermatrix is generated. This provides the basis for extraction from the limit supermatrix of the global weights $w_{ROA}, w_{AQ}, w_{E\&P}, w_{C\&L}, w_{F\&L}, w_{EQUITY}, w_{SIZE}, w_{GDP}, w_{INF}$. Thus, by applying fuzzy-ANP with PCA, we establish a mathematical framework for this bank performance model under the assumption of country risk, with the main scope of determining a performance score, considering the following:

$$BP_\beta = \begin{pmatrix} w_{ROA} \\ w_{AQ} \\ w_{E\&P} \\ w_{C\&L} \\ w_{F\&L} \\ w_{SIZE} \\ w_{EQUITY} \\ w_{GDP} \\ w_{INF} \end{pmatrix}^T \begin{pmatrix} U_{ROA_\beta} \\ U_{AQ_\beta} \\ U_{E\&P_\beta} \\ U_{C\&L_\beta} \\ U_{F\&L_\beta} \\ U_{SIZE_\beta} \\ U_{EQUITY_\beta} \\ U_{GDP_k} \\ U_{INF_k} \end{pmatrix} = \begin{pmatrix} w_{ROA} \\ w_{AQ} \\ w_{E\&P} \\ w_{C\&L} \\ w_{F\&L} \\ w_{SIZE} \\ w_{EQUITY} \\ w_{GDP} \\ w_{INF} \end{pmatrix}^T \begin{pmatrix} \frac{ROA_\beta - 7.83}{7.95} e^{-R_k} \\ \left(1 - \frac{AQ_\beta - 0.25}{13.75}\right) e^{-R_k} \\ \frac{E\&P_\beta + 0.25}{5.25} e^{-R_k} \\ \frac{C\&L_\beta - 6}{16} e^{-R_k} \\ \left(1 - \frac{F\&L_\beta - 45}{250}\right) e^{-R_k} \\ \frac{SIZE_\beta - 18.94}{0.2} e^{-R_k} \\ \frac{EQUITY_\beta - 2.46}{44.19} e^{-R_k} \\ \frac{GDP_k - 13.55}{29.25} e^{-R_k} \\ \left(1 - \frac{INF_k - 2}{62.27}\right) e^{-R_k} \end{pmatrix} \quad (49)$$

## 4. Empirical Analysis and Results

Based on the steps presented above and associated with this multi-analytic approach of fuzzy-ANP with PCA, a bank performance model under the assumption of country risk was proposed for validation. To obtain this overall model, first we developed the country risk model that provides the scores corresponding to the operating environment of the banks. Second, the country risk scores were associated with selected bank-related variables, resulting in a bank performance model and its associated scores.

*4.1. Country Risk Model*

4.1.1. Extracting the Country Risk Factors with PCA

As a first step, we utilized PCA to reduce our selected set of 17 variables (Table 4) to the lowest number of factors that could describe the highest level of variance observed in the empirical data [55,59,63–68]. According to Steps 2a–f with their corresponding Equations (1)–(18), the PCA procedure was applied in IBM SPSS Statistics v.26 (IBM Corp., Armonk, NY, USA), and the results are presented in Tables 3 and 4.

Table 4. Total variance explained for the country risk principal component analysis.

| Component ($\ell$) | Initial Eigenvalues | | | Extraction Sums of Squared Loading | | | Rotation Sums of Squared Loading | | |
|---|---|---|---|---|---|---|---|---|---|
| | Total | % of Variance | Cumulative % | Total | % of Variance | Cumulative % | $f_\ell$ | % of Variance | Cumulative % |
| 1 | 10.5550 | 62.0885 | 62.0885 | 10.5550 | 62.0885 | 62.0885 | 6.0475 | 35.5738 | 35.5738 |
| 2 | 1.6996 | 9.9978 | 72.0863 | 1.6996 | 9.9978 | 72.0863 | 4.6261 | 27.2126 | 62.7864 |
| 3 | 1.2309 | 7.2404 | 79.3267 | 1.2309 | 7.2404 | 79.3267 | 2.8119 | 16.5403 | 79.3267 |

Extraction method: principal component analysis.

PCA generated three factors that provided an understanding of the variables included in the country risk assessment model. The PCA results showcased adequacy according to the 0.951 score for the Kaiser–Meyer–Olkin measure of sampling adequacy (KMO higher than 0.7) [66] and the significant Bartlett's test ($\chi^2(300) = 22183.121$, $p < 0.001$) [59]. Pertaining to Table 4's results, all three resulting factors ($f_1, f_2, f_3$) had Eigenvalues greater than 0.7 [64] and total variance explained was 79.3267%, which exceeded the accepted 60% threshold [59].

Table 4 presents the matrix of rotated factors (using Varimax rotation), in accordance with Steps 2d–f. The values obtained and presented in Table 5 represent $\widetilde{\lambda}_{i\ell}$. We applied Equation (14) to obtain variables $v_{\ell_i}$, namely the values for variable $X_i$ with respect to factor $f_\ell$.

Table 5. Rotated factors matrix for country risk.

| Description | Variables | Communalities ($h_i$) | $f_1$ | $f_2$ | $f_3$ |
|---|---|---|---|---|---|
| Type of governance | $X_1 \rightarrow v_1$ | 0.8034 | 0.3881 | 0.7871 | 0.1824 |
| Civil liberties and political rights | $X_2 \rightarrow v_2$ | 0.8979 | 0.3195 | 0.8614 | 0.2319 |
| Freedom of the press | $X_3 \rightarrow v_3$ | 0.8739 | 0.2151 | 0.8821 | 0.2225 |
| Political stability | $X_4 \rightarrow v_4$ | 0.8039 | 0.5103 | 0.3823 | 0.6303 |
| Regulatory quality | $X_5 \rightarrow v_5$ | 0.8805 | 0.8325 | 0.4010 | 0.1633 |
| Rule of law | $X_6 \rightarrow v_6$ | 0.8500 | 0.7716 | 0.4262 | 0.2702 |
| Armed conflict | $X_7 \rightarrow v_7$ | 0.7570 | 0.3405 | 0.2769 | 0.7512 |
| Human rights | $X_8 \rightarrow v_8$ | 0.7735 | 0.2915 | 0.7078 | 0.4330 |
| Voice and accountability | $X_9 \rightarrow v_9$ | 0.9192 | 0.4076 | 0.8475 | 0.1865 |
| Average earnings | $X_{10} \rightarrow v_{10}$ | 0.7621 | 0.8271 | 0.1665 | 0.2242 |
| Economic freedom | $X_{11} \rightarrow v_{11}$ | 0.7516 | 0.7765 | 0.3111 | 0.2279 |
| Sovereign credit ratings | $X_{12} \rightarrow v_{12}$ | 0.5925 | 0.7043 | 0.2246 | 0.2143 |
| Competitiveness | $X_{13} \rightarrow v_{13}$ | 0.7506 | 0.8347 | 0.1936 | 0.1279 |
| Corruption | $X_{14} \rightarrow v_{14}$ | 0.8077 | 0.7149 | 0.4880 | 0.2417 |
| Natural resources industry controls | $X_{15} \rightarrow v_{15}$ | 0.7408 | 0.8082 | 0.2929 | 0.0436 |
| Terrorism | $X_{16} \rightarrow v_{16}$ | 0.7957 | −0.0102 | 0.1327 | 0.8820 |
| Absence of violence | $X_{17} \rightarrow v_{17}$ | 0.7252 | 0.4341 | 0.3846 | 0.6236 |

4.1.2. Constructing Pairwise Comparison Matrices, and Obtaining Local Weights for the Country Risk Model

The resulting factors $f_\ell$ (Table 4) and variables $v_{\ell_i}$ (Table 5) were further used for the next steps of fuzzy-ANP. Considering Step 3c and Section 3.2.2, we applied Equations (22)–(25) to construct the fuzzy pairwise comparison matrix of the country risk factors (Table 6).

Table 6. Fuzzy pairwise comparison matrix of country risk factors.

| Linguistic Pairwise Comparison | | | Corresponding TFNs | | | $\left(\sum_{j=1}^{3} l_{ij}, \sum_{j=1}^{3} m_{ij}, \sum_{j=1}^{3} u_{ij}\right)$ | $W_f$ |
|---|---|---|---|---|---|---|---|
| | $f_1$ | $f_2$ | $f_3$ | $f_1$ | $f_2$ | $f_3$ | |
| $f_1$ | 1 | 2 | 9 | (1, 1, 1) | (1, 2, 3) | (9, 9, 9) | (11, 12, 13) | 0.9489 |
| $f_2$ | 1/2 | 1 | 6 | (1/3, 1/2, 1) | (1, 1, 1) | (5, 6, 7) | (6.3333, 7.5, 9) | 0.0511 |
| $f_3$ | 1/9 | 1/6 | 1 | (1/9, 1/9, 1/9) | (1/7, 1/6, 1/5) | (1, 1, 1) | (1.254, 1.2778, 1.3111) | 0.0000 |
| Σ | | | | | | | (18.5873, 20.7778, 23.3111) | |

Note: Consistency ratio = 0.0089 < 0.1 [28,41,43,46,77].

The relative importance weights vector from the fuzzy pairwise comparison matrix was obtained using the extent analysis method [69] of the fuzzy-ANP. The result is shown in Table 6, and its compilation is based on the calculations explained below (based on Step 4 and Section 3.2.2):

$$S_{f_1} = (11, 12, 13) \otimes \left(\frac{1}{23.3111}, \frac{1}{20.7778}, \frac{1}{18.5873}\right) = (0.4719, 0.5775, 0.6994) \quad (50)$$

$$S_{f_2} = (6.3333, 7.5, 9) \otimes \left(\frac{1}{23.3111}, \frac{1}{20.7778}, \frac{1}{18.5873}\right) = (0.2717, 0.3610, 0.4842) \quad (51)$$

$$S_{f_3} = (1.2554, 1.2778, 1.3111) \otimes \left(\frac{1}{23.3111}, \frac{1}{20.7778}, \frac{1}{18.5873}\right) = (0.0538, 0.0615, 0.0705) \quad (52)$$

Then, we applied Equations (35) and (36) to compute the degree possibility:

$$V\left(S_{f_1} \geq S_{f_2}\right) = 1, V\left(S_{f_1} \geq S_{f_3}\right) = 1 \quad (53)$$

$$V\left(S_{f_2} \geq S_{f_1}\right) = \frac{0.4719 - 0.4842}{(0.3610 - 0.4842) - (0.5775 - 0.4719)} = 0.0538, V\left(S_{f_2} \geq S_{f_3}\right) = 1 \quad (54)$$

$$V\left(S_{f_3} \geq S_{f_1}\right) = 0, V\left(S_{f_3} \geq S_{f_2}\right) = 0 \quad (55)$$

Finally, Equations (37)–(39) were utilized to obtain the relative weight vector:

$$d'\left(S_{f_1}\right) = \min V\left(S_{f_1} \geq S_{f_2}, S_{f_3}\right) = \min(1, 1) = 1 \quad (56)$$

$$d'\left(S_{f_1}\right) = \min V\left(S_{f_2} \geq S_{f_1}, S_{f_3}\right) = \min(0.0538, 1) = 0.0538 \quad (57)$$

$$d'\left(S_{f_1}\right) = \min V\left(S_{f_3} \geq S_{f_1}, S_{f_2}\right) = \min(1, 0) = 0 \quad (58)$$

Therefore,

$$W' = (1, 0.0538, 0)^T \quad (59)$$

The normalized relative weight vector attained via normalization of $W'$ is as follows:

$$W_{\tilde{F}} = (0.9489, 0.0511, 0)^T \quad (60)$$

This algorithm was applied in the same manner to all pairwise comparison matrices. Appendix A shows the results for the pairwise matrices that are formed from the calculations of the relative importance weights of variables $v_{\ell_1}, v_{\ell_2}, \ldots, v_{\ell_{17}}$ with respect to each factor $f_\ell$ resulting from the country risk PCA. The normalized relative weight vectors are as follows:

$$W_{\tilde{V_1}} = (0.0002, 0, 0, 0.0441, 0.1321, 0.1056, 0, 0, 0.0096, 0.1290, 0.1117, 0.0897, 0.1351, 0.0941, 0.1215, 0, 0.0274)^T \quad (61)$$

$$W_{\widetilde{V}_2} = (0.1778, 0.2115, 0.2187, 0, 0, 0.0115, 0, 0.1375, 0.2010, 0, 0, 0, 0, 0.0421, 0, 0, 0)^T \tag{62}$$

$$W_{\widetilde{V}_3} = (0, 0, 0, 0.1867, 0, 0, 0.2651, 0.0325, 0, 0, 0, 0, 0, 0, 0, 0.3489, 0.1669)^T \tag{63}$$

### 4.1.3. Determining the Supermatrices for the Country Risk Model

According to Step 5 and Section 3.2.3, the weights derived from prior steps were used to populate the columns of the specific unweighted supermatrix for this country risk model. Applying Equations (41) and (42) from Step 6, we obtained the following weighted supermatrix (Table 7):

**Table 7.** Weighted supermatrix for the country risk model.

|  | Goal | $f_1$ | $f_2$ | $f_3$ | $v_1$ | $v_2$ | $v_3$ | $v_4$ | $v_5$ | $v_6$ | $v_7$ | $v_8$ | $v_9$ | $v_{10}$ | $v_{11}$ | $v_{12}$ | $v_{13}$ | $v_{14}$ | $v_{15}$ | $v_{16}$ | $v_{17}$ |
|---|---|---|---|---|---|---|---|---|---|---|---|---|---|---|---|---|---|---|---|---|---|
| Goal | 0 | 0 | 0 | 0 | 0 | 0 | 0 | 0 | 0 | 0 | 0 | 0 | 0 | 0 | 0 | 0 | 0 | 0 | 0 | 0 | 0 |
| $f_1$ | 0.9489 | 0 | 0 | 0 | 0 | 0 | 0 | 0 | 0 | 0 | 0 | 0 | 0 | 0 | 0 | 0 | 0 | 0 | 0 | 0 | 0 |
| $f_2$ | 0.0511 | 0 | 0 | 0 | 0 | 0 | 0 | 0 | 0 | 0 | 0 | 0 | 0 | 0 | 0 | 0 | 0 | 0 | 0 | 0 | 0 |
| $f_3$ | 0.0000 | 0 | 0 | 0 | 0 | 0 | 0 | 0 | 0 | 0 | 0 | 0 | 0 | 0 | 0 | 0 | 0 | 0 | 0 | 0 | 0 |
| $v_1$ | 0 | 0.0002 | 0.1778 | 0.0000 | 1 | 0 | 0 | 0 | 0 | 0 | 0 | 0 | 0 | 0 | 0 | 0 | 0 | 0 | 0 | 0 | 0 |
| $v_2$ | 0 | 0.0000 | 0.2115 | 0.0000 | 0 | 1 | 0 | 0 | 0 | 0 | 0 | 0 | 0 | 0 | 0 | 0 | 0 | 0 | 0 | 0 | 0 |
| $v_3$ | 0 | 0.0000 | 0.2187 | 0.0000 | 0 | 0 | 1 | 0 | 0 | 0 | 0 | 0 | 0 | 0 | 0 | 0 | 0 | 0 | 0 | 0 | 0 |
| $v_4$ | 0 | 0.0441 | 0.0000 | 0.1867 | 0 | 0 | 0 | 1 | 0 | 0 | 0 | 0 | 0 | 0 | 0 | 0 | 0 | 0 | 0 | 0 | 0 |
| $v_5$ | 0 | 0.1321 | 0.0000 | 0.0000 | 0 | 0 | 0 | 0 | 1 | 0 | 0 | 0 | 0 | 0 | 0 | 0 | 0 | 0 | 0 | 0 | 0 |
| $v_6$ | 0 | 0.1056 | 0.0115 | 0.0000 | 0 | 0 | 0 | 0 | 0 | 1 | 0 | 0 | 0 | 0 | 0 | 0 | 0 | 0 | 0 | 0 | 0 |
| $v_7$ | 0 | 0.0000 | 0.0000 | 0.2651 | 0 | 0 | 0 | 0 | 0 | 0 | 1 | 0 | 0 | 0 | 0 | 0 | 0 | 0 | 0 | 0 | 0 |
| $v_8$ | 0 | 0.0000 | 0.1375 | 0.0325 | 0 | 0 | 0 | 0 | 0 | 0 | 0 | 1 | 0 | 0 | 0 | 0 | 0 | 0 | 0 | 0 | 0 |
| $v_9$ | 0 | 0.0096 | 0.2010 | 0.0000 | 0 | 0 | 0 | 0 | 0 | 0 | 0 | 0 | 1 | 0 | 0 | 0 | 0 | 0 | 0 | 0 | 0 |
| $v_{10}$ | 0 | 0.1290 | 0.0000 | 0.0000 | 0 | 0 | 0 | 0 | 0 | 0 | 0 | 0 | 0 | 1 | 0 | 0 | 0 | 0 | 0 | 0 | 0 |
| $v_{11}$ | 0 | 0.1117 | 0.0000 | 0.0000 | 0 | 0 | 0 | 0 | 0 | 0 | 0 | 0 | 0 | 0 | 1 | 0 | 0 | 0 | 0 | 0 | 0 |
| $v_{12}$ | 0 | 0.0897 | 0.0000 | 0.0000 | 0 | 0 | 0 | 0 | 0 | 0 | 0 | 0 | 0 | 0 | 0 | 1 | 0 | 0 | 0 | 0 | 0 |
| $v_{13}$ | 0 | 0.1351 | 0.0000 | 0.0000 | 0 | 0 | 0 | 0 | 0 | 0 | 0 | 0 | 0 | 0 | 0 | 0 | 1 | 0 | 0 | 0 | 0 |
| $v_{14}$ | 0 | 0.0941 | 0.0421 | 0.0000 | 0 | 0 | 0 | 0 | 0 | 0 | 0 | 0 | 0 | 0 | 0 | 0 | 0 | 1 | 0 | 0 | 0 |
| $v_{15}$ | 0 | 0.1215 | 0.0000 | 0.0000 | 0 | 0 | 0 | 0 | 0 | 0 | 0 | 0 | 0 | 0 | 0 | 0 | 0 | 0 | 1 | 0 | 0 |
| $v_{16}$ | 0 | 0.0000 | 0.0000 | 0.3489 | 0 | 0 | 0 | 0 | 0 | 0 | 0 | 0 | 0 | 0 | 0 | 0 | 0 | 0 | 0 | 1 | 0 |
| $v_{17}$ | 0 | 0.0274 | 0.0000 | 0.1669 | 0 | 0 | 0 | 0 | 0 | 0 | 0 | 0 | 0 | 0 | 0 | 0 | 0 | 0 | 0 | 0 | 1 |

### 4.1.4. Establishing the Limit Supermatrix and the Global Weights of the Country Risk Model

Finally, according to Step 7 and Section 3.2.4, by multiplying the weighted supermatrix by itself, we obtained the limit supermatrix.

In the first column of limit supermatrix (Table 8), the relative importance weights of all variables with respect to the country risk are showcased.

**Table 8.** Limit supermatrix for country risk model.

|  | Goal | $f_1$ | $f_2$ | $f_3$ | $v_1$ | $v_2$ | $v_3$ | $v_4$ | $v_5$ | $v_6$ | $v_7$ | $v_8$ | $v_9$ | $v_{10}$ | $v_{11}$ | $v_{12}$ | $v_{13}$ | $v_{14}$ | $v_{15}$ | $v_{16}$ | $v_{17}$ |
|---|---|---|---|---|---|---|---|---|---|---|---|---|---|---|---|---|---|---|---|---|---|
| Goal | 0 | 0 | 0 | 0 | 0 | 0 | 0 | 0 | 0 | 0 | 0 | 0 | 0 | 0 | 0 | 0 | 0 | 0 | 0 | 0 | 0 |
| $f_1$ | 0 | 0 | 0 | 0 | 0 | 0 | 0 | 0 | 0 | 0 | 0 | 0 | 0 | 0 | 0 | 0 | 0 | 0 | 0 | 0 | 0 |
| $f_2$ | 0 | 0 | 0 | 0 | 0 | 0 | 0 | 0 | 0 | 0 | 0 | 0 | 0 | 0 | 0 | 0 | 0 | 0 | 0 | 0 | 0 |
| $f_3$ | 0 | 0 | 0 | 0 | 0 | 0 | 0 | 0 | 0 | 0 | 0 | 0 | 0 | 0 | 0 | 0 | 0 | 0 | 0 | 0 | 0 |
| $v_1$ | 0.0093 | 0.0002 | 0.1778 | 0.0000 | 1 | 0 | 0 | 0 | 0 | 0 | 0 | 0 | 0 | 0 | 0 | 0 | 0 | 0 | 0 | 0 | 0 |
| $v_2$ | 0.0108 | 0.0000 | 0.2115 | 0.0000 | 0 | 1 | 0 | 0 | 0 | 0 | 0 | 0 | 0 | 0 | 0 | 0 | 0 | 0 | 0 | 0 | 0 |
| $v_3$ | 0.0112 | 0.0000 | 0.2187 | 0.0000 | 0 | 0 | 1 | 0 | 0 | 0 | 0 | 0 | 0 | 0 | 0 | 0 | 0 | 0 | 0 | 0 | 0 |
| $v_4$ | 0.0418 | 0.0441 | 0.0000 | 0.1867 | 0 | 0 | 0 | 1 | 0 | 0 | 0 | 0 | 0 | 0 | 0 | 0 | 0 | 0 | 0 | 0 | 0 |
| $v_5$ | 0.1253 | 0.1321 | 0.0000 | 0.0000 | 0 | 0 | 0 | 0 | 1 | 0 | 0 | 0 | 0 | 0 | 0 | 0 | 0 | 0 | 0 | 0 | 0 |
| $v_6$ | 0.1008 | 0.1056 | 0.0115 | 0.0000 | 0 | 0 | 0 | 0 | 0 | 1 | 0 | 0 | 0 | 0 | 0 | 0 | 0 | 0 | 0 | 0 | 0 |
| $v_7$ | 0.0000 | 0.0000 | 0.0000 | 0.2651 | 0 | 0 | 0 | 0 | 0 | 0 | 1 | 0 | 0 | 0 | 0 | 0 | 0 | 0 | 0 | 0 | 0 |
| $v_8$ | 0.0070 | 0.0000 | 0.1375 | 0.0325 | 0 | 0 | 0 | 0 | 0 | 0 | 0 | 1 | 0 | 0 | 0 | 0 | 0 | 0 | 0 | 0 | 0 |
| $v_9$ | 0.0193 | 0.0096 | 0.2010 | 0.0000 | 0 | 0 | 0 | 0 | 0 | 0 | 0 | 0 | 1 | 0 | 0 | 0 | 0 | 0 | 0 | 0 | 0 |

Table 8. Cont.

| | Goal | $f_1$ | $f_2$ | $f_3$ | $v_1$ | $v_2$ | $v_3$ | $v_4$ | $v_5$ | $v_6$ | $v_7$ | $v_8$ | $v_9$ | $v_{10}$ | $v_{11}$ | $v_{12}$ | $v_{13}$ | $v_{14}$ | $v_{15}$ | $v_{16}$ | $v_{17}$ |
|---|---|---|---|---|---|---|---|---|---|---|---|---|---|---|---|---|---|---|---|---|---|
| $v_{10}$ | 0.1224 | 0.1290 | 0.0000 | 0.0000 | 0 | 0 | 0 | 0 | 0 | 0 | 0 | 0 | 0 | 1 | 0 | 0 | 0 | 0 | 0 | 0 | 0 |
| $v_{11}$ | 0.1060 | 0.1117 | 0.0000 | 0.0000 | 0 | 0 | 0 | 0 | 0 | 0 | 0 | 0 | 0 | 0 | 1 | 0 | 0 | 0 | 0 | 0 | 0 |
| $v_{12}$ | 0.0851 | 0.0897 | 0.0000 | 0.0000 | 0 | 0 | 0 | 0 | 0 | 0 | 0 | 0 | 0 | 0 | 0 | 1 | 0 | 0 | 0 | 0 | 0 |
| $v_{13}$ | 0.1282 | 0.1351 | 0.0000 | 0.0000 | 0 | 0 | 0 | 0 | 0 | 0 | 0 | 0 | 0 | 0 | 0 | 0 | 1 | 0 | 0 | 0 | 0 |
| $v_{14}$ | 0.0915 | 0.0941 | 0.0421 | 0.0000 | 0 | 0 | 0 | 0 | 0 | 0 | 0 | 0 | 0 | 0 | 0 | 0 | 0 | 1 | 0 | 0 | 0 |
| $v_{15}$ | 0.1153 | 0.1215 | 0.0000 | 0.0000 | 0 | 0 | 0 | 0 | 0 | 0 | 0 | 0 | 0 | 0 | 0 | 0 | 0 | 0 | 1 | 0 | 0 |
| $v_{16}$ | 0.0000 | 0.0000 | 0.0000 | 0.3489 | 0 | 0 | 0 | 0 | 0 | 0 | 0 | 0 | 0 | 0 | 0 | 0 | 0 | 0 | 0 | 1 | 0 |
| $v_{17}$ | 0.0260 | 0.0274 | 0.0000 | 0.1669 | 0 | 0 | 0 | 0 | 0 | 0 | 0 | 0 | 0 | 0 | 0 | 0 | 0 | 0 | 0 | 0 | 1 |

Thus, based on the weights from Tables 8 and 9, we obtained the country risk score ($R_k$ score) for each country $k$ by applying Equation (44).

Table 9. Relative importance weights of all variables with respect to country risk.

| Variables ($X_i$) | Corresponding to PCA | Description | $w_i$ |
|---|---|---|---|
| $X_1$ | $v_1$ | Type of governance | 0.0093 |
| $X_2$ | $v_2$ | Civil liberties and political rights | 0.0108 |
| $X_3$ | $v_3$ | Freedom of the press | 0.0112 |
| $X_4$ | $v_4$ | Political stability | 0.0418 |
| $X_5$ | $v_5$ | Regulatory quality | 0.1253 |
| $X_6$ | $v_6$ | Rule of law | 0.1008 |
| $X_7$ | $v_7$ | Armed conflict | 0.0000 |
| $X_8$ | $v_8$ | Human rights | 0.0070 |
| $X_9$ | $v_9$ | Voice and accountability | 0.0193 |
| $X_{10}$ | $v_{10}$ | Average earnings | 0.1224 |
| $X_{11}$ | $v_{11}$ | Economic freedom | 0.1060 |
| $X_{12}$ | $v_{12}$ | Sovereign credit ratings | 0.0851 |
| $X_{13}$ | $v_{13}$ | Competitiveness | 0.1282 |
| $X_{14}$ | $v_{14}$ | Corruption | 0.0915 |
| $X_{15}$ | $v_{15}$ | Natural resources industry controls | 0.1153 |
| $X_{16}$ | $v_{16}$ | Terrorism | 0.0000 |
| $X_{17}$ | $v_{17}$ | Absence of violence | 0.0260 |

Table 10 reflects the IMF country classification and the mean values for the identified groups, considering the country risk scores (calculated based on the novel fuzzy-ANP with the PCA method). Based on Table 10 and Figure 3, the results showed the lowest levels of country risk for the advanced economies. The mean scores of the advanced economies (1.5982 calculated for year 2022) and emerging Europe (2.8559 calculated for year 2022) were below the global mean (2.9574). The other country groups exhibited mean scores above the global mean. Notably, the Sub-Saharan Africa group reflected the highest mean country risk scores (3.7170 calculated for year 2022).

Table 10. Country risk scores based on economy type.

| Economy Type [a] | N | Indicator | 2022 | 2021 | 2020 | 2019 | 2018 | 2017 | 2016 |
|---|---|---|---|---|---|---|---|---|---|
| Advanced Economies | 37 | Mean | 1.5982 | 1.6326 | 1.6310 | 1.6128 | 1.6454 | 1.6622 | 1.6781 |
| | | SD | 0.4045 | 0.4020 | 0.4096 | 0.4397 | 0.4754 | 0.4698 | 0.4910 |
| Emerging and Developing Asia | 25 | Mean | 3.2304 | 3.2412 | 3.2049 | 3.2071 | 3.2430 | 3.2212 | 3.2664 |
| | | SD | 0.4059 | 0.4194 | 0.4334 | 0.4194 | 0.4224 | 0.4101 | 0.4687 |
| Emerging and Developing Europe | 13 | Mean | 2.8559 | 2.8198 | 2.8632 | 2.8923 | 2.9240 | 2.9268 | 2.9316 |
| | | SD | 0.4022 | 0.3669 | 0.3649 | 0.4092 | 0.4050 | 0.4466 | 0.4463 |
| Latin America and The Caribbean | 30 | Mean | 3.0005 | 3.0148 | 3.0659 | 3.0672 | 3.0527 | 3.0651 | 3.0691 |
| | | SD | 0.4715 | 0.4572 | 0.4515 | 0.4390 | 0.4301 | 0.4192 | 0.4050 |
| Middle East and Central Asia | 25 | Mean | 3.4207 | 3.3810 | 3.4185 | 3.4241 | 3.4306 | 3.3652 | 3.3473 |
| | | SD | 0.6272 | 0.6566 | 0.6931 | 0.6358 | 0.6191 | 0.6216 | 0.6519 |

Table 10. Cont.

| Economy Type [a] | N | Indicator | 2022 | 2021 | 2020 | 2019 | 2018 | 2017 | 2016 |
|---|---|---|---|---|---|---|---|---|---|
| Sub-Saharan Africa | 42 | Mean | 3.7170 | 3.7206 | 3.7119 | 3.7154 | 3.7024 | 3.6762 | 3.6689 |
|  |  | SD | 0.4844 | 0.4829 | 0.5013 | 0.4957 | 0.5052 | 0.4649 | 0.4449 |
| All countries | 172 | Mean | 2.9574 | 2.9612 | 2.9711 | 2.9716 | 2.9815 | 2.9684 | 2.9750 |
|  |  | SD | 0.8960 | 0.8848 | 0.8924 | 0.8950 | 0.8860 | 0.8639 | 0.8643 |

[a] International monetary fund classification.

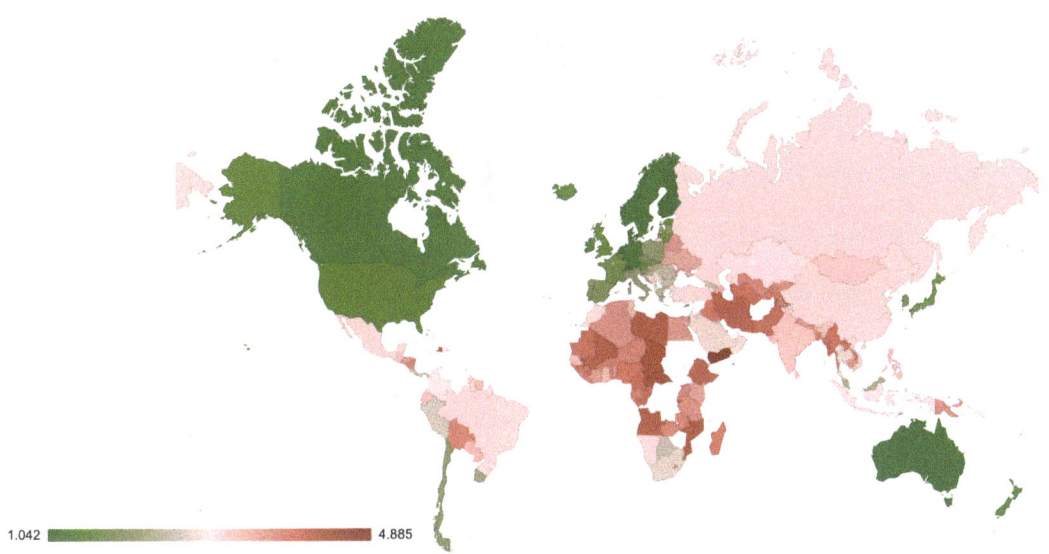

**Figure 3.** Map of country risk scores (source: own computation).

### 4.2. Bank Performance Model under the Assumption of Country Risk

The country risk scores obtained in the previous section (Section 4.1) were further incorporated in this second stage of the model. For this second stage, fuzzy-ANP with PCA provides a multicriteria model of bank performance under the assumption of country risk based on the steps presented in Section 3.3.2.

#### 4.2.1. Extracting Bank Performance Factors with PCA

Regarding the proposed method, at this stage, PCA was used to reduce the nine selected variables (Table 3). Considering Steps 2a–f, PCA was developed in IBM SPSS Statistics v.26 (IBM Corp., Armonk, NY, USA), and the results are presented in Tables 10 and 11.

**Table 11.** Total variance explained for the PCA of bank performance.

| Component ($\ell$) | Initial Eigenvalues | | | Extraction Sums of Squared Loading | | | Rotation Sums of Squared Loading | | |
|---|---|---|---|---|---|---|---|---|---|
|  | Total | % of Variance | Cumulative % | Total | % of Variance | Cumulative % | $f_\ell$ | % of Variance | Cumulative % |
| 1 | 6.520 | 72.439 | 72.439 | 6.520 | 72.439 | 72.439 | 3.921 | 43.572 | 43.572 |
| 2 | 0.859 | 9.545 | 81.984 | 0.859 | 9.545 | 81.984 | 3.457 | 38.412 | 81.984 |

Extraction method: principal component analysis.

The bank performance PCA generated two factors that helped understand the selected variables in a new framework. The PCA results showcased appropriateness according to the 0.839 score for KMO (>0.7) [66] and the significant Bartlett's test (23,045.334 with

$p<0.001$ [59]. As shown in Table 11, the newly generated factors highlighted Eigenvalues values that exceeded the recommended threshold of 0.7 [64], with a total variance explained of 81.984% (higher than the 60% level recommended by Hair [59]).

Table 11 presents the matrix of rotated factors, in accordance with Steps 2d–f. The values obtained and presented in Table 12 represent $\tilde{\lambda}_{i\ell}$. We used Equation (14) to obtain variables $v_{\ell_i}$, namely the values for variable $X_i$ with respect to factor $f_\ell$.

**Table 12.** Rotated factors matrix for PCA of bank performance.

| Variables | Corresponding in PCA | Communalities ($h_i$) | $f_1$ | $f_2$ |
|---|---|---|---|---|
| $u_{ROA}$ | $v_1$ | 0.8069 | 0.8714 | 0.2181 |
| $u_{AQ}$ | $v_2$ | 0.8609 | 0.6792 | 0.6321 |
| $u_{E\&P}$ | $v_3$ | 0.8155 | 0.4894 | 0.7590 |
| $u_{C\&L}$ | $v_4$ | 0.7491 | 0.4661 | 0.7293 |
| $u_{F\&L}$ | $v_5$ | 0.6545 | 0.6783 | 0.4409 |
| $u_{SIZE}$ | $v_6$ | 0.8541 | 0.1080 | 0.9179 |
| $u_{EQUITY}$ | $v_7$ | 0.8456 | 0.8918 | 0.2241 |
| $u_{GDP}$ | $v_8$ | 0.8518 | 0.6897 | 0.6133 |
| $u_{INF}$ | $v_9$ | 0.9401 | 0.7081 | 0.6624 |

### 4.2.2. Constructing the Pairwise Comparison Matrices and Obtaining Local Weights for the Bank Performance Model

The resulting factors $f_\ell$ (Table 11) and variables $v_{\ell_i}$ (Table 12) were further used in next steps of fuzzy-ANP to develop the pairwise comparison matrices for the factors and variables. Considering Step 3b and Section 3.3.2, the fuzzy pairwise comparison matrix of the bank performance factors was developed (Table 13).

**Table 13.** Fuzzy pairwise comparison matrix of the bank performance factors.

| Linguistic Pairwise Comparison | | | Corresponding TFNs | | Σ | $W_f$ |
|---|---|---|---|---|---|---|
| | $f_1$ | $f_2$ | $f_1$ | $f_2$ | | |
| $f_1$ | 1 | 9 | (1, 1, 1) | (9, 9, 9) | (10, 10, 10) | 1.0000 |
| $f_2$ | 1/9 | 1 | (1/9, 1/9, 1/9) | (1, 1, 1) | (1.1111, 1.1111, 1.1111) | 0.0000 |
| Σ | | | | | (11.1111, 11.1111, 11.1111) | |

Using the extent analysis method of fuzzy-ANP [69], the relative importance weights are available in Table 13 and the calculations are presented below:

$$S_{f_1} = (10, 10, 10) \otimes \left(\frac{1}{11.1111}, \frac{1}{11.1111}, \frac{1}{11.1111}\right) = (0.9, 0.9, 0.9) \quad (64)$$

$$S_{f_2} = (1.1111, 1.1111, 1.1111) \otimes \left(\frac{1}{11.1111}, \frac{1}{11.1111}, \frac{1}{11.1111}\right) = (0.1, 0.1, 0.1) \quad (65)$$

Considering Equations (35) and (36), the degree possibility was:

$$V\left(S_{f_1} \geq S_{f_2}\right) = 1, \ V\left(S_{f_2} \geq S_{f_1}\right) = 0 \quad (66)$$

Finally, considering Equations (37)–(39), the relative weight vector was as follows:

$$W_{\tilde{F}} = (1, 0)^T = \begin{pmatrix} 1 \\ 0 \end{pmatrix} \quad (67)$$

Based on this result, factor $f_1$ displayed a higher level of importance with respect to the goal to select the model's variables and determine their relative importance weights for the bank performance score. Corresponding to Step 5 and Section 3.3.2, the local weight vectors of variables $v_{1_i}$ with respect to $f_1$ were computed as follows (Tables 14 and 15):

**Table 14.** Linguistic pairwise comparison matrix of variables $v_{1_i}$ with respect to $f_1$.

| $f_1$ | $v_{1_1}$ | $v_{1_2}$ | $v_{1_3}$ | $v_{1_4}$ | $v_{1_5}$ | $v_{1_6}$ | $v_{1_7}$ | $v_{1_8}$ | $v_{1_9}$ |
|---|---|---|---|---|---|---|---|---|---|
| $v_{1_1}$ | 1 | 2 | 2 | 2 | 2 | 2 | 1/2 | 2 | 2 |
| $v_{1_2}$ | 1/2 | 1 | 2 | 2 | 2 | 2 | 1/2 | 1/2 | 1/2 |
| $v_{1_3}$ | 1/2 | 1/2 | 1 | 2 | 1/2 | 2 | 1/2 | 1/2 | 1/2 |
| $v_{1_4}$ | 1/2 | 1/2 | 1/2 | 1 | 1/2 | 2 | 1/2 | 1/2 | 1/2 |
| $v_{1_5}$ | 1/2 | 1/2 | 2 | 2 | 1 | 2 | 1/2 | 1/2 | 1/2 |
| $v_{1_6}$ | 1/2 | 1/2 | 1/2 | 1/2 | 1/2 | 1 | 1/3 | 1/2 | 1/2 |
| $v_{1_7}$ | 2 | 2 | 2 | 2 | 2 | 3 | 1 | 2 | 2 |
| $v_{1_8}$ | 1/2 | 2 | 2 | 2 | 2 | 2 | 1/2 | 1 | 1/2 |
| $v_{1_9}$ | 1/2 | 2 | 2 | 2 | 2 | 2 | 1/2 | 2 | 1 |

Note: Consistency ratio = 0.0409 < 0.1 [28,41,43,46,77].

**Table 15.** Fuzzy pairwise comparison matrix of variables $v_{1_i}$ with respect to $f_1$.

| $f_1$ | $v_{1_1}$ | $v_{1_2}$ | $v_{1_3}$ | $v_{1_4}$ | $v_{1_5}$ | $v_{1_6}$ | $v_{1_7}$ | $v_{1_8}$ | $v_{1_9}$ | Σ | $W_{v_1}$ |
|---|---|---|---|---|---|---|---|---|---|---|---|
| $v_{1_1}$ | (1, 1, 1) | (1, 2, 3) | (1, 2, 3) | (1, 2, 3) | (1, 2, 3) | (1, 2, 3) | (1/3, 1/2, 1) | (1, 2, 3) | (1, 2, 3) | (8.3333, 15.5, 23) | 0.1406 |
| $v_{1_2}$ | (1/3, 1/2, 1) | (1, 1, 1) | (1, 2, 3) | (1, 2, 3) | (1, 2, 3) | (1, 2, 3) | (1/3, 1/2, 1) | (1/3, 1/2, 1) | (1/3, 1/2, 1) | (6.3333, 11, 17) | 0.1157 |
| $v_{1_3}$ | (1/3, 1/2, 1) | (1/3, 1/2, 1) | (1, 1, 1) | (1, 2, 3) | (1/3, 1/2, 1) | (1, 2, 3) | (1/3, 1/2, 1) | (1/3, 1/2, 1) | (1/3, 1/2, 1) | (5, 8, 13) | 0.0928 |
| $v_{1_4}$ | (1/3, 1/2, 1) | (1/3, 1/2, 1) | (1/3, 1/2, 1) | (1, 1, 1) | (1/3, 1/2, 1) | (1, 2, 3) | (1/3, 1/2, 1) | (1/3, 1/2, 1) | (1/3, 1/2, 1) | (4.3333, 6.5, 11) | 0.0786 |
| $v_{1_5}$ | (1/3, 1/2, 1) | (1/3, 1/2, 1) | (1, 2, 3) | (1, 2, 3) | (1, 1, 1) | (1, 2, 3) | (1/3, 1/2, 1) | (1/3, 1/2, 1) | (1/3, 1/2, 1) | (5.6667, 9.5, 15) | 0.1051 |
| $v_{1_6}$ | (1/3, 1/2, 1) | (1/3, 1/2, 1) | (1/3, 1/2, 1) | (1/3, 1/2, 1) | (1/3, 1/2, 1) | (1, 1, 1) | (1/4, 1/3, 1/2) | (1/3, 1/2, 1) | (1/3, 1/2, 1) | (3.5833, 4.8333, 8.5) | 0.0578 |
| $v_{1_7}$ | (1, 2, 3) | (1, 2, 3) | (1, 2, 3) | (1, 2, 3) | (1, 2, 3) | (2, 3, 4) | (1, 1, 1) | (1, 2, 3) | (1, 2, 3) | (10, 18, 26) | 0.1512 |
| $v_{1_8}$ | (1/3, 1/2, 1) | (1, 2, 3) | (1, 2, 3) | (1, 2, 3) | (1, 2, 3) | (1, 2, 3) | (1/3, 1/2, 1) | (1, 1, 1) | (1/3, 1/2, 1) | (7, 12.5, 19) | 0.1250 |
| $v_{1_9}$ | (1/3, 1/2, 1) | (1, 2, 3) | (1, 2, 3) | (1, 2, 3) | (1, 2, 3) | (1, 2, 3) | (1/3, 1/2, 1) | (1, 2, 3) | (1, 1, 1) | (7.6667, 14, 21) | 0.1332 |
| Σ | | | | | | | | | | (57.9167, 99.8333, 153.5) | |

$$S_{v_{1_1}} = (8.3333, 15.5, 23) \otimes \left(\frac{1}{153.5}, \frac{1}{99.8333}, \frac{1}{57.9167}\right) = (0.0543, 0.1553, 0.3971) \quad (68)$$

$$S_{v_{1_2}} = (6.3333, 11, 17) \otimes \left(\frac{1}{153.5}, \frac{1}{99.8333}, \frac{1}{57.9167}\right) = (0.0413, 0.1102, 0.2935) \quad (69)$$

$$S_{v_{1_3}} = (5, 8, 13) \otimes \left(\frac{1}{153.5}, \frac{1}{99.8333}, \frac{1}{57.9167}\right) = (0.0326, 0.0801, 0.2245) \quad (70)$$

$$S_{v_{1_4}} = (4.3333, 6.5, 11) \otimes \left(\frac{1}{153.5}, \frac{1}{99.8333}, \frac{1}{57.9167}\right) = (0.0282, 0.0651, 0.1899) \quad (71)$$

$$S_{v_{1_5}} = (5.6667, 9.5, 15) \otimes \left(\frac{1}{153.5}, \frac{1}{99.8333}, \frac{1}{57.9167}\right) = (0.0369, 0.0952, 0.259) \quad (72)$$

$$S_{v_{1_6}} = (3.5833, 4.8333, 8.5) \otimes \left(\frac{1}{153.5}, \frac{1}{99.8333}, \frac{1}{57.9167}\right) = (0.0233, 0.0484, 0.1468) \quad (73)$$

$$S_{v_{1_7}} = (10, 18, 26) \otimes \left(\frac{1}{153.5}, \frac{1}{99.8333}, \frac{1}{57.9167}\right) = (0.0651, 0.1803, 0.4489) \quad (74)$$

$$S_{v_{18}} = (7, 12.5, 19) \otimes \left(\frac{1}{153.5}, \frac{1}{99.8333}, \frac{1}{57.9167}\right) = (0.0456, 0.1252, 0.3281) \quad (75)$$

$$S_{v_{19}} = (7.6667, 14, 21) \otimes \left(\frac{1}{153.5}, \frac{1}{99.8333}, \frac{1}{57.9167}\right) = (0.0499, 0.1402, 0.3626) \quad (76)$$

Equations (31) and (35) were applied to compute the degree possibility [69], and the results are presented in Table 16.

**Table 16.** Degree possibility.

| $V(S_{v_{1j}} \geq S_{v_{1i}})$ | $S_{v_{11}}$ | $S_{v_{12}}$ | $S_{v_{13}}$ | $S_{v_{14}}$ | $S_{v_{15}}$ | $S_{v_{16}}$ | $S_{v_{17}}$ | $S_{v_{18}}$ | $S_{v_{19}}$ |
|---|---|---|---|---|---|---|---|---|---|
| $S_{v_{11}}$ | - | 1 | 1 | 1 | 1 | 1 | 0.9299 | 1 | 1 |
| $S_{v_{12}}$ | 0.8415 | - | 1 | 1 | 1 | 1 | 0.7651 | 0.9429 | 0.8902 |
| $S_{v_{13}}$ | 0.6937 | 0.8591 | - | 1 | 0.9258 | 1 | 0.6140 | 0.7987 | 0.7438 |
| $S_{v_{14}}$ | 0.6007 | 0.7673 | 0.9128 | - | 0.8358 | 1 | 0.5200 | 0.7060 | 0.6508 |
| $S_{v_{15}}$ | 0.7730 | 0.9354 | 1 | 1 | - | 1 | 0.6948 | 0.8766 | 0.8226 |
| $S_{v_{16}}$ | 0.4639 | 0.6307 | 0.7826 | 0.8765 | 0.7015 | - | 0.3823 | 0.5685 | 0.5132 |
| $S_{v_{17}}$ | 1 | 1 | 1 | 1 | 1 | 1 | - | 1 | 1 |
| $S_{v_{18}}$ | 0.9011 | 1 | 1 | 1 | 1 | 1 | 0.8268 | - | 0.9487 |
| $S_{v_{19}}$ | 0.9535 | 1 | 1 | 1 | 1 | 1 | 0.8813 | 1 | - |

$$V(S_{v_{1j}} \geq S_{v_{1i}}) = \begin{cases} 1, & \text{if } m_j \geq m_i \\ 0, & \text{if } l_i \geq l_j \\ \frac{l_i - u_j}{(m_j - u_j) - (m_i - l_i)} \end{cases} \quad (77)$$

Finally, based on Equations (36)–(39), relative weight vector was established:

$$d'(S_{v_{11}}) = \min V(S_{v_{11}} \geq S_{v_{12}}, S_{v_{13}}, S_{v_{14}}, S_{v_{15}}, S_{v_{16}}, S_{v_{17}}, S_{v_{18}}, S_{v_{19}}) = \min(1, 1, 1, 1, 0.9299, 1, 1) = 0.9299 \quad (78)$$

$$d'(S_{v_{12}}) = \min V(S_{v_{12}} \geq S_{v_{11}}, S_{v_{13}}, S_{v_{14}}, S_{v_{15}}, S_{v_{16}}, S_{v_{17}}, S_{v_{18}}, S_{v_{19}}) = \min(0.8415, 1, 1, 1, 1, 0.7651, 0.9429, 0.8902) = 0.7651 \quad (79)$$

$$d'(S_{v_{13}}) = \min V(S_{v_{13}} \geq S_{v_{11}}, S_{v_{12}}, S_{v_{14}}, S_{v_{15}}, S_{v_{16}}, S_{v_{17}}, S_{v_{18}}, S_{v_{19}}) = \min(0.6937, 0.8591, 1, 0.9258, 1, 0.6140, 0.7987, 0.7438) = 0.6140 \quad (80)$$

$$d'(S_{v_{14}}) = \min V(S_{v_{14}} \geq S_{v_{11}}, S_{v_{12}}, S_{v_{13}}, S_{v_{15}}, S_{v_{16}}, S_{v_{17}}, S_{v_{18}}, S_{v_{19}}) = \min(0.6007, 0.7673, 0.9128, 0.8358, 1, 0.52, 0.706, 0.6508) = 0.5200 \quad (81)$$

$$d'(S_{v_{15}}) = \min V(S_{v_{15}} \geq S_{v_{11}}, S_{v_{12}}, S_{v_{13}}, S_{v_{14}}, S_{v_{16}}, S_{v_{17}}, S_{v_{18}}, S_{v_{19}}) = \min(0.7730, 0.9354, 1, 1, 1, 0.6948, 0.8766, 0.8226) = 0.6948 \quad (82)$$

$$d'(S_{v_{16}}) = \min V(S_{v_{16}} \geq S_{v_{11}}, S_{v_{12}}, S_{v_{13}}, S_{v_{14}}, S_{v_{15}}, S_{v_{17}}, S_{v_{18}}, S_{v_{19}}) = \min V(0.4639, 0.6307, 0.7826, 0.8765, 0.7015, 0.3823, 0.5685, 0.5132) = 0.3823 \quad (83)$$

$$d'(S_{v_{17}}) = \min V(S_{v_{17}} \geq S_{v_{11}}, S_{v_{12}}, S_{v_{13}}, S_{v_{14}}, S_{v_{15}}, S_{v_{16}}, S_{v_{18}}, S_{v_{19}}) = \min(1, 1, 1, 1, 1, 1, 1) = 1.0000 \quad (84)$$

$$d'(S_{v_{18}}) = \min V(S_{v_{18}} \geq S_{v_{11}}, S_{v_{12}}, S_{v_{13}}, S_{v_{14}}, S_{v_{15}}, S_{v_{16}}, S_{v_{17}}, S_{v_{19}}) = \min(0.9011, 1, 1, 1, 1, 0.8268, 0.9487) = 0.8268 \quad (85)$$

$$d'\left(S_{v_{1_9}}\right) = minV\left(S_{v_{1_9}} \geq S_{v_{1_1}}, S_{v_{1_2}}, S_{v_{1_3}}, S_{v_{1_4}}, S_{v_{1_5}}, S_{v_{1_6}}, S_{v_{1_7}}, S_{v_{1_8}}\right) = min(0.9535, 1, 1, 1, 1, 0.8813, 1) = 0.8813 \quad (86)$$

Therefore,

$$W' = (0.9299, 0.7651, 0.6140, 0.5200, 0.6948, 0.3823, 1.0000, 0.8268, 0.8813)^T \quad (87)$$

The normalized relative weight vector was obtained via the normalization of $W'$:

$$W_{\tilde{V_1}} = (0.1406, 0.1157, 0.0928, 0.0786, 0.1051, 0.0578, 0.1512, 0.1250, 0.1332)^T \quad (88)$$

This algorithm was applied in the same manner to the pairwise comparison matrix of variable $v_{2_i}$ with respect to $f_2$.

### 4.2.3. Determining Supermatrices for the Bank Performance Model

Considering Step 5 and Section 3.3.3, the weights derived from the previous steps were applied to populate the columns of the specific unweighted supermatrix for this bank performance model. Utilizing Equations (41) and (42) from Step 6, we achieved the weighted supermatrix presented in Table 17.

**Table 17.** Weighted supermatrix for the bank performance model.

|  | Goal | $f_1$ | $f_1$ | $v_1$ | $v_2$ | $v_3$ | $v_4$ | $v_5$ | $v_6$ | $v_7$ | $v_8$ | $v_9$ |
|---|---|---|---|---|---|---|---|---|---|---|---|---|
| Goal | 0 | 0 | 0 | 0 | 0 | 0 | 0 | 0 | 0 | 0 | 0 | 0 |
| $f_1$ | 1.0000 | 0 | 0 | 0 | 0 | 0 | 0 | 0 | 0 | 0 | 0 | 0 |
| $f_2$ | 0.0000 | 0 | 0 | 0 | 0 | 0 | 0 | 0 | 0 | 0 | 0 | 0 |
| $v_1$ | 0 | 0.1406 | 0.0651 | 1 | 0 | 0 | 0 | 0 | 0 | 0 | 0 | 0 |
| $v_2$ | 0 | 0.1157 | 0.1154 | 0 | 1 | 0 | 0 | 0 | 0 | 0 | 0 | 0 |
| $v_3$ | 0 | 0.0928 | 0.1386 | 0 | 0 | 1 | 0 | 0 | 0 | 0 | 0 | 0 |
| $v_4$ | 0 | 0.0786 | 0.1318 | 0 | 0 | 0 | 1 | 0 | 0 | 0 | 0 | 0 |
| $v_5$ | 0 | 0.1051 | 0.0941 | 0 | 0 | 0 | 0 | 1 | 0 | 0 | 0 | 0 |
| $v_6$ | 0 | 0.0578 | 0.1447 | 0 | 0 | 0 | 0 | 0 | 1 | 0 | 0 | 0 |
| $v_7$ | 0 | 0.1512 | 0.0808 | 0 | 0 | 0 | 0 | 0 | 0 | 1 | 0 | 0 |
| $v_8$ | 0 | 0.1250 | 0.1055 | 0 | 0 | 0 | 0 | 0 | 0 | 0 | 1 | 0 |
| $v_9$ | 0 | 0.1332 | 0.1241 | 0 | 0 | 0 | 0 | 0 | 0 | 0 | 0 | 1 |

### 4.2.4. Establishing the Limit Supermatrix and the Global Weights of the Bank Performance Model under Country Risk Assumption

Finally, pertaining to Step 7 of fuzzy-ANP and Section 3.3.4, the limit supermatrix was computed by multiplying the weighted supermatrix of model by itself, resulting in Table 18.

**Table 18.** Limiting supermatrix for the bank performance model.

|  | Goal | $f_1$ | $f_1$ | $v_1$ | $v_2$ | $v_3$ | $v_4$ | $v_5$ | $v_6$ | $v_7$ | $v_8$ | $v_9$ |
|---|---|---|---|---|---|---|---|---|---|---|---|---|
| Goal | 0 | 0 | 0 | 0 | 0 | 0 | 0 | 0 | 0 | 0 | 0 | 0 |
| $f_1$ | 0 | 0 | 0 | 0 | 0 | 0 | 0 | 0 | 0 | 0 | 0 | 0 |
| $f_2$ | 0 | 0 | 0 | 0 | 0 | 0 | 0 | 0 | 0 | 0 | 0 | 0 |
| $v_1$ | 0.1406 | 0.1406 | 0.0651 | 1 | 0 | 0 | 0 | 0 | 0 | 0 | 0 | 0 |
| $v_2$ | 0.1157 | 0.1157 | 0.1154 | 0 | 1 | 0 | 0 | 0 | 0 | 0 | 0 | 0 |
| $v_3$ | 0.0928 | 0.0928 | 0.1386 | 0 | 0 | 1 | 0 | 0 | 0 | 0 | 0 | 0 |
| $v_4$ | 0.0786 | 0.0786 | 0.1318 | 0 | 0 | 0 | 1 | 0 | 0 | 0 | 0 | 0 |
| $v_5$ | 0.1051 | 0.1051 | 0.0941 | 0 | 0 | 0 | 0 | 1 | 0 | 0 | 0 | 0 |
| $v_6$ | 0.0578 | 0.0578 | 0.1447 | 0 | 0 | 0 | 0 | 0 | 1 | 0 | 0 | 0 |
| $v_7$ | 0.1512 | 0.1512 | 0.0808 | 0 | 0 | 0 | 0 | 0 | 0 | 1 | 0 | 0 |
| $v_8$ | 0.1250 | 0.1250 | 0.1055 | 0 | 0 | 0 | 0 | 0 | 0 | 0 | 1 | 0 |
| $v_9$ | 0.1332 | 0.1332 | 0.1241 | 0 | 0 | 0 | 0 | 0 | 0 | 0 | 0 | 1 |

Considering the global weights (Table 18), the bank performance score ($BP_\beta$) for each bank $\beta$, under the assumption of country risk $R_k$, was obtained by applying the following:

$$BP_\beta = \begin{pmatrix} 0.1406 \\ 0.1157 \\ 0.0928 \\ 0.0786 \\ 0.1051 \\ 0.0578 \\ 0.1512 \\ 0.1250 \\ 0.1332 \end{pmatrix}^T \begin{pmatrix} U_{ROA_\beta} \\ U_{AQ_\beta} \\ U_{E\&P_\beta} \\ U_{C\&L_\beta} \\ U_{F\&L_\beta} \\ U_{SIZE_\beta} \\ U_{EQUITY_\beta} \\ U_{GDP_k} \\ U_{INF_k} \end{pmatrix} = \begin{pmatrix} 0.1406 \\ 0.1157 \\ 0.0928 \\ 0.0786 \\ 0.1051 \\ 0.0578 \\ 0.1512 \\ 0.1250 \\ 0.1332 \end{pmatrix}^T \begin{pmatrix} \frac{ROA_\beta - 7.83}{7.95} e^{-R_k} \\ \left(1 - \frac{AQ_\beta - 0.25}{13.75}\right) e^{-R_k} \\ \frac{E\&P_\beta + 0.25}{5.25} e^{-R_k} \\ \frac{C\&L_\beta - 6}{16} e^{-R_k} \\ \left(1 - \frac{F\&L_\beta - 45}{250}\right) e^{-R_k} \\ \frac{SIZE_\beta - 18.94}{0.2} e^{-R_k} \\ \frac{EQUITY_\beta - 2.46}{44.19} e^{-R_k} \\ \frac{GDP_k - 13.55}{29.25} e^{-R_k} \\ \left(1 - \frac{INF_k - 2}{62.27}\right) e^{-R_k} \end{pmatrix} \quad (89)$$

Considering the premises of Equation (89), an increase in country risk leads to a decrease in bank performance scores. Thus, after an overall assessment of the results, we noted that country risk reflected an indirect relationship with bank performance.

Table 19 portrays the bank performance scores calculated based on the fuzzy-ANP with the PCA method. Considering the IMF classification of countries and calculations from 2022, Table 19 and Figure 4 show that the advanced economies' bank performance scores (0.1243) highlighted the above mean results for the year 2022 (0.0933), whereas the emerging economies' banks exhibited scores below the mean for all regions. Considering emerging economies, the highest scores for bank performance were established for emerging and developing Europe (0.0365). On the opposite end, the lowest bank performance scores were determined for the analyzed group of 22 banks for Sub-Saharan Africa (0.0224).

Table 19. Bank performance scores according to the economy type.

| Bank Groups by Economy Type | N | | 2022 | 2021 | 2020 | 2019 |
|---|---|---|---|---|---|---|
| Advanced Economies | 331 | Mean | 0.1243 | 0.1183 | 0.1122 | 0.1320 |
| | | SD | 0.0297 | 0.0312 | 0.0300 | 0.0299 |
| | | Min | 0.0409 | 0.0393 | 0.0266 | 0.0241 |
| | | Max | 0.2292 | 0.2324 | 0.2172 | 0.2301 |
| Emerging and Developing Asia | 55 | Mean | 0.0307 | 0.0345 | 0.0345 | 0.0356 |
| | | SD | 0.0111 | 0.0104 | 0.0108 | 0.0124 |
| | | Min | 0.0091 | 0.0161 | 0.0176 | 0.0188 |
| | | Max | 0.0599 | 0.0628 | 0.0639 | 0.0691 |
| Emerging and Developing Europe | 20 | Mean | 0.0365 | 0.0395 | 0.0352 | 0.0393 |
| | | SD | 0.0179 | 0.0172 | 0.0185 | 0.0208 |
| | | Min | 0.0200 | 0.0227 | 0.0190 | 0.0221 |
| | | Max | 0.0712 | 0.0727 | 0.0729 | 0.0815 |
| Latin America and the Caribbean | 8 | Mean | 0.0290 | 0.0309 | 0.0259 | 0.0286 |
| | | SD | 0.0056 | 0.0072 | 0.0064 | 0.0064 |
| | | Min | 0.0211 | 0.0214 | 0.0178 | 0.0198 |
| | | Max | 0.0369 | 0.0402 | 0.0334 | 0.0372 |
| Middle East and Central Asia | 60 | Mean | 0.0329 | 0.0345 | 0.0337 | 0.0336 |
| | | SD | 0.0143 | 0.0154 | 0.0151 | 0.0161 |
| | | Min | 0.0095 | 0.0095 | 0.0074 | 0.0086 |
| | | Max | 0.0689 | 0.0753 | 0.0735 | 0.0756 |

Table 19. Cont.

| Bank Groups by Economy Type | N | | 2022 | 2021 | 2020 | 2019 |
|---|---|---|---|---|---|---|
| Sub-Saharan Africa | 22 | Mean | 0.0224 | 0.0217 | 0.0214 | 0.0224 |
| | | SD | 0.0119 | 0.0106 | 0.0100 | 0.0131 |
| | | Min | 0.0100 | 0.0107 | 0.0104 | 0.0089 |
| | | Max | 0.0427 | 0.0439 | 0.0435 | 0.0495 |
| All sample | 496 | Mean | 0.0933 | 0.0900 | 0.0856 | 0.0992 |
| | | SD | 0.0509 | 0.0482 | 0.0457 | 0.0534 |
| | | Min | 0.0091 | 0.0095 | 0.0074 | 0.0086 |
| | | Max | 0.2292 | 0.2324 | 0.2172 | 0.2301 |

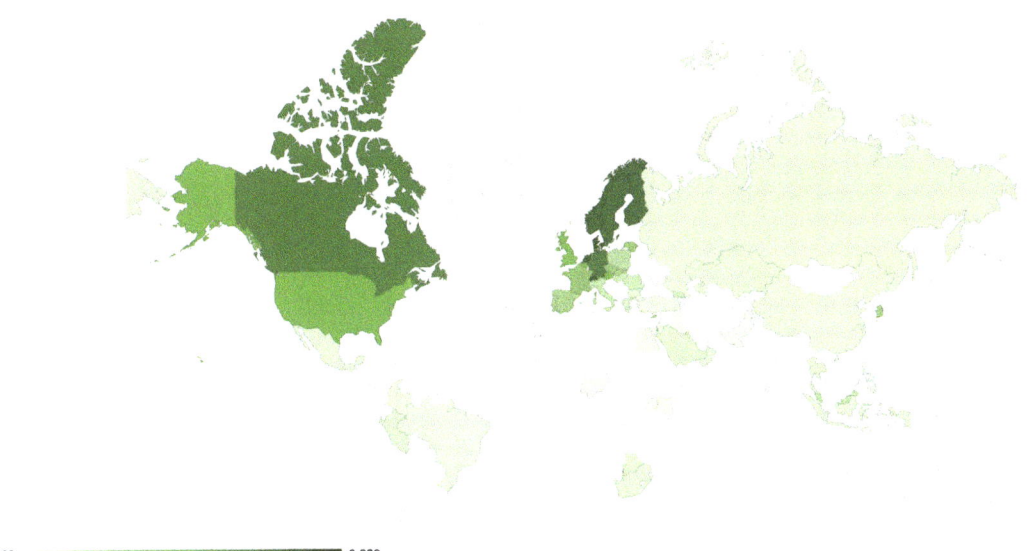

Figure 4. Map of countries based on bank performance scores under the assumption of country risk (source: own computation).

With regard to the main trends observed based on the calculations presented in Table 19, for the first pandemic year (2020), all banks registered downturn of their overall performance, regardless of their economy type. Furthermore, 2021 highlighted a recovery for all regions in terms of bank performance; however, this upward trend was continued only for the banks from advanced economies in 2022, while the banks from emerging economies reflected declines in their performance.

### 4.3. Exemplification of Bank Performance Model under the Assumption of Country Risk

This section validates the presented model of bank performance under the assumption of country risk considering an exemplification of three banks that are part of Groupe Societe Generale, namely Societe Generale from France, Komercni Banka from the Czech Republic, and BRD Groupe Societe Generale SA from Romania. Applying Equation (44) to the real bank data presented in Table 20, we obtained the following countries' risk scores (measured on a scale from 1 (very low risk) to 5 (very high risk)): 1.6840 for France, 1.8316 for the Czech Republic, and 2.5309 for Romania.

Table 20. Calculated country risk scores for France, the Czech Republic, and Romania (2022).

| Description | Variables | Weights ($w_i$) | France | Czech Republic | Romania |
|---|---|---|---|---|---|
| Type of governance | $X_1$ | 0.0093 | 2 | 1 | 2 |
| Civil liberties and political rights | $X_2$ | 0.0108 | 2 | 1 | 2 |
| Freedom of the press | $X_3$ | 0.0112 | 2 | 2 | 2 |
| Political stability | $X_4$ | 0.0418 | 2 | 2 | 2 |
| Regulatory quality | $X_5$ | 0.1253 | 2 | 2 | 3 |
| Rule of law | $X_6$ | 0.1008 | 2 | 2 | 3 |
| Armed conflict | $X_7$ | 0.0000 | 3 | 2 | 1 |
| Human rights | $X_8$ | 0.0070 | 1 | 1 | 2 |
| Voice & accountability | $X_9$ | 0.0193 | 2 | 2 | 2 |
| Average earnings | $X_{10}$ | 0.1224 | 2 | 2 | 2 |
| Economic freedom | $X_{11}$ | 0.1060 | 2 | 2 | 2 |
| Sovereign credit ratings | $X_{12}$ | 0.0851 | 2 | 2 | 3 |
| Competitiveness | $X_{13}$ | 0.1282 | 1 | 2 | 3 |
| Corruption | $X_{14}$ | 0.0915 | 1 | 2 | 3 |
| Natural resources industry controls | $X_{15}$ | 0.1153 | 1 | 1 | 2 |
| Terrorism | $X_{16}$ | 0.0000 | 4 | 3 | 3 |
| Absence of violence | $X_{17}$ | 0.0260 | 3 | 1 | 2 |
| Country Risk Scores ($R_k$) | - | - | 1.6840 | 1.8316 | 2.5309 |

By using the calculated country risk values from these three countries and real data for bank variables included in the model and presented in Table 21, Equation (89) was applied to calculate the bank performance scores for Societe Generale, Komercni Banka, and BRD Groupe Societe Generale SA.

Table 21. Calculated bank performance scores for Societe Generale, Komercni Banka, and BRD Groupe Societe Generale SA (2022).

| Variables | Weights | Societe Generale SA (France) | Komercni Banka as (Czech Republic) | BRD Groupe Societe Generale SA (Romania) |
|---|---|---|---|---|
| $R_k$ | - | 1.6840 | 1.8316 | 2.5309 |
| $ROA_\beta$ | 0.0108 | 0.2364 | 1.1579 | 2.0223 |
| $AQ_\beta$ | 0.0112 | 2.5514 | 2.4286 | 3.3305 |
| $E\&P_\beta$ | 0.0418 | 4.2502 | 9.2841 | 5.1919 |
| $C\&L_\beta$ | 0.1253 | 16.2900 | 18.9000 | 20.6400 |
| $F\&L_\beta$ | 0.1008 | 90.6945 | 77.9352 | 69.0012 |
| $SIZE_\beta$ | 0.0000 | 27.9937 | 24.5852 | 23.3242 |
| $EQUITY_\beta$ | 0.0070 | 4.4672 | 9.6728 | 13.2372 |
| $GDP_k$ | 0.0193 | 2.6060 | 2.4420 | 4.7910 |
| $INF_k$ | 0.1224 | 6.9580 | 15.7590 | 16.3710 |
| Bank Performance Scores | - | 0.1064 | 0.0965 | 0.0507 |

The scores of the banks from the advanced economies, namely Societe Generale (0.1064) from France and Komercni Banka (0.0965) from the Czech Republic, registered higher values than the bank from emerging and developing Europe, namely BRD Groupe Societe Generale SA (0.0507) from Romania. The findings from the bank performance scores' calculation reconfirm and provide additional validation to the results reported in Table 19 from Section 4.2.4.

## 5. Discussion

As an active research area of country risk assessment and bank performance, the authors have highlighted multiple mathematical techniques for multi-criteria decision making (MCDM) [85,86]. In this study, a new mathematical framework was proposed to expand MCDM by incorporating fuzzy-ANP and PCA for more effective risk assessment and performance analysis. The proposed method presented in Section 3.1. was explored through two studies: (1) country risk assessment and (2) bank performance model under the assumption of country risk.

In the first study, the country risk assessment model included an analysis of 172 countries, based on secondary data extracted from Refinitiv Thomson Reuters. This model showed that competitiveness (0.1282), regulatory quality (0.1253), and natural resources industry controls (0.1153) had the highest relative importance weights for determining the country risk scores (Table 9). Country risk scores were mainly influenced by economic dimensions, which had cumulated weights of 0.4417. All four of the economic dimensions included in the country risk assessments had significant weights: competitiveness (0.1282), average earnings (0.1224), economic freedom (0.1060), and sovereign credit ratings (0.0861). Considering the political dimensions of country risk assessment, they showcased cumulated weights of 0.3256, and the most important ones were regulatory quality (0.1253) and rule of law (0.1008). The criminal dimensions of country risk had cumulated weights of 0.2327 and the most notable ones were natural resources industry controls (0.1153) and corruption (0.0915). Based on these results, this study extends existing methodologies for determining country risk scores [1,27,29–31,33–35].

In the second study, this research examined a bank performance model under the assumption of country risk, considering a set of 496 banks. The data included for this analysis were extracted from Refinitiv Thomson Reuters and International Monetary Fund, but also incorporated the country risk scores from the previous study in the newly proposed fuzzy-ANP with the PCA method.

The bank performance model's weights are displayed in Table 18 and Equation (89). The most important bank variables for the performance score were EQUITY (0.1512) and ROA (0.1406). Additionally, macroeconomic indicators played a key role in establishing the bank performance score, based on the following weights: INF (0.1332) and GDP (0.1250). Based on the results of this model and considering the challenging operating environments of banks throughout the world, country risk has proven its relevancy in assessing the performance of banks. These results are in line with previous studies that have empirically examined bank performance in relation to country risk [1,20,27,39]. Moreover, for both studies, the fuzzy-ANP with PCA results were validated based on accuracy and consistency tests [59,64,65,69].

## 6. Conclusions

Because of challenging environments, country risk has proved its relevancy in assessing banks' performance and assisting decision-making. This study proposed a new bank performance model under the assumption of country risk, based on a multi-analytical effort that included PCA in a fuzzy-ANP model. Fuzzy applications [70,71,73,87] and ANPs [41,43,45–51] are valuable techniques due to their decision-making abilities. Nonetheless, certain authors have highlighted the need to address inconsistency issues associated with the complexity of the method [45,46], showcasing a gap in research. Based on this novel approach, this paper addressed this literature gap of proposing, applying, and validating unbiased perspectives in decision-making contexts.

From the perspective of mathematic methodology, this research contributes with an original approach that integrates fuzzy-ANP with PCA. The implementation of this new methodology involved multiple stages. In the initial stage, a Principal Component Analysis was developed based on a set of selected variables, collected based on secondary data. In the following stages, the PCA results were incorporated in the widely-known fuzzy-ANP method. By integrating secondary data in fuzzy-ANP with PCA mathematical methodology, this novel approach tackled the persistent issues of biases and inconsistencies associated with the general and commonly encountered implementation of fuzzy-ANP. Secondary data offers a broad and comprehensive perspective, showcasing accurate representation for complex-decision-making process. Moreover, PCA successfully reduces the dimensionality of the data while maintaining the efficiency of the analysis.

From the perspective of business and economic analysis, this research offers contributions in establishing a novel approach for bank performance evaluation considering country risk. The proposed methodology was applied and validated in two studies. The first study contributed to the development and validation of a new model for country risk assessment, considering the new fuzzy-ANP with PCA approach. The country risk assessment model considered a set of 17 variables. By applying fuzzy-ANP with PCA, a key finding of this model was reflected in the importance and prominence of the economic environment variables (competitiveness, average earnings, economic freedom, and sovereign credit ratings) affecting country risk, with cumulated weights of 0.4417.

The second study offered original contributions for evaluating and establishing a bank performance model, considering country risk scores (obtained in the previous study) within a set of nine bank-related variables. This second study offered additional support and validation for this novel fuzzy-ANP with PCA approach. Concerning the results of the second study, this model showed that bank performance was impacted by country risk. It is also important to note that the most relevant bank variables were equity and return-on-assets (ROA).

This study and its proposed methodology also highlight practical implications. The bank performance model can represent an effective instrument for decision making, risk management, and strategic planning, particularly in the context of modifying country risk settings. In practical settings, managers and decision makers have to identify key risk factors and the threat level of each factor. The findings provide guidelines for decision-making processes, such as choosing potential banking partners in different markets, investing in new markets, or establishing strategic investments from a strategic planning perspective, by delivering insights into the comparative risks connected to various countries.

Considering changing country risk circumstances, it is fundamental to understand bank performance for effective risk management. The model helps distinguish potential drawbacks and manage risk exposure by examining key risk factors and assessing institutions' risk management practices. These understandings assist in developing risk mitigation methods, strategic planning for diversification and competitive positioning in certain markets, as well as addressing the issues of appropriate resource allocation.

Thus, this research also provides decision makers with comprehensive insights into bank performance under the assumption of country risk, by showing the relative strengths and limits of banks, enabling informed choices and proactive measures to mitigate risks.

Additionally, this study provides certain implications for policymakers. Firstly, policymakers have to intervene in economies when country risk scores register an upward trend. This model provides useful insights for policymakers and aids them in deciding whether or not financial guarantees or liquidity support mechanisms are needed for banks. Secondly, this bank performance model can help policymakers to analyze and identify banks that may require directed assistance and support.

Although the research showcases many contributions, certain study limitations need to be addressed. Firstly, the proposed method was examined in the context of a predefined set of variables for the country risk assessment model and the bank performance model. Thus, future research could expand this framework and consider including additional variables. Secondly, a significant limitation of the study is reflected in the availability of the data. Although this study utilized data from an appreciated source of secondary data, namely Thomson Reuters Refinitiv, it is important to note that the model's reliability is dependent on relevant, comprehensive, and up-to-date data.

Thirdly, the bank performance model considered secondary data from listed and public companies. Thus, future research could extend this analysis with private companies. Fourthly, the bank performance model's effectiveness is conditional to the findings reflected in the country risk assessment. The interdependence of the two models should also be explored in the supplementary analyses.

Additionally, this newly proposed framework should also be tested in other contexts and other timeframes. Furthermore, this proposed mathematical method could also be amplified by employing additional decision-making frameworks (ELECTRE, DEMATEL, VIKOR, TOPSIS, or TODIM [88]) with distinct variables for further empirical investigations. Likewise, in future studies, the method of fuzzy-ANP could also be explored based on type-2 fuzzy sets for enhancing decision making [89] and by using the "trapezoidal type-2 intuitionistic fuzzy set [88].

**Author Contributions:** Conceptualization, A.O. and S.V.; methodology, A.O. and S.V.; software, A.O. and S.V.; validation, A.O., S.V., D.M.M., L.B. and R.-A.Ș.; formal analysis, A.O., S.V., D.M.M., L.B. and R.-A.Ș.; investigation, A.O.; resources, A.O., S.V., D.M.M., L.B. and R.-A.Ș.; data curation, A.O., D.M.M., L.B. and R.-A.Ș.; writing—original draft preparation, A.O. and S.V.; writing—review and editing, A.O., S.V., D.M.M., L.B. and R.-A.Ș.; visualization, A.O.; supervision, A.O.; project administration, A.O.; funding acquisition, A.O. All authors have read and agreed to the published version of the manuscript.

**Funding:** Project financed by Lucian Blaga University of Sibiu and Hasso Plattner Foundation research grants LBUS-IRG-2020-06.

**Data Availability Statement:** Third-party data restrictions apply to the availability of these data. Data were obtained from Thomson Reuters Eikon and are available at https://emea1-apps.platform.refinitiv.com/web/Apps/Homepage (accessed on 10 March 2023) with the permission of Thomson Reuters Eikon.

**Acknowledgments:** Project financed by Lucian Blaga University of Sibiu and Hasso Plattner Foundation research grants LBUS-IRG-2020-06.

**Conflicts of Interest:** The authors declare no conflict of interest.

## Appendix A

**Table A1.** Country risk model. Linguistic pairwise comparison matrix of variables $v_{1_i}$ with respect to $f_1$.

| $f_1$ | $v_{1_1}$ | $v_{1_2}$ | $v_{1_3}$ | $v_{1_4}$ | $v_{1_5}$ | $v_{1_6}$ | $v_{1_7}$ | $v_{1_8}$ | $v_{1_9}$ | $v_{1_{10}}$ | $v_{1_{11}}$ | $v_{1_{12}}$ | $v_{1_{13}}$ | $v_{1_{14}}$ | $v_{1_{15}}$ | $v_{1_{16}}$ | $v_{1_{17}}$ |
|---|---|---|---|---|---|---|---|---|---|---|---|---|---|---|---|---|---|
| $v_{1_1}$ | 1 | 2 | 2 | 1/2 | 1/4 | 1/3 | 2 | 2 | 1/2 | 1/4 | 1/3 | 1/3 | 1/4 | 1/3 | 1/4 | 3 | 1/2 |
| $v_{1_2}$ | 1/2 | 1 | 2 | 1/2 | 1/5 | 1/4 | 1/2 | 2 | 1/2 | 1/5 | 1/4 | 1/4 | 1/5 | 1/4 | 1/4 | 3 | 1/2 |
| $v_{1_3}$ | 1/2 | 1/2 | 1 | 1/3 | 1/6 | 1/6 | 1/2 | 1/2 | 1/2 | 1/6 | 1/6 | 1/5 | 1/6 | 1/5 | 1/6 | 2 | 1/3 |
| $v_{1_4}$ | 2 | 2 | 3 | 1 | 1/3 | 1/2 | 2 | 3 | 2 | 1/3 | 1/2 | 1/2 | 1/3 | 1/2 | 1/3 | 4 | 2 |
| $v_{1_5}$ | 4 | 5 | 6 | 3 | 1 | 2 | 4 | 5 | 4 | 2 | 2 | 2 | 1/2 | 2 | 2 | 9 | 3 |
| $v_{1_6}$ | 3 | 4 | 6 | 2 | 1/2 | 1 | 4 | 4 | 3 | 1/2 | 1/2 | 2 | 1/2 | 2 | 1/2 | 8 | 3 |
| $v_{1_7}$ | 1/2 | 2 | 2 | 1/2 | 1/4 | 1/4 | 1 | 2 | 1/2 | 1/4 | 1/4 | 1/3 | 1/4 | 1/3 | 1/4 | 3 | 1/2 |
| $v_{1_8}$ | 1/2 | 1/2 | 2 | 1/3 | 1/5 | 1/4 | 1/2 | 1 | 1/2 | 1/5 | 1/5 | 1/4 | 1/5 | 1/4 | 1/5 | 2 | 1/2 |
| $v_{1_9}$ | 2 | 2 | 2 | 1/2 | 1/4 | 1/3 | 2 | 2 | 1 | 1/4 | 1/3 | 1/3 | 1/4 | 1/3 | 1/3 | 3 | 1/2 |
| $v_{1_{10}}$ | 4 | 5 | 6 | 3 | 1/2 | 2 | 4 | 5 | 4 | 1 | 2 | 2 | 1/2 | 2 | 2 | 9 | 3 |
| $v_{1_{11}}$ | 3 | 4 | 6 | 2 | 1/2 | 2 | 4 | 5 | 3 | 1/2 | 1 | 2 | 1/2 | 2 | 1/2 | 8 | 3 |
| $v_{1_{12}}$ | 3 | 4 | 5 | 2 | 1/2 | 1/2 | 4 | 3 | 4 | 1/2 | 1/2 | 1 | 1/2 | 1/2 | 1/2 | 7 | 3 |
| $v_{1_{13}}$ | 4 | 5 | 6 | 3 | 2 | 2 | 4 | 5 | 4 | 2 | 2 | 2 | 1 | 2 | 2 | 9 | 3 |
| $v_{1_{14}}$ | 3 | 4 | 5 | 2 | 1/2 | 1/2 | 3 | 4 | 3 | 1/2 | 1/2 | 2 | 1/2 | 1 | 1/2 | 7 | 3 |
| $v_{1_{15}}$ | 4 | 4 | 6 | 3 | 1/2 | 2 | 4 | 5 | 3 | 1/2 | 2 | 2 | 1/2 | 2 | 1 | 9 | 3 |
| $v_{1_{16}}$ | 1/3 | 1/3 | 1/2 | 1/4 | 1/9 | 1/8 | 1/3 | 1/2 | 1/3 | 1/9 | 1/8 | 1/7 | 1/9 | 1/7 | 1/9 | 1 | 1/4 |
| $v_{1_{17}}$ | 2 | 2 | 3 | 1/2 | 1/3 | 1/3 | 2 | 2 | 2 | 1/3 | 1/3 | 1/3 | 1/3 | 1/3 | 1/3 | 4 | 1 |

Note: Consistency Ratio = 0.0266 < 0.1.

Table A2. Country risk model. Fuzzy pairwise comparison matrix of variables $v_{1_i}$ with respect to $f_1$ (part 1).

| $f_1$ | $v_{1_1}$ | $v_{1_2}$ | $v_{1_3}$ | $v_{1_4}$ | $v_{1_5}$ | $v_{1_6}$ | $v_{1_7}$ | $v_{1_8}$ | $v_{1_9}$ |
|---|---|---|---|---|---|---|---|---|---|
| $v_{1_1}$ | (1, 1, 1) | (1, 2, 3) | (1, 2, 3) | (1/3, 1/2, 1) | (1/5, 1/4, 1/3) | (1/4, 1/3, 1/2) | (1, 2, 3) | (1, 2, 3) | (1/3, 1/2, 1) |
| $v_{1_2}$ | (1/3, 1/2, 1) | (1, 1, 1) | (1, 2, 3) | (1/3, 1/2, 1) | (1/6, 1/5, 1/4) | (1/5, 1/4, 1/3) | (1/3, 1/2, 1) | (1, 2, 3) | (1/3, 1/2, 1) |
| $v_{1_3}$ | (1/3, 1/2, 1) | (1/3, 1/2, 1) | (1, 1, 1) | (1/4, 1/3, 1/2) | (1/7, 1/6, 1/5) | (1/7, 1/6, 1/5) | (1/3, 1/2, 1) | (1/3, 1/2, 1) | (1/3, 1/2, 1) |
| $v_{1_4}$ | (1, 2, 3) | (1, 2, 3) | (2, 3, 4) | (1, 1, 1) | (1/4, 1/3, 1/2) | (1/3, 1/2, 1) | (1, 2, 3) | (2, 3, 4) | (1, 2, 3) |
| $v_{1_5}$ | (3, 4, 5) | (4, 5, 6) | (5, 6, 7) | (2, 3, 4) | (1, 1, 1) | (1, 2, 3) | (3, 4, 5) | (4, 5, 6) | (3, 4, 5) |
| $v_{1_6}$ | (2, 3, 4) | (3, 4, 5) | (5, 6, 7) | (1, 2, 3) | (1/3, 1/2, 1) | (1, 1, 1) | (3, 4, 5) | (3, 4, 5) | (2, 3, 4) |
| $v_{1_7}$ | (1/3, 1/2, 1) | (1, 2, 3) | (1, 2, 3) | (1/3, 1/2, 1) | (1/5, 1/4, 1/3) | (1/5, 1/4, 1/3) | (1, 1, 1) | (1, 2, 3) | (1/3, 1/2, 1) |
| $v_{1_8}$ | (1/3, 1/2, 1) | (1/3, 1/2, 1) | (1, 2, 3) | (1/4, 1/3, 1/2) | (1/6, 1/5, 1/4) | (1/5, 1/4, 1/3) | (1/3, 1/2, 1) | (1, 1, 1) | (1/3, 1/2, 1) |
| $v_{1_9}$ | (1, 2, 3) | (1, 2, 3) | (1, 2, 3) | (1/3, 1/2, 1) | (1/5, 1/4, 1/3) | (1/4, 1/3, 1/2) | (1, 2, 3) | (1, 2, 3) | (1, 1, 1) |
| $v_{1_{10}}$ | (3, 4, 5) | (4, 5, 6) | (5, 6, 7) | (2, 3, 4) | (1/3, 1/2, 1) | (1, 2, 3) | (3, 4, 5) | (4, 5, 6) | (3, 4, 5) |
| $v_{1_{11}}$ | (2, 3, 4) | (3, 4, 5) | (5, 6, 7) | (1, 2, 3) | (1/3, 1/2, 1) | (1, 2, 3) | (3, 4, 5) | (4, 5, 6) | (2, 3, 4) |
| $v_{1_{12}}$ | (2, 3, 4) | (3, 4, 5) | (4, 5, 6) | (1, 2, 3) | (1/3, 1/2, 1) | (1/3, 1/2, 1) | (2, 3, 4) | (3, 4, 5) | (2, 3, 4) |
| $v_{1_{13}}$ | (3, 4, 5) | (4, 5, 6) | (5, 6, 7) | (2, 3, 4) | (1, 2, 3) | (1, 2, 3) | (3, 4, 5) | (4, 5, 6) | (3, 4, 5) |
| $v_{1_{14}}$ | (2, 3, 4) | (3, 4, 5) | (4, 5, 6) | (1, 2, 3) | (1/3, 1/2, 1) | (1/3, 1/2, 1) | (2, 3, 4) | (3, 4, 5) | (2, 3, 4) |
| $v_{1_{15}}$ | (3, 4, 5) | (3, 4, 5) | (5, 6, 7) | (2, 3, 4) | (1/3, 1/2, 1) | (1, 2, 3) | (3, 4, 5) | (4, 5, 6) | (2, 3, 4) |
| $v_{1_{16}}$ | (1/4, 1/3, 1/2) | (1/4, 1/3, 1/2) | (1/3, 1/2, 1) | (1/5, 1/4, 1/3) | (1/9, 1/9, 1/9) | (1/9, 1/8, 1/7) | (1/4, 1/3, 1/2) | (1/3, 1/2, 1) | (1/4, 1/3, 1/2) |
| $v_{1_{17}}$ | (1, 2, 3) | (1, 2, 3) | (2, 3, 4) | (1/3, 1/2, 1) | (1/4, 1/3, 1/2) | (1/4, 1/3, 1/2) | (1, 2, 3) | (1, 2, 3) | (1, 2, 3) |

Table A3. Country risk model. Fuzzy pairwise comparison matrix of variables $v_{1_i}$ with respect to $f_1$ (part 2).

| $f_1$ | $v_{1_{10}}$ | $v_{1_{11}}$ | $v_{1_{12}}$ | $v_{1_{13}}$ | $v_{1_{14}}$ | $v_{1_{15}}$ | $v_{1_{16}}$ | $v_{1_{17}}$ | Σ | $w_{\bar{v}_1}$ |
|---|---|---|---|---|---|---|---|---|---|---|
| $v_{1_1}$ | (1/5, 1/4, 1/3) | (1/4, 1/3, 1/2) | (1/4, 1/3, 1/2) | (1/5, 1/4, 1/3) | (1/4, 1/3, 1/2) | (1/4, 1/3, 1/2) | (2, 3, 4) | (1/3, 1/2, 1) | (9.8, 15.8333, 23.3333) | 0.0002 |
| $v_{1_2}$ | (1/6, 1/5, 1/4) | (1/5, 1/4, 1/3) | (1/5, 1/4, 1/3) | (1/6, 1/5, 1/4) | (1/5, 1/4, 1/3) | (1/5, 1/4, 1/3) | (2, 3, 4) | (1/3, 1/2, 1) | (8.1667, 12.35, 18.4167) | 0.0000 |
| $v_{1_3}$ | (1/7, 1/6, 1/5) | (1/7, 1/6, 1/5) | (1/6, 1/5, 1/4) | (1/7, 1/6, 1/5) | (1/6, 1/5, 1/4) | (1/7, 1/6, 1/5) | (1, 2, 3) | (1/4, 1/3, 1/2) | (5.3571, 7.5667, 11.7) | 0.0000 |
| $v_{1_4}$ | (1/4, 1/3, 1/2) | (1/3, 1/2, 1) | (1/3, 1/2, 1) | (1/4, 1/3, 1/2) | (1/3, 1/2, 1) | (1/4, 1/3, 1/2) | (3, 4, 5) | (1, 2, 3) | (15.3333, 24.3333, 35) | 0.0441 |
| $v_{1_5}$ | (1, 2, 3) | (1, 2, 3) | (1, 2, 3) | (1/3, 1/2, 1) | (1, 2, 3) | (1, 2, 3) | (9, 9, 9) | (2, 3, 4) | (42.3333, 56.5, 71) | 0.1321 |
| $v_{1_6}$ | (1/3, 1/2, 1) | (1/3, 1/2, 1) | (1, 2, 3) | (1/3, 1/2, 1) | (1, 2, 3) | (1/3, 1/2, 1) | (7, 8, 9) | (2, 3, 4) | (32.6667, 44.5, 58) | 0.1056 |
| $v_{1_7}$ | (1/5, 1/4, 1/3) | (1/5, 1/4, 1/3) | (1/4, 1/3, 1/2) | (1/5, 1/4, 1/3) | (1/4, 1/3, 1/2) | (1/5, 1/4, 1/3) | (2, 3, 4) | (1/3, 1/2, 1) | (9.0333, 14.1667, 21) | 0.0000 |
| $v_{1_8}$ | (1/6, 1/5, 1/4) | (1/6, 1/5, 1/4) | (1/5, 1/4, 1/3) | (1/6, 1/5, 1/4) | (1/5, 1/4, 1/3) | (1/6, 1/5, 1/4) | (1, 2, 3) | (1/3, 1/2, 1) | (6.35, 9.5833, 14.75) | 0.0000 |
| $v_{1_9}$ | (1/5, 1/4, 1/3) | (1/4, 1/3, 1/2) | (1/4, 1/3, 1/2) | (1/5, 1/4, 1/3) | (1/4, 1/3, 1/2) | (1/4, 1/3, 1/2) | (2, 3, 4) | (1/3, 1/2, 1) | (10.5167, 17.4167, 25.5) | 0.0096 |
| $v_{1_{10}}$ | (1, 1, 1) | (1, 2, 3) | (1, 2, 3) | (1/3, 1/2, 1) | (1, 2, 3) | (1, 2, 3) | (9, 9, 9) | (2, 3, 4) | (41.6667, 55, 69) | 0.1290 |
| $v_{1_{11}}$ | (1/3, 1/2, 1) | (1, 1, 1) | (1, 2, 3) | (1/3, 1/2, 1) | (1, 2, 3) | (1/3, 1/2, 1) | (7, 8, 9) | (2, 3, 4) | (34.3333, 47, 61) | 0.1117 |
| $v_{1_{12}}$ | (1/3, 1/2, 1) | (1/3, 1/2, 1) | (1, 1, 1) | (1/3, 1/2, 1) | (1/3, 1/2, 1) | (1/3, 1/2, 1) | (6, 7, 8) | (2, 3, 4) | (28.3333, 38.5, 51) | 0.0897 |
| $v_{1_{13}}$ | (1, 2, 3) | (1, 2, 3) | (1, 2, 3) | (1, 1, 1) | (1, 2, 3) | (1, 2, 3) | (9, 9, 9) | (2, 3, 4) | (43, 58, 73) | 0.1351 |
| $v_{1_{14}}$ | (1/3, 1/2, 1) | (1/3, 1/2, 1) | (1, 2, 3) | (1/3, 1/2, 1) | (1, 1, 1) | (1/3, 1/2, 1) | (6, 7, 8) | (2, 3, 4) | (29, 40, 53) | 0.0941 |
| $v_{1_{15}}$ | (1/3, 1/2, 1) | (1, 2, 3) | (1, 2, 3) | (1/3, 1/2, 1) | (1, 2, 3) | (1, 1, 1) | (9, 9, 9) | (2, 3, 4) | (39, 51.5, 65) | 0.1215 |
| $v_{1_{16}}$ | (1/9, 1/9, 1/9) | (1/9, 1/8, 1/7) | (1/8, 1/7, 1/6) | (1/9, 1/9, 1/9) | (1/8, 1/7, 1/6) | (1/9, 1/9, 1/9) | (1, 1, 1) | (1/5, 1/4, 1/3) | (3.9833, 4.8135, 6.7302) | 0.0000 |
| $v_{1_{17}}$ | (1/4, 1/3, 1/2) | (1/4, 1/3, 1/2) | (1/4, 1/3, 1/2) | (1/4, 1/3, 1/2) | (1/4, 1/3, 1/2) | (1/4, 1/3, 1/2) | (3, 4, 5) | (1, 1, 1) | (13.3333, 21.1667, 30) | 0.0274 |
| Σ | | | | | | | | | (371.2071, 518.2302, 687.4302) | |

Table A4. Country risk model. Linguistic pairwise comparison matrix of variables $v_{2_i}$ with respect to $f_2$.

| $f_2$ | $v_{2_1}$ | $v_{2_2}$ | $v_{2_3}$ | $v_{2_4}$ | $v_{2_5}$ | $v_{2_6}$ | $v_{2_7}$ | $v_{2_8}$ | $v_{2_9}$ | $v_{2_{10}}$ | $v_{2_{11}}$ | $v_{2_{12}}$ | $v_{2_{13}}$ | $v_{2_{14}}$ | $v_{2_{15}}$ | $v_{2_{16}}$ | $v_{2_{17}}$ |
|---|---|---|---|---|---|---|---|---|---|---|---|---|---|---|---|---|---|
| $v_{2_1}$ | 1 | 1/2 | 1/2 | 4 | 3 | 3 | 5 | 2 | 1/2 | 7 | 5 | 6 | 7 | 3 | 5 | 8 | 4 |
| $v_{2_2}$ | 2 | 1 | 1/2 | 4 | 4 | 4 | 6 | 2 | 2 | 8 | 5 | 7 | 8 | 3 | 6 | 9 | 4 |
| $v_{2_3}$ | 2 | 2 | 1 | 4 | 4 | 4 | 6 | 2 | 2 | 9 | 5 | 7 | 8 | 3 | 6 | 9 | 4 |
| $v_{2_4}$ | 1/4 | 1/4 | 1/4 | 1 | 1/2 | 1/2 | 2 | 1/3 | 1/4 | 3 | 2 | 2 | 2 | 1/2 | 2 | 3 | 1/2 |
| $v_{2_5}$ | 1/3 | 1/4 | 1/4 | 2 | 1 | 1/2 | 2 | 1/3 | 1/4 | 3 | 2 | 2 | 3 | 1/2 | 2 | 3 | 2 |
| $v_{2_6}$ | 1/3 | 1/4 | 1/4 | 2 | 2 | 1 | 2 | 1/3 | 1/4 | 3 | 2 | 3 | 3 | 1/2 | 2 | 3 | 2 |
| $v_{2_7}$ | 1/5 | 1/6 | 1/6 | 1/2 | 1/2 | 1/2 | 1 | 1/4 | 1/6 | 2 | 1/2 | 2 | 2 | 1/3 | 1/2 | 2 | 1/2 |
| $v_{2_8}$ | 1/2 | 1/2 | 1/2 | 3 | 3 | 3 | 4 | 1 | 1/2 | 6 | 4 | 5 | 6 | 2 | 4 | 7 | 3 |
| $v_{2_9}$ | 2 | 1/2 | 1/2 | 4 | 4 | 4 | 6 | 2 | 1 | 8 | 5 | 7 | 7 | 3 | 5 | 9 | 4 |
| $v_{2_{10}}$ | 1/7 | 1/8 | 1/9 | 1/3 | 1/3 | 1/3 | 1/2 | 1/6 | 1/8 | 1 | 1/2 | 1/2 | 1/2 | 1/4 | 1/2 | 2 | 1/3 |
| $v_{2_{11}}$ | 1/5 | 1/5 | 1/5 | 1/2 | 1/2 | 1/2 | 2 | 1/4 | 1/5 | 2 | 1 | 2 | 2 | 1/2 | 2 | 2 | 1/2 |
| $v_{2_{12}}$ | 1/6 | 1/7 | 1/7 | 1/2 | 1/2 | 1/3 | 1/2 | 1/5 | 1/7 | 2 | 1/2 | 1 | 2 | 1/3 | 1/2 | 2 | 1/2 |
| $v_{2_{13}}$ | 1/7 | 1/8 | 1/8 | 1/2 | 1/3 | 1/3 | 1/2 | 1/6 | 1/7 | 2 | 1/2 | 1/2 | 1 | 1/3 | 1/2 | 2 | 1/2 |
| $v_{2_{14}}$ | 1/3 | 1/3 | 1/3 | 2 | 2 | 2 | 3 | 1/2 | 1/3 | 4 | 2 | 3 | 3 | 1 | 2 | 4 | 2 |
| $v_{2_{15}}$ | 1/5 | 1/6 | 1/6 | 1/2 | 1/2 | 1/2 | 2 | 1/4 | 1/5 | 2 | 1/2 | 2 | 2 | 1/2 | 1 | 2 | 1/2 |
| $v_{2_{16}}$ | 1/8 | 1/9 | 1/9 | 1/3 | 1/3 | 1/3 | 1/2 | 1/7 | 1/9 | 1/2 | 1/2 | 1/2 | 1/2 | 1/4 | 1/2 | 1 | 1/3 |
| $v_{2_{17}}$ | 1/4 | 1/4 | 1/4 | 2 | 1/2 | 1/2 | 2 | 1/3 | 1/4 | 3 | 2 | 2 | 2 | 1/2 | 2 | 3 | 1 |

Note: Consistency Ratio = 0.0239 < 0.1.

Table A5. Country risk model. Fuzzy pairwise comparison matrix of variables $v_{2_i}$ with respect to $f_2$ (part 1).

| $f_2$ | $v_{2_1}$ | $v_{2_2}$ | $v_{2_3}$ | $v_{2_4}$ | $v_{2_5}$ | $v_{2_6}$ | $v_{2_7}$ | $v_{2_8}$ | $v_{2_9}$ |
|---|---|---|---|---|---|---|---|---|---|
| $v_{2_1}$ | (1, 1, 1) | (1/3, 1/2, 1) | (1/3, 1/2, 1) | (3, 4, 5) | (2, 3, 4) | (2, 3, 4) | (4, 5, 6) | (1, 2, 3) | (1/3, 1/2, 1) |
| $v_{2_2}$ | (1, 2, 3) | (1, 1, 1) | (1/3, 1/2, 1) | (3, 4, 5) | (3, 4, 5) | (3, 4, 5) | (5, 6, 7) | (1, 2, 3) | (1, 2, 3) |
| $v_{2_3}$ | (1, 2, 3) | (1, 2, 3) | (1, 1, 1) | (3, 4, 5) | (3, 4, 5) | (3, 4, 5) | (5, 6, 7) | (1, 2, 3) | (1, 2, 3) |
| $v_{2_4}$ | (1/5, 1/4, 1/3) | (1/5, 1/4, 1/3) | (1/5, 1/4, 1/3) | (1, 1, 1) | (1/3, 1/2, 1) | (1/3, 1/2, 1) | (1, 2, 3) | (1/4, 1/3, 1/2) | (1/5, 1/4, 1/3) |
| $v_{2_5}$ | (1/4, 1/3, 1/2) | (1/5, 1/4, 1/3) | (1/5, 1/4, 1/3) | (1, 2, 3) | (1, 1, 1) | (1/3, 1/2, 1) | (1, 2, 3) | (1/4, 1/3, 1/2) | (1/5, 1/4, 1/3) |
| $v_{2_6}$ | (1/4, 1/3, 1/2) | (1/5, 1/4, 1/3) | (1/5, 1/4, 1/3) | (1, 2, 3) | (1, 2, 3) | (1, 1, 1) | (1, 2, 3) | (1/4, 1/3, 1/2) | (1/5, 1/4, 1/3) |
| $v_{2_7}$ | (1/6, 1/5, 1/4) | (1/7, 1/6, 1/5) | (1/7, 1/6, 1/5) | (1/3, 1/2, 1) | (1/3, 1/2, 1) | (1/3, 1/2, 1) | (1, 1, 1) | (1/5, 1/4, 1/3) | (1/7, 1/6, 1/5) |
| $v_{2_8}$ | (1/3, 1/2, 1) | (1/3, 1/2, 1) | (1/3, 1/2, 1) | (2, 3, 4) | (2, 3, 4) | (2, 3, 4) | (3, 4, 5) | (1, 1, 1) | (1/3, 1/2, 1) |
| $v_{2_9}$ | (1, 2, 3) | (1/3, 1/2, 1) | (1/3, 1/2, 1) | (3, 4, 5) | (3, 4, 5) | (3, 4, 5) | (5, 6, 7) | (1, 2, 3) | (1, 1, 1) |
| $v_{2_{10}}$ | (1/8, 1/7, 1/6) | (1/9, 1/8, 1/7) | (1/9, 1/9, 1/9) | (1/4, 1/3, 1/2) | (1/4, 1/3, 1/2) | (1/4, 1/3, 1/2) | (1/3, 1/2, 1) | (1/7, 1/6, 1/5) | (1/9, 1/8, 1/7) |
| $v_{2_{11}}$ | (1/6, 1/5, 1/4) | (1/6, 1/5, 1/4) | (1/6, 1/5, 1/4) | (1/3, 1/2, 1) | (1/3, 1/2, 1) | (1/3, 1/2, 1) | (1, 2, 3) | (1/5, 1/4, 1/3) | (1/6, 1/5, 1/4) |
| $v_{2_{12}}$ | (1/7, 1/6, 1/5) | (1/8, 1/7, 1/6) | (1/8, 1/7, 1/6) | (1/3, 1/2, 1) | (1/3, 1/2, 1) | (1/4, 1/3, 1/2) | (1/3, 1/2, 1) | (1/6, 1/5, 1/4) | (1/8, 1/7, 1/6) |
| $v_{2_{13}}$ | (1/8, 1/7, 1/6) | (1/9, 1/8, 1/7) | (1/9, 1/8, 1/7) | (1/3, 1/2, 1) | (1/4, 1/3, 1/2) | (1/4, 1/3, 1/2) | (1/3, 1/2, 1) | (1/7, 1/6, 1/5) | (1/8, 1/7, 1/6) |
| $v_{2_{14}}$ | (1/4, 1/3, 1/2) | (1/4, 1/3, 1/2) | (1/4, 1/3, 1/2) | (1, 2, 3) | (1, 2, 3) | (1, 2, 3) | (2, 3, 4) | (1/3, 1/2, 1) | (1/4, 1/3, 1/2) |
| $v_{2_{15}}$ | (1/6, 1/5, 1/4) | (1/7, 1/6, 1/5) | (1/7, 1/6, 1/5) | (1/3, 1/2, 1) | (1/3, 1/2, 1) | (1/3, 1/2, 1) | (1, 2, 3) | (1/5, 1/4, 1/3) | (1/6, 1/5, 1/4) |
| $v_{2_{16}}$ | (1/9, 1/8, 1/7) | (1/9, 1/9, 1/9) | (1/9, 1/9, 1/9) | (1/4, 1/3, 1/2) | (1/4, 1/3, 1/2) | (1/4, 1/3, 1/2) | (1/3, 1/2, 1) | (1/8, 1/7, 1/6) | (1/9, 1/9, 1/9) |
| $v_{2_{17}}$ | (1/5, 1/4, 1/3) | (1/5, 1/4, 1/3) | (1/5, 1/4, 1/3) | (1, 2, 3) | (1/3, 1/2, 1) | (1/3, 1/2, 1) | (1, 2, 3) | (1/4, 1/3, 1/2) | (1/5, 1/4, 1/3) |

Table A6. Country risk model. Fuzzy pairwise comparison matrix of variables $v_{2_i}$ with respect to $f_2$ (part 2).

| $f_2$ | $v_{2_{10}}$ | $v_{2_{11}}$ | $v_{2_{12}}$ | $v_{2_{13}}$ | $v_{2_{14}}$ | $v_{2_{15}}$ | $v_{2_{16}}$ | $v_{2_{17}}$ | Σ | $w_{\tilde{v}_2}$ |
|---|---|---|---|---|---|---|---|---|---|---|
| $v_{2_1}$ | (6, 7, 8) | (4, 5, 6) | (5, 6, 7) | (6, 7, 8) | (2, 3, 4) | (4, 5, 6) | (7, 8, 9) | (3, 4, 5) | (51, 64.5, 79) | 0.1778 |
| $v_{2_2}$ | (7, 8, 9) | (4, 5, 6) | (6, 7, 8) | (7, 8, 9) | (2, 3, 4) | (5, 6, 7) | (9, 9, 9) | (3, 4, 5) | (61.3333, 75.5, 90) | 0.2115 |
| $v_{2_3}$ | (9, 9, 9) | (4, 5, 6) | (6, 7, 8) | (7, 8, 9) | (2, 3, 4) | (5, 6, 7) | (9, 9, 9) | (3, 4, 5) | (64, 78, 92) | 0.2187 |
| $v_{2_4}$ | (2, 3, 4) | (1, 2, 3) | (1, 2, 3) | (1, 2, 3) | (1/3, 1/2, 1) | (1, 2, 3) | (2, 3, 4) | (1/3, 1/2, 1) | (12.3833, 20.3333, 29.8333) | 0.0000 |
| $v_{2_5}$ | (2, 3, 4) | (1, 2, 3) | (1, 2, 3) | (2, 3, 4) | (1/3, 1/2, 1) | (1, 2, 3) | (2, 3, 4) | (1, 2, 3) | (14.7667, 24.4167, 35) | 0.0000 |
| $v_{2_6}$ | (2, 3, 4) | (1, 2, 3) | (2, 3, 4) | (2, 3, 4) | (1/3, 1/2, 1) | (1, 2, 3) | (2, 3, 4) | (1, 2, 3) | (16.4333, 26.9167, 38) | 0.0115 |
| $v_{2_7}$ | (1, 2, 3) | (1/3, 1/2, 1) | (1, 2, 3) | (1, 2, 3) | (1/4, 1/3, 1/2) | (1/3, 1/2, 1) | (1, 2, 3) | (1/3, 1/2, 1) | (8.0452, 13.2833, 20.6833) | 0.0000 |
| $v_{2_8}$ | (5, 6, 7) | (3, 4, 5) | (4, 5, 6) | (5, 6, 7) | (1, 2, 3) | (3, 4, 5) | (6, 7, 8) | (2, 3, 4) | (40.3333, 53, 67) | 0.1375 |
| $v_{2_9}$ | (7, 8, 9) | (4, 5, 6) | (6, 7, 8) | (6, 7, 8) | (2, 3, 4) | (4, 5, 6) | (9, 9, 9) | (3, 4, 5) | (58.6667, 72, 86) | 0.2010 |
| $v_{2_{10}}$ | (1, 1, 1) | (1/3, 1/2, 1) | (1/3, 1/2, 1) | (1/3, 1/2, 1) | (1/5, 1/4, 1/3) | (1/3, 1/2, 1) | (1, 2, 3) | (1/4, 1/3, 1/2) | (5.4679, 7.754, 12.0968) | 0.0000 |
| $v_{2_{11}}$ | (1, 2, 3) | (1, 1, 1) | (1, 2, 3) | (1, 2, 3) | (1/3, 1/2, 1) | (1, 2, 3) | (1, 2, 3) | (1/3, 1/2, 1) | (9.5333, 16.55, 25.3333) | 0.0000 |
| $v_{2_{12}}$ | (1, 2, 3) | (1/3, 1/2, 1) | (1, 1, 1) | (1, 2, 3) | (1/4, 1/3, 1/2) | (1/3, 1/2, 1) | (1, 2, 3) | (1/3, 1/2, 1) | (7.1845, 11.4619, 17.95) | 0.0000 |
| $v_{2_{13}}$ | (1, 2, 3) | (1/3, 1/2, 1) | (1/3, 1/2, 1) | (1, 1, 1) | (1/4, 1/3, 1/2) | (1/3, 1/2, 1) | (1, 2, 3) | (1/3, 1/2, 1) | (6.3651, 9.7024, 15.319) | 0.0000 |
| $v_{2_{14}}$ | (3, 4, 5) | (1, 2, 3) | (2, 3, 4) | (2, 3, 4) | (1, 1, 1) | (1, 2, 3) | (3, 4, 5) | (1, 2, 3) | (20.3333, 31.8333, 44) | 0.0421 |
| $v_{2_{15}}$ | (1, 2, 3) | (1/3, 1/2, 1) | (1, 2, 3) | (1, 2, 3) | (1/3, 1/2, 1) | (1, 1, 1) | (1, 2, 3) | (1/3, 1/2, 1) | (8.819, 14.9833, 23.2333) | 0.0000 |
| $v_{2_{16}}$ | (1/3, 1/2, 1) | (1/3, 1/2, 1) | (1/3, 1/2, 1) | (1/3, 1/2, 1) | (1/5, 1/4, 1/3) | (1/3, 1/2, 1) | (1, 1, 1) | (1/4, 1/3, 1/2) | (4.7694, 6.1845, 9.9762) | 0.0000 |
| $v_{2_{17}}$ | (2, 3, 4) | (1, 2, 3) | (1, 2, 3) | (1, 2, 3) | (1/3, 1/2, 1) | (1, 2, 3) | (2, 3, 4) | (1, 1, 1) | (13.05, 21.8333, 31.8333) | 0.0000 |
| Σ | | | | | | | | | (402.4845, 548.2528, 717.2587) | |

Table A7. Country risk model. Linguistic pairwise comparison matrix of variables $v_{3_i}$ with respect to $f_3$.

| $f_3$ | $v_{3_1}$ | $v_{3_2}$ | $v_{3_3}$ | $v_{3_4}$ | $v_{3_5}$ | $v_{3_6}$ | $v_{3_7}$ | $v_{3_8}$ | $v_{3_9}$ | $v_{3_{10}}$ | $v_{3_{11}}$ | $v_{3_{12}}$ | $v_{3_{13}}$ | $v_{3_{14}}$ | $v_{3_{15}}$ | $v_{3_{16}}$ | $v_{3_{17}}$ |
|---|---|---|---|---|---|---|---|---|---|---|---|---|---|---|---|---|---|
| $v_{3_1}$ | 1 | 1/2 | 1/2 | 1/4 | 2 | 1/2 | 1/6 | 1/3 | 1/2 | 1/2 | 1/2 | 1/2 | 2 | 1/2 | 2 | 1/7 | 1/4 |
| $v_{3_2}$ | 2 | 1 | 2 | 1/4 | 2 | 1/2 | 1/5 | 1/2 | 2 | 2 | 2 | 2 | 2 | 1/2 | 2 | 1/6 | 1/4 |
| $v_{3_3}$ | 2 | 1/2 | 1 | 1/4 | 2 | 1/2 | 1/5 | 1/2 | 2 | 1/2 | 1/2 | 2 | 2 | 1/2 | 2 | 1/7 | 1/4 |
| $v_{3_4}$ | 4 | 4 | 4 | 1 | 5 | 3 | 1/2 | 2 | 4 | 4 | 4 | 4 | 5 | 4 | 6 | 1/2 | 2 |
| $v_{3_5}$ | 1/2 | 1/2 | 1/2 | 1/5 | 1 | 1/2 | 1/6 | 1/3 | 1/2 | 1/2 | 1/2 | 1/2 | 2 | 1/2 | 2 | 1/8 | 1/4 |
| $v_{3_6}$ | 2 | 2 | 2 | 1/3 | 2 | 1 | 1/4 | 1/2 | 2 | 2 | 2 | 2 | 2 | 2 | 2 | 1/6 | 1/3 |
| $v_{3_7}$ | 6 | 5 | 5 | 2 | 6 | 4 | 1 | 3 | 6 | 5 | 5 | 5 | 6 | 5 | 7 | 1/2 | 2 |
| $v_{3_8}$ | 3 | 2 | 2 | 1/2 | 3 | 2 | 1/3 | 1 | 3 | 2 | 2 | 3 | 3 | 2 | 3 | 1/4 | 1/2 |
| $v_{3_9}$ | 2 | 1/2 | 1/2 | 1/4 | 2 | 1/2 | 1/6 | 1/3 | 1 | 1/2 | 1/2 | 1/2 | 2 | 1/2 | 2 | 1/7 | 1/4 |
| $v_{3_{10}}$ | 2 | 1/2 | 2 | 1/4 | 2 | 1/2 | 1/5 | 1/2 | 2 | 1 | 1/2 | 2 | 2 | 1/2 | 2 | 1/7 | 1/4 |
| $v_{3_{11}}$ | 2 | 1/2 | 2 | 1/4 | 2 | 1/2 | 1/5 | 1/2 | 2 | 2 | 1 | 2 | 2 | 1/2 | 2 | 1/6 | 1/4 |
| $v_{3_{12}}$ | 2 | 1/2 | 1/2 | 1/4 | 2 | 1/2 | 1/5 | 1/3 | 2 | 1/2 | 1/2 | 1 | 2 | 1/2 | 2 | 1/7 | 1/4 |
| $v_{3_{13}}$ | 1/2 | 1/2 | 1/2 | 1/5 | 1/2 | 1/2 | 1/6 | 1/3 | 1/2 | 1/2 | 1/2 | 1/2 | 1 | 1/2 | 2 | 1/8 | 1/5 |
| $v_{3_{14}}$ | 2 | 2 | 2 | 1/4 | 2 | 1/2 | 1/5 | 1/2 | 2 | 2 | 2 | 2 | 2 | 1 | 2 | 1/6 | 1/4 |
| $v_{3_{15}}$ | 1/2 | 1/2 | 1/2 | 1/6 | 1/2 | 1/2 | 1/7 | 1/3 | 1/2 | 1/2 | 1/2 | 1/2 | 1/2 | 1/2 | 1 | 1/9 | 1/5 |
| $v_{3_{16}}$ | 7 | 6 | 7 | 2 | 8 | 6 | 2 | 4 | 7 | 7 | 6 | 7 | 8 | 6 | 9 | 1 | 2 |
| $v_{3_{17}}$ | 4 | 4 | 4 | 1/2 | 4 | 3 | 1/2 | 2 | 4 | 4 | 4 | 4 | 5 | 4 | 5 | 1/2 | 1 |

Note: Consistency ratio = 0.0239 < 0.1.

**Table A8.** Country risk model. Fuzzy pairwise comparison matrix of variables $v_{3_i}$ with respect to $f_3$ (part 1).

| $f_3$ | $v_{3_1}$ | $v_{3_2}$ | $v_{3_3}$ | $v_{3_4}$ | $v_{3_5}$ | $v_{3_6}$ | $v_{3_7}$ | $v_{3_8}$ | $v_{3_9}$ |
|---|---|---|---|---|---|---|---|---|---|
| $v_{3_1}$ | (1, 1, 1) | (1/3, 1/2, 1) | (1/3, 1/2, 1) | (1/5, 1/4, 1/3) | (1, 2, 3) | (1/3, 1/2, 1) | (1/7, 1/6, 1/5) | (1/4, 1/3, 1/2) | (1/3, 1/2, 1) |
| $v_{3_2}$ | (1, 2, 3) | (1, 1, 1) | (1, 2, 3) | (1/5, 1/4, 1/3) | (1, 2, 3) | (1/3, 1/2, 1) | (1/6, 1/5, 1/4) | (1/3, 1/2, 1) | (1, 2, 3) |
| $v_{3_3}$ | (1, 2, 3) | (1/3, 1/2, 1) | (1, 1, 1) | (1/5, 1/4, 1/3) | (1, 2, 3) | (1/3, 1/2, 1) | (1/6, 1/5, 1/4) | (1/3, 1/2, 1) | (1, 2, 3) |
| $v_{3_4}$ | (3, 4, 5) | (3, 4, 5) | (3, 4, 5) | (1, 1, 1) | (4, 5, 6) | (2, 3, 4) | (1/3, 1/2, 1) | (1, 2, 3) | (3, 4, 5) |
| $v_{3_5}$ | (1/3, 1/2, 1) | (1/3, 1/2, 1) | (1/3, 1/2, 1) | (1/6, 1/5, 1/4) | (1, 1, 1) | (1/3, 1/2, 1) | (1/7, 1/6, 1/5) | (1/4, 1/3, 1/2) | (1/3, 1/2, 1) |
| $v_{3_6}$ | (1, 2, 3) | (1, 2, 3) | (1, 2, 3) | (1/4, 1/3, 1/2) | (1, 2, 3) | (1, 1, 1) | (1/5, 1/4, 1/3) | (1/3, 1/2, 1) | (1, 2, 3) |
| $v_{3_7}$ | (5, 6, 7) | (4, 5, 6) | (4, 5, 6) | (1, 2, 3) | (5, 6, 7) | (3, 4, 5) | (1, 1, 1) | (2, 3, 4) | (5, 6, 7) |
| $v_{3_8}$ | (2, 3, 4) | (1, 2, 3) | (1, 2, 3) | (1/3, 1/2, 1) | (2, 3, 4) | (1, 2, 3) | (1/4, 1/3, 1/2) | (1, 1, 1) | (2, 3, 4) |
| $v_{3_9}$ | (1, 2, 3) | (1/3, 1/2, 1) | (1/3, 1/2, 1) | (1/5, 1/4, 1/3) | (1, 2, 3) | (1/3, 1/2, 1) | (1/7, 1/6, 1/5) | (1/4, 1/3, 1/2) | (1, 1, 1) |
| $v_{3_{10}}$ | (1, 2, 3) | (1/3, 1/2, 1) | (1, 2, 3) | (1/5, 1/4, 1/3) | (1, 2, 3) | (1/3, 1/2, 1) | (1/6, 1/5, 1/4) | (1/3, 1/2, 1) | (1, 2, 3) |
| $v_{3_{11}}$ | (1, 2, 3) | (1/3, 1/2, 1) | (1, 2, 3) | (1/5, 1/4, 1/3) | (1, 2, 3) | (1/3, 1/2, 1) | (1/6, 1/5, 1/4) | (1/3, 1/2, 1) | (1, 2, 3) |
| $v_{3_{12}}$ | (1, 2, 3) | (1/3, 1/2, 1) | (1/3, 1/2, 1) | (1/5, 1/4, 1/3) | (1, 2, 3) | (1/3, 1/2, 1) | (1/6, 1/5, 1/4) | (1/4, 1/3, 1/2) | (1, 2, 3) |
| $v_{3_{13}}$ | (1/3, 1/2, 1) | (1/3, 1/2, 1) | (1/3, 1/2, 1) | (1/6, 1/5, 1/4) | (1/3, 1/2, 1) | (1/3, 1/2, 1) | (1/7, 1/6, 1/5) | (1/4, 1/3, 1/2) | (1/3, 1/2, 1) |
| $v_{3_{14}}$ | (1, 2, 3) | (1, 2, 3) | (1, 2, 3) | (1/5, 1/4, 1/3) | (1, 2, 3) | (1/3, 1/2, 1) | (1/6, 1/5, 1/4) | (1/3, 1/2, 1) | (1, 2, 3) |
| $v_{3_{15}}$ | (1/3, 1/2, 1) | (1/3, 1/2, 1) | (1/3, 1/2, 1) | (1/7, 1/6, 1/5) | (1/3, 1/2, 1) | (1/3, 1/2, 1) | (1/8, 1/7, 1/6) | (1/4, 1/3, 1/2) | (1/3, 1/2, 1) |
| $v_{3_{16}}$ | (6, 7, 8) | (5, 6, 7) | (6, 7, 8) | (1, 2, 3) | (7, 8, 9) | (5, 6, 7) | (1, 2, 3) | (3, 4, 5) | (6, 7, 8) |
| $v_{3_{17}}$ | (3, 4, 5) | (3, 4, 5) | (3, 4, 5) | (1/3, 1/2, 1) | (3, 4, 5) | (2, 3, 4) | (1/3, 1/2, 1) | (1, 2, 3) | (3, 4, 5) |

**Table A9.** Country risk model. Fuzzy pairwise comparison matrix of variables $v_{2_i}$ with respect to $f_3$ (part 2).

| $f_3$ | $v_{3_{10}}$ | $v_{3_{11}}$ | $v_{3_{12}}$ | $v_{3_{13}}$ | $v_{3_{14}}$ | $v_{3_{15}}$ | $v_{3_{16}}$ | $v_{3_{17}}$ | Σ | $W \sim V_3$ |
|---|---|---|---|---|---|---|---|---|---|---|
| $v_{3_1}$ | (1/3, 1/2, 1) | (1/3, 1/2, 1) | (1/3, 1/2, 1) | (1, 2, 3) | (1/3, 1/2, 1) | (1, 2, 3) | (1/8, 1/7, 1/6) | (1/5, 1/4, 1/3) | (7.5845, 12.1429, 19.5333) | 0.0000 |
| $v_{3_2}$ | (1, 2, 3) | (1, 2, 3) | (1, 2, 3) | (1, 2, 3) | (1/3, 1/2, 1) | (1, 2, 3) | (1/7, 1/6, 1/5) | (1/5, 1/4, 1/3) | (11.7095, 21.3667, 32.1167) | 0.0000 |
| $v_{3_3}$ | (1/3, 1/2, 1) | (1/3, 1/2, 1) | (1, 2, 3) | (1, 2, 3) | (1/3, 1/2, 1) | (1, 2, 3) | (1/8, 1/7, 1/6) | (1/5, 1/4, 1/3) | (9.6917, 16.8429, 26.0833) | 0.0000 |
| $v_{3_4}$ | (3, 4, 5) | (3, 4, 5) | (3, 4, 5) | (4, 5, 6) | (3, 4, 5) | (5, 6, 7) | (1/3, 1/2, 1) | (1, 2, 3) | (42.6667, 57, 72) | 0.1867 |
| $v_{3_5}$ | (1/3, 1/2, 1) | (1/3, 1/2, 1) | (1/3, 1/2, 1) | (1, 2, 3) | (1/3, 1/2, 1) | (1, 2, 3) | (1/9, 1/8, 1/7) | (1/5, 1/4, 1/3) | (6.8706, 10.575, 17.4262) | 0.0000 |
| $v_{3_6}$ | (1, 2, 3) | (1, 2, 3) | (1, 2, 3) | (1, 2, 3) | (1, 2, 3) | (1, 2, 3) | (1/7, 1/6, 1/5) | (1/4, 1/3, 1/2) | (13.1762, 24.5833, 36.5333) | 0.0000 |
| $v_{3_7}$ | (4, 5, 6) | (4, 5, 6) | (4, 5, 6) | (5, 6, 7) | (4, 5, 6) | (6, 7, 8) | (1/3, 1/2, 1) | (1, 2, 3) | (58.3333, 73.5, 89) | 0.2651 |
| $v_{3_8}$ | (1, 2, 3) | (1, 2, 3) | (2, 3, 4) | (2, 3, 4) | (1, 2, 3) | (2, 3, 4) | (1/5, 1/4, 1/3) | (1/3, 1/2, 1) | (20.1167, 32.5833, 45.8333) | 0.0325 |
| $v_{3_9}$ | (1/3, 1/2, 1) | (1/3, 1/2, 1) | (1/3, 1/2, 1) | (1, 2, 3) | (1/3, 1/2, 1) | (1, 2, 3) | (1/8, 1/7, 1/6) | (1/5, 1/4, 1/3) | (8.2512, 13.6429, 21.5333) | 0.0000 |
| $v_{3_{10}}$ | (1, 1, 1) | (1/3, 1/2, 1) | (1, 2, 3) | (1, 2, 3) | (1/3, 1/2, 1) | (1, 2, 3) | (1/8, 1/7, 1/6) | (1/5, 1/4, 1/3) | (10.3583, 18.3429, 28.0833) | 0.0000 |
| $v_{3_{11}}$ | (1, 2, 3) | (1, 1, 1) | (1, 2, 3) | (1, 2, 3) | (1/3, 1/2, 1) | (1, 2, 3) | (1/7, 1/6, 1/5) | (1/5, 1/4, 1/3) | (11.0429, 19.8667, 30.1167) | 0.0000 |
| $v_{3_{12}}$ | (1/3, 1/2, 1) | (1/3, 1/2, 1) | (1, 1, 1) | (1, 2, 3) | (1/3, 1/2, 1) | (1, 2, 3) | (1/8, 1/7, 1/6) | (1/5, 1/4, 1/3) | (8.9417, 15.1762, 23.5833) | 0.0000 |
| $v_{3_{13}}$ | (1/3, 1/2, 1) | (1/3, 1/2, 1) | (1/3, 1/2, 1) | (1, 1, 1) | (1/3, 1/2, 1) | (1, 2, 3) | (1/9, 1/8, 1/7) | (1/6, 1/5, 1/4) | (6.1706, 9.025, 15.3429) | 0.0000 |
| $v_{3_{14}}$ | (1, 2, 3) | (1, 2, 3) | (1, 2, 3) | (1, 2, 3) | (1, 1, 1) | (1, 2, 3) | (1/7, 1/6, 1/5) | (1/5, 1/4, 1/3) | (12.3762, 22.8667, 34.1167) | 0.0000 |
| $v_{3_{15}}$ | (1/3, 1/2, 1) | (1/3, 1/2, 1) | (1/3, 1/2, 1) | (1/3, 1/2, 1) | (1/3, 1/2, 1) | (1, 1, 1) | (1/9, 1/9, 1/9) | (1/6, 1/5, 1/4) | (5.4623, 7.454, 13.2278) | 0.0000 |
| $v_{3_{16}}$ | (6, 7, 8) | (5, 6, 7) | (6, 7, 8) | (7, 8, 9) | (5, 6, 7) | (9, 9, 9) | (1, 1, 1) | (1, 2, 3) | (80, 95, 110) | 0.3489 |
| $v_{3_{17}}$ | (3, 4, 5) | (3, 4, 5) | (3, 4, 5) | (4, 5, 6) | (3, 4, 5) | (4, 5, 6) | (1/3, 1/2, 1) | (1, 1, 1) | (40, 53.5, 68) | 0.1669 |
| Σ | | | | | | | | | (352.7524, 503.4683, 682.5302) | |

**Table A10.** List of countries.

| Economy Type | N | Countries |
|---|---|---|
| Advanced Economies | 331 | Australia, Austria, Belgium, Canada, Croatia, Cyprus, Czech Republic, Denmark, Estonia, Finland, France, Germany, Greece, Hong Kong, Iceland, Ireland, Israel, Italy, Japan, Latvia, Lithuania, Luxembourg, Malta, Netherlands, New Zealand, Norway, Portugal, Singapore, Slovakia, Slovenia, South Korea, Spain, Sweden, Switzerland, Taiwan, United Kingdom, and United States |
| Emerging and Developing Asia | 55 | Bangladesh, Bhutan, Brunei, Cambodia, China (Mainland), East Timor/Timor-Leste, Fiji, India, Indonesia, Kiribati, Laos, Malaysia, Maldives, Mongolia, Myanmar, Nepal, Papua New Guinea, Philippines, Samoa, Solomon Islands, Sri Lanka, Thailand, Tonga, Vanuatu, and Vietnam |
| Emerging and Developing Europe | 20 | Albania, Belarus, Bosnia and Herzegovina, Bulgaria, Hungary, Moldova, Montenegro, Poland, Romania, Russia, Serbia, Turkey, and Ukraine |
| Latin America and the Caribbean | 8 | Antigua and Barbuda, Bahamas, Barbados, Belize, Bolivia, Brazil, Chile, Colombia, Costa Rica, Dominica, Dominican Republic, Ecuador, El Salvador, Grenada, Guatemala, Guyana, Haiti, Honduras, Jamaica, Mexico, Nicaragua, Panama, Paraguay, Peru, Saint Kitts and Nevis, Saint Lucia, Saint Vincent and the Grenadines, Suriname, Trinidad and Tobago, and Uruguay |

Table A10. Cont.

| Economy Type | N | Countries |
|---|---|---|
| Middle East and Central Asia | 60 | Algeria, Armenia, Azerbaijan, Bahrain, Djibouti, Egypt, Georgia, Iran, Iraq, Jordan, Kazakhstan, Kuwait, Kyrgyzstan, Libya, Mauritania, Morocco, Oman, Pakistan, Qatar, Saudi Arabia, Tajikistan, Tunisia, Turkmenistan, Uzbekistan, and Yemen |
| Sub-Saharan Africa | 22 | Angola, Benin, Botswana, Burkina Faso, Burundi, Cameroon, Cape Verde, Central African Republic, Chad, Comoros, and Congo (DRC), Congo (RC), Equatorial Guinea, Eswatini, Ethiopia, Gabon, Gambia, Ghana, Guinea, Guinea-Bissau, Ivory Coast, Kenya, Lesotho, Liberia, Madagascar, Malawi, Mali, Mauritius, Mozambique, Namibia, Niger, Nigeria, Rwanda, Sao Tome and Principe, Senegal, Seychelles, Sierra Leone, South Africa, Tanzania, Togo, Uganda, and Zambia |

Table A11. Number of banks included in the bank performance model.

| Economy Type | Countries | No. of Banks | Countries | No. of Banks | Countries | No. of Banks |
|---|---|---|---|---|---|---|
| Advanced Economies | Austria | 5 | Greece | 1 | Portugal | 1 |
| | Belgium | 1 | Hong Kong | 5 | Singapore | 3 |
| | Canada | 1 | Israel | 5 | Slovakia | 1 |
| | Cyprus | 1 | Italy | 9 | Spain | 5 |
| | Czech Republic | 2 | South Korea | 3 | Sweden | 5 |
| | Denmark | 7 | Lithuania | 1 | Switzerland | 7 |
| | Finland | 3 | Netherlands | 2 | United Kingdom | 8 |
| | France | 14 | Norway | 18 | United States | 222 |
| | Germany | 1 | | | | |
| Emerging and Developing Asia | China (Mainland) | 33 | Malaysia | 7 | Sri Lanka | 1 |
| | Indonesia | 12 | Philippines | 1 | Thailand | 1 |
| Emerging and Developing Europe | Bulgaria | 2 | Poland | 4 | Russia | 2 |
| | Hungary | 1 | Romania | 2 | Turkey | 9 |
| Latin America and the Caribbean | Brazil | 3 | Mexico | 1 | Peru | 3 |
| | Colombia | 1 | | | | |
| Middle East and Central Asia | Bahrain | 4 | Jordan | 13 | Pakistan | 2 |
| | Egypt | 8 | Kazakhstan | 2 | Qatar | 7 |
| | Georgia | 1 | Kuwait | 7 | Saudi Arabia | 9 |
| | Iraq | 1 | Oman | 6 | Pakistan | 2 |
| Sub-Saharan Africa | Botswana | 3 | Mauritius | 1 | South Africa | 4 |
| | Kenya | 6 | Nigeria | 7 | Uganda | 1 |

## References

1. Lee, C.C.; Lin, C.W.; Lee, C.C. Globalization, government regulation, and country risk: International evidence. *J. Int. Trade Econ. Dev.* **2023**, *32*, 132–162. [CrossRef]
2. Sargen, N. Economic indicators and country risk appraisal. *Econ. Rev.* **1977**, 19–35.
3. Nagy, P. Quantifying country risk-system developed by economists at the bank of Montreal. *Columbia J. World Bus.* **1978**, *13*, 135–147.
4. Sun, X.; Feng, Q.; Li, J. Understanding country risk assessment: A historical review. *Appl. Econ.* **2021**, *53*, 4329–4341. [CrossRef]
5. Meier, S.; Strobl, E.; Elliott, R.J.; Kettridge, N. Cross-country risk quantification of extreme wildfires in Mediterranean Europe. *Risk Anal.* **2022**. online ahead of print. [CrossRef]
6. Lee, C.-C.; Chen, M.-P. Ecological footprint, tourism development, and country risk: International evidence. *J. Clean. Prod.* **2020**, *279*, 123671. [CrossRef]
7. Chaudhry, S.M.; Ahmed, R.; Shafiullah, M.; Huynh, T.L.D. The impact of carbon emissions on country risk: Evidence from the G7 economies. *J. Environ. Manag.* **2020**, *265*, 110533. [CrossRef]
8. Peiró-Signes, Á.; Cervelló-Royo, R.; Segarra-Oña, M. Can a country's environmental sustainability exert influence on its economic and financial situation? The relationship between environmental performance indicators and country risk. *J. Clean. Prod.* **2022**, *375*, 134121. [CrossRef]
9. Đukan, M.; Kitzing, L. A bigger bang for the buck: The impact of risk reduction on renewable energy support payments in Europe. *Energy Policy* **2023**, *173*, 113395. [CrossRef]
10. Li, Y.; Huang, J.; Zhang, H. The impact of country risks on cobalt trade patterns from the perspective of the industrial chain. *Resour. Policy* **2022**, *77*, 102641. [CrossRef]

11. Qazi, A.; Simsekler, M.C.E.; Formaneck, S. Impact assessment of country risk on logistics performance using a Bayesian Belief Network model. *Kybernetes* **2023**, *52*, 1620–1642. [CrossRef]
12. Filipović, S.; Radovanović, M.; Golušin, V. Macroeconomic and political aspects of energy security–Exploratory data analysis. *Renew. Sustain. Energy Rev.* **2018**, *97*, 428–435. [CrossRef]
13. Zhang, W.; Chiu, Y.B. Do country risks influence carbon dioxide emissions? A non-linear perspective. *Energy* **2020**, *206*, 118048. [CrossRef]
14. Zhang, H.; Wang, Y.; Yang, C.; Guo, Y. The impact of country risk on energy trade patterns based on complex network and panel regression analyses. *Energy* **2021**, *222*, 119979. [CrossRef]
15. Özkan, B.; Erdem, M.; Özceylan, E. Evaluation of Asian Countries using Data Center Security Index: A Spherical Fuzzy AHP-based EDAS Approach. *Comput. Secur.* **2022**, *122*, 102900. [CrossRef]
16. Angosto-Fernández, P.L.; Ferrández-Serrano, V. Independence day: Political risk and cross-sectional determinants of firm exposure after the Catalan crisis. *Int. J. Financ. Econ.* **2022**, *27*, 4318–4335. [CrossRef]
17. Lee, C.-C.; Lee, C.-C. Oil price shocks and Chinese banking performance: Do country risks matter? *Energy Econ.* **2019**, *77*, 46–53. [CrossRef]
18. Mascarenhas, B.; Christian Sand, O. Country-Risk Assessment System in Banks: Patterns and Performance. *J. Int. Bus. Stud.* **1985**, *16*, 19–35. [CrossRef]
19. Somerville, R.A.; Taffler, R.J. Banker judgement versus formal forecasting models: The case of country risk assessment. *J. Bank. Financ.* **1995**, *19*, 281–297. [CrossRef]
20. Simpson, J. An Empirical Economic Development Based Model of International Banking Risk and Risk Scoring. *Rev. Dev. Econ.* **2002**, *6*, 91–102. [CrossRef]
21. Cherubini, U.; Mulinacci, S. Contagion-based distortion risk measures. *Appl. Math. Lett.* **2014**, *27*, 85–89. [CrossRef]
22. Babayeva, S.; Rzayeva, I.; Babayev, T. Weighted Estimate of Country Risk Using a Fuzzy Method of Maxmin Convolution. *Adv. Intell. Syst. Comput.* **2018**, *896*, 559–567. [CrossRef]
23. Li, J.; Dong, X.; Jiang, Q.; Dong, K. Analytical Approach to Quantitative Country Risk Assessment for the Belt and Road Initiative. *Sustainability* **2021**, *13*, 423. [CrossRef]
24. Yim, J.; Mitchell, H. Comparison of country risk models: Hybrid neural networks, logit models, discriminant analysis and cluster techniques. *Expert Syst. Appl.* **2005**, *28*, 137–148. [CrossRef]
25. Coccia, M. A new taxonomy of country performance and risk based on economic and technological indicators. *J. Appl. Econ.* **2007**, *10*, 29–42. [CrossRef]
26. Xie, Y.; Wang, W.; Guo, Y.; Yang, J. Study on the country risk rating with distributed crawling system. *J. Supercomput.* **2019**, *75*, 6159–6177. [CrossRef]
27. Kouzez, M. Political environment and bank performance: Does bank size matter? *Econ. Syst.* **2023**, *47*, 101056. [CrossRef]
28. Niemira, M.P.; Saaty, T.L. An Analytic Network Process Model for Financial-Crisis Forecasting. *Int. J. Forecast.* **2004**, *20*, 573–587. [CrossRef]
29. Brown, C.L.; Cavusgil, S.T.; Lord, A.W. Country-risk measurement and analysis: A new conceptualization and managerial tool. *Int. Bus. Rev.* **2015**, *24*, 246–265. [CrossRef]
30. Albaity, M.; Mallek, R.S.; Bakather, A.; Al-Tamimi, H. Heterogeneity of the MENA region's bank stock returns: Does country risk matter? *J. Open Innov. Technol. Mark. Complex.* **2023**, *9*, 100057. [CrossRef]
31. Bouchet, M.H.; Clark, E.; Groslambert, B. *Country Risk Assessment: A Guide to Global Investment Strategy*; Wiley: Hoboken, NJ, USA, 2003.
32. Refinitiv Thomson Reuters. Available online: https://www.refinitiv.com/content/dam/marketing/en_us/documents/brochures/country-risk-ranking-brochure.pdf (accessed on 1 March 2023).
33. Gelemerova, L.; Harvey, J.; van Duyne, P.C. Banks assessing corruption risk: A risky undertaking. In *Corruption in Commercial Enterprise*; Routledge: London, UK, 2018; pp. 182–198.
34. Roe, M.J.; Siegel, J.I. Political instability: Effects on financial development, roots in the severity of economic inequality. *J. Comp. Econ.* **2011**, *39*, 279–309. [CrossRef]
35. Lehkonen, H.; Heimonen, K. Democracy, political risks and stock market performance. *J. Int. Money Financ.* **2015**, *59*, 77–99. [CrossRef]
36. Hayakawa, K.; Kimura, F.; Lee, H.H. How does country risk matter for foreign direct investment? *Dev. Econ.* **2013**, *51*, 60–78. [CrossRef]
37. Park, S.J.; Lee, K.M.; Yang, J.S. Calculating the country risk embedded in treaty-shopping networks. *Technol. Forecast. Soc. Chang.* **2023**, *189*, 122354. [CrossRef]
38. Ghirelli, C.; Gil, M.; Pérez, J.J.; Urtasun, A. Measuring economic and economic policy uncertainty and their macroeconomic effects: The case of Spain. *Empir. Econ.* **2021**, *60*, 869–892. [CrossRef]
39. Huang, J.C.; Lin, H.C. Country Risk and Bank Stability. *J. Econ. Forecast.* **2021**, *24*, 72–96.
40. Walter, I. Country risk, portfolio decisions and regulation in international bank lending. *J. Bank. Financ.* **1981**, *5*, 77–92. [CrossRef]
41. Aragonés-Beltrán, P.; Chaparro-González, F.; Pastor-Ferrando, J.P.; Pla-Rubio, A. An AHP (Analytic Hierarchy Process)/ANP (Analytic Network Process)-based multi-criteria decision approach for the selection of solar-thermal power plant investment projects. *Energy* **2014**, *66*, 222–238. [CrossRef]

42. Sun, C.C. A performance evaluation model by integrating fuzzy AHP and fuzzy TOPSIS methods. *Expert Syst. Appl.* **2010**, *37*, 7745–7754. [CrossRef]
43. Saaty, T.L. Decision making—The analytic hierarchy and network processes (AHP/ANP). *J. Syst. Sci. Syst. Eng.* **2004**, *13*, 1–35. [CrossRef]
44. Kumar, M.; Choubey, V.K.; Raut, R.D.; Jagtap, S. Enablers to achieve zero hunger through IoT and blockchain technology and transform the green food supply chain systems. *J. Clean. Prod.* **2023**, *405*, 136894. [CrossRef]
45. Büyüközkan, G.; Çifçi, G. A novel hybrid MCDM approach based on fuzzy DEMATEL, fuzzy ANP and fuzzy TOPSIS to evaluate green suppliers. *Expert Syst. Appl.* **2012**, *39*, 3000–3011. [CrossRef]
46. Ergu, D.; Kou, G.; Shi, Y.; Shi, Y. Analytic network process in risk assessment and decision analysis. *Comput. Oper. Res.* **2014**, *42*, 58–74. [CrossRef]
47. Uygun, Ö.; Kaçamak, H.; Kahraman, Ü.A. An integrated DEMATEL and Fuzzy ANP techniques for evaluation and selection of outsourcing provider for a telecommunication company. *Comput. Ind. Eng.* **2015**, *86*, 137–146. [CrossRef]
48. Mistarihi, M.Z.; Okour, R.A.; Mumani, A.A. An integration of a QFD model with Fuzzy-ANP approach for determining the importance weights for engineering characteristics of the proposed wheelchair design. *Appl. Soft Comput.* **2020**, *90*, 106136. [CrossRef]
49. Schulze-González, E.; Pastor-Ferrando, J.-P.; Aragonés-Beltrán, P. Testing a Recent DEMATEL-Based Proposal to Simplify the Use of ANP. *Mathematics* **2021**, *9*, 1605. [CrossRef]
50. Nguyen, T.S.; Chen, J.-M.; Tseng, S.-H.; Lin, L.-F. Key Factors for a Successful OBM Transformation with DEMATEL–ANP. *Mathematics* **2023**, *11*, 2439. [CrossRef]
51. Dincer, H. HHI-based evaluation of the European banking sector using an integrated fuzzy approach. *Kybernetes* **2019**, *48*, 1195–1215. [CrossRef]
52. Sánchez-Garrido, A.J.; Navarro, I.J.; García, J.; Yepes, V. An Adaptive ANP & ELECTRE IS-Based MCDM Model Using Quantitative Variables. *Mathematics* **2022**, *10*, 2009. [CrossRef]
53. Khalilzadeh, M.; Katoueizadeh, L.; Zavadskas, E.K. Risk identification and prioritization in banking projects of payment service provider companies: An empirical study. *Front. Bus. Res. China* **2020**, *14*, 1–27. [CrossRef]
54. Dincer, H.; Hacioglu, U.; Tatoglu, E.; Delen, D. Developing a hybrid analytics approach to measure the efficiency of deposit banks. *J. Bus. Res.* **2019**, *104*, 131–145. [CrossRef]
55. Pearson, K.F.R.S. LIII. On lines and planes of closest fit to systems of points in space. *Lond. Edinb. Dublin Philos. Mag. J. Sci.* **1901**, *2*, 559–572. [CrossRef]
56. Malhotra, N. *Marketing Research: An Applied Orientation*, 7th ed.; Pearson Education: Harlow, UK, 2020.
57. Ďuriš, V.; Bartková, R.; Tirpáková, A. Principal Component Analysis and Factor Analysis for an Atanassov IF Data Set. *Mathematics* **2021**, *9*, 2067. [CrossRef]
58. Abdi, H.; Williams, L.J. Principal component analysis. *Interdiscip. Rev. Comput. Stat.* **2010**, *2*, 433–459. [CrossRef]
59. Hair, J.F.; Black, W.C.; Babin, B.J.; Anderson, R.E.; Tatham, R.L. *Multivariate Data Analysis*; Prentice Hall: Upper Saddle River, NJ, USA, 2017.
60. Widaman, K.F. Common factor analysis versus principal component analysis: Differential bias in representing model parameters? *Multivar. Behav. Res.* **1993**, *28*, 263–311. [CrossRef] [PubMed]
61. IBM Corp. *IBM SPSS Statistics Algorithms*; IBM Corp.: Armonk, NY, USA, 2017.
62. Rummel, R.J. *Applied Factor Analysis*; Northwestern University Press: Evanston, IL, USA, 1988.
63. Kaiser, H.F. A second generation little jiffy. *Psychometrika* **1970**, *35*, 401–415. [CrossRef]
64. Jolliffe, I.T. *Principal Component Analysis for Special Types of Data*; Springer: New York, NY, USA, 2002; pp. 338–372.
65. Harman, H.H. *Modern Factor Analysis*; University of Chicago Press: Chicago, IL, USA, 1976.
66. Kaiser, H.F. The varimax criterion for analytic rotation in factor analysis. *Psychometrika* **1958**, *23*, 187–200. [CrossRef]
67. Kaiser, H.F. An index of factorial simplicity. *Psychometrika* **1974**, *39*, 31–36. [CrossRef]
68. Cerny, B.A.; Kaiser, H.F. A Study of a Measure of Sampling Adequacy For Factor-Analytic Correlation Matrices. *Multivar. Behav. Res.* **1977**, *12*, 43–47. [CrossRef]
69. Chang, D.Y. Applications of the extent analysis method on fuzzy AHP. *Eur. J. Oper. Res.* **1996**, *95*, 649–655. [CrossRef]
70. De Andrés-Sánchez, J. A systematic review of the interactions of fuzzy set theory and option pricing. *Expert Syst. Appl.* **2023**, *223*, 119868. [CrossRef]
71. de Andrés-Sánchez, J.; Puchades, L.G.V. Using fuzzy random variables in life annuities pricing. *Fuzzy Sets Syst.* **2012**, *188*, 27–44. [CrossRef]
72. Kheybari, S.; Rezaie, F.M.; Farazmand, H. Analytic network process: An overview of applications. *Appl. Math. Comput.* **2020**, *367*, 124780. [CrossRef]
73. Herrera, F.; Alonso, S.; Chiclana, F.; Herrera-Viedma, E. Computing with words in decision making: Foundations, trends and prospects. *Fuzzy Optim. Decis. Mak.* **2009**, *8*, 337–364. [CrossRef]
74. Han, J.; Pei, J.; Tong, H. *Data Mining: Concepts and Techniques*; Morgan Kaufmann: Cambridge, MA, USA, 2022.
75. Singh, D.; Singh, B. Investigating the impact of data normalization on classification performance. *Appl. Soft Comput.* **2020**, *97*, 105524. [CrossRef]

76. Arias-Oliva, M.; de Andrés-Sánchez, J.; Pelegrín-Borondo, J. Fuzzy Set Qualitative Comparative Analysis of Factors Influencing the Use of Cryptocurrencies in Spanish Households. *Mathematics* **2021**, *9*, 324. [CrossRef]
77. Míguez, J.L.; Rivo-López, E.; Porteiro, J.; Pérez-Orozco, R. Selection of non-financial sustainability indicators as key elements for multi-criteria analysis of hotel chains. *Sustain. Prod. Consum.* **2023**, *35*, 495–508. [CrossRef]
78. Yüksel, İ.; Dağdeviren, M. Using the fuzzy analytic network process (ANP) for Balanced Scorecard (BSC): A case study for a manufacturing firm. *Expert Syst. Appl.* **2010**, *37*, 1270–1278. [CrossRef]
79. Saaty, T.L.; Vargas, L.G. Diagnosis with dependent symptoms: Bayes theorem and the analytic hierarchy process. *Oper. Res.* **1998**, *46*, 491–502. [CrossRef]
80. Chen, H.K.; Liao, Y.C.; Lin, C.Y.; Yen, J.F. The effect of the political connections of government bank CEOs on bank performance during the financial crisis. *J. Financ. Stab.* **2018**, *36*, 130–143. [CrossRef]
81. Elyasiani, E.; Jia, J. Relative performance and systemic risk contributions of small and large banks during the financial crisis (Jane). *Q. Rev. Econ. Financ.* **2019**, *74*, 220–241. [CrossRef]
82. Fitch. Bank Rating Criteria. Available online: https://www.fitchratings.com/research/banks/bank-rating-criteria-07-09-2022 (accessed on 1 March 2023).
83. Bitar, M.; Kabir Hassan, M.; Hippler, W.J. The determinants of Islamic bank capital decisions. *Emerg. Mark. Rev.* **2018**, *35*, 48–68. [CrossRef]
84. Alraheb, T.H.; Nicolas, C.; Tarazi, A. Institutional environment and bank capital ratios. *J. Financ. Stab.* **2019**, *43*, 1–24. [CrossRef]
85. Chen, C.-Y.; Huang, J.-J. Integrating Dynamic Bayesian Networks and Analytic Hierarchy Process for Time-Dependent Multi-Criteria Decision-Making. *Mathematics* **2023**, *11*, 2362. [CrossRef]
86. Wang, C.-N.; Pan, C.-F.; Nguyen, H.-P.; Fang, P.-C. Integrating Fuzzy AHP and TOPSIS Methods to Evaluate Operation Efficiency of Daycare Centers. *Mathematics* **2023**, *11*, 1793. [CrossRef]
87. Peña, A.; Bonet, I.; Lochmuller, C.; Chiclana, F.; Góngora, M. Flexible inverse adaptive fuzzy inference model to identify the evolution of operational value at risk for improving operational risk management. *Appl. Soft Comput.* **2018**, *65*, 614–631. [CrossRef]
88. Shukla, A.K.; Prakash, V.; Nath, R.; Muhuri, P.K. Type-2 intuitionistic fuzzy TODIM for intelligent decision-making under uncertainty and hesitancy. *Soft Comput.* **2022**. *online ahead of print*. [CrossRef]
89. Runkler, T.; Coupland, S.; John, R. Interval type-2 fuzzy decision making. *Int. J. Approx. Reason.* **2017**, *80*, 217–224. [CrossRef]

**Disclaimer/Publisher's Note:** The statements, opinions and data contained in all publications are solely those of the individual author(s) and contributor(s) and not of MDPI and/or the editor(s). MDPI and/or the editor(s) disclaim responsibility for any injury to people or property resulting from any ideas, methods, instructions or products referred to in the content.

 *mathematics*

*Article*

# Fuzzy Assessment of Management Consulting Projects: Model Validation and Case Studies

Hongyi Sun [1], Wenbin Ni [2,*] and Lanxuan Huang [1]

1. Department of Systems Engineering, City University of Hong Kong, Hong Kong 999017, China; sun.3333@cityu.edu.hk (H.S.); lanxhuang2-c@my.cityu.edu.hk (L.H.)
2. School of Business Administration, Zhejiang University of Finance & Economics, Hangzhou 310018, China
* Correspondence: nwb@zufe.edu.cn

**Abstract:** Management consulting (MC) has been heavily involved in emerging business opportunities in mainland China. However, there are no well-known local MC project management models to help evaluate whether an MC project can be successful or not. This paper reports a model for the self-assessment of management consulting projects, which has been validated by 15 experts and 13 cases. The new model, with seven factors that are critical to the success of MC projects, was developed from a literature review. The model was then verified by developing a questionnaire that was sent to 15 experts and using Dempster–Shafer theory to obtain the weight of each part of the model. The model was applied to 13 real cases to verify its effectiveness in evaluating an MC project. This new MC model can help consulting teams to conduct assessments in the early and middle stages, and evaluate in the late stage, of consulting projects, and also can help teams improve the probability of project success and client satisfaction. It can be used by consultants, client companies, or both.

**Keywords:** management consulting; project management; fuzzy assessment; case study

**MSC:** 90B50

**Citation:** Sun, H.; Ni, W.; Huang, L. Fuzzy Assessment of Management Consulting Projects: Model Validation and Case Studies. *Mathematics* 2023, *11*, 4381. https://doi.org/10.3390/math11204381

Academic Editors: Jorge de Andres Sanchez and Laura González-Vila Puchades

Received: 29 August 2023
Revised: 14 October 2023
Accepted: 15 October 2023
Published: 21 October 2023

**Copyright:** © 2023 by the authors. Licensee MDPI, Basel, Switzerland. This article is an open access article distributed under the terms and conditions of the Creative Commons Attribution (CC BY) license (https://creativecommons.org/licenses/by/4.0/).

## 1. Introduction

In recent decades, virtually every enterprise has been engaged in the process of project development or system reform. The enterprise normally invites outside consultants when their internal experience and ability are insufficient. This has made management consulting (MC) increasingly popular as a management practice applicable to many industries and has prompted the need to develop better standards, technologies, and practices for MC [1]. However, managing an MC project is a complex endeavor. Finding a comprehensive and applicable process model that can help MC projects succeed has been a critical and challenging task in the study of MC projects. Several MC project models have been proposed, but a truly comprehensive one remains elusive.

The above issue is even more challenging for Hong Kong MC teams in exploring the mainland market of China. Backed by the mainland market, the MC industry in Hong Kong has a huge potential market. The central government of China and Hong Kong signed the Closer Economic Partnership Arrangement (CEPA) for the first time in 2003. The purpose of the CEPA is to promote the industrial restructuring and upgrading of the two sides to achieve mutual benefit and complementarity. Since then, a supplement to the CEPA has been signed each year with the aim of continuously expanding market liberalization measures to further facilitate Hong Kong service providers. In 2014, the two sides signed a sub-agreement under the CEPA, namely the agreement on fundamentally liberalizing the mainland's trade in services in Guangdong and Hong Kong (the Guangdong Agreement). In December 2015, the two sides signed the trade-in services agreement, delineating the liberalization measures that the mainland would undertake to open its doors to service providers and professionals from Hong Kong from June 2016. Furthermore, this agreement expanded the geographic scope of service trade liberalization to encompass the entirety of the mainland. The Chinese mainland has provided Hong Kong MC enterprises with a vast market place and unlimited growth potential. Hong Kong companies are the largest outside investors in mainland China, and mainland companies are significant investors in the Hong Kong economy.

MC is expected to provide a systematic approach to cover all phases of a management project and ensure that each phase is carefully planned, monitored, and measured [2]. While many researchers have solved the problems related to project management in large companies [3,4], more research should be conducted on project management in small and medium-sized enterprises (SMEs) [5].

At present, most of the international MC ideas have been widely accepted in the global scope. It is not difficult for entrepreneurs to accept advanced ideas, but helping them implement these theories in the local market remains a challenge. For the management consulting industry in mainland China, after 30 years of exploration, the dual transformation of the consulting subject and the consulting content is realized [6]. With the rapid development of local management consulting institutions in China, there is still a large-scale gap with international consulting companies, such as a lack of profitability and core competitiveness. Compared to mature international MC companies, Hong Kong's local consultants fully understand the local market environment, but in the face of strong competitors, there is not a good selection of MC companies in Hong Kong, and the use of the MC method lacks many innovative and targeted MC models.

This paper aims to report a proposal and validation of a more suitable model for Hong Kong MC enterprises, enabling them to conduct management consulting effectively in Hong Kong and/or mainland China. From the literature review, we identified seven factors that are critical to the success of MC projects. The model was then evaluated by 15 experts, and the Dempster–Shafer theory was used to obtain the weight of each factor. Thirteen case studies are reported to verify the application. Section 2 provides the development of the new model from the literature review. The model is then evaluated using the Dempster–Shafer theory in Sections 3 and 4 to obtain the weight of each part of the model, and in Section 5 is applied to 13 real cases to verify its effectiveness.

## 2. Literature Review and Model Development

### 2.1. Concepts and Terminologies

As a form of modern consulting, MC in contemporary society has rapidly developed and played a huge role. It is often referred to as a "brain industry" that helps managers identify and analyze problems, advise, and get out of trouble. However, there is still no unified definition of MC.

The Association of MC Engineers defines MC by stating: "a person with theoretical knowledge or experience in MC exposes problems in The Management of the enterprise and proposes practical solutions to help implement them". As defined by The International Council of Management Consulting Institutes, "an MC consultant is an individual responsible for Management who provides independent Consulting advice and guidance to clients". The International Labor Committee defines MC as "helping to solve management and business problems, to identify new opportunities, and to use it for the purpose of organizing administrative agencies to help continue and expand learning opportunities".

According to [7], MC is "dynamically facing new challenges because the management tools, methods and methods that make up the field are applied in different fields, for different purposes and in different cultures".

To sum up, MC refers to the management behavior in which natural persons or legal persons with professional knowledge and experience or training accept commissions, take operation and management as their primary business, and use management tools to provide knowledge, functions, planning, and other high-intelligence services in various fields for different purposes.

*2.2. Previous Models for Consultation Management*

While undeniably crucial, MC is fraught with challenges. Planning and implementing a successful MC project is not easy. It requires a criterion for success or a complete, comprehensive, and applicable process model. The ASQ team spent approximately 35 years and engaged numerous teams from over 30 countries, to create the International Team Excellence Award (ITEA) Criteria, and provide a framework for assessing team performance and project processes. On this basis, we searched the literature on MC and project management (PM) and reviewed the influencing factors and models related to MC.

From the literature, seven different MC models and seven associated factors were identified (see Table 1 below).

**Table 1.** Factors in previous MC models.

| Factors Affecting MC | Model 1 | Model 2 | Model 3 | Model 4 | Model 5 | Model 6 | Model 7 |
|---|---|---|---|---|---|---|---|
| 1. Project background and purpose | ✓ | ✓ | ✓ | ✓ | ✓ | ✓ | ✓ |
| 2. Project framework | ✓ | ✓ | ✓ | ✓ | ✓ |  | ✓ |
| 3. Project stakeholders and the project team | ✓ |  |  | ✓ |  | ✓ |  |
| 4. Project overview | ✓ |  | ✓ | ✓ | ✓ | ✓ | ✓ |
| 5. Project walkthrough | ✓ | ✓ | ✓ | ✓ | ✓ | ✓ |  |
| 6. Project tracking and control |  | ✓ | ✓ | ✓ |  | ✓ | ✓ |
| 7. Project presentation | ✓ |  |  |  | ✓ |  |  |

✓: indicates one model includes the factor.

In the following, the seven models will be elaborated from the following aspects: which factors will be included, to which fields and industries do they apply, whether to conduct quantitative analysis, whether there is empirical analysis or just a conceptual model, whether there is a flow chart, advantages and disadvantages, etc.

Model 1—The ASQ organization's ITEA model [8] provides a six-section framework to help organizations improve the results of their projects, providing guidance and repeatable benchmarks for projects of different organization sizes, industry types, or project types. This model starts from the identification and selection of the project and ends with a project presentation, which relatively clearly and fully presents the process of all parts of the project. Every part is responsible for the detailed and rich further subdivided activities and description. For each sub-part, this model provides scoring criteria of differing maturity. The scores range from 0 to 4, with each layer having to perform better based on covering the previous layer. At the same time, the model emphasizes the relevance of each phase, its importance to the long-term planning of an MC project, and the relevant planning of the organization to support the project. However, the model does not provide a process or sequence, leaving the user with many considerations but no idea where to start or what to do at a certain point in time. This model is only suitable for evaluating completed projects, but it cannot be used as a starting point for a project.

Model 2—Reference [9] provided four main phases of a project decision analysis process (PDAP): decision framing, modelling the alternatives, quantitative analysis, and actual performance tracking. The four phases run in sequence, while part of the actual performance trace is continuously fed back to the remaining three. These four stages correspond to the project framework, project walkthrough, project background and purpose, and project tracking and control. The PDAP model provides process guidance that requires both qualitative and quantitative analysis, and in which the quantitative analysis method can be adjusted according to different requirements. This model takes more account of process quality and relationships with the system organization and is effective and practical: it is practical because it is easy to integrate with existing processes; its effectiveness is reflected in the scalability and flexibility of the model to provide effective feedback and adaptability. At the same time, this model also considers the correlation degree and strength between its effectiveness and organizational effectiveness under the framework of competitive value. However, the model is implemented on the premise that there must be high-quality useful information, sufficient and accurate information about competitors, that the project leader or decision maker needs to be trained, and that the appropriate, but not all, project processes can be integrated.

Model 3—Reference [3] discussed how to establish a project organization in a telecommunications environment and developed a standardized project management process, which was divided into four steps: project initiation, project definition, project implementation, and project completion. These four stages correspond to the project background and purpose, the project framework, project overview, and project walkthrough. At each stage, validation was repeated until all conditions were met. The main purpose of this model is to provide a common operational framework and major control mechanisms for all project managers. The advantage is that the framework is relatively flexible and can accommodate and monitor the situation of each part while maintaining necessary system control. Second, the model facilitates stakeholder participation in each phase of the project lifecycle. In addition, the model's versatility makes it easy for new employees to start. However, this model is only a qualitative analysis and lacks a quantitative data analysis. In addition, the absence of risk anticipation and response procedures makes it difficult for project personnel or organizations to respond promptly to the changes in project requirements. At the same time, this model also lacks benchmarks as it is confined to individual project management and is not suitable for comparing or measuring different project management processes.

Model 4—Reference [5] identified six factors of successful project management with the greatest potential benefits for small and medium-sized businesses (SMEs). They are clear objectives, top management support, resource allocation, planning, monitoring and control, client consulting and risk management. The six success factors correspond to the project background and purpose, project framework, project stakeholders and project team, project overview, project walkthrough, project tracking and control. The six factors are based on a survey conducted asking managers of small and medium-sized enterprises their opinions on the six factors in their enterprises on a scale of 1 to 5. Each of the more than 200 small and medium-sized businesses in the survey had fewer than 250 employees, and they covered a wide range of sectors, including health care, telecommunications, electronics and engineering, and were mostly in high-tech industries. Although high-tech companies contribute a lot to society in terms of wealth creation and employment, these technical entrepreneurs have relatively poor business management skills, so this model is a good way to help these high tech SMEs. The model analyzed the questionnaire results using SPSS 27 software and ranked the importance of six influencing factors. Among these factors, clear objectives and support from senior management were identified as the most important success factors. The significance of this model lies in the in-depth study of its project management model based on the characteristics of small and medium-sized enterprises, but the scope of use is also limited to small and medium-sized enterprises, therefore, there is no way of it being widely promoted.

Model 5—Reference [10] proposed a comprehensive project management model that elaborated several stages of systematic management of university processes: the general concept of processes, environmental characteristics and internal accuracy, and the ability to plan, organize, implement, evaluate, adjust and improve. These stages correspond to the project background and purpose, project framework, project overview, project walkthrough, and project presentation. This model is applicable to general university management and is an effective method of substantive process management. It helps optimize human, material, technical, financial and information resources to improve the quality and impact of management results. Notably, this model is characterized by high interactivity, meaning the completion of each stage affects the entire process and depends on at least one other stage. This feature facilitates the guidance of the process and allows for recalibration when necessary. The system model was successfully implemented during the 2012–2013 academic year at the tested universities, resulting in improvement in all its selected indicators. By observing the process and communicating with the actors involved in the process, Aguilera found that all stakeholders had a high degree of satisfaction with the management of the substantive process. The limitation of this comprehensive project management model is that it only extends to the organization and functions of the university, and only applies to the management of the university.

Model 6—In the Project Excellence Model®, reference [11] proposed a series of critical key success factors, five project types and six organizational domains through a literature review. The critical factors for project success are organization, results, and feedback, respectively. These factors include (1) leadership and team, (2) policy and strategy, (3) stakeholder management, (4) resources, (5) contracting, (6) project management, (7) success criteria and (8) external factors, respectively. These factors are interrelated to form a coherent model.

Project types play a critical role in project management because the project objectives of different areas and types must match external factors. The five project types in the model include (1) product-oriented, (2) tool-oriented, (3) system-oriented, (4) process-oriented and (5) complete project management. The six result areas include (1) project results, (2) appreciation by the client, (3) appreciation by project personnel, (4) appreciation by users, (5) appreciation by contracting partners, and (6) appreciation by clients. This model includes the project background and purpose, project stakeholders and project team, project overview, project walkthrough, project tracking and control. At project startup, it is imperative to categorize the six resulting domain reads of the model and select the corresponding project type in each domain. This model has been successfully demonstrated in a medium-sized organization and is generally flexible in adapting to project objectives. Linking project outcome areas, organizational areas, and different project types can provide good insights into improving project organizational functions. However, the model has its limitations in terms of comprehensively covering all relevant success factors.

Model 7—Reference [12] proposed PRINCE2, a standard project management tool. PINS2 is a structured project management method that encompasses elements related to project organization, management, and control. It finds primary application with commercial, government and construction projects in the UK. The authors used it in clinical trial management and obtained good results. This model mainly has the following four characteristics: clear objectives, measurable conclusions, clearly defined resources and clearly defined organizational responsibilities. This model includes the project background and purpose, project framework, project overview, project tracking and control. This model can be used in different areas to improve management efficiency and reduce process costs. However, it should be noted that this approach comes with certain limitations. The tools and terminology employed may not be readily familiar to most participants, necessitating additional training to surmount the considerable learning curve.

Two gaps are identified from the above review of the seven MC models. First, these seven models identify seven factors that are important for MC. However, as shown in Table 1, they only cover some of the seven factors that are related to successful MC. All of them miss one or another factor. The following section will propose a new model that integrates all the seven factors identified from previous models.

Secondly, most of these models are qualitative, and only those involving maturity are quantitatively analyzed. The models rely more on managers' experience and judgment of subjective consciousness. There is no complete and systematic model to conduct both qualitative and quantitative analysis of these factors step by step. Even these MC factors have differences in partitioning and qualification between different models, as shown in Table 1 above. This study solves this problem by proposing and applying a new model to the MC project.

*2.3. The Proposal of a New Model*

The success of the MC project firstly depends on the manager who leads the project. Therefore, this study proposes an MC project manager-oriented model, as shown in Figure 1. Managers can use this model to have clear control over the overall project framework and direction. In this model, the initial three parts (part A to part C) are mainly dedicated to understanding and mastering the basic information of the project, part D to part F place emphasis on methods, processes and results of the project, part G underscores the notion that, as a management consulting project, the presentation of project results and the project's completion process should be conducted by consultants for the benefit of the client. This brings about the holistic process of management consultation. The subsequent section elaborates on the seven factors (categories) of this new model.

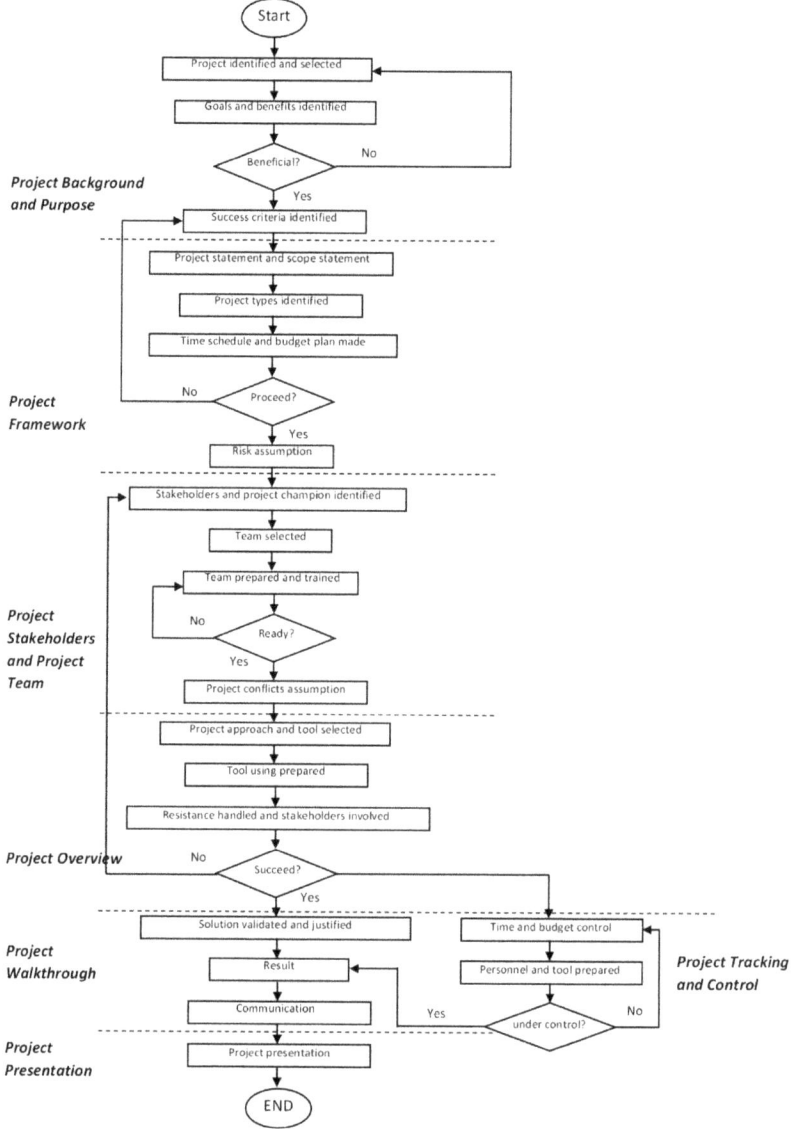

**Figure 1.** A new conceptual model for MC in Hong Kong and mainland China.

### 2.3.1. Project Background and Purpose

The project background and purpose include these parts: organizational approach to project planning, project identification process, project selection process, project goals and benefits, and success measures/criteria identified [8]. Before the start of an MC project, the manager should select and prioritize. Total resources resemble a pie, and they are limited. Each project cannot share the same amount of manpower, funds, equipment and other resources. It is the first step of the model, which is how to identify the scope of the project and allocate resources according to the project's revenue and requirements. In this step, the project needs to be evaluated and predicted in terms of cost, potential benefits, development risks, time to market and so on. Methods commonly used in project selection are the checklist model, scoring model and analytic hierarchy process (AHP) [13].

Secondly, success criteria are the criteria to measure the success or failure of a project, and an MC project manager should clearly distinguish between critical success factors and critical success criteria before starting.

### 2.3.2. Project Framework

This project framework section builds upon the project selection, goals, and success measures discussed in Factor 1. For maximum effectiveness, it is crucial that all team members have a clear understanding of both the "what" and the "why" (the significance) of their projects. Whether an organization follows a formal project charter process or not, team members should possess the ability to succinctly summarize their project, comprehend the type of project they are undertaking, grasp the scope of their work, and be aware of the project's timeline. The team should explicitly define the project type, which can include problem-solving, process/continuous improvement, design, or transformational, among other examples. Documenting basic assumptions and anticipated risks is important to prevent unexpected challenges during the project. Furthermore, the team should have a thorough understanding of the resources available to them. A project framework template is provided to ensure consistency in capturing and sharing the necessary information.

The project framework includes these parts: concise project statement, type of project, scope statement, assumptions/expectations, project schedule/high-level plan, budget (financial or resource) and risk management. The combination of project type and team is crucial, in particular because the personality and personal style of the project manager have a certain influence on the success of the project [14].

The project scope needs to state everything about the project, including all activities to perform, resources to consume, end products and quality standards. A scoping statement usually uses a work breakdown structure (WBS), an organization breakdown structure (OBS), and a linear responsibility chart. Gantt charts are a popular way of time scheduling which is crucial. Reference [5] proved that the completion schedule can make the project more likely to succeed.

### 2.3.3. Project Stakeholders and the Project Team

Project stakeholders include these elements: stakeholders and how they are identified, project champions, project team selection, team preparation, and team routines. Project stakeholders are significant. A successful operation of the MC project requires the support and cooperation of banks, governments, environmental groups, customers, employers, employees, the public, shareholders, suppliers, distributors and other groups. In a successful MC project, stakeholders can be involved throughout the whole process. Reference [11] also considered appreciation and other feedback from both the direct and indirect parties involved in the project.

In addition, as far as team development is concerned, there are generally four stages: forming, storming, cooperation, and performing [15]. Managers need to keep an eye on the development of the team and resolve internal and external conflicts.

Team preparation requires training in tools, techniques, and knowledge of the project. Consulting training has not been given sufficient concern [16]. The lack of training practice may be related to the lack of research on consulting training [17]. In the past, a project would provide consultation courses focused on the theoretical knowledge of consulting, the development of the intervention, the process, and the maintenance of the intervention through consultation [18]. After determining the background, purpose, framework and team members of the MC project, the manager needs to organize training and preparation for the members of the team in terms of content, culture, methodology, and development. This is a critical step. Sufficient training can improve the efficiency of project members and project completion. In terms of content, each member should be made aware of all information about the project. Regarding culture, members need to understand each other's cultural differences and the cultural backgrounds of other stakeholders. There are clear cultural elements in the consulting literature, such as "multicultural consulting" [19] and "cross-cultural consulting" [20], which can be regarded as the theoretical framework of consulting. Project participants usually spend much less time in the field of multiculturalism or diversity [18]. Skills and methods can be taught to engineers without many difficulties [21]. Only with simple and rapid training can project members continuously learn in action [22].

2.3.4. Project Overview

The project overview serves as a bridge between the background/preparation work and project execution/results. The project overview includes these parts: project approach, tools used throughout project, tool output at different stages of a project, how a team was prepared to use the tools, dealing with project risk, encountering and handling resistance as a risk and stakeholder involvement in a project. The project needs to be subdivided into more detailed work steps at each stage, and one or more project management tools must be used at each stage [10]. Project tools are many, such as project management maturity models (PMMMs) [23], critical path method (CPM), process evaluation and review techniques(PERT) [24], critical chain project management (CCPM) [25] and increasingly popular hybrid methods [26].

2.3.5. Project Walkthrough

The project walkthrough is the core of the project to demonstrate how they moved from decision to decision to complete their project. The project walkthrough includes these parts: data-driven project flow, solution validation, solution justification, results, maintaining the gains and project communication. Process improvement has been a top priority for the past decade [27]. Teams should validate and improve their solutions and always communicate with project stakeholders before implementing project solutions.

2.3.6. Project Tracking and Control

Project tracking and control is further discussions and implementation of the risks in the project overview. This must be a continuous process overseen by a designated individual.

Project tracking includes the implementation, monitoring and review of project [9]. Specifically, the team is implementing the best alternative, monitoring project execution, and reviewing the project experience. Project tracking and monitoring is a very important phase for the execution and management of an MC project. A previous study by [28] pointed out that proper tracking and monitoring practices are critical to successfully delivering a project.

Project control includes the control of time, process progress, capital use, risk and uncertainty factors, etc. Risk management is the most important part of project control. Uncertainty and risk are at the heart of all projects. Effective risk management is essential of successful project management [1]. Appropriate risk management can help project managers mitigate known and unexpected risks for various of projects [29].

2.3.7. Project Presentation

Although the project presentation is not a separate phase of a project, it is a collection of key points for the project team to share with stakeholders.

Project presentation includes slide readability, logical flow of information, use of graphics and illustrations, and narrative and visual text. In addition, the speaker's body language and eye contact with the audience are important.

Project presentation is the integration of everything, such as project purpose, team, stakeholders, method of use, process, end results and gap with expectations. The speaker needs to concisely explain these key points and key information to the internal and external groups. It is the final stage of completion of the project.

## 3. Model Evaluation Methodology

### 3.1. Data Collection Method

To verify the model shown in Figure 1, a questionnaire (assessment tool) was designed based on the seven factors in Figure 1 and supported by relevant literature. For each factor, about 6–12 questions were asked to measure the importance of the factor. Scores ranged from 1 to 10, from unimportant to very important. This questionnaire is supposed to be used for two purposes. The first is that the questionnaire will be used for the expert assessment of the seven factors and the questions under each factor, and the data analysis of the assessment results will be carried out. The weight of each factor will be determined based on the results of the expert assessment. The second is that the questionnaire will be used for the next phase of the case project evaluation.

The questionnaire (assessment tool) is attached in Appendix A.

### 3.2. Data Analysis Method

To quantitatively assess the model, integrate expert ratings, and enhance its applicability in real-world scenarios, the following seven factors should be evaluated to obtain their respective weights. The MC model proposed in this paper contains seven factors and dozens of problems, so we did not use methods like AHP (analytical hierarchical process), but adopted the combination method of Dempster–Shafer, based on upper and lower bound probability [30].

The D-S theory was proposed by Dempster in 1967. It belongs to artificial intelligence and the expert system. The method has the ability to cope with uncertain information by the expert scoring and represented in the data structure [31]. D-S evidence theory is a tool for decision making on multi-source data with uncertain information [32]. D-S theory has been widely used in many fields including sensor data, biometric recognition, and decision support systems [33–35].

Dempster–Shafer theory provides many combination rules for framework construction. This paper uses the combined Dempster–Shafer method, which is widely used, easy to implement, and emphasizes the consistency between multiple sources.

The process of determining the weight for each category is shown as follows. First, for each expert, we calculate the score of each category as the mean value of the questions in that category. Then, the category scores were normalized using the following formula:

$$m_i(X) = m_{ix}/sum_i$$

where $m_{ix}$ is the score of categories $X(X = A$ to $H)$ from expert $i$, and $sum_i$ is the sum of all category score by expert $i$.

Then, according to the Dempster–Shafer combination rule, to combines 2 experts' score.

$$[m_1 \oplus m_2](y) = \begin{cases} 0 & y = \varphi \\ \dfrac{\sum_{A \cap B = y} m_1(A) m_2(B)}{1 - \sum_{A \cap B = \varphi} m_1(A) m_2(B)} & y \neq \varphi \end{cases}$$

## 4. Model Evaluation Process

### 4.1. Experts Evaluation

We invited 15 experts who agreed to support this project, as listed in Table 2. They all have experience in management consultation for years in China. During the separate correspondence process with each expert, the information gathered reveals that the new MC model is comprehensive and can be used to evaluate an MC project relatively fully. The

15 experts were finally invited for the evaluation of the model according to the questionnaire (assessment tool) in Appendix A. The backgrounds of the 15 experts are listed in Table 2.

Table 2. The background of the 15 experts.

|    | Gender | Age Range | Work Area | Years of Experiences in MC | Industry of MC Projects Involved |
|----|--------|-----------|-----------|----------------------------|----------------------------------|
| 1  | Male   | 26~30     | East China | 10 | IT, Engineering and Construction |
| 2  | Male   | Over 60   | Hong Kong | 30 | Manufacturing |
| 3  | Female | 31~40     | East China | 8 | Quality Management |
| 4  | Male   | 51~60     | East China | 22 | Utilities, Enterprises, Hospitals |
| 5  | Female | 31~40     | Southwest of China | 5 | Communication, Transportation Industries |
| 6  | Male   | 31~40     | South China | 5 | Finance, State-owned Enterprises |
| 7  | Female | 26~30     | South China | 5 | Finance Industry |
| 8  | Male   | 26~30     | Greater Bay Area | 5 | Finance Industry |
| 9  | Male   | 51~60     | North China | 15 | Aviation Industry |
| 10 | Male   | 41~50     | Greater Bay Area | 20 | Technology, Mergers and Acquisitions, Marketing, Production |
| 11 | Male   | 51~60     | Hong Kong | 20 | Information Technology |
| 12 | Male   | Over 60   | Greater Bay Area | 24 | Manufacturing Industry |
| 13 | Male   | 51~60     | East China | 25 | Manufacturing Industry |
| 14 | Female | 26~30     | South China | 5 | Strategy Management, Human Resources |
| 15 | Male   | 26~30     | East China | 5 | Internet, Medical Industry |

### 4.2. Expert Evaluation Analysis via the Dempster–Shafer Combination Method

According to the expert scoring, we obtained 15 pieces of data with different weights. In order to obtain a more accurate and comprehensive weight, the data need to be normalized according to the principles and guidelines of the Delphi method to obtain a comprehensive evaluation of the model [36]. Through the D-S data processing method described above, 15 expert scores were combined one by one to obtain the D-S value.

The weight of each category is determined as follows. First, for each expert, we calculate the average of their response to the questions with each category. Subsequently, we calculate the sum of these averages across all specialists.

$$\text{Average score } (A) = (A_1 + A_2 + \ldots + A_i)/i;$$

$$\text{Average score } (B) = (B_1 + B_2 + \ldots + B_j)/j;$$

$$\ldots \ldots$$

$$\text{Average score } (G) = (G_1 + G_2 + \ldots + G_m)/m;$$

SUM of Average score = Average score $(A)$ + Average score $(B)$ + $\ldots \ldots$ + Average score $(G)$

As shown in Table 3, the scores of 15 experts on seven factors are processed.

Table 3. The average and sum scores from the 15 experts.

|     | 1      | 2      | 3      | 4      | 5      | 6      | 7      | 8      | 9      | 10     | 11     | 12     | 13     | 14     | 15     |
|-----|--------|--------|--------|--------|--------|--------|--------|--------|--------|--------|--------|--------|--------|--------|--------|
| A   | 8.167  | 8.000  | 8.000  | 8.500  | 8.000  | 8.500  | 8.167  | 9.667  | 8.000  | 9.167  | 8.833  | 6.667  | 7.667  | 8.333  | 8.500  |
| B   | 9.429  | 7.714  | 9.143  | 9.000  | 8.429  | 8.429  | 9.000  | 8.714  | 8.571  | 9.571  | 8.857  | 7.000  | 7.857  | 6.429  | 8.429  |
| C   | 7.286  | 6.857  | 8.857  | 8.429  | 8.571  | 7.714  | 8.429  | 7.571  | 7.571  | 9.429  | 8.857  | 6.714  | 8.571  | 3.571  | 7.714  |
| D   | 8.000  | 7.000  | 8.000  | 8.429  | 8.143  | 9.571  | 8.571  | 8.000  | 8.429  | 8.714  | 8.714  | 5.286  | 8.000  | 3.000  | 7.000  |
| E   | 8.167  | 7.000  | 9.000  | 8.667  | 9.000  | 8.667  | 7.667  | 7.667  | 7.667  | 9.000  | 9.167  | 6.167  | 7.000  | 3.833  | 9.000  |
| F   | 8.167  | 7.333  | 8.333  | 8.500  | 9.167  | 9.167  | 7.500  | 8.167  | 8.000  | 10.00  | 8.000  | 4.167  | 9.000  | 3.000  | 9.000  |
| G   | 6.250  | 6.917  | 8.083  | 8.167  | 9.667  | 7.083  | 8.000  | 8.083  | 7.500  | 8.083  | 8.667  | 5.833  | 7.833  | 4.333  | 8.333  |
| SUM | 55.464 | 50.821 | 59.417 | 59.690 | 60.976 | 59.131 | 57.333 | 57.869 | 55.738 | 63.964 | 61.095 | 41.833 | 55.929 | 32.500 | 57.976 |

Second, the following formula is used to standardize category scores:

$$m_i(X) = m_{ix}/sum_i$$

where $m_{ix}$ is the score of categories X (X = A to G) from expert $i$, and $sum_i$ is the sum of all category score by expert $i$.

As shown in Table 4, scores are standardized.

**Table 4.** The standard scores.

|   | m1    | m2    | m3    | m4    | m5    | m6    | m7    | m8    | m9    | m10   | m11   | m12   | m13   | m14   | m15   |
|---|-------|-------|-------|-------|-------|-------|-------|-------|-------|-------|-------|-------|-------|-------|-------|
| A | 0.147 | 0.157 | 0.135 | 0.142 | 0.131 | 0.144 | 0.142 | 0.167 | 0.144 | 0.143 | 0.145 | 0.159 | 0.137 | 0.256 | 0.147 |
| B | 0.170 | 0.152 | 0.154 | 0.151 | 0.138 | 0.143 | 0.157 | 0.151 | 0.154 | 0.150 | 0.145 | 0.167 | 0.140 | 0.198 | 0.145 |
| C | 0.131 | 0.135 | 0.149 | 0.141 | 0.141 | 0.130 | 0.147 | 0.131 | 0.136 | 0.147 | 0.145 | 0.161 | 0.153 | 0.110 | 0.133 |
| D | 0.144 | 0.138 | 0.135 | 0.141 | 0.134 | 0.162 | 0.150 | 0.138 | 0.151 | 0.136 | 0.143 | 0.126 | 0.143 | 0.092 | 0.121 |
| E | 0.147 | 0.138 | 0.151 | 0.145 | 0.148 | 0.147 | 0.134 | 0.132 | 0.138 | 0.141 | 0.150 | 0.147 | 0.125 | 0.118 | 0.155 |
| F | 0.147 | 0.144 | 0.140 | 0.142 | 0.150 | 0.155 | 0.131 | 0.141 | 0.144 | 0.156 | 0.131 | 0.100 | 0.161 | 0.092 | 0.155 |
| G | 0.113 | 0.136 | 0.136 | 0.137 | 0.159 | 0.120 | 0.140 | 0.140 | 0.135 | 0.126 | 0.142 | 0.139 | 0.140 | 0.133 | 0.144 |
| SUM | 1.000 | 1.000 | 1.000 | 1.000 | 1.000 | 1.000 | 1.000 | 1.000 | 1.000 | 1.000 | 1.000 | 1.000 | 1.000 | 1.000 | 1.000 |

Then, using the Dempster–Shafer combination rule to combine two experts' score.

To illustrate the combination rule, see the following example. If the normalized score from expert 1 is $[m_1(A), m_1(B), m_1(C)\ldots, m_1(F), m_1(G)]$ for category A to G, and the normalized score from expert 2 is $[m_2(A), m_2(B), m_2(C)\ldots, m_2(F), m_2(G)]$ for category A to G it would be optimized to calculate the Dempster–Shafer value for the expert 1 and expert 2 for category A as follows:

$$DS_2(A) = \frac{m_1(A)m_2(A)}{1 - (\sum m_1(A)m_1(B)m_1(C)\ldots m_1(H)m_2(A)m_2(B)m_2(C)\ldots m_2(G))}$$

$$= \frac{m_1(A)m_2(A)}{1 - ((1 - m_1(A)) \times m_2(A) + (1 - m_1(B)) \times m_2(B) + \ldots + (1 - m_1(G)) \times m_2(G))}$$

For category B:

$$DS_2(B) = \frac{m_1(B)m_2(B)}{1 - (\sum m_1(A)m_1(B)m_1(C)\ldots m_1(H)m_2(A)m_2(B)m_2(C)\ldots m_2(G))}$$

$$= \frac{m_1(B)m_2(B)}{1 - ((1 - m_1(A)) \times m_2(A) + (1 - m_1(B)) \times m_2(B) + \ldots + (1 - m_1(G)) \times m_2(G))}$$

For category C:

$$DS_2(C) = \frac{m_1(C)m_2(C)}{1 - (\sum m_1(A)m_1(B)m_1(C)\ldots m_1(H)m_2(A)m_2(B)m_2(C)\ldots m_2(G))}$$

$$= \frac{m_1(C)m_2(C)}{1 - ((1 - m_1(A)) \times m_2(A) + (1 - m_1(B)) \times m_2(B) + \ldots + (1 - m_1(G)) \times m_2(G))}$$

……

For category G:

$$DS_2(G) = \frac{m_1(G)m_2(G)}{1 - (\sum m_1(A)m_1(B)m_1(C)\ldots m_1(H)m_2(A)m_2(B)m_2(C)\ldots m_2(G))}$$

$$= \frac{m_1(G)m_2(G)}{1 - ((1 - m_1(A)) \times m_2(A) + (1 - m_1(B)) \times m_2(B) + \ldots + (1 - m_1(G)) \times m_2(G))}$$

where $DS_2$ means 2 experts' score are combined.

After the scores from expert 1 and expert 2 are combined, the result would be combined with score from expert 3, as follows:

For category A:

$$DS_3(A) = \frac{DS_2(A)m_3(A)}{1 - (\sum DS_2(A)DS_2(B)DS_2(C)\ldots DS_2(H)m_3(A)m_3(B)m_3(C)\ldots m_3(G))}$$

$$= \frac{DS_2(A)m_3(A)}{1 - ((1 - DS_2(A)) \times m_3(A) + (1 - DS_2(B)) \times m_3(B) + \ldots + (1 - DS_2(G)) \times m_3(G))}$$

For category B:

$$DS_3(B) = \frac{DS_2(B)m_3(B)}{1 - (\sum DS_2(A)DS_2(B)DS_2(C)\ldots DS_2(H)m_3(A)m_3(B)m_3(C)\ldots m_3(G))}$$

$$= \frac{DS_2(B)m_3(B)}{1 - ((1 - DS_2(A)) \times m_3(A) + (1 - DS_2(B)) \times m_3(B) + \ldots + (1 - DS_2(G)) \times m_3(G))}$$

......

For category G:

$$DS_3(G) = \frac{DS_2(G)m_3(G)}{1 - (\sum DS_2(A)DS_2(B)DS_2(C)\ldots DS_2(H)m_3(A)m_3(B)m_3(C)\ldots m_3(G))}$$

$$= \frac{DS_2(G)m_3(G)}{1 - ((1 - DS_2(A)) \times m_3(A) + (1 - DS_2(B)) \times m_3(B) + \ldots + (1 - DS_2(G)) \times m_3(G))}$$

where $DS_3$ means 3 experts' score are combined.

And then the result would be combined with expert 4. It would be repeated until all of the experts' score are combined.

As shown in Table 5, the D-S scores of 15 experts for seven factors are shown.

**Table 5.** The D-S value of 7 sections from expert 1 to expert 15 (weight of section).

|   | DS2 | DS3 | DS4 | DS5 | DS6 | DS7 | DS8 | DS9 | DS10 | DS11 | DS12 | DS13 | DS14 | DS15 |
|---|---|---|---|---|---|---|---|---|---|---|---|---|---|---|
| A | 0.162 | 0.152 | 0.151 | 0.139 | 0.139 | 0.139 | 0.161 | 0.160 | 0.159 | 0.161 | 0.176 | 0.171 | 0.276 | 0.280 |
| B | 0.180 | 0.193 | 0.203 | 0.198 | 0.196 | 0.215 | 0.225 | 0.240 | 0.248 | 0.252 | 0.290 | 0.288 | 0.359 | 0.362 |
| C | 0.124 | 0.129 | 0.126 | 0.125 | 0.114 | 0.117 | 0.106 | 0.100 | 0.102 | 0.104 | 0.114 | 0.124 | 0.086 | 0.079 |
| D | 0.139 | 0.130 | 0.128 | 0.120 | 0.136 | 0.142 | 0.136 | 0.143 | 0.135 | 0.134 | 0.117 | 0.118 | 0.069 | 0.057 |
| E | 0.141 | 0.150 | 0.151 | 0.157 | 0.160 | 0.150 | 0.138 | 0.131 | 0.128 | 0.135 | 0.136 | 0.121 | 0.090 | 0.096 |
| F | 0.148 | 0.145 | 0.144 | 0.152 | 0.164 | 0.150 | 0.147 | 0.147 | 0.159 | 0.145 | 0.100 | 0.113 | 0.066 | 0.071 |
| G | 0.107 | 0.102 | 0.097 | 0.108 | 0.090 | 0.088 | 0.085 | 0.080 | 0.070 | 0.069 | 0.066 | 0.066 | 0.055 | 0.055 |

The scores of DS 15 are the composite weight scores of 15 experts for 7 factors, also called weight of section.

After the weighting factor of each issue at organization readiness has been calculated, it is time to generate the weighting factor for each KPI in each section, which is the result of the multiplication of the MC factors' weight and the KPI weight of that related issue.

First, the same method is used to standardize the data. Subsequently, according to the Dempster–Shafer combination rule, the DS value of KPI in each section can be calculated in Table 6.

And the weight of each KPI is the result of the multiplication of the weight of the section and DS15 of KPI, the combined weight value of 15 experts in Table 7.

Table 6. The DS value of KPI in each section by 15 experts.

|   |   | DS2 | DS3 | DS4 | DS5 | DS6 | DS7 | DS8 | DS9 | DS10 | DS11 | DS12 | DS13 | DS14 | DS15 |
|---|---|---|---|---|---|---|---|---|---|---|---|---|---|---|---|
| A | A1 | 0.229 | 0.229 | 0.242 | 0.185 | 0.210 | 0.225 | 0.227 | 0.250 | 0.253 | 0.235 | 0.239 | 0.307 | 0.286 | 0.261 |
|   | A2 | 0.142 | 0.142 | 0.134 | 0.154 | 0.174 | 0.166 | 0.167 | 0.144 | 0.145 | 0.118 | 0.171 | 0.176 | 0.205 | 0.210 |
|   | A3 | 0.183 | 0.183 | 0.172 | 0.198 | 0.224 | 0.213 | 0.215 | 0.237 | 0.240 | 0.251 | 0.109 | 0.112 | 0.131 | 0.134 |
|   | A4 | 0.142 | 0.142 | 0.134 | 0.120 | 0.041 | 0.034 | 0.027 | 0.023 | 0.012 | 0.014 | 0.006 | 0.005 | 0.004 | 0.003 |
|   | A5 | 0.160 | 0.160 | 0.151 | 0.173 | 0.157 | 0.131 | 0.132 | 0.145 | 0.147 | 0.171 | 0.198 | 0.153 | 0.143 | 0.130 |
|   | A6 | 0.142 | 0.142 | 0.167 | 0.171 | 0.194 | 0.231 | 0.232 | 0.200 | 0.202 | 0.211 | 0.276 | 0.247 | 0.231 | 0.263 |
| B | B1 | 0.156 | 0.137 | 0.135 | 0.128 | 0.147 | 0.113 | 0.114 | 0.117 | 0.085 | 0.094 | 0.089 | 0.083 | 0.096 | 0.096 |
|   | B2 | 0.082 | 0.081 | 0.071 | 0.067 | 0.054 | 0.060 | 0.060 | 0.061 | 0.063 | 0.056 | 0.053 | 0.044 | 0.025 | 0.020 |
|   | B3 | 0.137 | 0.149 | 0.131 | 0.155 | 0.125 | 0.138 | 0.154 | 0.158 | 0.163 | 0.181 | 0.221 | 0.258 | 0.374 | 0.372 |
|   | B4 | 0.117 | 0.115 | 0.114 | 0.108 | 0.087 | 0.077 | 0.060 | 0.048 | 0.049 | 0.044 | 0.047 | 0.028 | 0.024 | 0.019 |
|   | B5 | 0.156 | 0.154 | 0.168 | 0.180 | 0.207 | 0.228 | 0.229 | 0.234 | 0.243 | 0.242 | 0.230 | 0.215 | 0.156 | 0.172 |
|   | B6 | 0.176 | 0.192 | 0.211 | 0.200 | 0.230 | 0.253 | 0.282 | 0.289 | 0.300 | 0.299 | 0.324 | 0.341 | 0.296 | 0.296 |
|   | B7 | 0.176 | 0.173 | 0.171 | 0.162 | 0.149 | 0.131 | 0.102 | 0.093 | 0.097 | 0.086 | 0.035 | 0.033 | 0.028 | 0.025 |
| C | C1 | 0.225 | 0.205 | 0.217 | 0.247 | 0.264 | 0.249 | 0.169 | 0.154 | 0.165 | 0.152 | 0.138 | 0.111 | 0.088 | 0.089 |
|   | C2 | 0.197 | 0.201 | 0.213 | 0.244 | 0.162 | 0.191 | 0.182 | 0.166 | 0.107 | 0.110 | 0.117 | 0.094 | 0.074 | 0.084 |
|   | C3 | 0.138 | 0.141 | 0.100 | 0.114 | 0.121 | 0.129 | 0.175 | 0.160 | 0.171 | 0.157 | 0.190 | 0.218 | 0.231 | 0.203 |
|   | C4 | 0.099 | 0.089 | 0.084 | 0.077 | 0.062 | 0.058 | 0.063 | 0.058 | 0.062 | 0.071 | 0.075 | 0.069 | 0.036 | 0.028 |
|   | C5 | 0.085 | 0.086 | 0.091 | 0.084 | 0.078 | 0.073 | 0.080 | 0.083 | 0.089 | 0.102 | 0.109 | 0.125 | 0.165 | 0.145 |
|   | C6 | 0.118 | 0.121 | 0.128 | 0.102 | 0.136 | 0.112 | 0.076 | 0.080 | 0.085 | 0.078 | 0.071 | 0.074 | 0.078 | 0.078 |
|   | C7 | 0.138 | 0.157 | 0.166 | 0.133 | 0.177 | 0.187 | 0.255 | 0.299 | 0.320 | 0.330 | 0.301 | 0.310 | 0.328 | 0.372 |
| D | D1 | 0.075 | 0.074 | 0.079 | 0.076 | 0.078 | 0.094 | 0.098 | 0.103 | 0.123 | 0.115 | 0.115 | 0.152 | 0.157 | 0.197 |
|   | D2 | 0.105 | 0.091 | 0.097 | 0.081 | 0.084 | 0.091 | 0.095 | 0.089 | 0.084 | 0.089 | 0.107 | 0.113 | 0.155 | 0.130 |
|   | D3 | 0.140 | 0.121 | 0.100 | 0.096 | 0.099 | 0.095 | 0.112 | 0.092 | 0.109 | 0.115 | 0.162 | 0.149 | 0.103 | 0.086 |
|   | D4 | 0.123 | 0.121 | 0.114 | 0.110 | 0.079 | 0.086 | 0.112 | 0.105 | 0.100 | 0.117 | 0.094 | 0.099 | 0.068 | 0.057 |
|   | D5 | 0.175 | 0.173 | 0.163 | 0.157 | 0.162 | 0.156 | 0.143 | 0.150 | 0.179 | 0.167 | 0.101 | 0.133 | 0.182 | 0.178 |
|   | D6 | 0.201 | 0.198 | 0.210 | 0.227 | 0.234 | 0.225 | 0.207 | 0.217 | 0.259 | 0.242 | 0.145 | 0.134 | 0.185 | 0.206 |
|   | D7 | 0.180 | 0.222 | 0.236 | 0.255 | 0.264 | 0.253 | 0.232 | 0.244 | 0.145 | 0.153 | 0.276 | 0.219 | 0.150 | 0.147 |
| E | E1 | 0.122 | 0.108 | 0.099 | 0.086 | 0.058 | 0.070 | 0.072 | 0.079 | 0.089 | 0.077 | 0.066 | 0.088 | 0.044 | 0.044 |
|   | E2 | 0.187 | 0.185 | 0.211 | 0.231 | 0.209 | 0.193 | 0.201 | 0.192 | 0.216 | 0.211 | 0.179 | 0.213 | 0.213 | 0.237 |
|   | E3 | 0.157 | 0.156 | 0.160 | 0.175 | 0.158 | 0.147 | 0.153 | 0.187 | 0.210 | 0.206 | 0.210 | 0.218 | 0.219 | 0.170 |
|   | E4 | 0.143 | 0.142 | 0.129 | 0.127 | 0.144 | 0.152 | 0.119 | 0.113 | 0.089 | 0.097 | 0.165 | 0.171 | 0.172 | 0.190 |
|   | E5 | 0.187 | 0.185 | 0.169 | 0.129 | 0.146 | 0.135 | 0.141 | 0.172 | 0.194 | 0.190 | 0.194 | 0.144 | 0.144 | 0.128 |
|   | E6 | 0.204 | 0.225 | 0.231 | 0.252 | 0.285 | 0.302 | 0.314 | 0.257 | 0.202 | 0.220 | 0.187 | 0.166 | 0.208 | 0.231 |
| F | F1 | 0.218 | 0.207 | 0.215 | 0.237 | 0.258 | 0.263 | 0.285 | 0.308 | 0.308 | 0.274 | 0.379 | 0.407 | 0.471 | 0.510 |
|   | F2 | 0.218 | 0.233 | 0.242 | 0.214 | 0.232 | 0.267 | 0.289 | 0.311 | 0.311 | 0.357 | 0.197 | 0.212 | 0.245 | 0.212 |
|   | F3 | 0.218 | 0.233 | 0.242 | 0.240 | 0.209 | 0.213 | 0.180 | 0.151 | 0.151 | 0.134 | 0.074 | 0.072 | 0.062 | 0.061 |
|   | F4 | 0.098 | 0.093 | 0.097 | 0.096 | 0.104 | 0.080 | 0.077 | 0.083 | 0.083 | 0.085 | 0.094 | 0.090 | 0.052 | 0.057 |
|   | F5 | 0.134 | 0.127 | 0.103 | 0.102 | 0.077 | 0.069 | 0.067 | 0.048 | 0.048 | 0.061 | 0.084 | 0.072 | 0.042 | 0.036 |
|   | F6 | 0.114 | 0.109 | 0.101 | 0.111 | 0.120 | 0.108 | 0.103 | 0.099 | 0.099 | 0.089 | 0.171 | 0.147 | 0.128 | 0.124 |
| G | G1 | 0.070 | 0.079 | 0.078 | 0.081 | 0.089 | 0.087 | 0.085 | 0.101 | 0.070 | 0.065 | 0.063 | 0.051 | 0.043 | 0.044 |
|   | G2 | 0.070 | 0.061 | 0.061 | 0.056 | 0.017 | 0.040 | 0.039 | 0.046 | 0.032 | 0.034 | 0.016 | 0.009 | 0.008 | 0.006 |
|   | G3 | 0.082 | 0.072 | 0.071 | 0.073 | 0.071 | 0.087 | 0.074 | 0.088 | 0.061 | 0.057 | 0.055 | 0.050 | 0.042 | 0.048 |
|   | G4 | 0.068 | 0.077 | 0.085 | 0.088 | 0.110 | 0.134 | 0.115 | 0.121 | 0.140 | 0.114 | 0.146 | 0.135 | 0.141 | 0.161 |
|   | G5 | 0.094 | 0.094 | 0.104 | 0.107 | 0.149 | 0.146 | 0.142 | 0.131 | 0.152 | 0.177 | 0.113 | 0.130 | 0.137 | 0.141 |
|   | G6 | 0.078 | 0.088 | 0.098 | 0.101 | 0.098 | 0.108 | 0.131 | 0.138 | 0.160 | 0.149 | 0.191 | 0.220 | 0.231 | 0.211 |
|   | G7 | 0.082 | 0.092 | 0.091 | 0.094 | 0.104 | 0.127 | 0.156 | 0.163 | 0.190 | 0.199 | 0.223 | 0.256 | 0.269 | 0.277 |
|   | G8 | 0.123 | 0.108 | 0.093 | 0.077 | 0.064 | 0.062 | 0.053 | 0.049 | 0.057 | 0.060 | 0.076 | 0.044 | 0.046 | 0.037 |
|   | G9 | 0.110 | 0.109 | 0.095 | 0.097 | 0.081 | 0.069 | 0.068 | 0.053 | 0.043 | 0.040 | 0.032 | 0.026 | 0.022 | 0.017 |
|   | G10 | 0.068 | 0.068 | 0.068 | 0.070 | 0.058 | 0.050 | 0.048 | 0.038 | 0.031 | 0.032 | 0.016 | 0.013 | 0.011 | 0.008 |
|   | G11 | 0.047 | 0.047 | 0.052 | 0.048 | 0.040 | 0.034 | 0.034 | 0.031 | 0.025 | 0.026 | 0.025 | 0.026 | 0.016 | 0.015 |
|   | G12 | 0.106 | 0.105 | 0.104 | 0.107 | 0.089 | 0.055 | 0.053 | 0.042 | 0.039 | 0.045 | 0.044 | 0.040 | 0.034 | 0.035 |

Table 7. The weight of KPI by 15 experts.

|   |   | DS15 | Weight of Section | Weight of KPI |
|---|---|---|---|---|
| A | A1 | 0.261 | 0.280 | 0.07295 |
|   | A2 | 0.210 |   | 0.05884 |
|   | A3 | 0.134 |   | 0.03752 |
|   | A4 | 0.003 |   | 0.00084 |
|   | A5 | 0.130 |   | 0.03631 |
|   | A6 | 0.263 |   | 0.07355 |
| B | B1 | 0.096 | 0.362 | 0.03475 |
|   | B2 | 0.020 |   | 0.00709 |
|   | B3 | 0.372 |   | 0.13466 |
|   | B4 | 0.019 |   | 0.00676 |
|   | B5 | 0.172 |   | 0.06233 |
|   | B6 | 0.296 |   | 0.10685 |
|   | B7 | 0.025 |   | 0.00908 |
| C | C1 | 0.089 | 0.079 | 0.00699 |
|   | C2 | 0.084 |   | 0.00667 |
|   | C3 | 0.203 |   | 0.01607 |
|   | C4 | 0.028 |   | 0.00218 |
|   | C5 | 0.145 |   | 0.01148 |
|   | C6 | 0.078 |   | 0.00620 |
|   | C7 | 0.372 |   | 0.02941 |
| D | D1 | 0.197 | 0.057 | 0.01131 |
|   | D2 | 0.130 |   | 0.00745 |
|   | D3 | 0.086 |   | 0.00493 |
|   | D4 | 0.057 |   | 0.00327 |
|   | D5 | 0.178 |   | 0.01022 |
|   | D6 | 0.206 |   | 0.01182 |
|   | D7 | 0.147 |   | 0.00842 |
| E | E1 | 0.044 | 0.096 | 0.00423 |
|   | E2 | 0.237 |   | 0.02283 |
|   | E3 | 0.170 |   | 0.01638 |
|   | E4 | 0.190 |   | 0.01835 |
|   | E5 | 0.128 |   | 0.01233 |
|   | E6 | 0.231 |   | 0.02229 |
| F | F1 | 0.510 | 0.071 | 0.03610 |
|   | F2 | 0.212 |   | 0.01504 |
|   | F3 | 0.061 |   | 0.00430 |
|   | F4 | 0.057 |   | 0.00401 |
|   | F5 | 0.036 |   | 0.00257 |
|   | F6 | 0.124 |   | 0.00881 |
| G | G1 | 0.044 | 0.055 | 0.00240 |
|   | G2 | 0.006 |   | 0.00034 |
|   | G3 | 0.048 |   | 0.00264 |
|   | G4 | 0.161 |   | 0.00885 |
|   | G5 | 0.141 |   | 0.00771 |
|   | G6 | 0.211 |   | 0.01156 |
|   | G7 | 0.277 |   | 0.01517 |
|   | G8 | 0.037 |   | 0.00202 |
|   | G9 | 0.017 |   | 0.00096 |
|   | G10 | 0.008 |   | 0.00046 |
|   | G11 | 0.015 |   | 0.00083 |
|   | G12 | 0.035 |   | 0.00190 |

## 5. Case Studies

### 5.1. Background of 13 Cases

With the help of several consulting firms, we found some real cases of MC projects. These companies are located in China's Hong Kong, Greater Bay Area, southwest, east and south, and they are all typical companies that meet the application conditions of the MC model (in China's market background and corresponding demand). As shown in Table 8, these projects cover different industries, have different application scopes and project sizes, which can verify that the MC model can effectively evaluate a management consulting project, regardless of organizational size, industry type or project type.

**Table 8.** Background of the 13 cases.

| | Industry | Type | Location/Area | The Number of Team | Estimated Project Duration | Actual Project Duration | The Rate of Time Overruns | Customer Satisfaction (0–10) |
|---|---|---|---|---|---|---|---|---|
| Case 1 | Energy | Strategy management | Southwest | 3 | 3 months | 3.5 months | 16.67% | 5 |
| Case 2 | Agriculture | Human resources | South | 3 | 5 months | 18 months | 260% | 3 |
| Case 3 | Finance | Strategy management | Southeast | 4 | 3 months | 3 months | 0 | 7 |
| Case 4 | Grid | Technology management | Northwest | 6 | 3 months | 2 months | −33.33% | 8 |
| Case 5 | Manufacture | Technology training management | North | 10 | 4 weeks | 4.5 weeks | 12.5% | 7 |
| Case 6 | Finance | Post-investment management | Southeast | 6 | 18 weeks | 18 months | 300% | 4 |
| Case 7 | Finance | Strategy management | Southeast | 11 | 14 weeks | 12 months | 242.86% | 7 |
| Case 8 | Food Manufacturing | ERP | Hong Kong | 6 | 14 months | 20 months | 42.86% | 8 |
| Case 9 | Wholesales | ERP | Hong Kong | 8 | 16 months | 18 months | 12.5% | 9 |
| Case 10 | Properties Management | Corporate Performance Management (CPM) | Hong Kong | 4 | 8 months | 9 months | 12.5% | 9 |
| Case 11 | Medicine | Performance Excellence Coaching | East | 3 | 3 weeks | 3 weeks | 0 | 9 |
| Case 12 | Grid | Performance Excellence Coaching | Northwest | 3 | 6 months | 5.5 months | −8.33% | 10 |
| Case 13 | Grid | Science and technology innovation | East | 4 | 5 months | 4 months | −20% | 10 |

### 5.2. The Process of Case Studies

The process is divided into the following four steps: project study (basic information acquisition and statement), project evaluation, weighted score calculation (combined with project evaluation scores and MC model weight scores), score comparison and conclusion. Project research mainly introduces the project background, including project type, industry involved, number of team members, expected completion time, actual completion time, client satisfaction, etc. Project scoring is to invite the consultant or the person in charge of the consultant to fill in the project measurement and evaluation questionnaire. Weighted score calculation is based on the score of the project and the weight of the experts.

### 5.3. Case Study One as an Example

Case 1 is from Team A, which is a management consulting team from a consulting firm in the Greater Bay Area. The total number in the team is 10. It has been established for eight years and has completed nearly 100 management consulting projects.

The project was carried out by Team A in Sichuan Province in March 2018. The project enterprise is a newly established provincial state-owned enterprise with more than 20 employees at its headquarters and six subordinate companies, each with about 30 employees. The purpose of this project is to establish an organizational structure and develop a performance appraisal plan for the enterprise. It was planned to be completed in three months, but it was actually delayed by two weeks. In this project, the participation of the senior management is high, but the cooperation between the middle management and the grassroots is not high, which leads to some resistance and affects the project schedule.

We obtained the project evaluation data according to the team leader's score of the project through the project measure and assessment tool (Appendix A).

In order to evaluate the project through the model, we combined the evaluation data provided by the team leader with KPI weight.

$$\text{KPI Score} = \text{Evaluation from Case} \times \text{Weight of KPI}$$

Weight% = $\sum$ of weight of each KPI, which shows the importance of that section, which also is weight of section (see Table 7).

$$\text{Score of Section} = \sum \text{of KPI score} / \sum \text{of weight of each KPI}$$

The project weight data processing of case 1 is shown in Table 9.

**Table 9.** Project weight data of case 1.

| Section | KPI | Weight of KPI | Evaluation from Case 1 | KPI Score 1 | Score 1 of Section | Weight % |
|---|---|---|---|---|---|---|
| A | A1 | 0.07295 | 3 | 0.219 | | |
| | A2 | 0.05884 | 1 | 0.059 | | |
| | A3 | 0.03752 | 1 | 0.038 | | |
| | A4 | 0.00084 | 2 | 0.002 | 1.787 | 28.00% |
| | A5 | 0.03631 | 1 | 0.036 | | |
| | A6 | 0.07355 | 2 | 0.147 | | |
| | sub-sum | | 10 | 0.500 | | |
| B | B1 | 0.03475 | 3 | 0.104 | | |
| | B2 | 0.00709 | 2 | 0.014 | | |
| | B3 | 0.13466 | 2 | 0.269 | | |
| | B4 | 0.00676 | 0 | 0.000 | 2.476 | 36.15% |
| | B5 | 0.06233 | 3 | 0.187 | | |
| | B6 | 0.10685 | 3 | 0.321 | | |
| | B7 | 0.00908 | 0 | 0.000 | | |
| | sub-sum | | 13 | 0.895 | | |
| C | C1 | 0.00699 | 2 | 0.014 | | |
| | C2 | 0.00667 | 0 | 0.000 | | |
| | C3 | 0.01607 | 1 | 0.016 | | |
| | C4 | 0.00218 | 2 | 0.004 | 0.816 | 7.90% |
| | C5 | 0.01148 | 1 | 0.011 | | |
| | C6 | 0.00620 | 3 | 0.019 | | |
| | C7 | 0.02941 | 0 | 0.000 | | |
| | sub-sum | | 9 | 0.064 | | |
| D | D1 | 0.01131 | 3 | 0.034 | | |
| | D2 | 0.00745 | 3 | 0.022 | | |
| | D3 | 0.00493 | 3 | 0.015 | | |
| | D4 | 0.00327 | 1 | 0.003 | 2.090 | 5.74% |
| | D5 | 0.01022 | 1 | 0.010 | | |
| | D6 | 0.01182 | 3 | 0.035 | | |
| | D7 | 0.00842 | 0 | 0.000 | | |
| | sub-sum | | 14 | 0.120 | | |

Table 9. Cont.

| Section | KPI | Weight of KPI | Evaluation from Case 1 | KPI Score 1 | Score 1 of Section | Weight % |
|---|---|---|---|---|---|---|
| E | E1 | 0.00423 | 1 | 0.004 | | |
| | E2 | 0.02283 | 3 | 0.068 | | |
| | E3 | 0.01638 | 1 | 0.016 | | |
| | E4 | 0.01835 | 1 | 0.018 | 1.601 | 9.64% |
| | E5 | 0.01233 | 2 | 0.025 | | |
| | E6 | 0.02229 | 1 | 0.022 | | |
| | sub-sum | | 9 | 0.154 | | |
| F | F1 | 0.03610 | 2 | 0.072 | | |
| | F2 | 0.01504 | 2 | 0.030 | | |
| | F3 | 0.00430 | 1 | 0.004 | | |
| | F4 | 0.00401 | 1 | 0.004 | 1.634 | 7.08% |
| | F5 | 0.00257 | 2 | 0.005 | | |
| | F6 | 0.00881 | 0 | 0.000 | | |
| | sub-sum | | 8 | 0.116 | | |
| G | G1 | 0.00240 | 1 | 0.002 | | |
| | G2 | 0.00034 | 1 | 0.000 | | |
| | G3 | 0.00264 | 2 | 0.005 | | |
| | G4 | 0.00885 | 1 | 0.009 | | |
| | G5 | 0.00771 | 1 | 0.008 | | |
| | G6 | 0.01156 | 3 | 0.035 | | |
| | G7 | 0.01517 | 1 | 0.015 | 1.470 | 5.48% |
| | G8 | 0.00202 | 1 | 0.002 | | |
| | G9 | 0.00096 | 1 | 0.001 | | |
| | G10 | 0.00046 | 1 | 0.000 | | |
| | G11 | 0.00083 | 1 | 0.001 | | |
| | G12 | 0.00190 | 1 | 0.002 | | |
| | sub-sum | 0.07295 | 15 | 0.081 | | |
| SUM | | | | | 11.875 | 1.000 |

### 5.4. Comparison of the 13 Cases

Due to page limitations, we will not report the application of the other 12 cases. Through the project evaluation of 13 management consulting cases of 6 consulting companies by the new MC model, we can obtain the weight score of these 13 cases as shown in Table 10.

Table 10. Comparison of weight scores and client satisfaction of 13 cases.

| Case | A | B | C | D | E | F | G | SUM | Client Satisfaction (0–10) |
|---|---|---|---|---|---|---|---|---|---|
| 1 | 1.787 | 2.478 | 0.816 | 2.090 | 1.601 | 1.634 | 1.470 | 11.876 | 5 |
| 2 | 1.997 | 1.778 | 1.189 | 2.090 | 1.601 | 1.124 | 1.470 | 11.249 | 3 |
| 3 | 2.526 | 2.975 | 1.737 | 2.090 | 1.601 | 2.004 | 1.470 | 14.403 | 7 |
| 4 | 2.729 | 2.141 | 1.710 | 0.551 | 1.342 | 2.722 | 1.470 | 12.665 | 8 |
| 5 | 2.605 | 2.249 | 1.129 | 1.092 | 1.549 | 2.846 | 1.048 | 12.519 | 7 |
| 6 | 2.081 | 1.755 | 1.680 | 1.315 | 1.829 | 1.742 | 0.815 | 11.219 | 4 |
| 7 | 2.003 | 2.313 | 2.651 | 2.558 | 2.956 | 1.062 | 1.455 | 14.998 | 7 |
| 8 | 0.263 | 0.879 | 0.346 | 0.635 | 0.872 | 0.305 | 0.863 | 4.153 | 8 |
| 9 | 1.736 | 2.706 | 2.478 | 2.372 | 2.555 | 2.305 | 1.161 | 15.315 | 9 |
| 10 | 3.000 | 3.000 | 3.000 | 2.943 | 3.000 | 2.876 | 1.209 | 19.028 | 9 |
| 11 | 2.870 | 3.000 | 2.855 | 3.000 | 3.000 | 3.000 | 1.470 | 19.195 | 9 |
| 12 | 3.000 | 3.000 | 3.000 | 3.000 | 3.000 | 3.000 | 1.470 | 19.470 | 10 |
| 13 | 3.000 | 2.980 | 2.743 | 3.000 | 3.000 | 3.000 | 1.470 | 19.193 | 10 |

As can be seen from Table 10, it is evident that projects with evaluation scores above 12 are generally more recognized and satisfied by clients, while projects with evaluation scores below 12 are generally less successful and less satisfactory.

We can divide the project into the following fractional sections. From the perspective of different sections, the individual scores of the first six sections also impact the success of the project, as shown in Table 11.

Table 11. The benchmarks for assessing MC projects.

| SUM Score Range | The Number of Section Points > 2 (Section A–F) | Project Degree of Success |
| --- | --- | --- |
| <12 | <2 | Failure projects |
| 12–15 | 3–4 | Projects with fair performance and client satisfaction |
| >15 | 5–6 | Projects with outstanding performance |

According to the classification in Table 11, among the 13 cases found in this paper, there are 4 failure cases, namely, cases 1, 2, 6 and 8; there are 4 common cases (with general performance), namely, cases 3, 4, 5 and 7; and there are 5 success cases, namely, cases 9, 10, 11, 12 and 13. This is shown in Table 12. Feedback was provided to the case projects and mostly matched the client satisfaction measure except for case 8.

Table 12. The assessment results for 13 cases under 3 categories.

| Degrees of Success | Case | A | B | C | D | E | F | G | SUM | Customer Satisfaction (0–10) |
| --- | --- | --- | --- | --- | --- | --- | --- | --- | --- | --- |
| Unsatisfied cases | 1 | 1.787 | 2.478 | 0.816 | 2.090 | 1.601 | 1.634 | 1.470 | 11.876 | 5 |
| | 2 | 1.997 | 1.778 | 1.189 | 2.090 | 1.601 | 1.124 | 1.470 | 11.249 | 3 |
| | 6 | 2.081 | 1.755 | 1.680 | 1.315 | 1.829 | 1.742 | 0.815 | 11.219 | 4 |
| | 8 | 0.263 | 0.879 | 0.346 | 0.635 | 0.872 | 0.305 | 0.863 | 4.153 | 8 |
| Fair cases | 3 | 2.526 | 2.975 | 1.737 | 2.090 | 1.601 | 2.004 | 1.470 | 14.403 | 7 |
| | 4 | 2.729 | 2.141 | 1.710 | 0.551 | 1.342 | 2.722 | 1.470 | 12.665 | 8 |
| | 5 | 2.605 | 2.249 | 1.129 | 1.092 | 1.549 | 2.846 | 1.048 | 12.519 | 7 |
| | 7 | 2.003 | 2.313 | 2.651 | 2.558 | 2.956 | 1.062 | 1.455 | 14.998 | 7 |
| Satisfactory cases | 9 | 1.736 | 2.706 | 2.478 | 2.372 | 2.555 | 2.305 | 1.161 | 15.315 | 9 |
| | 10 | 3.000 | 3.000 | 3.000 | 2.943 | 3.000 | 2.876 | 1.209 | 19.028 | 9 |
| | 11 | 2.870 | 3.000 | 2.855 | 3.000 | 3.000 | 3.000 | 1.470 | 19.195 | 9 |
| | 12 | 3.000 | 3.000 | 3.000 | 3.000 | 3.000 | 3.000 | 1.470 | 19.470 | 10 |
| | 13 | 3.000 | 2.980 | 2.743 | 3.000 | 3.000 | 3.000 | 1.470 | 19.193 | 10 |

## 6. Discussions and Implications

### 6.1. Theoretical Implications

Using models to help manage consulting projects is not a novel approach. There are many such models, but some parts of these models need to be improved. The ITEA model of the ASQ organization only carries out post-project evaluations and lacks the weight analysis and process analysis of each part, so it cannot be used as a reference model in the early stages of the project. Reference [9] provided the project decision analysis process (PDAP), and reference [3] presented the project organization model, providing only a process guide. Reference [5] only proposed six management factors for successful projects. References [10–12] proposed a qualitative conceptual model without quantifying the model.

Compared with previous models, this new management consulting model explains the relationship between the factors and processes. It covers the tracking and control part of the project. It is convenient for the consulting team to follow the D-S theory, and it can help the consulting team to predict, track and evaluate the consulting project in the early, middle and late stages, thereby helping the team to improve the success of a project and client satisfaction.

The new management consulting model was validated through the professional evaluation by 15 experts with 5–30 years of experience and Dempster–Shafer theory. This allows the new model to perform both qualitative and quantitative analysis of management consulting projects. This was not possible in all the previous models.

*6.2. Practical Implications*

The new model can help the project team to conduct guidance, self-tests and correction in the early and middle stages of the project. The process-based model and the maturity scale with clear levels can help the project team to conduct self-assessment and improvement in the early stage of a project, and improve the success probability and client satisfaction of the project through clear standards. In the middle of the project, it can be based on the model to fill in the missing pieces of the successful factors.

A good management consulting model can be applied to different stages and situations in a project [12]. This model can be used for project establishment, management and evaluation, providing a transparent and powerful tool for managing the risk, budget and more aspects of consulting projects [11].

## 7. Conclusions

Based on the review of the previous management consulting models, this paper discovered the existing deficiencies and proposed a new MC model. A total of 15 experts with 5–30 years of experience were invited to assess the importance of the seven factors of the new model. The Dempster–Shafer algorithm was used to summarize the 15 expert scores and obtain the weight of each part of the model. Then, the MC model was proved to be effective in the evaluation of management consulting projects in Hong Kong and mainland China through 13 cases. This new MC model can help the consulting team to conduct an assessment in early stage, track in the middle stage and evaluate in the late stage of the consulting project, and also can help the team improve the probability of project success, and client satisfaction.

The contribution of the new model can be summarized as follows. (1) the model covers all seven important factors identified from the literature review, providing a more integrated and systematic model to evaluate an MC project; (2) the model is evaluated by D-S theory and verified by case study, providing a complete and systematic model to conduct qualitative and quantitative analysis for an MC project; (3) the model can be applied to different stages of an MC project, allow flexibility in real-world applications and improve both project success and client satisfaction.

The research is not without limitations. First, the study was conducted in the Chinese context. As the success of an MC project may be related to cultural factors, the effectiveness of the proposed model beyond the boundary of China is questionable. Second, this model was only applied in a relatively small sample size of 13 cases. In the future, the model should be verified in an international context to see its validation across cultures and verified by more real cases.

**Author Contributions:** Conceptualization, H.S. and W.N.; formal analysis, L.H.; writing—original draft preparation, L.H. and H.S.; writing—review and editing, H.S. and W.N. All authors have read and agreed to the published version of the manuscript.

**Funding:** The report is supported by a project (92399046) from City University of Hong Kong.

**Data Availability Statement:** The data presented in this study are available on request from the corresponding author. The data are not publicly available for business reasons.

**Conflicts of Interest:** The authors declare no conflict of interest.

## Appendix A. A Quantitative Assessment Tool for Management Consultation Model

| | Pls. rate the importance of the following factors for MC | Not important ←→ Important | | | | | | | | | |
|---|---|---|---|---|---|---|---|---|---|---|---|
| Part A | Project Background and Purpose | 1 | 2 | 3 | 4 | 5 | 6 | 7 | 8 | 9 | 10 |
| A1 | Should organizations have a general approach to selecting projects? | 1 | 2 | 3 | 4 | 5 | 6 | 7 | 8 | 9 | 10 |
| A2 | Should the team understand how the need for projects is identified in their organization? | 1 | 2 | 3 | 4 | 5 | 6 | 7 | 8 | 9 | 10 |
| A3 | Should the team understand how project prioritization/selection be done? | 1 | 2 | 3 | 4 | 5 | 6 | 7 | 8 | 9 | 10 |
| A4 | Should the project selection process be data-based? | 1 | 2 | 3 | 4 | 5 | 6 | 7 | 8 | 9 | 10 |
| A5 | Are project goals and benefits well-documented? | 1 | 2 | 3 | 4 | 5 | 6 | 7 | 8 | 9 | 10 |
| A6 | Are project goals and benefits evaluated? | 1 | 2 | 3 | 4 | 5 | 6 | 7 | 8 | 9 | 10 |
| | | Not important ←→ Important | | | | | | | | | |
| Part B | Project Framework | 1 | 2 | 3 | 4 | 5 | 6 | 7 | 8 | 9 | 10 |
| B1 | Does the project have concise project statement which includes three parts (the current state, desired future state and the gap)? | 1 | 2 | 3 | 4 | 5 | 6 | 7 | 8 | 9 | 10 |
| B2 | Are the type of project specified? | 1 | 2 | 3 | 4 | 5 | 6 | 7 | 8 | 9 | 10 |
| B3 | Are the project scope stated? | 1 | 2 | 3 | 4 | 5 | 6 | 7 | 8 | 9 | 10 |
| B4 | Are the assumptions/expectations documented? (Assumptions typically include timing, resource availability, or products or services that will come from outside the group.) | 1 | 2 | 3 | 4 | 5 | 6 | 7 | 8 | 9 | 10 |
| B5 | Is there a project schedule or high-level plan? | 1 | 2 | 3 | 4 | 5 | 6 | 7 | 8 | 9 | 10 |
| B6 | Is there a financial or resource budget? | 1 | 2 | 3 | 4 | 5 | 6 | 7 | 8 | 9 | 10 |
| B7 | Is there a risk management plan? | 1 | 2 | 3 | 4 | 5 | 6 | 7 | 8 | 9 | 10 |
| | | Not important ←→ Important | | | | | | | | | |
| Part C | Project Stakeholders and the Project Team | 1 | 2 | 3 | 4 | 5 | 6 | 7 | 8 | 9 | 10 |
| C1 | Are stakeholders or stakeholder groups identified? | 1 | 2 | 3 | 4 | 5 | 6 | 7 | 8 | 9 | 10 |
| C2 | Is project champion who is the primary stakeholder identified? | 1 | 2 | 3 | 4 | 5 | 6 | 7 | 8 | 9 | 10 |
| C3 | Should skills be required during project team selection? | 1 | 2 | 3 | 4 | 5 | 6 | 7 | 8 | 9 | 10 |
| C4 | Are there any team preparation activities? | 1 | 2 | 3 | 4 | 5 | 6 | 7 | 8 | 9 | 10 |
| C5 | Is there any team training (such as skill, tool, or project background)? | 1 | 2 | 3 | 4 | 5 | 6 | 7 | 8 | 9 | 10 |
| C6 | Are the team routines discussed and be understood? | 1 | 2 | 3 | 4 | 5 | 6 | 7 | 8 | 9 | 10 |
| C7 | Are internal and external conflicts considered? | 1 | 2 | 3 | 4 | 5 | 6 | 7 | 8 | 9 | 10 |
| | | Not important ←→ Important | | | | | | | | | |
| Part D | Project Overview | 1 | 2 | 3 | 4 | 5 | 6 | 7 | 8 | 9 | 10 |
| D1 | Is there a formal project approach or structure? | 1 | 2 | 3 | 4 | 5 | 6 | 7 | 8 | 9 | 10 |
| D2 | Is there a tools selection and explanation? | 1 | 2 | 3 | 4 | 5 | 6 | 7 | 8 | 9 | 10 |
| D3 | Is there tool output at different stages of project? | 1 | 2 | 3 | 4 | 5 | 6 | 7 | 8 | 9 | 10 |
| D4 | How team was prepared to use the tools? | 1 | 2 | 3 | 4 | 5 | 6 | 7 | 8 | 9 | 10 |
| D5 | Are there some mitigation plans for common risk ahead of time? | 1 | 2 | 3 | 4 | 5 | 6 | 7 | 8 | 9 | 10 |
| D6 | Are there ways to identified and addressed risk of stakeholder resistance? | 1 | 2 | 3 | 4 | 5 | 6 | 7 | 8 | 9 | 10 |
| D7 | Are stakeholders or stakeholder groups involved throughout the whole project? | 1 | 2 | 3 | 4 | 5 | 6 | 7 | 8 | 9 | 10 |
| | | Not important ←→ Important | | | | | | | | | |
| Part E | Project Walkthrough | 1 | 2 | 3 | 4 | 5 | 6 | 7 | 8 | 9 | 10 |
| E1 | Is there a data-driven project flow? | 1 | 2 | 3 | 4 | 5 | 6 | 7 | 8 | 9 | 10 |
| E2 | Is there a statement of solution validation? | 1 | 2 | 3 | 4 | 5 | 6 | 7 | 8 | 9 | 10 |
| E3 | Is there a statement of solution justification (to show the final solution's appropriateness)? | 1 | 2 | 3 | 4 | 5 | 6 | 7 | 8 | 9 | 10 |
| E4 | Is there is a statement of project results which can show how the gap has been closed? | 1 | 2 | 3 | 4 | 5 | 6 | 7 | 8 | 9 | 10 |
| E5 | Is there a need to ensure that the changes remain in place and that the results are maintained? | 1 | 2 | 3 | 4 | 5 | 6 | 7 | 8 | 9 | 10 |
| E6 | Are results communicated during stakeholders? | 1 | 2 | 3 | 4 | 5 | 6 | 7 | 8 | 9 | 10 |

|  |  |  | Not important ←→ Important | | | | | | | | | |
|---|---|---|---|---|---|---|---|---|---|---|---|---|
| Part F | Project Tracking and Control | 1 | 2 | 3 | 4 | 5 | 6 | 7 | 8 | 9 | 10 |
| F1 | Is there any plan for tracking process (time control)? | 1 | 2 | 3 | 4 | 5 | 6 | 7 | 8 | 9 | 10 |
| F2 | Is there any plan for tracking finance (budget control)? | 1 | 2 | 3 | 4 | 5 | 6 | 7 | 8 | 9 | 10 |
| F3 | Are there any tools for project tracking and control? | 1 | 2 | 3 | 4 | 5 | 6 | 7 | 8 | 9 | 10 |
| F4 | Is there any specific person who response for project tracking? | 1 | 2 | 3 | 4 | 5 | 6 | 7 | 8 | 9 | 10 |
| F5 | Is there any adjustment during project? | 1 | 2 | 3 | 4 | 5 | 6 | 7 | 8 | 9 | 10 |
| F6 | Is there a review or summary of the project? | 1 | 2 | 3 | 4 | 5 | 6 | 7 | 8 | 9 | 10 |
|  |  | Not important ←→ Important | | | | | | | | | |
| Part G | Project Presentation | 1 | 2 | 3 | 4 | 5 | 6 | 7 | 8 | 9 | 10 |
| G1 | Are slide numbers mostly visible or readable? | 1 | 2 | 3 | 4 | 5 | 6 | 7 | 8 | 9 | 10 |
| G2 | Are items numbers mostly visible or readable? | 1 | 2 | 3 | 4 | 5 | 6 | 7 | 8 | 9 | 10 |
| G3 | Are most slide contents visible and easy to read? | 1 | 2 | 3 | 4 | 5 | 6 | 7 | 8 | 9 | 10 |
| G4 | Is the presentation easy to follow logically? | 1 | 2 | 3 | 4 | 5 | 6 | 7 | 8 | 9 | 10 |
| G5 | Do the item numbers and slide labeling mostly matched material being presented? | 1 | 2 | 3 | 4 | 5 | 6 | 7 | 8 | 9 | 10 |
| G6 | Are graphics, illustrations and narrative used as presentation tools? | 1 | 2 | 3 | 4 | 5 | 6 | 7 | 8 | 9 | 10 |
| G7 | Are graphics, illustrations and narrative integrated to support the presentation and emphasize key points? | 1 | 2 | 3 | 4 | 5 | 6 | 7 | 8 | 9 | 10 |
| G8 | Are there any errors on English grammar, spelling or sentence structure? | 1 | 2 | 3 | 4 | 5 | 6 | 7 | 8 | 9 | 10 |
| G9 | Is presenter volume acceptable? | 1 | 2 | 3 | 4 | 5 | 6 | 7 | 8 | 9 | 10 |
| G10 | Is pace of narration acceptable? | 1 | 2 | 3 | 4 | 5 | 6 | 7 | 8 | 9 | 10 |
| G11 | Do written and spoken narratives match? | 1 | 2 | 3 | 4 | 5 | 6 | 7 | 8 | 9 | 10 |
| G12 | Is there any body language or eye contact to help the presentation and interaction? | 1 | 2 | 3 | 4 | 5 | 6 | 7 | 8 | 9 | 10 |

## References

1. Hugo, F.D.; Pretorius, L.; Benade, S.J. Some aspects of the use and usefulness of quantitative risk analysis tools in project management. *S. Afr. J. Ind. Eng.* **2018**, *29*, 116–128. [CrossRef]
2. Picciotto, R. Towards a 'New Project Management' movement? An international development perspective. *Int. J. Proj. Manag.* **2020**, *38*, 474–485. [CrossRef]
3. Bryde, D.J. Establishing a project organization and a project-management process for telecommunications project management. *Int. J. Proj. Manag.* **1995**, *13*, 25–31. [CrossRef]
4. White, D.; Fortune, J. Current practice in project management—An empirical study. *Int. J. Proj. Manag.* **2002**, *20*, 1–11. [CrossRef]
5. Murphy, A.; Ledwith, A. Project management tools and techniques in high-technology SMEs. *Manag. Res. News* **2007**, *30*, 153–166. [CrossRef]
6. Chong, K. *Best Practice: Management Consulting and the Ethics of Financialization in China*; Duke University Press: London, UK, 2018.
7. Crawford, L.; Pollack, J.; England, D. Uncovering the trends in project management: Journal emphases over the last 10 years. *Int. J. Proj. Manag.* **2006**, *24*, 175–184. [CrossRef]
8. Zilbershtein, D. International Team Excellence Award: A Judge's Behind-the-Scenes Perspective of the Teams. *J. Qual. Particip.* **2010**, *33*, 30.
9. Virine, L.; Trumper, M. *Project Decisions: The Art and Science*; Berrett-Koehler Publishers: San Francisco, CA, USA, 2019.
10. Aguilera, N.P.; Zaldivar, M.A.B.; Aguilera, S.P. The Integrated Management for Projects. A method for systemic management of university processes. *Dilemas Contemp. Educ. Política Y Valore* **2017**, *4*, 1–28.
11. Westerveld, E. The Project Excellence Model®: Linking success criteria and critical success factors. *Int. J. Proj. Manag.* **2003**, *21*, 411–418. [CrossRef]
12. Gist, P.; Langley, D. Application of Standard Project Management Tools to Research--A Case Study from a Multi-National Clinical Trial. *J. Res. Adm.* **2007**, *38*, 51–58.
13. Basheer, M.F.; Imran, M.; Hamid, S.N.A.; Azelin, A.Z.I.Z. Project selection for group decision making: A multiple project perspective from Pakistan. *Bus. Manag. Stud. Int. J.* **2018**, *6*, 190–203. [CrossRef]
14. Herath, S.; Chong, S. Key components and critical success factors for project management success: A literature review. *Oper. Supply Chain Manag. Int. J.* **2021**, *14*, 431–443. [CrossRef]
15. Verma, V.K. *Managing the Project Team*; Project Management Institute: New Town Square, PA, USA, 1997; pp. 102–103.
16. Meyers, J. Training in consultation. *Am. J. Community Psychol.* **1984**, *12*, 233–239. [CrossRef] [PubMed]
17. Newman, D.S. A grounded theory study of supervision of preservice consultation training. *J. Educ. Psychol. Consult.* **2012**, *22*, 247–279. [CrossRef]

18. Anton-LaHart, J.; Rosenfield, S. A survey of preservice consultation training in school psychology programs. *J. Educ. Psychol. Consult.* **2004**, *15*, 41–62. [CrossRef]
19. Ingraham, C.L. Studying multicultural aspects of consultation. In *Handbook of Research in School Consultation*; Routledge: Milton Park, UK, 2014; pp. 281–304.
20. Sander, J.B.; Hernández Finch, M.E.; Pierson, E.E.; Bishop, J.A.; German, R.L.; Wilmoth, C.E. School-based consultation: Training challenges, solutions and building cultural competence. *J. Educ. Psychol. Consult.* **2016**, *26*, 220–240. [CrossRef]
21. Sun, H.; Wong, S.Y.; Zhao, Y.; Yam, R. A systematic model for assessing innovation competence of Hong Kong/China manufacturing companies: A case study. *J. Eng. Technol. Manag.* **2012**, *29*, 546–565. [CrossRef]
22. Wu, S.H.; Coughlan, P.; Coghlan, D.; McNabola, A.; Novara, D. Developing green process innovation through network action learning. *Creat. Innov. Manag.* **2022**, *31*, 248–259. [CrossRef]
23. Fabbro, E.; Tonchia, S. Project management maturity models: Literature review and new developments. *J. Mod. Proj. Manag.* **2021**, *8*, 31–43.
24. Shiue, F.J.; Lee, H.Y.; Zheng, M.C.; Khitam, A.F.; Assefa, S. An estimation model of construction project segmentation for optimum project pricing. *Eng. Constr. Archit. Manag.* **2021**, *28*, 2361–2380. [CrossRef]
25. Ordoñez, R.E.C.; Vanhoucke, M.; Coelho, J.; Anholon, R.; Novaski, O. A study of the critical chain project management method applied to a multi-project system. *Proj. Manag. J.* **2019**, *50*, 322–334. [CrossRef]
26. Cameron, R.; Sankaran, S.; Scales, J. Mixed methods use in project management research. *Proj. Manag. J.* **2015**, *46*, 90–104. [CrossRef]
27. Harmon, P.; Wolf, C. The State of Business Process Management. 2016. Available online: https://www.club-bpm.com/Contenido/Estudios/BPT-Survey-Report.pdf (accessed on 28 August 2023).
28. Kissi, E.; Agyekum, K.; Baiden, B.K.; Tannor, R.A.; Asamoah, G.E.; Andam, E.T. Impact of project monitoring and evaluation practices on construction project success criteria in Ghana. *Built Environ. Proj. Asset Manag.* **2019**, *9*, 364–382. [CrossRef]
29. Ghadage, Y.D.; Narkhede, B.E.; Raut, R.D. Risk management of innovative projects using FMEA; a case study. *Int. J. Bus. Excell.* **2020**, *20*, 70–97. [CrossRef]
30. Sentz, K.; Ferson, S. *Combination of Evidence in Dempster-Shafer Theory*; Sandia National Laboratories: Albuquerque, Mexico, 2002; Volume 4015.
31. Dutta, P. An uncertainty measure and fusion rule for conflict evidences of big data via Dempster–Shafer theory. *Int. J. Image Data Fusion* **2018**, *9*, 152–169. [CrossRef]
32. Brodzik, A.K.; Enders, R.H. Semigroup structure of singleton Dempster–Shafer evidence accumulation. *IEEE Trans. Inf. Theory* **2009**, *55*, 5241–5250. [CrossRef]
33. Blackman, S.; Popoli, R. *Design and Analysis of Modern Tracking Systems*; Artech House: Norwood, MA, USA, 1999.
34. Le Hegarat-Mascle, S.; Bloch, I.; Vidal-Madjar, D. Application of Dempster-Shafer evidence theory to unsupervised classification in multisource remote sensing. *IEEE Trans. Geosci. Remote Sens.* **1997**, *35*, 1018–1031. [CrossRef]
35. Rey, M.; Tunaley, J.K.; Sibbald, T. Use of the Dempster-Shafer algorithm for the detection of SAR ship wakes. *IEEE Trans. Geosci. Remote Sens.* **1993**, *31*, 1114–1118. [CrossRef]
36. Barrios, M.; Guilera, G.; Nuño, L.; Gómez-Benito, J. Consensus in the delphi method: What makes a decision change? *Technol. Forecast. Soc. Chang.* **2021**, *163*, 120484. [CrossRef]

**Disclaimer/Publisher's Note:** The statements, opinions and data contained in all publications are solely those of the individual author(s) and contributor(s) and not of MDPI and/or the editor(s). MDPI and/or the editor(s) disclaim responsibility for any injury to people or property resulting from any ideas, methods, instructions or products referred to in the content.

Article

# Research on the Improvement Path of Total Factor Productivity in the Industrial Software Industry: Evidence from Chinese Typical Firms

Xiaoxiang Wang [1,2,*], Songling Wu [3] and Lixiang Zhao [1]

1. College of Economics and Management, Beijing University of Technology, Beijing 100124, China; b201811002@emails.bjut.edu.cn
2. School of Economics and Management, Wenzhou University of Technology, Wenzhou 325035, China
3. Business School, Henan University of Science and Technology, Luoyang 471023, China; 9901658@haust.edu.cn
* Correspondence: wangxiaoxiang626@163.com

**Abstract:** The high-quality development of the industrial software industry is of strategic significance to enhancing the core competitiveness of the manufacturing industry and promoting the high-quality development of China's industrial economy. By integrating the "capital-technology-environment-human" production factor theory and configuration perspective, this paper constructs a comprehensive analysis framework that drives the total factor productivity (TFP) of the industrial software industry. This paper uses 40 typical industrial software firms in 2018–2020 as case samples and uses fuzzy set Qualitative Comparative Analysis (fsQCA) to empirically explore the influencing factors and complex mechanisms that achieve high-quality development of the industrial software industry. It is found that: (1) a single industrial factor is hardly a necessary condition to drive the industrial software industry; (2) there are four paths to achieving high TFP, which are summarized as "technical-human-environmental" balanced driving type, "capital-human-environmental" balanced driving type, "technical-capital" dual driving type, and "capital" single driving type. There are four driving mechanisms. There are also four not-high TFP configurations with asymmetric characteristics; (3) under certain conditions, the combination of capital factors, technical factors, environmental factors, and human factors can drive TFP in an "all roads lead to Rome". In this process, the government's attention plays a more universal role. The study not only expands the application scenarios of fsQCA but also provides decision guidelines for the practice of strategic emerging industrialization represented by the industrial software industry.

**Keywords:** industrial software industry; total factor productivity; fsQCA; path

**MSC:** 03E75; 91B86

## 1. Introduction

At present, many world manufacturing powers, such as "Made in China 2025" in China, "Industrial Internet" in the United States, and "Industry 4.0" in Germany, have implemented the development strategy of "intelligent manufacturing" at the national level. Although China's industrial capacity and export scale have been at the world's leading level, and its industrial added value as the world's largest manufacturing country accounts for about 30% of the world's total, China is the only country with all industrial categories (41 major categories, 207 medium categories, and 666 subcategories) in the United Nations Industrial Classification, and has been leading other manufacturing economies in the world for many consecutive years. However, even though China has such a huge industrial scale, it is still facing "industrial software", which cannot be bypassed by "intelligent manufacturing" so far [1]. In 2021, at the General Assembly of the China Association for Science and Technology and the General Assembly of the academicians of the Chinese

Academy of Sciences and the Chinese Academy of Engineering, China's scientific and technological breakthroughs should be based on the urgent needs of current and long-term development, and focus on breakthroughs in core technologies in high-end chip fields and industrial software. Industrial software is considered to be the most urgent problem to be solved today, which is related to the country's current economic development needs and highlights the important strategic value of industrial software [2]. In 2021, industrial software was included in the "National Key Research and Development Plan—the first batch of key special research plan" of the Ministry of Science and Technology for the first time, which represents that it has become the highest level of strategic deployment in the domestic science and technology field, and also marks that China's domestic industrial software will step into a new stage of vigorous development. Academite Ni Guangnan (2019) pointed out that China is facing the transformation from a "manufacturing power" to a "manufacturing power", and vigorously developing industrial software is the key support for "intelligent manufacturing" and an important foundation for realizing high-quality development of manufacturing [3]. Promoting the development of China's "intelligent manufacturing" to industrial "intelligent digitalization" can not only give priority to the layout of the transformation and upgrading of "manufacturing power", but also achieve the purpose of rapidly occupying the middle- and high-end global market [4].

According to the statistics of the White Paper on China's Industrial Software Industry (2020), the market size of China's industrial software in 2020 was 197.4 billion CNY, accounting for only 6% of the global industrial software market size, with a year-on-year growth rate of up to 15% (see Figure 1). In 2020, for example, China's industrial-added value exceeded 31.3 trillion CNY, accounting for nearly 30% of the world's total. Although the scale of the industrial added value industry is huge, the proportion of China's industrial software market in the world is too low, resulting in a very strong domestic demand for industrial software [5,6]. Since 2020, with the continuous spread of COVID-19 worldwide and the increased risk of anti-globalization in the international situation, China's economic development environment has undergone great changes, and the policy of "new pattern of internal circulation" has become the main line of our future economic and social development. In the process of high-quality development into a "manufacturing power", China is also facing a series of problems from the "bottleneck" of industrial software in Europe and the United States. As shown in Figure 2, such as the United States banned ZTE and Huawei from using industrial software related to chip design of integrated circuit Electronic Design Automation (EDA), and then prohibited some domestic universities from using MATLAB software (MATLAB Campus Edition) in course teaching [7]. Based on the above research background, we find that the state attaches special importance to the development of the industrial software industry and has formulated promotion policies through relevant departments, which also shows that the government recognizes the important role of industrial software in promoting the growth of the industrial economy. In October 2022, China's "Report to the 20th National Congress" emphasized the need to "accelerate the construction of a modern economic system, strive to improve total factor productivity, and strive to improve the resilience and safety level of industrial and supply chains. In addition, the "14th Five-Year Plan for the Development of Software and Information Technology Service Industry" issued by the Ministry of Industry and Information Technology of China in November 2021 has a more detailed plan for the future development of industrial software.

**Figure 1.** (a) 2012–2022 Global industrial software market size and growth rate; (b) 2012–2020 China industrial software market size and growth rate.

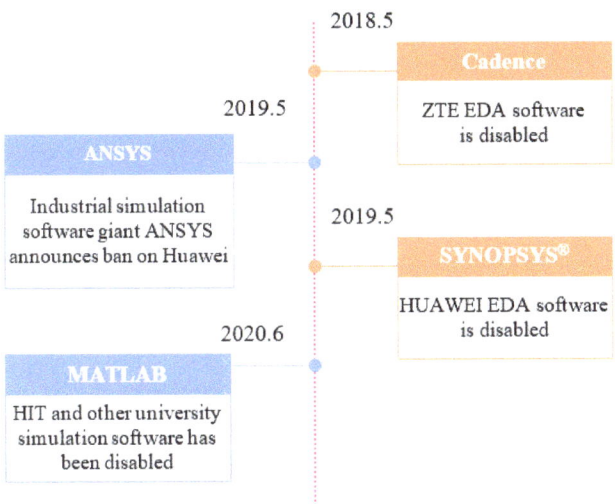

Figure 2. Industrial software disablement event.

Why study total factor productivity (TFP) and improvement paths in the industrial software industry? First, China's industrial software affects the high-quality development of intelligent manufacturing. The way to achieve high-quality development of the industrial software industry is to optimize the allocation efficiency of the industry. Therefore, improving the total factor productivity (TFP) of the industrial software industry is an effective means to achieve development of the industrial software industry. The total factor productivity (TFP) of the industrial software industry is a measure of the high-quality development of the industrial software industry. Second, when analyzing the influencing factors of the industrial software industry, capital, technology, environment, and human factors cannot fully explain the impact on the industrial software industry. Therefore, it is necessary to study the path to improving the total factor productivity (TFP) of the software industry through the configuration and combination of production factors. Finally, in the process of China's intelligent manufacturing transformation, a considerable number of industrial enterprises have low efficiency due to low intelligence and informatization, and the industrial software industry directly affects the transformation and upgrading of the manufacturing industry. Therefore, it is necessary to study whether China's industrial software industry can develop with high quality. The high-quality development of the industrial software industry is measured by the total factor productivity (TFP) of the industrial software industry. The improvement of the total factor productivity (TFP) of China's industrial software industry depends to a large extent on the R&D investment of domestic industrial software companies, government support, and corporate R&D personnel investment. How to improve the total factor productivity (TFP) of the industry has become an extremely realistic issue.

In summary, this paper starts with the total factor productivity (TFP) of the industrial software industry, quantitatively measures the total factor productivity of my country's industrial software industry, analyzes the influencing factors of the total factor productivity of the industrial software industry, and uses the fsQCA method to study its improvement path. From the perspective of the overall analysis, we explore the best path for different factors to improve the total factor productivity of the industrial software industry [8].

The main purposes of this study mainly include the following aspects: Firstly, using fsQCA to study the improvement of TFP in China's industrial software industry is to enrich the literature and efficiency methods of China's industrial software industry, especially for the specific path to improve TFP in the industrial software industry [9,10]. Secondly, explore the relationship between influencing factor variables and outcome variables from a system perspective and use fsQCA to explain the outcome achieved by multiple different path configurations. The research results of this paper not only conform to fuzzy logic but are also more critical to the high-quality development of China's industrial software industry [9,11]. Thirdly, the fsQCA method is used to focus on the asymmetric causal relationship between cause and effect, which makes up for the limitations of symmetric thinking based on correlation coefficients in traditional quantitative linear regression research [9,12,13].

The rest of the paper is structured as follows: This article continues with Section 2, which presents the relevant theoretical basis and analytical framework. In Section 3, we discuss the materials and methods. Section 4 exhibits the empirical analysis of the TFP of the Chinese industrial software industry and also conducts a fsQCA to explore the configurations of TFP improvement [14]. Conclusions and discussion are presented in Section 5.

## 2. Theoretical Basis and Analytical Framework

Existing research has conducted preliminary and useful explorations on the topic of industrial software industry development, which has laid a certain foundation for subsequent related research. However, there is still room for improvement in existing research. On the one hand, existing research still lacks direct empirical evidence to explore the relationship between relevant industry factors and industrial software industrialization. Compared with traditional industries, the industrial software industry is a strategic emerging industry. The differences in industrial attributes may lead to certain differences in the elements of its industrialization. Therefore, it is very necessary to summarize the supporting factors related to the industrial software industry with the help of theory. On the other hand, existing industrialization research is mostly one-dimensional and prefers to explore the single impact of industrial factors on the level of industrialization. However, the industrialization of industrial software itself is a highly complex phenomenon. During the development process, there will definitely be the joint action of multiple factors and the coordinated interaction of multiple factors. At the same time, there may also be situations where the combination of factors is equivalent. In this context, multi-dimensional research is more in line with the reality of high-quality development of industrial software. In addition, there are certain limitations and mismatches in the methods adopted by existing studies. First, quantitative methods based on regression ideas can only explain linear relationships or net effects but cannot reveal the nonlinear relationship between industrial factors, the level of industrial software industrialization, or the underlying mechanism. Second, the application of qualitative methods represented by case analysis has always faced doubts about the representativeness of the sample and the validity of the generalization of the results.

In view of this, this paper attempts to creatively introduce the production factor theory of "capital-technical-environmental-human" into the field of industrial development and combines the configuration perspective to build an integrated analysis framework. It uses the fuzzy set qualitative comparative analysis method to analyze China's typical industrial software companies, which are used as case samples to empirically analyze the influencing factors and implementation mechanisms of industrial software industrialization. Therefore, on the basis of this theory, this paper introduces the configuration perspective for modification and finally forms an integrated analysis framework including six influencing factors at the four levels of technology, capital, human resources, and environment (as shown in Figure 3).

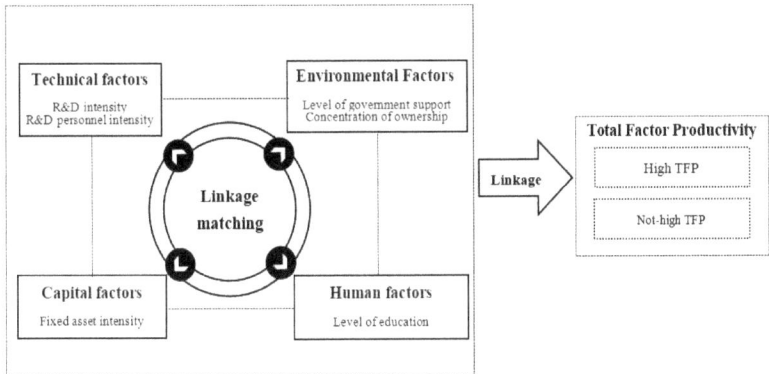

**Figure 3.** Analysis framework of total factor productivity driving mechanism in the industrial software industry.

### 2.1. In Terms of Capital Factors

The development of the industrial software industry requires a large amount of capital investment, and capital investment plays an important role in the production process of the industrial software industry. Capital investment is support for the stable development of the industrial software industry, which is conducive to improving the development environment of the industrial software industry and the infrastructure level of the industrial software industry. The intensity of fixed asset investment can reflect the development in the industrial software industry, so the amount of fixed asset investment is also closely related to the total factor productivity of the industrial software industry. When Bai Wen studied the factors affecting the efficiency of my country's provincial software industry through Tobit model regression analysis, he found that increasing fixed asset investment is conducive to improving industrial efficiency [15]. He Xiong used empirical analysis of soft packaging industry data from 28 provinces in China and found that industry scale, human input level, capital investment level, etc. are the main factors affecting total factor productivity, and believed that the level of capital investment can improve soft packaging industrial efficiency [16]. Based on the availability of data on China's software industry from 2000 to 2015, Guo Rengui and Qiao Yongzhong believe that the software industry is affected by factors such as the intensity of copyright protection, income quota, fixed asset investment, number of employees, export quota, etc. The intensity of copyright protection A significant negative impact occurs, fixed asset investment has a significant negative impact, and other remaining influencing factors are not significant [17].

## 2.2. In Terms of Technical Factors

Li Xu analyzed the relationship between the technological innovation of software companies and the performance of listed companies. The use of R&D funds and personnel investment levels can reflect technological innovation capabilities. The higher the level of R&D investment, the higher the technological innovation capabilities and corporate performance levels [18]. Shao Jinju and Wang Pei measured the input and output efficiency of China's domestic software service industry. The key influencing factor, R&D investment, is significantly positively correlated with the efficiency of the software service industry [19]. Jiao Yunxia [20] used the SFA method to analyze the factors that affect the efficiency of China's software industry. The influencing factors include the level of informatization (represented by the informatization development index), the level of specialization (represented by the proportion of R&D personnel), and the level of R&D investment (represented by the proportion of R&D funds) (represented by ratio), government support level (represented by the proportion of government funding), and enterprise size (represented by the ratio of total business income to the number of regional enterprises). Among them, investment in R&D personnel can improve the efficiency level of the software industry, but the level of R&D investment has a negative impact on the efficiency of the software industry. Chen Guanju (2015) used the SFA method to study relevant data from 31 national-level software industry bases from 2008 to 2012. The results showed that science and technology funding can promote efficiency improvement, and science and technology funding is a key factor affecting innovation efficiency [21]. Jiao Yunxia [22] used the SFA method to analyze the factors that affect the efficiency of the software industry. The influencing factors include the level of specialization (represented by the proportion of R&D personnel), the level of R&D investment (represented by the proportion of R&D funds), and the degree of industrial trade openness (represented by the proportion of export revenue) (represented by ratio), enterprise size (represented by the ratio of total business revenue to the number of regional enterprises), and these factors have a very significant impact. Among them, the level of R&D personnel investment can improve the efficiency of the software industry, and the level of R&D investment has a negative impact on the efficiency of the software industry. Du Qiaoqiao (2019) analyzed the dimensions of production factors (indicating human capital and innovation capabilities), industry dimension (indicating the development in related industries), urban dimension (indicating city scale), and institutional dimension (indicating government support) that affect the agglomeration level of the information service industry. Five-dimensional factors include intensity (indicating intensity) and international dimension (indicating the level of opening up to the outside world) [23]. Ye Hongyun (2020) obtained two main factors that affect the performance of the industrial software industry through a literature review: technological innovation capability factors and resource integration factors. The study also found that technological innovation has a significant positive impact on the performance of enterprises, and resource integration also has a significant positive impact on performance [24]. When Guo Chaoxian, Miao Yufei, et al. (2022) analyzed the current competitiveness level of China's industrial software industry, the study believed that increasing R&D investment can improve the development level of the industrial software industry [25]. Dai Xiaolong (2022) believes that industrial software technology innovation and R&D investment are the keys to the development of industrial software companies and are the key factors that promote high-quality development of industrial software companies [26].

## 2.3. In Terms of Environmental Factors

When Chen Na (2013) analyzed the operating performance of China's listed software companies, she found that the company's performance was positively correlated with the proportion of the top five shareholders' shareholdings to the company's total shares [27]. When Zhiguang Li (2020) analyzed industrial ownership concentration, he believed that there was a negative relationship between company performance and the shareholding ratio of the company's largest shareholder [28]. When Liao Mingyan et al. (2018) studied the efficiency of software industry clusters, they used the four-stage DEA method to measure the decomposition of TFP. Their study found that environmental factors are the key influencing factors that limit the improvement of cluster efficiency [29]. Yan Xiaochang and Huang Guitian (2019) used the software industry base as a research data sample and used a panel regression model to measure the influencing factors on the development of the software industry. The results concluded that enterprises and central government funds, tax incentives, land incentives, and the preferential policies available to talents are significantly positive. Therefore, they believe that government support policies are the main influencing factor [30]. Tao Zhuo and Huang Weidong (2021) sorted out a series of relevant policies at the national level and major provinces and cities regarding the domestic industrial software industry, analyzed the specific current situation of the industrial chain, R&D chain, and market chain, and distinguished between foreign and domestic representative provinces (Jiangsu, Guangdong) industry development trends. It is proposed to improve the government support environment (policies, tax incentives) [31]. Long Yuntao, Huang Tingting, and others (2021) analyzed the root causes of bottlenecks that restrict the development of domestic industrial software in China and proposed that improving the innovative ecological environment (intellectual property protection, government tax exemptions) can improve the development of industrial software [32]. When Zhou Yong, Zhao Dan, et al. (2022) analyzed the development of China's industrial software industry, they believed that preferential tax policies, support for software trade, and other forms could enhance the development of China's industrial software [33]. When Guo Chaoxian, Miao Yufei, and others (2022) analyzed the current competitiveness level of China's industrial software industry, they proposed ways to increase government loan support, insurance subsidy support, application reward and subsidy support, and intellectual property protection to improve industrial software industrial development [25].

*2.4. In Terms of Human Factors*

Shao Jinju and Wang Pei (2013) used the SFA method to measure the input and output efficiency of China's domestic software service industry and the Tobit model to empirically test the key factors affecting the efficiency of the software service industry. The key influencing factors include scientific and technological innovation capabilities (represented by R&D investment), urbanization level (represented by the proportion of the tertiary industry to GDP and the proportion of non-agricultural population), human resource levels (represented by the cost of employees with college or above and labor costs), infrastructure level (represented by the number of Internet accounts), and industrial accumulation degree (represented by location entropy). However, the results found that human capital has a positive but not significant impact on efficiency [19]. Wu Lei et al. (2013) studied 12 software industry cities in China. They believed that factors such as the number of high-tech talents, R&D investment, and government support policies were important influencing factors. Among them, the number of high-tech talents as a human capital factor can improve efficiency levels [34]. Chen Guanju (2015) used the SFA method to study relevant data from 31 national-level software industry bases from 2008 to 2012. The results showed that human capital stock can promote efficiency improvement; human capital structure is a key factor affecting innovation efficiency [21]. Tao Zhuo and Huang Weidong (2021) sorted out a series of relevant policies at the national level and major provinces and cities (Beijing, Guangdong, Shanghai, Jiangsu) about the domestic industrial software industry and analyzed the specific status of the industrial chain, R&D chain, and market chain. The development trend of the industry in foreign and domestic representative provinces (Jiangsu and Guangdong) was analyzed, and it was pointed out that the talent structure of industrial software practitioners is a key factor affecting the development of the industrial software industry [31]. When Zhou Yong, Zhao Dan, et al. (2022) analyzed the breakthrough path of industrial software development, based on the development situation of China's industrial software industry, they believed that supporting the training of industrial software talents could improve the development of China's industrial software [33]. Guo

Chaoxian, Miao Yufei, and others (2022) found that the competitiveness level of China's industrial software industry needs to be improved compared with European and American countries; they believe that paying attention to the talents of industrial software companies can improve the development level of the industrial software industry [25].

## 3. Materials and Methods
### 3.1. Data Collection

After combing through the relevant literature of domestic scholars in China, it was found that there is currently no sample data for the industrial software industry, and no scholars have empirically studied how to obtain it because there is no statistical yearbook or related database on the industrial software industry in China. Therefore, this paper refers to the data acquisition methods of Ma Hong and Wang Yuanyue, Chu Deyin et al. (2016) [35], and Ye Hongyun (2020) [24]. This paper considers the development of listed firms in the industrial software industry or firms that have received IPO GEM acceptance. It is relatively good. These typical firms are basically within 100 in the industrial software ranking list and can represent the current development level of China's domestic industrial software industry. Therefore, this paper conducts sample screening and analysis of 848 domestic industrial software firms in the "Directory of Chinese Industrial Software and Service Firms" and collects and compiles available relevant data on industrial software firms.

As shown in Figure 4 above, judging from the distribution of industrial software firms in various provinces in China, the development of China's industrial software industry is extremely uneven. About 80% of the total number of industrial software firms is concentrated in five provinces, namely Beijing, Shanghai, Guangdong, Jiangsu, and Zhejiang. The industry in these provinces is relatively developed, with a relatively large number of firms in the industrial field, and the operating efficiency of industrial firms is relatively good. Compared with other regions, they pay more attention to digital transformation. These regions have a greater demand for industrial software. Therefore, this paper chooses to study the basic situation of typical enterprises in the industrial software industry at the micro-level.

This paper collects and collates the relevant data of industrial software firms and takes the listed firms or IPO firms accepted by GEM among 848 industrial software firms as samples, mainly including R&D and design industrial software firms, operation and management industrial software firms, production control industrial software firms, industrial Internet platform, and industrial APP industrial software firms. For the purpose of empirical research, the data of the above firms is processed:

- First of all, the input-output data of the DEA model cannot be negative. However, due to the characteristics of some indicators, there may be situations where the original data of some indicators is negative. This requires dimensionless processing of these indicator data so that the processed original data is scaled to be within the positive range.
- Secondly, firms with missing enterprise indicator data or input-output indicators of 0 are eliminated. In order to ensure the research sample size, industrial software accounts for the main business firms or certain comparable firms in the listed annual reports of category firms are also used as supplementary samples.
- Finally, after processing, relevant data of 40 typical industrial software firms from 2018 to 2020 were obtained (because the listing of typical industrial software firms in the R&D and design category or the platform category is relatively late; even ZW Software will be launched in 2021, resulting in a short time interval for data acquisition, so only data from 2018 to 2020 can be selected in a limited manner).

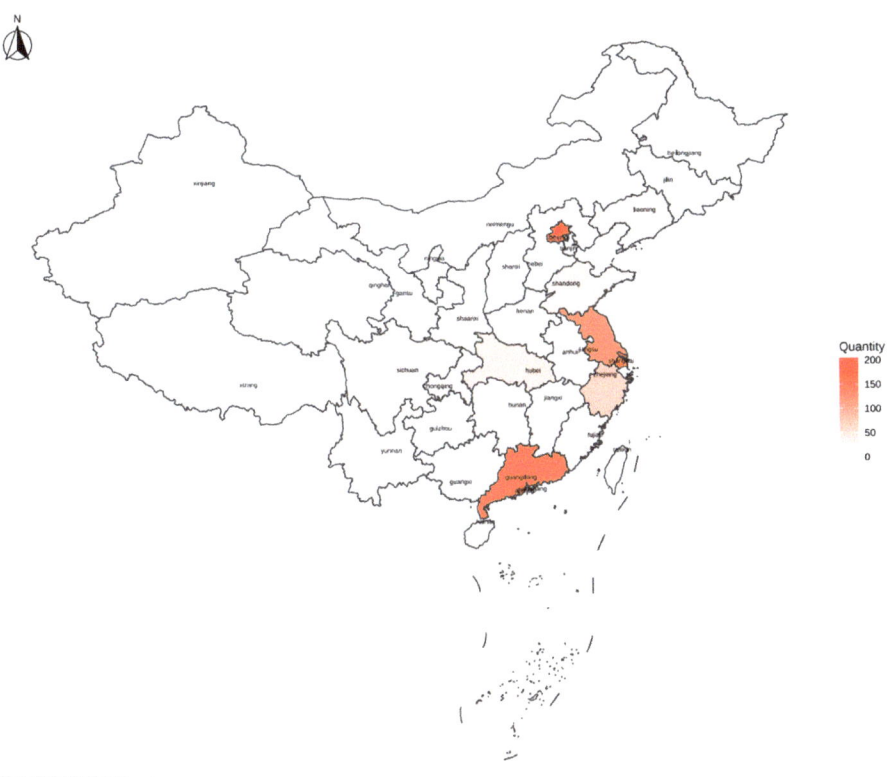

**Figure 4.** Distribution of Chinese industrial software firms in 2021.

### 3.2. Variable Selection: Input-Output

The investment indicators selected by the industrial software industry are in line with Bai Wen (2015) [15], Wang Zhen et al. (2016) [36], Wang Zhe et al. (2017) [37], and Wang Huanfang et al. (2020) [35]. For research and analysis in the field, the number of industry personnel at the end of the year is selected to represent the labor input index; in line with the research of Zhou Jing (2011) [38], Liao Jing (2016) [39], and others, fixed asset investment is taken as a capital investment; fixed asset investment can indirectly reflect the scale of the firm and its development, etc. It is generally considered to be the material guarantee for innovation and development; it is in line with the views of Ren Yousheng and Qiu Xiaodong (2017) [40], Wang Huanfang et al. (2020) [35], etc., who choose R&D investment as the capital investment indicator of the industrial software industry.

This paper takes the main business income and net profit of industrial software firms as output indicators. Refer to the research of Li Zhifeng (2018), Yang Ruoxia (2018) [41], and Wang Huanfang et al. (2020) [35]. Corporate performance can generally be measured by corporate net profit indicators. Obtaining net profits is the purpose of corporate participation in economic activities. Drawing on the research of Bai Wen (2015) [15], Liao Jing (2016) [39], and others, they classified each enterprise into software. The main operating income is used as an output indicator to measure the efficiency of software firms.

Based on the above analysis, according to the characteristics of the industrial software industry and the common ground of industrial development in related fields, and referring to the empirical research of scholars in related fields, the final selected input indicators are the number of employees at the end of the year, investment in fixed assets, and investment in R&D funds. The output indicators are the operating income and net profit of each software business owner (see Table 1). By processing the relevant data collected and collated, this paper selects the input-output indicators of data. First of all, it fully considers their availability, and second, it also refers to the index selection of other scholars to verify the effectiveness of the index selection of the paper.

Table 1. Input-output indicators of typical industrial software firms.

| Category | Indicators | Indicators Meaning |
|---|---|---|
| Input | Labor input | Number of employees at the end of the year (person) |
| | Capital input | R&D expenditure (10,000 CNY) |
| | | Investment in Fixed Assets (10,000 CNY) |
| Output | Industry revenue | Operating income of each business owner (10,000 CNY) |
| | Total net profit | Total net profit of each firm (10,000 CNY) |

### 3.3. Measurement Methods of TFP in China's Industrial Software Industry

This paper chooses to use the DEA-Malmquist index method to measure the TFP of typical firms in China's industrial software industry for the following reasons:

- First, this method does not require certain constraints or specific forms for the function. The real development time of China's industrial software industry is not long, and the specific development situations of each category of industrial software are also different, which makes it difficult to set a consistent production function suitable for different types of industrial software. In this field, using the DEA-Malmquist index method can avoid measurement deviations caused by setting different functional forms to the greatest extent possible.
- Second, the study uses relevant data from typical industrial software firms in China from 2018 to 2020, which can analyze the overall TFP changes of the industrial software industry and the TFP changes of sub-categories from the perspective of time and category.
- Third, this method is not affected by the selected input-output data unit, and it can incorporate multiple input and output indicators.
- Fourth, the TFP change index obtained by this method is the product of the technical efficiency change index (EFFCH) and the technological progress rate change index (TECHCH), and EFFCH is the change index of pure technical efficiency (PECH) and the scale efficiency change index. EFFCH can be used to empirically analyze TFP from the aspects of technological innovation level, capital investment status, R&D funds, and changes in the number of employees in related industries, and explore the sources of dynamic changes in TFP and the internal influencing mechanisms.

This section discusses methods of measuring TFP. Malmquist proposed the Malmquist index for analyzing the consumption domain, and then the application of the Malmquist index was extended to the production domain and combined with the data envelopment method (DEA) to calculate the TFP [9,42]. At present, the DEA-Malmquist index method based on output constructed by Fare et al. [9] is generally adopted to measure TFP. Its formula is expressed as follows:

$$TFPCH = M_0(x^{t+1}, y^{t+1}, x^t, y^t) = \sqrt{\frac{D_0^t(x^{t+1}, y^{t+1})}{D_0^t(x^t, y^t)} \times \frac{D_0^{t+1}(x^{t+1}, y^{t+1})}{D_0^{t+1}(x^t, y^t)}} \quad (1)$$

Among them, $D_0^t(x^t, y^t)$, $D_0^{t+1}(x^{t+1}, y^{t+1})$, respectively, represent the production efficiency distance function of period $t$ with the technology of period $t$ as a reference and the production efficiency distance function of period $t + 1$ with the technology of period $t + 1$ as a reference; $(x^t, y^t), (x^{t+1}, y^{t+1})$ represents the input-output combination of period $t$ and $t + 1$ [9]. Formula (1) expresses the change in total factor production efficiency of the input-output combination of the software industry in period t to the input-output mix of the software industry in period $t + 1$ [9,42]. When $M_0 < 1$, it means that the total factor productivity from period $t$ to period $t + 1$ is decreasing; when $M_0 = 1$, it means that the TFP from period $t$ to period $t + 1$ remains unchanged; when $M_0 > 1$, it means that the total factor productivity from period $t$ to period $t + 1$ is increasing [9,42]. Formula (1) can be further decomposed into the following:

$$M_0(x^{t+1}, y^{t+1}, x^t, y^t) = \frac{D_0^{t+1}(x^{t+1}, y^{t+1})}{D_0^t(x^t, y^t)} \times \sqrt{\frac{D_0^t(x^t, y^t)}{D_0^{t+1}(x^t, y^t)} \times \frac{D_0^{t+1}(x^{t+1}, y^{t+1})}{D_0^t(x^{t+1}, y^{t+1})}} \quad (2)$$

In Formula (2), the first term $\frac{D_0^{t+1}(x^{t+1}, y^{t+1})}{D_0^t(x^t, y^t)}$ on the right side of the equal sign represents the change index of technical efficiency from period $t$ to period $t + 1$, denoted as *EFFCH*; The second term $\sqrt{\frac{D_0^t(x^t, y^t)}{D_0^{t+1}(x^t, y^t)} * \frac{D_0^{t+1}(x^{t+1}, y^{t+1})}{D_0^t(x^{t+1}, y^{t+1})}}$ represents the change index of technological progress from period $t$ to period $t + 1$, denoted as *TECHCH* [9,42].

It can be seen that, under the condition of constant returns to scale [9], the equation of TFP is as follows:

$$TFPCH = EFFCH \times TECHCH \quad (3)$$

### 3.4. Methodology: Apply fsQCA to Improvement Paths

This paper uses qualitative comparative analysis (QCA) to analyze the factors and mechanisms that drive total factor productivity in the industrial software industry. There are three main reasons: First, the improvement of TFP in industrial software is a complex issue caused by multiple concurrent causes and effects. QCA can use configuration thinking to test the linkage-matching effect of multiple factors, identify multiple equivalent paths that drive the improvement of total factor productivity in the industrial software industry, and explore potential substitute relationships between various factors. Second, the QCA method can accurately locate The typical enterprise cases covered by each equivalent path helping this article provide an in-depth explanation of the industrial development paths of different types of industrial software enterprises. At the same time, QCA follows the assumption of causality asymmetry, which can help this paper discover the differences and reasons for the combination of conditions that produce high and non-high levels of total factor productivity in the industrial software industry. Third, the variables selected in this study are all continuous variables, and it is more suitable to adopt fuzzy set qualitative comparative analysis (fsQCA) to reflect the changes in the degree and level of variables [42].

The QCA method set operation logical relationship is expressed in the form of Boolean algebra, stipulating that the ~ symbol represents "not", the * symbol represents "and", and the + symbol represents "or". This method is to obtain different paths with strong explanatory power for the outcome variables by screening and optimizing the consistency value and coverage level of the antecedent condition configuration [43]. The consistency value represents the similarity between the corresponding sample configuration combination and the original data, and the coverage represents the extent to which the sample result variable can be explained by a specific configuration. The following are formulas representing consistency value and coverage, respectively:

$$Consistency(Y \leq X) = \sum min(x_i, y_i) / \sum x_i \quad (4)$$

$$Converage(Y \leq X) = \sum min(x_i, y_i) / \sum y_i \quad (5)$$

Research steps of fsQCA method:
- Step 1: Select research case objects. Based on determining the content of the research, delineate a scope according to attributes, such as category or subdivision level, and then select the case objects to be studied based on the standards.

- Step 2: Determine the antecedent conditions and outcome variables. The outcome variable of the research content is the core point, and the antecedent condition variables are selected from the influencing factors involved in the previous research by scholars to further construct the antecedent condition variable configuration. In the fsQCA antecedent condition variable selection process, the range of the number of antecedent condition variables is usually relatively small; generally, 4–6 are selected. Too many antecedent condition variables will make the case objects "individualized," which cannot fully explain the regularity and integrity of cross-case objects [44].
- Step 3: Quantify each variable and obtain case data. Based on the clarified variables, combined with available case data, each variable is quantified, and relevant data values are obtained using databases, corporate yearbooks, survey prospectuses, etc.
- Step 4: Variable data calibration. Three calibration anchor points are set for each variable to transform the original case data into a membership value between 0 and 1. The membership includes complete membership (membership value = 1), fuzzy intersection point (membership value = 0.50), and complete non-membership. (Membership value = 0), drawing on the research experience of relevant scholars, 95% is selected as the complete membership point, 5% as the incomplete membership point, and 0.5 as the fuzzy intersection point. The original case data for each variable is calibrated to fuzzy membership values [45].
- Step 5: Test the sufficiency and necessity of a single variable. The adequacy test of fsQCA can tell whether a single factor as an antecedent condition variable is a subset of the outcome variable. If the test is not ideal, it means that improving total factor productivity is the result of the interaction of multiple factors. Multiple different antecedent condition variables are important for improving total factor productivity. There is a complex relationship between factor productivity. fsQCA analysis tests the necessity of a single factor and can determine whether the outcome variable is a subset of the antecedent condition variables. The fsQCA method explores the impact of different configurations of antecedent condition variables on outcome variables under non-essential conditions. The antecedent condition variables are selected by eliminating variables that pass the necessity test. According to scholars' research, if the consistency value exceeds 0.9, it is deemed that the test result is sufficient or necessary [45].
- Step 6: Construct a truth table. The calibrated case sample data is converted into a set membership value, and a $2^k$ row truth table can be generated, where $k$ represents the number of antecedent conditions, and the antecedent condition variable configuration in each row is a path that promotes the outcome variable. Set reasonable case sample frequencies and consistency threshold values, eliminate configurations that do not meet the set conditions, and finally build a truth table. Considering that the sample size of domestic industrial software enterprise cases is relatively small, the frequency threshold is set to 1 and the consistency threshold is 0.85 in this paper, which also satisfies the requirement that the selected configuration samples account for more than 75% of the total case samples [46].
- Step 7: Conditional combination configuration analysis. After calibration and analysis of this method, complex solutions, simple solutions, and intermediate solutions can be obtained. The complex solution does not consider the logical remainder, and its analysis is more complicated and cumbersome. The simple solution completely takes into account all the logical remainders, and it is definitely inconsistent with the actual situation. The intermediate solution is to add the consistent part of the logical remainder to the configuration without removing the necessary conditions for the outcome variable. Researchers generally believe that the intermediate solution is better than the other two solutions. The analysis of the paper is an intermediate solution adopted to obtain the consistency value, original coverage, and unique coverage values under each configuration. At the same time, this method also needs to judge and analyze the antecedent condition variables. If the antecedent condition

variables in the configuration all appear in the configuration of the intermediate and parsimonious solutions, then this variable is considered to be the core variable, which has an important influence on the outcome variable. It has a super strong influence; if the antecedent condition variable only appears in the intermediate plan configuration, then the variable is considered a non-core variable, and its impact on the outcome variable is relatively weak [47].

## 4. Results
### 4.1. Results from the Measurement Model

From the perspective of the industrial software industry as a whole, the DEA-Malmquist index analysis was conducted on the relevant data of listed companies or IPO GEM-accepting companies in China's industrial software industry from 2018 to 2020 to measure the total factor productivity change index and its decomposition of typical companies in the industrial software industry. The summary of results shows (see Table 2) that the average annual total factor productivity of typical enterprises in China's industrial software industry is 0.965 and the average annual growth rate is −3.5%. After decomposing the average total factor productivity of typical enterprises in China's industrial software industry, we get the annual average technical efficiency is 0.793, the annual average growth rate of technical efficiency is −20.7%, the annual average technical progress rate is 1.216, and the annual average growth rate is 21.6%, which shows the annual average growth rate of typical enterprises in China's industrial software industry. The reason for the decline in total factor productivity comes from the decline in the annual average technical efficiency growth rate. Further decomposing the technical efficiency of typical industrial software enterprises in China, it can be seen that the annual average growth rate of pure technical efficiency and scale efficiency has declined. The annual average growth rate of pure technical efficiency is 0.814, and the average annual growth rate is −18.6%. The annual average value of scale efficiency is 0.975, and the average annual growth rate is −2.5%. From the above analysis, it can be seen that the decline in the annual average growth rate of technical efficiency is due to the decrease in the annual average value of pure technical efficiency and the annual average value of scale efficiency. As a result, the total factor productivity of China's industrial software industry has declined, resulting in a low-end development trend. This is due to the low level of optimal allocation efficiency of typical industrial software enterprises; that is, the scale of the enterprise is too small, the daily management capabilities of the enterprise are too weak, and the utilization of enterprise resources is too low. Problems such as low levels are the main bottlenecks in improving the total factor productivity of the industrial software industry.

Table 2. 2018–2020 Industrial software TFP change index and its decomposition.

| Year | EFFCH=PECH * SECH | TECHCH | PECH | SECH | TFPCH |
|---|---|---|---|---|---|
| 2018–2019 | 0.612 | 1.473 | 0.683 | 0.896 | 0.901 |
| 2019–2020 | 1.029 | 1.004 | 0.969 | 1.061 | 1.033 |
| Mean value | 0.793 | 1.216 | 0.814 | 0.975 | 0.965 |

The analysis of the measurement model was done in Appendix A and quantitative results are summarized in Tables A1 and A2 of Appendix A.

From the index change from 2018 to 2019 (see Table A1), the technological progress rate index is 1.473, and the technical efficiency, pure technical efficiency, and scale efficiency are 0.612, 0.683, and 0.896, respectively, indicating that the decline in TFP of typical enterprises in China's industrial software industry from 2018 to 2019 is mainly caused by the decline in technical efficiency. Although enterprises have improved in technology update and iteration, technology introduction, and other aspects, the utilization efficiency of production factors in industrial software enterprises has been greatly reduced. From the index change from 2019 to 2020 (see Table A2), the TFP of typical industrial software enterprises is 1.033, which indicates that the TFP of typical industrial software enterprises has increased by 3.3%, and its technical efficiency, pure technical efficiency, scale efficiency, and technological progress rate are 1.029, 0.969, 1.061, and 1.004, respectively. Technical efficiency and technological progress rates have changed significantly. It can be seen that although the technological innovation and technological progress of industrial software enterprises have not improved much from 2019 to 2020, the scale efficiency and daily management level of industrial software enterprises have greatly improved from 2019 to 2020. This shows that the combined effect of technical efficiency and technological progress rate promotes the positive growth of TFP in the industrial software industry.

### 4.2. Results from fsQCA

#### 4.2.1. Variable Selection and Descriptive Statistics

Wang and Jiang et al. [48] pointed out that the sample size of the fsQCA method should be at least greater than or equal to 10. In this paper, the DEA-Malmquist index analysis method is used to measure the TFP of the industrial software industry, and the TFP of the industrial software industry in 2020 is used as the outcome variable of fsQCA [9]. Considering the time lag of the input and output of the industrial software industry, six variables under the four dimensions that affect the TFP of the industrial software industry in 2019 are selected, and the level of government support, fixed asset investment intensity, R&D investment level, R&D personnel investment level, ownership concentration, and education level are the antecedent condition variables (see Table 3).

Table 3. Descriptive statistics.

| Variable | Measurement Variables | | Variable | Mean | SD | Max | Min |
|---|---|---|---|---|---|---|---|
| Outcome | Total factor productivity of industrial software industry | | TFP | 1.134 | 0.510 | 3.004 | 0.136 |
| Condition | Capital factors | Fixed asset intensity (%) | FIX | 8.781 | 8.410 | 38.300 | 0.100 |
| | Technical factors | R&D intensity (%) | RD | 16.644 | 12.227 | 54.550 | 0.330 |
| | | R&D personnel intensity (%) | RDP | 41.857 | 19.593 | 90.280 | 11.400 |
| | Environmental factors | Government support (‰) | GOV | 50.190 | 64.560 | 287.400 | 0.100 |
| | | Ownership concentration (%) | OC | 56.145 | 19.325 | 97.750 | 23.330 |
| | Human factors | Higher education (year) | HE | 16.349 | 0.619 | 18.329 | 15.332 |

#### 4.2.2. Calibration of Variables

Unlike traditional variables, the dataset must be calibrated before it can be analyzed by fuzzy set software. In the current version of the fsQCA 3.0 software, the calibration is automatic and easy to perform once the three qualitative anchors are defined: full membership, full non-membership, and crossover point [9]. This paper uses fsQCA to analyze the relationship between the causal conditions (namely, the intensity of fixed asset investment, the level of R&D investment, the level of R&D personnel investment, the level of government support, and the level of education) and the outcome (TFP of industrial software firms). In this paper, fsQCA is used to set the three qualitative anchors of fuzzy sets of outcome variables and condition variables as full membership (95%), full non-membership (5%), and crossover point (0.50) [49]. All variable calibration anchors are shown in Table 4. Through qualitative anchors of outcome variables and condition variables, the original values of all variables are transformed into fuzzy membership scores (values between 0 and 1) by using the "calibrate" calibration command in fsQCA 3.0 software. However, there is a problem with the calibration in that it can produce a fuzzy set membership score of exactly 0.5, which makes it difficult to analyze this situation due to the ambiguity of the case member set. Therefore, the use of an exact membership score of 0.5 for causal conditions should be avoided. According to the research practices of previous scholars, this paper adds a constant of 0.01 to the score of all fuzzy set members. Doing so ensures that no cases are removed from the fuzzy set analysis [50]. Finally, the membership scores of fuzzy sets are obtained.

Table 4. Summary of the calibration of all variables.

| Variable | Measurement Variables | | Calibration Anchors | | |
|---|---|---|---|---|---|
| | | | Full Membership | Crossover | Full Non-Membership |
| Outcome | TFP | | 2.09 | 0.99 | 0.58 |
| Condition | Capital factors | FIX | 17.40 | 6.95 | 0.30 |
| | Technical factors | RD | 40.45 | 13.26 | 2.31 |
| | | RDP | 78.08 | 38.49 | 12.86 |
| | Environmental factors | GOV | 211.10 | 29.35 | 0.40 |
| | | OC | 93.4 | 52.11 | 26.26 |
| | Human factors | HE | 17.44 | 16.22 | 15.56 |

4.2.3. Analysis of Necessity Conditions

Although the analysis of sufficient condition combinations is the most critical part of the fsQCA study, the necessity of each condition must be tested before constructing the truth table [9]. As suggested by researchers such as Xie, X., Wang, H. (2020) [49], and Ragin, C. C. (2008) [51], if a single condition variable is required, the consistency and coverage of each condition variable must be above the recommended threshold of 0.9; otherwise, it is not a requirement. This study analyzes several condition variables of production factors such as FIX, RD, RDP, and GOV, as well as the prerequisites for OC and HE to produce TFP in the industrial software industry. In order to determine whether any of these 6 conditions are required for total factor productivity in the industrial software industry, this paper analyzes whether this antecedent condition variable always exists (does not exist) in all cases where the outcome variable exists (does not exist). The results in Table 5 show that the necessary consistency of all individual variables is less than 0.9, which is not enough to constitute a necessary condition for TFP in the industrial software industry. No antecedent condition variable can independently improve the TFP of the industrial software industry. One possible reason is that TFP in the industrial software industry is caused by multiple factors, and therefore, no single factor is necessary for high or not-high TFP in the industrial software industry [9].

Table 5. Necessity analysis on TFP and ~TFP.

| Outcome/Condition | TFP | | ~TFP | |
|---|---|---|---|---|
| | Consistency | Coverage | Consistency | Coverage |
| FIX | 0.678659 | 0.701478 | 0.588534 | 0.590932 |
| ~FIX | 0.604238 | 0.601865 | 0.702689 | 0.679922 |
| RD | 0.719073 | 0.752450 | 0.651953 | 0.662713 |
| ~RD | 0.677674 | 0.667152 | 0.756469 | 0.723435 |
| RDP | 0.650074 | 0.666835 | 0.714865 | 0.712336 |
| ~RDP | 0.719566 | 0.722057 | 0.665652 | 0.648863 |
| GOV | 0.643174 | 0.769004 | 0.592085 | 0.687684 |
| ~GOV | 0.738787 | 0.650890 | 0.801116 | 0.685627 |
| OC | 0.705274 | 0.704926 | 0.714865 | 0.694089 |
| ~OC | 0.693938 | 0.714721 | 0.696093 | 0.696447 |
| HE | 0.676195 | 0.701432 | 0.705226 | 0.710634 |
| ~HE | 0.721045 | 0.715753 | 0.703704 | 0.678571 |

4.2.4. Constructing the Truth Table

In order to identify combinations of conditions that are logically sufficient for the existence of an outcome, it is necessary to construct a truth table. The truth table needs to be preliminary refined according to three criteria of frequency threshold, original consistency, and proportional reduction in inconsistency (PRI) consistency before analysis [9,49].

Although some recent scholars have shown that the fsQCA method is a very useful tool for analyzing large N (i.e., more than 50 cases) case situations, most previous scholars' studies using the fsQCA method mostly involve relatively small N case situations (i.e., 10–50 cases) [9,52]. Ragin (2008) [51] and Jin et al. (2020) [50] suggested that for the case of small N, the frequency cutoff of 1 is the most appropriate. However, for case scenarios with large N, the frequency cutoff should be set higher with the number of cases. This paper studies 40 cases of typical Chinese industrial software companies, which are consistent with the situation of small N. Therefore, the frequency cutoff value is set to 1 in this paper. In addition, the main representative scholar studies of the fsQCA approach suggest [9,53] that at least 75–80% of all empirical cases should be included as part of the analysis [9,54].

In the study presented in this paper, we rely on both original consistency and PRI consistency. This paper adopts the two rules suggested by Park (2020) [55] and other scholars on the QCA method to determine the critical value of original consistency. Firstly, the raw consistency should be higher than 0.85 for combinations/rows that reliably produce high or non-high TFP [52]. Second, if there is a breakpoint in which agreement between two rows decreases significantly from the row with a high level of raw consistency to the row with the next level of raw consistency, then the breakpoint can be either high TFP or not-high TFP [9]. For example, in the high TFP of the industrial software industry, there is a significant decrease in consistency from line 29 with a consistency of 0.851163 to line 30 with a consistency of 0.845343 at the next level (see Table 6). For the not-high TFP of the industrial software industry, there is a breakpoint between the consistency of 0.852252 in line 27 and 0.846875 in line 28 (see Table 6); therefore, we can decide to use 0.85 as the original consistency cutoff. Therefore, the critical value selection to determine the original consistency of the result column values in the truth table ultimately depends on the context, and researchers should consider some decision criteria to determine the critical value cutoff value based on their knowledge of the case and context [55]. In fsQCA fuzzy set analysis, it is also important to consider PRI consistency scores. PRI consistency scores should be high and ideally not too far from raw consistency scores (e.g., 0.75), Current best practice further recommends that each solution meet a PRI consistency cutoff of 0.65 [9].

In summary, this paper excluded from the subsequent analysis the leading combinations that did not satisfy the frequency (1 or above), raw consistency (above 0.85), and PRI consistency (above 0.60) criteria. As a result, the retained truth table contains 31 rows of high TFP and 31 rows of not-high TFP [9]. Tables of truth values are shown in Appendix B (see Tables A3 and A4).

4.2.5. Path Configuration Analysis

After obtaining the truth table in the previous section, this paper uses Ragin's truth table algorithm to conduct sufficiency analysis in this step so as to identify the attribute combination that is always associated with the outcome and can obtain the complex solution, parsimonious solution and intermediate solution of TFP and ~TFP, respectively. Generally speaking, most researchers use an intermediate solution that is both general and heuristic. This paper uses the intermediate solution to analyze the specific configuration and combination model to improve the TFP of the industrial software industry, including the configuration of each path, the raw coverage, unique coverage, consistency value, as well as the coverage of the overall solution and the consistency value of the overall solution in the configuration mode.

Table 6. Path configurations for achieving a high TFP.

| Condition | Outcome = TFP | | | | | | |
|---|---|---|---|---|---|---|---|
| | H1a | H1b | H1c | H2a | H2b | H3 | H4 |
| FIX | ● | ● | ● | ● | ● | | ● |
| RD | | ⊕ | ⊕ | | ⊕ | ● | ● |
| RDP | ⊕ | ⊕ | ⊕ | ⊕ | ⊕ | ● | ⊕ |
| GOV | ⊕ | | ⊕ | ⊕ | | • | • |
| OC | ⊕ | ⊕ | ⊕ | ● | ● | ● | • |
| HE | ⊕ | ⊕ | | ● | ● | ● | ⊕ |
| Raw Coverage | 0.4032 | 0.3800 | 0.3849 | 0.2765 | 0.2666 | 0.3760 | 0.2755 |
| Unique Coverage | 0.0276 | 0.0079 | 0.0039 | 0.0074 | 0.0030 | 0.1774 | 0.0237 |
| Consistency | 0.9317 | 0.9256 | 0.9029 | 0.9525 | 0.9508 | 0.8760 | 0.9459 |
| Overall solution Coverage | | | | 0.723016 | | | |
| Overall solution Consistency | | | | 0.830221 | | | |

Fiss (2011) defined the antecedent conditions for the overlap between the intermediate solution configuration and the simple solution configuration as core conditions, recorded as "●" or "⊕" [9]; the antecedent conditions and parsimonious solutions that appear in the intermediate solution are excluded the antecedent condition is defined as a peripheral condition, represented by a small "•" or "⊕", and a blank indicates that the condition variable is insignificant [45]. Under the conditions of satisfying the consistency and coverage of path configurations, the results show that there are 4 path configurations with core conditions that can be used to evaluate the high TFP (i.e., paths H1–H4) and 4 path configurations with core conditions that can be used to evaluate the not-high TFP (i.e., paths L1–L4). The specific path configuration of TFP in China's industrial software industry is shown in Tables 6 and 7 [9].

Table 7. Path configurations for achieving a not-high TFP.

| Condition | Outcome = ~TFP | | | | | | | |
|---|---|---|---|---|---|---|---|---|
| | L1a | L1b | L1c | L1d | L2a | L2b | L3 | L4 |
| FIX | • | • | | ⊕ | ⊕ | ⊕ | | ⊕ |
| RD | ⊕ | ⊕ | • | • | ⊕ | ⊕ | ● | ● |
| RDP | ● | ● | ● | ● | ⊕ | • | • | ⊕ |
| GOV | ⊕ | ⊕ | ⊕ | ⊕ | ⊕ | | • | ⊕ |
| OC | | ⊕ | ⊕ | ⊕ | • | • | ⊕ | ● |
| HE | ⊕ | | ⊕ | | ● | ● | ● | ⊕ |
| Raw Coverage | 0.3415 | 0.3333 | 0.3699 | 0.3338 | 0.3470 | 0.3409 | 0.3125 | 0.2268 |
| Unique Coverage | 0.0178 | 0.0091 | 0.0036 | 0.0091 | 0.0223 | 0.0213 | 0.0036 | 0.0320 |
| Consistency | 0.9479 | 0.9467 | 0.9251 | 0.9777 | 0.9072 | 0.9573 | 0.9319 | 0.9293 |
| Overall solution Coverage | | | | 0.645358 | | | | |
| Overall solution Consistency | | | | 0.888268 | | | | |

The path configuration of China's industrial software industry with high TFP as the outcome variable is shown in Table 6. Through the analysis of intermediate solutions and parsimonious solutions, four path configurations with core conditions were obtained to improve the TFP of China's industrial software industry. The overall solution consistency score of the high TFP improvement path configuration of the industrial software industry is 0.830221. The consistency scores of specific path configurations are 0.9317 (for path configuration H1a), 0.9256 (for path configuration H1b), 0.9029 (for path configuration

H1c), 0.9525 (for path configuration H2a), 0.9508 (for path configuration H2b), 0.8760 (for path configuration H3), 0.9459 (for path configuration H4) [9]. Therefore, it can be seen that the consistency value of each path configuration exceeds 0.85, and the consistency value of the overall solution exceeds 0.80. This shows that the four path configurations have a good explanation for the industrial software industry with high TFP. The TFP of the industrial software industry can be improved through these four paths. The overall solution coverage is 0.723016. Among the four path configurations, path configuration H1 (H1a raw coverage value 0.4032, H1b raw coverage value 0.3800, H1c raw coverage value 0.3849) achieved better performance than other path configurations (H2a raw coverage value 0.2765, H2b raw coverage value 0.2666, H3 raw coverage value 0.3760, H4 raw coverage value 0.2755), which indicates a higher relative empirical correlation [56]. Among them, H1 has higher coverage, and most industrial software firms with high TFP achieve TFP improvement through H1 path configuration. The above is in line with the qualitative comparative analysis standards proposed by Woodside (2017) [53].

The detailed analysis of these four path configurations is as follows:

- The capital path takes high fixed asset investment intensity, low R&D personnel investment, and low equity concentration as the main adjustment means. High TFP path configuration H1 includes path H1a (FIX*~RDP*~GOV*~OC*~HE), path H1b (FIX*~RD*~RDP*~OC*~HE), and path H1c (FIX*~RD*~RDP*~GOV*~OC). Paths H1a, H1b, and H1c show that high fixed asset investment intensity, low R&D personnel investment, and low equity concentration are the core conditions for improving the TFP efficiency of the industrial software industry. The auxiliary conditions of path H1a are low government support and low education level. In path H1b, the other two auxiliary conditions are a low R&D investment level and a low education level. In path H1c, the other two auxiliary conditions are a low R&D investment level and low government support. Path H1a describes that when the level of R&D personnel investment is low, the degree of ownership concentration is low, but the fixed asset investment intensity of industrial software companies is high, the TFP of the industrial software industry can be improved even if there is a lack of high government support and good education. Path H1b describes that when the level of R&D personnel investment is low, the degree of ownership concentration is low, but when the fixed asset investment intensity of industrial software companies is high, the TFP of the industrial software industry can be improved even if there is a lack of high R&D investment levels and good education levels. Path H1c describes that when the level of R&D personnel investment is low, the degree of equity concentration is low, but the fixed asset investment intensity of industrial software companies is high, the TFP of the industrial software industry can be improved even if there is a lack of high R&D investment levels and higher levels of government support. High TFP path configuration H1 includes path H1a, path H1b, and path H1c. The case firms represented by paths H1a, H1b, and H1c are Runhe Software firm, Jinzhi Technology firm, and Dingjie Software firm, respectively.

- The capital-human-environmental path takes high fixed asset investment intensity, high equity concentration, and high educational attainment as the main adjustment means. The high total factor productivity path configuration H2 includes path H2a (FIX*~RDP*~GOV*OC*HE) and path H2b (FIX*~RD*~RDP*OC*HE). Paths H2a and H2b show that high fixed asset investment intensity, high ownership concentration, and high educational level are the core conditions for improving the total factor productivity efficiency of the industrial software industry. The auxiliary conditions for path H2a are low government support and low R&D personnel investment. In path H2b, the other two auxiliary conditions are low R&D investment level and low R&D personnel investment level. Path H2a describes that when the intensity of fixed asset investment, ownership concentration, and educational level are high, the TFP of the industrial software industry can be improved even if there is a lack of high government support and R&D personnel investment. Path H2b describes that when the intensity of fixed asset investment, ownership concentration, and educational level are all high, the TFP of the industrial software industry can be improved even if there is a lack of higher R&D investment levels and R&D personnel investment levels. The high TFP path configuration H2 includes path H2a and path H2b. The case firms represented by paths H2a and H2b are Qingyun Technology firm and Baoxin Software firm, respectively.

- The technical-human-environmental path is based on high R&D investment levels, high R&D personnel investment levels, high equity concentration, and high education levels as the main adjustment means. High TFP path configuration H3 (RD*RDP*GOV*OC*HE). Path H3 shows that high R&D investment levels, high R&D personnel investment levels, high ownership concentration, and high education levels are the core conditions for improving the total factor productivity efficiency of the industrial software industry. The auxiliary condition of path H3 is higher government support. Path H3 describes that when there is a high level of R&D investment, a high level of R&D personnel investment, a high degree of equity concentration, and a high level of education, the TFP of the industrial software industry can be improved even if there is a lack of high government support. The case firm represented by path H3 is Zhongwang Software firm.

- The technical-capital path is based on high fixed asset investment intensity, high R&D investment level, and low R&D personnel investment level as the main adjustment means [9]. High TFP path H4 (FAI*RD*~RDP*GOV*OC*~HE). Path H4 shows that high fixed asset investment intensity, high R&D investment level, and low R&D personnel investment level are the core conditions for improving the total factor productivity efficiency of the industrial software industry. The auxiliary conditions of path H4 are higher government support, higher ownership concentration, and lower educational level. Path H4 describes when there is high fixed asset investment intensity, high R&D investment level, and low R&D personnel investment level [9]. Even in the absence of higher government support, higher ownership concentration, and lower education levels, the TFP of the industrial software industry can be improved. The case firm represented by path H4 is Yonyou Software firm.

The path configuration of China's industrial software industry with not-high TFP as the outcome variable is shown in Table 7. The overall solution consistency score of not-high TFP path configuration in the industrial software industry is 0.888268. It can be seen that the consistency value of each path configuration exceeds 0.85 and the overall solution consistency value exceeds 0.80, which indicates that there are 4 path configurations with a good explanation for the industrial software industry with low TFP, and the analysis of the not-high TFP of the industrial software industry can be realized through these four paths. The overall solution coverage is 0.645358, and most industrial software companies without high TFP are configured for the L1c path.

The detailed analysis of these four path configurations is as follows:

- External Environmental constrained path. The not-high TFP path configuration L1 includes L1a "FIX*~RD*RDP*~GOV*~HE", L1b "FIX*~RD*RDP*~GOV*~OC", and L1c "RD*RDP*~GOV*~OC*~HE", L1d "~FIX*RD*RDP*~GOV*~OC". Paths L1a, L1b, L1c, and L1d show that high levels of personnel investment and low levels of government support are core conditions that are not conducive to improving the TFP of the industrial software industry.

- Capital-technical constrained path. The not-high TFP path configuration L2 includes path L2a (~FIX*~RD*~GOV*OC*HE), and (~FIX*~RD*RDP*OC*HE). Paths L2a and L2b show that low fixed asset investment intensity, low R&D investment level, and high education level are core conditions that are not conducive to improving the TFP of the industrial software industry.

- Internal environmental-constrained path. Not-high TFP path configuration L3 (RD*RDP* GOV*~OC*HE). Path H3 shows that high R&D investment levels, low ownership

concentration, and high education levels are core conditions that are detrimental to the TFP of the industrial software industry.
- Environmental-human-constrained path. Not-high total factor productivity path L4 (~FIX*RD*~RDP*~GOV*OC*~HE). Path L4 shows that high R&D investment levels, low government support, high ownership concentration, and low education levels are core conditions that are unfavorable to the TFP of the industrial software industry.

## 5. Discussion and Conclusions

There are not many empirical studies on the TFP of the industrial software industry at the micro-level, which provides a new perspective for studying the TFP of the industrial software industry. Apply fsQCA to the analysis of the high-quality development path of industrial software in the field of economics and obtain the synergistic path of multiple variable factors, providing reference suggestions for industrial software companies to choose a higher TFP path. Scholars' current research using the fsQCA method is mostly applied in management, sociology, and other fields. In recent years, some researchers have begun to extend the application of the fsQCA method to the field of economics. Based on the analysis of the configuration principle and the applicability of this method, this paper uses the fsQCA method to obtain the path configuration of each factor to improve the TFP of the industrial software industry [57].

This study has four findings: first, the necessity test finds that the six factors, including technological innovation, cannot constitute the necessary conditions for promoting high-quality development of the industrial software industry alone. Secondly, the configuration analysis finds that there are four paths to drive high-quality development in the industrial software industry, which can be summed up as four driving modes: "technical-human-environmental" balanced driving type, "capital-human-environmental" balanced driving type, "technical-capital" dual driving type, and "capital" single driving type. These four configurations and four modes reflect the multiple implementation methods of typical enterprises in different industrial software industries. In addition, there are four paths that produce non-high industrialization, and there is an obvious asymmetric relationship between the two types of configurations. Finally, the analysis of the potential substitution relationship finds that under specific objective endowment conditions, the combination of technology, capital, human resources, and environmental factors can promote high-quality development of the industrial software industry through equivalent substitution. Among them, the government attaches importance to the significance of more important values. Based on industrial development theory, the balanced drive of "technical-capital-environmental-human" is an ideal implementation model. Industrial economics points out that industrial development is a process of absorbing and integrating resource elements. The balanced driving model of ideality means that the intensity of fixed asset investment, the level of R&D investment, the level of R&D personnel investment, the degree of government support, the degree of ownership concentration, and the level of education in the path allocation, as the production demand factors supporting the development of relevant industries, together become the influencing factors to promote the improvement of total factor productivity [58].

Based on the above conclusions, this paper makes four suggestions:
- Implementing the technological innovation-driven strategy and implementing the classification policy: Increase investment in R&D funds and human capital in the industrial software industry, implement a strategy centered on technological innovation, and improve the utilization of R&D funds and human capital based on technological innovation. In the early stages of technological innovation, a large amount of human capital, R&D funds, etc. are required to be invested. Since the transformation of technological innovation results is extremely slow, a long-term mechanism must be established to ensure the sustainable operation of technological innovation. In October 2021, the 34th collective study session of the Political Bureau of the Chinese Central Committee pointed out that it is necessary to comprehensively promote industrializa-

tion and large-scale application, focus on breakthroughs in key software, promote the software industry to become bigger and stronger, and enhance key software technology innovation and supply capabilities.
- Increase government support and accurately formulate government support policies: The government and relevant industry participants should follow the development rules of strategic emerging industries, gain insight into the internal correlations and conflicts between various factors that affect industrial development, explore the key factors and paths that restrict industrial development, and use information and intelligent means for good industry whole-process management.
- Coordinate efforts to support the training of industrial software talents through multiple channels: Give full play to the open nature of the open source community, based on national conditions, gather talents from multiple parties, promote the construction of industrial software open-source ecosystem, technical community construction, open-source project cultivation, open-source group standard formulation, open source technology promotion and application, open-source talent training, etc., and explore the formation of an Internet environment. A new model for open source development of industrial software. Provide policy guidance, intellectual property protection, open source community construction, relevant standard formulation, data asset protection, and other services for talent targets at all levels. It is necessary to improve the industrial innovation distribution system and incentive mechanism, improve the development evaluation system that is consistent with the characteristics of various talents, and fully stimulate the motivation of talents to innovate. Respect human input and wisdom output, reasonably ensure personnel treatment, and increase the proportion of personnel costs in project implementation. Promote the "industry-university-research-application" coordination mechanism and encourage industrial software companies to collaborate with universities and scientific research institutions to cultivate the industry. Add industrial software courses in colleges and universities, strengthen the construction of domestic industrial software training systems, and improve the level of human-related industrial software applications.
- The promotion of industrial software classification creates a good environment for the development of China's domestic industrial software industry. Promote the combination of effective markets and promising governments around the industrial software development environment, start from the market demand driven by industrial enterprise software products and industrial enterprise application scenarios, implement policies by coordinating and integrating the policy resources of all parties, and rationally allocate taxation and finance in the domestic manufacturing market, financial support, and other resource support, forming an "internal circulation" and "internal and external dual circulation" pattern for the development of the industrial software industry.

This research had some limitations. This paper has shortcomings and issues worthy of future research. This paper only uses relevant data from 40 industrial software firms, which may lead to less than ideal accuracy of TFP and its decomposition indicators. Since the development cycle of industrial software is relatively long and may be interfered with by random factors, this paper uses the DEA-Malmquist index method, which is only suitable for non-parametric estimation. This method ignores the impact of random factors on TFP and attempts to use the SFA method to explore these factors.

**Author Contributions:** Conceptualization, X.W., S.W. and L.Z.; Methodology, X.W.; Software, X.W.; Validation, X.W. and L.Z.; Formal analysis, X.W.; Investigation, X.W.; Resources, L.Z.; Data curation, X.W.; Writing, original draft preparation, X.W.; Writing, review and editing, X.W., S.W. and L.Z.; Supervision X.W. and L.Z.; Project administration, X.W., S.W. and L.Z.; Funding acquisition, L.Z. All authors have read and agreed to the published version of the manuscript.

**Funding:** This research was supported by the National Social Science Foundation of China (Grant No. 20BJY097).

**Data Availability Statement:** Survey supporting the study can be obtained by demanding it from any author.

**Acknowledgments:** Authors acknowledge the helpful comments of anonymous reviewers.

**Conflicts of Interest:** The authors declare no conflict of interest.

## Appendix A

Table A1. 2018–2019 Industrial software industry TFP change index and its decomposition.

| Category | Firm Name | EFFCH | TECHCH | PECH | SECH | TFPCH |
|---|---|---|---|---|---|---|
| R&D and design | ZWsoft | 0.612 | 1.449 | 0.753 | 0.812 | 0.886 |
| | Glodon | 0.476 | 1.557 | 0.231 | 2.055 | 0.741 |
| | General electron | 0.056 | 1.687 | 0.507 | 0.110 | 0.094 |
| | Gstarsoft | 0.258 | 1.254 | 0.649 | 0.398 | 0.324 |
| | Anwise | 0.462 | 1.634 | 0.942 | 0.490 | 0.754 |
| | S2C | 0.802 | 1.217 | 1.000 | 0.802 | 0.977 |
| | Empyrean | 0.706 | 1.362 | 0.820 | 0.861 | 0.962 |
| | Semitronix | 1.289 | 1.634 | 0.933 | 1.381 | 2.106 |
| | YJK Building | 1.000 | 1.139 | 1.000 | 1.000 | 1.139 |
| | Hollywave | 0.668 | 1.417 | 1.000 | 0.668 | 0.946 |
| Business management | Yonyou Network | 0.942 | 1.404 | 1.430 | 0.658 | 1.323 |
| | Neusoft | 0.568 | 1.581 | 0.384 | 1.478 | 0.898 |
| | Dahua Technology | 0.763 | 1.534 | 1.000 | 0.763 | 1.171 |
| | BMsoft | 0.675 | 1.307 | 0.499 | 1.351 | 0.882 |
| | YGsoft | 0.805 | 1.248 | 0.519 | 1.551 | 1.005 |
| | QM information | 1.087 | 1.268 | 1.346 | 0.808 | 1.378 |
| | DHC Software | 0.562 | 1.692 | 0.577 | 0.975 | 0.952 |
| | HAND Enterprise | 0.168 | 1.615 | 0.081 | 2.072 | 0.272 |
| | HopeRun | 0.140 | 1.452 | 0.112 | 1.253 | 0.203 |
| | DigiwinSoft | 0.979 | 1.284 | 1.092 | 0.896 | 1.257 |
| Production control | Baosight | 0.787 | 1.501 | 0.998 | 0.789 | 1.182 |
| | Taiji Computer | 0.624 | 1.713 | 0.670 | 0.933 | 1.070 |
| | Supcon | 0.834 | 1.239 | 0.865 | 0.964 | 1.034 |
| | Friendess Electronic | 1.000 | 1.344 | 1.000 | 1.000 | 1.344 |
| | Wiscom System | 0.716 | 1.713 | 0.776 | 0.922 | 1.226 |
| | Sifang Automation | 0.564 | 1.703 | 0.498 | 1.132 | 0.961 |
| | Integrated Electronic | 0.518 | 1.618 | 0.695 | 0.745 | 0.839 |
| | HITE | 0.698 | 1.830 | 0.756 | 0.924 | 1.277 |
| | SCIYON | 0.738 | 1.253 | 0.838 | 0.882 | 0.925 |
| | HuazhongCNC | 0.599 | 1.861 | 0.779 | 0.769 | 1.115 |
| Industrial Internet and industrial app | Nancal | 0.800 | 1.486 | 0.874 | 0.916 | 1.189 |
| | Yonyou auto | 0.793 | 1.331 | 0.578 | 1.373 | 1.056 |
| | QingCloud Tech | 0.585 | 1.861 | 0.860 | 0.680 | 1.089 |
| | Thunder Soft | 0.746 | 1.550 | 0.548 | 1.362 | 1.157 |
| | Autel | 0.590 | 1.243 | 0.594 | 0.994 | 0.734 |
| | Seeyon | 0.833 | 1.468 | 0.879 | 0.947 | 1.222 |
| | BONC | 0.595 | 1.248 | 0.553 | 1.076 | 0.743 |
| | FII | 0.763 | 1.474 | 1.000 | 0.763 | 1.125 |
| | GUOLIAN | 1.000 | 1.581 | 1.000 | 1.000 | 1.581 |
| | UNIS | 0.606 | 1.681 | 1.000 | 0.606 | 1.019 |
| | mean value | 0.612 | 1.473 | 0.683 | 0.896 | 0.901 |

Table A2. 2019–2020 Industrial software industry TFP change index and its decomposition.

| Category | Firm Name | EFFCH | TECHCH | PECH | SECH | TFPCH |
|---|---|---|---|---|---|---|
| R&D and design | ZWsoft | 1.219 | 0.828 | 1.120 | 1.089 | 1.010 |
| | Glodon | 0.763 | 1.471 | 0.715 | 1.067 | 1.122 |
| | General electron | 2.944 | 0.867 | 1.181 | 2.493 | 2.552 |
| | Gstarsoft | 2.285 | 0.916 | 1.131 | 2.020 | 2.093 |
| | Anwise | 1.175 | 0.492 | 1.714 | 0.686 | 0.578 |
| | S2C | 0.179 | 0.760 | 0.835 | 0.215 | 0.136 |
| | Empyrean | 1.034 | 1.242 | 0.994 | 1.040 | 1.284 |
| | Semitronix | 1.337 | 1.208 | 0.958 | 1.396 | 1.615 |
| | YJK Building | 1.000 | 0.925 | 1.000 | 1.000 | 0.925 |
| | Hollywave | 0.770 | 1.139 | 1.000 | 0.770 | 0.877 |
| Business management | Yonyou Network | 1.061 | 0.963 | 0.926 | 1.146 | 1.021 |
| | Neusoft | 0.535 | 1.394 | 0.348 | 1.539 | 0.746 |
| | Dahua Technology | 0.784 | 1.263 | 1.000 | 0.784 | 0.990 |
| | BMsoft | 0.897 | 1.077 | 0.684 | 1.312 | 0.966 |
| | YGsoft | 1.454 | 0.763 | 1.480 | 0.982 | 1.109 |
| | QM information | 0.759 | 1.038 | 0.728 | 1.042 | 0.788 |
| | DHC Software | 1.533 | 0.601 | 0.758 | 2.021 | 0.921 |
| | HAND Enterprise | 1.947 | 0.491 | 1.761 | 1.106 | 0.956 |
| | HopeRun | 2.958 | 1.015 | 1.872 | 1.580 | 3.004 |
| | DigiwinSoft | 0.985 | 1.052 | 1.083 | 0.910 | 1.036 |
| Production control | Baosight | 1.063 | 1.262 | 1.120 | 0.949 | 1.341 |
| | Taiji Computer | 0.640 | 1.538 | 0.372 | 1.722 | 0.984 |
| | Supcon | 1.190 | 0.828 | 0.750 | 1.587 | 0.986 |
| | Friendess Electronic | 1.000 | 0.954 | 1.000 | 1.000 | 0.954 |
| | Wiscom System | 0.544 | 1.731 | 0.773 | 0.704 | 0.942 |
| | Sifang Automation | 1.131 | 1.455 | 1.129 | 1.002 | 1.646 |
| | Integrated Electronic | 0.889 | 1.097 | 1.028 | 0.864 | 0.975 |
| | HITE | 1.424 | 1.285 | 1.473 | 0.967 | 1.830 |
| | SCIYON | 0.835 | 1.085 | 0.931 | 0.897 | 0.906 |
| | HuazhongCNC | 0.754 | 1.952 | 1.053 | 0.717 | 1.472 |
| Industrial Internet and industrial app | Nancal | 0.805 | 1.358 | 0.940 | 0.856 | 1.094 |
| | Yonyou auto | 1.314 | 0.725 | 1.329 | 0.989 | 0.952 |
| | QingCloud Tech | 0.491 | 2.073 | 1.166 | 0.421 | 1.019 |
| | Thunder Soft | 1.419 | 0.771 | 1.899 | 0.748 | 1.094 |
| | Autel | 0.985 | 0.865 | 0.737 | 1.335 | 0.851 |
| | Seeyon | 1.383 | 0.736 | 1.341 | 1.032 | 1.018 |
| | BONC | 0.748 | 0.788 | 0.278 | 2.691 | 0.590 |
| | FII | 1.447 | 0.647 | 1.000 | 1.447 | 0.936 |
| | GUOLIAN | 1.000 | 0.998 | 1.000 | 1.000 | 0.998 |
| | UNIS | 1.345 | 0.777 | 1.000 | 1.345 | 1.045 |
| | mean value | 1.029 | 1.004 | 0.969 | 1.061 | 1.033 |

## Appendix B

Table A3. Truth table (Outcome = TFP).

| FIX | RD | RDP | GOV | OC | HE | NUMBER | TFP | RAW CONSIST | PRI CONSIST | SYM CONSIST |
|---|---|---|---|---|---|---|---|---|---|---|
| 1 | 1 | 1 | 1 | 1 | 1 | 1 | 1 | 0.966229 | 0.810527 | 0.810527 |
| 1 | 1 | 0 | 0 | 1 | 1 | 1 | 1 | 0.965251 | 0.766233 | 0.766234 |
| 1 | 0 | 0 | 1 | 1 | 1 | 1 | 1 | 0.961621 | 0.766234 | 0.766234 |
| 1 | 1 | 0 | 0 | 0 | 0 | 1 | 1 | 0.951563 | 0.75969 | 0.75969 |
| 1 | 0 | 0 | 0 | 1 | 1 | 1 | 1 | 0.949549 | 0.745454 | 0.745455 |
| 1 | 1 | 0 | 1 | 1 | 0 | 2 | 1 | 0.945854 | 0.776223 | 0.776224 |

**Table A3.** *Cont.*

| FIX | RD | RDP | GOV | OC | HE | NUMBER | TFP | RAW CONSIST | PRI CONSIST | SYM CONSIST |
|---|---|---|---|---|---|---|---|---|---|---|
| 1 | 0 | 0 | 0 | 0 | 1 | 1 | 1 | 0.937407 | 0.65 | 0.661018 |
| 1 | 0 | 0 | 1 | 0 | 0 | 1 | 1 | 0.937288 | 0.637255 | 0.637255 |
| 1 | 0 | 0 | 1 | 0 | 0 | 2 | 1 | 0.93426 | 0.727749 | 0.727749 |
| 0 | 0 | 0 | 1 | 1 | 0 | 1 | 0 | 0.930328 | 0.507247 | 0.507247 |
| 0 | 0 | 0 | 0 | 0 | 7 | 2 | 0 | 0.927565 | 0.5 | 0.571429 |
| 0 | 0 | 0 | 0 | 0 | 0 | 1 | 0 | 0.915398 | 0.468086 | 0.468085 |
| 0 | 1 | 0 | 1 | 1 | 1 | 1 | 0 | 0.913481 | 0.537634 | 0.537635 |
| 0 | 0 | 0 | 0 | 1 | 0 | 1 | 0 | 0.912162 | 0.469389 | 0.469389 |
| 1 | 1 | 1 | 1 | 1 | 0 | 1 | 0 | 0.910985 | 0.548076 | 0.548077 |
| 1 | 1 | 1 | 1 | 0 | 0 | 1 | 0 | 0.907873 | 0.59854 | 0.59854 |
| 1 | 0 | 0 | 1 | 1 | 0 | 1 | 0 | 0.906621 | 0.583333 | 0.583334 |
| 1 | 1 | 1 | 0 | 0 | 0 | 2 | 0 | 0.902208 | 0.392157 | 0.392157 |
| 1 | 0 | 1 | 0 | 0 | 0 | 1 | 0 | 0.894188 | 0.342593 | 0.342593 |
| 1 | 1 | 1 | 1 | 0 | 1 | 1 | 0 | 0.893855 | 0.366667 | 0.366666 |
| 0 | 0 | 1 | 1 | 1 | 1 | 2 | 0 | 0.886364 | 0.076923 | 0.086206 |
| 0 | 1 | 0 | 0 | 1 | 0 | 1 | 0 | 0.883576 | 0.377779 | 0.377778 |
| 1 | 0 | 1 | 0 | 1 | 0 | 1 | 0 | 0.879859 | 0.352381 | 0.352381 |
| 0 | 1 | 1 | 1 | 1 | 1 | 4 | 1 | 0.879357 | 0.623431 | 0.680365 |
| 1 | 0 | 1 | 0 | 0 | 1 | 1 | 0 | 0.877388 | 0.197916 | 0.197916 |
| 0 | 1 | 0 | 0 | 0 | 0 | 1 | 0 | 0.872381 | 0.417392 | 0.417392 |
| 0 | 1 | 1 | 1 | 0 | 1 | 1 | 0 | 0.86907 | 0.233334 | 0.233334 |
| 0 | 1 | 1 | 0 | 0 | 0 | 1 | 0 | 0.859247 | 0.148514 | 0.148515 |
| 0 | 0 | 1 | 0 | 1 | 1 | 2 | 0 | 0.851163 | 0.119266 | 0.131313 |
| 0 | 0 | 0 | 0 | 1 | 1 | 1 | 0 | 0.845343 | 0.278689 | 0.278689 |
| 0 | 1 | 1 | 0 | 0 | 1 | 1 | 0 | 0.84168 | 0.066667 | 0.066667 |

**Table A4.** Truth table (Outcome = ~TFP).

| FIX | RD | RDP | GOV | OC | HE | NUMBER | TFP | RAW CONSIST | PRI CONSIST | SYM CONSIST |
|---|---|---|---|---|---|---|---|---|---|---|
| 1 | 1 | 1 | 1 | 1 | 1 | 1 | 1 | 0.988691 | 0.933333 | 0.933333 |
| 1 | 1 | 0 | 0 | 1 | 1 | 1 | 1 | 0.977273 | 0.815384 | 0.913793 |
| 1 | 0 | 0 | 1 | 1 | 1 | 1 | 1 | 0.97545 | 0.851484 | 0.851485 |
| 1 | 1 | 0 | 0 | 0 | 0 | 1 | 1 | 0.969745 | 0.802083 | 0.802084 |
| 1 | 0 | 0 | 0 | 1 | 1 | 1 | 1 | 0.964341 | 0.788991 | 0.868687 |
| 1 | 1 | 0 | 1 | 1 | 0 | 2 | 1 | 0.960152 | 0.766666 | 0.766666 |
| 1 | 0 | 0 | 0 | 0 | 1 | 1 | 1 | 0.944858 | 0.657407 | 0.657407 |
| 1 | 0 | 0 | 1 | 0 | 0 | 1 | 1 | 0.940246 | 0.721312 | 0.721311 |
| 1 | 0 | 0 | 1 | 0 | 0 | 2 | 1 | 0.938548 | 0.633334 | 0.633334 |
| 0 | 0 | 0 | 1 | 1 | 0 | 1 | 1 | 0.936909 | 0.607843 | 0.607843 |
| 0 | 0 | 0 | 0 | 0 | 7 | 2 | 1 | 0.934629 | 0.647618 | 0.647619 |
| 0 | 0 | 0 | 0 | 0 | 0 | 1 | 1 | 0.929314 | 0.622223 | 0.622222 |
| 0 | 1 | 0 | 1 | 1 | 1 | 1 | 0 | 0.928279 | 0.492754 | 0.492753 |
| 0 | 0 | 0 | 0 | 1 | 0 | 1 | 0 | 0.92555 | 0.531914 | 0.531915 |
| 1 | 1 | 1 | 1 | 1 | 0 | 1 | 0 | 0.922297 | 0.530611 | 0.530611 |
| 1 | 1 | 1 | 1 | 0 | 0 | 1 | 0 | 0.909457 | 0.375 | 0.428571 |
| 1 | 0 | 0 | 1 | 1 | 0 | 1 | 0 | 0.908571 | 0.582609 | 0.582608 |
| 1 | 1 | 1 | 0 | 0 | 0 | 2 | 0 | 0.899396 | 0.462365 | 0.462365 |
| 1 | 0 | 1 | 0 | 0 | 0 | 1 | 0 | 0.892045 | 0.451923 | 0.451923 |
| 1 | 1 | 1 | 1 | 0 | 1 | 1 | 0 | 0.889831 | 0.362745 | 0.362745 |
| 0 | 0 | 1 | 1 | 1 | 1 | 2 | 0 | 0.8861 | 0.233766 | 0.233766 |
| 0 | 1 | 0 | 0 | 1 | 0 | 1 | 0 | 0.880775 | 0.333333 | 0.338983 |
| 1 | 0 | 1 | 0 | 1 | 0 | 1 | 0 | 0.8742 | 0.233766 | 0.233766 |
| 0 | 1 | 1 | 1 | 1 | 1 | 4 | 0 | 0.86927 | 0.416666 | 0.416667 |
| 1 | 0 | 1 | 0 | 0 | 1 | 1 | 0 | 0.862647 | 0.40146 | 0.40146 |
| 0 | 1 | 0 | 0 | 0 | 0 | 1 | 0 | 0.855535 | 0.189473 | 0.189473 |
| 0 | 1 | 1 | 1 | 0 | 1 | 1 | 0 | 0.852252 | 0.254545 | 0.254545 |
| 0 | 1 | 1 | 0 | 0 | 0 | 1 | 0 | 0.846875 | 0.24031 | 0.24031 |
| 0 | 0 | 1 | 0 | 1 | 1 | 2 | 0 | 0.824273 | 0.272251 | 0.272251 |
| 0 | 0 | 0 | 0 | 1 | 1 | 1 | 0 | 0.812183 | 0.223776 | 0.223776 |
| 0 | 1 | 1 | 0 | 0 | 1 | 1 | 0 | 0.773458 | 0.292887 | 0.319635 |

## References

1. Zhou, Q. Development status and bottleneck breakthrough gradient of China's industrial software firms. *China Indu. Inform.* **2020**, *3*, 56–61. [CrossRef]
2. Wang, H. Pay attention to the high-quality development of the domestic industrial software industry from the perspective of national strategy. *China Dev. Obs.* **2021**, *14*, 13–18. [CrossRef]
3. Ni, G. Vigorously develop industrial software. *Civil-Milit. Integ. Cyber.* **2019**, *6*, 14–16.
4. Wang, L.; Zhang, C.; Cai, E.; Shi, H.; Wang, D. Knowledge extraction and knowledge base construction method from industrial software packages. *J. Tsinghua Univer. Nat. Sci. Ed.* **2022**, *62*, 978–986. [CrossRef]
5. China Industrial Technology Software Industry Alliance. *China Industrial Software Industry White Paper (2020)*; China Industrial Technology Software Industry Alliance: Beijing, China, 2021.
6. Chen, L.; Bian, M.; Liu, J. *Search: Strategies for the Development of China's Industrial Software Industry*; Machinery Industry Press: Beijing, China, 2021.
7. Tang, Z.; Li, Y.; Zhang, L. Identification Method and Breakthrough Path of "Neck- jamming" Technologies under the Background of Sino-US Trade Friction: A Case of the Electronic Information Industry. *Sci. Tech. Pro. Pol.* **2021**, *38*, 1–9.
8. Zhang, W. Research on the Way to Promote Scientific Research Productivity in Analysis (fsQCA) Based on 31 Provinces Chinese Universities: A Fuzzy Set Qualitative Comparative. *China High. Edu. Res.* **2019**, *7*, 78–84. [CrossRef]
9. Zhao, L.; Wang, X.; Wu, S. The Total Factor Productivity of China's Software Industry and its Promotion Path. *IEEE Access* **2021**, *9*, 96039–96055. [CrossRef]
10. Peiró-Signes, Á.; Trull, Ó.; Segarra-Oña, M.; García-Díaz, J.C. Attitudes Towards Statistics in Secondary Education: Findings from fsQCA. *Mathematics* **2020**, *8*, 804. [CrossRef]
11. Arias-Oliva, M.; de Andrés-Sánchez, J.; Pelegrín-Borondo, J. Fuzzy Set Qualitative Comparative Analysis of Factors Influencing the Use of Cryptocurrencies in Spanish Households. *Mathematics* **2021**, *9*, 324. [CrossRef]
12. Castelló-Sirvent, F.; Pinazo-Dallenbach, P. Corruption Shock in Mexico: fsQCA Analysis of Entrepreneurial Intention in University Students. *Mathematics* **2021**, *9*, 1702. [CrossRef]
13. de Andres-Sanchez, J.; Almahameed, A.A.; Arias-Oliva, M.; Pelegrin-Borondo, J. Correlational and Configurational Analysis of Factors Influencing Potential Patients' Attitudes toward Surgical Robots: A Study in the Jordan University Community. *Mathematics* **2022**, *10*, 4319. [CrossRef]
14. Akhmedova, A.; Marimon, F.; Mas-Machuca, M. Winning strategies for customer loyalty in the sharing economy: A mixedmethods study. *J. Bus. Res.* **2020**, *112*, 33–44. [CrossRef]
15. Bai, W. *Research on the Efficiency of My Country's Provincial Software Industry Based on DEA*; Jiangxi University of Finance and Economics: Nanchang, China, 2015.
16. He, X. *Research on Input-Output Efficiency Evaluation of Software Outsourcing Industry in Our Country*; South Central University for Nationalities: Wuhan, China, 2018.
17. Guo, R.; Qiao, Y. An empirical study on the relationship between the intensity of copyright protection and the development of software industry. *Stud. Sci. Sci.* **2019**, *37*, 1013–1021. [CrossRef]
18. Li, X. *Research on Performance Evaluation of Chinese Software Listed Companies Based on DEA*; Nanchang University: Nanchang, China, 2012.
19. Shao, J.; Wang, P. Empirical analysis of input-output efficiency and influencing factors of China's software service industry. *J. Manag. World* **2013**, *7*, 176–177. [CrossRef]
20. Jiao, Y. Research on regional differences and influencing factors of software industry Efficiency in China. In *Proceedings 21st Century Quantitative Economics*; China Economic and Management Press: Beijing, China, 2015; pp. 365–382.
21. Chen, G. Innovation Efficiency of National Software Industry Bases from Human Capital Perspective. *For. Sci. Tech. China* **2015**, *9*, 97–102. [CrossRef]
22. Jiao, Y. Research on efficiency of China's software industry. In *Proceedings 21st Century Quantitative Economics*; China Economic and Management Press: Beijing, China, 2016; pp. 355–372.
23. Du, Q. *Research on Agglomeration Level of Information Service Industry and Its Influencing Factors in Beijing*; Beijing Jiaotong University: Beijing, China, 2019.
24. Ye, H. *Research on the Influencing Factors of Technological Innovation Capability to Innovation Performance of Industrial Software Enterprises*; University of International Business and Economics: Beijing, China, 2020.
25. Guo, C.; Miao, Y.; Xu, T. Global Industrial Software Ecosystem and Evaluation of China's Industrial Software Competitiveness. *J. Xi'an Jiaotong Univ. Soc. Sci.* **2022**, *2*, 22–30. [CrossRef]
26. Dai, X. Analysis of the Current Situation and Trend of Chinese Industrial Software Development. *Soft. Gui.* **2022**, *21*, 31–35. [CrossRef]
27. Chen, N. *Evaluation on Efficiency of China's Listed Software Companies Based on DEA*; Northwest A&F University: Xianyang, China, 2013.
28. Li, Z.; Li, Y.; Long, D. Research on the improvement of technical efficiency of China's property insurance industry: A fuzzy-set qualitative comparative analysis. *Int. J. Emerg. Mark.* **2021**, *16*, 1077–1104. [CrossRef]
29. Liao, M.; Cao, X.; Qu, J. A study of regional difference of environmental factors for software industry cluster efficiency. *Sci. Res. Manag.* **2018**, *33*, 74–82.

30. Yan, X.; Huang, G. Government support effect in the development of high-tech industry: Based on the data of software industry base of National Torch Program. *Econo. Sci.* **2019**, *6*, 5–16.
31. Tao, Z.; Huang, W. Research on the Development Path of Industrial Software Industry in China. *J. Tech. Econo. Manag.* **2021**, *4*, 78–82. [CrossRef]
32. Long, Y.; Huang, T.; Luo, X. How to break through the domestic industrial software. *Insi. China* **2021**, *4*, 22–23.
33. Zhou, Y.; Zhao, D.; Liu, Z. Development Practice and Breakthrough Path of China's Intelligent Manufacturing. *Strateg. Study CAE* **2022**, *24*, 48–55. [CrossRef]
34. Wu, L.; Shi, X. Analysis and empirical research on influencing factors of Chinese software industry development. *Eco. Visi.* **2013**, *30*, 39–40.
35. Wang, H.; Zhang, X.; He, Z.; Bin, H. Research on Measurement and Influence Factors of Total Factor Productivity in Strategic Emerging Industries. *China Soft Sci.* **2020**, *11*, 143–153. [CrossRef]
36. Wang, Z.; Gao, Y. Total Factor Productivity of Chinese Strategic Emerging Industry: Based on DEA-Malmquist Index Model. *J. Harbin Univ. Commer. Soci. Sci. Ed.* **2016**, *5*, 65–70. [CrossRef]
37. Wang, Z.; Sha, G.; Hu, W. Measurement of total factor productivity of strategic emerging industries in Anhui Province: Based on DEA-malmquist Index Method. *East China Econ. Manag.* **2017**, *31*, 25–30. [CrossRef]
38. Zhou, J.; He, J. Study on Standards for Emerging Industries of Strategic Importance Statistics. *Stat. Res.* **2011**, *28*, 3–8. [CrossRef]
39. Liao, J. *A Study on the Factors Affecting the Total Factor Productivity of Software and Information Technology Services Industry in China*; South Central University for Nationalities: Wuhan, China, 2016.
40. Ren, Y.; Qiu, X. Can Government Subsidies and Enterprise R&D Inputs Promote Strategic Emerging Industries to Enhance Productivity. *J. Shanxi Univ. Financ. Econ.* **2017**, *39*, 55–69.
41. Shen, J.; Yang, R. Total Factor Productivity of Strategic Emerging Industries in Yangtze River Delta and Its Influencing Factors. *Fina. Tra. Res.* **2017**, *28*, 29–33.
42. Muoz-Pascual, L.; Curado, C.; Galende, J. Fuzzy Set Qualitative Comparative Analysis on the Adoption of Environmental Practices: Exploring Technological-and Human-Resource-Based Contributions. *Mathematics* **2021**, *9*, 1553. [CrossRef]
43. Berné-Martínez, J.; Arnal-Pastor, M.; Llopis-Amorós, M. Reacting to the paradigm shift: QCA study of the factors shaping innovation in publishing, information services, advertising and market research activities in the European Union. *Technol. Forecast. Soc. Change* **2021**, *162*, 120340. [CrossRef]
44. Park, Y.K.; Fiss, P.C.; El Sawy, O.A. Theorizing the Multiplicity of Digital Phenomena: The Ecology of Configurations, Causal Recipes, and Guidelines for Applying QCA. *MIS Q.* **2020**, *44*, 1493–1520. [CrossRef]
45. Fiss, P.C. Building Better Causal Theories: A Fuzzy Set Approach to Typologies in Organization Research. *Acad. Manag. J.* **2011**, *54*, 393–420. [CrossRef]
46. Veríssimo, J.M.C. Enablers and restrictors of mobile banking app use: A fuzzy set qualitative comparative analysis (fsQCA). *J. Bus. Res.* **2016**, *69*, 5456–5460. [CrossRef]
47. Oyemomi, O.; Liu, S.; Neaga, I.; Alkhuraiji, A. How knowledge sharing and business process contribute to organizational performance: Using the fsQCA approach. *J. Bus. Res.* **2016**, *69*, 5222–5227.
48. Wang, F.; Jiang, H.; Wang, C. The Evolution of the Control Framework China's Central SOEs: Is it Strategy Determined, Institution Driven, or Dependence on the Path?—An Attempt of a Quality Comparative Analysis. *J. Manag. World* **2014**, *12*, 92–114.
49. Xie, X.; Wang, H. How can open innovation ecosystem modes push product innovation forward? an fsqca analysis. *J. Bus. Res.* **2020**, *108*, 29–41. [CrossRef]
50. Jin, X.L.; Zhou, Z.; Tian, Y. A Configurational Analysis of the Causes of Consumer Indirect Misbehaviors in Access-Based Consumption. *J. Bus. Ethics* **2022**, *175*, 135–166. [CrossRef]
51. Ragin, C.C. *Redesigning Social Inquiry: Fuzzy Sets and Beyond*; University of Chicago Press: Chicago, IL, USA, 2008.
52. Ragin, C.C. Set relations in social research: Evaluating their consistency and coverage. *Political Anal.* **2006**, *14*, 291–310. [CrossRef]
53. Woodside, A.G. Moving beyond multiple regression analysis to algorithms: Calling for adoption of a paradigm shift from symmetric to asymmetric thinking in data analysis and crafting theory. *J. Bus. Res.* **2013**, *66*, 463–472. [CrossRef]
54. Cervelló-Royo, R.; Moya-Clemente, I.; Perelló-Marín, M.R.; Ribes-Giner, G. Sustainable development, economic and financial factors, that influence the opportunity-driven entrepreneurship: An fsQCA approach. *J. Bus. Res.* **2020**, *115*, 393–402. [CrossRef]
55. Park, Y.K.; Mithas, S. Organized Complexity of Digital Business Strategy: A Configurational Perspective. *MIS Q.* **2020**, *44*, 85–127. [CrossRef]
56. Leischnig, A.; Woodside, A.G. Who Approves Fraudulence? Configurational Causes of Consumers' Unethical Judgments. *J. Bus. Ethics* **2019**, *158*, 713–726. [CrossRef]
57. Carmona, P.; Momparler, A.; Climent, F. A Fuzzy-Set Qualitative Comparative Analysis of Causal Configurations Influencing Mutual Fund Performance: The Role of Fund Manager Skill. *Mathematics* **2023**, *11*, 4500. [CrossRef]
58. Dong, L.; Liang, H.; Gao, Z.; Luo, X.; Ren, J. Spatial distribution of China's renewable energy industry: Regional features and implications for a harmonious development future. *Renew. Sustain. Ener. Rev.* **2016**, *58*, 1521–1531. [CrossRef]

**Disclaimer/Publisher's Note:** The statements, opinions and data contained in all publications are solely those of the individual author(s) and contributor(s) and not of MDPI and/or the editor(s). MDPI and/or the editor(s) disclaim responsibility for any injury to people or property resulting from any ideas, methods, instructions or products referred to in the content.

Article

# Analyzing Primary Sector Selection for Economic Activity in Romania: An Interval-Valued Fuzzy Multi-Criteria Approach

Alina Elena Ionașcu [1,*], Shankha Shubhra Goswami [2,*], Alexandra Dănilă [1], Maria-Gabriela Horga [3], Corina Aurora Barbu [4] and Adrian Șerban-Comănescu [4]

1. Department of Finance and Accounting, Faculty of Economic Sciences, Ovidius University of Constanta, 900001 Constanța, Romania; alexandra.danila@365.univ-ovidius.ro
2. Abacus Institute of Engineering and Management, West Bengal 712148, India
3. UNESCO Department, The Faculty of Business Administration in Foreign Languages (FABIZ), Bucharest University of Economic Studies, 010374 Bucharest, Romania; maria.horga@fabiz.ase.ro
4. Department of Business Administration, Faculty of Economic Studies, Ovidius University of Constanta, 900001 Constanța, Romania; corina.barbu@365.univ-ovidius.ro (C.A.B.); adrian.serban-comanescu@365.univ-ovidius.ro (A.Ș.-C.)
* Correspondence: alina.ionascu@365.univ-ovidius.ro (A.E.I.); ssg.mech.official@gmail.com (S.S.G.)

**Citation:** Ionașcu, A.E.; Goswami, S.S.; Dănilă, A.; Horga, M.-G.; Barbu, C.A.; Șerban-Comănescu, A. Analyzing Primary Sector Selection for Economic Activity in Romania: An Interval-Valued Fuzzy Multi-Criteria Approach. *Mathematics* 2024, 12, 1157. https://doi.org/10.3390/math12081157

Academic Editors: Jorge de Andres Sanchez and Laura González-Vila Puchades

Received: 25 February 2024
Revised: 9 April 2024
Accepted: 10 April 2024
Published: 11 April 2024

**Copyright:** © 2024 by the authors. Licensee MDPI, Basel, Switzerland. This article is an open access article distributed under the terms and conditions of the Creative Commons Attribution (CC BY) license (https://creativecommons.org/licenses/by/4.0/).

**Abstract:** This study presents an in-depth analysis of the selection process for primary sectors impacting the economic activity in Romania, employing an interval-valued fuzzy (IVF) approach combined with multi-criteria decision-making (MCDM) methodologies. This research aims to identify eight key criteria influencing the selection of Romanian primary sectors, including technology adaptation, infrastructure development and investment, gross domestic product (GDP), sustainability, employment generation, market demand, risk management and government policies. The current analysis evaluates eight primary sector performances against these eight criteria through the application of three MCDM methods, namely, Simple Additive Weighting (SAW), Weighted Product Model (WPM), and Weighted Aggregated Sum Product Assessment (WASPAS). Ten economic experts comprising a committee have been invited to provide their views on the criteria's importance and the alternatives' performance. Based on the decision-maker's qualitative judgement, GDP acquires the highest weightage, followed by environmental impact and sustainability, thus indicating the most critical factors among the group. The IVF-MCDM hybrid model indicates the energy sector as Romanian primary sector with the most potential, followed by the agriculture and forestry sector among the list of eight alternatives. It also explores the robustness of results by considering sensitivity analysis and the potential impacts of political and international factors, such as pandemics or armed conflicts, on sector selection. The findings indicate consistency in sector rankings across the different methodologies employed, underscoring the importance of methodological choice and criteria weighting. Additionally, this study sheds light on the potential influence of political and international dynamics on sector prioritization, emphasizing the need for comprehensive decision-making frameworks in economic planning processes.

**Keywords:** interval-valued fuzzy sets (IVFS); multi-criteria decision-making (MCDM); SAW; WPM; WASPAS; primary sector; Romanian economy

**MSC:** 03B52; 90B50; 91B06; 62C86; 97M40

## 1. Introduction

The primary sector (PS), a cornerstone of Romania's economic activity, significantly shapes its economic landscape. Situated in south-eastern Europe with abundant natural resources, fertile lands, and a favorable climate for agriculture, Romania's primary sector, including agriculture, forestry, fishing, and mining, has historically driven economic growth and sustainability [1]. The primary sector selection process holds critical significance for

Romania's economic development, given its pivotal role in driving growth, employment, and sustainability. Against a backdrop of evolving economic challenges and opportunities, understanding the dynamics of primary sector selection becomes imperative. Romania, as an emerging market economy, faces distinct challenges in optimizing its primary sector activities to maximize economic productivity and resilience. This section delves into the crucial role the primary sector plays in Romania's economy, encompassing its historical significance and implications for economic development [2]. From the lush fields of Transylvania to the mineral-rich Carpathian Mountains, Romania's dynamic primary sector continues to mold the nation's economic destiny. The significance of this study lies in its exploration of the nuanced factors influencing primary sector selection and the methodologies employed to address them. Romania's economic landscape is characterized by a diverse range of primary sector activities, spanning agriculture, manufacturing, energy, and natural resource extraction. However, navigating the complexities of sectoral prioritization amidst fluctuating market dynamics, technological advancements, and geopolitical uncertainties presents a formidable challenge [3]. The significance of this research can be described as follows.

- Economic development: The primary sector plays a crucial role in Romania's economy, contributing significantly to GDP, employment, and overall economic activity. Understanding which primary sectors drive economic activity in Romania is important for fostering economic growth and development [4]. By identifying key sectors and understanding their contributions, policymakers can formulate targeted strategies to strengthen these sectors and enhance overall economic performance.
- Resource allocation: Effective resource allocation is essential for maximizing productivity and efficiency within primary sectors [5]. This research identifies key criteria influencing sector selection and evaluates sector performance against these criteria, allowing policymakers and stakeholders to optimize resources more strategically, directing investments, subsidies, and support towards sectors with the greatest potential for growth and impact on the economy.
- Diversification: Romania's economy may benefit from diversifying its primary sector activities to reduce dependence on a narrow range of industries [6]. Studying sector selection can reveal opportunities for diversification into new sectors or value chains, thereby spreading risk and enhancing economic resilience against external shocks or market fluctuations.
- Employment opportunities: The primary sector is a significant source of employment in Romania, particularly in rural areas [7]. Understanding which sectors contribute most to job creation and income generation can inform policies aimed at promoting employment growth and improving livelihoods, especially in regions with high unemployment rates or limited economic opportunities.
- Sustainability: As sustainability becomes increasingly important globally, studying the selection of primary sectors can help identify opportunities to promote environmentally friendly practices and sustainable development. By prioritizing sectors with lower environmental impacts and higher resource efficiency, Romania can contribute to environmental protection and meet its international commitments towards sustainable development goals [8]. This research evaluates primary sector performance with respect to criteria such as environmental impact and income distribution, facilitating the identification of sustainable development pathways and the promotion of green growth strategies.
- Policy formulation: Insights from studying sector selection can inform the formulation of economic policies and strategies at the national and regional levels [9]. Decision-makers can use this knowledge to design policies that support the growth and competitiveness of priority sectors, foster innovation and technological advancement, and create an enabling environment for business development and investment.

Hence, it is very important to study the primary sectors that directly or indirectly influence the Romanian economy. This research aims to identify the potential primary sectors and rate them according to their effect on the Romanian economy. Romania faces unique challenges and opportunities in its primary sector activities, ranging from agricultural modernization and industrial diversification to environmental sustainability and technological innovation [10]. This research seeks to address these challenges and leverage opportunities by providing insights into sectoral performance and identifying areas for improvement. In an increasingly globalized and uncertain economic landscape, enhancing the resilience of primary sectors is essential for mitigating risks and adapting to changing market conditions. By analyzing sectoral performance under different scenarios and considering external factors such as political events or international trade dynamics, this research aims to contribute to the development of robust and adaptive economic strategies. Moreover, the selection of primary sectors involves complex decision-making processes that consider various economic, social, environmental, and political factors. By employing an IVF-MCDM approach, this research aims to provide a structured framework for analyzing and prioritizing primary sectors effectively [11]. Therefore, the motivation behind this research is to provide actionable insights and decision support tools that can inform strategic interventions aimed at strengthening Romania's primary sector activities, driving economic growth, and promoting sustainable development.

*1.1. Historical Significance of the Primary Sector in Romania*

Centuries of agrarian and extractive activities form the historical foundation of Romania's primary sector [3]. Agriculture, a cornerstone of the country's culture and economy, thrived owing to its fertile plains, extensive river systems, and temperate climate, enabling the cultivation of crops like wheat, corn, barley, and sunflowers. Romania's historical agricultural output played a crucial role in sustaining its population and establishing its prominence as a regional agricultural producer. Simultaneously, the Carpathian Mountains' vast forests provided timber and forest products, supporting local communities and serving as valuable resources for construction, fuel, and export [4]. Forestry activities became more regulated during the late medieval period. Additionally, Romania's rich mining history involved the extraction of gold, silver, salt, coal, and other minerals. This mining heritage expanded during the 19th century industrialization, contributing significantly to Romania's primary sector and its broader European importance. The historical significance of the eight primary sectors in Romania highlights their pivotal roles in shaping the country's economy, society, and identity over time. Let us delve deeper into historical information about each of the primary sectors in Romania.

- Energy sector: Romania's energy sector has historical significance dating back to the late 19th century, when oil fields were discovered in Ploiești. This discovery propelled Romania into the ranks of major oil-producing nations, fueling industrialization and economic growth. Throughout the 20th century, Romania invested in expanding its energy infrastructure, including the development of hydropower plants, coal mines, and nuclear reactors. The energy sector played a crucial role during periods of political change, providing a source of national revenue and energy independence.
- Agriculture and forestry: Agriculture and forestry have been central to Romania's economy and culture for centuries. Historically, Romania's fertile plains and favorable climate supported diverse agricultural activities, including wheat, corn, grapes, and orchards. Traditional farming methods, such as crop rotation and transhumance, were practiced for generations. Similarly, Romania's vast forests have been a vital source of timber, fuel, and biodiversity, contributing to rural livelihoods and environmental conservation efforts.
- Manufacturing and construction: Romania's manufacturing and construction sectors have undergone significant transformations throughout history. Industrialization gained momentum in the late 19th and early 20th centuries, with the establishment of textile mills, metallurgical plants, and machinery factories. The construction industry boomed during periods of urbanization and infrastructure development, with notable

projects including roads, railways, and buildings. These sectors played pivotal roles in shaping Romania's modern economy and urban landscape.

- Information technology: The Information Technology (IT) sector in Romania has evolved rapidly since the late 20th century. Following the fall of communism, Romania embarked on economic reforms and invested in technology and telecommunications infrastructure. The IT industry experienced exponential growth, driven by a skilled workforce, favorable business environment, and government support. Today, Romania is known for its thriving IT sector, with strengths in software development, IT services, and innovation.
- Mining: Romania's mining industry has ancient origins, with evidence of mining activities dating back to Roman times. Throughout history, Romania has been known for its rich mineral deposits, including gold, silver, copper, salt, and coal. Mining played a vital role in the country's economy, attracting investment, generating revenue, and supporting industrialization. However, the mining sector also faced challenges related to environmental degradation, labor conditions, and economic fluctuations.
- Automobile industry: The automobile industry in Romania emerged in the mid-20th century, with the establishment of manufacturing plants and assembly lines. Initially focused on producing vehicles for domestic consumption, Romania later attracted foreign investment from multinational automakers. This led to the expansion of the automobile industry, with the production of passenger cars, commercial vehicles, and automotive components. The sector became a significant contributor to Romania's GDP and exports.
- Textile industry: Romania's textile industry has a long history dating back centuries, rooted in traditional craftsmanship and artisanal production. Textile manufacturing flourished during the Industrial Revolution, with the establishment of factories and mills in urban centers. Romania's textile sector boomed in the 20th century, producing a wide range of fabrics, garments, and textiles for domestic and international markets. The industry provided employment opportunities and contributed to Romania's export earnings.
- Fishing industry: Romania's fishing industry has ancient origins, supported by its extensive coastline along the Black Sea and numerous rivers and lakes. Historically, fishing was a vital source of food, trade, and livelihoods for coastal communities and inland regions. Traditional fishing techniques and practices were passed down through generations, sustaining local economies and cultural traditions. Today, the fishing industry continues to play a significant role in Romania's coastal regions, albeit facing challenges related to overfishing, environmental degradation, and regulatory issues.

These historical insights highlight the enduring importance of Romania's primary sectors, reflecting a rich tapestry of traditions, innovations, and socio-economic developments over the centuries.

*1.2. The Current State of Romania's Primary Sector*

In contemporary Romania, the primary sector remains vital to the economy, especially agriculture, which constitutes a major part of the GDP and employs a significant portion of the population. The fertile plains yield diverse crops, and Romania is renowned for its quality wine, sunflower oil, and maize production [5,8]. Despite these strengths, the agricultural sector grapples with modern challenges, such as the imperative for increased mechanization and technological advancements to boost productivity and sustainability. Historical land reforms have left a legacy of land fragmentation, hindering economies of scale in agriculture. Ongoing efforts focus on modernizing the sector, adopting sustainable farming practices, and promoting rural development to enhance competitiveness in the global market.

Forestry is pivotal in Romania's primary sector, contributing to domestic and export revenues. The country's diverse forests, prized for biodiversity and esthetics, serve as both a tourist attraction and a timber resource. Emphasis on sustainable forest management aims to balance economic gains with environmental conservation. Mining remains a significant economic force, leveraging Romania's wealth in minerals like coal, salt, copper, and industrial minerals [3,4]. Despite facing environmental and modernization challenges, the mining industry remains crucial for GDP and export revenue [6]. In the primary sector, the fishing industry, though less prominent than agriculture and forestry, utilizes Romania's extensive Black Sea coastline and inland waters for sustainable freshwater fishing. However, Romania also faces several specific challenges in primary sector selection, which may include the following points.

- Romania's transition from a centrally planned to a market economy has left a legacy of inefficiencies and structural challenges in its primary sectors [7]. The legacy of state-owned enterprises, outdated infrastructure, and bureaucratic barriers can hinder effective sector selection and impede the competitiveness of certain industries.
- Agriculture is a significant primary sector in Romania, but the prevalence of small-scale farming and land fragmentation presents challenges for modernization and efficiency [8]. Fragmented land ownership makes it difficult to implement large-scale agricultural projects, adopt modern technologies, and achieve economies of scale.
- Access to financing is a challenge for many primary sector businesses in Romania, particularly small and medium-sized enterprises (SMEs) [5,6]. Limited access to capital constrains investment in modernization, technology adoption, and value-added activities, hindering the competitiveness of primary sectors.
- Many primary sector industries in Romania lag behind in terms of technology adoption and innovation [10,11]. Outdated equipment, inadequate infrastructure, and limited investment in research and development (R&D) hamper productivity and competitiveness, making it challenging to compete in global markets.
- Ensuring the environmental sustainability of primary sector activities is a growing challenge for Romania. Agriculture, forestry, and mining activities can have significant environmental impacts, including soil degradation, deforestation, and pollution [12]. Balancing economic development with environmental protection requires careful sector selection and the implementation of sustainable practices.
- Romania's primary sectors, including agriculture, forestry, and mining, are heavily dependent on natural resources [8,9]. Overexploitation of natural resources can lead to environmental degradation, resource depletion, and vulnerability to external shocks such as climate change and fluctuations in commodity prices.
- Primary sector businesses in Romania face challenges in accessing international markets due to trade barriers, tariffs, and non-tariff barriers [1,2]. Limited market access restricts export opportunities and exposes primary sector industries to competition from imports, affecting their competitiveness and profitability.

Addressing these challenges requires targeted policies and interventions to promote modernization, technological innovation, access to finance, environmental sustainability, and market access for Romania's primary sectors. By overcoming these challenges, Romania can enhance the competitiveness and sustainability of its primary sector activities and drive economic growth and development.

### 1.3. Implications for Romania's Economic Development

Romania's evolving primary sector, while maintaining historical significance, plays a multifaceted role in economic development. It remains a crucial source of employment, especially in rural areas, supporting communities and contributing to regional development and stability. The sector, encompassing agriculture and mining, generates valuable export revenue, with agricultural products like grains and sunflower oil contributing to foreign exchange earnings. Sustainable resource management practices are increasingly prioritized, emphasizing responsible agriculture, forestry, and mining for long-term viability [7]. Investment in the primary sector aligns with rural development initiatives, focusing on improving infrastructure, education, and healthcare to enhance living conditions and encourage community residency. Modernizing agriculture and mining through technology adoption is essential for productivity and competitiveness, prompting Romania's investments in research and innovation to stay abreast of global trends. Balancing economic interests with environmental conservation is a vital concern, emphasizing the need for sustainable practices and responsible resource management to preserve natural beauty and biodiversity.

Romania's primary sector, rooted in a rich historical legacy, remains pivotal in shaping the country's present-day economic activity. Agriculture, forestry, mining, and fishing contribute significantly to employment, export earnings, and rural development [8]. In the pursuit of sustainable growth and development, the primary sector serves as a cornerstone, harmonizing tradition with innovation and economic progress with environmental responsibility. Let us discuss in detail the key important roles that the primary sector plays in developing the Romanian economy.

- The primary sector, which includes agriculture, forestry, mining, and fishing, contributes significantly to Romania's gross domestic product (GDP) [4]. Although the share of the primary sector in GDP has declined over the years due to industrialization and the service sector growth, it remains an essential component of the economy.
- The primary sector is a major source of employment in Romania, particularly in rural areas where agriculture and forestry activities are prevalent [5,6]. The sector provides livelihoods for a significant portion of the population, contributing to poverty reduction and rural development.
- Agriculture plays a crucial role in ensuring food security for Romania's population. The country has fertile agricultural land and favorable climatic conditions for crop cultivation and livestock rearing [7]. The primary sector contributes to domestic food production, reducing reliance on imports and enhancing food self-sufficiency.
- Romania's primary sector generates export revenue through the export of agricultural products, timber, minerals, and other natural resources [10]. Export earnings from primary sector commodities contribute to the country's trade balance and foreign exchange reserves, supporting economic stability and growth.
- The primary sector is closely linked to rural development in Romania, where many agricultural and forestry activities take place [11]. Investment in primary sector infrastructure, agricultural extension services, and rural development programs can stimulate economic growth, improve living standards, and reduce regional disparities.
- Romania's natural landscapes, traditional agriculture, and rural way of life attract tourists and contribute to cultural heritage preservation [4,5]. Agriculture-related tourism, agro-tourism, and eco-tourism activities in rural areas provide additional income opportunities for farmers and support local economies.
- The primary sector plays a role in environmental stewardship and biodiversity conservation in Romania [12]. Sustainable agriculture practices, reforestation efforts, and responsible mining practices help mitigate environmental degradation and preserve natural habitats and ecosystems.

The primary sector is of paramount importance to the Romanian economy, contributing to GDP, employment, food security, export earnings, rural development, tourism, cultural heritage preservation, and environmental sustainability. Ensuring the viability and competitiveness of the primary sector is essential for achieving balanced and sustainable economic development in Romania.

*1.4. Outlining the Issue for Solution*

The primary sector, which includes agriculture, forestry, fishing, and mining, is crucial in shaping a nation's economic landscape. In Romania, with its rich agricultural heritage and diverse resource base, understanding the selection of primary sector activities and their impact on economic activity is paramount [9]. This research paper aims to explore the multifaceted relationship between the primary sector and economic activity in Romania, utilizing advanced MCDM techniques, specifically the IVF version of SAW, WPM, and

WASPAS. It is the firm belief of the authors that the developed model of IVF integrated with SAW, WPM, and WASPAS MCDM techniques can significantly contribute to addressing the challenges that Romania faces in primary sector selection in the following ways.

- These techniques incorporate IVF sets to represent uncertainty and imprecision in decision-making. In the context of challenges such as land fragmentation, limited access to capital, and environmental sustainability, where data may be uncertain or imprecise, interval-valued fuzzy techniques provide a robust framework for analyzing and prioritizing primary sectors.
- Primary sector selection involves evaluating multiple criteria, including economic, social, environmental, and technological factors. IVF integrated with SAW, WPM, and WASPAS techniques allow for the integration of diverse criteria and their respective importance weights, enabling a comprehensive assessment of sector performance against multiple dimensions.
- These techniques offer flexibility in modeling decision-making preferences and adapting to different decision contexts. In the face of challenges such as technological obsolescence and market access barriers, where decision criteria may evolve over time, interval-valued fuzzy techniques allow decision-makers to update criteria weights and adjust their decision models accordingly.
- IVF-MCDM techniques facilitate sensitivity analysis to assess the robustness of decision outcomes to changes in criteria weights and input data [13]. This capability is particularly valuable in addressing challenges such as dependence on natural resources and environmental sustainability, where uncertainties and fluctuations in input parameters may affect decision outcomes.
- IVF-MCDM techniques allow for the incorporation of expert judgment and subjective preferences into decision-making processes. In the context of challenges such as the legacy of communism and bureaucratic barriers, where qualitative insights and expert knowledge play a crucial role in decision-making, these techniques enable decision-makers to capture and integrate expert opinions effectively.
- IVF-MCDM techniques provide transparent and interpretable decision models, enabling decision-makers to understand the rationale behind decision outcomes and identify areas for improvement. This transparency is essential for building consensus among stakeholders and gaining buy-in for primary sector selection decisions.

IVF integrated with SAW, WPM, and WASPAS MCDM techniques offer a comprehensive and flexible framework for addressing the challenges that Romania faces in primary sector selection [12,13]. By providing robust decision support tools that handle uncertainty, integrate multiple criteria, facilitate sensitivity analysis, and incorporate expert judgment, these techniques empower decision-makers to make informed and effective decisions that drive economic growth and development in Romania's primary sectors.

1.4.1. Problem Statement

The selection and development of Romania's primary sector depends on different critical determinants of the nation's economic stability and growth. Despite ongoing policy initiatives and economic reforms, effective allocation of resources, investments, and attention to the primary sector remains a significant challenge [10]. The primary sector selection process in Romania lacks a systematic framework for evaluating sectoral performance and guiding strategic decisions. This deficiency hinders the country's ability to optimize resource allocation, promote sustainable development, and enhance overall economic prosperity. Specifically, the lack of clarity regarding which primary sectors to prioritize and the criteria for evaluating their performance poses challenges for policymakers, investors, and stakeholders. Eight sectors have been identified in this research that are believed to have the greatest influence on the Romanian economy. These primary sectors include Fishing (A1), Automobile (A2), Agriculture and Forestry (A3), Energy (A4), Manufacturing and Construction (A5), Textile (A6), Information Technology (A7) and Mining (A8). The central question guiding this research is as follows: "To what extent does the strategic choice of primary sector activities impact economic activity in Romania, and how can advanced MCDM methods, specifically IVF combined with techniques such as SAW, WPM and WASPAS, assist in assessing and optimizing resource allocation and policy interventions in this sector?"

This research paper proposes investigating the use of interval-valued fuzzy MCDM to address the primary sector selection challenge, emphasizing inclusivity in economic activity. IVF logic allows decision-makers to express preferences as intervals, accommodates imprecision and diverse perspectives [11]. This approach effectively navigates the complexity and uncertainty inherent in economic problems, defining primary sector options within a desirability range. IVF logic provides a flexible and precise framework, aligning with the nuanced nature of the economy and incorporating uncertainty and subjectivity into decision-making. This research aims to improve primary sector selection decision-making, promoting economic inclusivity and robustness in Romania. The main objective involves facilitating a multi-criteria discussion with ten economic experts assessing eight primary sectors based on eight factors including Technological Adaptation and Innovation (TAI), Infrastructure Development and Investment (IDI), Gross Domestic Product Contribution (GDP), Environmental Impact and Sustainability (EIS), Employment Generation (EG), Market Demand and Export Opportunities (MDE), Risk Management and Resilience (RMR), and Government Policies and Subsidies (GPS).

The primary sectors under examination form the foundation for the selection criteria in shaping the evaluation framework meticulously identified through expert discussions and an extensive literature review. Figure 1 depicts a hierarchical structure, visually conveying interrelationships and relative importance among these criteria [12]. These parameters have garnered favorable feedback, indicating strong economic preferences for their inclusion. By synthesizing insights from decision-makers and the existing literature, this research aims to create an economic framework aligned with objectives and positively resonant with the populace, enhancing engagement and effectiveness in economic processes for the benefit of the nation.

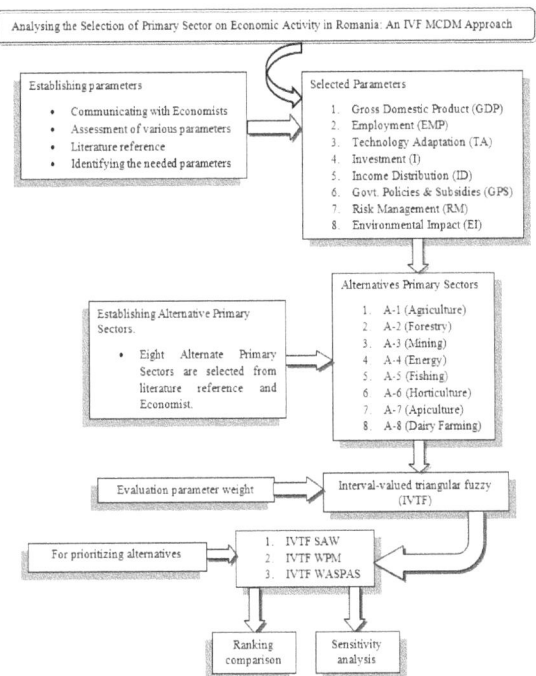

**Figure 1.** Flow chart of the proposed study. (Source: author's own elaboration).

1.4.2. Research Objectives

The objectives of the current research can be formulated as follows.

1. To identify the key factors and criteria influencing the selection and performance of the primary sector in Romania, encompassing economic, environmental, and policy-related dimensions.
2. To apply advanced MCDM techniques, including IVF-embedded SAW, WPM, and WASPAS, to evaluate the performance of eight primary sectors based on eight economic factors in Romania while considering the inherent uncertainty and imprecision in decision-making.
3. Assess the robustness of decision outcomes and the sensitivity of results to changes in criteria weights, input data, and external factors such as geopolitical uncertainties, market dynamics, and environmental regulations.
4. To develop a decision support framework that can assist policymakers and investors in making informed decisions related to the development, resource allocation and driving economic growth in Romania's primary sector.

By addressing these objectives, this research aims to contribute to a deeper understanding of the dynamics of primary sector selection and development in Romania and provide practical guidance for policymakers, stakeholders, and researchers involved in economic planning and decision-making processes.

## 2. Literature Review

Since the end of communism in 1989, Romania's south-eastern European economy has transformed significantly, transitioning from a centrally planned to a market-oriented system and joining the EU in 2007, shaping its economic landscape [13]. Key indicators, including GDP growth, inflation rates, and employment trends, reflect its economic performance, influenced by foreign direct investment, government policies, and external factors.

Understanding Romania's economic dynamics is crucial for assessing its growth prospects and evolving role in broader European and global contexts.

## 2.1. Past Studies on Economical Role of Primary Sectors

Throughout history, the primary sector has been a vital aspect of human economies, serving as the main livelihood for early agrarian societies and playing a pivotal role in their development. Scholars like Siksnelyte-Butkiene et al. [14] emphasize agriculture's central role in transitioning from nomadic lifestyles to settled communities, enabling food surplus, population growth, and complex societies. The Industrial Revolution witnessed a significant shift away from agriculture toward industrialization in Western countries, leading to structural transformation. Nasri et al. [15] note the declining share of agriculture in national income and employment during this period. Despite these shifts, the primary sector remains crucial, especially in low-income and developing nations, with agriculture seen as a pathway out of poverty. Hsueh et al.'s [16] research underscores the link between agricultural productivity and poverty reduction, highlighting the importance of modernizing agricultural practices.

The primary sector acts as a catalyst for economic growth by supplying inputs to other sectors, such as the mining sector, and providing raw materials to manufacturing industries, thus fostering industrialization [17]. The interdependence between the primary and secondary sectors underscores its significance in economic development. However, it faces challenges, particularly in environmental sustainability. Agriculture, linked to deforestation and soil erosion, prompts discussions on sustainable practices [18]. The mining sector faces concerns like resource depletion and environmental degradation, emphasizing the need for sustainable resource management [19]. Globalization brings opportunities for new markets and increased demand but exposes primary sector producers to international competition and market fluctuations.

The global agricultural trade regime, marked by subsidies and tariffs, sparks debate about its impact on the primary sector's development [20]. Technological advancements, like the Green Revolution and innovations in farming and mining, have boosted productivity [21]. However, these innovations pose challenges, such as declining employment in the primary sector, especially in transitioning economies. Urbanization raises concerns about the sustainability of rural communities [22]. Some propose policies that create non-farm jobs in rural areas to alleviate pressure on urban centers [23]. Despite challenges, the primary sector remains a critical component of the modern economy, playing a pivotal role in development, sustaining livelihoods, and addressing food needs. Technological advancements reshape the sector, and rural–urban dynamics continue to evolve.

## 2.2. Past Studies on Interval-Valued Fuzzy MCDM Method Application

MCDM is essential in diverse fields like engineering, economics, environmental science, and management, helping decision-makers choose the best alternative from multiple criteria. Interval-valued fuzzy MCDM, an extension dealing with uncertainty, uses interval-valued fuzzy numbers for effective handling of imprecise information. Researchers, including Opreana et al. [24] in 2023, have extensively explored its application, leading to various methodologies and practical uses. IVF sets have become a prominent tool due to their ability to capture uncertainty. The widely used Interval-Valued Fuzzy Analytic Hierarchy Process (IVF-AHP) method, introduced by Martín et al. [25] in 2020, extends AHP by utilizing interval-valued fuzzy numbers for more realistic and flexible decision modeling.

Another notable method is the Technique for Order of Preference by Similarity to Ideal Solution (IVF-TOPSIS) developed by Makarevic and Stavrou [26] in 2022, integrating fuzzy set theory and TOPSIS to rank alternatives based on their closeness to the ideal solution. Interval-valued fuzzy preference relations have led to the IVF Preference Programming (IVFPP) method, enabling comprehensive representation of decision-makers' preferences. Interval-valued fuzzy MCDM methods find applications in various domains, addressing uncertain decision-making problems. In environmental decision-making, they assess the impact of projects, considering fuzzy intervals to account for uncertainties in input data. In healthcare, these methods optimize medical treatment and provider selection, considering both qualitative and quantitative factors to inform decisions amid uncertainties in patient preferences and medical outcomes.

IVF-MCDM is pivotal in energy planning and resource allocation, evaluating alternatives considering economic, environmental, and social criteria for sustainable energy development [27]. In transportation planning, IVF-MCDM assesses complex trade-offs in infrastructure projects, aiding decision-makers in making robust choices amid uncertainties [28]. Financial decision-making, particularly in portfolio selection and risk assessment, benefits from IVF-MCDM by incorporating fuzzy intervals for better risk management [29]. As a potent tool for dealing with complex problems characterized by uncertainty, IVF-MCDM finds applications in various domains, including environmental management, healthcare, energy planning, transportation, and financial management [30]. The continual development and refinement of these methods have the potential to significantly contribute to more informed and robust decision-making processes across diverse fields.

## 2.3. Comparative Studies on SAW, WPM, WASPAS MCDM Method

MCDM methods play a pivotal role in addressing complex decision problems by considering multiple criteria simultaneously. Among the various MCDM techniques, SAW, WPM and WASPAS are widely recognized and applied in diverse decision-making contexts. These methods offer distinct approaches to evaluating alternatives based on their performance across multiple criteria, each with its own strengths and limitations [19]. In recent years, there has been growing interest in the application of SAW, WPM, and WASPAS to better understand their relative merits and applicability in different decision scenarios. Such studies aim to provide insights into the performance, robustness, transparency, and computational efficiency of these methods, thereby aiding decision-makers in selecting the most suitable approach for their specific needs. This section presents a comprehensive review and comparative analysis of SAW, WPM, and WASPAS MCDM methods. By examining key characteristics such as ease of implementation, transparency, flexibility, consideration of criteria interactions, robustness, and computational efficiency, this discussion seeks to elucidate the strengths and weaknesses of each method [22]. Additionally, it also discusses real-world applications and case studies where these methods have been successfully employed, highlighting their effectiveness in addressing practical decision-making challenges. Through a systematic comparison of SAW, WPM, and WASPAS, this argument aims to provide valuable insights for decision-makers, researchers, and practitioners involved in MCDM applications. By understanding the unique features and performance attributes of each method, stakeholders can make informed choices and enhance the effectiveness of their decision-making processes.

To provide a detailed comparative analysis of SAW, WPM and WASPAS methods with other MCDM methodologies, let us consider several key aspects.

- Complexity and ease of use: SAW, WPM, and WASPAS are relatively simple and easy to understand compared to some other MCDM techniques such as AHP, TOPSIS, and ELECTRE (Elimination and Choice Translating Reality). These three methods typically involve straightforward calculations and do not require complex pairwise comparisons or extensive data manipulation, making them more accessible to practitioners and decision-makers with limited technical expertise. They also offer a balance between computational complexity and analytical rigor, making them suitable choices for the research context [23].
- Transparency and interpretability: SAW, WPM, and WASPAS provide transparent results that are easy to interpret, as they directly assign weights to criteria and alternatives based on predetermined preferences or performance metrics [15]. In contrast, methods like AHP and ELECTRE involve subjective judgments in pairwise comparisons or complex mathematical formulations, which can introduce ambiguity and make it challenging to understand the rationale behind the final rankings.

- Flexibility and adaptability: SAW, WPM, and WASPAS offer flexibility in handling various types of criteria and decision contexts. They can accommodate both quantitative and qualitative data and allow for the incorporation of stakeholder preferences through adjustable weighting schemes [20,21]. Some MCDM methods like PROMETHEE (Preference Ranking Organization Method for Enrichment Evaluations) and AHP may have more rigid structures or require specific data formats, limiting their applicability in diverse decision-making scenarios.
- Computational efficiency: SAW, WPM, and WASPAS are computationally efficient and can be implemented using simple spreadsheet-based tools or software packages. They require minimal computational resources and are suitable for analyzing large datasets or conducting sensitivity analyses [6,7]. By contrast, methods like PROMETHEE and AHP may involve iterative calculations or complex algorithms, leading to longer processing times and potentially higher computational costs.
- Robustness and stability: SAW, WPM, and WASPAS are robust methods that generally produce consistent results across different decision scenarios and datasets. They rely on additive or multiplicative aggregation principles, which are mathematically well-founded and less sensitive to variations in input parameters. These methods are more preferable because they are well-established and widely used in the MCDM literature, indicating their robustness and stability in decision-making contexts [17,18]. Researchers may have confidence in the reliability of results obtained using these methods. Other MCDM techniques such as TOPSIS and ELECTRE may be more sensitive to changes in criteria weights or alternative rankings, leading to greater variability in outcomes and potentially less reliable decision support.
- Applicability to real-world problems: SAW, WPM, and WASPAS have been widely used in various practical applications across industries and domains, ranging from project selection and supplier evaluation to resource allocation and strategic planning [10,11]. While other MCDM methodologies offer specialized features or address specific decision contexts (e.g., uncertainty handling in Fuzzy TOPSIS or group decision-making in Group ELECTRE), SAW, WPM, and WASPAS are versatile techniques that can be applied effectively in a wide range of decision problems.

While each MCDM method has its strengths and weaknesses, SAW, WPM, and WASPAS stand out for their simplicity, transparency, flexibility, computational efficiency, robustness, and broad applicability, making them preferred choices in many decision-making situations. However, a detailed comparison of SAW, WPM and WASPAS with other widely used MCDM methodologies is provided in Table 1.

Table 1. Comparative analysis among different MCDM tools.

| Criteria | SAW | WPM | WASPAS | TOPSIS | AHP | ELECTRE | PROMETHEE | ANP | TOPSIS | GRA |
|---|---|---|---|---|---|---|---|---|---|---|
| Methodology | Weighted sum | Weighted product | Weighted sum & weighted product | Ideal and anti-ideal | Pair-wise comparisons | Outranking | Outranking | Network of interdependent criteria | Ideal solution | Similarity to ideal solution |
| Weighting | Equal/preassigned | Equal/preassigned | Expert opinion | Equal/importance hierarchy | Pair-wise comparisons | Importance ranks | Pair-wise comparisons | Pairwise and interactions | Equal/preassigned | Correlation between factors |
| Sensitivity to weighting | Sensitive | Sensitive | Sensitive | Sensitive | Sensitive | Sensitive | Sensitive | Sensitive | Sensitive | Sensitive |
| Computation complexity | Low | Moderate | Moderate | Low | Moderate | Moderate | Moderate | Moderate | Low | Moderate |
| Handling of objective functions | Linear/Nonlinear | Linear/Nonlinear | Linear/Nonlinear | Linear/Nonlinear | Pair-wise comparisons | Not applicable | Not applicable | Linear/Nonlinear | Linear/Nonlinear | Linear/Nonlinear |
| Transparency and interpretability | Transparent | Transparent | Transparent | Transparent | Transparent | Interpretation may vary | Interpretation may vary | Interpretation may vary | Transparent | Interpretation may vary |
| Scalability | Small to medium | Small to medium | Small to medium | Small to medium | Small to medium | Small to medium | Small to medium | Small to medium | Small to medium | Small to medium |
| Decision space representation | Additive | Multiplicative | Additive | Geometric | Hierarchy | Relationship matrices | Preference functions | Network | Geometric | Relational |
| Ease of implementation | Relatively easy | Moderate | Moderate | Moderate | Moderate | Moderate | Moderate | Moderate | Relatively easy | Moderate |
| Flexibility | Limited | Moderate | Moderate | Limited | High | Moderate | Moderate | High | Limited | Moderate |
| Consideration of Criteria Interactions | Limited | Limited | Limited | Limited | Limited | Yes | Yes | Yes | Limited | Yes |
| Consideration of performance and Importance | Yes | Yes | Yes | Yes | Yes | Yes | Yes | Yes | Yes | Yes |
| Robustness | Moderate | Moderate | Moderate | Moderate | High | Moderate | Moderate | High | Moderate | Moderate |
| Computational efficiency | Low | Moderate | Moderate | Low | Moderate | Moderate | Moderate | Moderate | Low | Moderate |
| Applicability | Generalized | Generalized | Generalized | Generalized | Generalized | Specialized | Specialized | Generalized | Generalized | Generalized |

(Source: author's own elaboration.)

SAW, introduced in the early 1980s, is a widely applied MCDM method that assigns weights to criteria and calculates the weighted sum for each alternative. The highest sum identifies the best choice, and SAW is valued for its simplicity and ease of implementation. However, it has limitations in handling non-commensurate criteria and lacks consideration for trade-offs [31,32]. Another model from the same period, WPM, calculates the product of each alternative's performance raised to the power of the corresponding weight. WPM is useful for emphasizing deviations from the ideal solution, allowing for non-linear relationship modeling and flexible weight assignment. However, it assumes criteria independence and does not capture interactions.

WASPAS, a recent MCDM method addressing SAW and WPM limitations, combines the weighted sum and product to calculate the overall performance, accommodating additive and multiplicative interactions between criteria [33]. It is valuable for complex problems with significant criteria interactions, allowing for trade-offs' consideration while accounting for overall performance. SAW, WPM, and WASPAS are vital MCDM methods widely applied in various contexts. SAW is simple but may overlook interactions. WPM models non-linear relationships but assumes criterion independence. WASPAS combines SAW and WPM strengths, considering interactions and offering flexibility in decision modeling. The advantages and limitations of the three applied techniques SAW, WPM and WASPAS are summarized in Table 2.

Table 2. Strengths and weaknesses of SAW, WPM and WASPAS.

| MCDM Tools | Strengths | | Weakness | |
|---|---|---|---|---|
| | Criteria | Explanation | Criteria | Explanation |
| SAW | Ease of implementation | SAW is straightforward to implement and understand. It involves assigning weights to criteria and then calculating the overall performance score for each alternative by summing the weighted scores. | Subjectivity in weight assignment | SAW relies on the assignment of subjective weights to criteria, which can introduce bias and uncertainty into the decision-making process. If the weights are not assigned appropriately, it may lead to skewed results. |
| | Scalability | SAW is highly scalable, making it suitable for decision problems with a large number of alternatives and criteria. Its straightforward nature allows for efficient scaling without significant increases in computational complexity. | | |
| | Transparency | The method provides transparent results, as the decision-making process is based on explicit criteria weights and performance scores. This transparency facilitates understanding and acceptance of the decision outcomes. | No consideration of criteria interactions | SAW assumes that criteria are independent of each other, ignoring potential interactions or dependencies among them. This simplification may not accurately reflect real-world decision scenarios where criteria may influence each other. |
| | Flexibility | SAW can accommodate various types of criteria, whether quantitative or qualitative, making it adaptable to different decision contexts. | | |
| | Computational efficiency | SAW requires minimal computational resources, making it suitable for analyzing large datasets or conducting sensitivity analyses. | Scoring inconsistencies | Inconsistencies in scoring across different criteria or decision-makers can affect the reliability and validity of the results obtained through SAW. |
| | Versatility | SAW can be applied to a wide range of decision problems, including project selection, supplier evaluation, and performance assessment. | | |

Table 2. Cont.

| MCDM Tools | Strengths | | Weakness | |
|---|---|---|---|---|
| | Criteria | Explanation | Criteria | Explanation |
| WPM | Consideration of criteria interactions | WPM accounts for interactions between criteria by multiplying the normalized scores of alternatives across all criteria, weighted by their respective importance. | Difficulty in determining weights | Like SAW, WPM requires the assignment of weights to criteria, which can be challenging and subjective. Determining appropriate weights for each criterion may be difficult, especially when stakeholders have differing opinions or preferences. |
| | Emphasis on dominant alternatives | WPM tends to highlight dominant alternatives that perform exceptionally well across all criteria. This emphasis can help decision-makers identify and prioritize alternatives that excel in multiple aspects, leading to more robust decisions. | | |
| | Transparency | Similar to SAW, WPM provides transparent results, enabling stakeholders to understand how each criterion contributes to the overall evaluation of alternatives. | Complexity with many criteria | WPM becomes increasingly complex and computationally intensive as the number of criteria increases. Calculating the weighted product of performance scores across numerous criteria may lead to computational challenges and longer processing times. |
| | Flexibility | WPM allows for the incorporation of stakeholder preferences through adjustable weighting schemes, providing flexibility in decision-making. | | |
| | Robustness | WPM tends to produce stable and consistent results, as it considers both the importance of criteria and the performance of alternatives across all criteria. | Risk of oversimplification | WPM assumes that the relationship between criteria is purely multiplicative, which may oversimplify the decision problem and fail to capture more nuanced relationships among criteria. |
| | Applicability | WPM is applicable to decision problems where criteria interactions are significant, such as product selection, project prioritization, and resource allocation. | | |
| WASPAS | Consideration of performance and importance | WASPAS integrates both the performance and importance of criteria in the decision-making process, ensuring a comprehensive evaluation of alternatives. | Difficulty in setting decision thresholds | WASPAS requires the specification of decision thresholds for each criterion, which can be arbitrary and difficult to determine objectively. Setting appropriate thresholds may require significant expertise and stakeholder input. |
| | Integration of qualitative and quantitative data | WASPAS effectively integrates qualitative and quantitative data in the decision-making process. This integration allows decision-makers to incorporate both objective performance metrics and subjective expert judgments, resulting in a more holistic assessment of alternatives. | | |

Table 2. Cont.

| MCDM Tools | Strengths | | Weakness | |
|---|---|---|---|---|
| | Criteria | Explanation | Criteria | Explanation |
| | Flexibility | Similar to SAW and WPM, WASPAS offers flexibility in handling diverse types of criteria and decision contexts. | Sensitivity to threshold selection | The choice of decision thresholds in WASPAS can significantly impact the ranking and selection of alternatives. Small variations in threshold values may lead to different outcomes, making the method sensitive to threshold selection. |
| | Robustness | WASPAS tends to produce robust results by aggregating weighted sums and products of criteria performance scores, reducing sensitivity to variations in criteria importance. | | |
| | Ability to handle non-linear relationships | WASPAS can capture non-linear relationships between criteria and alternatives, allowing for more nuanced evaluations in complex decision problems. | Complexity in parameter setting | WASPAS involves multiple parameters, such as weights, decision thresholds, and aggregation functions, which need to be set appropriately. The complexity of parameter setting may pose challenges, particularly in decision problems with high uncertainty or ambiguity. |
| | Applicability | WASPAS is suitable for decision problems where both the performance and importance of criteria need to be considered, such as supplier selection, investment decision-making, and technology assessment. | | |

Source: Author's own elaboration.

While SAW, WPM, and WASPAS are valuable MCDM methods, it is important to recognize their limitations and consider them carefully when applying these techniques in real-world decision-making contexts [29]. The authors have made full efforts to address the limitations by integrating the interval-valued fuzzy concept, which can enhance the reliability and effectiveness of these three methods. Moreover, this study engages with a diverse group of experts through consultative workshops, interviews, and structured surveys to elicit their judgments on criteria weights and performance scores. By aggregating and synthesizing expert judgments, this analysis aims to capture a broad range of perspectives and insights while mitigating individual biases and uncertainties. Fuzzy logic and IVF numbers have been utilized to represent uncertainties associated with criteria weights and performance scores. Fuzzy numbers allow for the representation of imprecise or uncertain information, enabling us to capture the vagueness and ambiguity inherent in expert judgments. This approach acknowledges the uncertainty surrounding criteria assessments and provides a formal framework for their representation and analysis. The significances of the IVF concept towards the ongoing analysis may be interpreted as follows.

- Enhanced representation of uncertainty: IVF sets provide a robust framework and flexible representation of uncertainty compared to other fuzzy variants [34]. While triangular or trapezoidal fuzzy sets represent uncertainty with single membership values, interval-valued fuzzy sets capture uncertainty through intervals of membership values. This allows for a more flexible representation of vague or imprecise information.
- Better Handling of Ambiguity: The IVF concept excels in handling ambiguity by allowing for a broader range of membership possibilities [35]. Unlike other fuzzy variants that assign a single membership value to each element, IVF sets accommodate multiple membership degrees within an interval, providing a more comprehensive characterization of uncertainty.

- Increased expressiveness: IVF sets offer increased expressiveness in representing complex and multifaceted uncertainty [36]. By capturing the variability and fuzziness inherent in real-world data more accurately, the IVF concept enables richer and more in-depth descriptions of uncertain phenomena.
- Greater robustness: The IVF concept is often more robust in the face of noise or imprecision in data [15,16]. The interval-based representation allows for a degree of tolerance to fluctuations or errors in the input, enhancing the stability and reliability of fuzzy inference systems.
- Improved decision-making: The IVF concept facilitates more informed decision-making by providing decision-makers with a more comprehensive understanding of uncertainty [30,31]. The interval-based representation allows decision-makers to explore a wider range of possible outcomes and assess the robustness of their decisions under different scenarios.
- Flexibility in modeling: IVF concept offers greater flexibility in modeling complex systems and phenomena. It can accommodate varying degrees of uncertainty and ambiguity, making them suitable for a wide range of applications across different domains, including engineering, finance, and decision sciences [24]. It can also capture the gradual transition between membership degrees, allowing for a more detailed representation of uncertainty compared to binary approaches.
- Adaptability to changing conditions: IVF concepts are well-suited for dynamic environments where conditions and preferences may change over time [25]. Their flexible nature allows for an easy adaptation to evolving circumstances, ensuring that fuzzy models remain relevant and effective in dynamic decision-making scenarios. It also ensures decision-makers to update and revise fuzzy sets as new information becomes available.
- Handling of incomplete information: In many practical situations, information may be incomplete or ambiguous [11]. The IVF concept enables decision-makers to handle such incomplete information by allowing for partial memberships to different categories, thereby facilitating more informed decisions.
- Integration of multiple criteria: IVF concepts are well-suited for integrating multiple criteria or attributes in decision-making processes [11,12]. These provide a unified framework for aggregating diverse sources of information, including qualitative judgments, expert opinions, and quantitative data.

It is evident from the overall comparative analysis that the three applied tools are chosen for specific purposes, and offer significant benefits over the other available MCDM tools. After conducting profound research on these three tools, the decision-makers were impressed by their merits and found it suitable for the present analysis. All the expert members also agreed to integrate the IVF concept to overcome the challenges offered by SAW, WPM and WASPAS. Therefore, the hybrid model of IVF integrated with SAW-WPM-WASPAS is capable of making effective decisions under vague conditions, thereby improving the quality and reliability of decisions across diverse applications and domains.

*2.4. Research Gaps and Novelty*

Despite notable contributions, this research addresses critical gaps. While MCDM techniques are widely used, their application in analyzing the primary sector's role in a national economy is sparse. This study bridges this gap by applying advanced MCDM techniques to a specific economic context. Previous applications of fuzzy MCDM in economics often focused on individual techniques or methodologies. However, this study integrates the IVF concept with the MCDM frameworks, to provide a comprehensive approach. This integration allows for a more holistic analysis of primary sector selection in Romania, considering both qualitative and quantitative aspects in decision-making. Fuzzy logic is an underexplored topic in economic studies designed to handle uncertainty and imprecision in decision-making. However, previous applications have struggled to effectively model and incorporate uncertainty, leading to less robust decision outcomes. By employing an

IVF approach, this study addresses this limitation by representing uncertainty as IVF numbers, allowing for a more accurate representation of decision-maker preferences and uncertainties. Moreover, economic decision-making often involves evaluating multiple criteria or objectives. Previous applications of fuzzy MCDM have focused on a limited set of criteria or failed to adequately consider the interrelationships among criteria. This study addresses this limitation by incorporating a comprehensive set of criteria influencing primary sector selection in Romania and evaluating sector performance against these criteria using multiple MCDM techniques. Additionally, there is a lack of research on the primary sector's role in Romania's economic development. Choosing Romania as a case study, this research fills a literature gap on MCDM applications in a country-specific context. Many previous applications of fuzzy MCDM in economics have been theoretical or hypothetical in nature, lacking practical relevance or applicability to real-world decision problems. This study addresses the limitation by applying IVF-MCDM techniques to analyze the selection of primary sectors influencing the economic activity in Romania, a context of significant importance and relevance to policymakers, stakeholders, and researchers.

This research makes unique contributions by integrating three advanced MCDM approaches, SAW, WPM, and WASPAS, to analyze the primary sector's role in the Romanian economy. The interdisciplinary approach offers a novel perspective on decision-making. The incorporation of IVF logic addresses the uncertainty in economic activity analysis, where data can be imprecise. Focusing on the Romanian economy adds a specific and valuable dimension, contributing to understanding the role of the primary sector in a transitioning economy. This research aims to fill gaps by combining advanced MCDM techniques with fuzzy logic, providing insights into economic decision-making in a transitioning economy. In addition, the present research also aims at providing actionable insights and decision support tools that can inform strategic interventions aimed at strengthening Romania's primary sector activities and driving economic growth and development.

## 3. Listing of Primary Sectors and the Factors Influencing Them

In this section, let us discuss in detail the significance of the eight identified primary sectors and their contribution towards the development of Romanian economy. Simultaneously, this section also sheds light on the significance of eight chosen factors and their influence on the Romanian primary sectors. Let us begin with the eight primary sector alternatives.

1. Fishing: Fishing contributes to food security, employment, and economic development in coastal areas. While Romania's fishing industry is relatively small compared to other sectors, it provides employment opportunities, particularly in coastal regions [37]. Additionally, it contributes to domestic food supply and exports, supporting economic growth. Pandemics can disrupt fishing activities due to restrictions on movement, labor shortages, and changes in consumer behavior. Reduced demand for seafood products and logistical challenges may affect Romania's fishing industry. Armed conflict may restrict fishing activities in coastal areas or maritime zones due to security concerns. Damage to infrastructure and displacement of coastal populations may further impact the fishing sector.

2. Automobile: The automobile industry plays a crucial role in manufacturing, employment generation, and technological advancement. Romania has emerged as an important player in the European automobile manufacturing sector [2,3]. The presence of major automobile manufacturers and supply chain companies has boosted exports, provided employment opportunities, and attracted foreign direct investment, contributing significantly to the country's GDP. Pandemics can impact the automobile industry through reduced consumer demand, supply chain disruptions, and factory closures. Economic uncertainty may also affect purchasing power and consumer confidence, leading to lower vehicle sales. Armed conflict can disrupt automobile supply chains, hinder cross-border trade, and lead to market volatility. Security con-

cerns and geopolitical tensions may impact consumer sentiment and investment in the automotive sector.

3. Agriculture and Forestry: The agriculture and forestry sectors provide food security, raw materials, employment, and contribute to rural development. Agriculture and forestry are traditional sectors in Romania, supporting rural livelihoods and contributing to GDP [35,36]. These sectors provide employment, ensure food security, and supply raw materials for various industries such as food processing and wood products. Pandemics can disrupt agricultural supply chains, labor availability, and export markets, affecting Romania's agricultural exports and revenues. Reduced demand and logistical challenges may also impact forestry operations. Armed conflict in neighboring countries can lead to disruptions in trade routes and market access for Romanian agricultural products. Additionally, land degradation and displacement may affect agricultural productivity and rural livelihoods.

4. Energy: Energy is essential for economic activities, industrial production, and improving living standards. Romania has diverse energy resources including coal, natural gas, oil, and renewable energy sources such as hydro and wind [23]. The energy sector contributes significantly to GDP through energy production, exports, and investment in infrastructure, supporting industrial growth and domestic consumption. During pandemics, energy demand may fluctuate due to changes in industrial activity, transportation, and commercial sectors. Reduced economic activity can lead to lower energy consumption, affecting revenues for energy companies. In times of armed conflict, energy supply routes may be disrupted, affecting Romania's energy imports and exports. Geopolitical tensions can also impact energy prices and investment in the sector.

5. Manufacturing and Construction: The manufacturing and construction sectors drive industrialization, infrastructure development, and economic growth. Manufacturing and construction are key contributors to Romania's GDP, providing employment and generating revenue through exports [38]. These sectors encompass a wide range of industries including machinery, electronics, chemicals, and building materials, supporting economic diversification and development. Pandemics can disrupt manufacturing operations due to workforce shortages, supply chain disruptions, and reduced demand for goods. Construction projects may face delays or cancellations due to economic uncertainty and logistical challenges. Armed conflict can disrupt manufacturing supply chains, damage infrastructure, and pose risks to worker safety. Uncertainty and security concerns may deter investment in construction projects, affecting sectoral growth.

6. Textile: The textile industry is important for providing clothing, employment, and supporting local economies. The textile industry in Romania contributes to employment generation, exports, and value addition to raw materials [39]. It provides opportunities for small and medium enterprises (SMEs) and supports the country's integration into global supply chains. Pandemics can disrupt textile manufacturing operations due to workforce shortages, supply chain disruptions, and changes in consumer behavior. Reduced demand for apparel and textile products may affect Romania's textile exports. Armed conflict may disrupt textile supply chains, damage manufacturing facilities, and lead to workforce displacement. Security concerns may also impact access to raw materials and export markets.

7. Information Technology: Information technology drives innovation, productivity, and competitiveness in the digital age. Romania has a growing IT sector known for software development, outsourcing, and IT services [40]. The IT industry contributes to GDP growth, exports, and job creation, attracting foreign investment and fostering entrepreneurship and innovation. Pandemics can accelerate digital transformation and increase demand for IT solutions such as remote work technologies, online education platforms, and telemedicine services. However, economic downturns may lead to reduced IT spending by businesses and consumers. Armed conflict

may disrupt IT infrastructure, cybersecurity measures, and data centers, posing risks to digital operations and online services. Geopolitical tensions can also impact technology exports and collaborations.

8. Mining: Mining provides essential raw materials for industrial production and infrastructure development. Although the mining sector in Romania has declined in recent years, it still contributes to GDP through the extraction of minerals such as coal, metals, and salt. Mining activities support industrial sectors, provide employment in mining regions, and generate revenue through exports [41]. Additionally, efforts to modernize and diversify the mining sector can contribute to sustainable economic development. Pandemics can affect mining operations through workforce shortages, supply chain disruptions, and fluctuations in commodity prices. Reduced global demand for minerals and metals may impact Romania's mining exports and revenues. Armed conflict may disrupt mining operations and lead to damage to infrastructure, affecting production and exports. Geopolitical tensions can also impact mining investment decisions and trade relations.

Let us now focus on why the eight identified factors are considered significant for influencing the primary factors in Romania. These eight factors are considered to collectively shape a country's economic performance and development.

1. Technological Adaptation and Innovation (TAI): It helps to drive efficiency and competitiveness by enabling the adoption of modern technologies, improving production processes, and enhancing product quality. It also fosters innovation and leads to the development of new products, services, and business models, which can stimulate growth and create new market opportunities [2,3]. Political and international factors also influence TAI through policies, collaborations, and trade relations. For example, during pandemics or conflicts, governments may prioritize technological innovation in healthcare, cybersecurity, or defense industries to address emerging challenges or threats.

2. Infrastructure Development and Investment (IDI): It enhances connectivity, logistics efficiency, and transportation networks, reducing costs and improving accessibility to markets. It also attracts investment, stimulates economic growth, and improves living standards through better access to essential services such as energy, water, and telecommunications [6]. Political stability and international relations also play a crucial role in IDI. Conflicts or geopolitical tensions can disrupt infrastructure projects, while diplomatic relations and international agreements can facilitate cross-border investments and infrastructure development initiatives.

3. Gross Domestic Product Contribution (GDP): It reflects the overall economic health and size of the sectors, providing a crucial indicator for assessing economic performance and guiding policymaking. It also serves as a measure of the sector's contribution to national income and its importance in driving economic growth and development [16]. Moreover, political stability, trade policies, and international economic conditions impact GDP contribution. Pandemics or armed conflicts can disrupt economic activities, trade flows, and supply chains, affecting GDP growth rates and overall economic performance.

4. Environmental Impact and Sustainability (EIS): It mitigates environmental degradation, conserves natural resources, and protects ecosystems, ensuring the long-term viability of sectors and promoting sustainable development. It also responds to consumer demand for environmentally friendly products and practices, enhancing reputation and market competitiveness [14,15]. Political decisions and international agreements help to shape environmental policies and sustainability initiatives. Conflicts or geopolitical tensions may exacerbate environmental degradation, while international cooperation and agreements promote sustainable development goals and environmental conservation efforts.

5. Employment Generation (EG): It alleviates poverty, reduces inequality, and promotes social cohesion by providing job opportunities and income generation. It also stim-

ulates economic activity and consumption, driving demand for goods and services and contributing to overall economic growth [22]. Additionally, political stability, economic policies, and international relations influence EG. Pandemics or armed conflicts can lead to job losses, displacement, and labor market disruptions, while government policies and international assistance programs may support employment recovery and livelihood restoration efforts.

6. Market Demand and Export Opportunities (MDE): It drives revenue growth and expansion opportunities for sectors by responding to consumer preferences and accessing new markets. It also enhances competitiveness and diversifies revenue streams, reducing dependency on domestic demand and improving resilience to economic fluctuations [29]. Political stability, trade policies, and geopolitical dynamics also affect MDE opportunities. Conflicts or diplomatic tensions can disrupt trade relations and market access, while international cooperation and trade agreements open up new export markets and opportunities for economic growth.

7. Risk Management and Resilience (RMR): It helps to mitigate risks associated with market volatility, natural disasters, and regulatory changes, ensuring business continuity and sectoral stability. It also enhances resilience by implementing risk management strategies, diversifying operations, and building adaptive capacity to withstand disruptions [19,20]. Furthermore, political stability, crisis management capabilities, and international alliances determine RMR strategies. Pandemics or armed conflicts pose significant risks to sectors and economies, requiring effective risk mitigation measures, contingency planning, and international cooperation to enhance resilience.

8. Government Policies and Subsidies (GPS): These help to shape sectoral development, stimulate investment, and address market failures through targeted policies, regulations, and financial incentives. These also support innovation, research and development, and capacity building, fostering competitiveness and sustainable growth across sectors [8,9]. Political decisions, regulatory frameworks, and international agreements assist in shaping GPS. During pandemics or conflicts, governments may implement emergency measures, stimulus packages, or subsidies to support affected sectors, promote recovery, and mitigate socio-economic impacts.

These parameters collectively shape a country's economic landscape. A well-rounded economy aims for balance, fostering growth, job creation, technological advancement, income equality, and environmental sustainability. Government policies play a vital role in influencing and regulating these factors for a healthy economy [40]. In addition, incorporating political and international factors into the analysis allows decision-makers to assess the broader context in which primary sector selection occurs. By considering these factors alongside the eight criteria, policymakers can develop more robust strategies, policies, and interventions to navigate complex geopolitical dynamics, mitigate risks, and promote sustainable economic development in Romania.

## 4. Methodology

The expected primary sector platforms, with eight competing criteria, are listed in the following subsection. Using the IVF tool, parameter weights are calculated to rank the primary sectors, representing fuzzy values to address decision-making uncertainty. The IVF SAW, WPM, and WASPAS processes, and MCDM techniques are employed to determine the ranking of primary sectors based on set standards.

### 4.1. Brainstorming Session

The following research work starts with the formation of an expert committee comprising ten economists who can offer their relevant views on the topic. The formation of this committee comprising ten economists from various fields aims to identify the most important Romanian sectors and to evaluate different factors influencing the respective primary sectors and their impact on Romanian economic activity. The evaluation criteria and their respective weights are determined through a structured process involving expert consultations, a literature review, and stakeholder engagement. Initially, we conduct interviews and workshops with a diverse group of experts, including economists, industry professionals, and policymakers, to identify and prioritize the key criteria relevant to each primary sector. These criteria are then refined through iterative discussions and consensus-building exercises to ensure their relevance and comprehensiveness. The weighting of criteria is achieved through a combination of expert judgment, where experts assign relative importance to each criterion based on their expertise and experience. The committee will conduct cross-sectoral analysis to identify interdependencies and synergies among different primary sectors and factors influencing them. In addition, the committee will also provide insights and recommendations to policymakers and stakeholders to optimize resource allocation and promote sustainable development in primary sectors. Experts with a minimum of ten years of relevant experience are selected based on their expertise in specific sectors related to the Romanian economy. Diversity in specialization ensures a comprehensive understanding of the factors influencing primary sectors. The demographic details of the ten expert committee members are provided in Table 3. The names of the experts are kept completely anonymous to avoid any future conflict of interest issues.

**Table 3.** Demographic details of the expert members.

| Expert Groups | Experts | Field | Experience (In Years) | Description |
|---|---|---|---|---|
| EG-1 | Expert 1 | Agricultural economist | 13 | With extensive experience in agricultural economics, expert 1 specializes in analyzing factors affecting crop production, land use, and agricultural policy. |
| | Expert 2 | Forestry economist | 12 | Expert 2 is a leading expert in forestry economics, focusing on sustainable forest management, timber production, and environmental conservation. |
| EG-2 | Expert 3 | Mining economist | 15 | Expert 3 brings expertise in mining economics, including mineral resource extraction, mine development, and regulatory frameworks. |
| | Expert 4 | Energy economist | 14 | Expert 5's expertise lies in energy economics, including energy production, consumption patterns, renewable energy adoption, and energy policy. |
| EG-3 | Expert 5 | Manufacturing economist | 13 | Expert 4 specializes in manufacturing economics, analyzing factors such as industrial production, technology adoption, and supply chain management. |
| | Expert 6 | Construction economist | 13 | Expert 6 focuses on construction economics, examining factors influencing building construction, infrastructure development, and real estate markets. |
| EG-4 | Expert 7 | Information Technology economist | 11 | Expert 7 brings expertise in information technology economics, focusing on factors influencing technology adoption, digital innovation, and IT industry competitiveness. |
| | Expert 8 | Environmental economist | 15 | Expert 8's expertise lies in environmental economics, examining factors such as resource utilization, pollution control, and sustainable development strategies. |
| EG-5 | Expert 9 | Fisheries economist | 11 | Expert 9 specializes in fisheries economics, analyzing factors affecting fishery management, aquaculture development, and marine resource conservation. |
| | Expert 10 | Textile economist | 12 | Expert 10 specializes in textile economics, focusing on factors influencing textile production, supply chain dynamics, and international trade in textiles. |

Source: Author's own elaboration.

The first stage of the session began with a discussion to identify the primary sectors that have the most significant influence on the Romanian economy. Data for this analysis were sourced from reputable sources, including government statistics, industry reports, academic publications, and expert assessments. Quantitative and qualitative data on various indicators related to the evaluation criteria were gathered, such as production volumes, employment rates, technological adoption levels, environmental impact assessments, and socioeconomic indicators. The experts' panel mainly relied on the Scopus and WoS databases to access numerous research articles on the field. After applying various filters and a thorough analysis of the abstracts, the committee found 200 research articles that suited the best related to the main theme, "Romanian economy". The list of 200 articles was further narrowed down by eliminating some of the irrelevant research articles after in-depth research and discussions. Finally, around 100 research papers were short-listed and considered for the ongoing analysis. After detailed investigation, the panel members agreed that the sectors listed in Table 4 have the greatest contribution towards the Romanian economy.

Table 4. Mapping of the selected factors to different sectors.

| Factors → / Alternatives ↓ | Technological Adaptation and Innovation (TAI) | Infrastructure Development and Investment (IDI) | Gross Domestic Product Contribution (GDP) | Environmental Impact and Sustainability (EIS) | Employment Generation (EG) | Market Demand and Export Opportunities (MDE) | Risk Management and Resilience (RMR) | Govt. Policies & Subsidies (GPS) |
|---|---|---|---|---|---|---|---|---|
| Fishing (A1) |  | ✓ | ✓ | ✓ | ✓ | ✓ | ✓ |  |
| Automobile (A2) | ✓ |  | ✓ | ✓ | ✓ | ✓ | ✓ |  |
| Agriculture and forestry (A3) | ✓ | ✓ | ✓ | ✓ | ✓ | ✓ | ✓ | ✓ |
| Energy (A4) | ✓ | ✓ | ✓ | ✓ | ✓ | ✓ | ✓ | ✓ |
| Manufacturing and construction (A5) | ✓ | ✓ | ✓ | ✓ | ✓ |  |  |  |
| Textile (A6) | ✓ |  | ✓ | ✓ | ✓ | ✓ |  |  |
| Information technology (A7) | ✓ |  | ✓ | ✓ | ✓ |  |  |  |
| Mining (A8) | ✓ | ✓ | ✓ | ✓ | ✓ | ✓ |  | ✓ |

Source: Panel of expert members.

In the second stage of the session, each participant was asked to brainstorm factors that have the greatest effect on these primary sectors. The facilitator recorded and refined the suggestions from past studies. After thorough deliberation, the eight factors listed in Table 4 were identified. The group then mapped each factor to the primary sectors, considering their relevance and impact, as shown in Table 4. It should be noted that for the current analysis of Romanian primary sector selection, political and international factors were implicitly taken into consideration through the eight factors considered in the analysis. The expert committee systematically explored how these factors intersect with political and international dynamics, particularly in the context of pandemics and armed conflicts, such as the conflict in Ukraine or the Israel/Gaza conflict.

In the final stage, the facilitator reviewed and summarized all the factors and their mapping to the primary sectors, ensuring alignment with the objectives of the brainstorming session. The experts were encouraged to provide any additional feedback or insights before concluding the session.

*4.2. Interval-Valued Fuzzy WSM Method*

The IVF-SAW method combines interval-valued fuzzy sets with the SAW method to address decision-making issues. It employs interval-valued fuzzy numbers to represent ambiguous information. The decision issue involves alternatives and criteria, each with specific aims or traits [30,31]. The goal is to rate options for overall effectiveness considering all criteria. The process begins with a decision matrix, where rows represent courses of action and columns represent criteria, using IVF numbers to convey ambiguity and imprecision in performance assessments. IVF numbers are a representation of uncertainty in expert judgments, particularly in situations where qualitative assessments are made. Gathering IVF numbers from qualitative judgments of experts involves a systematic process to translate linguistic expressions or qualitative assessments into fuzzy numbers that capture the uncertainty associated with the judgments.

Step 1: Establish language-based criteria for performance assessment and weight. In a MCGDM problem, create a fuzzy decision matrix $X_{ij}^k$ using linguistic specifications for criteria weights and performance ratings outlined in Table 5.

Table 5. Known linguistic specifications (criteria and alternative ratings).

| Language Standards for Criteria | | Language Standards for Alternatives | |
| --- | --- | --- | --- |
| Linguistic Specifications | TFNs | Linguistic Specifications | TFNs |
| Very Low (VL) | (0.0, 0.0, 0.1) | Very Poor (VP) | (0.0, 0.0, 0.1) |
| Low (L) | (0.0, 0.1, 0.3) | Poor (P) | (0.0, 0.1, 0.3) |
| Medium Low (ML) | (0.1, 0.3, 0.5) | Medium Poor (MP) | (0.1, 0.3, 0.5) |
| Medium (M) | (0.3, 0.5, 0.7) | Fair (F) | (0.3, 0.5, 0.7) |
| Medium High (MH) | (0.5, 0.7, 0.9) | Medium Good (MG) | (0.5, 0.7, 0.9) |
| High (H) | (0.7, 0.7, 1.0) | Good (G) | (0.7, 0.7, 1.0) |
| Very High (VH) | (0.9, 1.0, 1.0) | Very Good (VG) | (0.9, 1.0, 1.0) |

Source: Panel of expert members.

Step 2: This will help to determine the fuzzy decision matrix X's weight and its 'm' alternative possibilities with 'n' features, and E-1, E-2, E-3, E-4,..., $E_j$ economist experts (or groups) related to linguistic variables PA-1, PA-2, PA-3, PA-4,... $PA_m$. Therefore, as seen in Equation (1), the performance of alternative $PA_m$ with regard to decision matrix is denoted by $X_{ij}^k$.

$$X_{ij}^k = \begin{pmatrix} X_{11}^k & \cdots & X_{1n}^k \\ \vdots & \ddots & \vdots \\ X_{m1}^k & \cdots & X_{mn}^k \end{pmatrix} \quad (1)$$

Linguistic variables serve the mentioned objectives but are not directly transformed into IVF integers. In this work [32], they are converted into conventional TFNs for better utilization of the opportunities presented by IVF numbers.

The linguistic specification set-1 = "Very low (VL), Low (L), Medium Low (ML), Medium (M), Medium High (MH), High (H), and Very High (VH)" shown in Table 5 is used to rate the criteria performances and the linguistic specification set-2 = "Very poor (VP), Poor (P), Medium Poor (MP), Fair (F), Medium Good (MG), Good (G), and Very Good (VG)" represented in Table 5 is used by the economy experts to determine the alternatives performances with respect to each criteria. Experts are asked to provide their qualitative judgments using linguistic expressions such as "very low", "low", "medium", "high", and "very high" to describe the degree of membership or fulfillment of a criterion by an alternative. Each linguistic expression is mapped to a fuzzy linguistic term, typically represented by a triangular or trapezoidal membership function. However, Triangular Fuzzy Numbers (TFNs) were used in this article, which contains lower, middle and upper bound values as depicted in Table 5. The linguistic specification value of an expert opinion is converted into triangular fuzzy integers with interval values using Equations (2)–(6).

$$l = min_d\left(l^d\right) \quad (2)$$

$$l' = \left(\prod_{d=1}^{d} l^d\right)^{1/d} \quad (3)$$

$$m = \left(\prod_{d=1}^{d} m^d\right)^{1/d} \quad (4)$$

$$u' = \left(\prod_{d=1}^{d} u^d\right)^{1/d} \quad (5)$$

$$u = max_d \left(u^d\right) \tag{6}$$

where $\bar{x} = [(l, l'), m, (u', u)]$ represents the corresponding interval-valued triangular fuzzy number; $\bar{x}^d = \left(l^d, m^d, u^d\right)$ represents the triangular fuzzy number obtained on the basis of opinion of $d^{th}$ decision maker, $d = 1.\ldots.D$; and $D$ is the number of decision makers.

Eight criteria are considered, and the ten economists clustered into five groups offered opinions regarding the criteria importance based on linguistic specifications $\bar{x}^d = \left(l^d, m^d, u^d\right)$ for each factor, as shown in Table 6. The linguistic values were converted to respective TFNs in Table 6 using scores from Table 5. Experts were able to discuss and calibrate their judgments to ensure consistency and coherence across the assessments. This could involve averaging or aggregating individual judgments or adjusting fuzzy numbers based on group consensus. The resulting fuzzy linguistic terms represent the uncertainty inherent in the qualitative judgments. The width of the fuzzy numbers reflects the degree of uncertainty or vagueness associated with the experts' assessments. The TFNs were then transformed into IVF numbers using Equations (2)–(6), as illustrated in Table 7. These weights were implemented in the SAW method to rank different pedagogy methods.

Table 6. Criteria rating by the expert members.

| Specification | Criteria Rating Linguistic Specifications into TFNs | | | | | | | |
|---|---|---|---|---|---|---|---|---|
| Criteria | TAI | IDI | GDP | EIS | EG | MDE | RMR | GPS |
| EG-1 | (0.7,0.7,1.0) H | (0.7,0.7,1.0) H | (0.7,0.7,1.0) H | (0.7,0.7,1.0) H | (0.5,0.7,0.9) MH | (0.9,1.0,1.0) VH | (0.3,0.5,0.7) M | (0.5,0.7,0.9) MH |
| EG-2 | (0.5,0.7,0.9) MH | (0.5,0.7,0.9) MH | (0.7,0.7,1.0) H | (0.9,1.0,1.0) VH | (0.7,0.7,1.0) H | (0.7,0.7,1.0) H | (0.5,0.7,0.9) MH | (0.5,0.7,0.9) MH |
| EG-3 | (0.5,0.7,0.9) MH | (0.7,0.7,1.0) H | (0.9,1.0,1.0) VH | (0.7,0.7,1.0) H | (0.5,0.7,0.9) MH | (0.5,0.7,0.9) MH | (0.3,0.5,0.7) M | (0.3,0.5,0.7) M |
| EG-4 | (0.7,0.7,1.0) H | (0.5,0.7,0.9) MH | (0.7,0.7,1.0) H | (0.5,0.7,0.9) MH | (0.7,0.7,1.0) H | (0.7,0.7,1.0) H | (01,0.3,0.5) ML | (0.3,0.5,0.7) M |
| EG-5 | (0.5,0.7,0.9) MH | (0.3,0.5,0.7) M | (0.7,0.7,1.0) H | (0.5,0.7,0.9) MH | (0.7,0.7,1.0) H | (0.3,0.5,0.7) M | (0.7,0.7,1.0) H | (01,0.3,0.5) ML |

Source: Panel of expert members.

Table 7. Interval-valued triangular fuzzy weights of criteria.

| Criteria | l | l' | m | u' | u | $DNC_j$ |
|---|---|---|---|---|---|---|
| TAI | 0.5000 | 0.5720 | 0.7000 | 0.9387 | 1.0000 | 0.1345 |
| IDI | 0.3000 | 0.5165 | 0.6544 | 0.8927 | 1.0000 | 0.1219 |
| GDP | 0.7000 | 0.7361 | 0.7518 | 1.0000 | 1.0000 | 0.1518 |
| EIS | 0.5000 | 0.6434 | 0.7518 | 0.9587 | 1.0000 | 0.1397 |
| EG | 0.5000 | 0.6119 | 0.7000 | 0.9587 | 1.0000 | 0.1367 |
| MDE | 0.3000 | 0.5809 | 0.7028 | 0.9117 | 1.0000 | 0.1267 |
| RMR | 0.1000 | 0.3160 | 0.5165 | 0.7391 | 1.0000 | 0.0968 |
| GPS | 0.1000 | 0.2954 | 0.5165 | 0.7237 | 0.9000 | 0.0919 |

Source: Panel of expert members.

Step 3: Rate optimum performance for each category by selecting the performance rating that best meets each criterion. Optimal performance ratings should be expressed as IVF numbers instead of precise ones. The formula below is used to determine these ratings.

$$\bar{x}_j = [(l_j, l'_j), m_j, (u'_j, u_j)] \tag{7}$$

Here, $\bar{x}_j$ stands for the $j_{th}$ criterion's interval-valued fuzzy best performance rating.

$$l_j = \begin{cases} max_i l_{ij}; \ j \in \omega_{max} \\ min_i l_{ij}; \ j \in \omega_{min} \end{cases} \quad (8)$$

$$l'_j = \begin{cases} max_i l'_{ij}; \ j \in \omega_{max} \\ min_i l'_{ij}; \ j \in \omega_{min} \end{cases} \quad (9)$$

$$m_j = \begin{cases} max_i m_{ij}; \ j \in \omega_{max} \\ min_i m_{ij}; \ j \in \omega_{min} \end{cases} \quad (10)$$

$$u'_j = \begin{cases} max_i u'_{ij}; \ j \in \omega_{max} \\ min_i u'_{ij}; \ j \in \omega_{min} \end{cases} \quad (11)$$

$$u_j = \begin{cases} max_i u_{ij}; \ j \in \omega_{max} \\ min_i u_{ij}; \ j \in \omega_{min} \end{cases} \quad (12)$$

Maximum for benefit criteria (prefer higher values) and minimum for cost criteria (prefer lower values).

The five expert groups use the linguistic specifications from Table 5 to evaluate the performances of the eight primary sectors with respect to each factor, as shown in Table 8. Fuzzy numbers obtained from multiple experts for each criterion and alternative are aggregated using fuzzy arithmetic operations from Equations (2)–(6) to receive the alternative performance scores with respect to each criterion in terms of IVF values. These aggregated fuzzy numbers provide a comprehensive representation of the overall expert judgments, considering both the central tendency and the variability of the assessments. The final decision matrix, presented in Table 9 as IVF numbers, undergoes assessment using Equations (7)–(6) for the IVF extension of the SAW model. The initial step in this approach is to obtain the suitable performance ratings using Equation (7).

Table 8. Alternative performance rating of group discussion in linguistic terms.

| PS | TAI | IDI | GDP | EIS | EG | MDE | RMR | GPS |
|---|---|---|---|---|---|---|---|---|
| A1 | MG, G, M, MP, M | G, MG, M, M, MG | M, M, MG, MG, M | MP, M, P, G, MG | G, VG, G, MG, MG | MG, M, MP, P, M | M, MP, G, MG, MP | P, VP, VP, MP, MP |
| A2 | G, MP, MG, G, MP | MP, MP, M, M, MG | MP, P, MP, MP, P | MP, MP, P, P, MP | M, MG, M, MG, MG | MG, M, MP, M, M | M, MP, M, MG.MP | MG, M, MP, M, M |
| A3 | VG, G, VG, G, G | M, MG, MG, M, MG | M, M, MG, MG, M | MG, G, M, MG, G | MG, G, M, MP, MG | G, MG, G, MG, M | G, MG, G, G, G | VG, G, VG, VG, G |
| A4 | MG, G, MG, MP, MG | MP, M, MG, MG, M | MG, G, G, G, G | M, MG, M, MG, MG | G, VG, G, G, MG | MG, G, G, MG, G | MG, G, MG, VG, G | G, MG, MG, MG, MG |
| A5 | P, VP, VP, MP, P | P, P, VP, VP, P | M, MP, MP, M, M | MP, MP, P, P, VP | MP, P, VP, P, VP | M, MP, P, M, MP | MP, P, MP, M, MP | M, VP, MP, MP, MP |
| A6 | MP, MP, M, MP, M | M, MG, M, MP, M | VP, VP, P, P, VP | MP, M, M, MP, M | P, MP, P, MP, P | VP, P, MP, MP, MP | MP, VP, P, MP, P | VP, P, MP, MP, P |
| A7 | P, VP, MP, VP, P | VP, P, MP, MP, VP | MP, MP, VP, MP, P | MP, MP, VP, VP, P | VP, MP, MP, P, VP | P, MP, MP, VP, VP | VP, P, VP, MP, VP | VP, MP, P, MP, P |
| A8 | M, M, MG, MG, G | M, MG, M, M, MG | MP, MP, M, M, MP | G, MG, G, MG, M | MG, M, MG, G, VG | G, MG, MG, MG, G | MG, G, M, G, MG | MP, MP, MP, MP, MP |

Source: Author's own elaboration.

Table 9. Interval-valued performance ratings of the primary sectors.

| PS | TAI | IDI | GDP | EIS | EG | MDE | RMR | GPS |
|---|---|---|---|---|---|---|---|---|
| A1 | 0.1000 | 0.3000 | 0.3000 | 0.0000 | 0.5000 | 0.0000 | 0.1000 | 0.0000 |
| | 0.3160 | 0.4360 | 0.3680 | 0.0000 | 0.6434 | 0.0000 | 0.2537 | 0.0000 |
| | 0.5165 | 0.6119 | 0.5720 | 0.3743 | 0.7518 | 0.3500 | 0.4663 | 0.0000 |
| | 0.7391 | 0.8313 | 0.7740 | 0.6239 | 0.9587 | 0.5809 | 0.6910 | 0.2371 |
| | 1.0000 | 1.0000 | 0.9000 | 1.0000 | 1.0000 | 0.9000 | 1.0000 | 0.5000 |

Table 9. Cont.

| PS | TAI | IDI | GDP | EIS | EG | MDE | RMR | GPS |
|---|---|---|---|---|---|---|---|---|
| A2 | 0.1000<br>0.3005<br>0.4988<br>0.7421<br>1.0000 | 0.1000<br>0.2141<br>0.4360<br>0.6434<br>0.9000 | 0.0000<br>0.0000<br>0.1933<br>0.4076<br>0.5000 | 0.0000<br>0.0000<br>0.1933<br>0.4076<br>0.5000 | 0.3000<br>0.5186<br>0.7028<br>0.8741<br>0.9000 | 0.1000<br>0.2667<br>0.4829<br>0.6882<br>0.9000 | 0.1000<br>0.2141<br>0.4360<br>0.6434<br>0.9000 | 0.1000<br>0.2667<br>0.4829<br>0.6882<br>0.9000 |
| A3 | 0.7000<br>0.7740<br>0.8073<br>1.0000<br>1.0000 | 0.3000<br>0.4076<br>0.6119<br>0.8139<br>0.9000 | 0.3000<br>0.3680<br>0.5720<br>0.7740<br>0.9000 | 0.3000<br>0.5165<br>0.6544<br>0.8927<br>1.0000 | 0.1000<br>0.3500<br>0.5524<br>0.7772<br>1.0000 | 0.3000<br>0.5165<br>0.6544<br>0.8927<br>1.0000 | 0.5000<br>0.6544<br>0.7000<br>0.9791<br>1.0000 | 0.7000<br>0.8139<br>0.8670<br>1.0000<br>1.0000 |
| A4 | 0.1000<br>0.3876<br>0.5909<br>0.8172<br>1.0000 | 0.1000<br>0.2954<br>0.5165<br>0.7237<br>0.9000 | 0.5000<br>0.6544<br>0.7000<br>0.9791<br>1.0000 | 0.3000<br>0.4076<br>0.6119<br>0.8139<br>0.9000 | 0.5000<br>0.6882<br>0.7518<br>0.9791<br>1.0000 | 0.5000<br>0.6119<br>0.7000<br>0.9587<br>1.0000 | 0.5000<br>0.6434<br>0.7518<br>0.9587<br>1.0000 | 0.5000<br>0.5348<br>0.7000<br>0.9192<br>1.0000 |
| A5 | 0.0000<br>0.0000<br>0.0000<br>0.2141<br>0.5000 | 0.0000<br>0.0000<br>0.0000<br>0.1933<br>0.3000 | 0.1000<br>0.1933<br>0.4076<br>0.6119<br>0.7000 | 0.0000<br>0.0000<br>0.0000<br>0.2954<br>0.5000 | 0.0000<br>0.0000<br>0.0000<br>0.2141<br>0.5000 | 0.0000<br>0.0000<br>0.2954<br>0.5165<br>0.7000 | 0.0000<br>0.0000<br>0.2667<br>0.4829<br>0.7000 | 0.0000<br>0.0000<br>0.0000<br>0.3876<br>0.7000 |
| A6 | 0.1000<br>0.1552<br>0.3680<br>0.5720<br>0.7000 | 0.1000<br>0.2667<br>0.4829<br>0.6882<br>0.9000 | 0.0000<br>0.0000<br>0.0000<br>0.1552<br>0.3000 | 0.1000<br>0.1933<br>0.4076<br>0.6119<br>0.7000 | 0.0000<br>0.0000<br>0.1552<br>0.3680<br>0.5000 | 0.0000<br>0.0000<br>0.0000<br>0.3272<br>0.5000 | 0.0000<br>0.0000<br>0.0000<br>0.2954<br>0.5000 | 0.0000<br>0.0000<br>0.0000<br>0.2954<br>0.5000 |
| A7 | 0.0000<br>0.0000<br>0.0000<br>0.2141<br>0.5000 | 0.0000<br>0.0000<br>0.0000<br>0.2371<br>0.5000 | 0.0000<br>0.0000<br>0.0000<br>0.3272<br>0.5000 | 0.0000<br>0.0000<br>0.0000<br>0.2371<br>0.5000 | 0.0000<br>0.0000<br>0.0000<br>0.3758<br>0.5000 | 0.0000<br>0.0000<br>0.0000<br>0.2371<br>0.5000 | 0.0000<br>0.0000<br>0.0000<br>0.2724<br>0.5000 | 0.0000<br>0.0000<br>0.0000<br>0.2954<br>0.5000 |
| A8 | 0.3000<br>0.4360<br>0.6119<br>0.8313<br>1.0000 | 0.3000<br>0.3680<br>0.5720<br>0.7740<br>0.9000 | 0.1000<br>0.1552<br>0.3680<br>0.5720<br>0.7000 | 0.3000<br>0.5165<br>0.6544<br>0.8927<br>1.0000 | 0.3000<br>0.5431<br>0.7028<br>0.8927<br>1.0000 | 0.5000<br>0.5720<br>0.7000<br>0.9387<br>1.0000 | 0.3000<br>0.5165<br>0.6544<br>0.8927<br>1.0000 | 0.1000<br>0.1000<br>0.3000<br>0.5000<br>0.5000 |

Source: Author's own elaboration.

Step 4: Normalize the decision matrix with Equations (13) and (14) based on parameter nature. Equation (13) is applied for benefit criteria, where larger values are expected.

$$N_{ij} = \left\{ \left( \frac{l_j}{max(l_j)}, \frac{l'_j}{max(l'_j)} \right), \frac{m_j}{max(m_j)} \cdot \left( \frac{u'_j}{max(u'_j)}, \frac{u_j}{max(u_j)} \right) \right\} \quad (13)$$

Use the following Equation (14) for non-benefit criterion (minimum parameter) whose smaller values are anticipated.

$$N_{ij} = \left\{ \left( \frac{min(l_j)}{l_j}, \frac{min(l_j)}{l'_j} \right), \frac{min(l_j)}{m_j} \cdot \left( \frac{min(l_j)}{u'_j}, \frac{min(l_j)}{u_j} \right) \right\} \quad (14)$$

Step 5: Determine the weighted normalized matrix using Equations (15) and (16).

$$WN_{ij} = N_{ij} \times DNC_j \quad (15)$$

$$DNC_j = \frac{l_c + l'_c + m_c + u'_c + u_c}{5} \quad (16)$$

Step 6: Defuzzification of IVF-weighted normalized performance rating using Equation (17) to calculate the defuzzification (DFW) and weighted sum ($W_i^S$) using Equation (18). The ranking of primary sectors and the corresponding values of ($W_i^S$) are shown in Table 10.

$$DFW_i = \frac{l + l' + m + u' + u}{5} \quad (17)$$

$$W_iP = W_i^S = DF_{GDPi} + DF_{EMPi} + DF_{TAi} + DF_{IVTi} + DF_{IDi} + DF_{GPSi} + DF_{RMi} + DF_{EIi} \quad (18)$$

Table 10. Prescribed rankings using IVF-SAW, IVF-WSM and IVF-WASPAS.

| PS | WSM ($W_i^s$) | Rank | WPM ($W_i^p$) | Rank | WASPAS ($Q_i$) | Rank |
|---|---|---|---|---|---|---|
| A1 | 0.6063 | 4 | 0.0411 | 4 | 0.3237 | 4 |
| A2 | 0.4304 | 5 | 0.0281 | 5 | 0.2293 | 5 |
| A3 | 0.7220 | 2 | 0.1126 | 2 | 0.4173 | 2 |
| A4 | 0.7427 | 1 | 0.1149 | 1 | 0.4288 | 1 |
| A5 | 0.2350 | 7 | 0.0010 | 7 | 0.1180 | 7 |
| A6 | 0.3451 | 6 | 0.0069 | 6 | 0.1760 | 6 |
| A7 | 0.1994 | 8 | 0.0003 | 8 | 0.0999 | 8 |
| A8 | 0.6907 | 3 | 0.1114 | 3 | 0.4010 | 3 |

Source: Author's own elaboration.

*4.3. Interval-Valued Fuzzy WPM Method*

In fuzzy MCDM problems, relative weights are often represented by fuzzy numbers. A fuzzy number is defined as a convex fuzzy set with a given interval of real numbers, each with a membership value between 0 and 1. To accommodate a situation where determining precise values is challenging, membership values can be expressed as an interval of real values. In this study, criteria weights are treated as linguistic variables, which is particularly useful for complex or poorly defined circumstances. These linguistic variables can be transformed into triangular fuzzy numbers with interval values [32]. Considering the difficulty in determining precise criteria levels in the physical world, we modify the WPM approach to address the MCGDM problem using linguistic criteria values.

Step 1: Define linguistic parameters for criteria weight and performance rating of eight alternatives in a fuzzy decision matrix for group decision, as outlined in Tables 6 and 8.

Step 2: Convert expert judgment to IVF numbers, following the same process as in IVF-SAW Step 2. IVF-WPM method uses the exact same data from IVF-SAW step 2.

Step 3: Rate optimal performance for each category, following the same process as in IVF-SAW Step 3. IVF-WPM method uses the data from IVF-SAW Step 3.

Step 4: Determine the normalized decision matrix, which is the same as in IVF-SAW Step 4. The same value is used for this step.

Step 5: Determine the weighted normalized matrix using Equation (19).

$$WN_{ij} = N_{ij}^{DNC_j} \quad (19)$$

Step 6: Defuzzify IVF-weighted normalized performance ratings using the same method as in IVF-SAW with Equations (17) and (18). The rank of pedagogy methods and corresponding values '$W_i^p$' are presented in Table 10.

*4.4. Interval-Valued Fuzzy WASPAS Method*

Combining IVF-SAW and IVF-WPM creates IVF-WASPAS, ranking alternatives using the aggregated sum product weightage ($Q_i$). This method integrates the weighted summation ($W_i^s$) and multiplication ($W_i^p$) procedures, as shown in Equation (20).

$$Q_i = 0.5 W_i^s + 0.5 W_i^p = 0.5 \sum_{j=1}^{n} N_{ij} W_j + 0.5 \sum_{j=1}^{n} N_{ij}^{W_j} \quad (20)$$

where, $Q_i$ is the aggregated sum product weightage of the $i_{th}$ alternative ($i = 1, 2, 3\ldots, m$; $j = 1, 2, 3\ldots, n$)

## 5. Result and Discussion

Using the IVF-SAW, IVF-WPM, and IVF-WASPAS methodologies, the primary sectors are evaluated and compared. Defuzzified IVF values for SAW, WPM, and WASPAS are established for each model. The subsequent section provides a detailed discussion on the impact of these strategies. A-4 (Energy sector) receives the highest preference score in all three techniques, while the A-7 (Information Technology) alternative scores the lowest as per the expert judgements and opinions. The preferred order for various primary sector options is as follows.

- IVF-SAW: A-4 > A-3 > A-8 > A-1 > A-2 > A-6 > A-5 > A-7
- IVF-WPM: A-4 > A-3 > A-8 > A-1 > A-2 > A-6 > A-5 > A-7
- IVF-WASPAS: A-4 > A-3 > A-8 > A-1 > A-2 > A-6 > A-5 > A-7

The discussion of the Romanian primary sectors ratings prescribed by the three MCDM methods offers valuable insights into the relative importance and performance of each sector. Let us discuss and justify these rankings in the context of the Romanian economy and real-world considerations with the help of Table 11, provided below.

Table 11. Aligning the alternatives' rating with the real-world application.

| Rank | Primary Sectors | Justifications |
|---|---|---|
| 1 | Energy | Energy consistently ranks highest across all three MCDM methods. This ranking is justified by the sector's significant contributions to technological adaptation and innovation through advancements in renewable energy technologies and efficiency measures. Furthermore, energy infrastructure development and investment, such as power plants and transmission networks, play crucial roles in supporting economic growth and industrial activities. The energy sector also contributes substantially to GDP, employment generation, and market demand, while government policies and subsidies encourage investment in sustainable energy sources, further solidifying its top-ranking position. |
| 2 | Agriculture and Forestry | Agriculture and forestry consistently rank second among the primary sectors. These sectors contribute to technological adaptation and innovation through the adoption of modern farming practices and sustainable forestry management techniques. Infrastructure development and investment in rural areas, such as irrigation systems and forest management facilities, support agricultural and forestry activities. Moreover, agriculture and forestry make significant contributions to GDP, employment generation, and environmental sustainability by preserving ecosystems and providing renewable resources. Government policies and subsidies further promote growth in these sectors through incentives for sustainable practices and rural development initiatives. |
| 3 | Mining | Mining consistently ranks third across all MCDM methods. While the sector may lag behind in technological adaptation compared to other industries, it still contributes to innovation through advancements in mining technologies and extraction methods. Infrastructure development and investment in mining operations, such as mine infrastructure and transportation networks, support economic activities in mining regions. Mining contributes significantly to GDP through mineral extraction and processing, albeit with potential environmental impacts that require sustainable practices and mitigation measures. Employment generation, market demand, and government policies also influence the sector's ranking, with subsidies aimed at promoting responsible mining practices and community development. |

Table 11. *Cont.*

| Rank | Primary Sectors | Justifications |
|---|---|---|
| 4 | Fishing | Fishing consistently ranks fourth among the primary sectors. While the sector may have limited technological innovation compared to other industries, infrastructure development and investment in fishing fleets and processing facilities support maritime activities. Fishing contributes to GDP through seafood production and export opportunities, while employment generation and market demand drive the sector's importance in coastal communities. Environmental sustainability is crucial for the fishing industry, with regulations and conservation efforts aimed at preserving marine ecosystems. Government policies and subsidies support sustainable fishing practices and resource management, influencing the sector's ranking. |
| 5 | Automobile | The automobile industry consistently ranks fifth across all MCDM methods. Technological adaptation and innovation are significant drivers in the automotive sector, with advancements in electric vehicles and autonomous driving technologies. Infrastructure development and investment in automotive manufacturing plants and transportation networks support industry growth. The automobile industry contributes significantly to GDP through manufacturing and exports, while employment generation and market demand influence its importance in the economy. Government policies and subsidies incentivize investment in research and development, emission reduction measures, and automotive production, impacting the sector's ranking. |
| 6 | Textile | The textile industry consistently ranks sixth among the primary sectors. While the sector may have limited technological innovation compared to other industries, infrastructure development and investment in textile manufacturing facilities support production activities. Textile manufacturing contributes to GDP through domestic production and export opportunities, while employment generation and market demand drive industry dynamics. Environmental sustainability is a growing concern, with initiatives aimed at reducing water consumption and promoting sustainable textile production. Government policies and subsidies support industry competitiveness and sustainability, influencing its ranking. |
| 7 | Manufacturing and Construction | The manufacturing and construction sectors consistently rank seventh across all MCDM methods. While these sectors may exhibit some technological adaptation and innovation, infrastructure development and investment in manufacturing facilities and construction projects support economic activities. Manufacturing and construction contribute significantly to GDP through industrial production and infrastructure development, while employment generation and market demand drive sector dynamics. Environmental sustainability considerations are important, with regulations and green building initiatives aimed at reducing environmental impact. Government policies and subsidies support industry growth and sustainability, impacting the sector's ranking. |
| 8 | Information Technology | Information technology consistently ranks lowest among the primary sectors. While the sector excels in technological adaptation and innovation, infrastructure development and investment in IT infrastructure and digital connectivity support industry growth. Information technology contributes to GDP through software development, IT services, and digital innovation, while employment generation and market demand drive sector dynamics. Environmental sustainability considerations are relevant, with initiatives aimed at reducing e-waste and promoting energy-efficient technologies. Government policies and subsidies support digital transformation and innovation, influencing the sector's ranking. |

Source: Author's own elaboration.

The rankings of Romanian primary sectors prescribed by the IVF-SAW, IVF-WPM, and IVF-WASPAS MCDM tools shown in Figure 2 align with real-world considerations across various factors. These rankings provide valuable insights for policymakers, investors, and stakeholders in strategic decision-making and resource allocation to promote sustainable economic development in Romania.

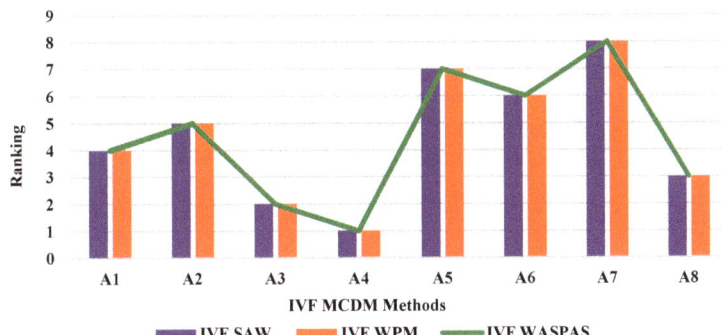

**Figure 2.** Ranking comparison of IVF-SAW, IVF-WPM, IVF-WASPAS. (Source: Author's own elaboration).

## 5.1. Sensitivity Analysis

Incorporating the diffusion coefficient (λ) into choice frameworks reflects the economic experts' views on uncertainty. Ensuring model stability requires a sensitivity analysis, varying λ from 0 to 1 and fine-tuning values. Probing the parameter's impact assesses the framework's responsiveness to changes in expert's perspective. This iterative process aligns the model with the intended pedagogical approach and enhances reliability in accommodating uncertainty. Sensitivity analysis validates stability and exhibits adaptability to the experts' evolving viewpoint on uncertainty in education.

### 5.1.1. Sensitivity Analysis on IVF-SAW Method

To determine the weighted sum score, convert overall performance ratings into exact IVF values. The choice of defuzzification techniques may impact outcomes, making it crucial to decide which technique to use and when to use it. Adjusting 'λ' in Equation (21) provides more options than Equation (17), allowing for a flexible weighting of lower (l, l') and upper (u, u') bounds. Table 12 presents results from Equation (21) for various coefficient values.

$$DF_\lambda = \frac{(1-\lambda)l + \lambda l' + m + \lambda u' + (1-\lambda)u}{3} \quad (21)$$

**Table 12.** Ranking for various parameters λ on IVF-SAW and IVF-WPM method.

| PS | λ = 0 | | | | λ = 0.5 | | | | λ = 1 | | | |
|----|-------|---|-------|---|---------|---|-------|---|-------|---|-------|---|
|    | $W_i^s$ | Rank | $W_i^p$ | Rank | $W_i^s$ | Rank | $W_i^p$ | Rank | $W_i^s$ | Rank | $W_i^p$ | Rank |
| A1 | 1.2162 | 4 | 0.0356 | 4 | 0.5993 | 4 | 0.0346 | 4 | 1.2162 | 4 | 3.8220 | 4 |
| A2 | 0.8534 | 5 | 0.0241 | 5 | 0.4262 | 5 | 0.0236 | 5 | 0.8534 | 5 | 2.5410 | 5 |
| A3 | 1.6117 | 2 | 0.0822 | 2 | 0.7178 | 2 | 0.0785 | 2 | 1.6117 | 2 | 11.8604 | 2 |
| A4 | 1.6728 | 1 | 0.0826 | 3 | 0.7395 | 1 | 0.0803 | 1 | 1.6728 | 1 | 12.3922 | 1 |
| A5 | 0.3008 | 7 | 0.0004 | 7 | 0.2157 | 7 | 0.0004 | 7 | 0.3008 | 7 | 0.0014 | 7 |
| A6 | 0.5850 | 6 | 0.0040 | 6 | 0.3287 | 6 | 0.0036 | 6 | 0.5850 | 6 | 0.0802 | 6 |
| A7 | 0.1348 | 8 | 0.0001 | 8 | 0.1662 | 8 | 0.0001 | 8 | 0.1348 | 8 | 0.0001 | 8 |
| A8 | 1.4834 | 3 | 0.0820 | 1 | 0.6828 | 3 | 0.0775 | 3 | 1.4834 | 3 | 11.4447 | 3 |

Source: Author's own elaboration.

The rankings in Table 12 and Figure 3 demonstrate that the proposed IVF integrated with SAW approach is a valuable tool for assessing decision-making scenarios and selecting the best alternative.

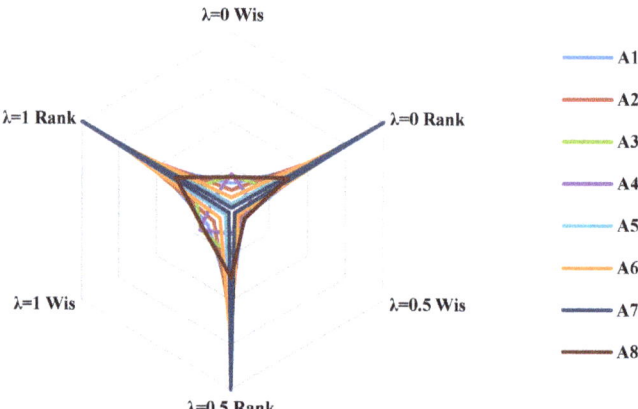

**Figure 3.** Ranking with change of λ for IVF-SAW. Source: Author's own elaboration.

5.1.2. Sensitivity Analysis on IVF-WPM Method

The same process is followed here as in IVF-SAW. By using Equation (21) and adjusting 'λ', it is possible to give more weight to the lower (l, l') or upper (u, u') bounds, allowing for sensitivity analysis. The weighted product of each alternative considering varying the 'λ' values is presented in Table 12. The rankings in Table 12 and Figure 4 demonstrate that the proposed IVF integrated with WPM approach is a valuable tool for assessing decision-making scenarios and selecting the best alternative.

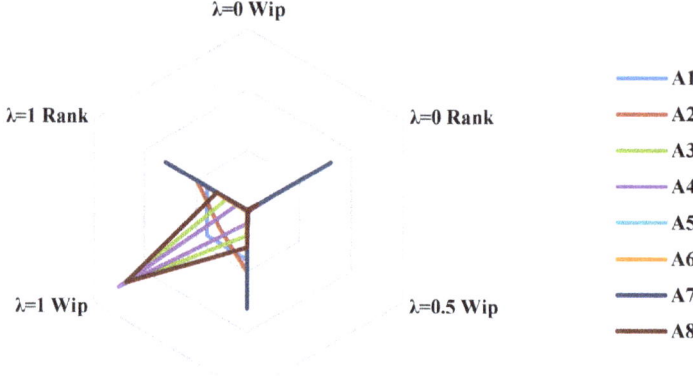

**Figure 4.** Ranking with change of λ for IVF-WPM. (Source: Author's own elaboration).

5.1.3. Sensitivity Analysis on IVF-WASPAS Method

A more generalized equation represented by Equation (22) is used to improve the efficacy and ranking accuracy. The corresponding values are shown in Table 13 and the alternative's ranking deviations are illustrated using Figure 5. Where, λ = 0, 0.1, 0.2, 0.3..., 1.

$$Q_i = \lambda W_i^s + (1-\lambda)W_i^p = \lambda \sum_{j=1}^{n} N_{ij}W_j + (1-\lambda)\sum_{j=1}^{n} N_{ij}^{W_j} \tag{22}$$

Table 13. Ranking of IVF-WASPAS method for varying 'λ'.

| PS | λ = 0 | λ = 0.1 | λ = 0.2 | λ = 0.3 | λ = 0.4 | λ = 0.5 | λ = 0.6 | λ = 0.7 | λ = 0.8 | λ = 0.9 | λ = 1 |
|---|---|---|---|---|---|---|---|---|---|---|---|
| A1 | 4 | 4 | 4 | 4 | 4 | 4 | 4 | 4 | 4 | 4 | 4 |
| A2 | 5 | 5 | 5 | 5 | 5 | 5 | 5 | 5 | 5 | 5 | 5 |
| A3 | 2 | 2 | 2 | 2 | 2 | 2 | 2 | 2 | 2 | 2 | 2 |
| A4 | 1 | 1 | 1 | 1 | 1 | 1 | 1 | 1 | 1 | 1 | 1 |
| A5 | 7 | 7 | 7 | 7 | 7 | 7 | 7 | 7 | 7 | 7 | 7 |
| A6 | 6 | 6 | 6 | 6 | 6 | 6 | 6 | 6 | 6 | 6 | 6 |
| A7 | 8 | 8 | 8 | 8 | 8 | 8 | 8 | 8 | 8 | 8 | 8 |
| A8 | 3 | 3 | 3 | 3 | 3 | 3 | 3 | 3 | 3 | 3 | 3 |

Source: Author's own elaboration.

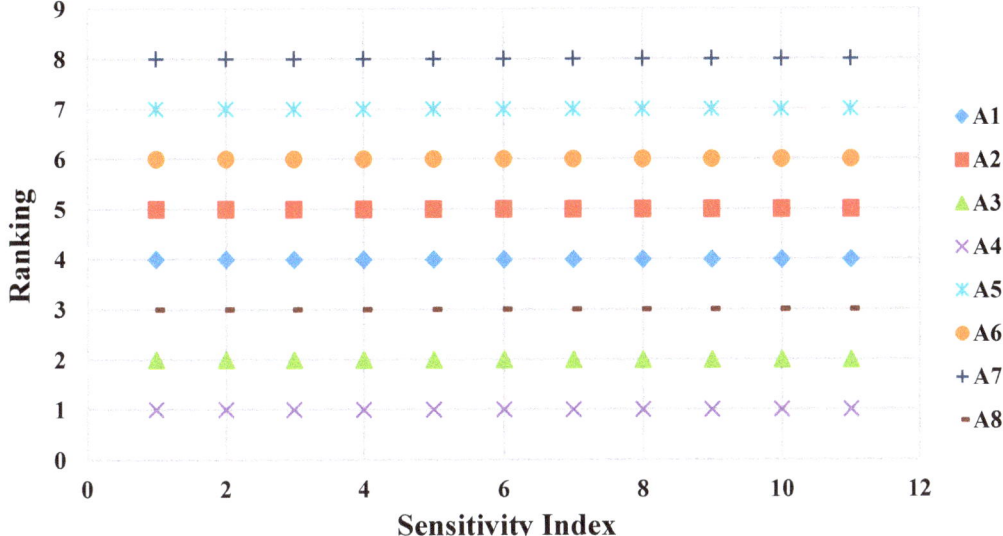

Figure 5. Ranking with change of λ for IVF-WASPAS. (Source: Author's own elaboration).

In conclusion, varying the variables from 0 to 1 in intervals of 0.1 does not impact the ranking order of alternatives. This suggests that, without changes, A-4 remains the top choice. This study highlights the reliability and robustness of the evaluation model, recommending the optimal method from a range of options. Overall, it is evident from Tables 12 and 13 that for every value of 'λ' variation, the exact same rankings have been obtained for every case, thus indicating the robustness and stability in the final output rankings.

The findings from the rankings of Romanian primary sectors can provide valuable guidance to decision-makers in selecting and prioritizing sectors for investment, policy intervention, and development initiatives. By leveraging sectoral strengths, addressing challenges, and promoting sustainability and resilience, decision-makers can foster inclusive and sustainable economic growth in Romania. Table 14 provides more concrete insights into how the findings from the rankings of Romanian primary sectors prescribed by the IVF-SAW, IVF-WPM, and IVF-WASPAS MCDM tools could influence primary sector selection and guide decision-making.

Table 14. Implications and recommendation of the experts.

| Area of Implications | | Implications and Recommendation |
|---|---|---|
| Strategic investment prioritization | Implications | The consistent top rankings of the energy, agriculture, and forestry sectors indicate their significant contributions to economic development and sustainability. |
| | Recommendations | Decision-makers should prioritize strategic investments in these sectors to capitalize on their strengths and potential for growth. This could involve allocating resources for infrastructure development, research and development, and capacity-building initiatives to enhance productivity and competitiveness. |
| Diversification and innovation | Implications | While certain sectors like energy and agriculture perform well across all MCDM methods, others like information technology and manufacturing show variability in their rankings. |
| | Recommendations | Decision-makers should focus on diversifying the economy and fostering innovation in sectors with lower rankings. This could involve implementing policies to support technology adoption, research and development, and entrepreneurship to stimulate growth and competitiveness in these sectors. |
| Environmental sustainability | Implications | The rankings provide insights into the environmental impact and sustainability practices of different sectors, with sectors like mining and manufacturing potentially facing challenges. |
| | Recommendations | Decision-makers should prioritize environmental sustainability in sector selection by promoting sustainable practices, implementing stricter regulations, and investing in clean technologies and renewable energy sources. This would not only mitigate environmental risks but also enhance long-term resilience and competitiveness. |
| Market demand and export opportunities | Implications | Sectors with high rankings in market demand and export opportunities, such as energy and agriculture, indicate their potential for driving economic growth through international trade. |
| | Recommendations | Decision-makers should leverage these sectors' strengths by promoting exports, facilitating market access, and fostering international partnerships. This could involve implementing trade policies, providing export incentives, and supporting market intelligence and export promotion initiatives. |
| Employment generation and rural development | Implications | Sectors like agriculture and forestry play a crucial role in employment generation and rural development, as indicated by their high rankings. |
| | Recommendations | Decision-makers should prioritize sectors with strong potential for job creation and rural development through targeted investments, skills training programs, and entrepreneurship support. This could help address unemployment, reduce rural-urban disparities, and stimulate inclusive economic growth. |
| Policy alignment and coordination | Implications | Government policies and subsidies can significantly influence sector performance and competitiveness. |
| | Recommendations | Decision-makers should ensure alignment and coordination of policies across sectors to create a conducive business environment and address sector-specific challenges. This could involve developing sectoral strategies, establishing policy coherence mechanisms, and enhancing stakeholder engagement to maximize policy effectiveness and impact. |
| Resilience and risk management | Implications | Sectors with lower rankings may face challenges related to resilience and risk management, such as technological disruptions, market volatility, and environmental risks. |
| | Recommendations | Decision-makers should assess and address sector-specific risks by implementing proactive measures, diversifying revenue streams, and enhancing adaptive capacity. This could involve establishing risk management frameworks, promoting innovation and flexibility, and providing targeted support to vulnerable sectors. |

Source: Author's own elaboration.

## 5.2. Ranking Comparisons

The following section highlights the comparisons of the present rankings with other methods to observe any differences in the outcome results. To prove the robustness of the present hybrid model, traditional SAW, WPM and WASPAS without considering fuzzy were further applied and the alterations in the output rankings were observed. It is to be noted from Table 15 that the alternative rankings vary across the three traditional MCDM tools. Although conventional SAW and WASPAS prescribe the same ranking order, the ranking proposed by traditional WPM is completely different, thus indicating the instability and lack of cooperation among these three traditional methods. On the other hand, when IVF is integrated with SAW, WPM and WASPAS, the ranking order is modified and the stability is further enhanced, thus producing the same ranking across the three methods as evident from Table 15. The variations in the ranking order among the applied MCDM methods are also illustrated graphically in Figure 6.

**Table 15.** Ranking comparisons among different MCDM models.

| PS | IVF-Fuzzy | | | Non-Fuzzy | | |
|---|---|---|---|---|---|---|
| | WSM | WPM | WASPAS | WSM | WPM | WASPAS |
| A1 | 4 | 4 | 4 | 4 | 1 | 4 |
| A2 | 5 | 5 | 5 | 5 | 5 | 5 |
| A3 | 2 | 2 | 2 | 2 | 4 | 2 |
| A4 | 1 | 1 | 1 | 1 | 2 | 1 |
| A5 | 7 | 7 | 7 | 8 | 8 | 8 |
| A6 | 6 | 6 | 6 | 6 | 6 | 6 |
| A7 | 8 | 8 | 8 | 7 | 7 | 7 |
| A8 | 3 | 3 | 3 | 3 | 3 | 3 |

Source: Author's own elaboration.

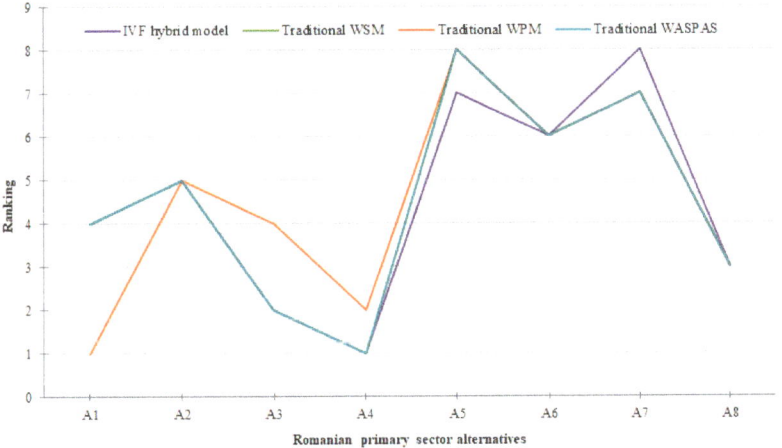

**Figure 6.** Graphical representation of the ranking comparisons. (Source: Author's own elaboration.)

Some other insights can be derived from this comparative analysis. Across both analyses, alternatives A2, A6 and A8 maintain the same ranks. This suggests that these alternatives possess a consistent performance across both IVF and traditional methods. Notably, there are differences in the rankings of alternatives A1, A3, A4, A5 and A7 between the two analyses. In the IVF analysis, all the alternatives are consistently ranked at the same positions for all three methods, respectively. In the second analysis of traditional methods, alternatives A2, A5, A6, A7 and A8 remain at positions 5, 8, 6, 7, and 3, but A1, A3 and A4 swap positions with ranks 1, 2 and 4, respectively. Hence, from the traditional methods, it would be contradictory to accomplish the first and second-rank alternatives since different methods suggest different ranking orders to the alternatives A1, A3 and A4. The discrepancies in rankings could be attributed to the handling of uncertainty and fuzziness in the IVF methods. IVF techniques allow for a more nuanced representation of uncertainty, which may lead to different rankings compared to traditional methods that do not account for fuzziness. Fuzzy methods tend to capture the imprecision and ambiguity present in decision-making processes more effectively, potentially resulting in better prioritization of alternatives.

In conclusion, the ranking comparisons between the two MCDM analyses reveal both consistencies and differences, primarily driven by the inclusion of fuzziness in IVF methods. The performance and the robustness of the results of any MCDM tools can be enhanced by integrating the fuzzy concept. However, it can be observed that fuzzy-embedded hybrid MCDM tools perform better compared to the traditional MCDM methodologies. Fuzzy models can produce consistent rankings and their stability is also better compared to other alternative models. Therefore, if decision-makers want to prioritize a more nuanced handling of uncertainty and are willing to accept potentially different rankings due to fuzziness, IVF methods might be preferred. Conversely, if decision-makers prefer straightforward, deterministic rankings without considering fuzziness, traditional methods could be more suitable.

## 6. Conclusions

This research delves into a comprehensive analysis of the primary sector's role in shaping the economic activity in Romania. Using advanced decision-making methodologies like IVF-SAW, IVF-WPM, and IVF-WASPAS within the MCDM framework, this study emphasizes the pivotal role of the energy sector compared to other alternatives. The findings underscore the critical significance of the energy sector in driving economic growth and development. Rigorous evaluation demonstrates its superior performance, indicating its capacity to generate economic value, create employment opportunities, and contribute significantly to overall prosperity in Romania. This research highlights the importance of prioritizing investments and initiatives in the energy sector for sustainable economic progress and increased resilience to economic fluctuations.

While the success of the energy sector is crucial, it does not diminish the importance of other primary sectors in Romania's economic landscape. These sectors play vital roles and must be nurtured alongside the energy sector for a balanced and diversified economy. This research provides a solid foundation for future studies and policy decisions related to the primary sector's selection in Romania. Acknowledging the central role of the energy sector and adopting a holistic approach to economic development can guide Romania towards greater prosperity and resilience in the evolving global economic landscape.

### 6.1. Managerial Implications

The present research on the selection of Romanian primary sectors using an integrated SAW, WPM, and WASPAS approach provides valuable insights for managers involved in sectoral development and investment decisions. By leveraging the findings and implications of this research, managers can make informed decisions that support the growth, competitiveness, and sustainability of primary sectors in Romania. The following research has several managerial implications that may be discussed as follows.

- Managers can use the integrated approach to allocate resources effectively across different primary sectors in Romania. By considering the strengths and weaknesses of each sector identified through the integrated SAW, WPM, and WASPAS approach, managers can allocate resources such as funding, manpower, and technology to maximize sectoral performance.
- The integrated approach provides a systematic framework for evaluating the performance of primary sectors. Managers can use the findings to identify areas for improvement within each sector and develop strategies to enhance performance. This

may involve implementing process improvements, adopting new technologies, or investing in workforce training and development.
- Managers can use the integrated approach to assess and mitigate risks associated with sectoral selection and investment decisions. By considering the uncertainties inherent in the decision-making process, managers can identify potential risks and develop contingency plans to manage them effectively.
- The integrated approach can facilitate collaboration and partnerships between different stakeholders within the primary sectors. Managers can leverage the findings to identify complementary strengths and opportunities for collaboration, such as joint research initiatives, supply chain partnerships, or market development efforts.
- This research's findings can inform policy formulation and advocacy efforts aimed at supporting the growth and development of primary sectors in Romania. Managers can use the insights gained from the integrated approach to advocate for policies that address sector-specific challenges, promote innovation, and create a conducive business environment.
- Managers can use the integrated approach to inform long-term planning and investment decisions within the primary sectors. By considering the sectoral priorities and opportunities identified through the approach, managers can develop strategic plans and investment strategies that support sustainable growth and development over the long term.
- Effective stakeholder engagement and communication are essential for the successful implementation of sectoral development initiatives. Managers can use the integrated approach to engage stakeholders such as government agencies, industry associations, and local communities in the decision-making process and communicate the rationale behind sectoral selection and investment decisions.

*6.2. Limitations of the Present Research*

Despite numerous positive interpretations, every decision-making analysis involving different factors involves certain limitations that need to be addressed properly to enhance the robustness and applicability of the MCDM models. Below are some of the identified limitations that may be associated with this research.

- The accuracy and reliability of the decision-making process heavily rely on the availability and quality of the data used in the analysis. Limitations in data availability or inaccuracies in data collection may introduce biases or uncertainties into the results.
- The integration of expert judgments in assigning criteria weights or assessing performance scores may introduce subjectivity and bias into the decision-making process. Differences in expertise, perspectives, or preferences among experts may influence the outcomes of the analysis.
- This research may involve simplifying assumptions or constraints to facilitate the decision-making process. These assumptions may not fully capture the complexities and nuances of the primary sector selection problem, potentially leading to oversimplification or unrealistic conclusions.
- The integrated SAW, WPM, and WASPAS decision-making approach may be complex and computationally intensive, particularly when dealing with a large number of criteria and alternatives. This complexity may limit the practical applicability of the approach or require significant computational resources and expertise for implementation.
- While interval-valued fuzzy sets offer a flexible framework for handling uncertainty, their validity and effectiveness depend on the appropriateness of the membership functions and the accuracy of interval assignments. Inaccurate or arbitrary assignments of interval values may undermine the reliability of the analysis.
- The findings and recommendations derived from this research may be specific to the context of the Romanian primary sector and may not be directly applicable to other regions or sectors. Factors such as cultural, economic, or institutional differences may limit the generalizability of the results.

- The primary sector selection problem is inherently dynamic, with evolving trends, preferences, and external factors influencing decision outcomes over time. This research may not adequately capture the dynamic nature of the decision context, leading to static or outdated recommendations.

*6.3. Future Directions*

Future work stemming from this research could focus on several areas to enhance the understanding and applicability of the decision-making process. By addressing these areas in future research, the understanding and applicability of the decision-making approach for selecting primary sectors in Romania can be further advanced, leading to more informed and effective decision outcomes.

- Further research could refine the methodology for defining and using interval-valued fuzzy sets in the decision-making process. This includes exploring alternative approaches for assigning interval values and membership functions to better capture the uncertainty and variability in criteria weights and performance scores.
- Future work could explore the integration of additional MCDM models beyond SAW, WPM, and WASPAS. Incorporating other models such as PROMETHEE, ELECTRE, or TOPSIS could provide alternative perspectives and enhance the robustness of the decision-making process.
- Developing dynamic decision-making frameworks that account for changes and uncertainties over time could be a promising avenue for future research. This includes exploring methods for updating criteria weights and performance scores in response to evolving conditions and preferences within the primary sectors.
- Extending this research to other sectors and regions beyond the Romanian primary sector could broaden the scope and impact of the decision-making approach. This includes adapting the methodology to address sector-specific challenges and priorities in different contexts and geographical areas.

**Author Contributions:** Conceptualization, S.S.G. and A.E.I.; methodology, S.S.G.; software, A.D. and C.A.B.; validation, S.S.G., A.E.I. and M.-G.H.; formal analysis, M.-G.H. and A.Ș.-C.; investigation, C.A.B.; resources, A.Ș.-C.; data curation, S.S.G. and M.-G.H.; writing—original draft preparation, S.S.G.; writing—review and editing, A.E.I. and A.D.; visualization, A.D.; supervision, M.-G.H.; project administration, A.Ș.-C.; funding acquisition, A.E.I. and C.A.B. All authors have read and agreed to the published version of the manuscript.

**Funding:** This research received no external funding.

**Data Availability Statement:** Data are contained within the article.

**Acknowledgments:** We extend our heartfelt appreciation to all individuals and organizations whose contributions made this research possible. Special thanks to the reviewers and editor whose expertise, support, and review comments significantly enriched this work. We are also grateful to our co-authors and colleagues, without whom this research would not have been feasible. Lastly, we express our gratitude to the expert team members who generously shared their time and insights. Their invaluable contributions are deeply appreciated.

**Conflicts of Interest:** The authors declare no conflicts of interest.

## References

1. Ban, A.I.; Ban, O.I.; Bogdan, V.; Popa, D.C.S.; Tuse, D. Performance evaluation model of Romanian manufacturing listed companies by fuzzy AHP and TOPSIS. *Technol. Econ. Dev. Econ.* **2020**, *26*, 808–836. [CrossRef]
2. Pamucar, D.; Iordache, M.; Deveci, M.; Schitea, D.; Iordache, I. A new hybrid fuzzy multi-criteria decision methodology model for prioritizing the alternatives of the hydrogen bus development: A case study from Romania. *Int. J. Hydrogen Energy* **2021**, *46*, 29616–29637. [CrossRef]
3. Magableh, G.M. Evaluating wheat suppliers using fuzzy MCDM technique. *Sustainability* **2023**, *15*, 10519. [CrossRef]
4. Büyüközkan, G.; Mukul, E.; Kongar, E. Health tourism strategy selection via SWOT analysis and integrated hesitant fuzzy linguistic AHP-MABAC approach. *Socio-Econ. Plan. Sci.* **2021**, *74*, 100929. [CrossRef]
5. Hajduk, S. Multi-criteria analysis of smart cities on the example of the Polish cities. *Resources* **2021**, *10*, 44. [CrossRef]

6. Broniewicz, E.; Ogrodnik, K. A comparative evaluation of multi-criteria analysis methods for sustainable transport. *Energies* **2021**, *14*, 5100. [CrossRef]
7. Xu, M.; Bai, C.; Shi, L.; Puška, A.; Štilić, A.; Stević, Ž. Assessment of mountain tourism sustainability using integrated fuzzy MCDM model. *Sustainability* **2023**, *15*, 14358. [CrossRef]
8. Xuanling, M.A.; Meng, J.I. Analysis on liquidity risk management of monetary and financial services based on the goal of financial stability. *Rom. J. Econ. Forecast.* **2023**, *26*, 72. Available online: https://ipe.ro/new/rjef/rjef2_2023/rjef2_2023p72-91.pdf (accessed on 14 January 2024).
9. Ghasemi, P.; Mehdiabadi, A.; Spulbar, C.; Birau, R. Ranking of sustainable medical tourism destinations in Iran: An integrated approach using fuzzy SWARA-PROMETHEE. *Sustainability* **2021**, *13*, 683. [CrossRef]
10. Tanveer, U.; Kremantzis, M.D.; Roussinos, N.; Ishaq, S.; Kyrgiakos, L.S.; Vlontzos, G. A fuzzy TOPSIS model for selecting digital technologies in circular supply chains. *Supply Chain Anal.* **2023**, *4*, 100038. [CrossRef]
11. Ghaffar, A.R.A.; Nadeem, M.R.; Hasan, M.G. Cost-benefit analysis of shale development in India: A best-worst method based MCDM approach. *J. King Saud Univ.-Sci.* **2021**, *33*, 101591. [CrossRef]
12. Mallick, J. Municipal solid waste landfill site selection based on fuzzy-AHP and geoinformation techniques in Asir region Saudi Arabia. *Sustainability* **2021**, *13*, 1538. [CrossRef]
13. Baydaş, M. Comparison of the performances of MCDM methods under uncertainty: An analysis on bist SME industry index. *OPUS J. Soc. Res.* **2022**, *19*, 308–326. [CrossRef]
14. Siksnelyte-Butkiene, I.; Karpavicius, T.; Streimikiene, D.; Balezentis, T. The achievements of climate change and energy policy in the European Union. *Energies* **2022**, *15*, 5128. [CrossRef]
15. Nasri, S.A.; Safaie, N.; Sarabi, A.; Eghbali, A.; Barkhordari, G. Performance evaluation of ICT companies using hybrid MCDM method in Iran. *Math. Probl. Eng.* **2022**, *2022*, 5308343. [CrossRef]
16. Hsueh, S.L.; Feng, Y.; Sun, Y.; Jia, R.; Yan, M.R. Using AI-MCDM model to boost sustainable energy system development: A case study on solar energy and rainwater collection in guangdong province. *Sustainability* **2021**, *13*, 12505. [CrossRef]
17. Candan, G.; Toklu, M.C. Evaluating security performances of EU countries in the context of sustainable development using fuzzy SMART and ARAS approaches. *Environ. Dev. Sustain.* **2024**, *26*, 1645–1671. [CrossRef]
18. Avram, S.; Cipu, C.; Corpade, A.M.; Gheorghe, C.A.; Manta, N.; Niculae, M.I.; Pascu, I.S.; Szep, R.E.; Rodino, S. GIS-based multi-criteria analysis method for assessment of lake ecosystems degradation—Case study in Romania. *Int. J. Environ. Res. Public Health* **2021**, *18*, 5915. [CrossRef] [PubMed]
19. Rehman, O.; Ali, Y.; Sabir, M. Risk assessment and mitigation for electric power sectors: A developing country's perspective. *Int. J. Crit. Infrastruct. Prot.* **2022**, *36*, 100507. [CrossRef]
20. Inamdar, Z.; Raut, R.; Narwane, V.S.; Gardas, B.; Narkhede, B.; Sagnak, M. A systematic literature review with bibliometric analysis of big data analytics adoption from period 2014 to 2018. *J. Enterp. Inf. Manag.* **2021**, *34*, 101–139. [CrossRef]
21. Brodny, J.; Tutak, M. Assessing the energy and climate sustainability of European Union member states: An MCDM-based approach. *Smart Cities* **2023**, *6*, 339–367. [CrossRef]
22. Hassan, M.S.; Ali, Y.; Petrillo, A.; De Felice, F. Risk assessment of circular economy practices in construction industry of Pakistan. *Sci. Total Environ.* **2023**, *868*, 161418. [CrossRef] [PubMed]
23. Rezaei, M. Prioritization of biodiesel development policies under hybrid uncertainties: A possibilistic stochastic multi-attribute decision-making approach. *Energy* **2022**, *260*, 125074. [CrossRef]
24. Opreana, A.; Vinerean, S.; Mihaiu, D.M.; Barbu, L.; Șerban, R.A. Fuzzy analytic network process with principal component analysis to establish a bank performance model under the assumption of country risk. *Mathematics* **2023**, *11*, 3257. [CrossRef]
25. Martín, J.C.; Moreira, P.; Roman, C. A hybrid-fuzzy segmentation analysis of residents' perception towards tourism in Gran Canaria. *Tour. Econ.* **2020**, *26*, 1282–1304. [CrossRef]
26. Makarevic, M.; Stavrou, S. Location selection of a manufacturing unit using BWM and ELECTRE III. *J. Supply Chain Manag. Sci.* **2022**, *3*, 113–130. [CrossRef]
27. Škrinjarić, T. Empirical assessment of the circular economy of selected European countries. *J. Clean. Prod.* **2020**, *255*, 120246. [CrossRef]
28. Albu, L.L.; Chivu, L.; Marinescu, A.C. Medium and long term convergence in EU. *Rom. J. Econ. Forecast.* **2023**, *26*, 5. Available online: https://ipe.ro/new/rjef/rjef3_2023/rjef3_2023p5-16.pdf (accessed on 14 January 2024).
29. Ma, C.; Li, H.; Saleem, S.F.; Mone, F. Balancing progress and sustainability: Industrial innovation's impact on Europe's emission management, economic expansion, and financial growth. *Rom. J. Econ. Forecast.* **2023**, *26*, 129. Available online: https://ipe.ro/new/rjef/rjef3_2023/rjef3_2023p129-147.pdf (accessed on 14 January 2024).
30. Barişik, S.; Ergen, K. Heterogenous effects of the determinants of pro-market reforms: Panel quantile estimation for OECD countries. *Rom. J. Econ. Forecast.* **2023**, *26*, 36. Available online: https://ipe.ro/rjef/rjef2_2023/rjef2_2023p36-51.pdf (accessed on 14 January 2024).
31. Yenugula, M.; Sahoo, S.; Goswami, S. Cloud computing for sustainable development: An analysis of environmental, economic and social benefits. *J. Future Sustain.* **2024**, *4*, 59–66. [CrossRef]
32. Goswami, S.S.; Behera, D.K.; Mitra, S. A comprehensive study of weighted product model for selecting the best product in our daily life. *Braz. J. Oper. Prod. Manag.* **2020**, *17*, 1–18. [CrossRef]

33. Goswami, S.S.; Behera, D.K. An overview of multiple criteria decision making techniques in the selection of best laptop model. *Adv. Syst. Sci. Appl.* **2023**, *23*, 11–23. [CrossRef]
34. Kordsofla, M.M.; Sorourkhah, A. Strategic adaptation in travel agencies: Integrating MARA with SWOT for uncertainty navigation. *J. Oper. Strateg. Anal.* **2023**, *1*, 173–189. [CrossRef]
35. Kiptum, C.K.; Bouraima, M.B.; Badi, I.; Zonon, B.I.P.; Ndiema, K.M.; Qiu, Y. Assessment of the challenges to urban sustainable development using an interval-valued fermatean fuzzy approach. *Syst. Anal.* **2023**, *1*, 11–26. [CrossRef]
36. Wang, W.; Yao, J.; Zhao, D.; Huang, C. Integration research of blockchain and social networks in rural management systems under fuzzy cognitive environment. *J. Fuzzy Ext. Appl.* **2024**, *5*, 16–34.
37. Khanaposhtani, G.F. A new multi-attribute decision-making method for interval data using support vector machine. *Big Data Comput. Vis.* **2023**, *3*, 137–145.
38. Toptancı, Ş. Ergonomic performance evaluation in türkiye's metal industry: Occupational health and safety indicators through VIKOR methodology. *J. Oper. Strateg. Anal.* **2023**, *1*, 140–146. [CrossRef]
39. Adak, A.; Gunjan, M. Profitable portfolio using fermatean fuzzy numbers. *J. Fuzzy Ext. Appl.* **2024**, *5*, 60–68. [CrossRef]
40. Sahoo, S.K.; Das, A.K.; Samanta, S.; Goswami, S.S. Assessing the role of sustainable development in mitigating the issue of global warming. *J. Process Manag. New Technol.* **2023**, *11*, 1–21. [CrossRef]
41. Yenugula, M.; Sahoo, S.K.; Goswami, S.S. Cloud computing in supply chain management: Exploring the relationship. *Manag. Sci. Lett.* **2023**, *13*, 193–210. [CrossRef]

**Disclaimer/Publisher's Note:** The statements, opinions and data contained in all publications are solely those of the individual author(s) and contributor(s) and not of MDPI and/or the editor(s). MDPI and/or the editor(s) disclaim responsibility for any injury to people or property resulting from any ideas, methods, instructions or products referred to in the content.

MDPI
St. Alban-Anlage 66
4052 Basel
Switzerland
www.mdpi.com

*Mathematics* Editorial Office
E-mail: mathematics@mdpi.com
www.mdpi.com/journal/mathematics

Disclaimer/Publisher's Note: The statements, opinions and data contained in all publications are solely those of the individual author(s) and contributor(s) and not of MDPI and/or the editor(s). MDPI and/or the editor(s) disclaim responsibility for any injury to people or property resulting from any ideas, methods, instructions or products referred to in the content.

www.ingramcontent.com/pod-product-compliance
Lightning Source LLC
LaVergne TN
LVHW070206100526
838202LV00015B/2006